T0322066

ENGLISH

FOR EVERYONE

ILLUSTRATED ENGLISH DICTIONARY

FREE AUDIO
website and app
www.dkefe.com

Author

Thomas Booth worked for 10 years as an English teacher in Poland, Romania, and Russia. He now lives in England, where he works as an editor and English-language materials writer. He has contributed to a number of books in the *English for Everyone* series.

ENGLISH

FOR EVERYONE

ILLUSTRATED ENGLISH DICTIONARY

123

DK

PRODUCED BY
Author / Editor Thomas Booth
Senior Art Editor Sunita Gahir
Art Editors Ali Jayne Scrivens, Samantha Richiardi
Illustrators Edward Byrne, Gus Scott
Project Manager Sunita Gahir / bigmetalfish design

DK UK
Senior Editor Amelia Petersen
Senior Designer Clare Shedden
Managing Art Editor Anna Hall
Managing Editors Christine Stroyan, Carine Tracanelli
Jacket Editors Stephanie Cheng Hui Tan, Juhi Sheth
Jacket Development Manager Sophia MTT
Production Editors Gillian Reid, Robert Dunn
Production Controller Sian Cheung
Publisher Andrew Macintyre
Art Director Karen Self
Publishing Director Jonathan Metcalf

First published in Great Britain in 2022 by
Dorling Kindersley Limited
DK, One Embassy Gardens, 8 Viaduct Gardens,
London, SW11 7BW

The authorized representative in the EEA is
Dorling Kindersley Verlag GmbH. Arnulfstr. 124,
80636 Munich, Germany

13 12 11 10
010–299755–Mar/2022

A CIP catalogue record for this book is available from the British Library
ISBN: 978-0-2415-4378-8

Printed and bound in China

www.dk.com

MIX
Paper | Supporting responsible forestry
FSC
www.fsc.org
FSC™ C018179

This book was made with Forest Stewardship Council™ certified paper – one small step in DK's commitment to a sustainable future.
Learn more at
www.dk.com/uk/information/sustainability

Contents

How to use this book 10

PEOPLE

01 Parts of the body 12

02 Hands and feet 14

03 Muscles and skeleton 16

04 Internal organs 18

05 Family 20

06 Feelings and moods 22

07 Life events 24

08 Pregnancy and childhood 26

09 Daily routines 28

10 Personality traits 30

11 Abilities and actions 32

APPEARANCE

12 Appearance and hair 34

13 Clothes 36

14 Clothes continued 38

15 Clothes continued 40

16 Accessories 42

17 Shoes 44

18 Beauty 46

HEALTH

19 Illness and injury 48

20 Visiting the doctor 50

21 The hospital 52

22 The dentist and optician 54

23 Diet and nutrition 56

24 Healthy body, healthy mind 58

HOME

25 A place to live 60

26 Living room and dining room 62

27 Kitchen and tableware 64

28 Kitchenware 66

29 Cooking 68

30 Bedroom 70

31 Bathroom 72

32 House and home 74

33 Electrics and plumbing 76

34 Household chores 78

35 Home improvements 80

36 Tools 82

37 Decorating 84

38 Garden plants and houseplants 86

39 Practical gardening 88

40 Garden tools 90

41 Garden features 92

CITY LIFE

42 In town 94

43 In town continued 96

44 Buildings and architecture 98

45 The bank and post office 100

46 Shopping 102

47 The shopping mall 104

48 The supermarket 106

49 The pharmacy 108

50 Emergency services 110

51 Energy and power supply 112

FOOD

52 Drinking and eating 114

53 Meat 116

54 Fish and seafood 118

55 Vegetables 120

56 Vegetables continued 122

57 Fruit 124

58 Fruit and nuts 126

59 Herbs and spices 128

60 In the pantry 130

61 Dairy produce 132

62 The bakery 134

63 The bakery continued 136

64 The delicatessen 138

65 At the café 140

66 At the café continued 142

67 Candy (US) / Sweets (UK) 143

68 At the bar 144

69 At the restaurant 146

70 Fast food 148

71 Breakfast 150

72 Lunch and dinner 152

STUDY

73 At school 154

74 Mathematics 156

75 Physics 158

76 Chemistry 160

77 Biology 162

78 The periodic table 164

79 History 166

80 At college 168

WORK

81 At work 170
82 In the office 172
83 Computers and technology 174
84 Media 176
85 Law 178
86 Farming 180
87 Construction 182
88 Military 184
89 Jobs 186
90 Jobs continued 188
91 Industries and departments 190
92 Applying for a job 192
93 Workplace skills 194
94 Money and finance 196
95 Meeting and presenting 198

GETTING AROUND

96 Roads 200
97 Cars 202
98 Cars continued 204
99 Cars and buses 206
100 Motorcycles 208
101 Cycling 210
102 Trains 212
103 Aircraft 214
104 At the airport 216
105 Sea vessels 218
106 The port 220

SPORTS

107 American football 222
108 Rugby 224
109 Soccer (US) / Football (UK) 226
110 Hockey and lacrosse 228
111 Cricket 230
112 Basketball and volleyball 232
113 Baseball 234
114 Tennis 236
115 Golf 238
116 Athletics 240
117 Combat sports 242
118 Swimming 244
119 Sailing and watersports 246
120 Horse riding 248

121 Fishing 250
122 Winter sports 252
123 Motorsports 254
124 At the gym 256
125 Other sports 258

LEISURE

126 On stage 260
127 Movies (US) / Films (UK) 262
128 Music 264
129 Music continued 266
130 Museums and galleries 268
131 Travel and accommodation 270
132 Sightseeing 272
133 Outdoor activities 274
134 On the beach 276
135 Camping 278
136 Home entertainment 280
137 Television 282
138 Books and reading 284
139 Fantasy and myth 286
140 Games 288
141 Arts and crafts 290
142 Arts and crafts continued 292

ENVIRONMENT

143 Space 294
144 Space continued 296
145 Planet Earth 298
146 Geography 300
147 Geography continued 302
148 Maps and directions 304
149 Countries 306
150 Countries continued 308
151 Countries continued 310
152 Nationalities 312
153 Nationalities continued 314
154 Weather 316
155 Climate and the environment 318
156 Rocks and minerals 320

NATURAL WORLD

157 Natural history 322
158 Mammals 324
159 Mammals continued 326
160 Birds 328
161 Birds continued 330

162	Insects and bugs	332
163	Amphibians and reptiles	334
164	Pets	336
165	Farm animals	338
166	Ocean life	340
167	Plants and trees	342
168	Plants and trees continued	344
169	Plants and trees continued	346
170	Fungi	348

REFERENCE

171	Time	350
172	The calendar	352
173	Numbers	354
174	Weights and measures	356
175	Writing	358
176	Describing things	360
177	Describing things continued	362
178	Common phrasal verbs	364
179	Useful expressions	366
180	Useful expressions continued	368

WORD LIST 370

Acknowledgments 400

Let's learn some words for bugs!

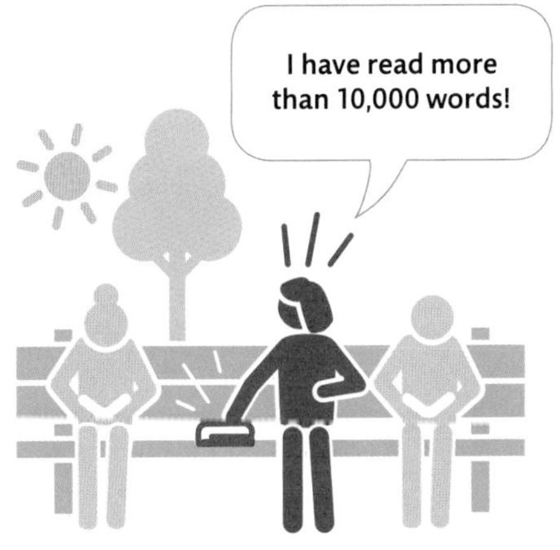
I have read more than 10,000 words!

How to use this book

English for Everyone: Illustrated Dictionary will help you to understand and remember more than 10,000 of the most useful words and phrases in English. Each of the 180 units in the dictionary covers a practical or everyday topic (such as health, food, or the natural world), and words are shown in a visual context to fix them in your memory. Listen to the audio provided online and in the app, and repeat each entry in the dictionary to help you remember new vocabulary.

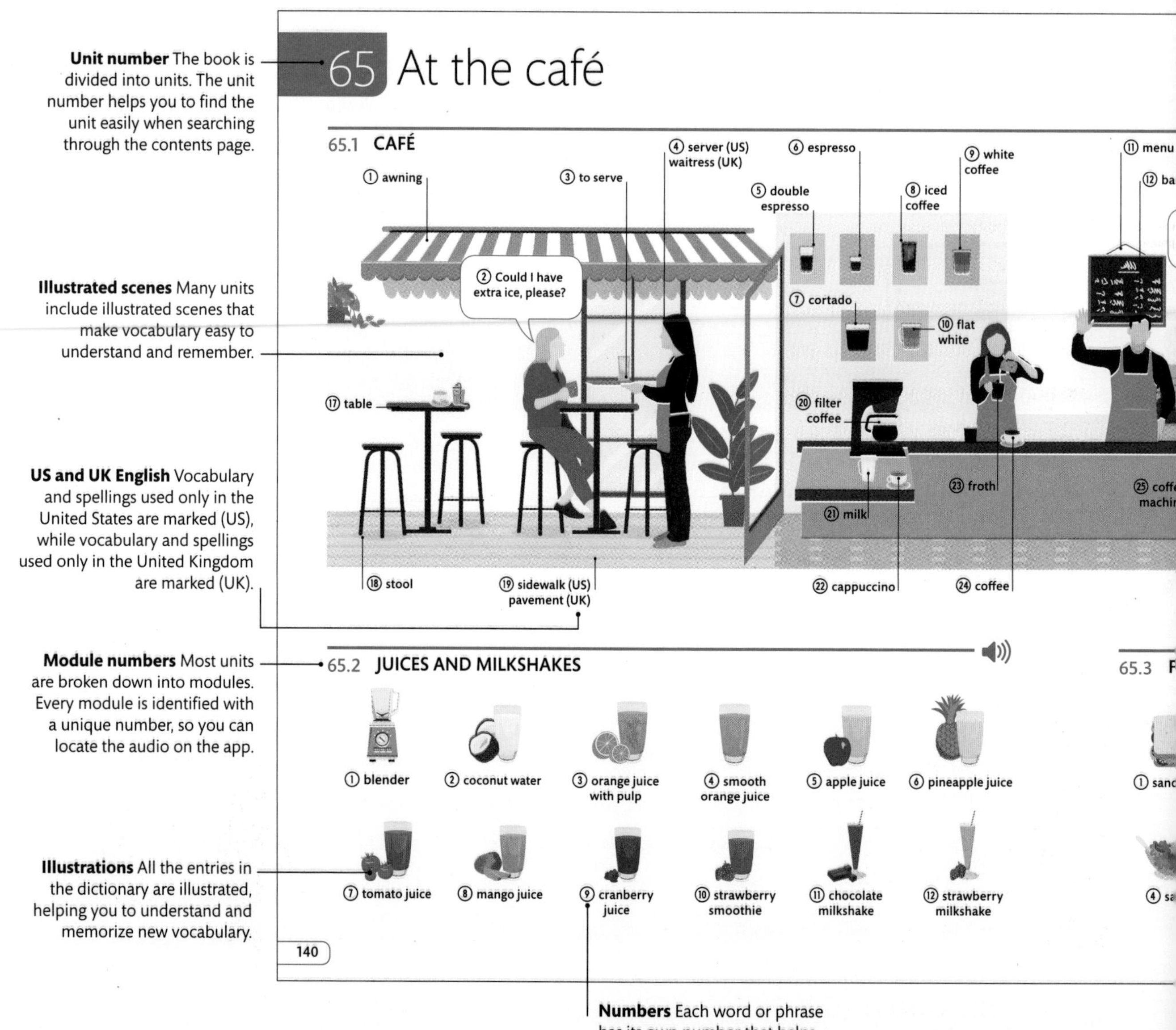

65 At the café
65.1 CAFÉ
① awning
② Could I have extra ice, please?
③ to serve
④ server (US) waitress (UK)
⑤ double espresso
⑥ espresso
⑦ cortado
⑧ iced coffee
⑨ white coffee
⑩ flat white
⑪ menu
⑰ table
⑱ stool
⑲ sidewalk (US) pavement (UK)
⑳ filter coffee
㉑ milk
㉒ cappuccino
㉓ froth
㉔ coffee
65.2 JUICES AND MILKSHAKES
① blender
② coconut water
③ orange juice with pulp
④ smooth orange juice
⑤ apple juice
⑥ pineapple juice
⑦ tomato juice
⑧ mango juice
⑨ cranberry juice
⑩ strawberry smoothie
⑪ chocolate milkshake
⑫ strawberry milkshake
65.3
140

Unit number The book is divided into units. The unit number helps you to find the unit easily when searching through the contents page.

Illustrated scenes Many units include illustrated scenes that make vocabulary easy to understand and remember.

US and UK English Vocabulary and spellings used only in the United States are marked (US), while vocabulary and spellings used only in the United Kingdom are marked (UK).

Module numbers Most units are broken down into modules. Every module is identified with a unique number, so you can locate the audio on the app.

Illustrations All the entries in the dictionary are illustrated, helping you to understand and memorize new vocabulary.

Numbers Each word or phrase has its own number that helps you to find the audio on the app.

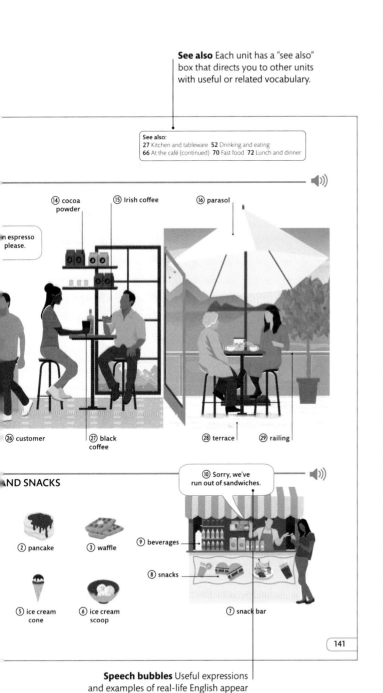

See also Each unit has a "see also" box that directs you to other units with useful or related vocabulary.

See also:
27 Kitchen and tableware 52 Drinking and eating
66 At the café (continued) 70 Fast food 72 Lunch and dinner

⑭ cocoa powder ⑮ Irish coffee ⑯ parasol

n espresso please.

㉖ customer ㉗ black coffee ㉘ terrace ㉙ railing

ND SNACKS

⑩ Sorry, we've run out of sandwiches.

② pancake ③ waffle ⑨ beverages

⑧ snacks

⑤ ice cream cone ⑥ ice cream scoop ⑦ snack bar

141

Speech bubbles Useful expressions and examples of real-life English appear in speech bubbles throughout the book.

Word list

The word list at the back of the book contains every entry from the dictionary. All the vocabulary is listed in alphabetical order, and each entry is followed by the unit number or numbers in which it is found. The part of speech (such as noun, verb, or adjective) is listed next to the word.

A

à la carte menu *n* **69**
A&E (UK) *n* **21, 50**
aardvark *n* **158**
ab wheel (US) *n* **124**
abandoned building (US) *n* **44**
abdomen *n* **01, 162**
abdominals *n* **03**
abilities *n* **11**
ability to drive *n* **93**
abseiling *n* **125**
Abyssinian *n* **164**
acacia *n* **47**
accelerator (UK) *n* **99**
access road *n* **106**
accessories *n* **16**
accident *n* **19**

Unit number The number in the word list matches the unit number in the dictionary.

Multiple units When an entry appears more than once, each unit number is listed.

Audio

English for Everyone: Illustrated Dictionary features extensive supporting audio resources. Every word and phrase in the dictionary is recorded, and you are encouraged to listen to the audio and repeat the words and phrases out loud, until you are confident you understand and can pronounce what has been said. The app can be found by searching for "DK English for Everyone".

FREE AUDIO
website and app
www.dkefe.com

Audio symbol This symbol indicates that audio recordings of the words and phrases in a module are available for you to listen to.

01 Parts of the body

1.1 THE HUMAN BODY

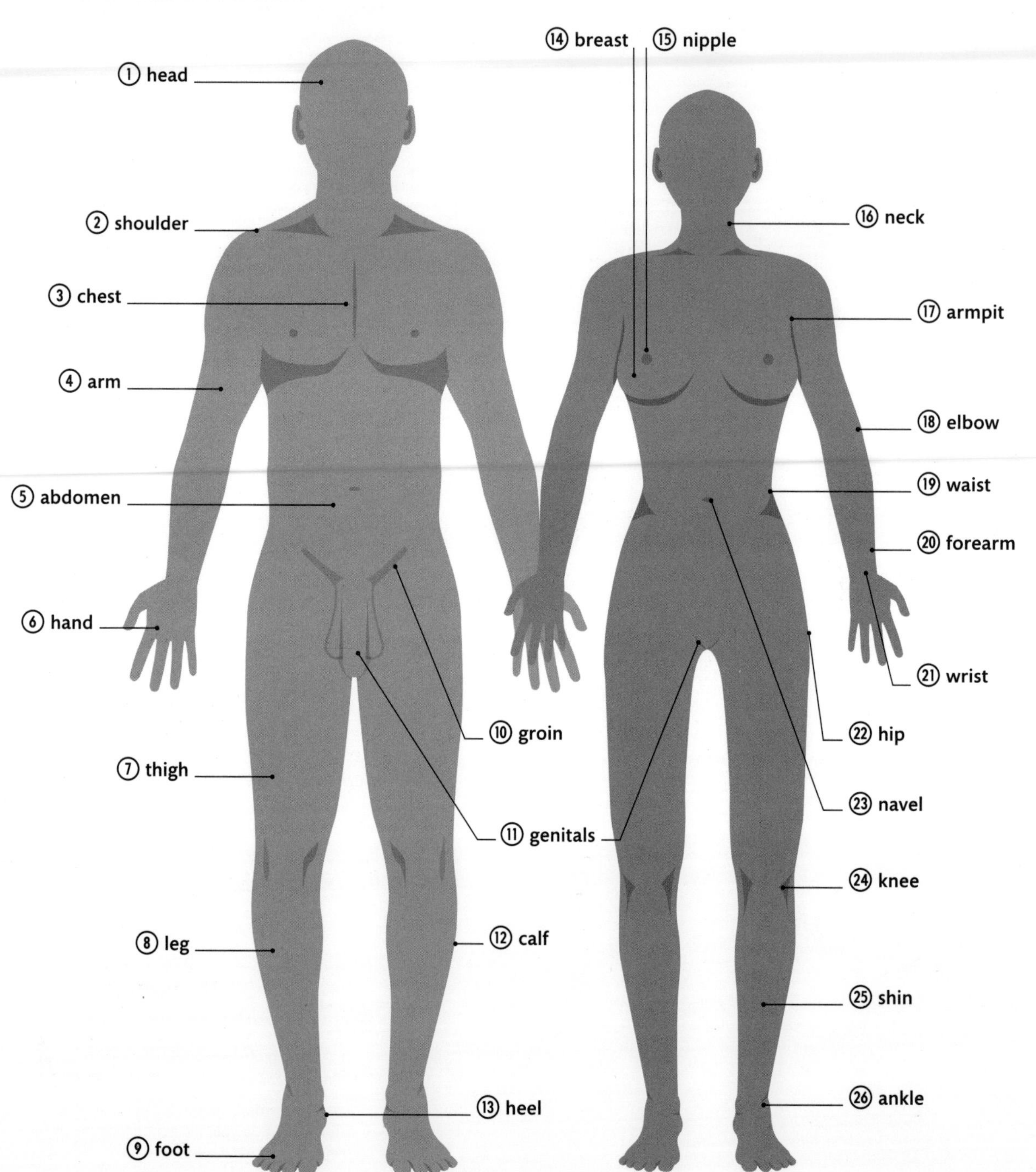

① head
② shoulder
③ chest
④ arm
⑤ abdomen
⑥ hand
⑦ thigh
⑧ leg
⑨ foot
⑩ groin
⑪ genitals
⑫ calf
⑬ heel
⑭ breast
⑮ nipple
⑯ neck
⑰ armpit
⑱ elbow
⑲ waist
⑳ forearm
㉑ wrist
㉒ hip
㉓ navel
㉔ knee
㉕ shin
㉖ ankle

See also:
02 Hands and feet **03** Muscles and skeleton **04** Internal organs
19 Illness and injury **20** Visiting the doctor **22** The dentist and optician

1.2 FACE

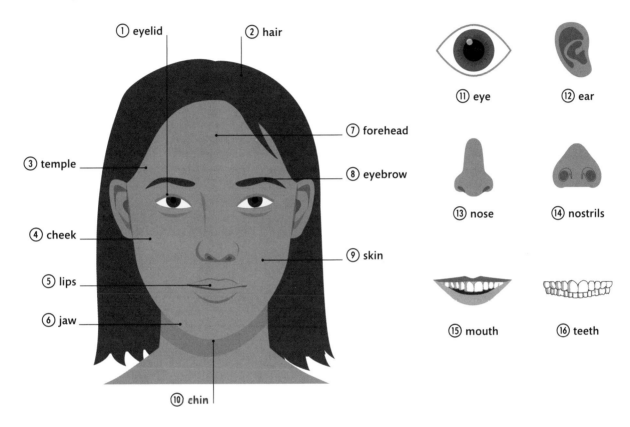

① **eyelid**
② **hair**
③ **temple**
④ **cheek**
⑤ **lips**
⑥ **jaw**
⑦ **forehead**
⑧ **eyebrow**
⑨ **skin**
⑩ **chin**
⑪ **eye**
⑫ **ear**
⑬ **nose**
⑭ **nostrils**
⑮ **mouth**
⑯ **teeth**

1.3 EYES

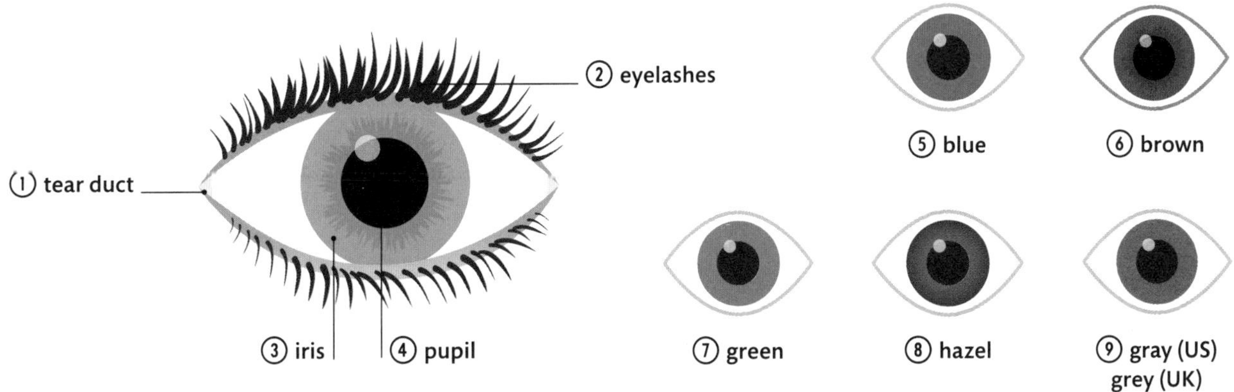
① tear duct
② eyelashes
③ iris
④ pupil
⑤ blue
⑥ brown
⑦ green
⑧ hazel
⑨ gray (US)
grey (UK)

02 Hands and feet

2.1 HANDS

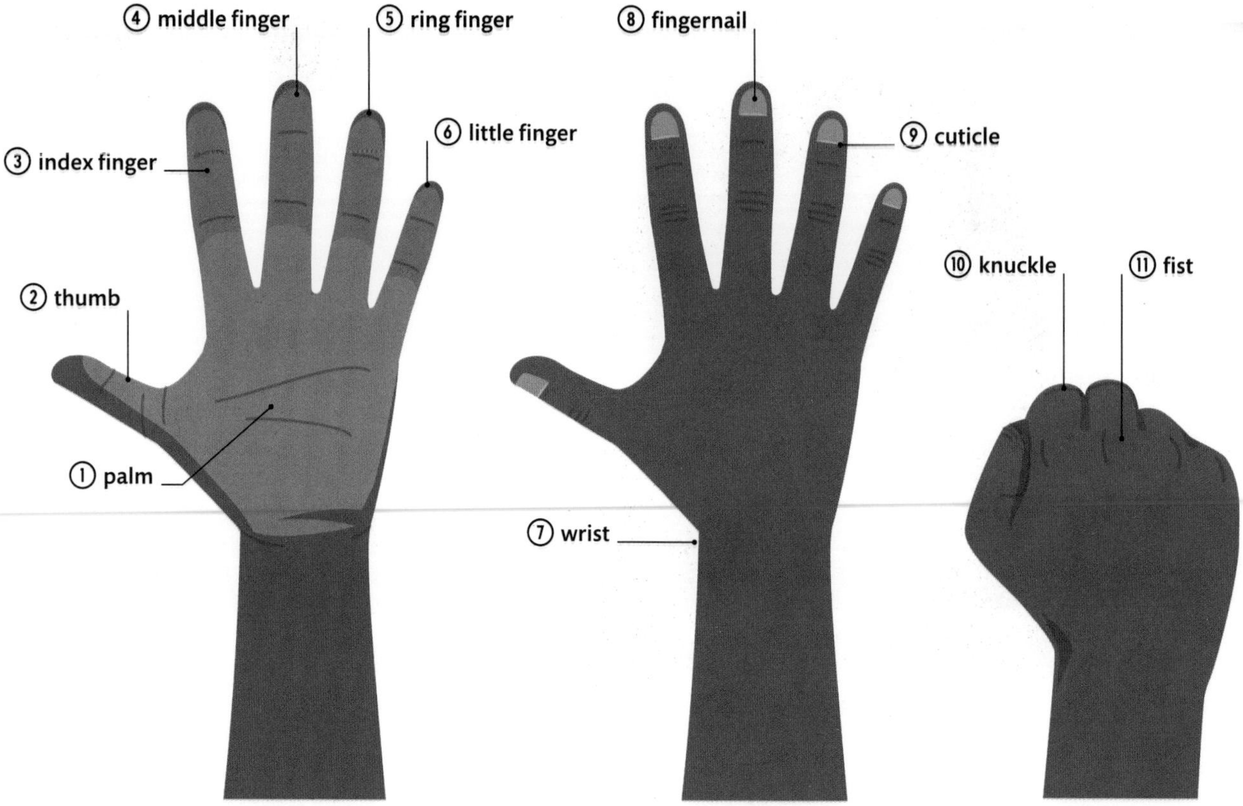

① palm
② thumb
③ index finger
④ middle finger
⑤ ring finger
⑥ little finger
⑦ wrist
⑧ fingernail
⑨ cuticle
⑩ knuckle
⑪ fist

2.2 BODY VERBS

① to smile

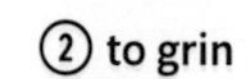
② to grin

③ to frown

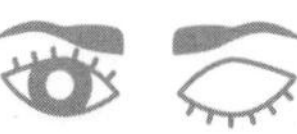
④ to wink

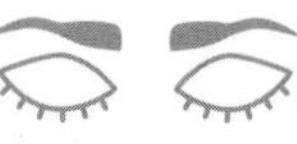
⑤ to blink

⑥ to blush

⑦ to yawn

⑧ to snore

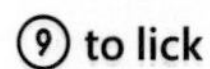
⑨ to lick

⑩ to suck

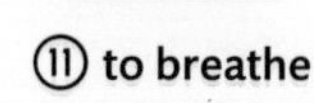
⑪ to breathe

⑫ to hold your breath

See also:
01 Parts of the body **03** Muscles and skeleton
19 Illness and injury **20** Visiting the doctor **21** The hospital

2.3 FEET

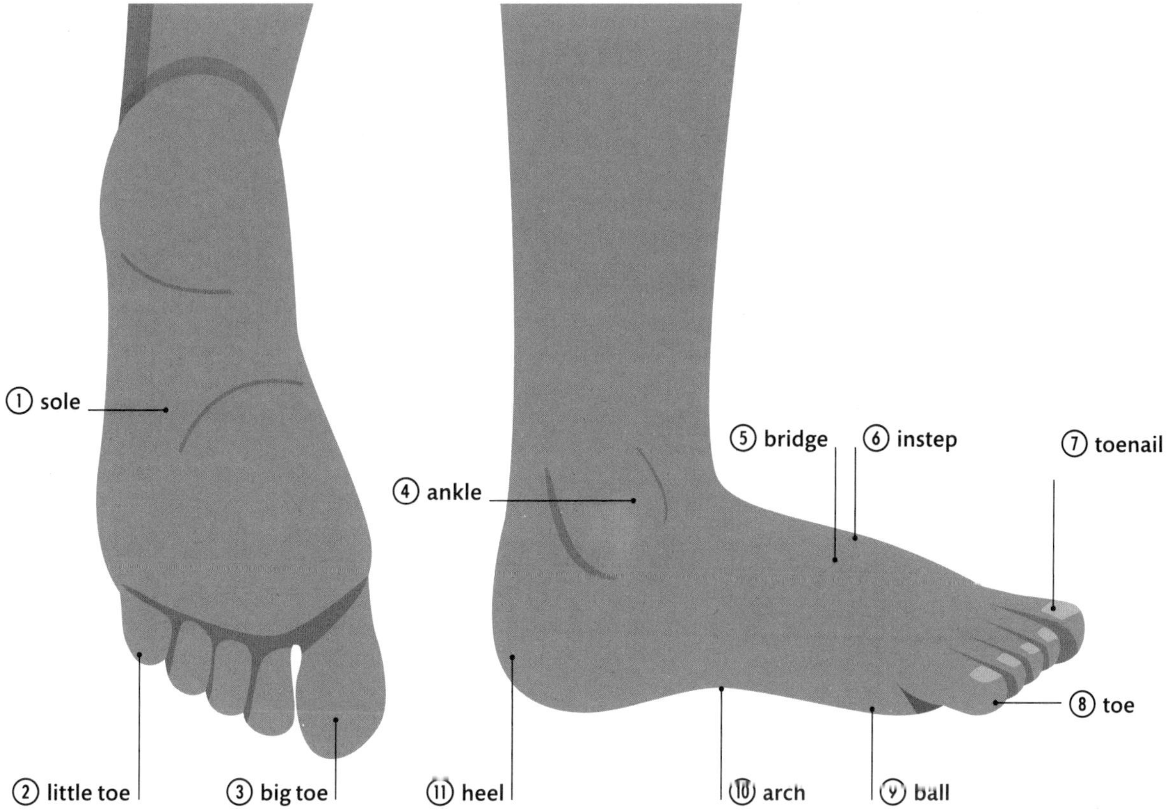

1. sole
2. little toe
3. big toe
4. ankle
5. bridge
6. instep
7. toenail
8. toe
9. ball
10. arch
11. heel

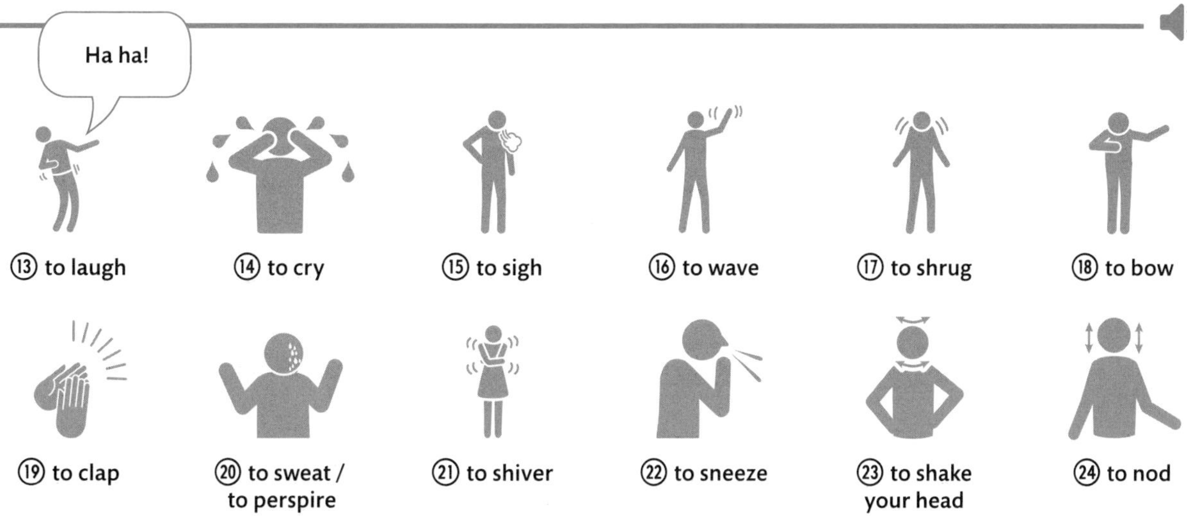

Ha ha!

13. to laugh

14. to cry

15. to sigh

16. to wave

17. to shrug

18. to bow

19. to clap

20. to sweat / to perspire

21. to shiver

22. to sneeze

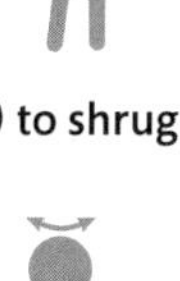

23. to shake your head

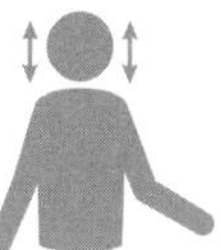

24. to nod

03 Muscles and skeleton

3.1 MUSCLES

3.2 TEETH

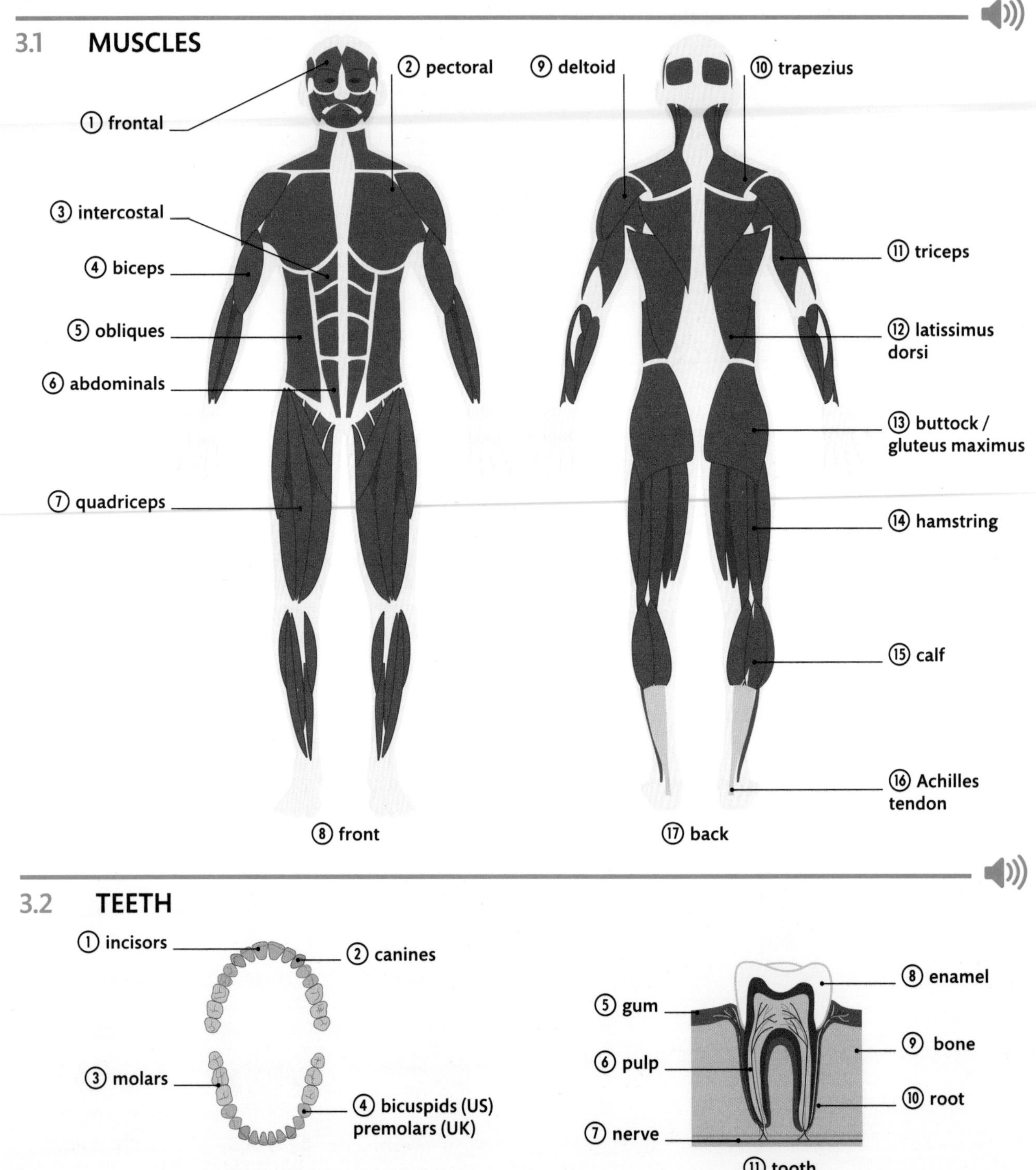

① frontal
② pectoral
③ intercostal
④ biceps
⑤ obliques
⑥ abdominals
⑦ quadriceps
⑧ front
⑨ deltoid
⑩ trapezius
⑪ triceps
⑫ latissimus dorsi
⑬ buttock / gluteus maximus
⑭ hamstring
⑮ calf
⑯ Achilles tendon
⑰ back
① incisors
② canines
③ molars
④ bicuspids (US) premolars (UK)
⑤ gum
⑥ pulp
⑦ nerve
⑧ enamel
⑨ bone
⑩ root
⑪ tooth

See also:
01 Parts of the body **02** Hands and feet **04** Internal organs
19 Illness and injury **20** Visiting the doctor **21** The hospital

3.3 SKELETON

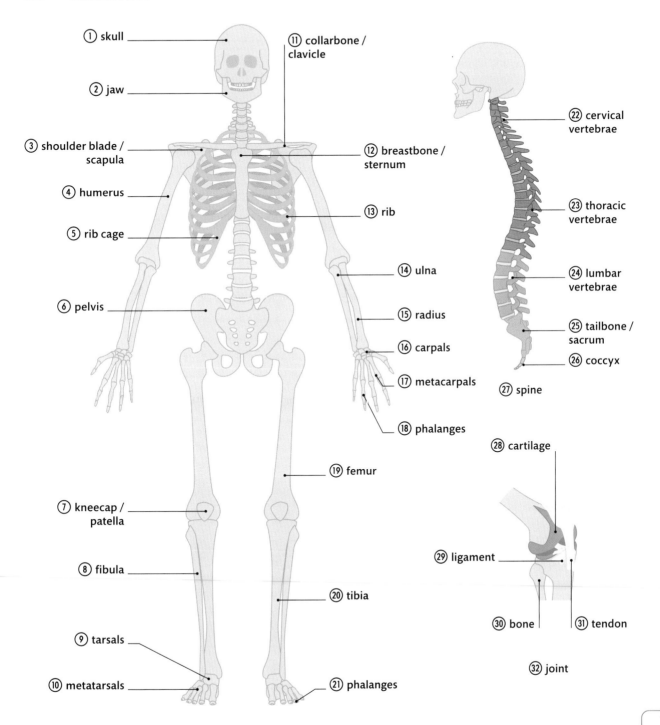

① skull
② jaw
③ shoulder blade / scapula
④ humerus
⑤ rib cage
⑥ pelvis
⑦ kneecap / patella
⑧ fibula
⑨ tarsals
⑩ metatarsals
⑪ collarbone / clavicle
⑫ breastbone / sternum
⑬ rib
⑭ ulna
⑮ radius
⑯ carpals
⑰ metacarpals
⑱ phalanges
⑲ femur
⑳ tibia
㉑ phalanges
㉒ cervical vertebrae
㉓ thoracic vertebrae
㉔ lumbar vertebrae
㉕ tailbone / sacrum
㉖ coccyx
㉗ spine
㉘ cartilage
㉙ ligament
㉚ bone
㉛ tendon
㉜ joint

04 Internal organs

4.1 INTERNAL ORGANS

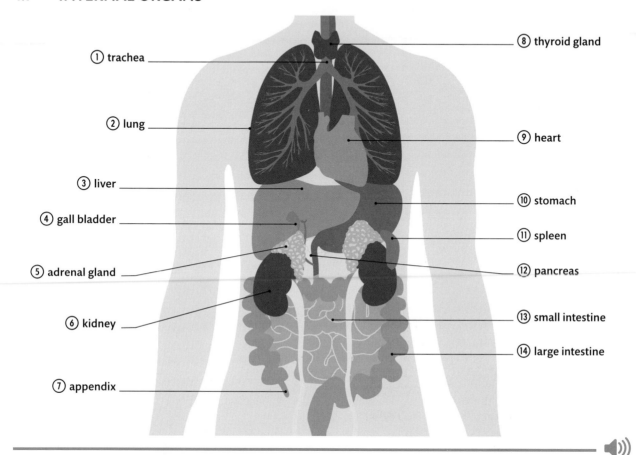

① trachea
② lung
③ liver
④ gall bladder
⑤ adrenal gland
⑥ kidney
⑦ appendix
⑧ thyroid gland
⑨ heart
⑩ stomach
⑪ spleen
⑫ pancreas
⑬ small intestine
⑭ large intestine

4.2 BODY SYSTEMS

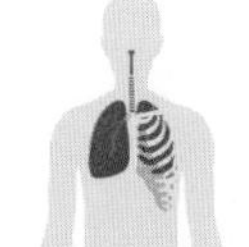
① respiratory

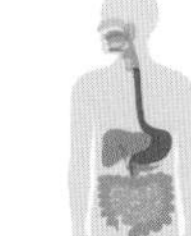
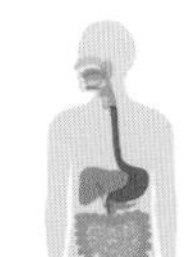
② digestive

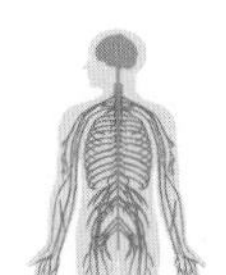
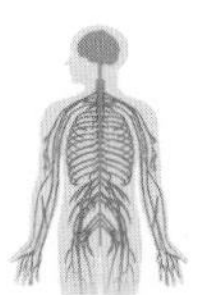
③ nervous

④ urinary

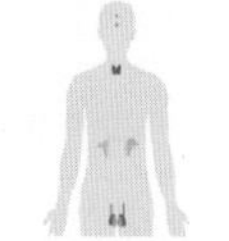
⑤ endocrine

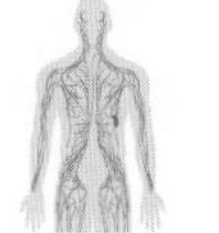
⑥ lymphatic

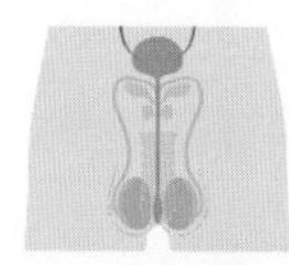
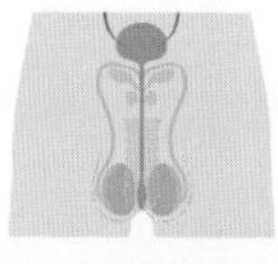
⑦ reproductive

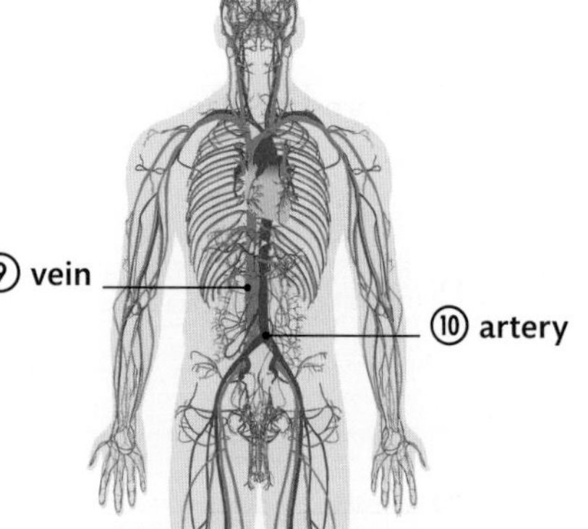
⑨ vein
⑩ artery
⑧ cardiovascular

See also:
01 Parts of the body **03** Muscles and skeleton
19 Illness and injury **20** Visiting the doctor **21** The hospital

4.3 HEAD

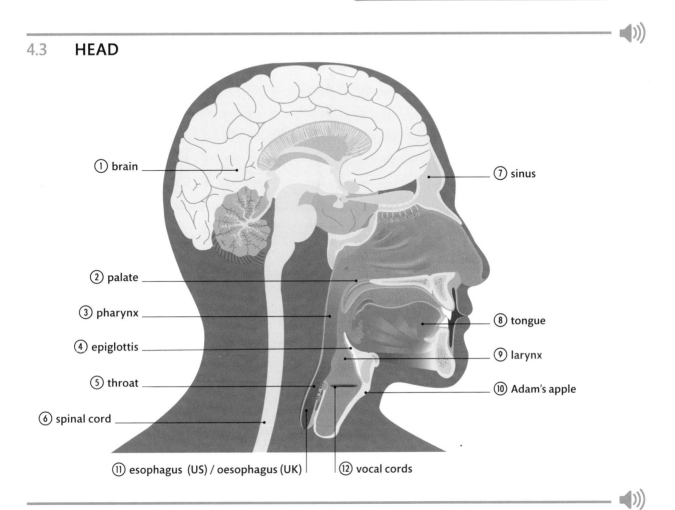

① brain
② palate
③ pharynx
④ epiglottis
⑤ throat
⑥ spinal cord
⑦ sinus
⑧ tongue
⑨ larynx
⑩ Adam's apple
⑪ esophagus (US) / oesophagus (UK)
⑫ vocal cords

4.4 REPRODUCTIVE ORGANS

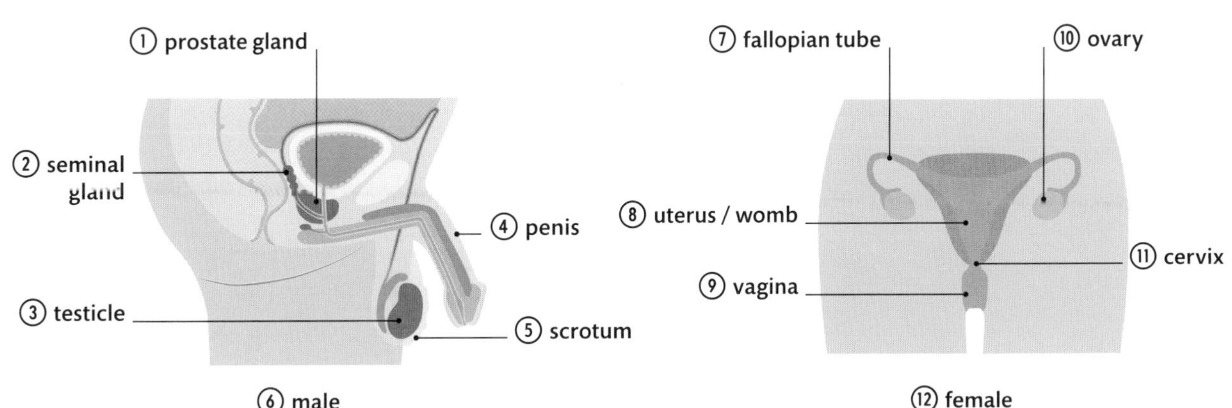
① prostate gland
② seminal gland
③ testicle
④ penis
⑤ scrotum
⑥ male
⑦ fallopian tube
⑧ uterus / womb
⑨ vagina
⑩ ovary
⑪ cervix
⑫ female

05 Family

5.1 CARLO'S FAMILY

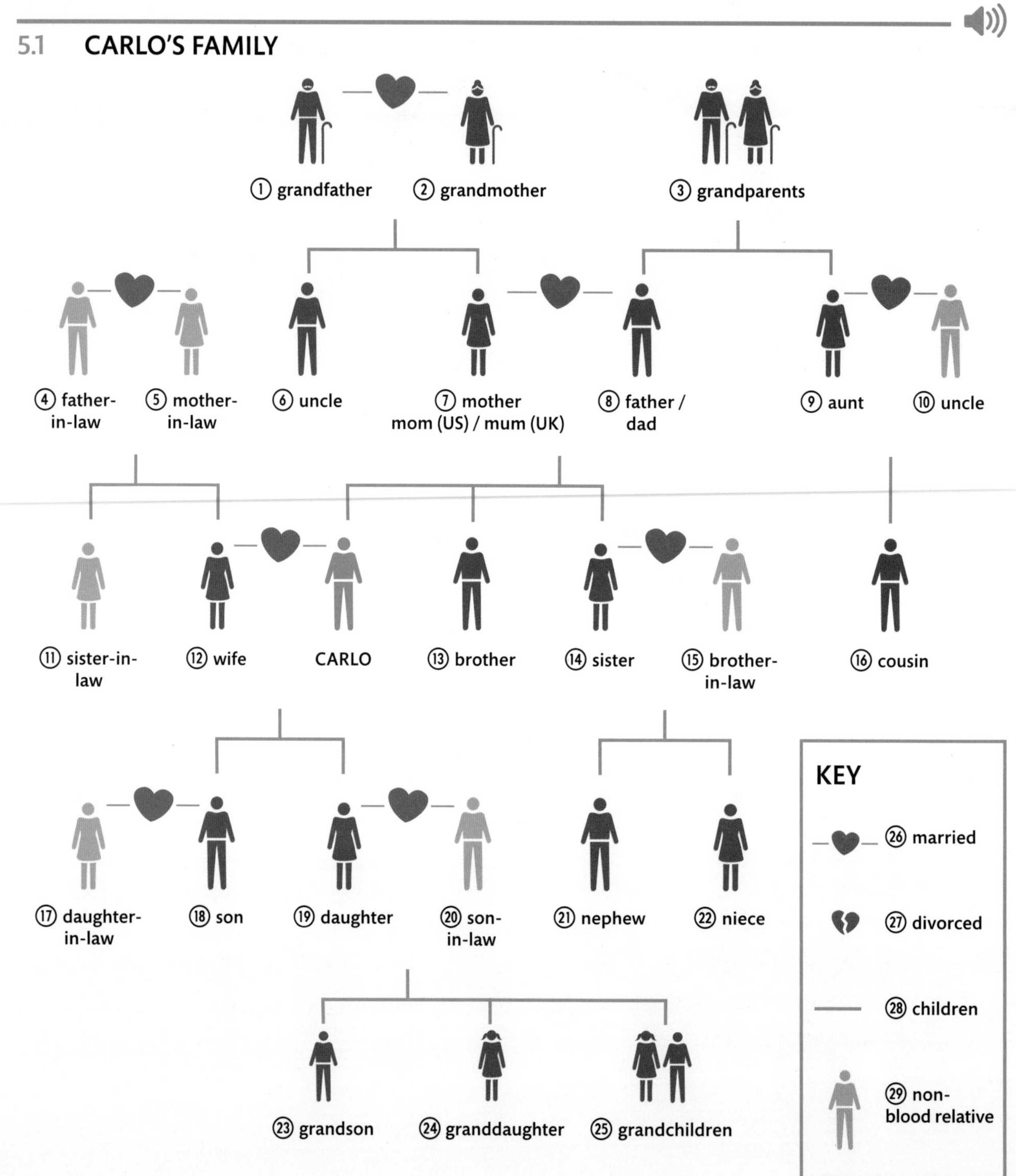

① grandfather
② grandmother
③ grandparents
④ father-in-law
⑤ mother-in-law
⑥ uncle
⑦ mother
mom (US) / mum (UK)
⑧ father / dad
⑨ aunt
⑩ uncle
⑪ sister-in-law
⑫ wife
CARLO
⑬ brother
⑭ sister
⑮ brother-in-law
⑯ cousin
⑰ daughter-in-law
⑱ son
⑲ daughter
⑳ son-in-law
㉑ nephew
㉒ niece
㉓ grandson
㉔ granddaughter
㉕ grandchildren
KEY
㉖ married
㉗ divorced
㉘ children
㉙ non-blood relative

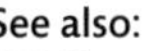

See also:
07 Life events
08 Pregnancy and childhood

5.2 SARAH'S FAMILY

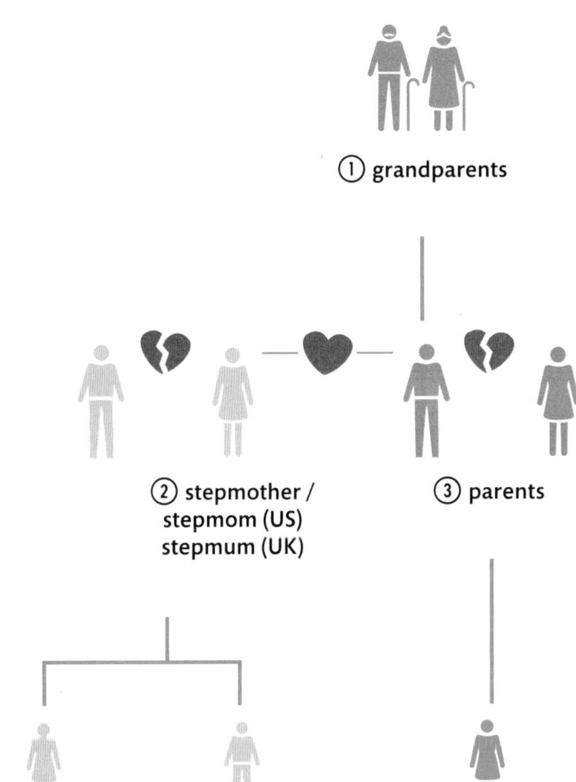
① grandparents
② stepmother / stepmom (US) stepmum (UK)
③ parents
④ stepsister
⑤ stepbrother
SARAH

5.3 RELATIONSHIPS

① boyfriend / girlfriend

② partner

③ single parent

④ widow

⑥ husband
⑦ wife

⑤ married

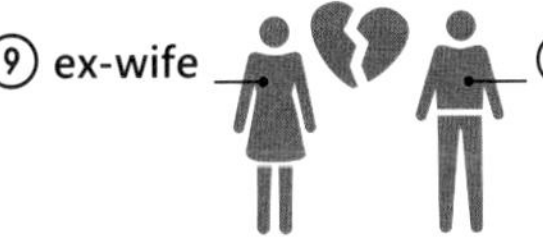
⑨ ex-wife
⑩ ex-husband

⑧ divorced

⑪ siblings

⑫ twins

⑬ triplets

⑭ only child

5.4 GROWING UP

① baby

② toddler

④ girl
⑤ boy

③ child

⑥ teenagers

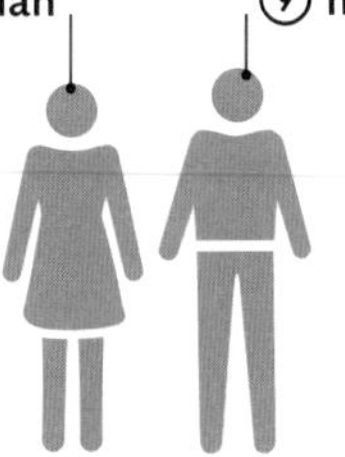
⑧ woman
⑨ man

⑦ adults

⑩ elderly

06 Feelings and moods

6.1 FEELINGS AND MOODS

① pleased

② cheerful

③ happy

④ delighted

⑤ ecstatic

Ha Ha!
⑥ amused

⑦ grateful

⑧ lucky

⑨ interested

?
⑩ curious

??
⑪ intrigued

⑫ amazed

⑬ surprised

⑭ proud

⑮ excited

⑯ thrilled

⑰ calm

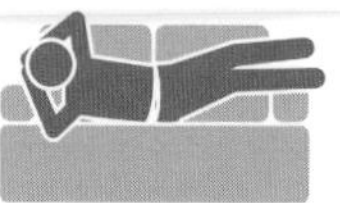
⑱ relaxed

⑳ Thank you. I really enjoyed the meal.

⑲ appreciative

㉑ confident

㉒ hopeful

㉓ sympathetic

㉔ annoyed

㉕ jealous

㉖ embarrassed

See also:
10 Personality traits **24** Healthy body, healthy mind
93 Workplace skills

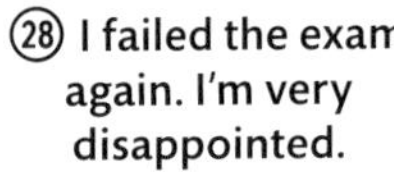
(28) I failed the exam again. I'm very disappointed.

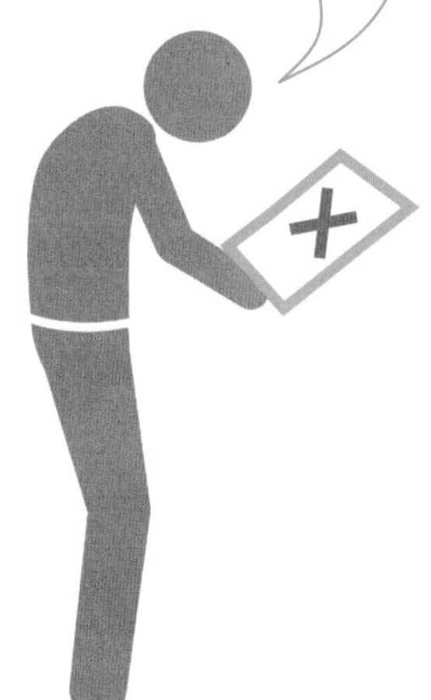
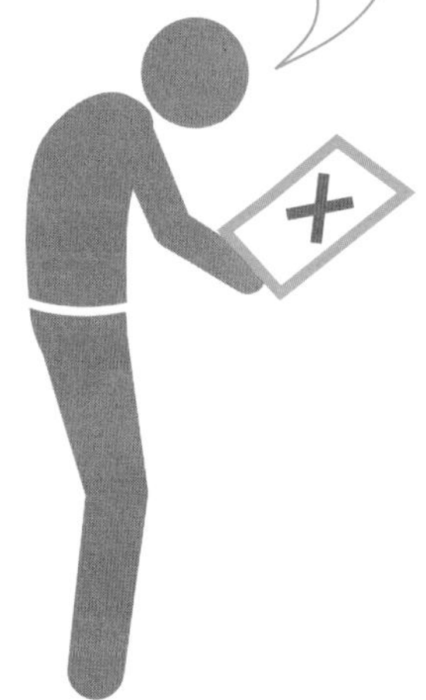
(27) disappointed

(29) worried

(30) anxious

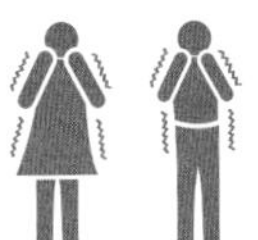
(31) nervous

(32) frightened

(33) scared

(34) terrified

(35) sad

(36) unhappy

(37) tearful

(38) miserable

(39) depressed

(40) lonely

(41) irritated

(42) frustrated

(43) angry / mad (US)

(44) furious

(45) disgusted

(46) unenthusiastic

(47) tired

z z z
(48) exhausted

?
(49) confused

(50) bored

(51) distracted

(52) serious

?
(53) indifferent

(54) stressed

(55) guilty

(56) unimpressed

(57) upset

(58) shocked

07 Life events

7.1 RELATIONSHIPS

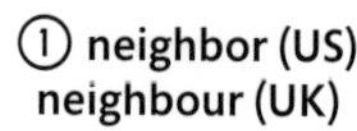

① neighbor (US) neighbour (UK)

② friend

③ acquaintance

④ colleague

⑤ pen pal

⑥ couple

⑦ best friend

⑧ partner

⑨ Will you marry me?

⑩ fiancée

⑪ fiancé

⑫ engaged couple

⑬ bride

⑭ groom

⑮ married couple

7.2 LIFE EVENTS

① to be born

② birth certificate

③ to go to preschool (US) to go to nursery (UK)

④ to start school

⑤ to make friends

⑥ to win a prize

⑦ to graduate

⑧ to emigrate

⑨ to get a job

⑩ to fall in love

⑪ to get married

See also:
05 Family 08 Pregnancy and childhood 19 Illness and injury 73 At school
80 At college 92 Applying for a job 131 Travel and accommodation

7.3 FESTIVALS AND CELEBRATIONS

① birthday

② present

③ birthday card

④ Christmas

⑤ New Year

⑥ carnival

⑦ Thanksgiving

⑧ Easter

⑨ Halloween

⑩ Kwanzaa

⑪ Passover

⑫ Diwali

⑬ Day of the Dead

⑭ Eid al-Fitr

⑮ Holi

⑯ Hanukkah

⑰ Baisakhi / Vaisakhi

⑫ wedding

⑬ honeymoon

⑭ anniversary

⑮ to have a baby

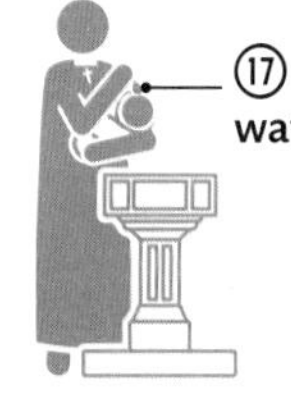
⑰ holy water
⑯ christening / baptism

⑱ bar mitzvah / bat mitzvah

⑲ to go on Hajj

⑳ to retire

㉑ divorce

㉒ to write a will (US) to make a will (UK)

㉓ to die

㉔ funeral

08 Pregnancy and childhood

8.1 PREGNANCY AND CHILDBIRTH

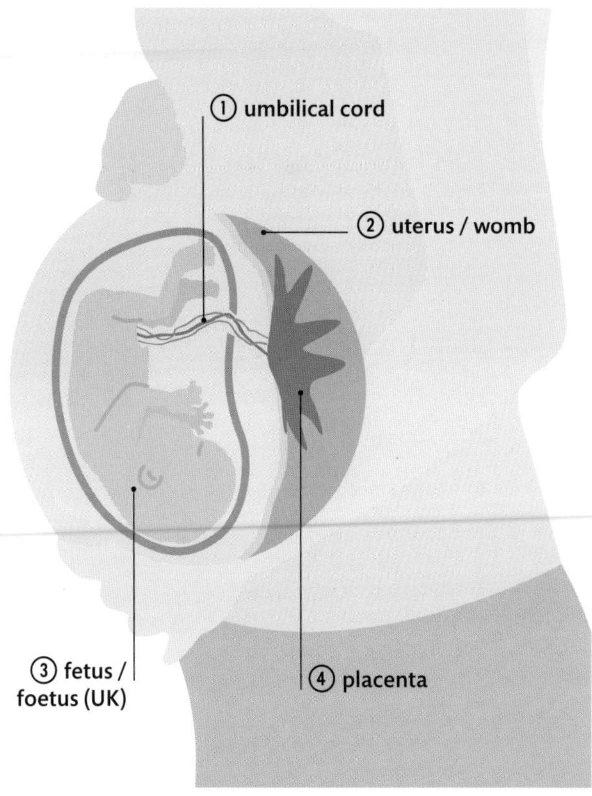

① umbilical cord
② uterus / womb
③ fetus / foetus (UK)
④ placenta

⑤ pregnancy test

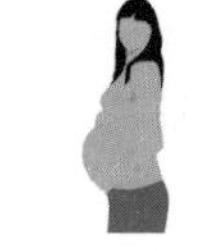
⑥ pregnant

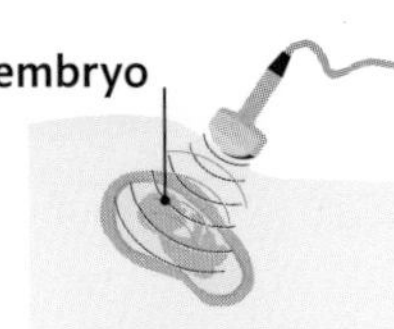

⑧ embryo

⑦ ultrasound

⑨ due date

⑩ midwife

⑪ obstetrician

⑫ birth

⑬ newborn baby

⑭ vaccination

⑮ incubator

8.2 TOYS AND GAMES

① doll

② dollhouse (US) doll's house (UK)

③ plush toy (US) soft toy (UK)

④ board game

⑤ building blocks / building bricks

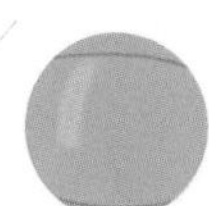
⑥ ball

⑦ top (US) spinning top (UK)

⑧ yo-yo

⑨ jump rope (US) skipping rope (UK)

⑩ trampoline

⑪ jigsaw puzzle

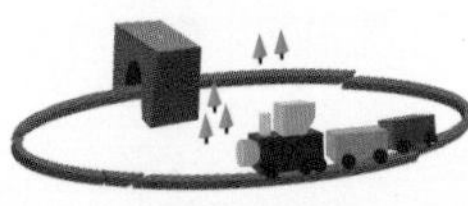
⑫ train set

See also:
05 Family **13** Clothes **20** Visiting the doctor
21 The hospital **30** Bedroom

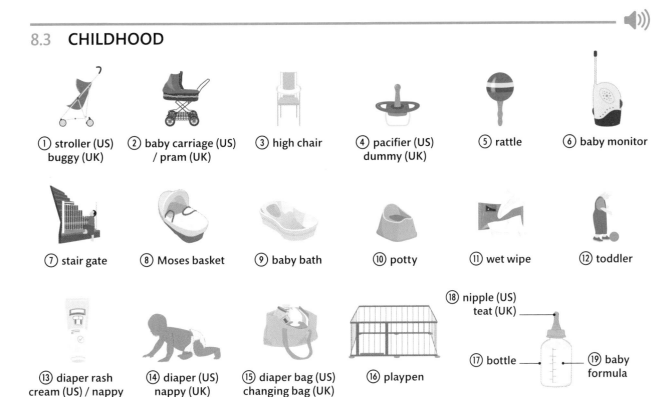

8.3 CHILDHOOD

1. stroller (US) buggy (UK)
2. baby carriage (US) / pram (UK)
3. high chair
4. pacifier (US) dummy (UK)
5. rattle
6. baby monitor
7. stair gate
8. Moses basket
9. baby bath
10. potty
11. wet wipe
12. toddler
13. diaper rash cream (US) / nappy rash cream (UK)
14. diaper (US) nappy (UK)
15. diaper bag (US) changing bag (UK)
16. playpen
17. bottle
18. nipple (US) teat (UK)
19. baby formula

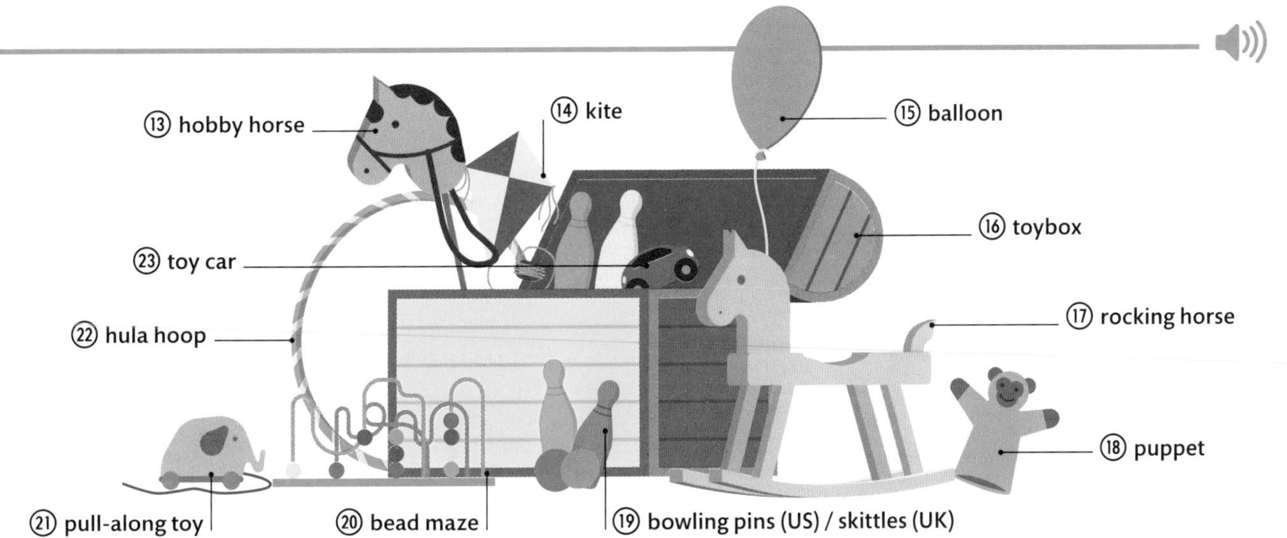
13 hobby horse
14 kite
15 balloon
16 toybox
23 toy car
17 rocking horse
22 hula hoop
18 puppet
21 pull-along toy
20 bead maze
19 bowling pins (US) / skittles (UK)

09 Daily routines

9.1 MORNING AND AFTERNOON

① alarm goes off

② to wake up

③ to get up

④ to take (or have) a shower

⑤ to take (or have) a bath

⑥ to put on makeup

⑦ to shave

⑧ to wash your hair

⑨ to dry your hair

⑩ to iron a shirt

⑪ to get dressed

⑫ to brush your teeth

⑬ to wash your face

⑭ to brush your hair

⑮ to make the bed

⑯ to have (or eat) breakfast

⑰ to pack your lunch

⑱ to leave the house

⑲ to go to work

⑳ to go to school

㉑ to drive

㉒ to catch the bus

㉓ to catch the train

㉔ to read a newspaper

㉕ to arrive

㉖ to arrive early

㉗ to arrive on time

㉜ I'm sorry I'm late again.

㉛ to arrive late / to be late

㉘ to have (or eat) lunch

㉙ to check your emails

㉚ to take a break (US) to have a break (UK)

See also:
11 Abilities and actions 29 Cooking 81 At work
82 In the office 171 Time 178 Common phrasal verbs

9.2 EVENING

① to finish work

④ There's no place like home!

② to leave work

③ to work overtime

⑤ to arrive home

⑥ to cook dinner

⑦ to have (or eat) dinner

⑧ to clear the table

⑨ to do the dishes (US) to wash up (UK)

⑩ to listen to the radio

⑪ to watch TV

⑫ to drink tea or coffee

⑬ to take out the trash (US) / rubbish (UK)

⑭ to put the children to bed

⑮ to go to bed

⑯ to set the alarm

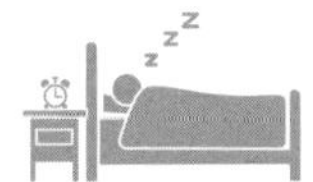
⑰ to go to sleep

9.3 OTHER ACTIVITIES

① to do homework

② to walk the dog

③ to feed the dog / cat

④ to buy groceries

⑤ to go out with friends

⑥ to go to a café

⑦ to call a friend / to call your family

⑧ to mow the lawn

⑨ to exercise

⑩ to play with your kids

⑪ to pay the bills

⑫ to take a nap

⑬ to clean the car

⑭ to play a musical instrument

⑮ to chat with friends

⑯ to chat online

⑰ to water the plants

⑱ to send a package / to send a parcel (UK)

10 Personality traits

10.1 DESCRIBING PERSONALITIES

① friendly

② unfriendly

③ talkative

④ enthusiastic

⑤ serious

⑥ assertive

⑦ critical

⑧ caring

⑨ sensitive

⑩ insensitive

⑪ reasonable

⑫ unreasonable

⑬ kind

⑭ unkind

⑮ secretive

⑯ mature

⑰ immature

⑱ cautious

⑲ generous

⑳ brave

Ha Ha!
Ha Ha!
㉑ funny

㉒ mean

㉓ patient

㉔ impatient

㉕ lazy

㉖ optimistic

㉗ outgoing

㉘ passionate

㉙ polite

㉚ rude

㉛ shy

㉜ intelligent

㉝ nervous

㉞ confident

㉟ silly

㊱ selfish

See also:
05 Family 06 Feelings and moods
11 Abilities and actions 93 Workplace skills

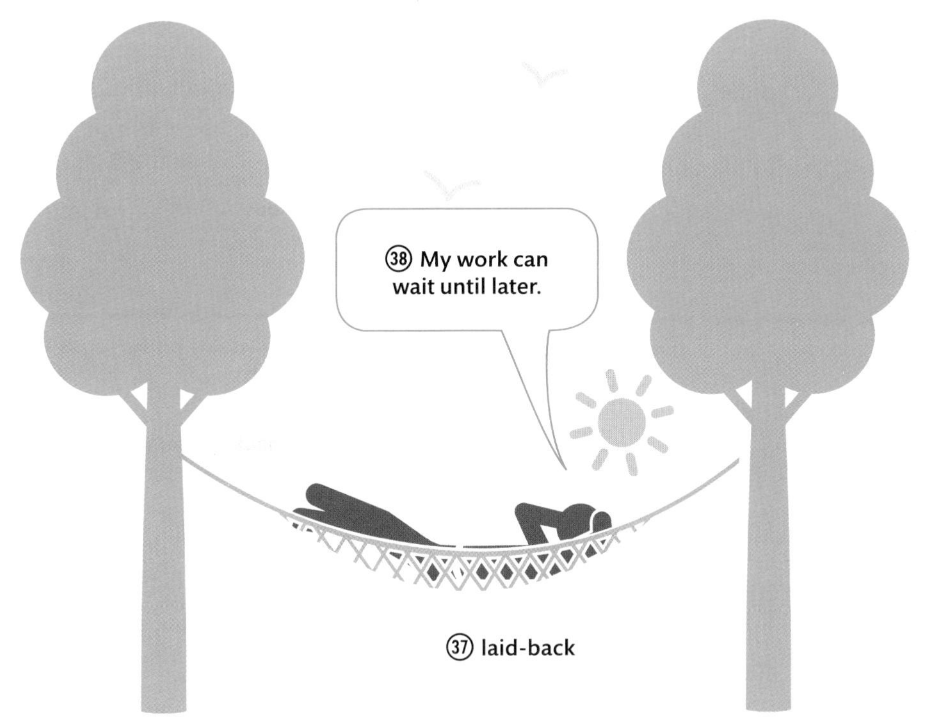
38 My work can wait until later.

37 laid-back

39 ambitious

40 spontaneous

41 romantic

42 calm

43 eccentric

44 honest

45 dishonest

46 supportive

47 impulsive

48 reliable

49 unreliable

50 talented

51 arrogant

52 considerate

53 adventurous

54 approachable

55 unapproachable

56 decisive

57 meticulous

58 clumsy

59 thoughtless

11 Abilities and actions

11.1 DESCRIBING ABILITIES AND ACTIONS

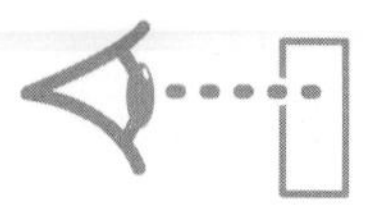
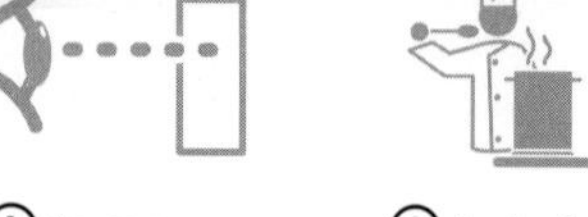

⑩ I love to dance.
⑪ Me too!

① to see 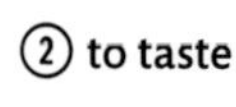 ② to taste 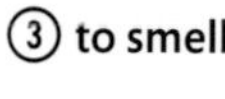 ③ to smell ④ to crawl

⑤ to hit ⑥ to play ⑦ to kick ⑧ to throw ⑨ to dance

⑫ to catch ⑬ to run ⑭ to hop ⑮ to jump ⑯ to creep ⑰ to shake

⑱ to work ⑲ to blow ⑳ to make (a snowman) ㉑ to spell ㉒ to do (homework) ㉓ to copy

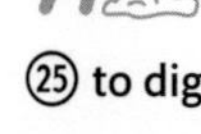

㉔ to build ㉕ to dig ㉖ to repair ㉗ to fix ㉘ to sit down ㉙ to stand up

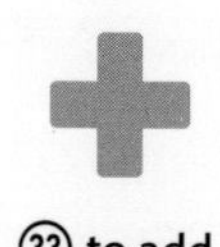

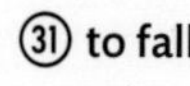

㉚ to understand ㉛ to fall ㉜ to lift ㉝ to add ㉞ to subtract ㉟ to count

See also:
09 Daily routines **93** Workplace skills
178 Common phrasal verbs

(36) to listen

(37) to talk

(38) to speak

(39) to shout

(40) to sing

(41) to act

(42) to whisper

(43) to think

(44) to decide

(45) to remember

(46) to forget

(47) to help

(48) to point

(49) to pack

(50) to unpack

(51) to fly

(52) to ride

(53) to climb

(54) to lick

(55) to take

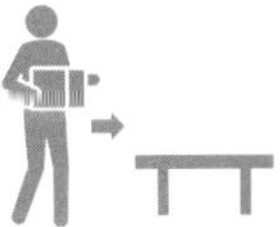
(56) to bring

(57) to pick up / to collect (UK)

(58) to enter

(59) to exit

(60) to win

(61) to raise

(62) to carry

(63) to juggle

(64) to hold

(65) to move

(66) to push

(67) to pull

12 Appearance and hair

12.1 GENERAL APPEARANCE

① medium height
② tall
③ short

④ beautiful

⑤ handsome

⑥ young

⑦ middle-aged

⑧ old

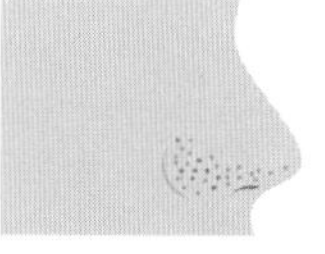

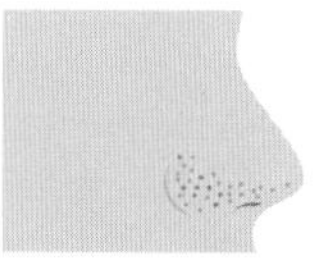

⑨ pores

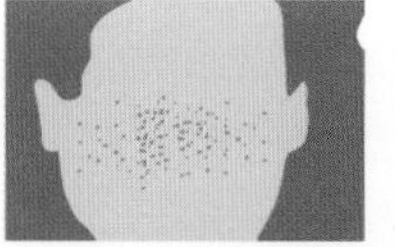

⑩ freckles

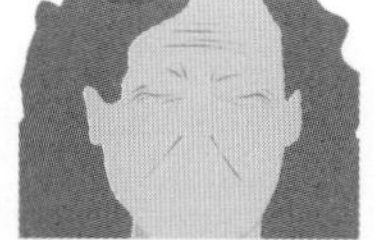

⑪ wrinkles

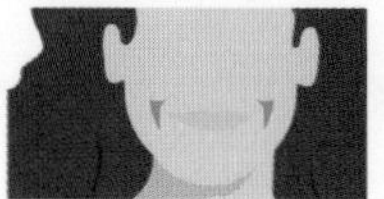

⑫ dimples

⑬ mole

12.2 HAIR

① to style your hair

② to wash your hair

③ to have (or get) your hair cut

④ to tie your hair back

JUNE

⑤ to grow your hair

⑥ to shave

⑦ long hair

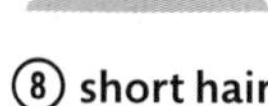

⑧ short hair

⑨ shoulder-length hair

⑩ side part (US) side parting (UK)

⑪ center part (US) centre parting (UK)

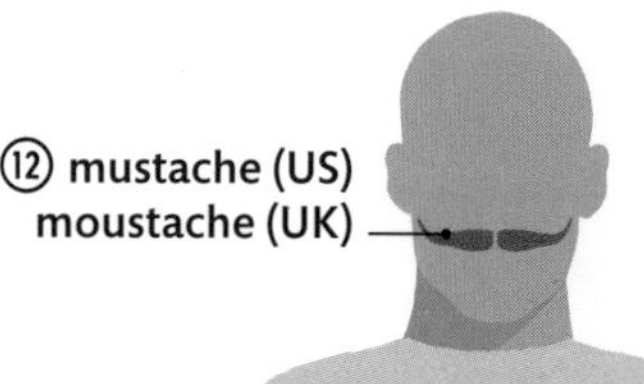

⑫ mustache (US) moustache (UK)

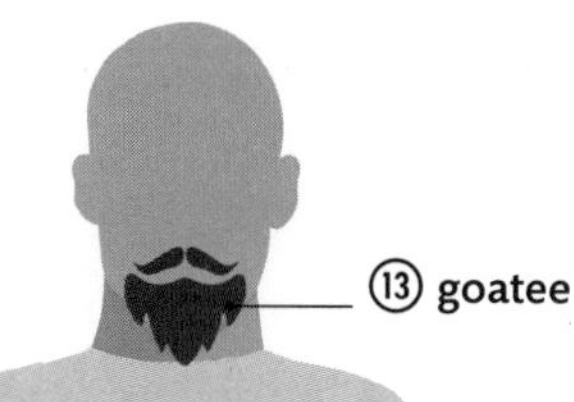

⑬ goatee

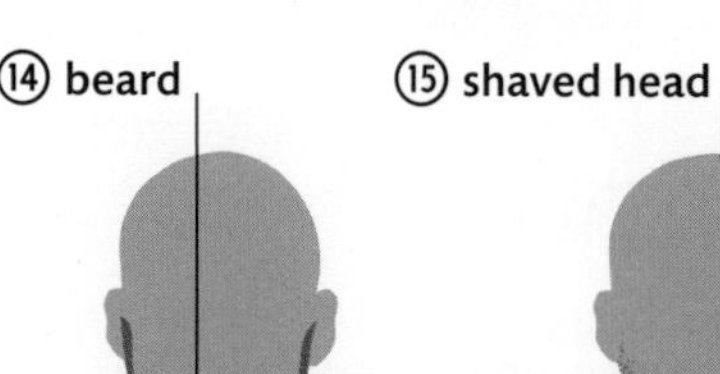

⑭ beard
⑮ shaved head
⑯ stubble

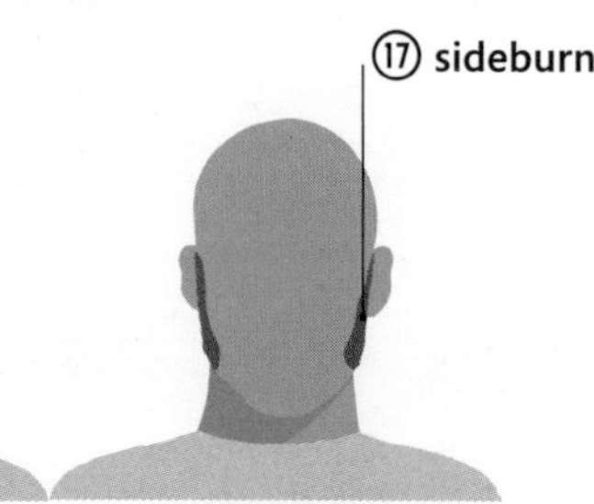

⑰ sideburns

⑱ facial hair

See also:
13-15 Clothes 16 Accessories
17 Shoes 18 Beauty

⑲ crew cut

⑳ bald

㉑ straight hair

㉒ wavy hair

㉓ curly hair

㉔ frizzy hair

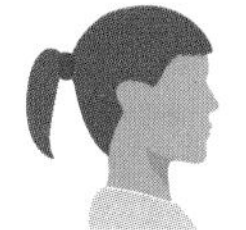
㉕ ponytail

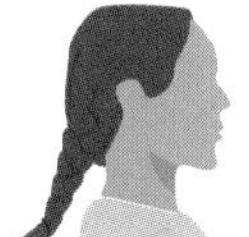
㉖ braid (US)
plait (UK)

㉗ pigtails

㉘ bob

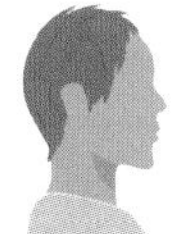
㉙ crop

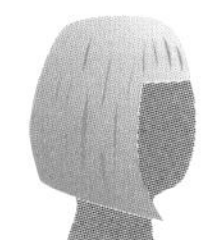
㉚ wig

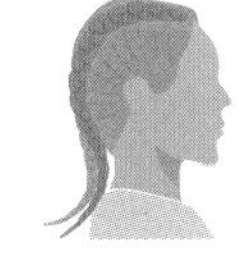
㉛ French braid (US)
French plait (UK)

㉜ bun

㉝ highlights

㉞ Afro

㉟ braids

㊱ cornrows

㊲ normal hair

㊳ greasy hair

㊴ dry hair

㊵ dandruff

㊶ hair gel

Hair Spray
㊷ hair spray

㊸ black hair

㊹ brown hair

㊺ blond / blonde hair

㊻ red hair

㊼ auburn hair

㊽ gray hair (US)
grey hair (UK)

㊾ straightening iron (US) / hair straightener (UK)

㊿ curling iron (US)
hair curler (UK)

(51) hairbrush

(52) comb

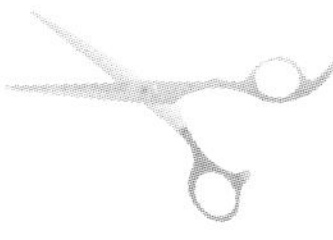
(53) hair scissors

(54) hair dryer

13 Clothes

13.1 DESCRIBING CLOTHES

① leather

② cotton

③ woolen (US)
woollen (UK)

④ silk

⑤ synthetic

⑥ denim

⑦ plain

⑧ striped

⑨ checkered (US)
checked (UK)

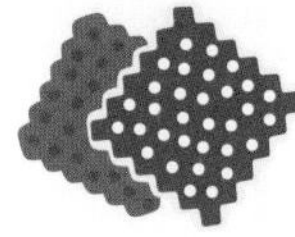
⑩ polka dot (US)
spotted (UK)

⑪ paisley

⑫ plaid

⑬ loose / baggy

⑭ fitted

⑮ tight

⑯ crumpled

⑰ cropped

⑱ vintage

13.2 WORK CLOTHES AND UNIFORMS

① chef's hat
② chef's coat
③ chef's uniform

④ apron

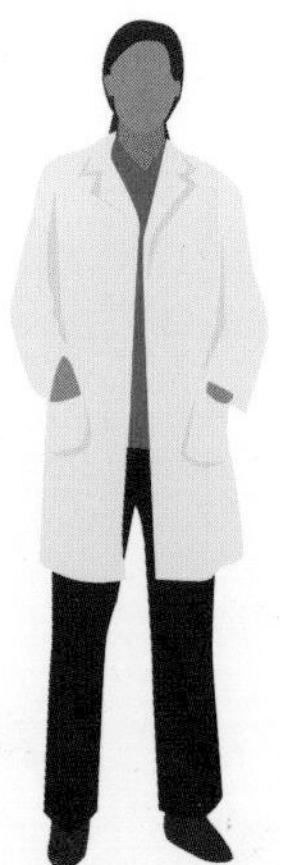
⑤ lab coat

⑥ firefighter's uniform

⑦ coveralls (US)
overalls (UK)

See also:
12 Appearance and hair **14-15** Clothes (continued)
16 Accessories **17** Shoes

13.3 KIDS' AND BABIES' CLOTHES

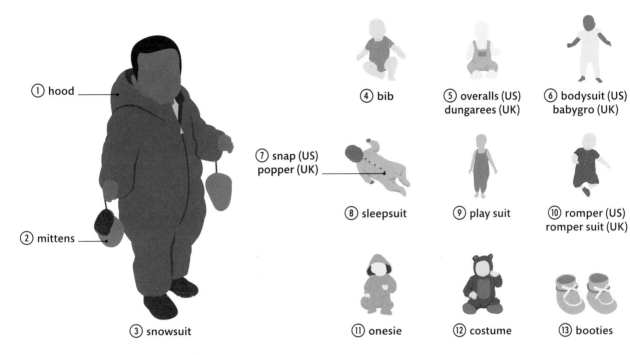

① hood
② mittens
③ snowsuit
④ bib
⑤ overalls (US) dungarees (UK)
⑥ bodysuit (US) babygro (UK)
⑦ snap (US) popper (UK)
⑧ sleepsuit
⑨ play suit
⑩ romper (US) romper suit (UK)
⑪ onesie
⑫ costume
⑬ booties

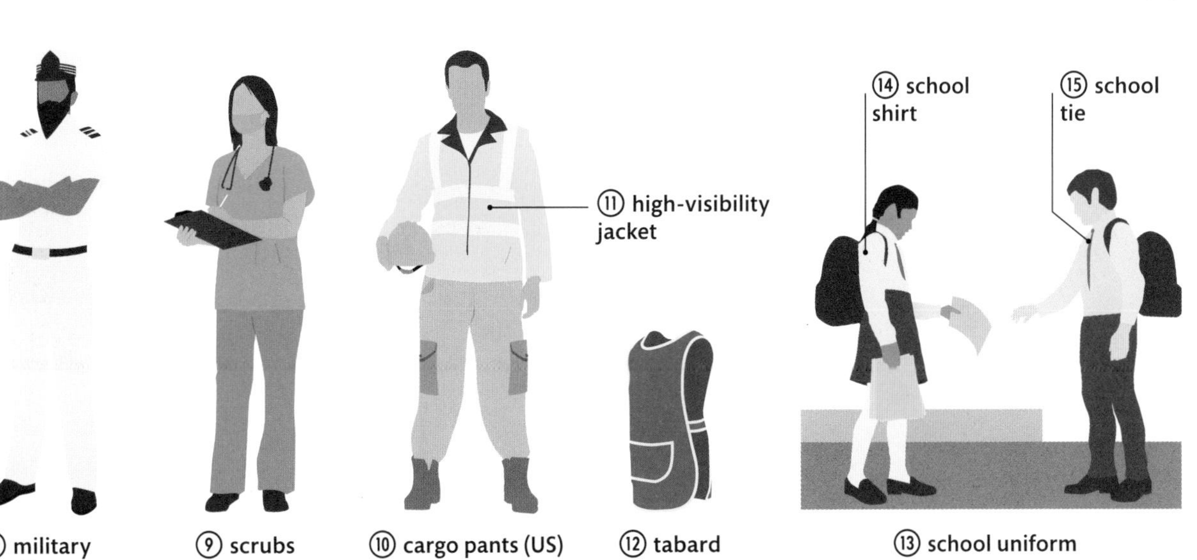
⑭ school shirt
⑮ school tie
⑪ high-visibility jacket
⑧ military uniform
⑨ scrubs
⑩ cargo pants (US) cargo trousers (UK)
⑫ tabard
⑬ school uniform

14 Clothes continued

14.1 CASUAL CLOTHES

① I prefer this casual outfit to my formal work clothes.
② blouse
③ sweater / jumper (UK)
④ skirt
⑤ pleat
⑥ hem
⑦ After work, I like to change into jeans and a T-shirt.
⑧ T-shirt
⑨ stripes
⑩ jeans
⑪ sweatshirt
⑫ shorts
⑬ Bermuda shorts
⑭ cardigan
⑮ tank top
⑯ dress
⑰ leggings
⑱ short-sleeved shirt
⑲ polo shirt
⑳ sun hat
㉑ V-neck
㉒ round neck

See also:
12 Appearance and hair 15 Clothes (continued)
16 Accessories 17 Shoes

14.2 NIGHTWEAR

① camisole

② slippers

③ eye mask

④ pajamas (US)
pyjamas (UK)

⑤ nightgown /
nightie

⑥ bathrobe (US)
dressing gown (UK)

14.3 UNDERWEAR

① panties (US)
knickers (UK)

② briefs (US)
pants (UK)

③ boxer shorts

④ socks

⑤ bra

⑥ slip (US)
slip dress (UK)

⑦ undershirt (US)
vest (UK)

⑧ pantyhose (US)
tights (UK)

⑨ stockings

⑩ corset (US)
basque (UK)

⑪ garter

⑫ garter belt (US)
suspenders (UK)

14.4 VERBS FOR CLOTHES

① to wear

② to fit

③ to put on

④ to take off

⑤ to fasten

⑥ to unfasten

⑦ to suit
(someone)

⑧ to change / to
get changed

⑨ to hang up

⑩ to fold

⑪ to turn up

⑫ to try
something on

15.1 FORMAL WEAR

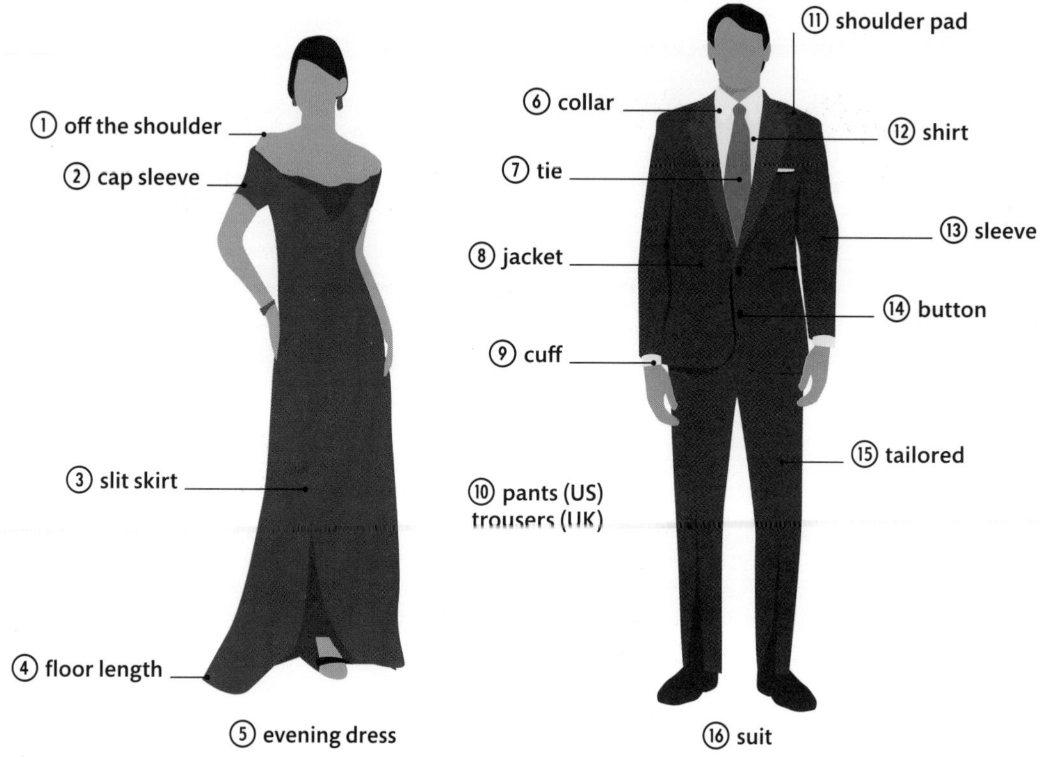
① off the shoulder
② cap sleeve
③ slit skirt
④ floor length
⑤ evening dress
⑥ collar
⑦ tie
⑧ jacket
⑨ cuff
⑩ pants (US)
trousers (UK)
⑪ shoulder pad
⑫ shirt
⑬ sleeve
⑭ button
⑮ tailored
⑯ suit

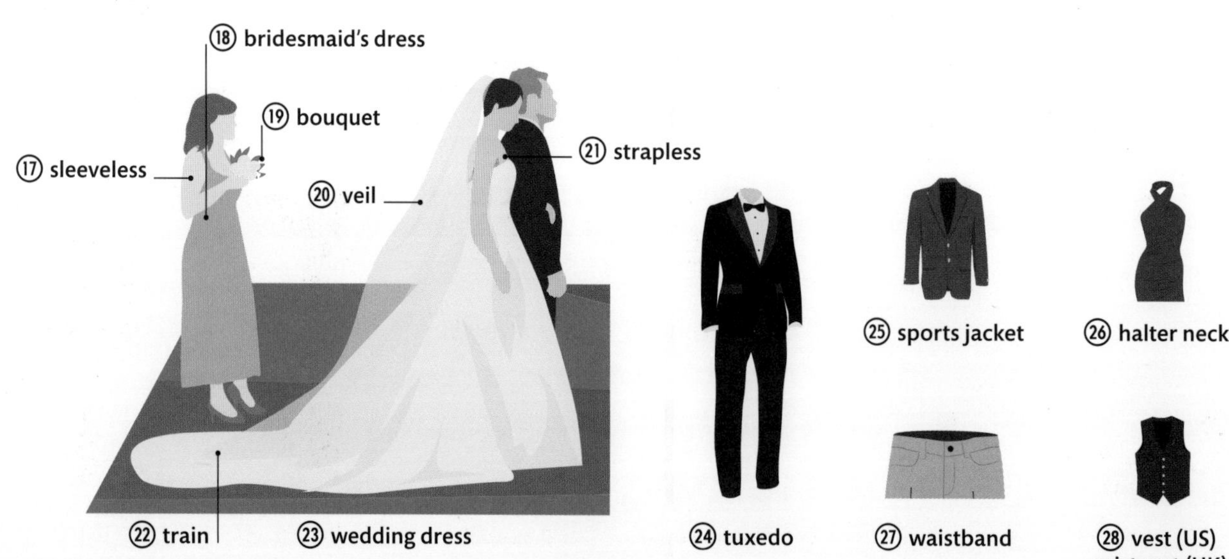
⑰ sleeveless
⑱ bridesmaid's dress
⑲ bouquet
⑳ veil
㉑ strapless
㉒ train
㉓ wedding dress
㉔ tuxedo
㉕ sports jacket
㉖ halter neck
㉗ waistband
㉘ vest (US)
waistcoat (UK)

See also:
12 Appearance and hair
16 Accessories 17 Shoes

15.2 COATS

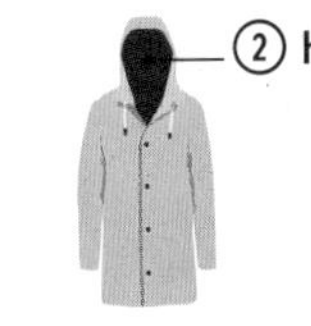
② hood

① raincoat

③ anorak

④ duffle coat

⑤ poncho

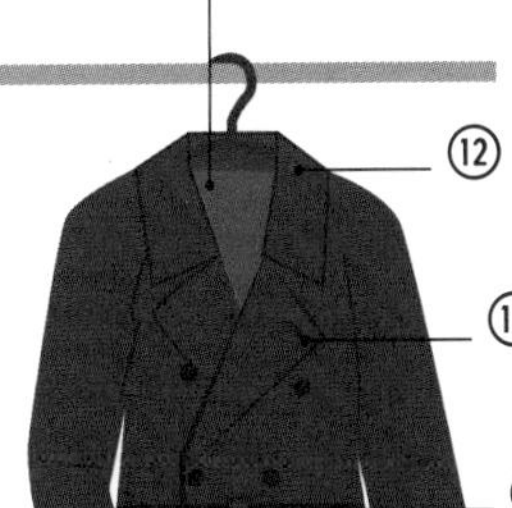
⑪ lining
⑫ lapel
⑬ buttonhole
⑭ belt
⑮ pocket

⑥ denim jacket

⑦ quilted jacket

⑧ bomber jacket

⑨ cloak

⑩ trench coat

15.3 SPORTSWEAR

① tracksuit

② sports bra

③ sweatpants

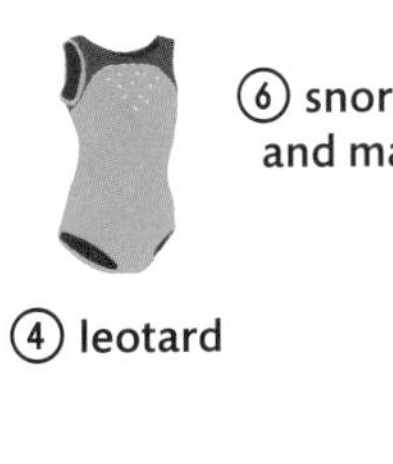

④ leotard

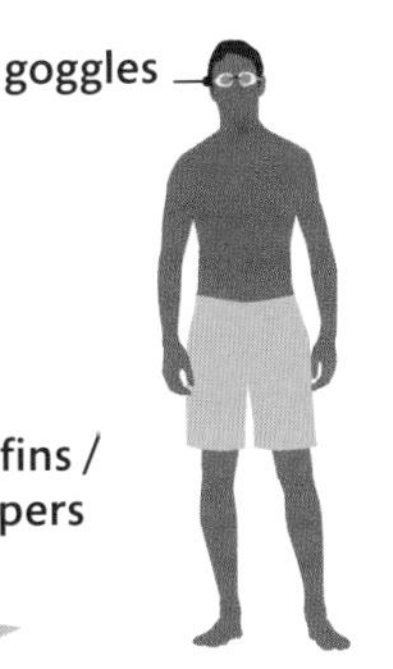
⑥ snorkel and mask
⑨ goggles
⑦ fins / flippers

⑤ soccer jersey (US) football shirt (UK)

⑧ swimsuit

⑩ swim trunks (US) swimming trunks (UK)

15.4 TRADITIONAL CLOTHES

① agbada

② flamenco dress

③ lederhosen

④ kimono

⑤ thawb

⑥ sari

⑦ kilt

⑧ sarong

⑨ folk blouse

16 Accessories

16.1 FASHION ACCESSORIES

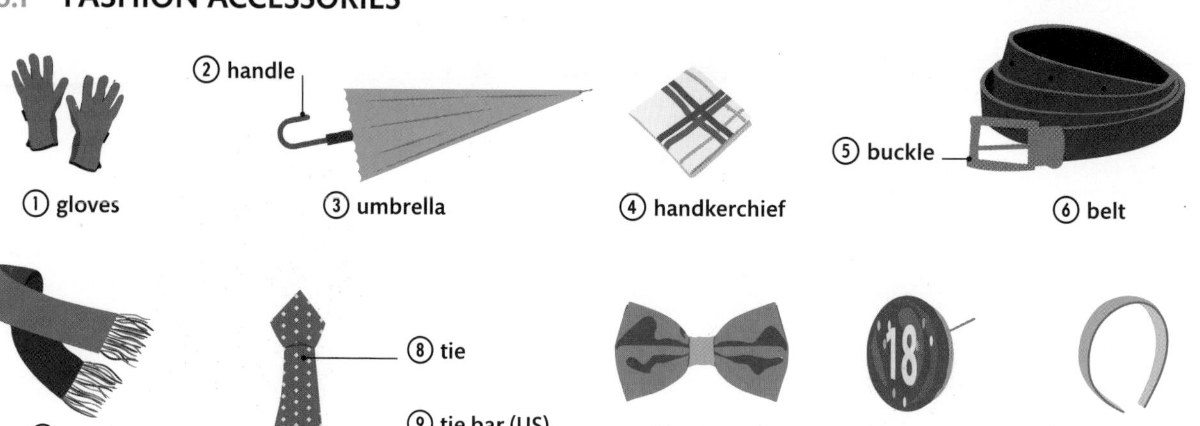

② handle
⑤ buckle
① gloves
③ umbrella
④ handkerchief
⑥ belt
⑧ tie
18

⑦ scarf

⑨ tie bar (US)
tie-pin (UK)

⑩ bow tie

⑪ pin (US)
badge (UK)

⑫ headband (US)
Alice band (UK)

16.2 JEWELRY (US) / JEWELLERY (UK)

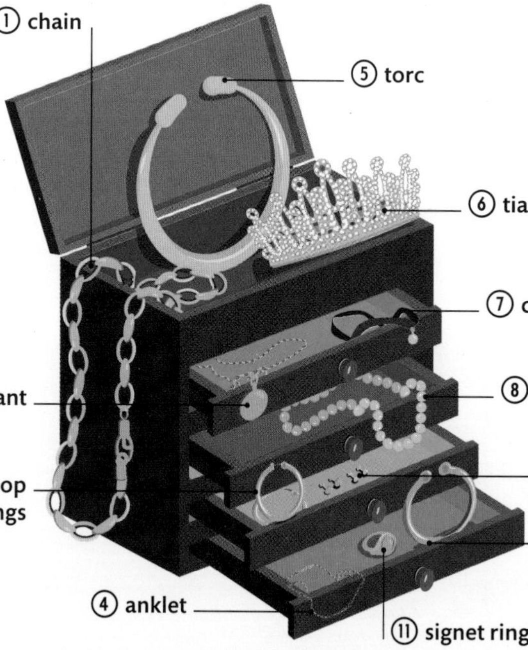

① chain
⑤ torc
⑥ tiara
⑦ choker
② pendant
⑧ string of pearls
③ hoop earrings
⑨ studs
⑩ bangle
④ anklet
⑪ signet ring
⑫ jewelry box (US) / jewellery box (UK)

⑬ watch 
⑭ stone
⑮ ring
⑯ earrings 
⑰ cufflinks 
⑱ brooch 
⑲ bracelet 
⑳ necklace

See also:
12 Appearance and hair
13-15 Clothes 17 Shoes

16.3 HEADWEAR

① flat cap

② baseball cap

③ pom pom beanie (US) bobble hat (UK)

④ hijab

⑤ yarmulke

⑥ turban

⑦ beret

⑧ fedora

⑨ deerstalker

⑩ fez

⑪ cowboy hat

⑫ sombrero

⑬ sun hat

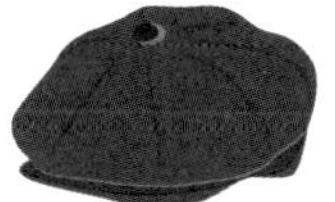
⑭ newsboy cap

⑮ panama

⑯ boater

⑰ beanie

⑱ cloche

16.4 BAGS

① briefcase

② backpack / rucksack (UK)

③ wallet (US) purse (UK)

④ duffel (US) holdall (UK)

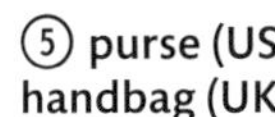
⑤ purse (US) handbag (UK)

⑥ suitcase

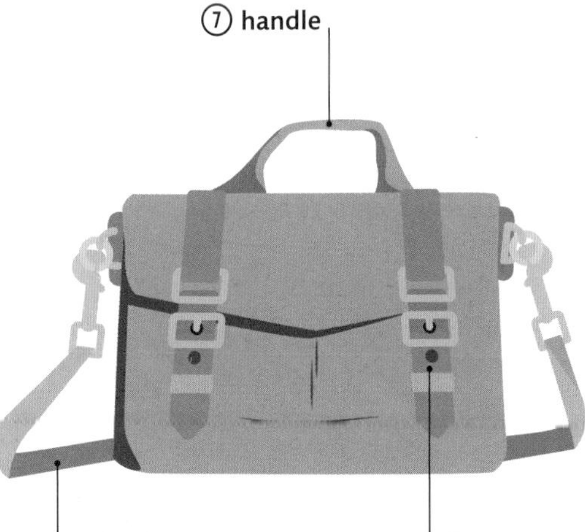
⑦ handle
⑧ shoulder strap
⑨ fastening
⑩ shoulder bag

17 Shoes

17.1 SHOES AND ACCESSORIES

① high-heeled shoes

② flats

③ flip-flops

④ espadrilles

⑤ kitten heels

⑥ stilettos

⑦ sandals

⑧ jelly sandals

⑨ gladiator sandals

⑩ wedge sandals

⑪ T-strap heels

⑫ platforms

⑬ ankle strap heels

⑭ peep toes

⑮ slingback heels

⑯ ballet flats

⑰ mules

⑱ Mary Janes

17.2 BOOTS

① work boots

② Chelsea boots

③ hiking boots

④ ankle boots

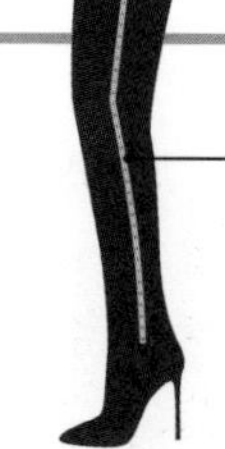
⑥ zipper (US) / zip (UK)
⑤ thigh-high boot

⑦ chukka boots / desert boots

⑧ lace
⑩ eyelet
⑨ sole
⑪ heel
⑫ lace-up boots

⑬ knee-high boots

⑭ rain boots (US) wellington boots (UK)

⑮ cowboy boots

See also:
12 Appearance and hair 13-15 Clothes
16 Accessories 40 Garden tools

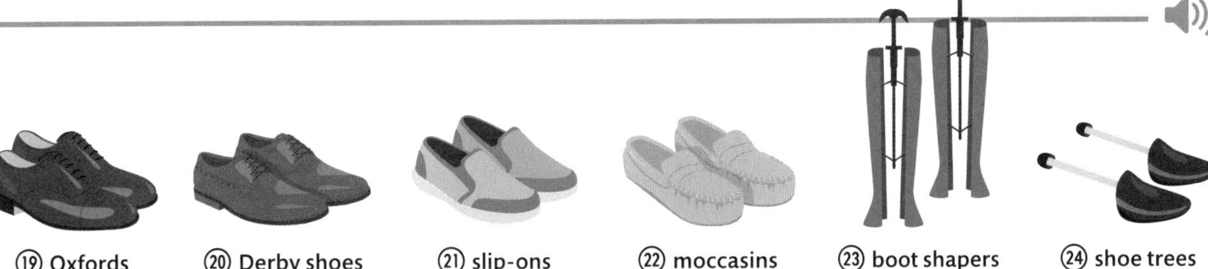

(19) Oxfords

(20) Derby shoes

(21) slip-ons

(22) moccasins

(23) boot shapers

(24) shoe trees

(25) clogs

(26) buckled shoes

(27) slides

(28) slippers

(29) shoelaces

(30) insoles

(31) loafers

(32) boat shoes

(33) kids' shoes

(34) brogues

(35) shoe polish

(36) shoe brush

17.3 SPORTS SHOES

(1) running spikes

(2) baseball cleats

(3) running shoes

(4) high-tops

(5) golf shoes

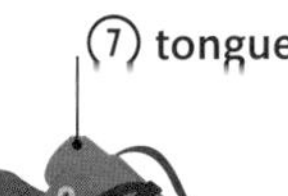
(7) tongue

(6) sneaker (US)
trainer (UK)

(8) cycling shoe

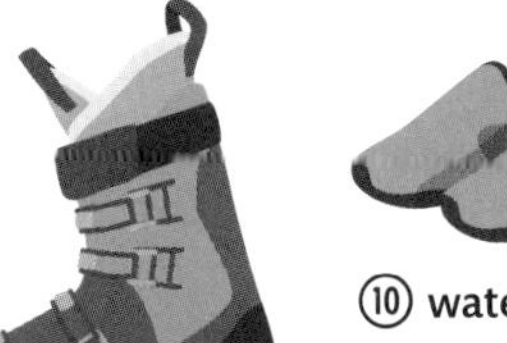
(10) water shoes

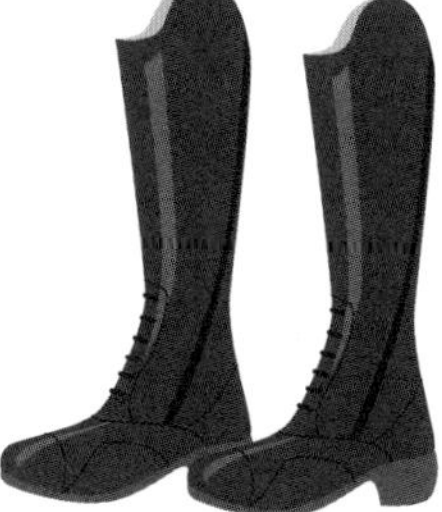
(11) riding boots

(9) ski boot

(12) tabi boots

(13) soccer cleats (US)
football boots (UK)

18 Beauty

18.1 MAKEUP

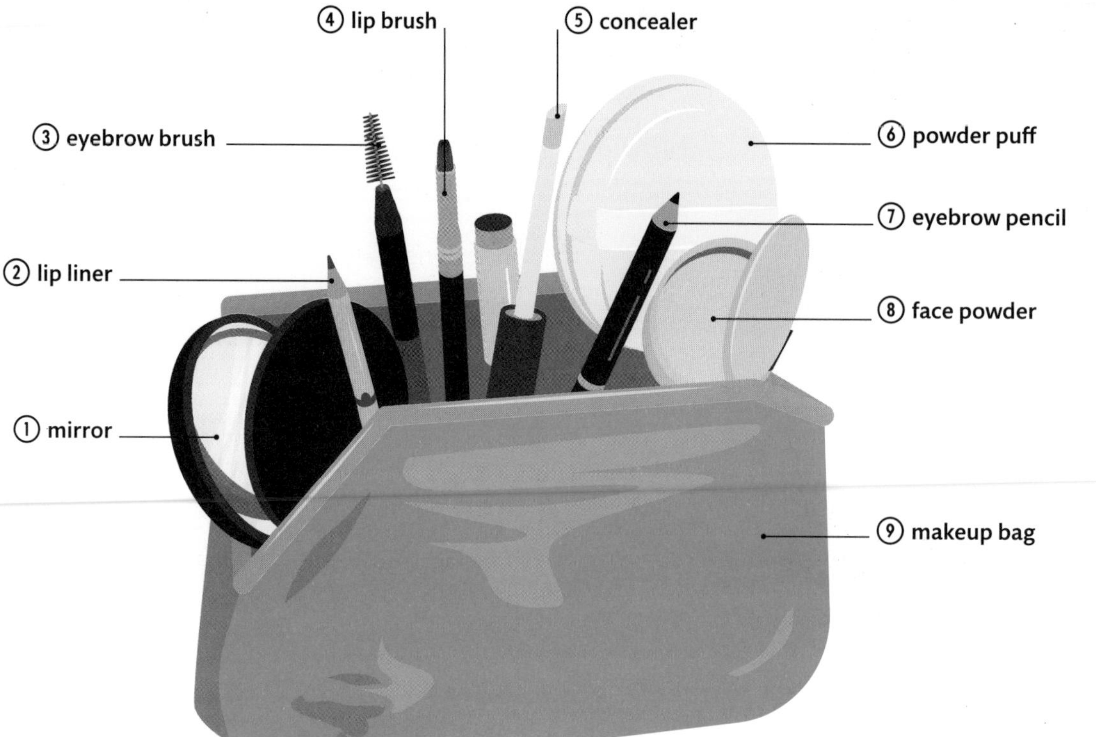

① mirror
② lip liner
③ eyebrow brush
④ lip brush
⑤ concealer
⑥ powder puff
⑦ eyebrow pencil
⑧ face powder
⑨ makeup bag

⑩ blush (US)
blusher (UK)

⑪ eyeliner

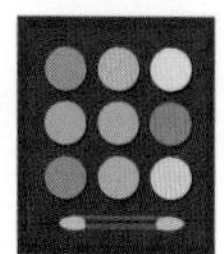
⑫ eyeshadow

⑬ foundation

⑭ mascara

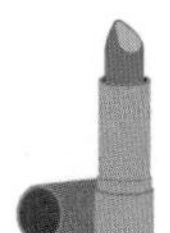
⑮ lipstick

18.2 SKIN TYPE

① normal

② dry

③ oily

④ sensitive

⑤ combination

See also:
12 Appearance and hair **13-15** Clothes
16 Accessories **17** Shoes **31** Bathroom

18.3 MANICURE

① nail scissors

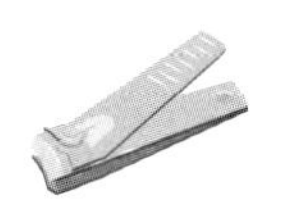

② nail clippers

③ nail polish / nail varnish (UK)

④ nail polish remover

⑤ nail file

⑥ hand cream

18.4 TOILETRIES AND BEAUTY TREATMENTS

① moisturizer

② toner

③ face wash

④ cleanser

⑤ perfume

⑥ aftershave

⑦ lip balm

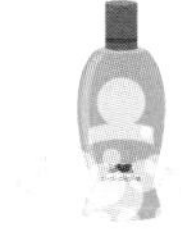

⑧ bubble bath

⑨ cotton balls

⑩ hair dye

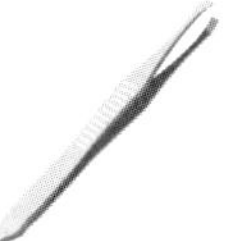

⑪ tweezers

⑫ wax

⑬ pedicure

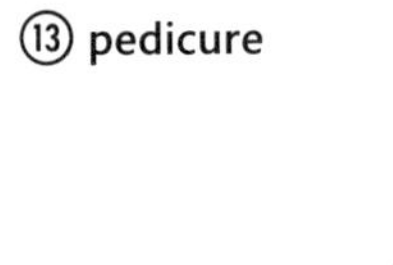

⑭ self tanner (US)
self-tanning lotion (UK)

⑮ tanning mitt

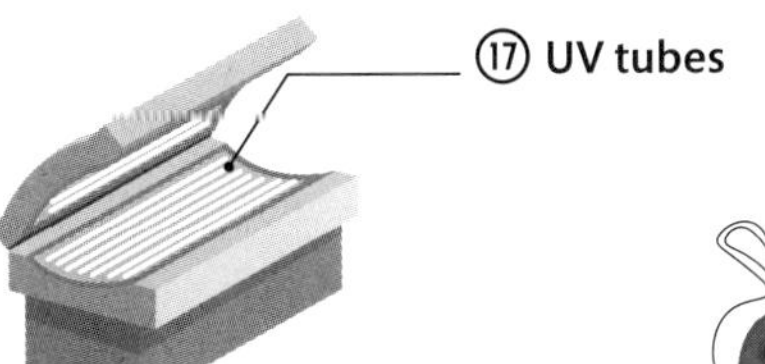

⑰ UV tubes

⑯ tanning bed (US) / sun bed (UK)

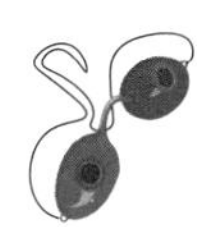

⑱ tanning goggles

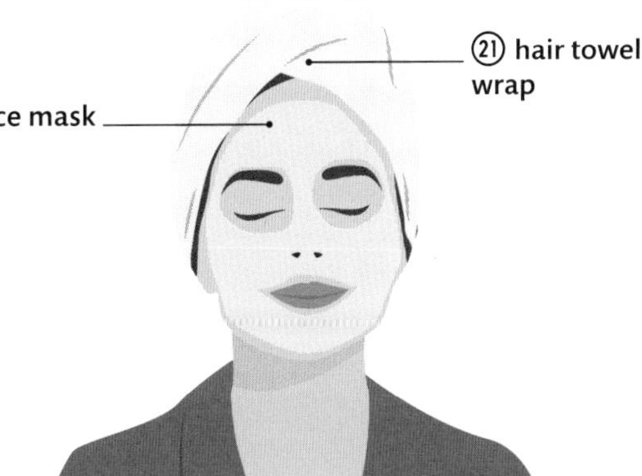

⑳ face mask

㉑ hair towel wrap

⑲ facial

19 Illness and injury

19.1 ILLNESS

① flu

② cold

③ cough

④ runny nose

⑤ virus

⑥ fever

⑦ chills (US) chill (UK)

⑧ sore throat

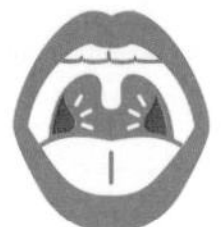
⑨ tonsillitis

⑩ headache

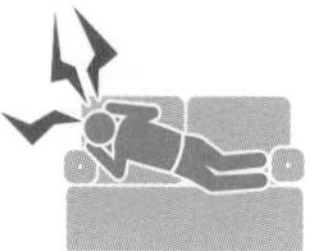
⑪ migraine

⑫ dizzy

⑬ food poisoning

⑭ poisoning

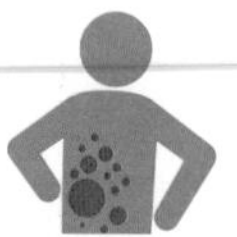
⑮ rash

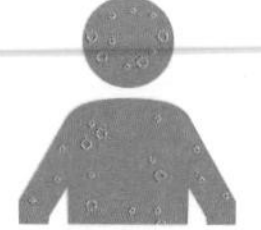
⑯ chickenpox

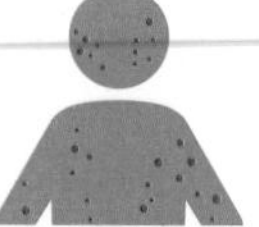
⑰ measles

⑱ mumps

⑲ eczema

⑳ asthma

㉑ allergy

㉒ hay fever

㉓ infection

㉔ diabetes

㉕ stress

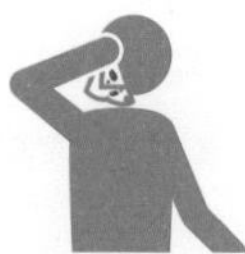
㉖ nosebleed

㉗ nausea

㉘ appendicitis

㉙ high blood pressure

㉚ symptoms

㉛ cramp

㉜ backache

㉝ pain

㉞ stomachache (US) stomach ache (UK)

㉟ insomnia

㊱ diarrhea (US) diarrhoea (UK)

See also:
01 Parts of the body **03** Muscles and skeleton
04 Internal organs **20** Visiting the doctor **21** The hospital

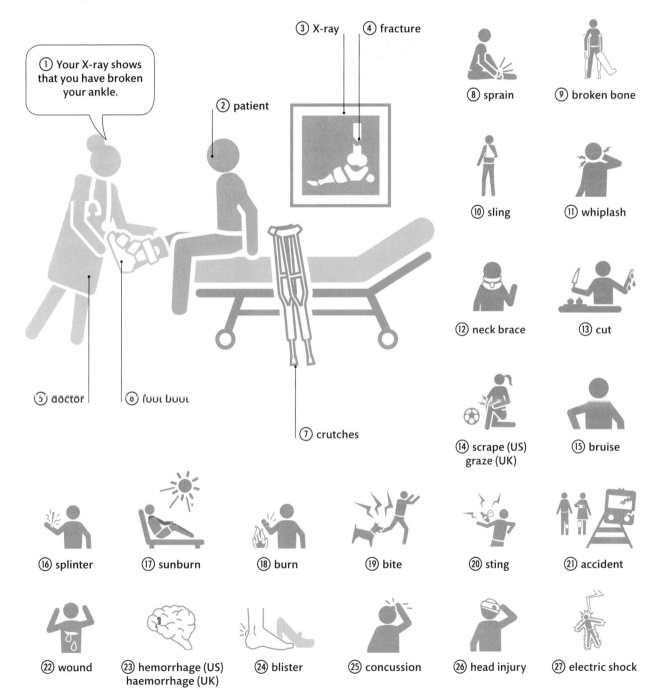

19.2 INJURY

① Your X-ray shows that you have broken your ankle.

② patient

③ X-ray

④ fracture

⑤ doctor

⑥ foot boot

⑦ crutches

⑧ sprain

⑨ broken bone

⑩ sling

⑪ whiplash

⑫ neck brace

⑬ cut

⑭ scrape (US) graze (UK)

⑮ bruise

⑯ splinter

⑰ sunburn

⑱ burn

⑲ bite

⑳ sting

㉑ accident

㉒ wound

㉓ hemorrhage (US) haemorrhage (UK)

㉔ blister

㉕ concussion

㉖ head injury

㉗ electric shock

20 Visiting the doctor

20.1 TREATMENT

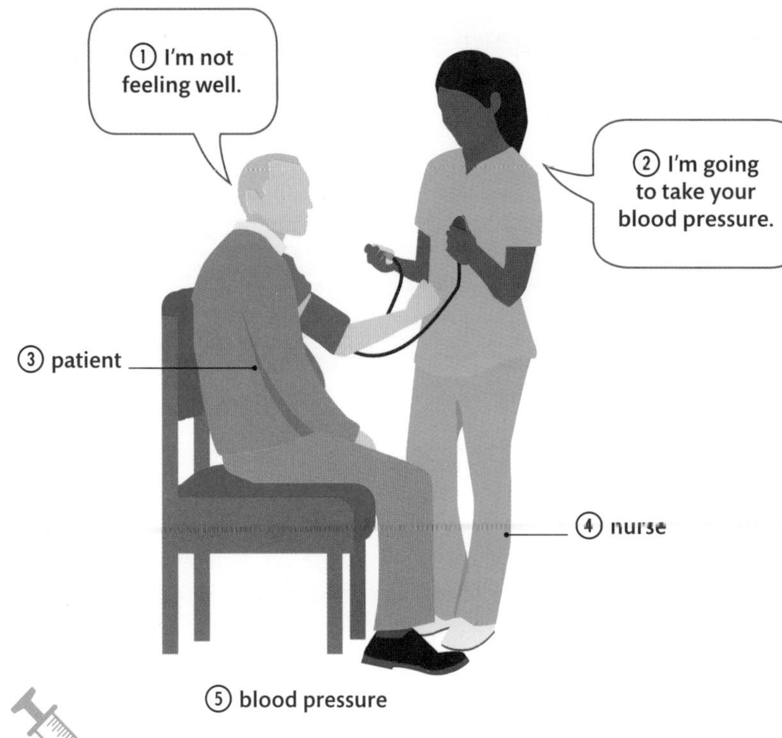

① I'm not feeling well.
② I'm going to take your blood pressure.
③ patient
④ nurse
⑤ blood pressure

⑥ doctor

⑦ doctor's office (US) doctor's surgery (UK)

⑧ waiting room

JUL
17

⑨ appointment

⑩ medical examination

⑪ inoculation / vaccination

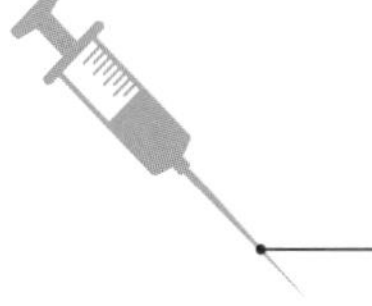
⑬ needle

⑫ syringe

⑭ blood test

⑮ test results

⑯ prescription

⑰ medicine / medication

⑱ pills / tablets

⑲ scale (US) scales (UK)

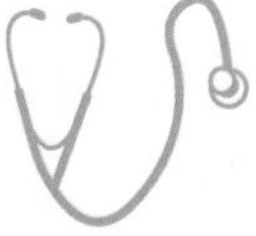
⑳ stethoscope

㉑ inhaler

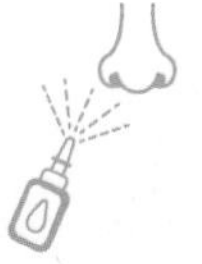
㉒ nasal spray

㉓ face mask

㉔ sling

㉕ dressing

㉖ gauze

㉗ tape

㉘ thermometer

㉙ ear thermometer

See also:
01 Parts of the body **02** Hands and feet **03** Muscles and skeleton
04 Internal organs **19** Illness and injury **21** The hospital

20.2 FIRST-AID KIT

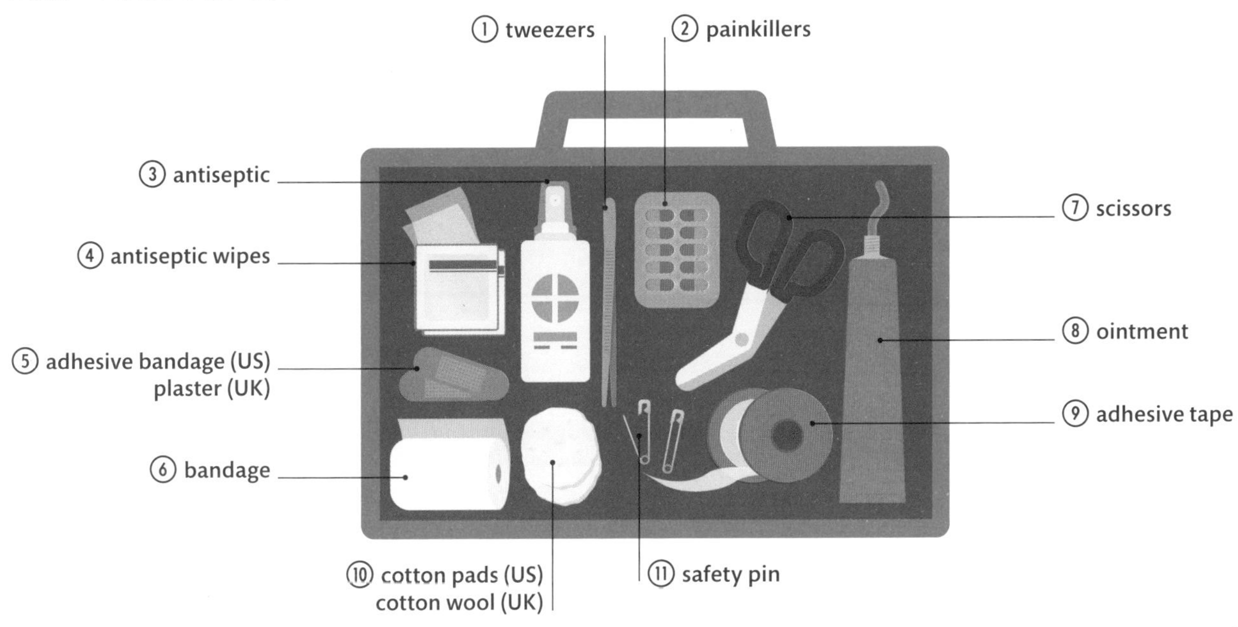
① tweezers
② painkillers
③ antiseptic
④ antiseptic wipes
⑤ adhesive bandage (US)
plaster (UK)
⑥ bandage
⑦ scissors
⑧ ointment
⑨ adhesive tape
⑩ cotton pads (US)
cotton wool (UK)
⑪ safety pin

20.3 VERBS TO DESCRIBE ILLNESS

① to vomit

② to sneeze

③ to cough

④ to hurt / to ache

⑤ to bleed

⑥ to faint

⑦ to lie down

⑧ to rest

⑨ to lose weight

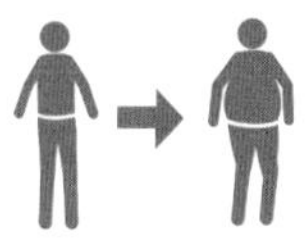
⑩ to gain weight

⑪ to drink water

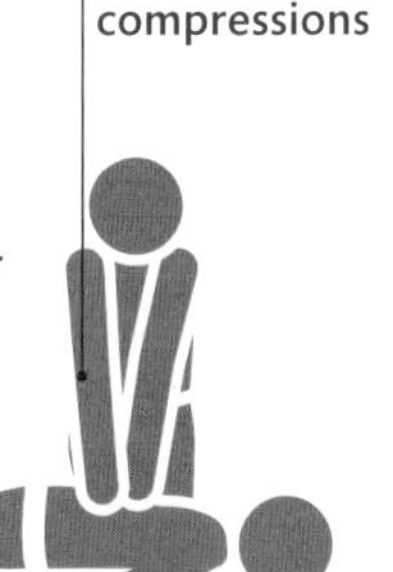
⑰ chest compressions

⑫ to exercise

⑬ to heal

⑭ to recover

⑮ to feel better

⑯ to resuscitate

21 The hospital

21.1 AT THE HOSPITAL

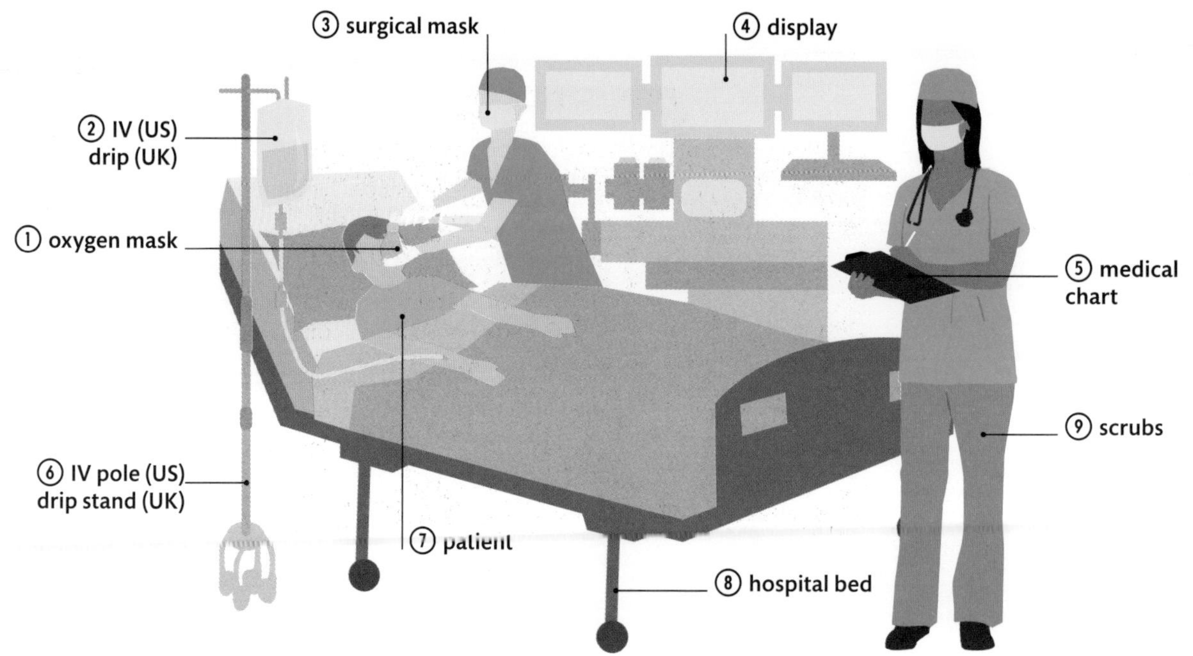

③ surgical mask
④ display
② IV (US)
drip (UK)
① oxygen mask
⑤ medical
chart
⑨ scrubs
⑥ IV pole (US)
drip stand (UK)
⑦ patient
⑧ hospital bed

⑩ hospital

⑪ ambulance

⑫ paramedic

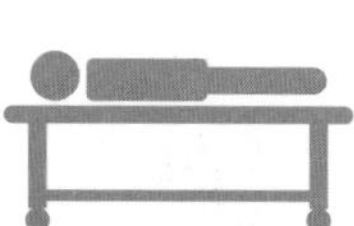
⑬ stretcher

⑭ surgeon

⑮ doctor

⑯ nurse

⑰ porter

⑱ wheelchair

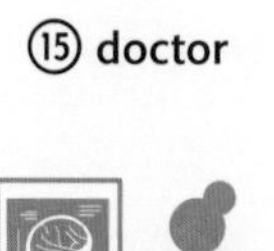
⑲ scan

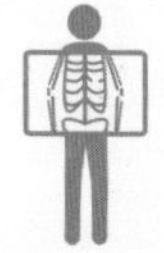
⑳ X-ray

㉑ blood test

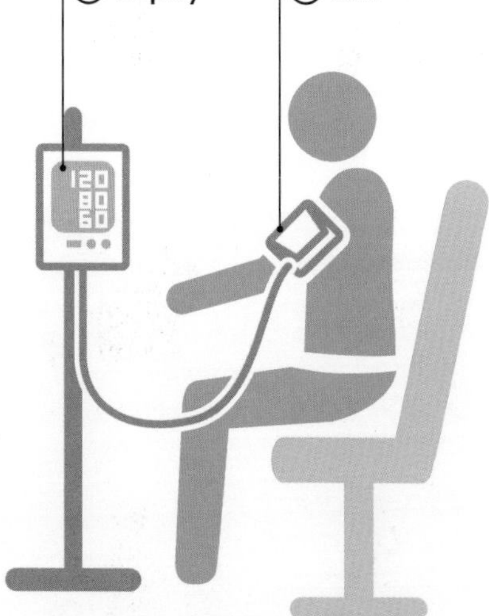

㉓ display
㉔ cuff
120
80
60

㉒ blood
pressure monitor

See also:
01 Parts of the body 03 Muscles and skeleton
04 Internal organs 19 Illness and injury 20 Visiting the doctor

㉕ scalpel

㉖ stitches

㉗ plastic surgery

㉘ treatment

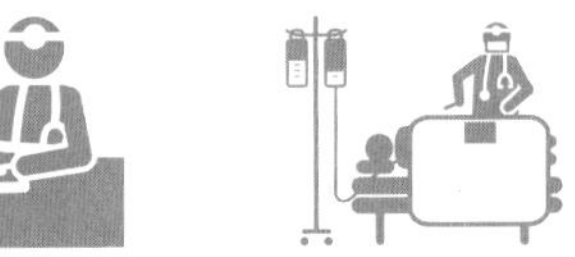
㉙ operation

㉚ operating table

㉛ operating room (US)
theatre (UK)

㉜ emergency room (US)
A&E (UK)

㉝ intensive care unit

㉞ recovery room

㉟ private room

㊱ ward

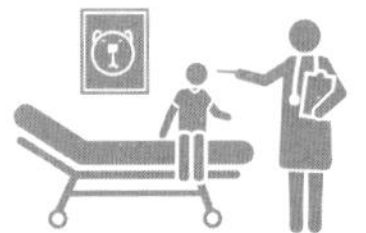
㊲ children's ward

㊳ maternity ward

㊴ to admit

㊵ to discharge

㊶ outpatient

21.2 DEPARTMENTS

① ENT (ear, nose, and throat)

② cardiology

③ orthopedics (US)
orthopaedics (UK)

④ neurology

⑤ radiology

⑥ pathology

⑦ pediatrics (US)
paediatrics (UK)

⑧ dermatology

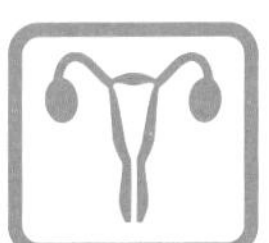
⑨ gynecology (US)
gynaecology (UK)

⑩ surgery

⑪ physical therapy (US)
physiotherapy (UK)

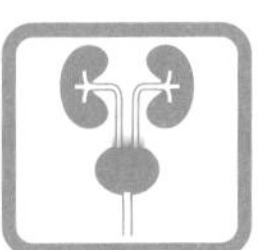
⑫ urology

⑬ maternity

⑭ psychiatry

⑮ ophthalmology

⑯ endocrinology

⑰ oncology

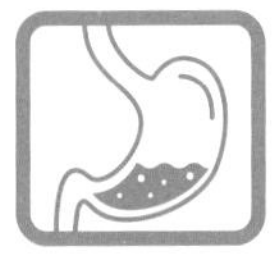
⑱ gastroenterology

22 The dentist and optician

22.1 DENTIST'S OFFICE (US) / DENTAL SURGERY (UK)

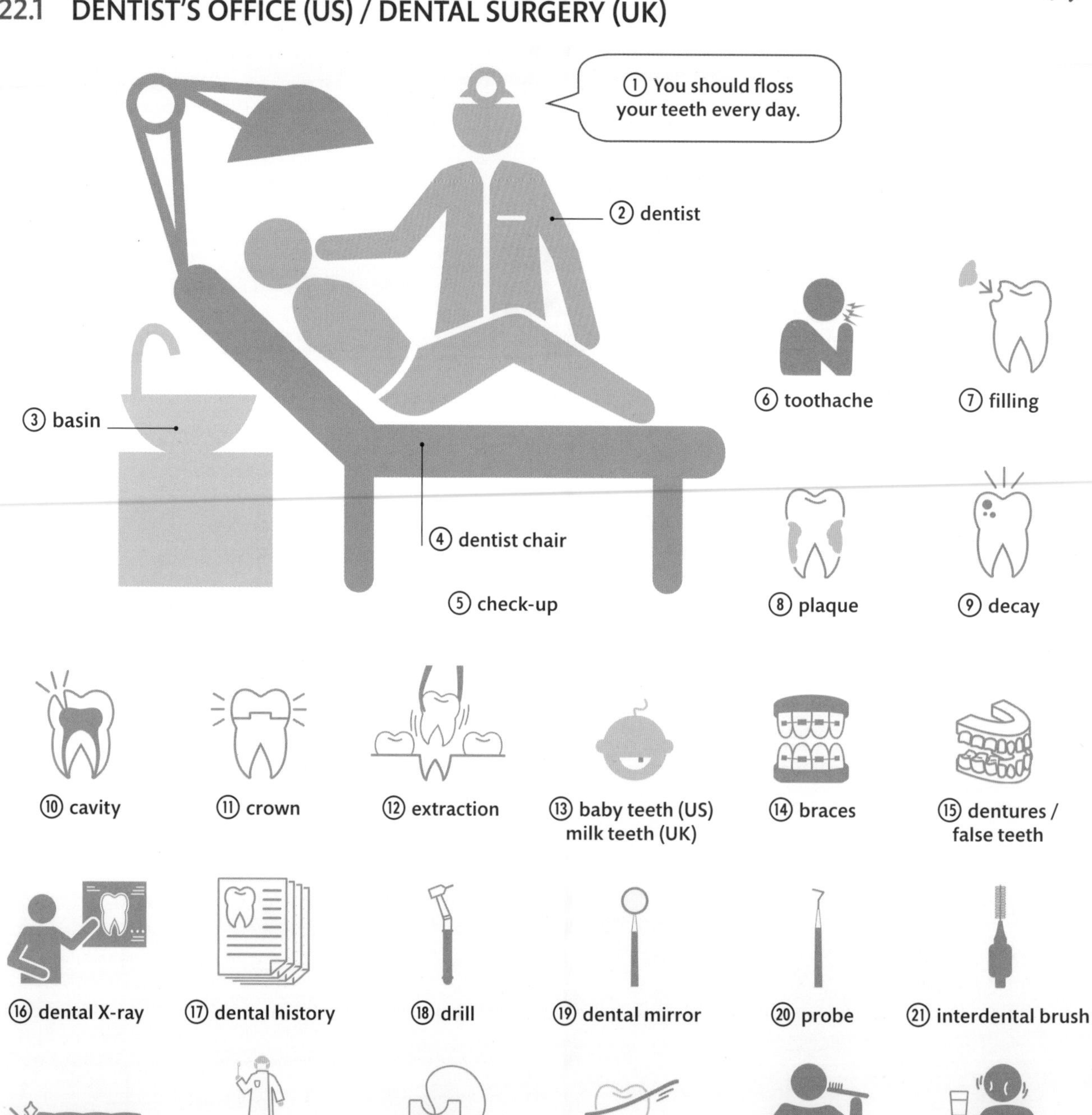

① You should floss your teeth every day.
② dentist
③ basin
④ dentist chair
⑤ check-up
⑥ toothache
⑦ filling
⑧ plaque
⑨ decay
⑩ cavity
⑪ crown
⑫ extraction
⑬ baby teeth (US) milk teeth (UK)
⑭ braces
⑮ dentures / false teeth
⑯ dental X-ray
⑰ dental history
⑱ drill
⑲ dental mirror
⑳ probe
㉑ interdental brush
㉒ whitening
㉓ dental hygienist
㉔ dental floss
㉕ to floss
㉖ to brush
㉗ to rinse

See also:
01 Parts of the body 03 Muscles and skeleton
20 Visiting the doctor 21 The hospital 31 Bathroom

22.2 OPTICIAN

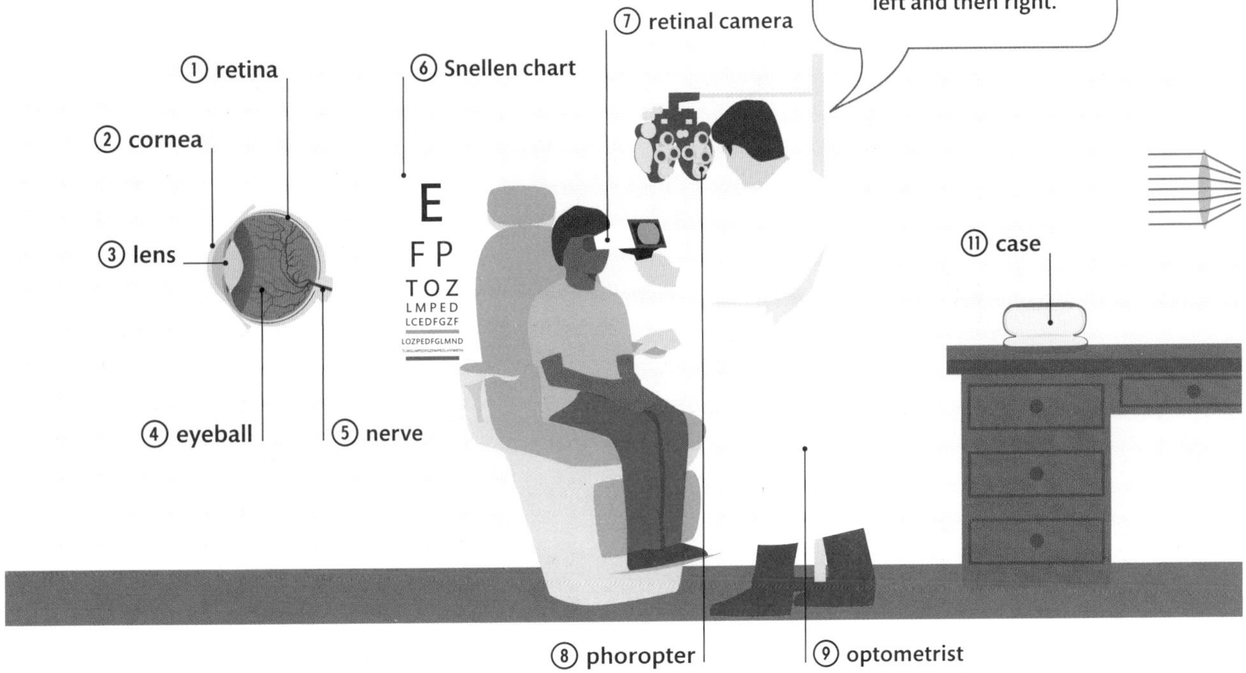

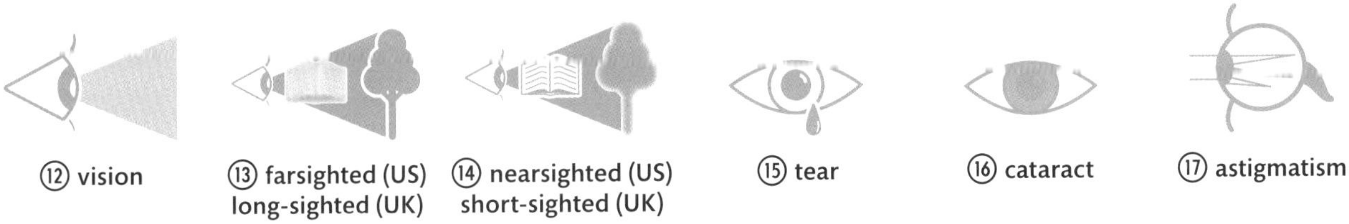

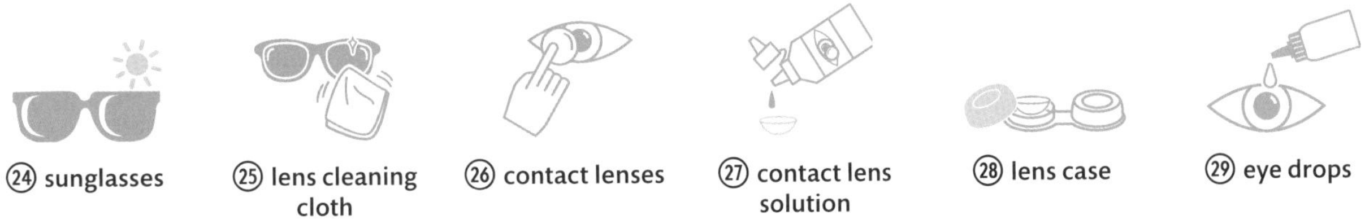

① retina
② cornea
③ lens
④ eyeball
⑤ nerve
⑥ Snellen chart
E
F P
T O Z
L M P E D
L C E D F G Z F
⑦ retinal camera
⑧ phoropter
⑨ optometrist
⑩ I'm going to check your retina. Please look left and then right.
⑪ case

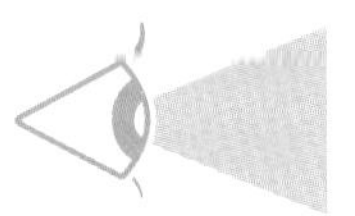

⑫ vision

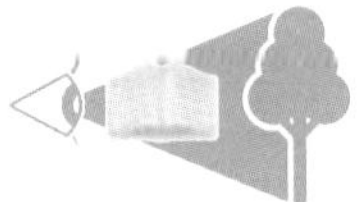

⑬ farsighted (US) long-sighted (UK)

⑭ nearsighted (US) short-sighted (UK)

⑮ tear

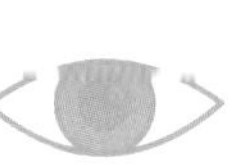

⑯ cataract

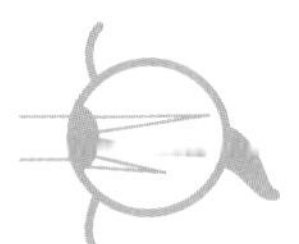

⑰ astigmatism

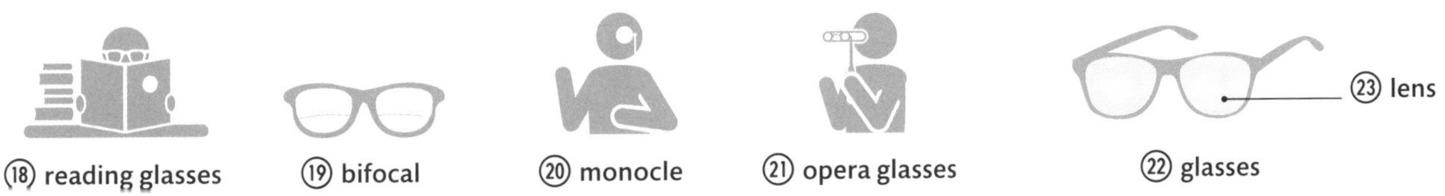

⑱ reading glasses

⑲ bifocal

⑳ monocle

㉑ opera glasses

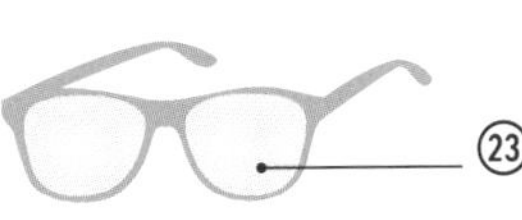

㉓ lens

㉒ glasses

㉔ sunglasses

㉕ lens cleaning cloth

㉖ contact lenses

㉗ contact lens solution

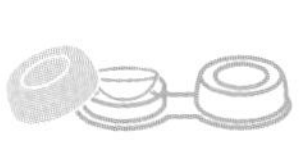

㉘ lens case

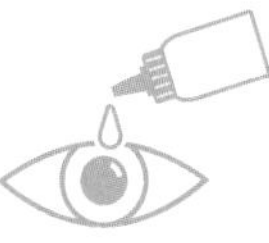

㉙ eye drops

23 Diet and nutrition

23.1 HEALTHY LIVING

(1) protein

(2) carbohydrates

(3) fiber (US)
fibre (UK)

(4) dairy

(5) legumes (US)
pulses (UK)

(6) sugar

(7) salt

(8) saturated fat

(9) unsaturated fat

(10) calories / energy

A
C
E
D

(11) vitamins

Ca
Zn
P
Fe
Co
Mn

(12) minerals

(13) calcium

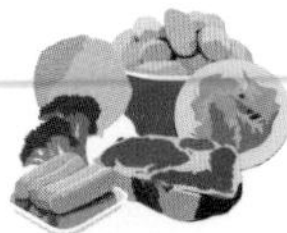

(14) iron

(15) cholesterol

(16) detox

(17) balanced diet

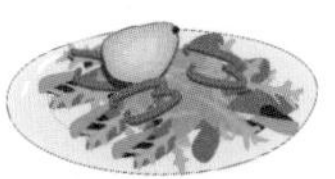

(18) calorie-controlled diet

HEALTH FOOD
(22) I like to buy organic fruit and vegetables.

(19) health food store (US)
health food shop (UK)

(20) organic food section

(21) local produce

(23) farmers' market

See also:
03 Muscles and skeleton **19** Illness and injury
24 Healthy body, healthy mind **29** Cooking **48** The supermarket **52-72** Food

(24) processed food

(25) superfoods

(26) organic

(27) supplement

(28) additives

(29) dairy-free

(30) vegetarian

(31) vegan

(32) pescatarian

(33) gluten-free

(34) to lose weight

(35) convenience food

(36) high-calorie

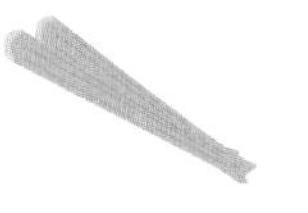
(37) low-calorie

(38) to cut down on

(39) to give up

(40) to go on a diet

(41) to overeat

23.2 FOOD ALLERGIES

(1) nut allergy

(2) peanut allergy

(3) seafood allergy

(4) lactose intolerant

(5) gluten intolerant

(6) dairy allergy

(7) wheat allergy

(8) egg allergy

(9) sesame allergy

(10) soy allergy (US) soya allergy (UK)

(11) celery allergy

(12) sulfite allergy (US) sulphite allergy (UK)

(13) allergic

(14) mustard allergy

(15) intolerant

24 Healthy body, healthy mind

24.1 YOGA

① yoga pants
② mat
③ headstand
④ yoga class
⑤ Take a deep breath in, and then breathe out.

⑥ child's pose

⑦ cobra pose

⑧ warrior pose

⑨ seated twist

⑩ triangle pose

⑪ seated forward fold

⑫ corpse pose

⑬ crow pose

⑭ chair pose

⑮ mountain pose

⑯ bridge pose

⑰ plank pose

⑱ bow pose

⑲ pigeon pose

⑳ tree pose

㉑ downward dog

㉒ bound ankle pose

㉓ camel pose

㉔ wheel pose

㉕ half moon pose

㉖ dolphin pose

See also:
03 Muscles and skeleton **04** Internal organs **19** Illness and injury
20 Visiting the doctor **21** The hospital **23** Diet and nutrition **29** Cooking

24.2 TREATMENTS AND THERAPY

① massage

② shiatsu

③ chiropractic

④ osteopathy

⑤ reflexology

⑥ meditation

⑦ reiki

⑧ acupuncture

⑨ ayurveda

⑩ hypnotherapy

⑪ hydrotherapy

⑫ aromatherapy

⑬ herbalism

⑭ essential oils

⑮ homeopathy

⑯ acupressure

⑰ crystal healing

⑱ naturopathy

⑲ feng shui

⑳ poetry therapy

㉑ art therapy

㉒ pet therapy

㉓ nature therapy

㉔ music therapy

㉕ relaxation

㉖ mindfulness

㉗ counselor (US)
counsellor (UK)

㉘ psychotherapy

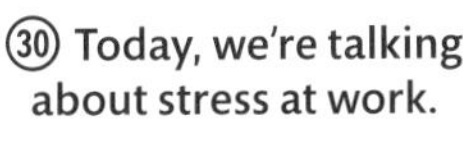
㉚ Today, we're talking about stress at work.

㉙ group therapy

25 A place to live

25.1 HOUSES

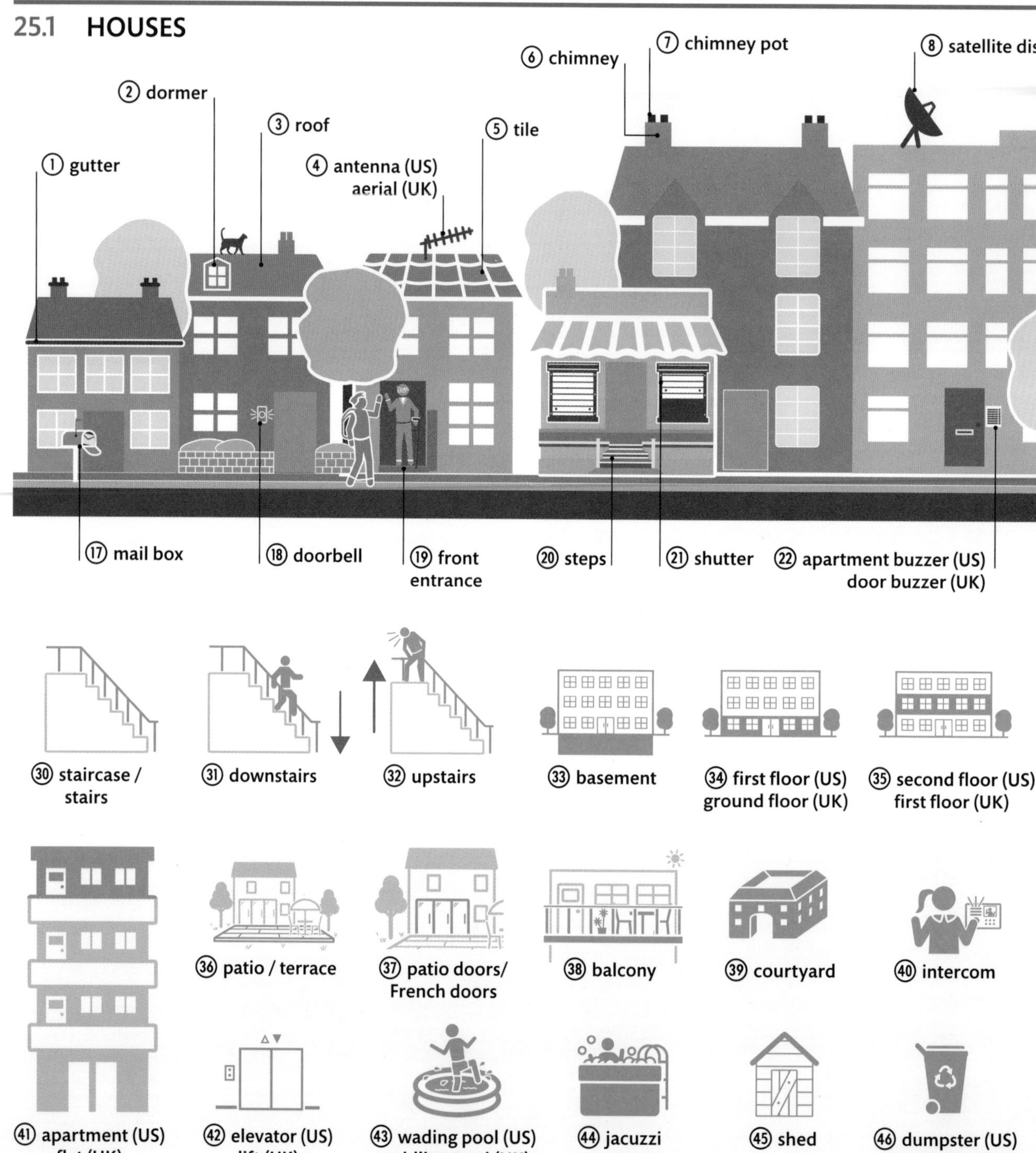

① gutter
② dormer
③ roof
④ antenna (US)
aerial (UK)
⑤ tile
⑥ chimney
⑦ chimney pot
⑧ satellite dish
⑰ mail box
⑱ doorbell
⑲ front entrance
⑳ steps
㉑ shutter
㉒ apartment buzzer (US)
door buzzer (UK)
㉚ staircase / stairs
㉛ downstairs
㉜ upstairs
㉝ basement
㉞ first floor (US)
ground floor (UK)
㉟ second floor (US)
first floor (UK)
㊱ patio / terrace
㊲ patio doors/
French doors
㊳ balcony
㊴ courtyard
㊵ intercom
㊶ apartment (US)
flat (UK)
㊷ elevator (US)
lift (UK)
㊸ wading pool (US)
paddling pool (UK)
㊹ jacuzzi
㊺ shed
㊻ dumpster (US)
wheelie bin (UK)

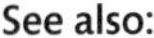

See also:
32 House and home 34 Household chores
37 Decorating 42-43 In town 44 Buildings and architecture

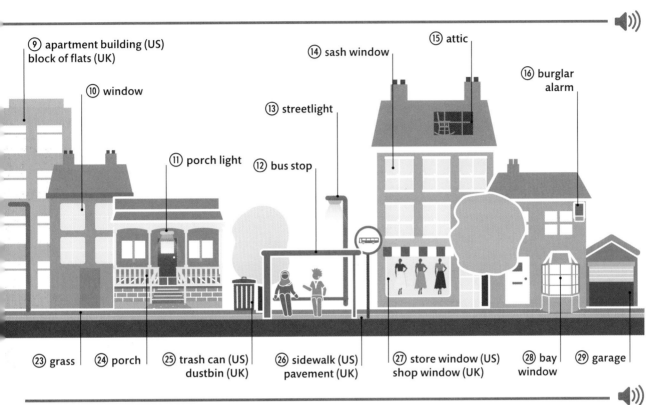

⑨ apartment building (US) block of flats (UK)

⑩ window

⑪ porch light

⑫ bus stop

⑬ streetlight

⑭ sash window

⑮ attic

⑯ burglar alarm

㉓ grass

㉔ porch

㉕ trash can (US) dustbin (UK)

㉖ sidewalk (US) pavement (UK)

㉗ store window (US) shop window (UK)

㉘ bay window

㉙ garage

25.2 HALLWAY

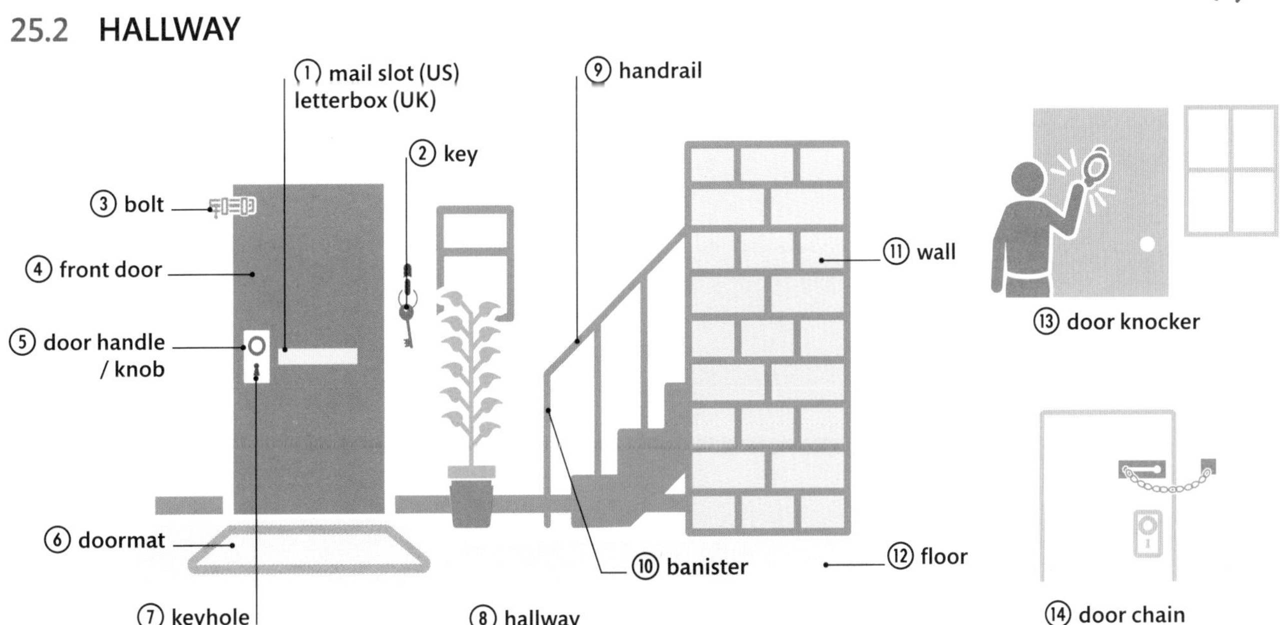
① mail slot (US)
letterbox (UK)
② key
③ bolt
④ front door
⑤ door handle / knob
⑥ doormat
⑦ keyhole
⑧ hallway
⑨ handrail
⑩ banister
⑪ wall
⑫ floor
⑬ door knocker
⑭ door chain

26 Living room and dining room

26.1 LIVING ROOM

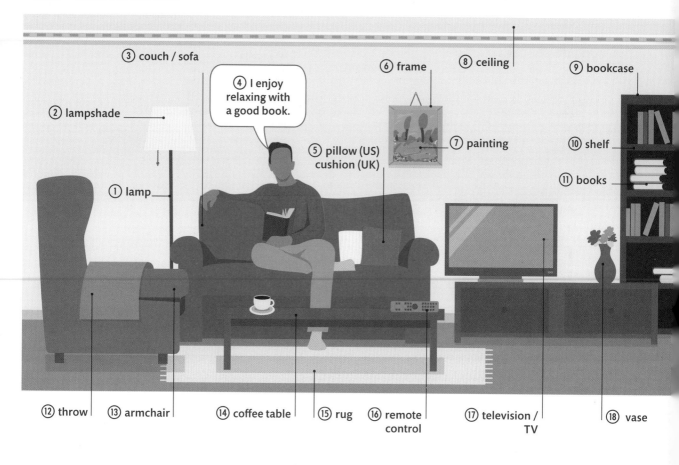

① lamp
② lampshade
③ couch / sofa
④ I enjoy relaxing with a good book.
⑤ pillow (US) cushion (UK)
⑥ frame
⑦ painting
⑧ ceiling
⑨ bookcase
⑩ shelf
⑪ books
⑫ throw
⑬ armchair
⑭ coffee table
⑮ rug
⑯ remote control
⑰ television / TV
⑱ vase

⑲ fireplace

⑳ mantlepiece

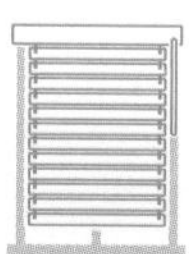

㉑ Venetian blinds

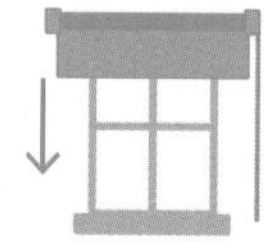

㉒ roller shade (US) roller blind (UK)

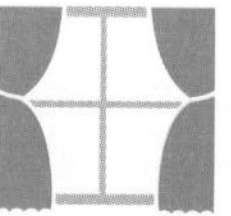

㉓ curtains

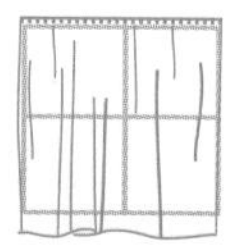

㉔ sheer curtain (US) net curtain (UK)

㉕ sofa bed

㉖ rocking chair

㉗ foot stool

㉘ sconce (US) wall light (UK)

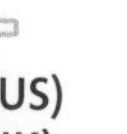

㉙ home office (US) / study (UK)

See also:
25 A place to live 27 Kitchen and tableware 34 Household chores
71 Breakfast 72 Lunch and dinner 136 Home entertainment

26.2 DINING ROOM

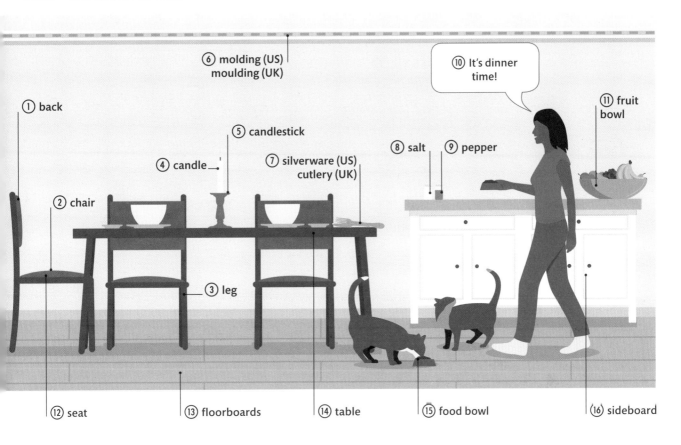

① back
② chair
③ leg
④ candle
⑤ candlestick
⑥ molding (US) moulding (UK)
⑦ silverware (US) cutlery (UK)
⑧ salt
⑨ pepper
⑩ It's dinner time!
⑪ fruit bowl
⑫ seat
⑬ floorboards
⑭ table
⑮ food bowl
⑯ sideboard

⑰ to set the table

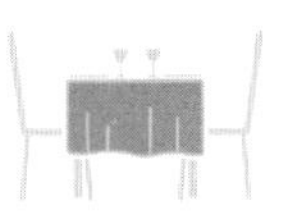

⑱ tablecloth

⑲ place mat

⑳ breakfast

㉑ lunch

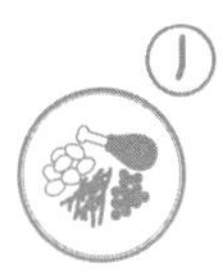

㉒ dinner

㉓ host / hostess

㉔ hungry

㉕ full

㉖ portion

㉘ guest

㉗ dinner party

27 Kitchen and tableware

27.1 KITCHEN APPLIANCES

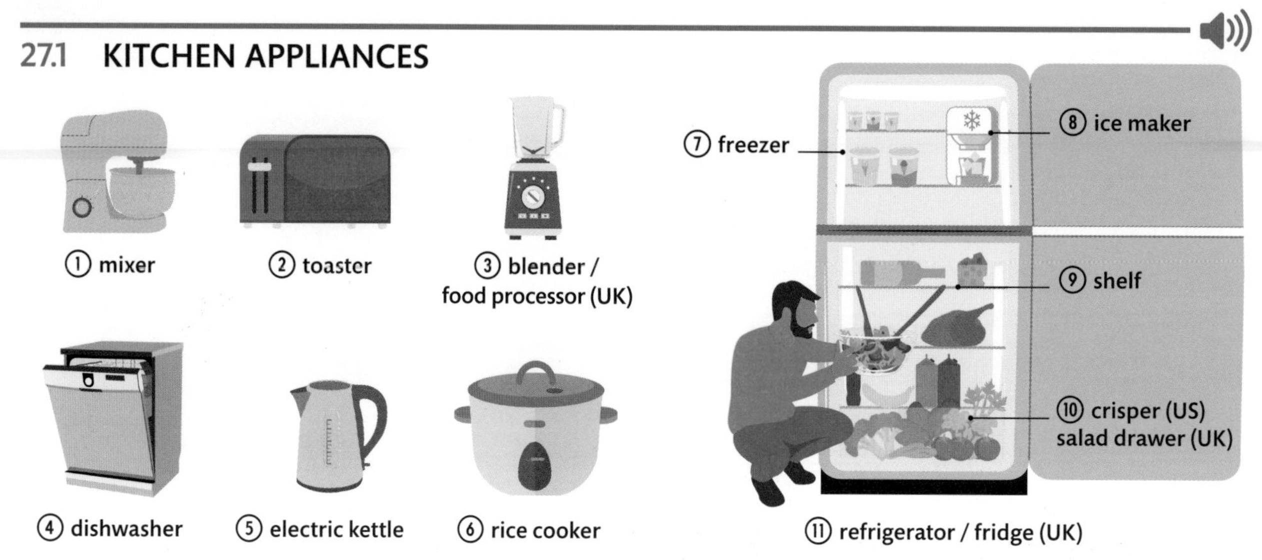

① mixer
② toaster
③ blender / food processor (UK)
④ dishwasher
⑤ electric kettle
⑥ rice cooker
⑦ freezer
⑧ ice maker
⑨ shelf
⑩ crisper (US) salad drawer (UK)
⑪ refrigerator / fridge (UK)

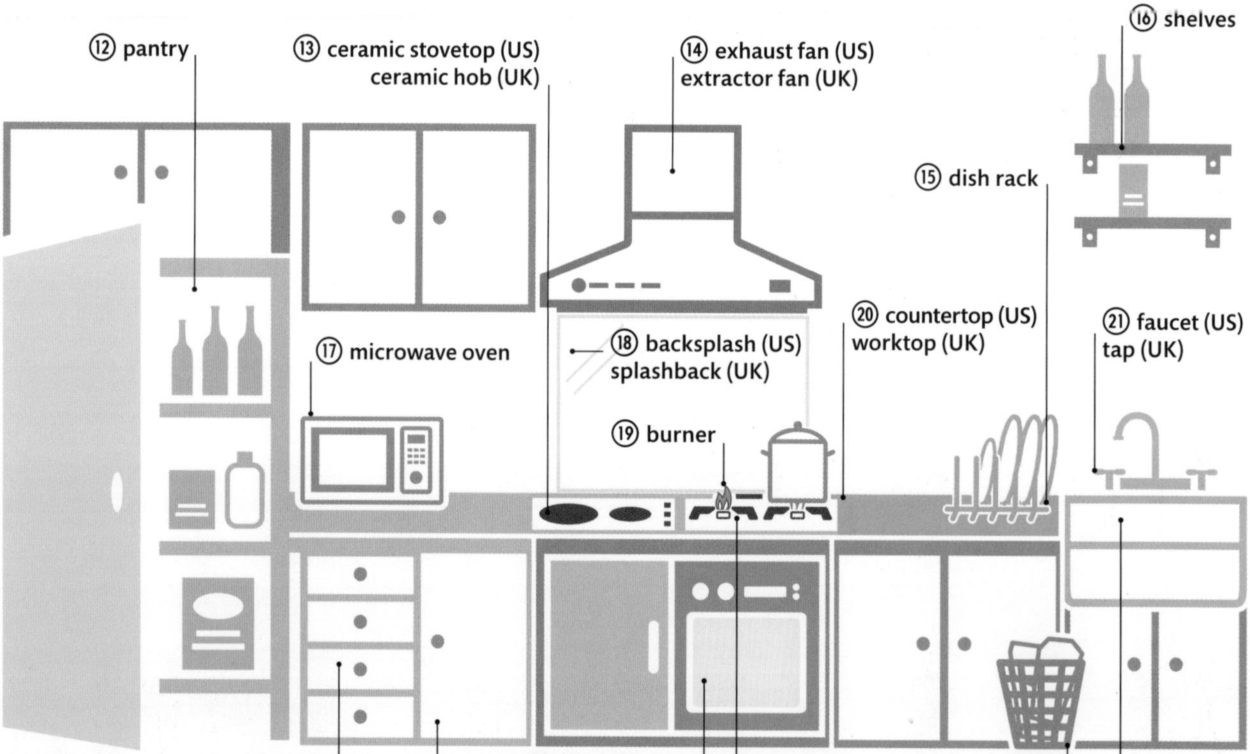

⑫ pantry

⑬ ceramic stovetop (US) ceramic hob (UK)

⑭ exhaust fan (US) extractor fan (UK)

⑮ dish rack

⑯ shelves

⑰ microwave oven

⑱ backsplash (US) splashback (UK)

⑲ burner

⑳ countertop (US) worktop (UK)

㉑ faucet (US) tap (UK)

㉒ drawer

㉓ cabinet

㉔ oven

㉕ stove (US) hob (UK)

㉖ trash can (US) rubbish bin (UK)

㉗ sink

See also:
28 Kitchenware 29 Cooking 59 Herbs and spices
60 In the pantry 71 Breakfast 72 Lunch and dinner

27.2 TABLEWARE

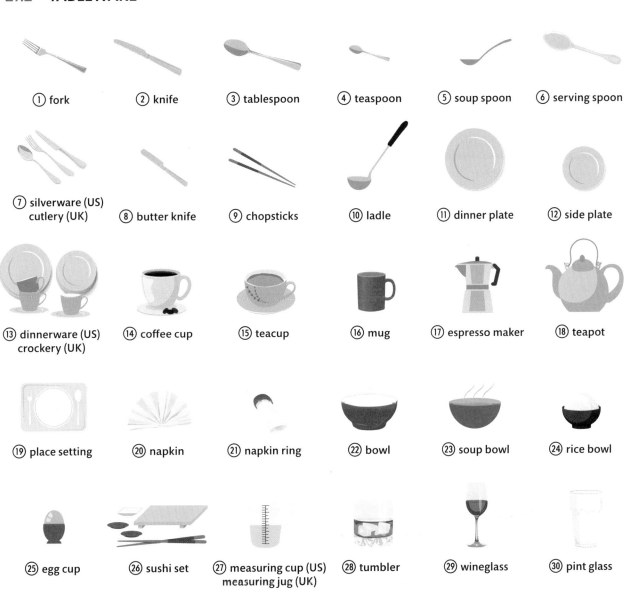

① fork ② knife ③ tablespoon ④ teaspoon ⑤ soup spoon ⑥ serving spoon

⑦ silverware (US) cutlery (UK) ⑧ butter knife ⑨ chopsticks ⑩ ladle ⑪ dinner plate ⑫ side plate

⑬ dinnerware (US) crockery (UK) ⑭ coffee cup ⑮ teacup ⑯ mug ⑰ espresso maker ⑱ teapot

⑲ place setting ⑳ napkin ㉑ napkin ring ㉒ bowl ㉓ soup bowl ㉔ rice bowl

㉕ egg cup ㉖ sushi set ㉗ measuring cup (US) measuring jug (UK) ㉘ tumbler ㉙ wineglass ㉚ pint glass

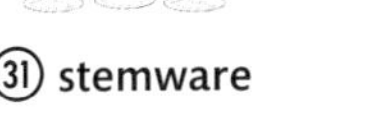

㉛ stemware ㉜ glasses / glassware ㉝ jar ㉞ sippy cup (US) beaker (UK) ㉟ sake cup ㊱ coaster

28 Kitchenware

28.1 KITCHEN EQUIPMENT

① grater
② peeler
③ whisk
④ kitchen knife
⑤ bread knife
⑥ kitchen scissors
⑦ cleaver
⑧ knife sharpener
⑨ meat tenderizer
⑩ skewer
⑪ can opener (US) tin opener (UK)
⑫ cutting board (US) chopping board (UK)
⑬ bottle opener
⑭ corkscrew
⑮ wooden spoon
⑯ slotted spoon
⑰ spatula
⑱ apple corer
⑲ masher
⑳ garlic press
㉑ carving fork
㉒ scoop
㉓ handle
㉔ lid
㉕ saucepan
㉖ frying pan
㉗ grill pan (US) griddle pan (UK)
㉘ wok
㉙ colander
㉚ turner / flipper (US) fish slice (UK)
㉛ sieve
㉜ measuring spoons
㉝ mortar
㉞ pestle
㉟ mortar and pestle

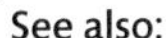

See also:
27 Kitchen and tableware 29 Cooking 59 Herbs and spices
60 In the pantry 71 Breakfast 72 Lunch and dinner

36 tagine
37 mixing bowl
38 soufflé dish
39 ramekin
40 casserole dish
41 frying basket
42 butter dish
43 timer
44 egg timer
45 lemon squeezer
46 coffee press / cafetière
47 meat thermometer

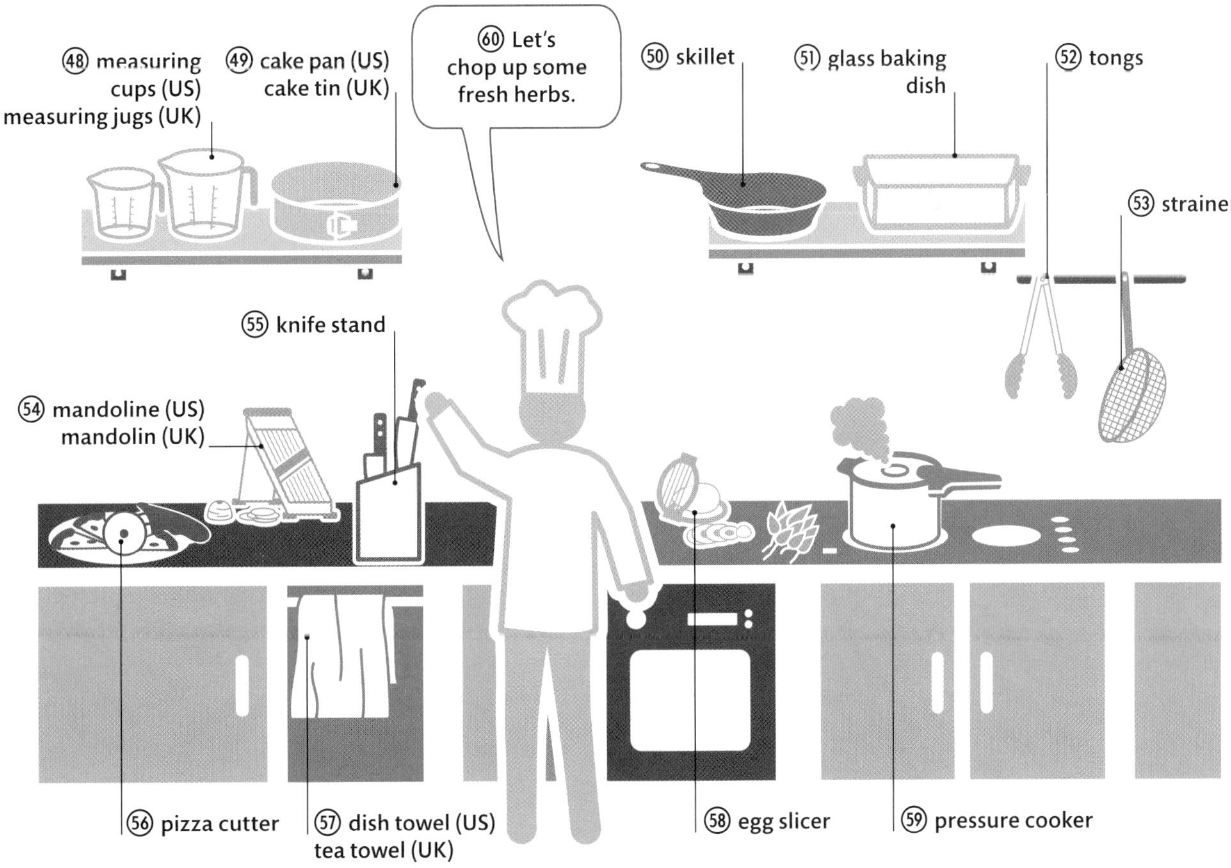

48 measuring cups (US) measuring jugs (UK)

49 cake pan (US) cake tin (UK)

60 Let's chop up some fresh herbs.

50 skillet

51 glass baking dish

52 tongs

53 strainer

55 knife stand

54 mandoline (US) mandolin (UK)

56 pizza cutter

57 dish towel (US) tea towel (UK)

58 egg slicer

59 pressure cooker

29 Cooking

29.1 COOKING VERBS

① to sprinkle
② to bake
③ to garnish
④ to grease
⑤ to roll
⑥ to taste
⑫ to stir-fry
⑬ I'll garnish this with some fresh herbs.
⑭ to chop

⑳ to broil (US)
to grill (UK)

㉑ to roast

㉒ to fry

㉓ to poach

㉔ to simmer

㉕ to boil

㉖ to freeze

㉗ to add

㉘ to mix

㉙ to stir

㉚ to whisk

㉛ to mash

㉜ to slice

㉝ a pinch

㉞ a dash

㉟ a handful

㊵ to pour

㊱ to mince

㊲ to peel

㊳ to cut

㊴ to grate

See also:
27 Kitchen and tableware **28** Kitchenware **59** Herbs and spices
60 In the pantry **62-63** The bakery **71** Breakfast **72** Lunch and dinner

⑦ to steam

⑧ Can you dice a carrot for me, please?

⑨ to beat eggs

⑩ I've burned the onions. They are ruined!

⑪ to microwave

⑮ to melt butter

⑯ to carve

⑰ to dice

⑱ to burn

⑲ to sauté

29.2 BAKING

① apron

② oven mitt (US)
oven glove (UK)

③ cake pan (US)
cake tin (UK)

④ flan pan (US)
flan tin (UK)

⑤ pie pan (US)
pie dish (UK)

⑥ pastry brush

⑦ rolling pin

⑧ baking pan (US)
baking tray (UK)

⑨ muffin tin (US)
muffin tray (UK)

⑩ cooling rack

⑪ icing

⑫ piping bag

⑬ scale (US)
scales (UK)

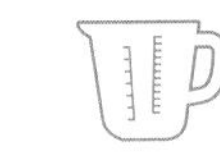
⑭ measuring cup (US)
measuring jug (UK)

⑮ to decorate

30 Bedroom

30.1 BEDROOM

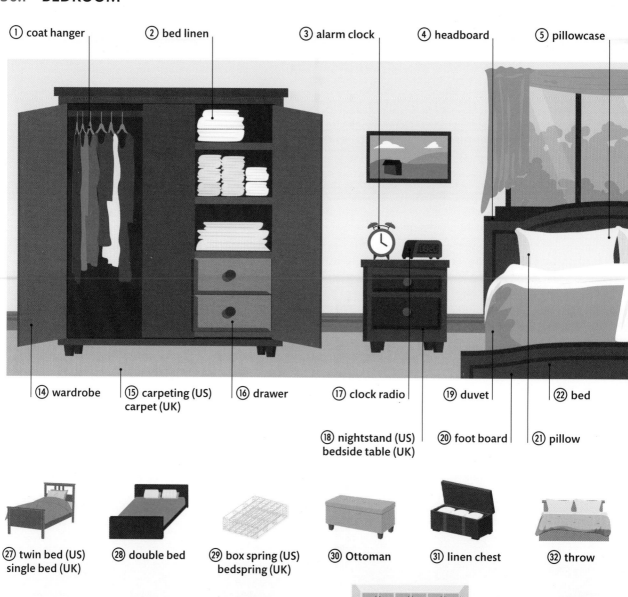

① coat hanger
② bed linen
③ alarm clock
④ headboard
⑤ pillowcase

⑭ wardrobe
⑮ carpeting (US) carpet (UK)
⑯ drawer
⑰ clock radio
⑱ nightstand (US) bedside table (UK)
⑲ duvet
⑳ foot board
㉑ pillow
㉒ bed

㉗ twin bed (US) single bed (UK)

㉘ double bed

㉙ box spring (US) bedspring (UK)

㉚ Ottoman

㉛ linen chest

㉜ throw

㉝ quilt

㉞ blanket

㉟ electric blanket

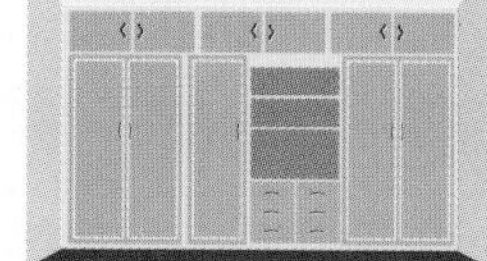
㊱ closet (US) / built-in wardrobe (UK)

㊲ hot-water bottle

See also:
08 Pregnancy and childhood 13-15 Clothes
25 A place to live 32 House and home

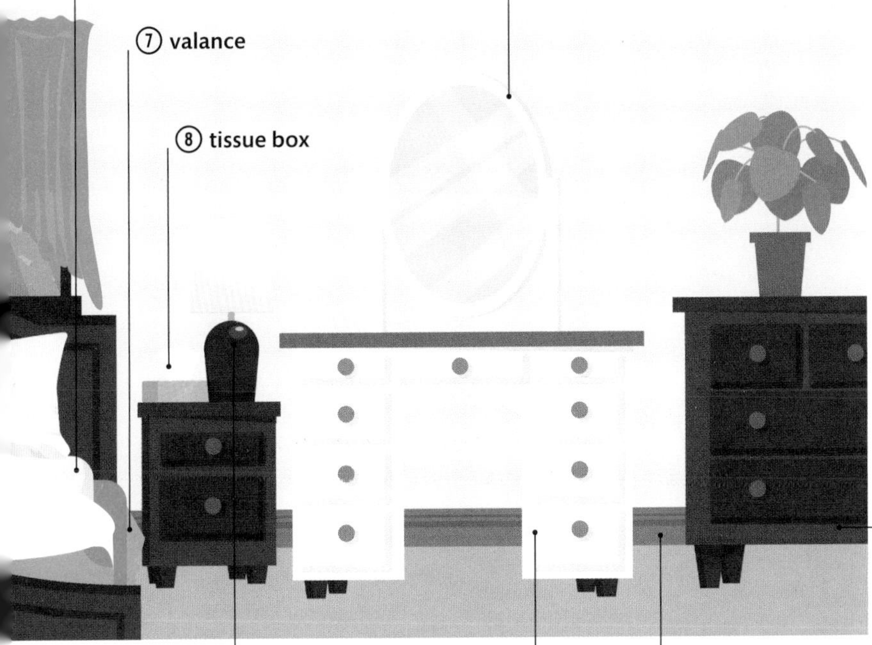

⑥ mattress

⑦ valance

⑧ tissue box

⑨ mirror

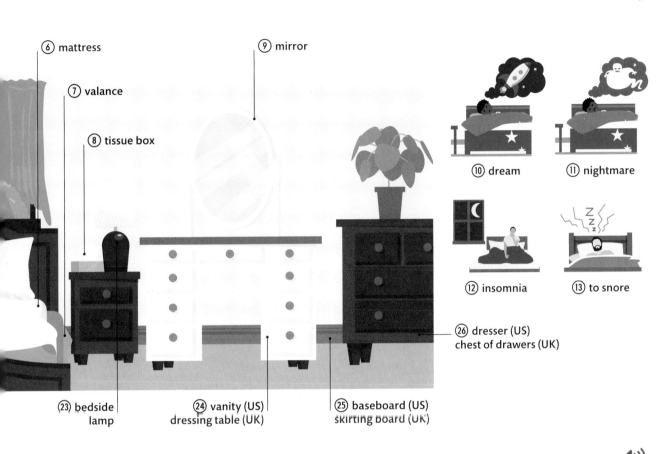

⑩ dream

⑪ nightmare

⑫ insomnia

⑬ to snore

㉓ bedside lamp

㉔ vanity (US)
dressing table (UK)

㉕ baseboard (US)
skirting board (UK)

㉖ dresser (US)
chest of drawers (UK)

30.2 NURSERY

① baby monitor
② crib (US) / cot (UK)
③ bars
④ sheet
⑤ Moses basket
⑥ night-light (US)
night light (UK)
⑦ mobile
⑧ changing mat
⑨ changing table
⑩ teddy bear
⑪ floor

31 Bathroom

31.1 IN THE BATHROOM

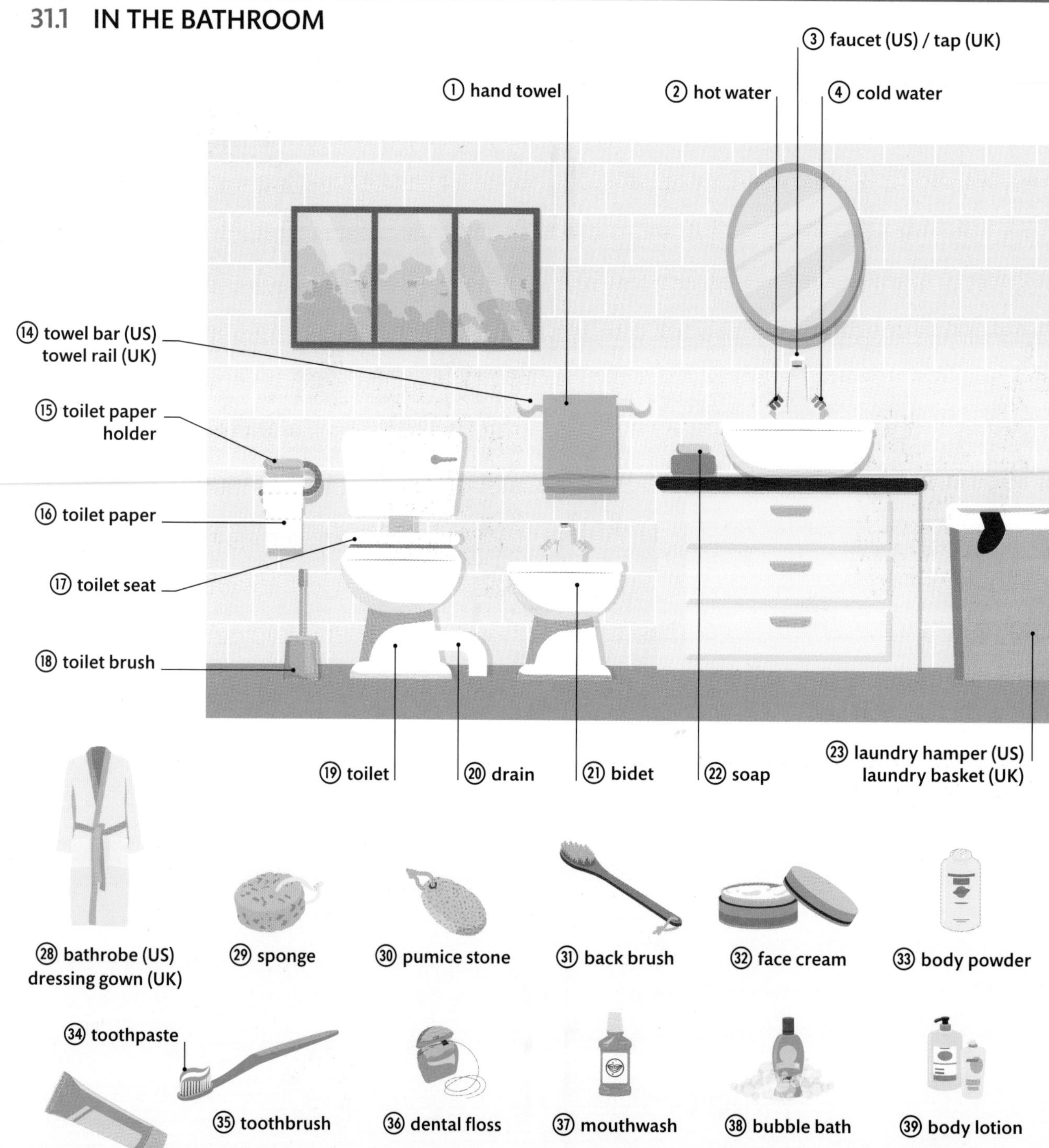

③ faucet (US) / tap (UK)
① hand towel
② hot water
④ cold water
⑭ towel bar (US)
towel rail (UK)
⑮ toilet paper
holder
⑯ toilet paper
⑰ toilet seat
⑱ toilet brush
⑲ toilet
⑳ drain
㉑ bidet
㉒ soap
㉓ laundry hamper (US)
laundry basket (UK)
㉘ bathrobe (US)
dressing gown (UK)
㉙ sponge
㉚ pumice stone
㉛ back brush
㉜ face cream
㉝ body powder
㉞ toothpaste
㉟ toothbrush
㊱ dental floss
㊲ mouthwash
㊳ bubble bath
㊴ body lotion

See also:
18 Beauty 25 A place to live
32 House and home 33 Electrics and plumbing

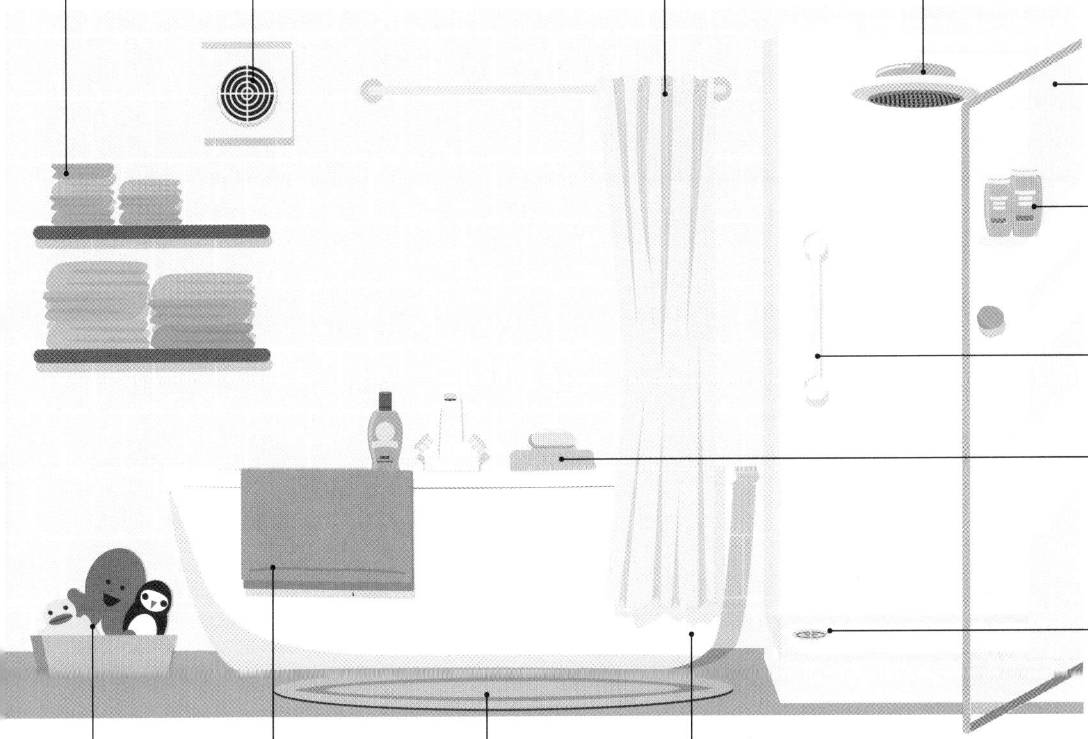

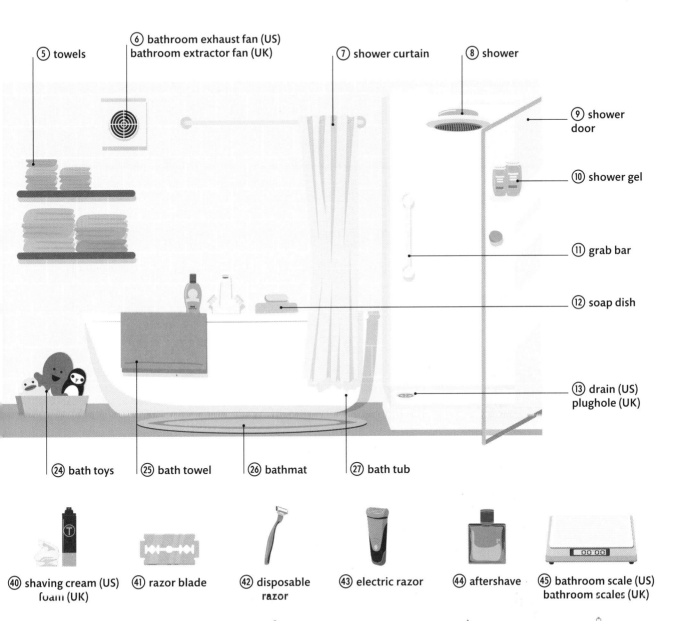

⑤ towels

⑥ bathroom exhaust fan (US)
bathroom extractor fan (UK)

⑦ shower curtain

⑧ shower

⑨ shower door

⑩ shower gel

⑪ grab bar

⑫ soap dish

⑬ drain (US)
plughole (UK)

㉔ bath toys

㉕ bath towel

㉖ bathmat

㉗ bath tub

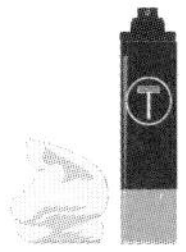

㊵ shaving cream (US)
foam (UK)

㊶ razor blade

㊷ disposable razor

㊸ electric razor

㊹ aftershave

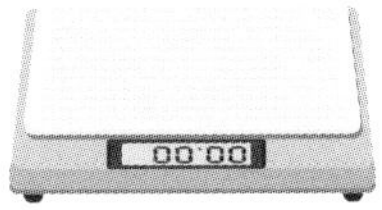

㊺ bathroom scale (US)
bathroom scales (UK)

㊻ plunger

㊼ plug

㊽ to dry yourself

㊾ to shave

㊿ to take (or have) a shower

51 to take (or have) a bath

32 House and home

32.1 TYPES OF HOUSES

① detached house

② duplex (US) semi-detached (UK)

③ row house (US) terraced house (UK)

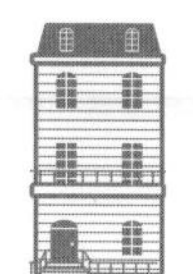

④ town house

⑤ cottage

⑥ villa

⑦ ranch house (US) bungalow (UK)

⑧ mansion

⑨ mobile home (US) caravan (UK)

⑩ cabin

⑪ tree house

⑫ chalet

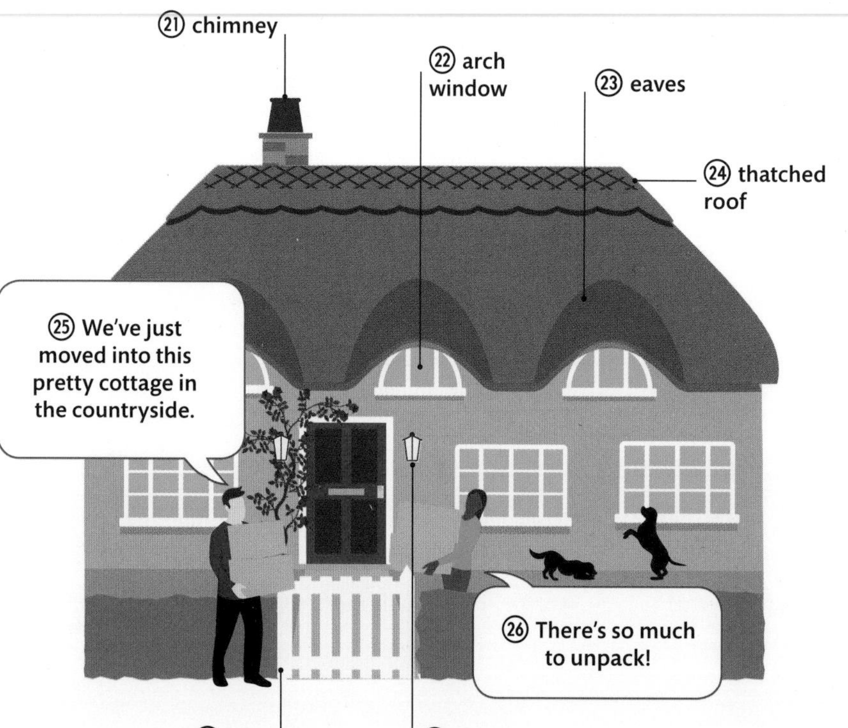
㉑ chimney
㉒ arch window
㉓ eaves
㉔ thatched roof
㉕ We've just moved into this pretty cottage in the countryside.
㉖ There's so much to unpack!
㉘ gate
㉗ light

㉙ thatched cottage

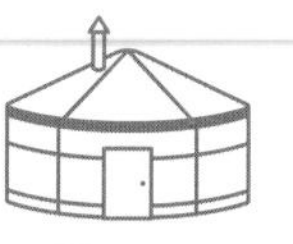

⑬ yurt

⑭ hut

⑮ wigwam

⑯ igloo

⑰ teepee

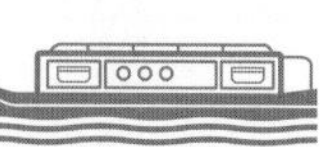

⑱ houseboat

⑲ prefab house

⑳ stilt house

See also:
25 A place to live **33** Electrics and plumbing **35** Home improvements
37 Decorating **42-43** In town **44** Buildings and architecture

32.2 BUYING AND RENTING A HOUSE

$$$

① realtor (US)
estate agent (UK)

② real estate (US)
property (UK)

$$

③ to view
a house

④ furnished

⑤ unfurnished

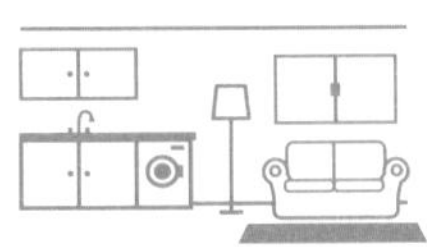

⑥ open-plan

P

⑦ parking space

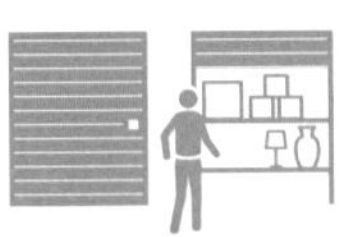

⑧ storage

⑨ to save up

$$$

⑩ to buy

⑪ to own

⑫ boxes

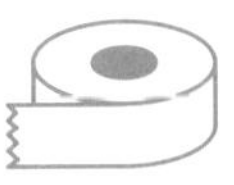

⑬ tape

⑭ keys

⑮ to pack

⑯ moving truck (US)
removal van (UK)

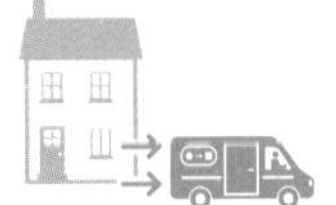

⑰ to move out

⑱ to move in

⑲ to unpack

⑳ to rent out

MAY

㉑ to rent

㉒ lease / tenancy
agreement (UK)

㉓ tenant

㉔ landlord

㉕ deposit

㉖ to give notice

㉗ mortgage

㉘ bills

㉙ roomer (US)
lodger (UK)

㉚ roommate (US)
housemate (UK)

㉛ residential area

33 Electrics and plumbing

33.1 ELECTRICITY

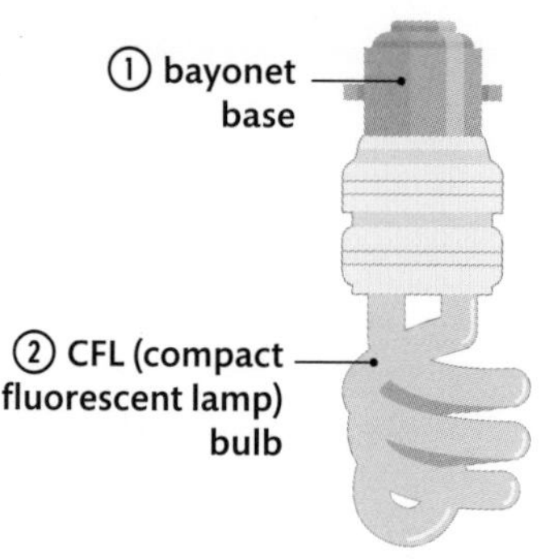

① bayonet base
② CFL (compact fluorescent lamp) bulb

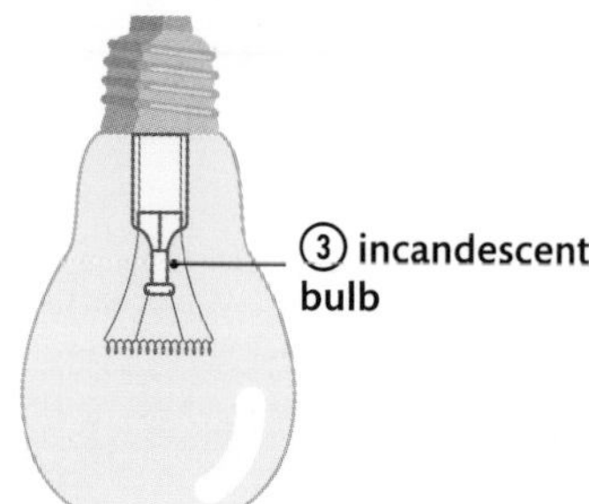

③ incandescent bulb

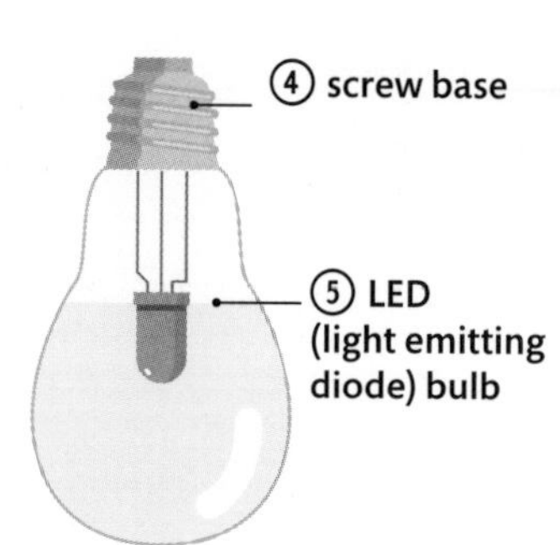

④ screw base
⑤ LED (light emitting diode) bulb

⑥ light bulbs

⑦ socket

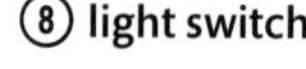
⑧ light switch

⑨ direct current

⑩ alternating current

⑪ generator

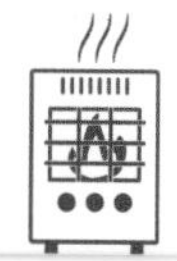
⑫ gas space heater

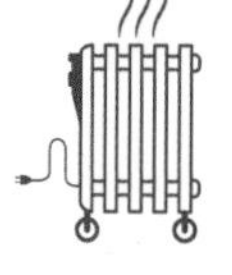
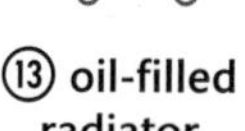
⑬ oil-filled radiator

⑭ fan space heater

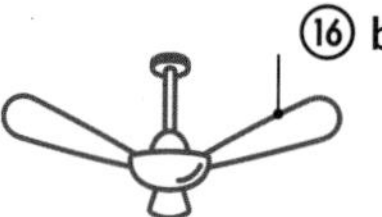

⑯ blade

⑮ ceiling fan

⑰ fan

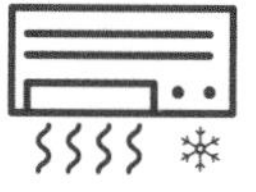
⑱ air conditioning

⑲ power

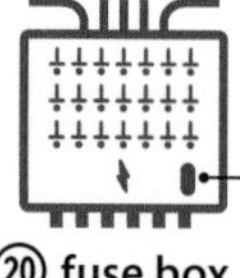

㉑ breaker (US) trip switch (UK)

⑳ fuse box

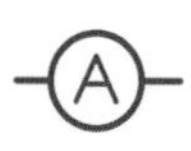
㉒ amp

㉓ live

㉔ neutral

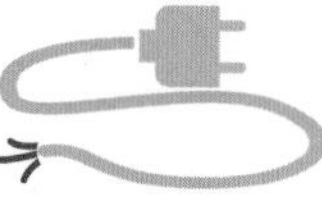
㉕ wires

㉖ ground (US) earthing (UK)

㉗ voltage

㉘ plug

㉙ pin

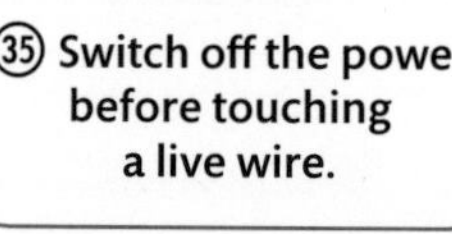

㉟ Switch off the power before touching a live wire.

㉚ electricity meter

㉛ transformer

㉜ power outage (US) power cut (UK)

㉝ utility power (US) mains supply (UK)

㉞ wiring

See also:
31 Bathroom 35 Home improvements
36 Tools 37 Decorating 87 Construction

33.2 PLUMBING

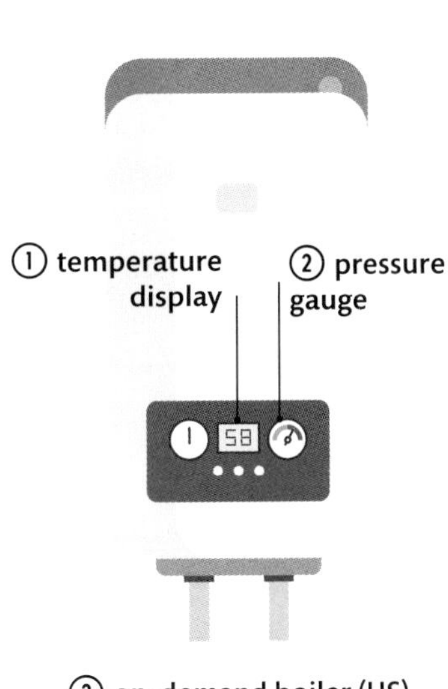
58

① temperature display
② pressure gauge
③ on-demand boiler (US) boiler (UK)

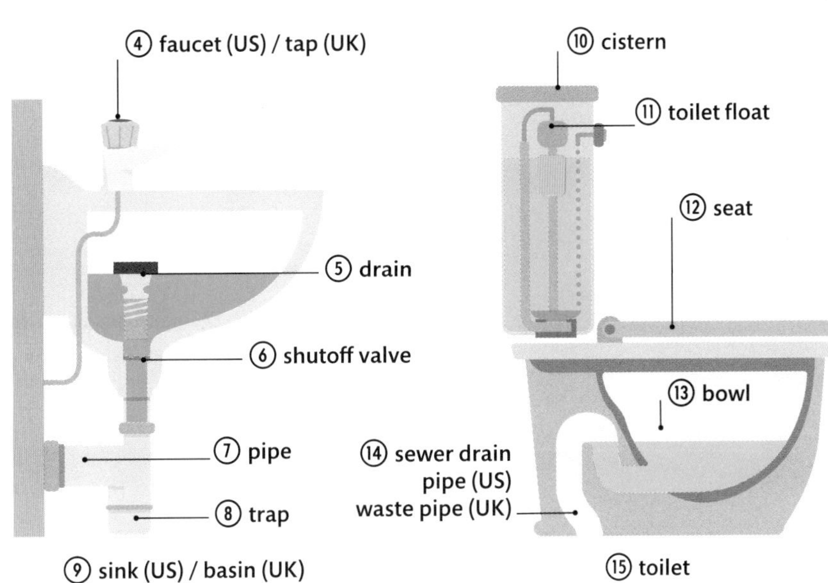

④ faucet (US) / tap (UK)
⑤ drain
⑥ shutoff valve
⑦ pipe
⑧ trap
⑨ sink (US) / basin (UK)
⑩ cistern
⑪ toilet float
⑫ seat
⑬ bowl
⑭ sewer drain pipe (US) waste pipe (UK)
⑮ toilet

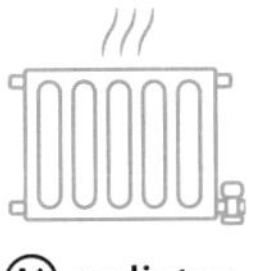

⑯ radiator

⑰ faucet (US) tap (UK)

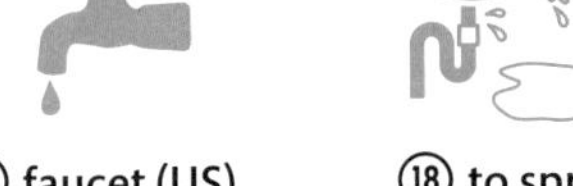

⑱ to spring a leak

⑲ to call a plumber

⑳ to repair

㉑ to install

33.3 WASTE

① trash can (US) / rubbish bin (UK)

② recycling bin

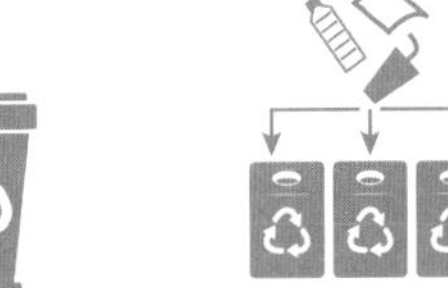

③ sorting unit

④ food compost bin

⑤ trash bag (US) bin liner (UK)

⑥ biodegradable waste

⑦ hazardous waste

⑧ electrical waste

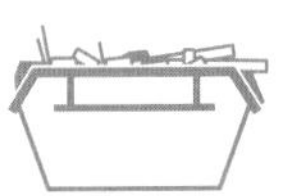

⑨ construction waste

34 Household chores

34.1 HOUSEHOLD TASKS

① to change the sheets

② to make the bed

③ to feed the pets

④ to water the plants

⑤ to wash the car

⑥ to sweep the floor

⑦ to scrub the floor

⑧ to clean the oven

⑨ to clean the windows

⑩ to defrost the freezer

⑪ to vacuum the carpet

⑫ to dust

⑬ to clean the bathroom

⑭ to clean up (US) to tidy (UK)

⑮ to buy groceries

⑯ to do the laundry

⑰ to hang clothes (US) to hang out clothes (UK)

⑱ to do the ironing

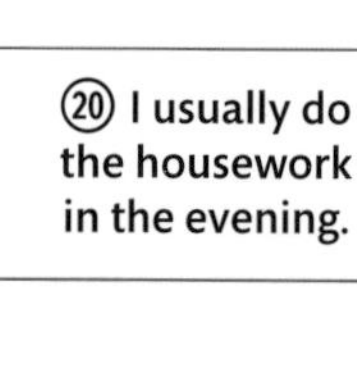

⑳ I usually do the housework in the evening.

⑲ to mop the floor

㉑ to fold clothes

㉒ to set the table

㉓ to clear the table

㉔ to load the dishwasher

㉕ to unload the dishwasher

㉖ to wipe the surfaces

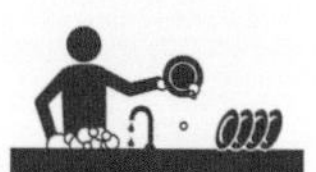

㉗ to do the dishes

㉘ to dry the dishes

㉙ to take out the trash (US) to take out the rubbish (UK)

See also:
09 Daily routines 25 A place to live 33 Electrics and plumbing
35 Home improvements 37 Decorating 39 Practical gardening

34.2 LAUNDRY AND CLEANING

① scouring pad

② sponge

③ cloth

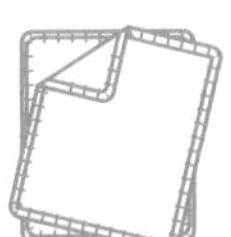
④ duster

⑤ feather duster

⑥ squeegee

⑦ bucket

⑧ mop

⑨ scrubbing brush

⑩ dustpan

⑪ brush

⑫ broom

⑬ recycling bin

⑭ trash bag (US)
bin liner (UK)

⑮ polish

⑯ surface cleaner

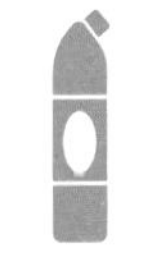
⑰ toilet cleaner

⑱ automatic toilet cleaner (US)
toilet block (UK)

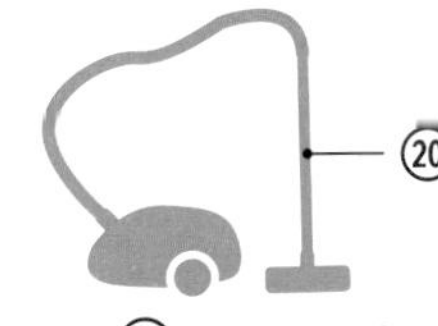
⑳ suction hose
⑲ vacuum cleaner

㉑ rubber gloves

㉒ white vinegar

㉓ dirty clothes (US)
dirty washing (UK)

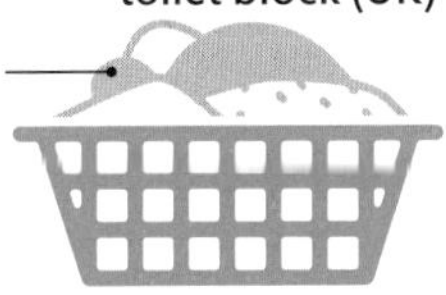
㉔ laundry hamper (US)
laundry basket (UK)

㉕ washing machine

㉖ tumble dryer

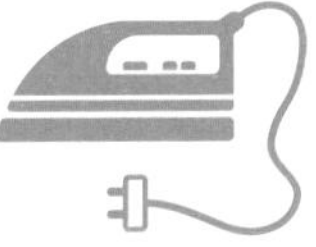
㉗ iron

㉘ ironing board

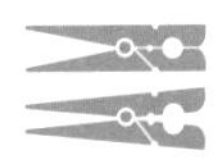
㉙ clothes pin (US)
clothes peg (UK)

㉚ clothesline /
washing line (UK)

㉛ laundry detergent

㉜ fabric softener

㉝ dishwasher

㉞ dishwasher tablets

㉟ dishwashing liquid (US)
washing-up liquid (UK)

㊱ bleach

35 Home improvements

35.1 TOOLS AND DIY EQUIPMENT

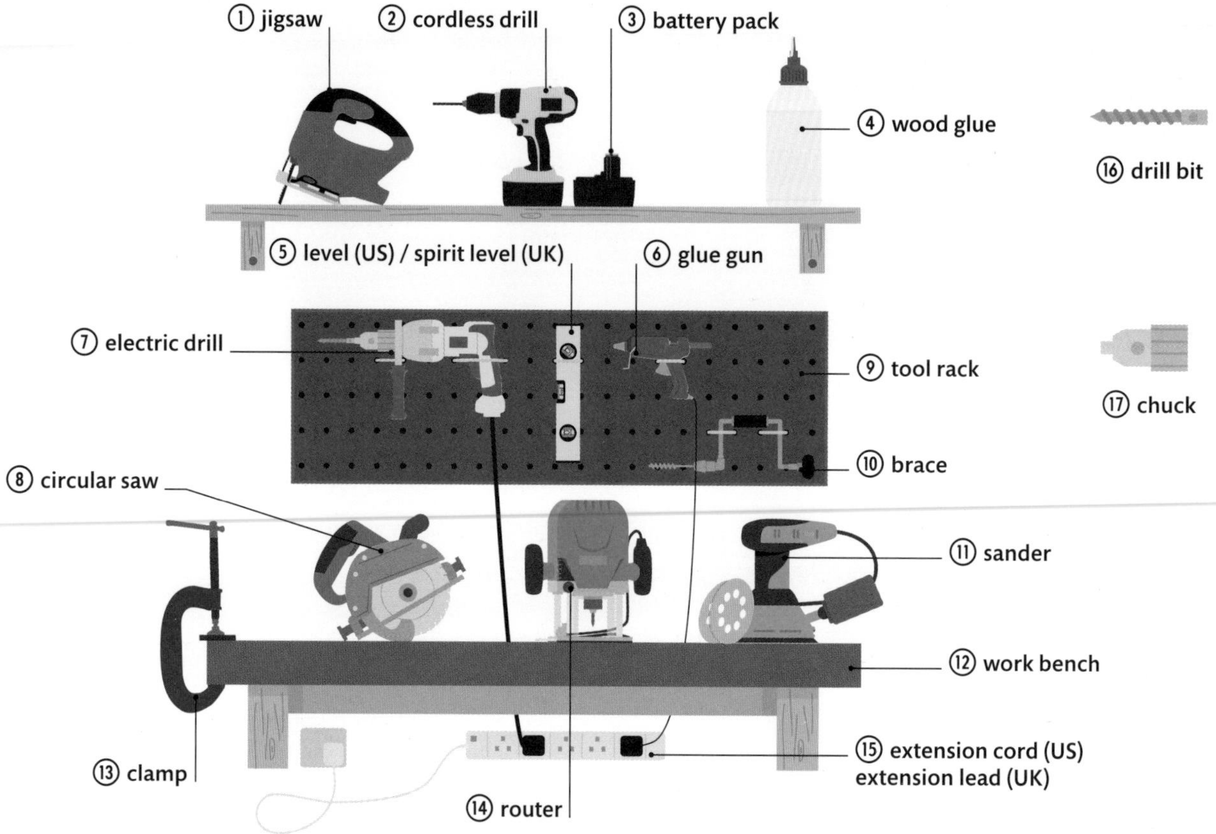

① jigsaw
② cordless drill
③ battery pack
④ wood glue
⑤ level (US) / spirit level (UK)
⑥ glue gun
⑦ electric drill
⑧ circular saw
⑨ tool rack
⑩ brace
⑪ sander
⑫ work bench
⑬ clamp
⑭ router
⑮ extension cord (US)
extension lead (UK)
⑯ drill bit
⑰ chuck

35.2 DIY VERBS

① to cut
② to saw
③ to drill
④ to hammer
⑤ to plane
⑥ to turn
⑦ to carve
⑧ to tile
⑨ to solder
⑩ solder
⑪ soldering iron

See also:
33 Electrics and plumbing 36 Tools
37 Decorating 87 Construction

35.3 MATERIALS

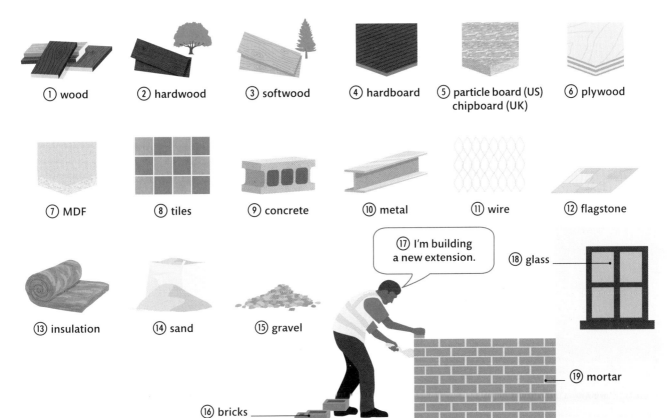

① wood
② hardwood
③ softwood
④ hardboard
⑤ particle board (US) chipboard (UK)
⑥ plywood
⑦ MDF
⑧ tiles
⑨ concrete
⑩ metal
⑪ wire
⑫ flagstone
⑬ insulation
⑭ sand
⑮ gravel
⑯ bricks
⑰ I'm building a new extension.
⑱ glass
⑲ mortar

⑫ to install a carpet (US) to fit (UK) a carpet

⑬ to unclog the sink (US) unblock the sink (UK)

⑭ to rewire the house

⑮ to lay bricks

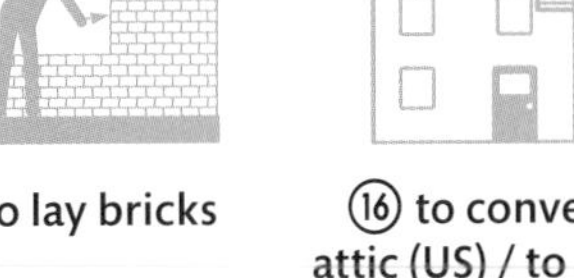

⑯ to convert the attic (US) / to convert the loft (UK)

⑰ to make curtains

⑱ to put up shelves

⑲ to change a light bulb

⑳ to unclog the toilet (US) unblock the toilet (UK)

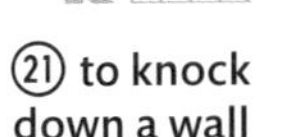

㉑ to knock down a wall

㉒ to paint a wall

㉓ to fix a fence

36 Tools

36.1 TOOLBOX

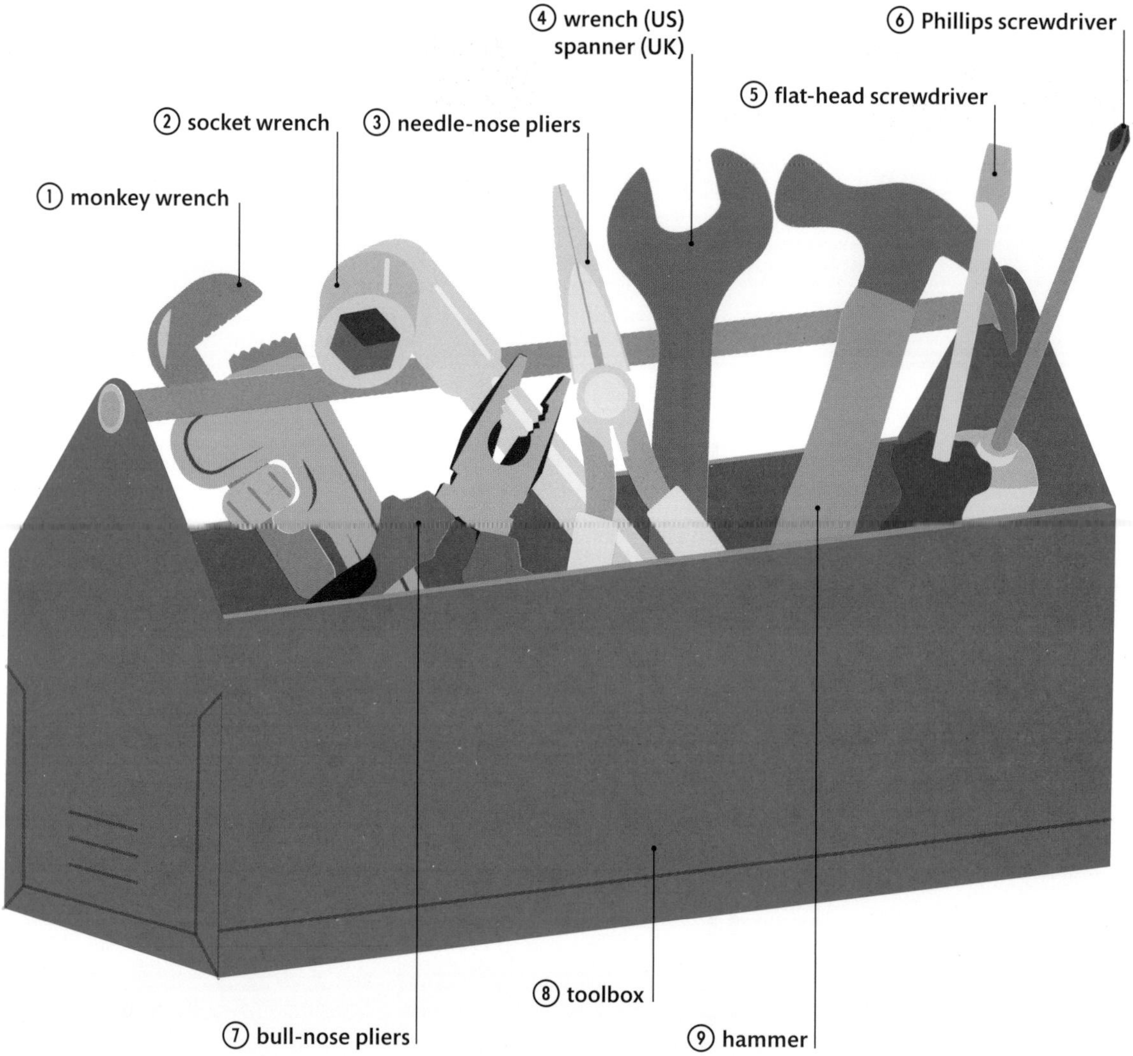

① monkey wrench
② socket wrench
③ needle-nose pliers
④ wrench (US) spanner (UK)
⑤ flat-head screwdriver
⑥ Phillips screwdriver
⑦ bull-nose pliers
⑧ toolbox
⑨ hammer

36.2 DRILL BITS

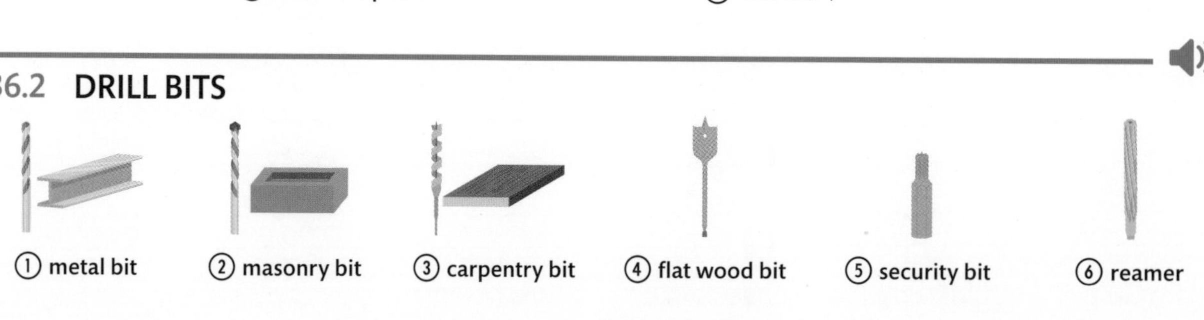
① metal bit
② masonry bit
③ carpentry bit
④ flat wood bit
⑤ security bit
⑥ reamer

See also:
33 Electrics and plumbing 35 Home improvements
37 Decorating 87 Construction

36.3 TOOLS

① tool belt

② nail

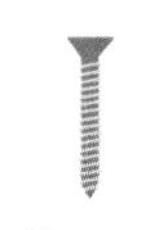
③ screw

④ bolt

⑤ washer

⑥ nut

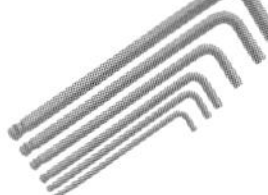
⑦ hex keys / Allen keys (UK)

⑧ tape measure

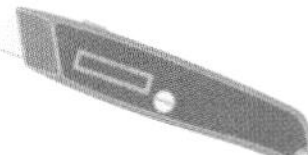
⑨ utility knife

⑩ hacksaw

⑪ tenon saw

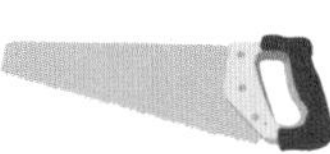
⑫ handsaw

⑬ plane

⑭ hand drill

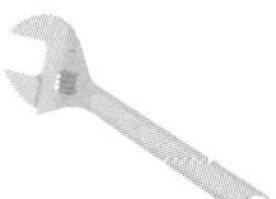
⑮ wrench (US) spanner (UK)

⑯ chisel

⑰ file

⑱ sharpening stone

⑳ rung

⑲ ladder

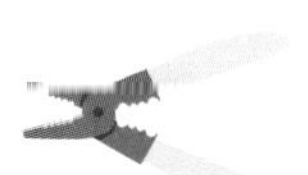
㉑ wire strippers

㉒ wire cutters

㉓ insulating tape

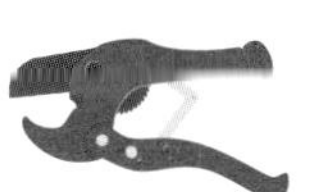
㉔ pipe cutter

㉕ plunger

㉖ mallet

㉗ ax (US) axe (UK)

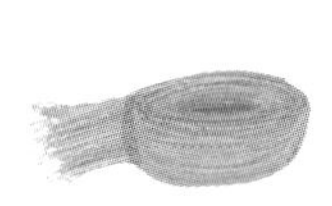
㉘ steel wool (US) wire wool (UK)

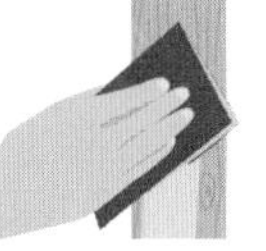
㉙ sandpaper

㉚ safety goggles

㉛ soldering iron

㉜ solder

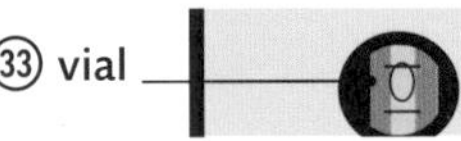

㉝ vial

㉞ level (US) spirit level (UK)

37 Decorating

37.1 HOUSEHOLD RENOVATION

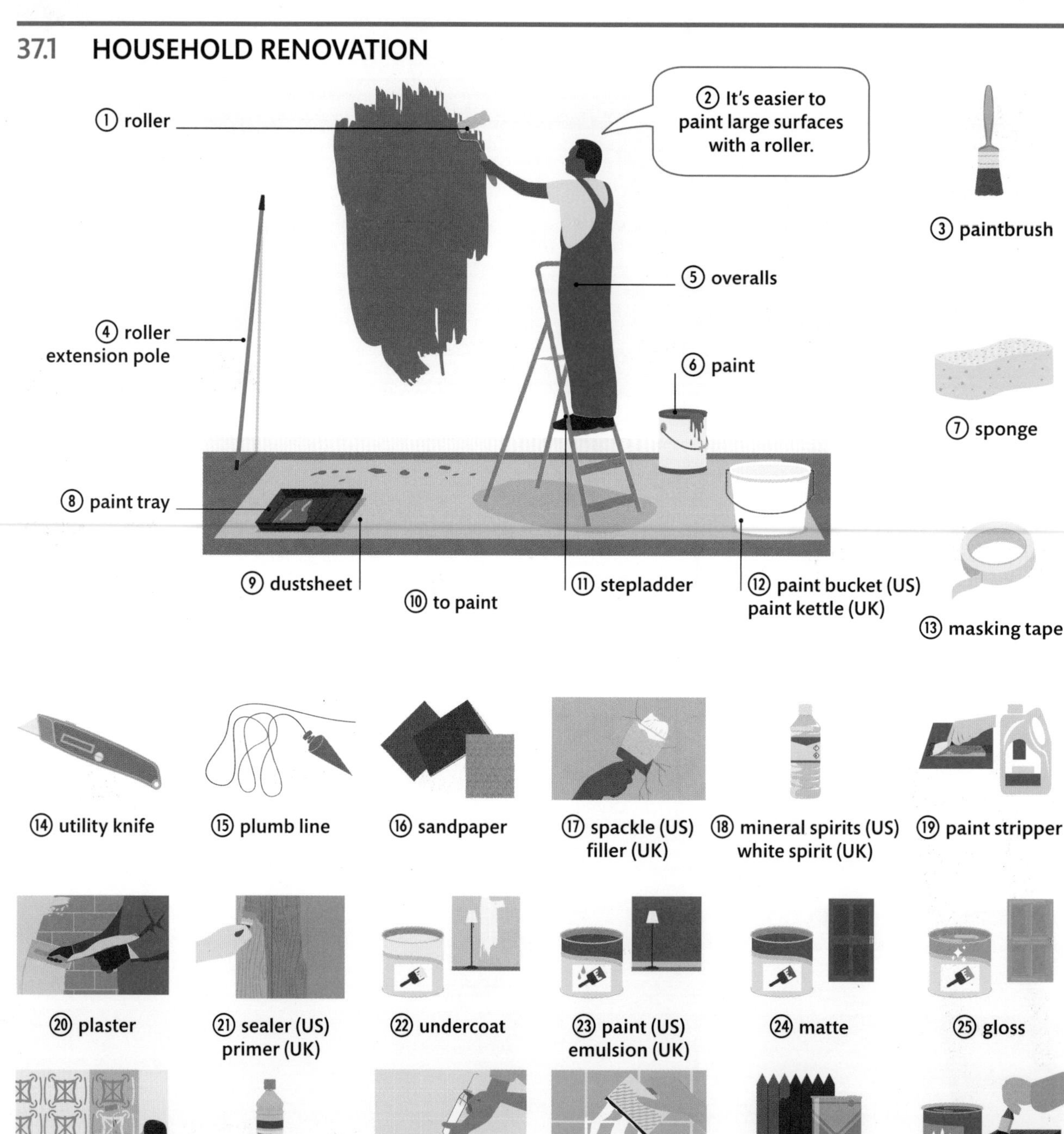

① roller
② It's easier to paint large surfaces with a roller.
③ paintbrush
④ roller extension pole
⑤ overalls
⑥ paint
⑦ sponge
⑧ paint tray
⑨ dustsheet
⑩ to paint
⑪ stepladder
⑫ paint bucket (US) paint kettle (UK)
⑬ masking tape
⑭ utility knife
⑮ plumb line
⑯ sandpaper
⑰ spackle (US) filler (UK)
⑱ mineral spirits (US) white spirit (UK)
⑲ paint stripper
⑳ plaster
㉑ sealer (US) primer (UK)
㉒ undercoat
㉓ paint (US) emulsion (UK)
㉔ matte
㉕ gloss
㉖ stencil
㉗ solvent
㉘ sealant / caulk
㉙ grout
㉚ wood preserver
㉛ varnish

See also:
32 House and home 33 Electrics and plumbing
34 Household chores 35 Home improvements

(32) scissors

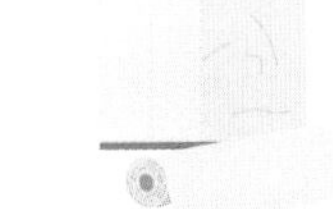

(33) lining paper

(34) wallpaper stripper

(35) scraper

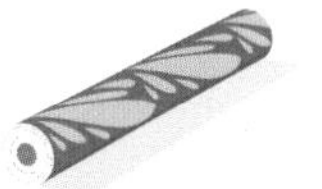

(36) wallpaper roll

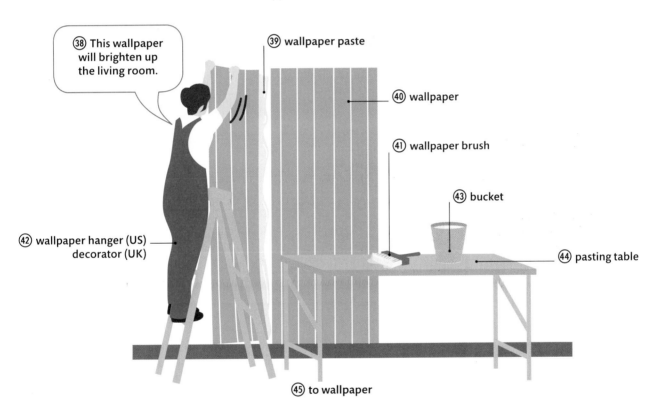

(37) wallpaper border

(38) This wallpaper will brighten up the living room.

(39) wallpaper paste

(40) wallpaper

(41) wallpaper brush

(43) bucket

(42) wallpaper hanger (US)
decorator (UK)

(44) pasting table

(45) to wallpaper

37.2 VERBS FOR DECORATING

(1) to strip

(2) to spackle (US)
to fill (UK)

(3) to sand

(4) to plaster

(5) to hang

(6) to tile

38 Garden plants and houseplants

38.1 GARDEN PLANTS AND FLOWERS

① dandelion

② evening primrose

③ thistle

④ tulip

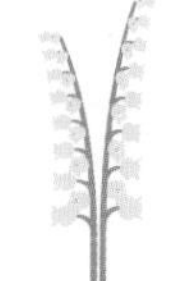
⑤ lily of the valley

⑥ carnation

⑧ daisy

⑨ buttercup

⑩ poppy

⑪ pansy

⑫ geranium

⑬ foxglove

⑮ lupin

⑯ rose

⑰ sunflower

⑱ orchid

⑲ begonia

⑳ lily

㉒ violet

㉓ crocus

㉔ daffodil

㉕ lilac

㉖ gardenia

㉗ lavender

㉙ marigold

㉚ azalea

㉛ chrysanthemum

㉜ rhododendron

㉝ rose of Sharon / hibiscus

㉟ honeysuckle

㊱ iris

㊲ lotus

㊳ wisteria

㊴ African daisy

㊵ hydrangea

See also:
39 Practical gardening **40** Garden tools
41 Garden features **167-169** Plants and trees

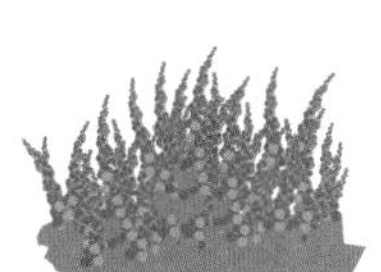

⑦ heather

⑭ camellia

㉑ pampas grass

㉘ protea

㉞ rosemary

㊶ bay tree

38.2 HOUSEPLANTS

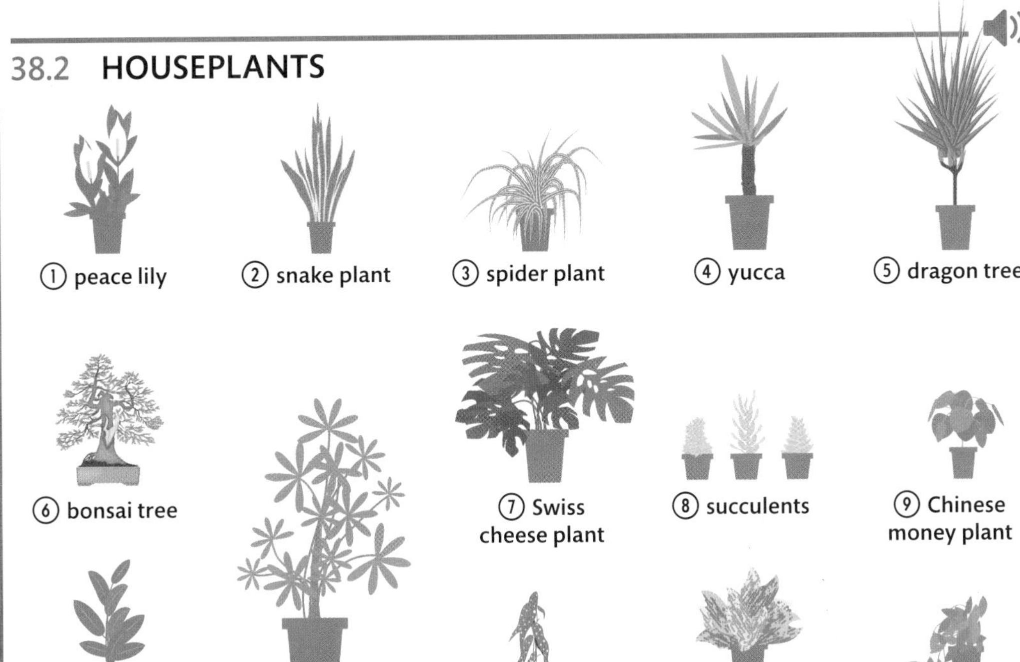
① peace lily
② snake plant
③ spider plant
④ yucca
⑤ dragon tree
⑥ bonsai tree
⑦ Swiss cheese plant
⑧ succulents
⑨ Chinese money plant
⑩ rubber plant
⑪ umbrella plant
⑫ polka dot plant
⑬ marble queen
⑭ jade pothos

38.3 FLOWER ANATOMY

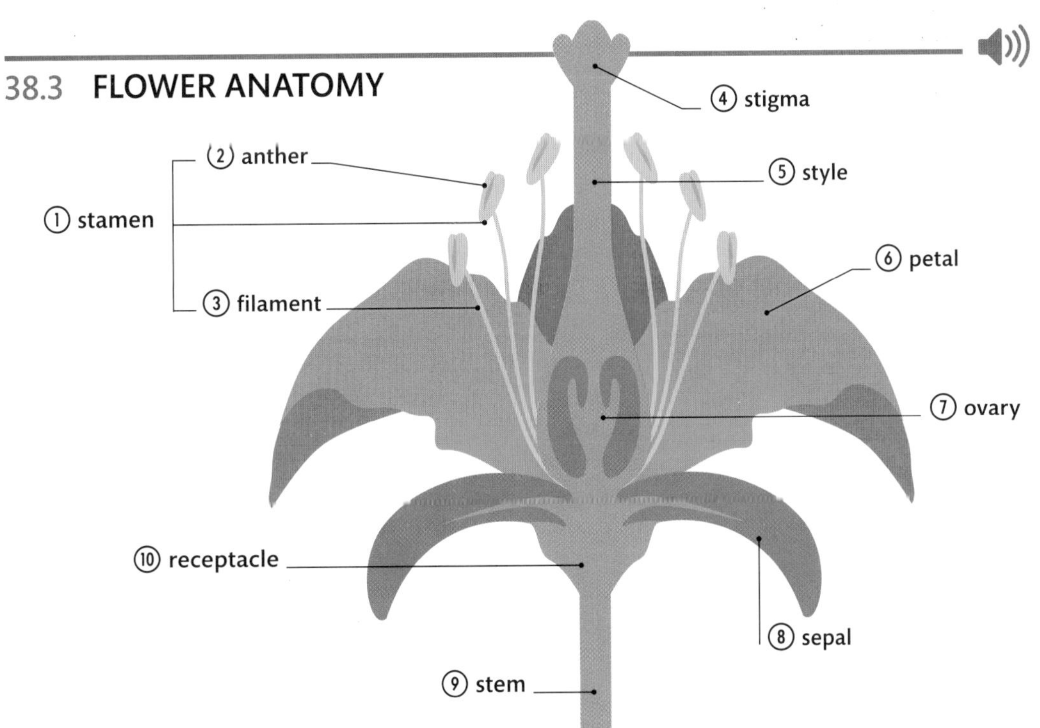
① stamen
② anther
③ filament
④ stigma
⑤ style
⑥ petal
⑦ ovary
⑧ sepal
⑨ stem
⑩ receptacle

39 Practical gardening

39.1 GARDENING VERBS

① My family and I enjoy gardening in the summer.
② to stake
③ to sow
⑥ to deadhead
⑦ to water
⑧ to harvest
⑮ to mow the lawn
⑯ to lay sod (US) to lay turf (UK)
⑰ to rake (soil)
⑱ to rake (leaves)
⑲ to aerate
⑳ cold frame
㉔ to graft
㉕ to propagate
㉖ to plant
㉗ to mulch
㉘ to do the weeding
㉙ to transplant
㉞ to cultivate
㉟ to trim
㊱ to prune
㊲ to chop
㊳ to sieve
㊴ to landscape

See also:
38 Garden plants and houseplants 40 Garden tools
41 Garden features 167-69 Plants and trees

④ potting shed

⑤ to dig

⑨ to pot (US)
to pot up (UK)

⑩ bone meal

⑪ plant cutting

⑫ greenhouse

⑬ shed

⑭ drainage

㉑ to top dress

㉒ to tend

㉓ to train

㉚ to spray

㉛ plant food

㉜ organic

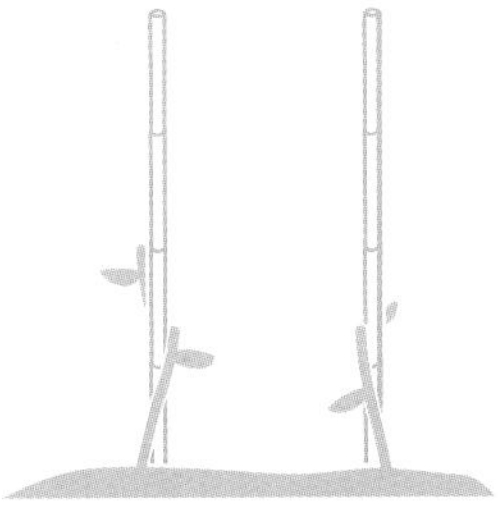

㉝ training / support cane

㊵ fertilizer

㊶ to fertilize

㊷ weedkiller

39.2 TYPES OF SOIL

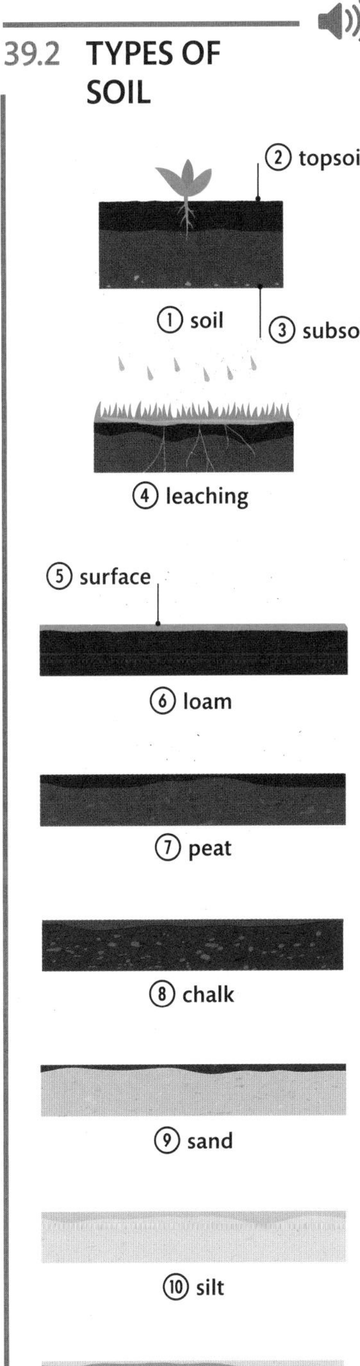
② topsoil
① soil
③ subsoil
④ leaching
⑤ surface
⑥ loam
⑦ peat
⑧ chalk
⑨ sand
⑩ silt 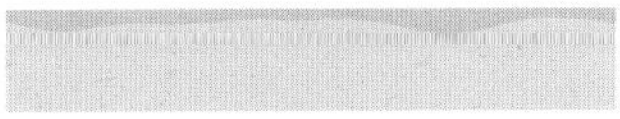
⑪ clay

40 Garden tools

40.1 GARDENING EQUIPMENT

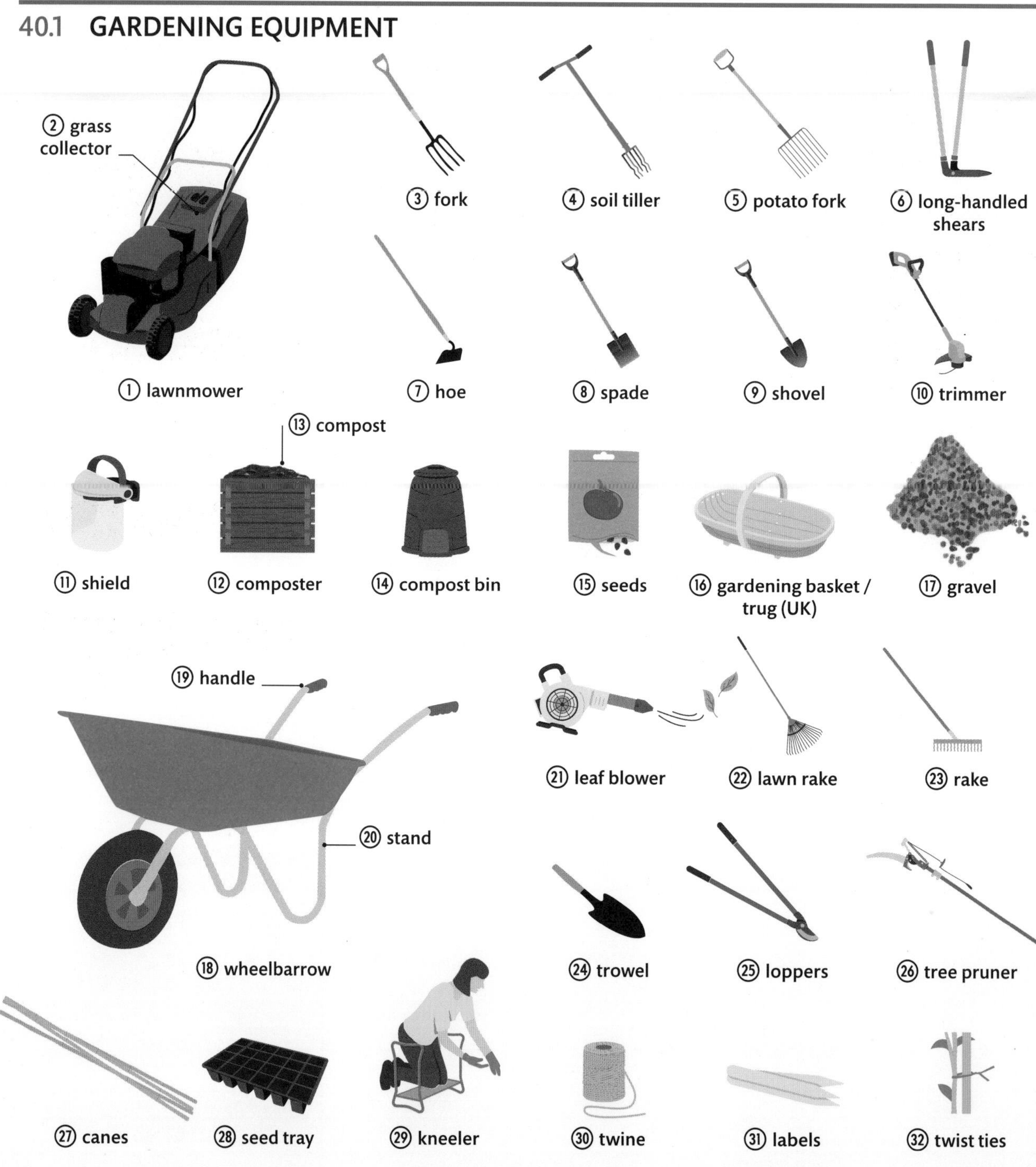

② grass collector
③ fork
④ soil tiller
⑤ potato fork
⑥ long-handled shears
① lawnmower
⑦ hoe
⑧ spade
⑨ shovel
⑩ trimmer
⑬ compost
⑪ shield
⑫ composter
⑭ compost bin
⑮ seeds
⑯ gardening basket / trug (UK)
⑰ gravel
⑲ handle
⑳ stand
㉑ leaf blower
㉒ lawn rake
㉓ rake
⑱ wheelbarrow
㉔ trowel
㉕ loppers
㉖ tree pruner
㉗ canes
㉘ seed tray
㉙ kneeler
㉚ twine
㉛ labels
㉜ twist ties

See also:
38 Garden plants and houseplants **39** Practical gardening
41 Garden features **167-169** Plants and trees

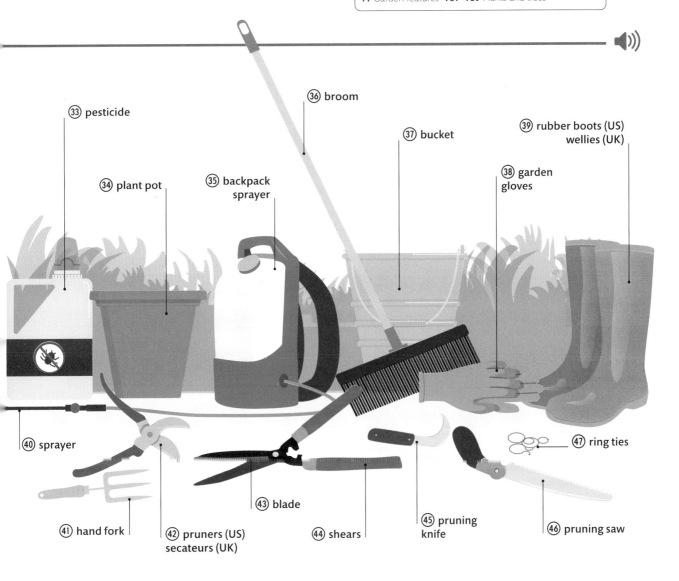

(33) pesticide

(34) plant pot

(35) backpack sprayer

(36) broom

(37) bucket

(38) garden gloves

(39) rubber boots (US)
wellies (UK)

(40) sprayer

(41) hand fork

(42) pruners (US)
secateurs (UK)

(43) blade

(44) shears

(45) pruning knife

(46) pruning saw

(47) ring ties

40.2 WATERING

(1) watering can

(2) spray nozzle

(3) sprinkler

(4) hose reel

(5) nozzle

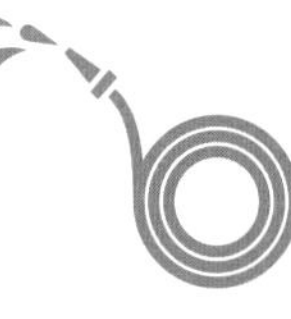

(6) garden hose

41 Garden features

41.1 GARDEN TYPES AND FEATURES

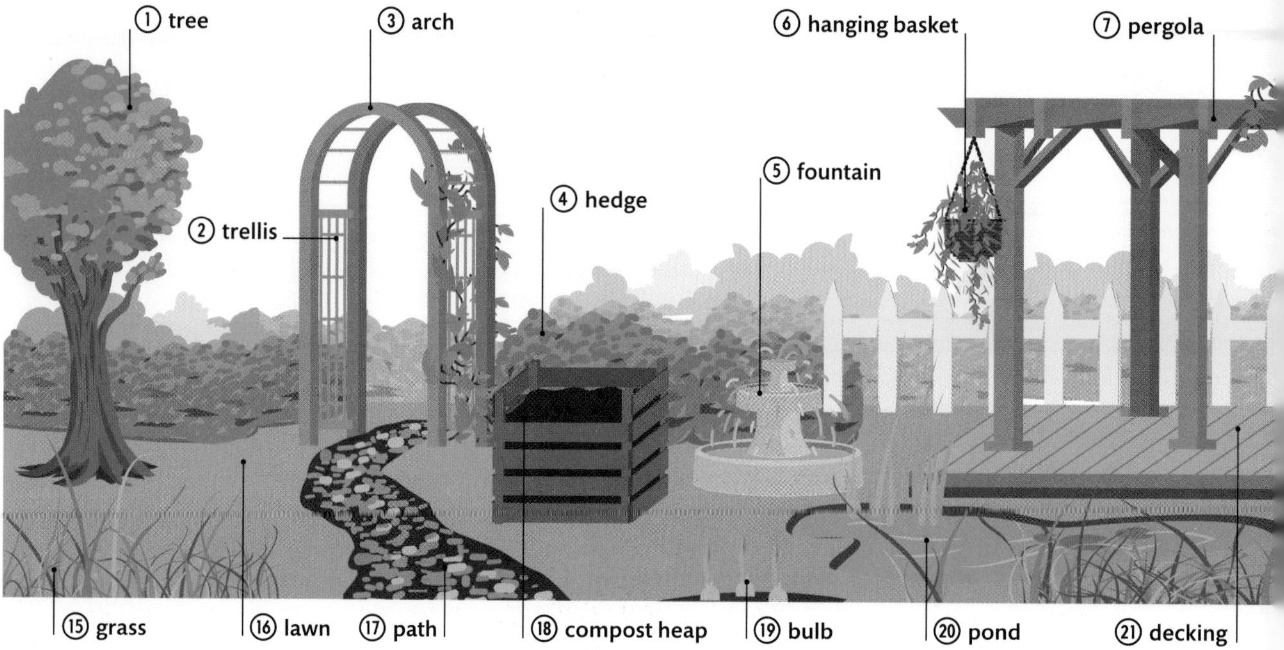

① tree
③ arch
⑥ hanging basket
⑦ pergola
② trellis
④ hedge
⑤ fountain
⑮ grass
⑯ lawn
⑰ path
⑱ compost heap
⑲ bulb
⑳ pond
㉑ decking

㉖ patio garden

㉗ roof garden

㉘ rock garden

㉙ formal garden

41.2 TYPES OF PLANTS

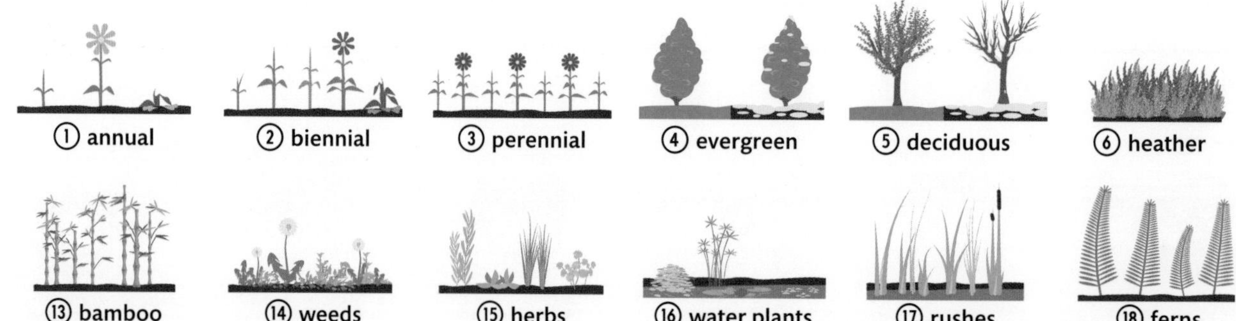
① annual
② biennial
③ perennial
④ evergreen
⑤ deciduous
⑥ heather
⑬ bamboo
⑭ weeds
⑮ herbs
⑯ water plants
⑰ rushes
⑱ ferns

See also:
38 Garden plants and houseplants **39** Practical gardening
40 Garden tools **167-169** Plants and trees

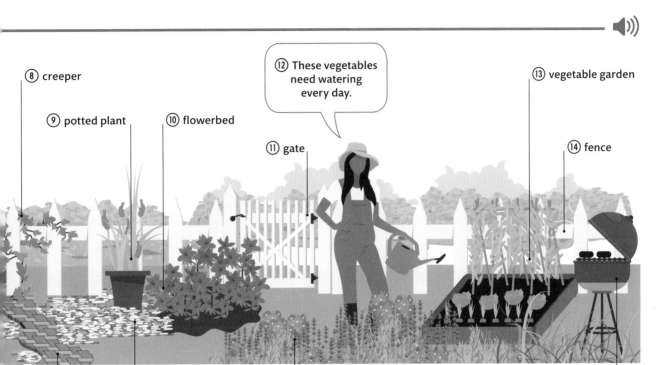

⑧ creeper

⑨ potted plant

⑩ flowerbed

⑪ gate

⑫ These vegetables need watering every day.

⑬ vegetable garden

⑭ fence

㉒ paving

㉓ ground cover

㉔ herbaceous border

㉕ grill (US) / barbecue (UK)

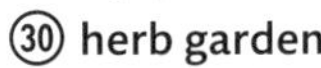

㉚ herb garden

㉛ water garden

㉜ cottage garden

㉝ courtyard

⑦ palms

⑧ conifers

⑨ topiary

⑩ climber

⑪ ornamental plants

⑫ shade plants

⑲ alpine plants

⑳ succulents

㉑ cacti

㉒ shrubs

㉓ flowering shrub

㉔ grasses

42 In town

42.1 BUILDINGS AND OTHER FEATURES

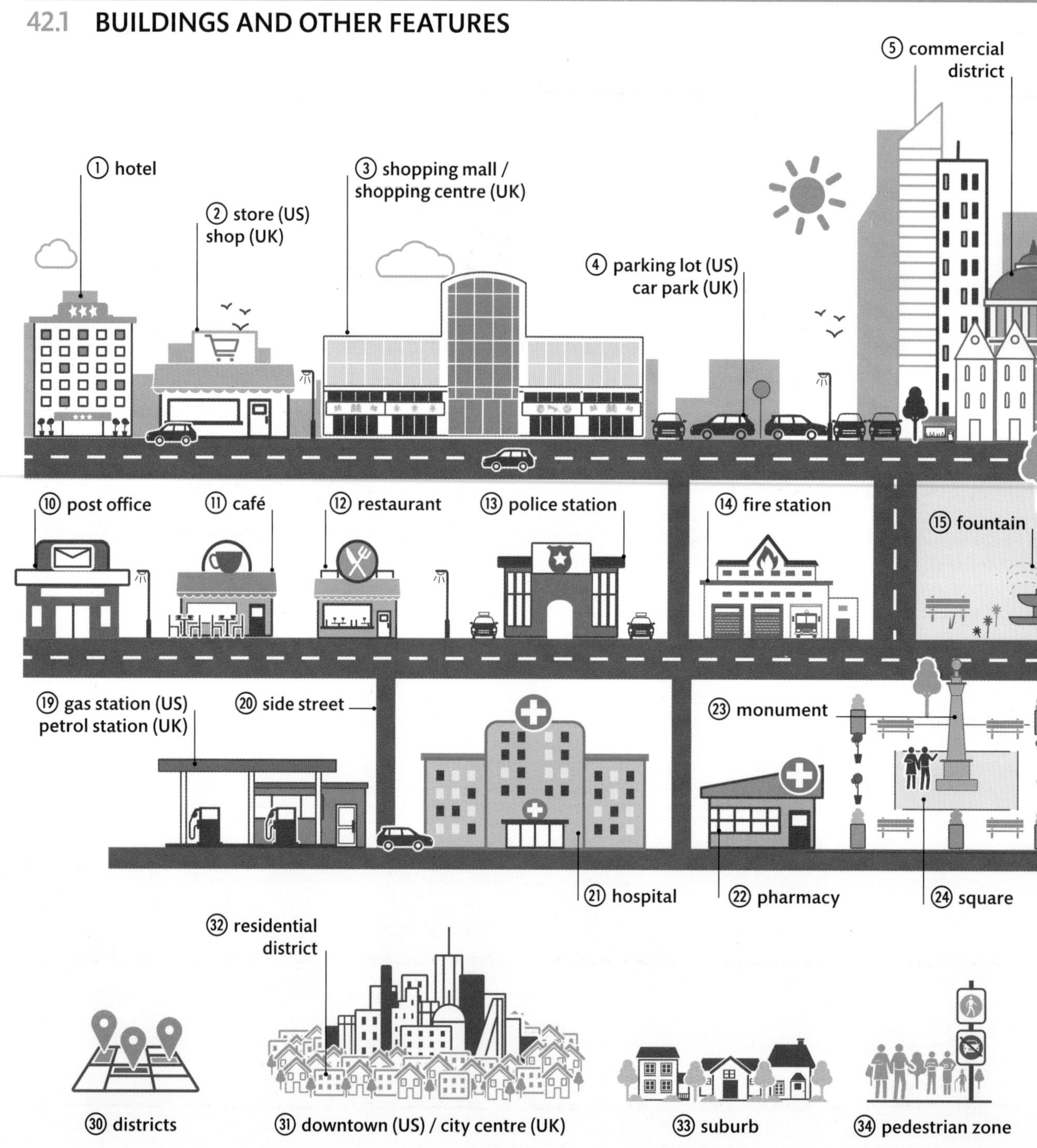

① hotel
② store (US)
shop (UK)
③ shopping mall /
shopping centre (UK)
④ parking lot (US)
car park (UK)
⑤ commercial
district
⑩ post office
⑪ café
⑫ restaurant
⑬ police station
⑭ fire station
⑮ fountain
⑲ gas station (US)
petrol station (UK)
⑳ side street
㉓ monument
㉑ hospital
㉒ pharmacy
㉔ square
㉜ residential
district
㉚ districts
㉛ downtown (US) / city centre (UK)
㉝ suburb
㉞ pedestrian zone

See also:
25 A place to live **43** In town (continued) **44** Buildings and architecture
46 Shopping **47** The shopping mall **102** Trains **104** At the airport **106** The port

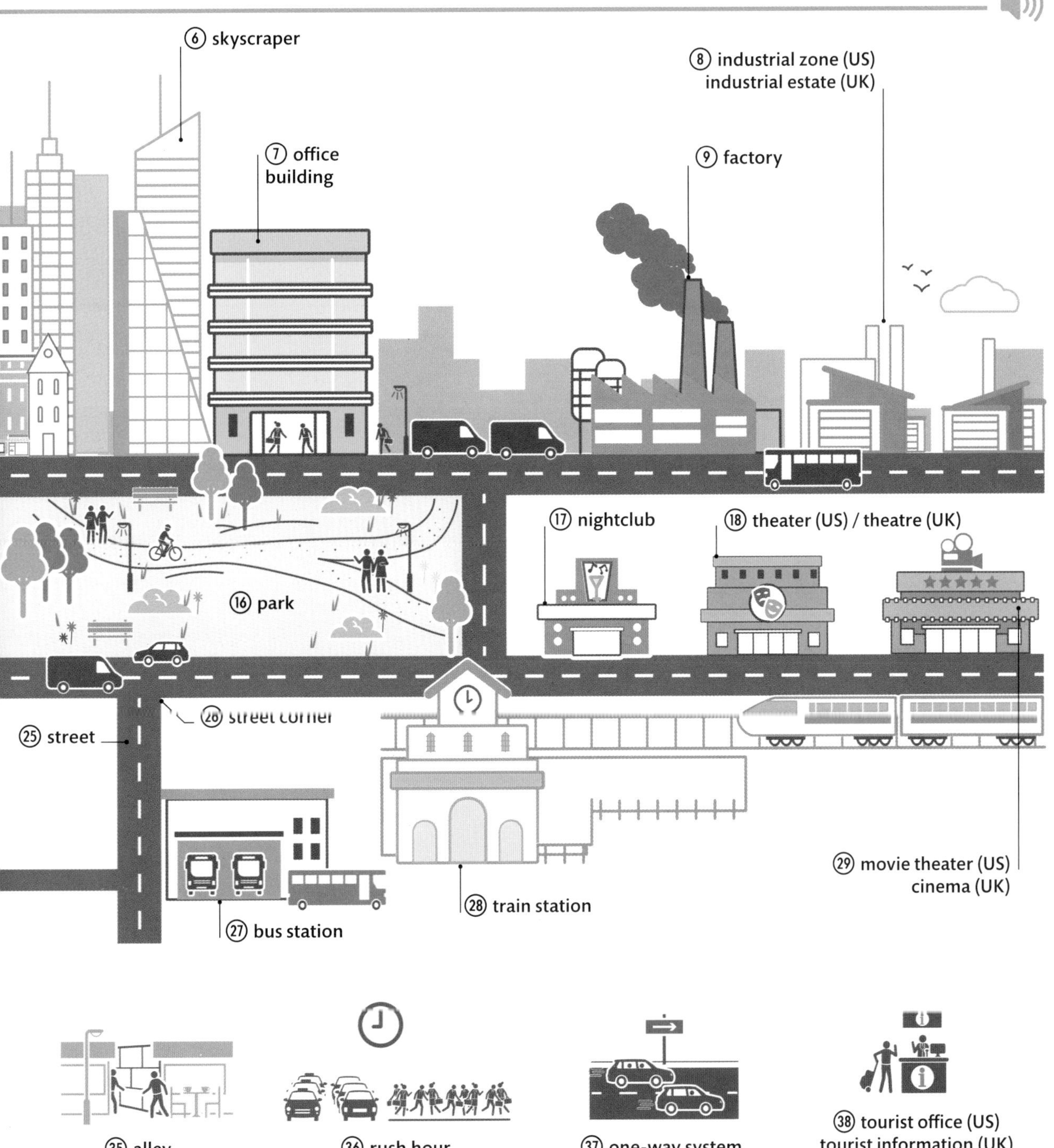
6 skyscraper
7 office building
8 industrial zone (US) industrial estate (UK)
9 factory
16 park
17 nightclub
18 theater (US) / theatre (UK)
25 street
26 street corner
27 bus station
28 train station
29 movie theater (US) cinema (UK)
35 alley
36 rush hour
37 one-way system
38 tourist office (US) tourist information (UK)

43 In town continued

43.1 BUILDINGS AND OTHER FEATURES

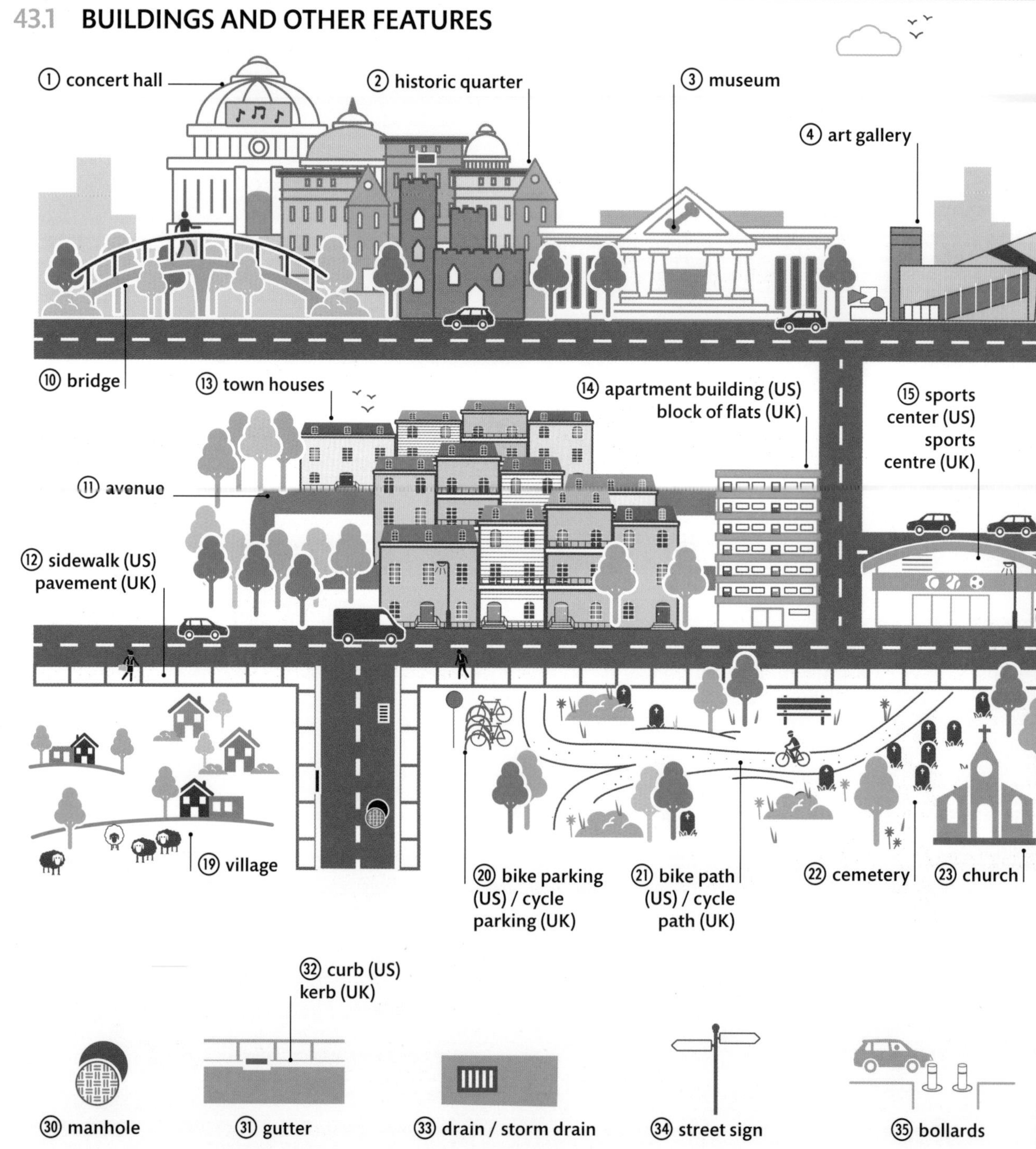

① concert hall
② historic quarter
③ museum
④ art gallery
⑩ bridge
⑪ avenue
⑫ sidewalk (US)
pavement (UK)
⑬ town houses
⑭ apartment building (US)
block of flats (UK)
⑮ sports
center (US)
sports
centre (UK)
⑲ village
⑳ bike parking
(US) / cycle
parking (UK)
㉑ bike path
(US) / cycle
path (UK)
㉒ cemetery
㉓ church

㉜ curb (US)
kerb (UK)

㉚ manhole
㉛ gutter
㉝ drain / storm drain
㉞ street sign
㉟ bollards

See also:
25 A place to live **44** Buildings and architecture **46** Shopping
47 The shopping mall **102** Trains **104** At the airport **106** The port

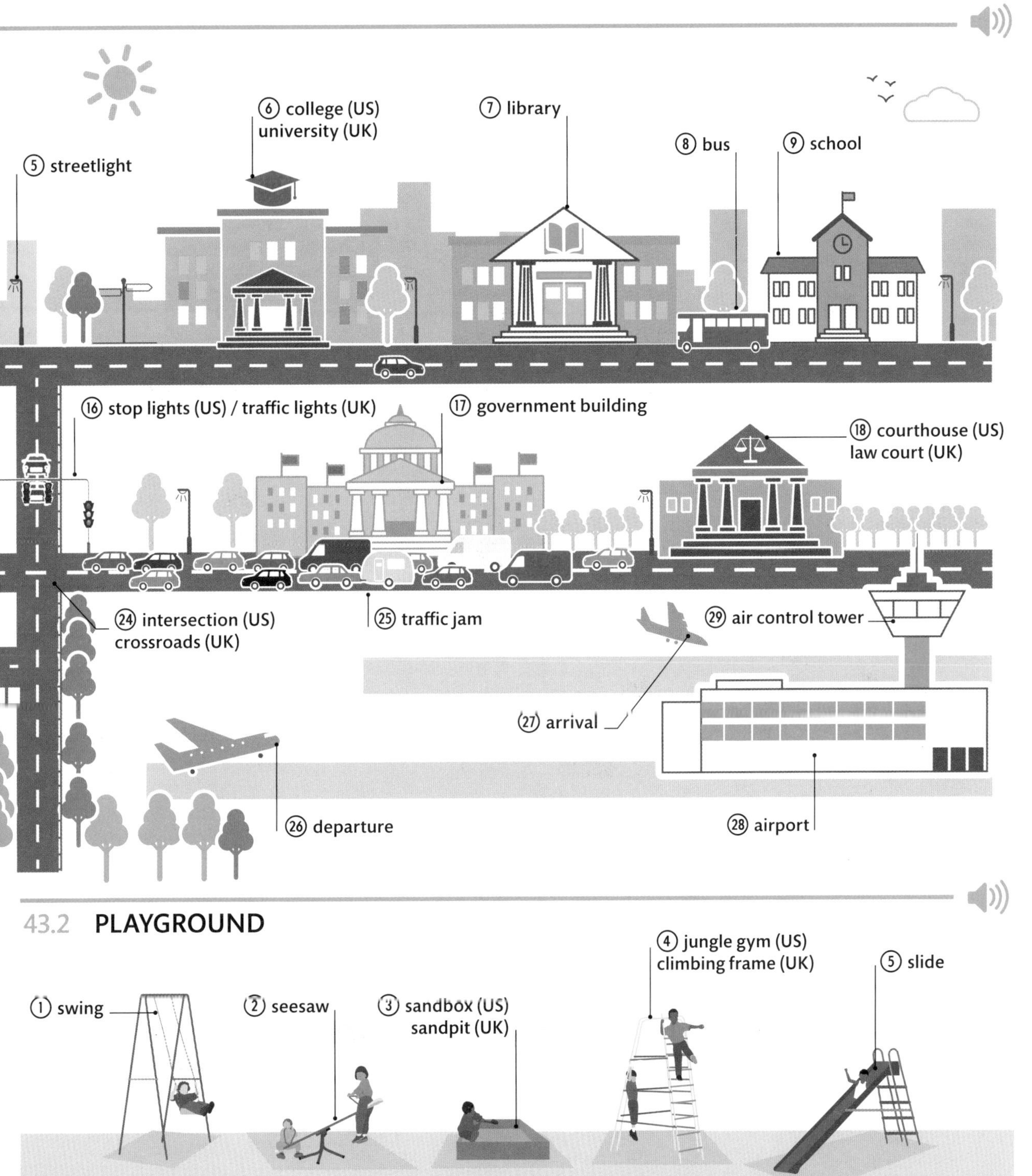
⑤ streetlight
⑥ college (US)
university (UK)
⑦ library
⑧ bus
⑨ school
⑯ stop lights (US) / traffic lights (UK)
⑰ government building
⑱ courthouse (US)
law court (UK)
㉔ intersection (US)
crossroads (UK)
㉕ traffic jam
㉙ air control tower
㉗ arrival
㉖ departure
㉘ airport
① swing
② seesaw
③ sandbox (US)
sandpit (UK)
④ jungle gym (US)
climbing frame (UK)
⑤ slide

43.2 PLAYGROUND

44 Buildings and architecture

44.1 TYPES OF BUILDINGS

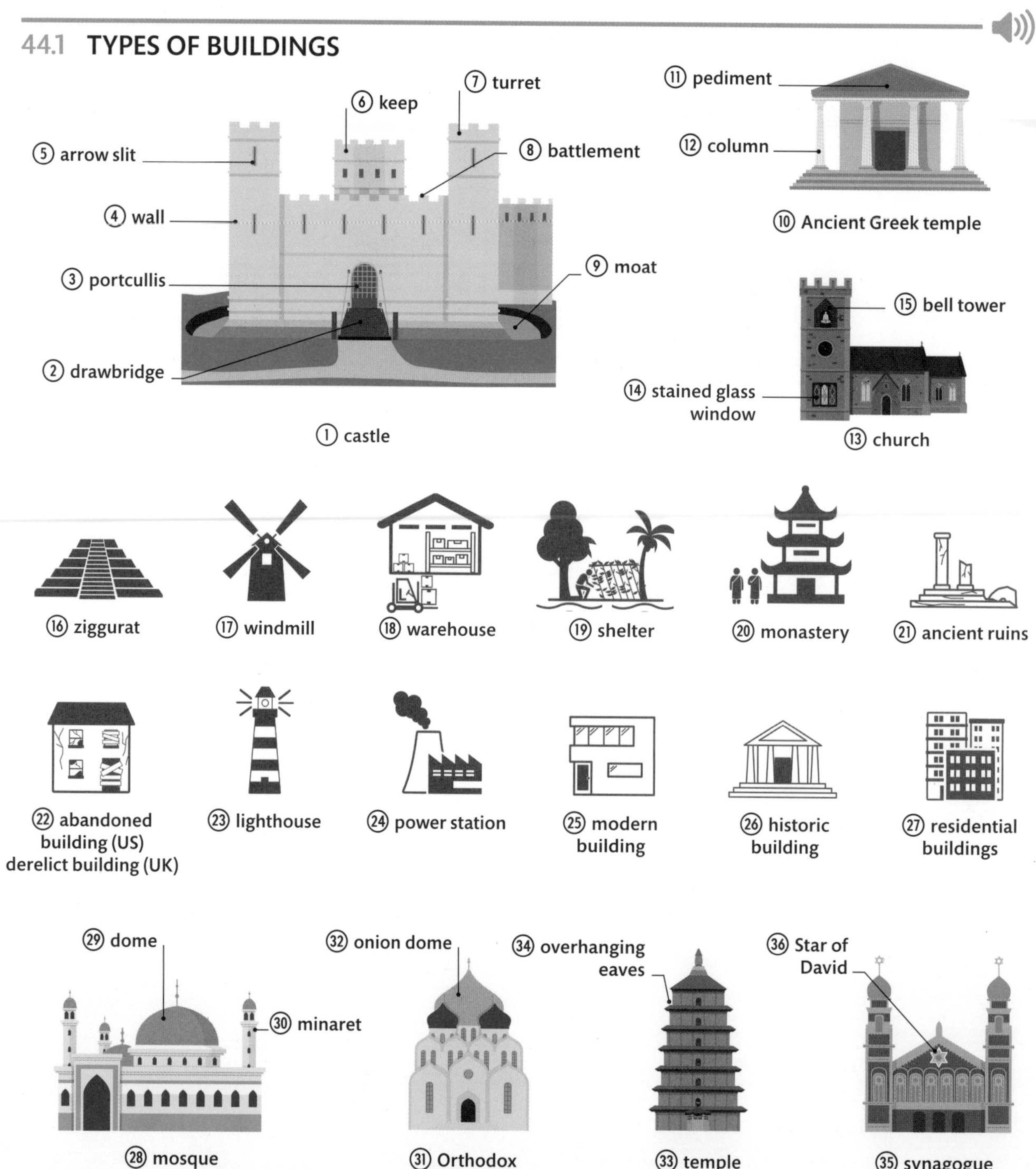

⑦ turret
⑥ keep
⑤ arrow slit
⑧ battlement
④ wall
③ portcullis
⑨ moat
② drawbridge
① castle
⑪ pediment
⑫ column
⑩ Ancient Greek temple
⑮ bell tower
⑭ stained glass window
⑬ church
⑯ ziggurat
⑰ windmill
⑱ warehouse
⑲ shelter
⑳ monastery
㉑ ancient ruins
㉒ abandoned building (US) derelict building (UK)
㉓ lighthouse
㉔ power station
㉕ modern building
㉖ historic building
㉗ residential buildings
㉙ dome
㉚ minaret
㉘ mosque
㉜ onion dome
㉛ Orthodox church
㉞ overhanging eaves
㉝ temple
㊱ Star of David
㉟ synagogue

See also:
25 A place to live 32 House and home
42-43 In town 132 Sightseeing

44.2 FAMOUS BUILDINGS AND MONUMENTS

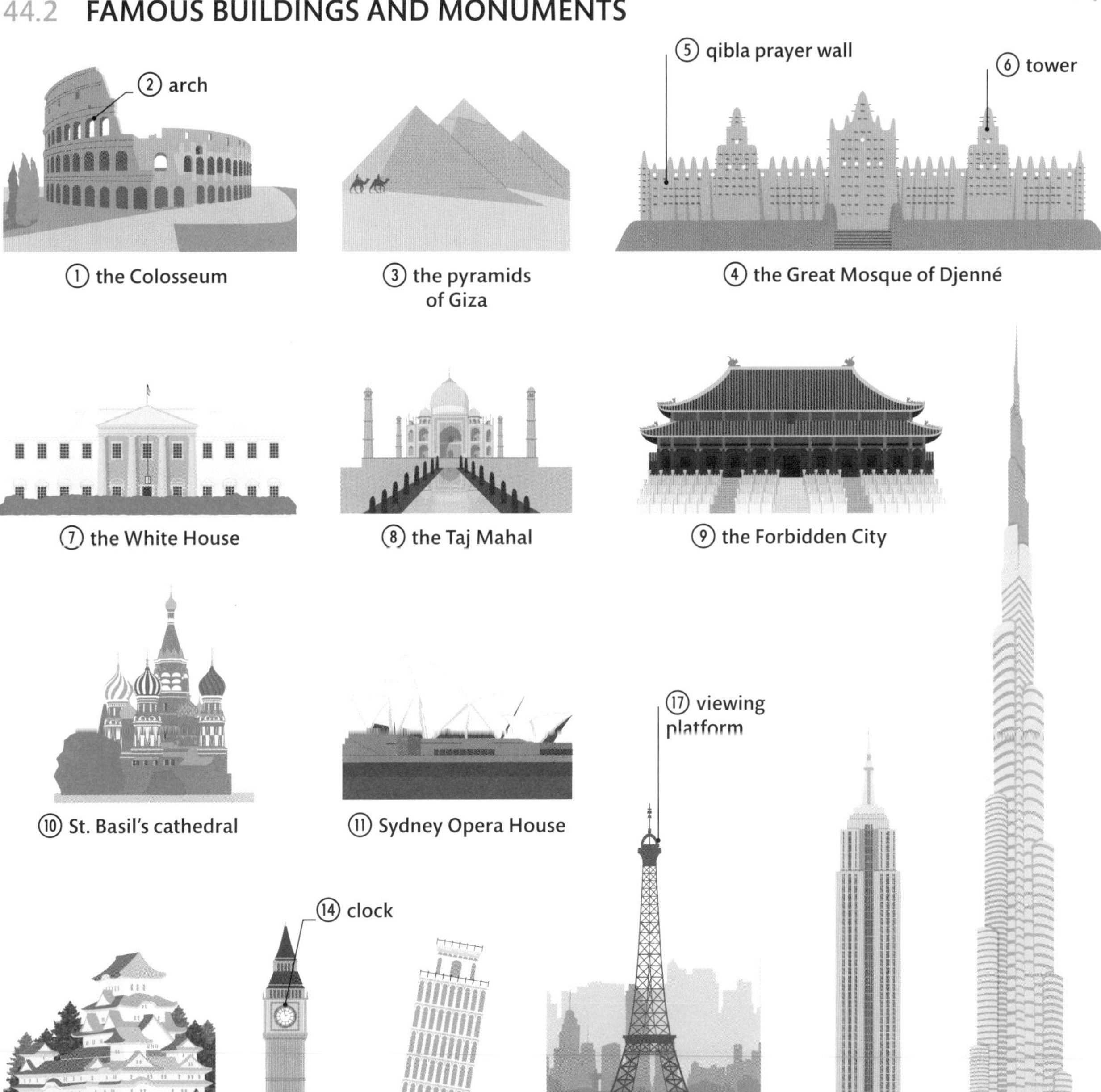
② arch
⑤ qibla prayer wall
⑥ tower
⑰ viewing platform
⑭ clock

① the Colosseum
③ the pyramids of Giza
④ the Great Mosque of Djenné
⑦ the White House
⑧ the Taj Mahal
⑨ the Forbidden City
⑩ St. Basil's cathedral
⑪ Sydney Opera House
⑫ Himeji Castle
⑬ Big Ben
⑮ the Leaning Tower of Pisa
⑯ the Eiffel Tower
⑱ the Empire State Building
⑲ Burj Khalifa

45 The bank and post office

45.1 BANK

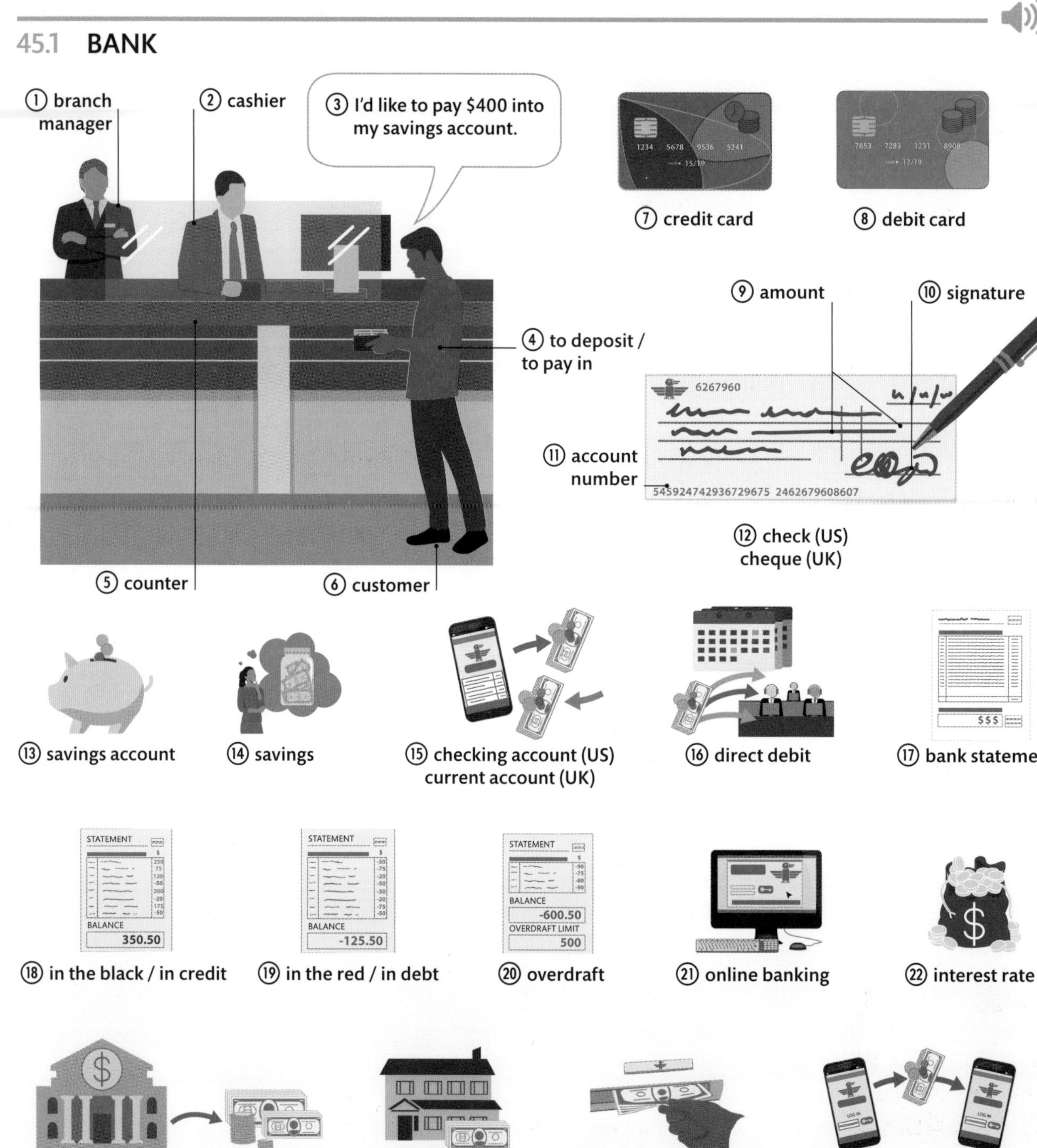

① branch manager
② cashier
③ I'd like to pay $400 into my savings account.
④ to deposit / to pay in
⑤ counter
⑥ customer
⑦ credit card
⑧ debit card
⑨ amount
⑩ signature
⑪ account number
⑫ check (US) cheque (UK)
⑬ savings account
⑭ savings
⑮ checking account (US) current account (UK)
⑯ direct debit
⑰ bank statement
⑱ in the black / in credit
⑲ in the red / in debt
⑳ overdraft
㉑ online banking
㉒ interest rate
㉓ bank loan
㉔ mortgage
㉕ to withdraw money
㉖ to transfer money

See also:
94 Money and finance
131 Travel and accommodation

45.2 MONEY

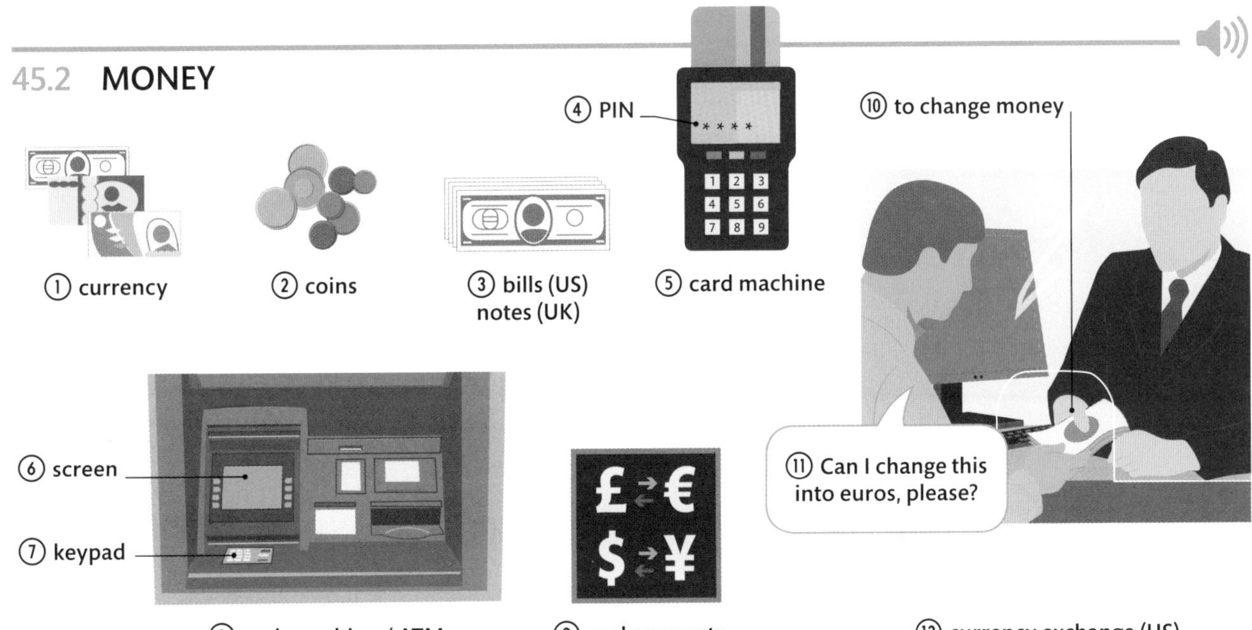

① currency
② coins
③ bills (US)
notes (UK)
④ PIN
⑤ card machine
⑥ screen
⑦ keypad
⑧ cash machine / ATM
⑨ exchange rate
⑩ to change money
⑪ Can I change this into euros, please?
⑫ currency exchange (US)
bureau de change (UK)

45.3 POST OFFICE

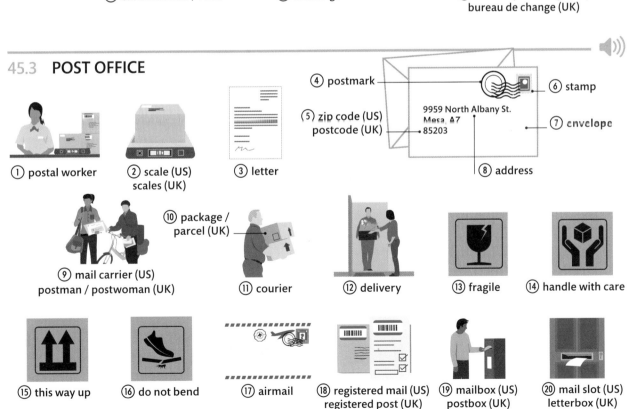

① postal worker

② scale (US)
scales (UK)

③ letter

④ postmark

⑤ zip code (US)
postcode (UK)

⑥ stamp

⑦ envelope

⑧ address

9959 North Albany St.
Mesa, AZ
85203

⑨ mail carrier (US)
postman / postwoman (UK)

⑩ package /
parcel (UK)

⑪ courier

⑫ delivery

⑬ fragile

⑭ handle with care

⑮ this way up

⑯ do not bend

⑰ airmail

⑱ registered mail (US)
registered post (UK)

⑲ mailbox (US)
postbox (UK)

⑳ mail slot (US)
letterbox (UK)

46 Shopping

46.1 ON THE MAIN STREET (US) / HIGH STREET (UK)

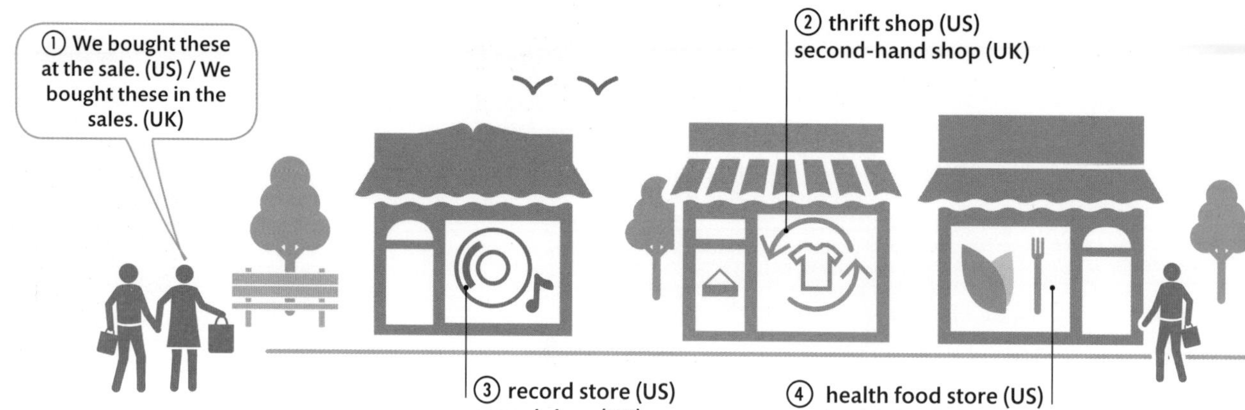

① We bought these at the sale. (US) / We bought these in the sales. (UK)
② thrift shop (US) second-hand shop (UK)
③ record store (US) record shop (UK)
④ health food store (US) health food shop (UK)

⑤ gift shop

⑥ boutique

⑦ jeweler (US) jeweller's (UK)

⑧ art store (US) art shop (UK)

⑨ antiques store (US) antiques shop (UK)

⑩ toy store (US) toy shop (UK)

⑪ optician

⑫ hardware store

⑬ key cutting shop

⑭ electronics store

⑮ pet store (US) pet shop (UK)

⑯ travel agent

⑰ street market

⑱ fishmonger

⑲ butcher

⑳ bakery

㉑ grocery store (US) greengrocer (UK)

㉒ delicatessen

㉓ bakery (US) cake shop (UK)

㉔ café / coffee shop

㉕ liquor store (US) off licence (UK)

㉖ newsstand / kiosk

㉗ bookstore (US) bookshop (UK)

㉘ shoe store (US) shoe shop (UK)

See also:
42-43 In town **47** The shopping mall
48 The supermarket

(29) garden center (US) garden centre (UK)

(30) florist

(31) tailor

(32) photo booth

(33) Laundromat (US) launderette (UK)

(34) dry cleaner's

(35) shopping spree

(36) window shopping

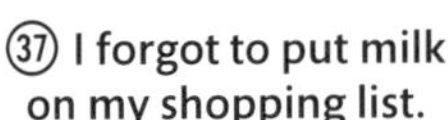
(37) I forgot to put milk on my shopping list.

(38) shopping list

46.2 SHOPPING VERBS

(1) to choose

(2) to sell

(3) to buy

(4) to want

(5) to fit

(6) to pay

(7) to try on

(8) to haggle

(9) to complain

(10) to exchange

(11) to refund

(12) to return

46.3 ORDERING ONLINE

(1) to add to the cart

(2) to add to wishlist

(3) to proceed to checkout

(4) to order

(5) to track your order

47 The shopping mall

47.1 SHOPPING MALL (US) / SHOPPING CENTRE (UK)

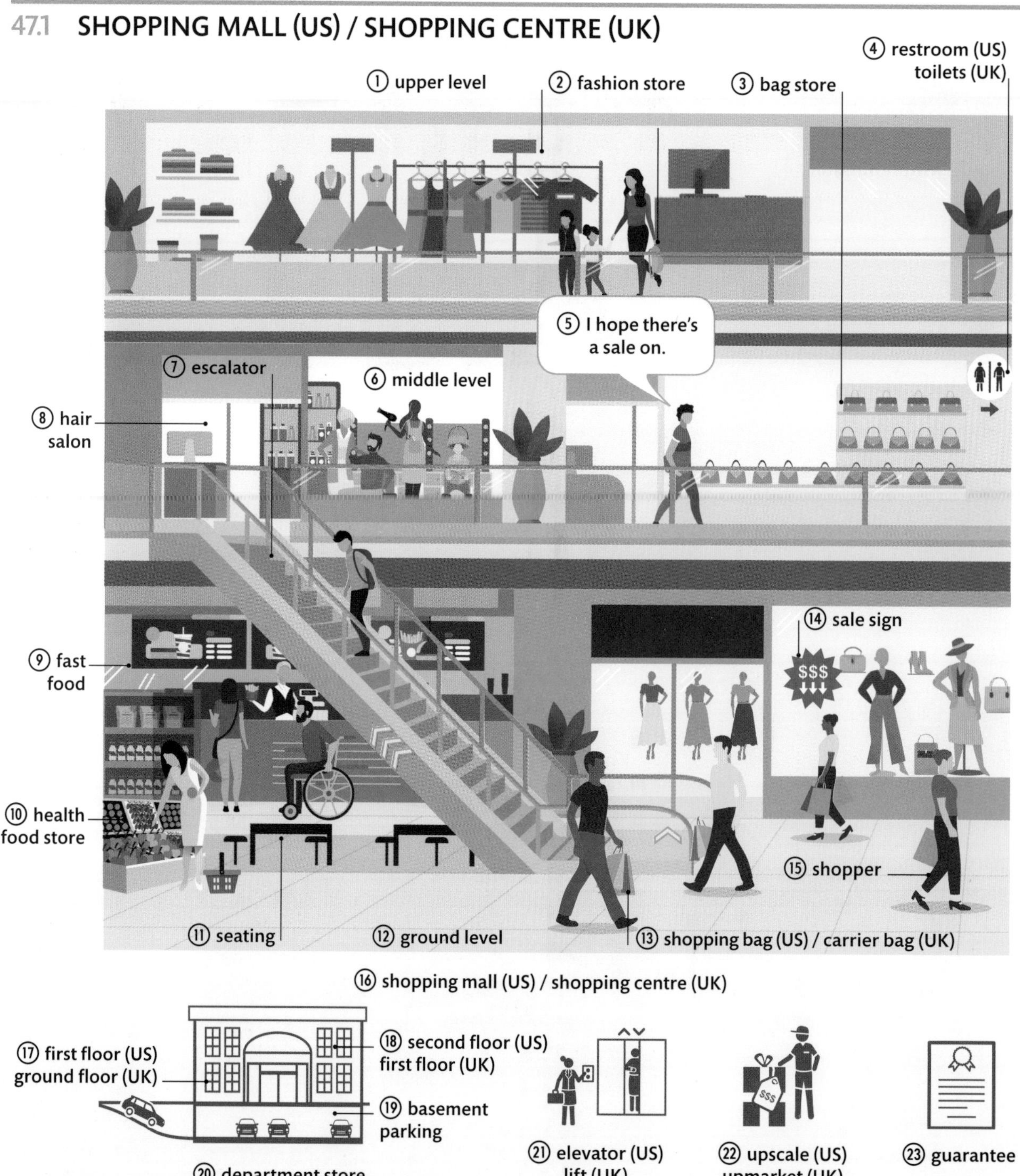

① upper level
② fashion store
③ bag store
④ restroom (US)
toilets (UK)
⑤ I hope there's a sale on.
⑥ middle level
⑦ escalator
⑧ hair salon
⑨ fast food
⑩ health food store
⑪ seating
⑫ ground level
⑬ shopping bag (US) / carrier bag (UK)
⑭ sale sign
$$$
⑮ shopper
⑯ shopping mall (US) / shopping centre (UK)
⑰ first floor (US)
ground floor (UK)
⑱ second floor (US)
first floor (UK)
⑲ basement parking
⑳ department store
㉑ elevator (US)
lift (UK)
$$$
㉒ upscale (US)
upmarket (UK)
㉓ guarantee

See also:
13-15 Clothes **16** Accessories **17** Shoes
18 Beauty **42-43** In town **46** Shopping

(24) changing rooms

(25) womenswear

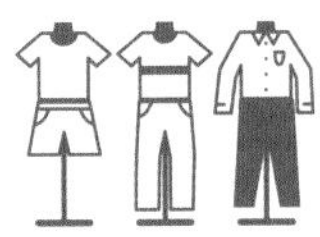
(26) menswear

(27) baby changing facilities

(28) children's department

(29) designer labels

↓%
(30) sale

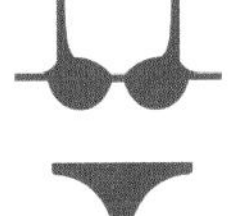
(31) lingerie

(32) home furnishings

(33) price tag

(34) lighting

(35) electrical appliances

(36) loyalty card

(37) DIY (do it yourself)

(38) beauty

(39) customer service

(40) cosmetics (US) perfumery (UK)

(41) food court

47.2 FLOWER STALL

(1) stall / kiosk
(2) florist
(3) garland
(4) bunch
(5) gladiolus
(6) pot plant
(7) foliage
(8) gerbera
(9) peony
(10) gypsophila
(11) bouquet
(12) acacia
(13) orchid
(14) stocks
(15) freesia

48 The supermarket

48.1 SUPERMARKET

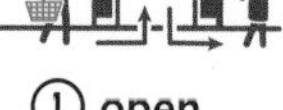
① open

② closed

③ customer

④ receipt

⑤ special offer

$$
$$$

⑥ bargain

⑦ wide range

⑧ line (US)
queue (UK)

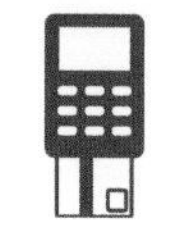
⑨ card machine

⑩ online shopping

⑪ delivery man

⑫ home delivery

48.2 CHECKOUT

① exit

② cashier

③ cash register (US)
till (UK)

④ shelves

⑤ self checkout

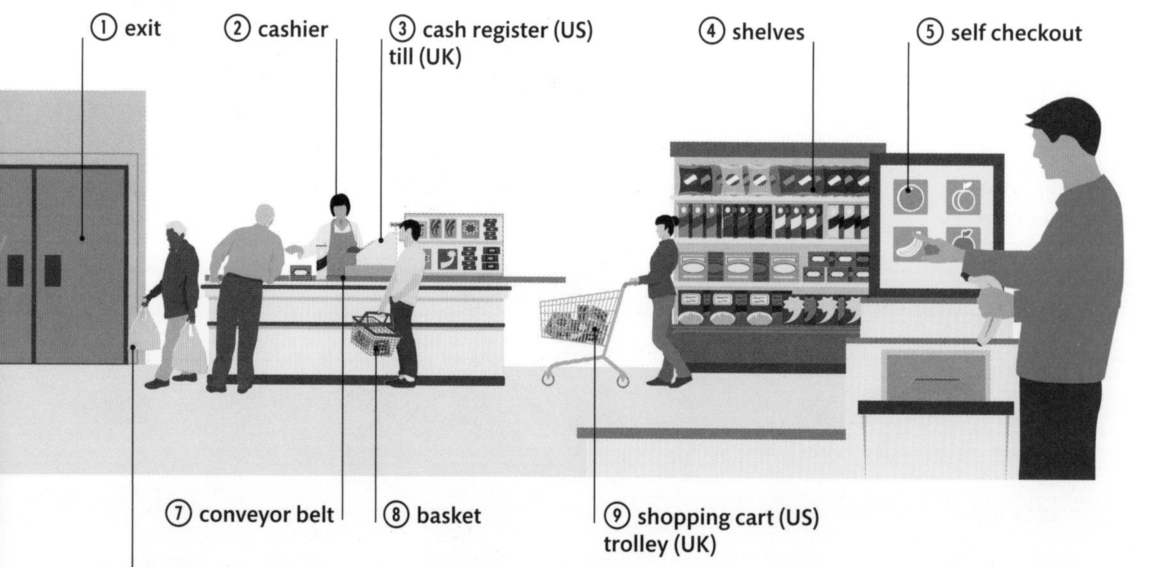

⑪ barcode

⑫ scanner

⑦ conveyor belt

⑧ basket

⑨ shopping cart (US)
trolley (UK)

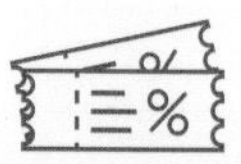
⑬ coupon (US)
discount voucher (UK)

⑥ shopping bag (US)
carrier bag (UK)

⑩ checkout

See also:
46 Shopping **53** Meat **54** Fish and seafood **55-56** Vegetables **57** Fruit **58** Fruit and nuts
59 Herbs and spices **60** In the pantry **61** Dairy produce **62-63** The bakery

48.3 AISLES / SECTIONS

① bakery

② dairy

③ breakfast cereals

④ canned food (US) tinned food (UK)

⑤ candy (US) confectionery (UK)

⑥ vegetables

⑦ fruit

⑧ meat and poultry

⑨ fish

⑩ deli

⑪ frozen food

⑫ convenience food

⑬ drinks

⑭ household products

⑮ toiletries

⑯ baby products

⑰ electrical goods

⑱ pet food

48.4 NEWSSTAND / KIOSK

① newspaper

② magazine

③ comic

④ postcard

⑤ tourist map

1
2
⑥ stamps

⑦ travel card

⑧ sim card

⑨ snack bar

⑩ chips (US) crisps (UK)

⑪ water

49 The pharmacy

49.1 PHARMACY

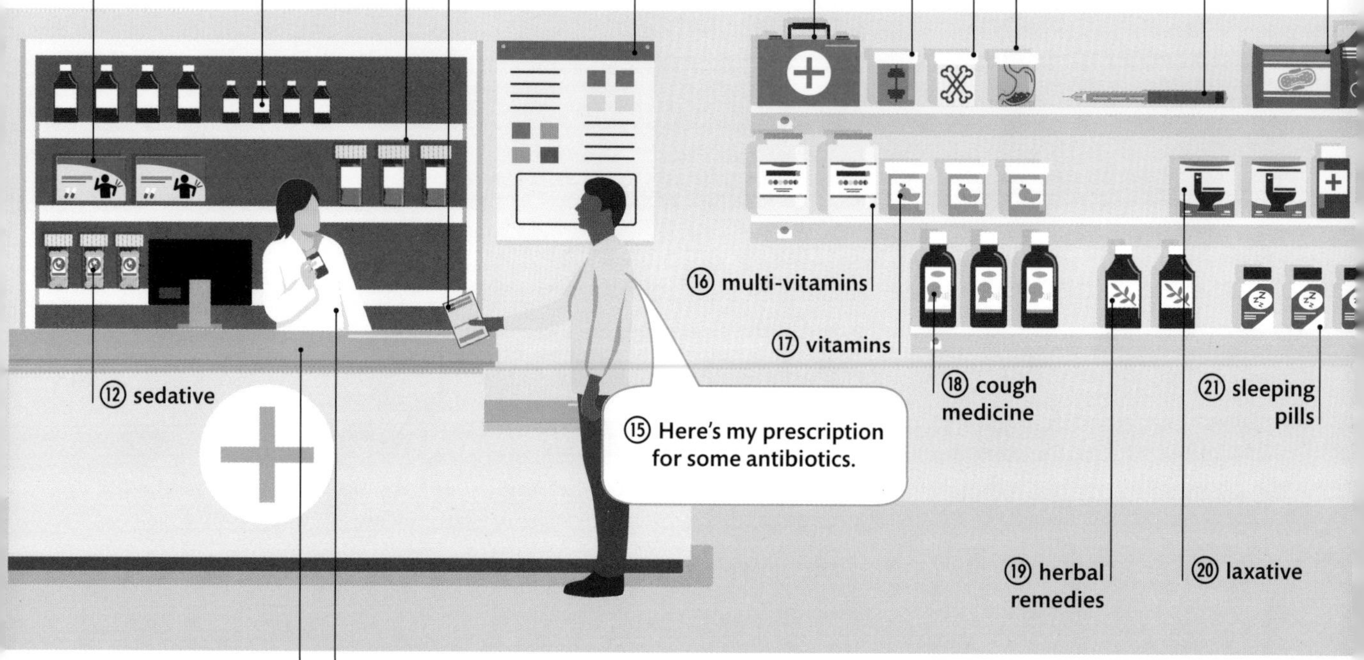

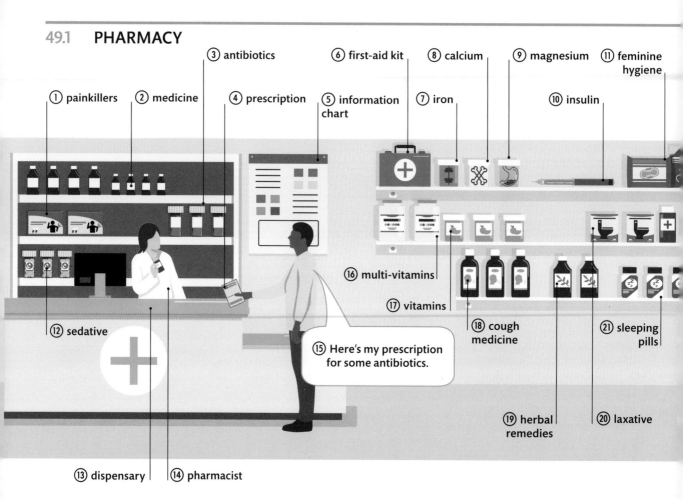

1. painkillers
2. medicine
3. antibiotics
4. prescription
5. information chart
6. first-aid kit
7. iron
8. calcium
9. magnesium
10. insulin
11. feminine hygiene
12. sedative
13. dispensary
14. pharmacist
15. Here's my prescription for some antibiotics.
16. multi-vitamins
17. vitamins
18. cough medicine
19. herbal remedies
20. laxative
21. sleeping pills

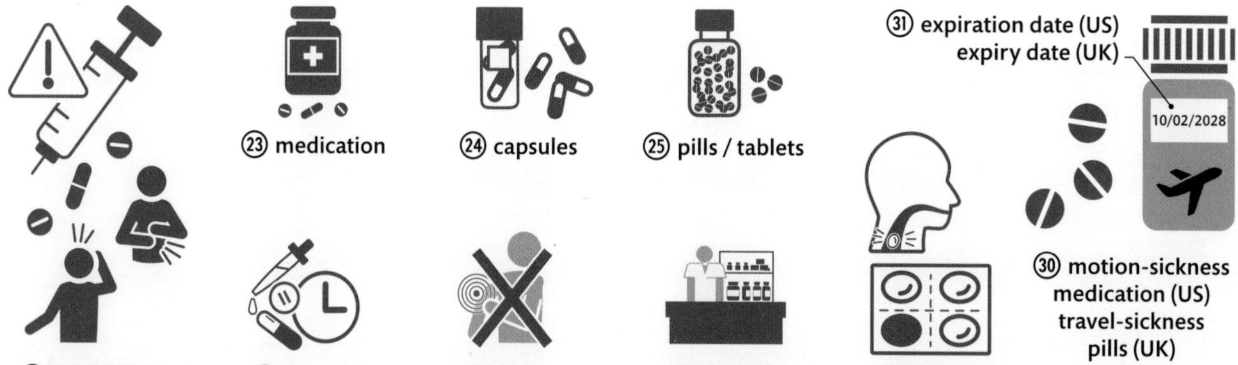

(22) side effects

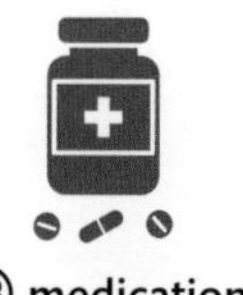

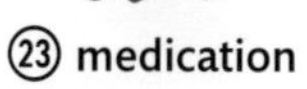

(23) medication

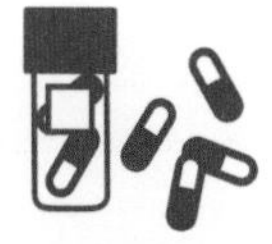

(24) capsules

(25) pills / tablets

(26) dosage

(27) anti-inflammatory

(28) over-the-counter drugs

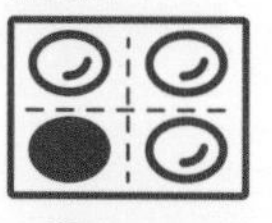

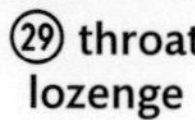

(29) throat lozenge

10/02/2028

(31) expiration date (US) expiry date (UK)

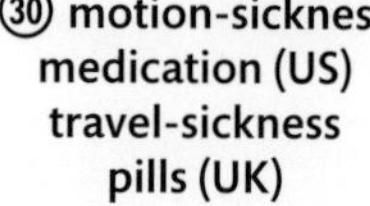

(30) motion-sickness medication (US) travel-sickness pills (UK)

See also:
19 Illness and injury 20 Visiting the doctor
21 The hospital 46 Shopping

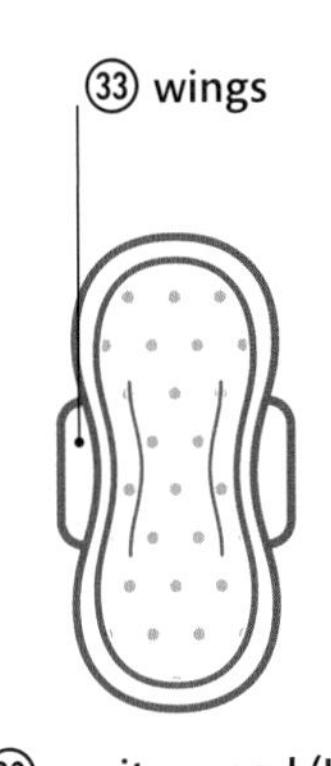
33 wings

32 sanitary pad (US) sanitary towel (UK)

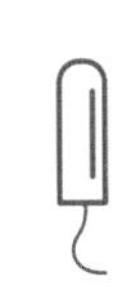

34 tampon

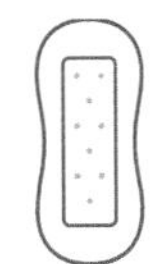

35 panty liner

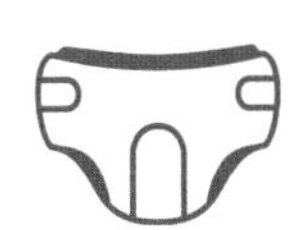

36 incontinence pads

37 suppository

38 deodorant

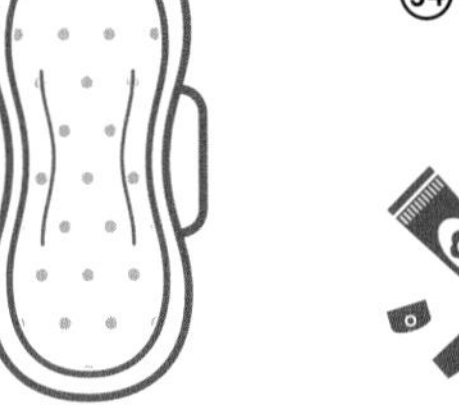

39 skin care

40 sunscreen (US) sun cream (UK)

41 sunblock

42 bandage

43 adhesive bandage (US) / plaster (UK)

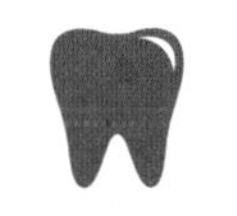

44 dental care

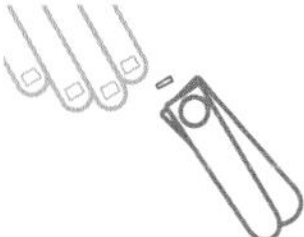

45 nail clippers

46 wet wipes

47 tissue

48 insoles

49 reading glasses

50 insect repellent

51 contact lens

52 lens solution

53 syringe

54 inhaler

55 drops

56 supplement

57 soluble

58 ointment

59 powder

60 spray

61 gel

62 cream

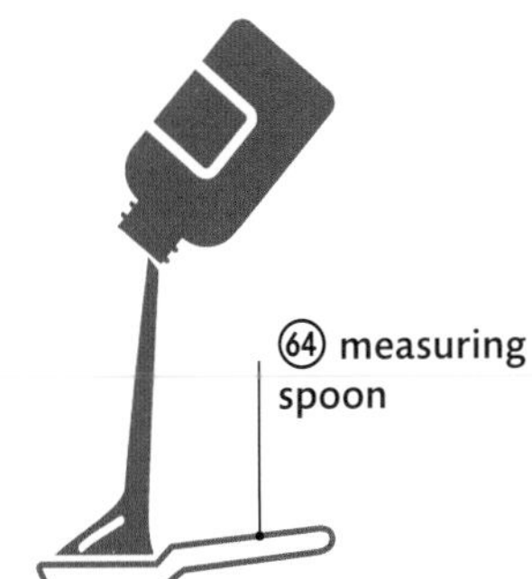
64 measuring spoon

63 syrup

50 Emergency services

50.1 ACCIDENT AND EMERGENCY

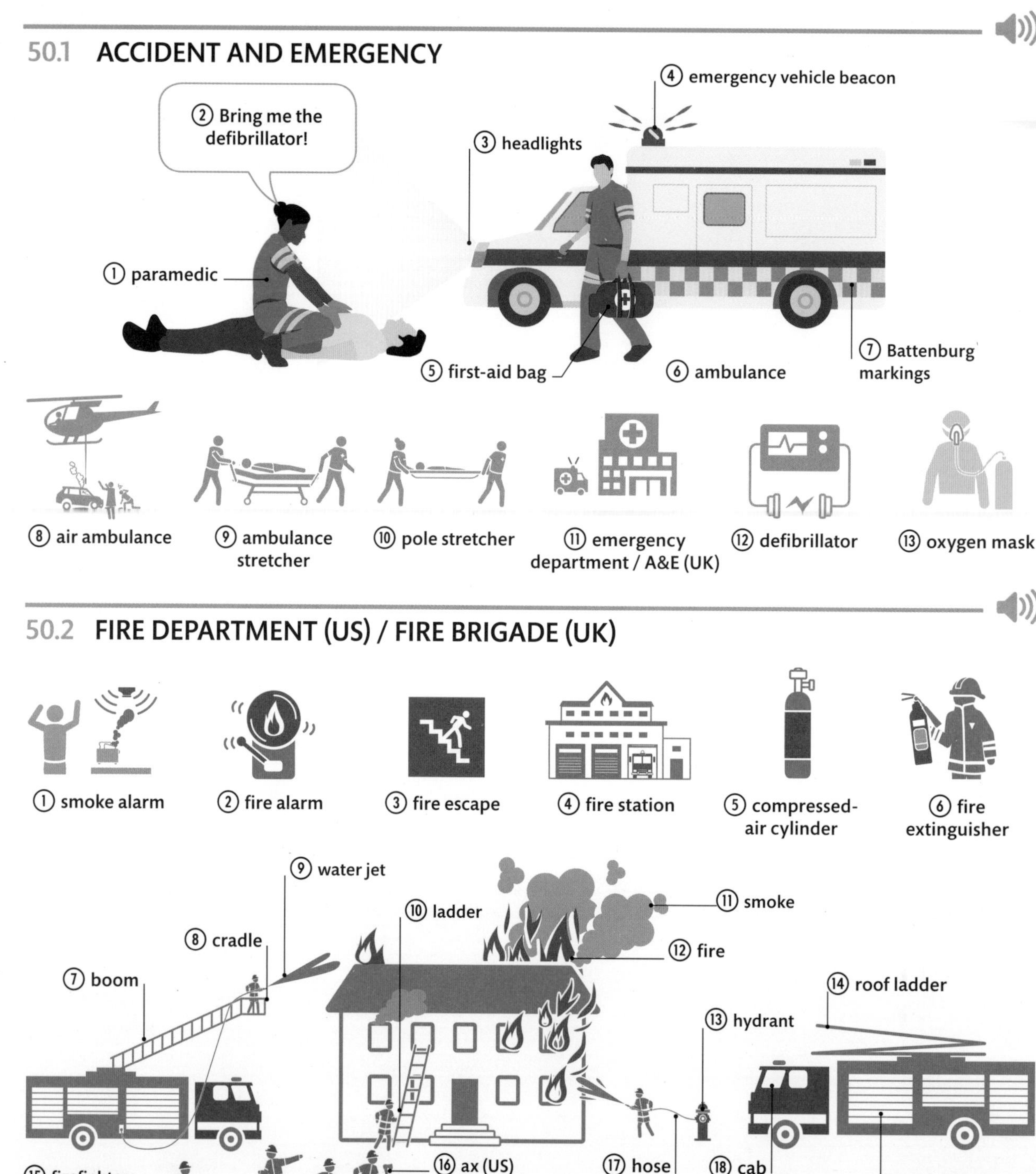

② Bring me the defibrillator!
① paramedic
③ headlights
④ emergency vehicle beacon
⑤ first-aid bag
⑥ ambulance
⑦ Battenburg markings
⑧ air ambulance
⑨ ambulance stretcher
⑩ pole stretcher
⑪ emergency department / A&E (UK)
⑫ defibrillator
⑬ oxygen mask
50.2 FIRE DEPARTMENT (US) / FIRE BRIGADE (UK)
① smoke alarm
② fire alarm
③ fire escape
④ fire station
⑤ compressed-air cylinder
⑥ fire extinguisher
⑦ boom
⑧ cradle
⑨ water jet
⑩ ladder
⑪ smoke
⑫ fire
⑬ hydrant
⑭ roof ladder
⑮ firefighters
⑯ ax (US) axe (UK)
⑰ hose
⑱ cab
⑲ fire engine

See also:
19 Illness and injury
21 The hospital 85 Law

50.3 POLICE

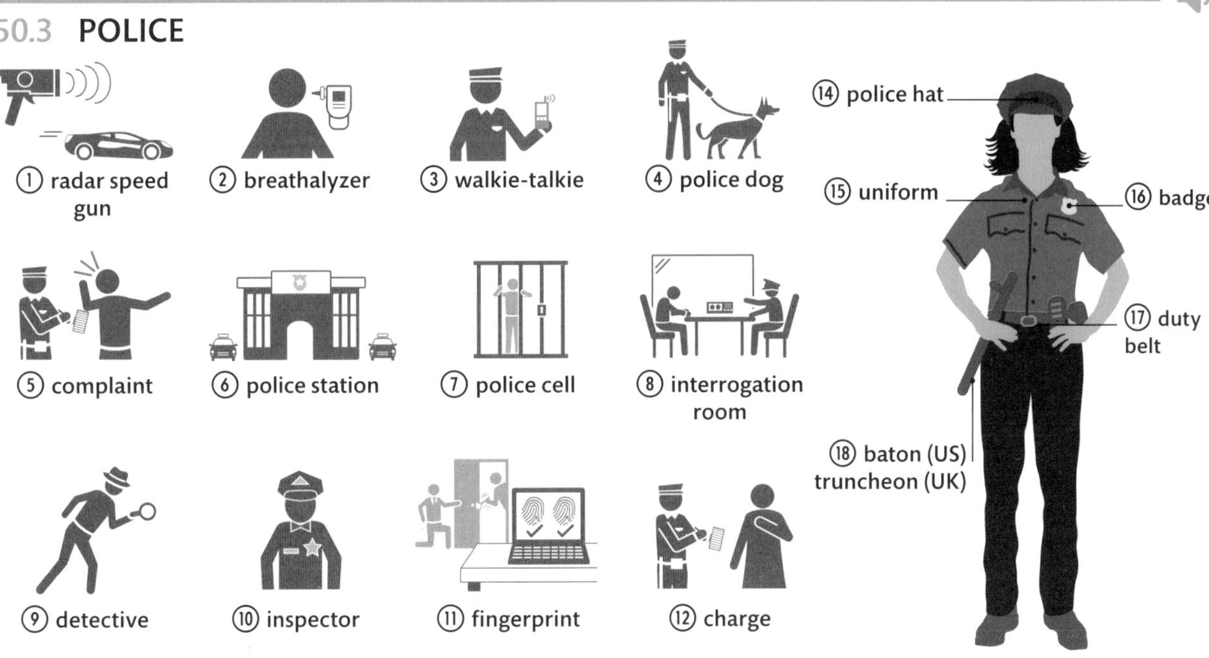
① radar speed gun
② breathalyzer
③ walkie-talkie
④ police dog
⑤ complaint
⑥ police station
⑦ police cell
⑧ interrogation room
⑨ detective
⑩ inspector
⑪ fingerprint
⑫ charge
⑬ police officer 
⑭ police hat
⑮ uniform
⑯ badge
⑰ duty belt
⑱ baton (US) truncheon (UK)

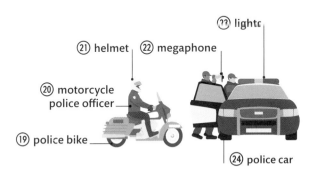

⑲ police bike
⑳ motorcycle police officer
㉑ helmet
㉒ megaphone
㉓ lights
㉔ police car

BANK

㉕ robbery
㉖ alarm
㉗ break in
㉘ robbers

㉙ crime scene
㉚ investigation
㉛ evidence
㉜ radio

㉝ arrest
㉞ suspect
㉟ handcuffs
㊱ You're under arrest!

51 Energy and power supply

51.1 NUCLEAR ENERGY AND FOSSIL FUELS

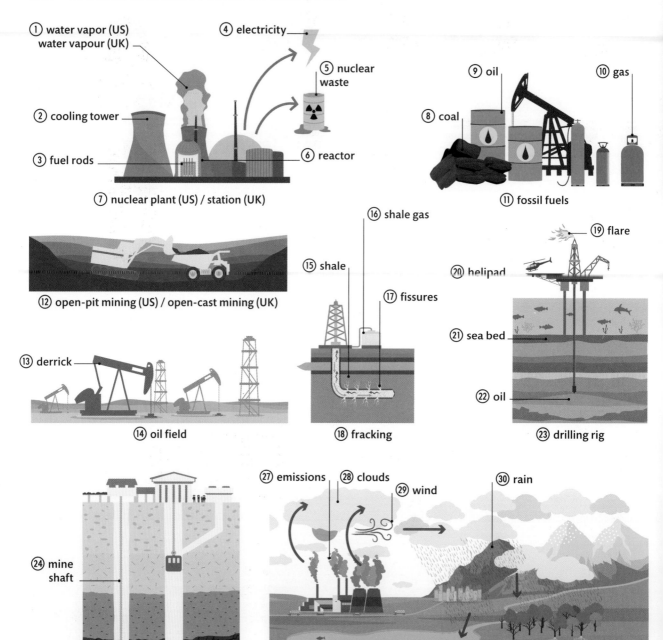

① water vapor (US) water vapour (UK)
② cooling tower
③ fuel rods
④ electricity
⑤ nuclear waste
⑥ reactor
⑦ nuclear plant (US) / station (UK)

⑧ coal
⑨ oil
⑩ gas
⑪ fossil fuels

⑫ open-pit mining (US) / open-cast mining (UK)

⑬ derrick
⑭ oil field

⑮ shale
⑯ shale gas
⑰ fissures
⑱ fracking

⑲ flare
⑳ helipad
㉑ sea bed
㉒ oil
㉓ drilling rig

㉔ mine shaft
㉕ miners
㉖ coal mine

㉗ emissions
㉘ clouds
㉙ wind
㉚ rain
㉛ acid rain

See also:
33 Electrics and plumbing **42-43** In town
145 Planet Earth **155** Climate and the environment

51.2 RENEWABLE ENERGY

① solar farm

② solar panel

③ tidal energy

④ wind farm

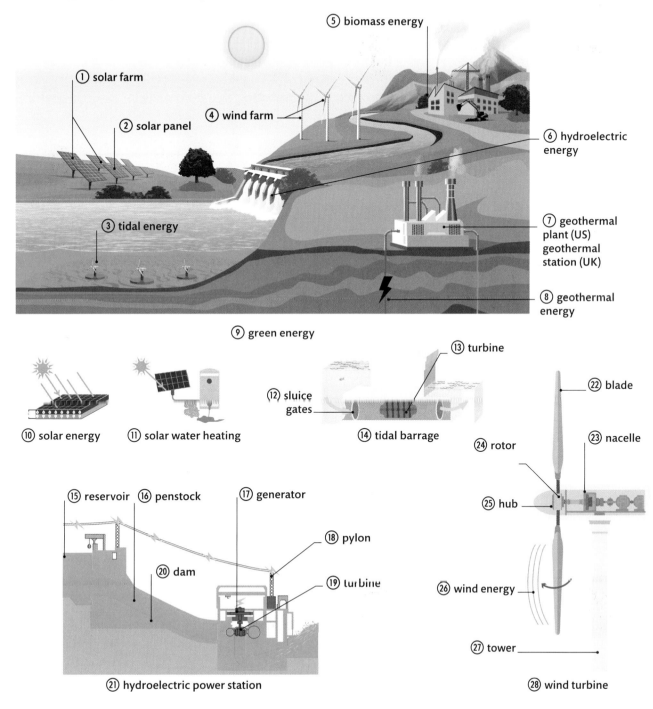

⑤ biomass energy

⑥ hydroelectric energy

⑦ geothermal plant (US) geothermal station (UK)

⑧ geothermal energy

⑨ green energy

⑩ solar energy

⑪ solar water heating

⑫ sluice gates

⑬ turbine

⑭ tidal barrage

⑮ reservoir

⑯ penstock

⑰ generator

⑱ pylon

⑲ turbine

⑳ dam

㉑ hydroelectric power station

㉒ blade

㉓ nacelle

㉔ rotor

㉕ hub

㉖ wind energy

㉗ tower

㉘ wind turbine

52 Drinking and eating

52.1 DRINKS

① coffee

② tea

③ hot chocolate

④ herbal tea

⑤ iced tea

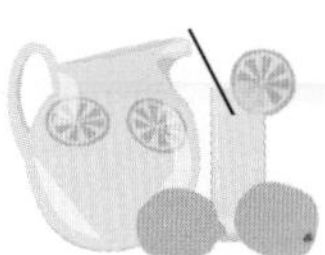
⑥ lemonade

⑦ juice

⑧ mineral water

⑨ tap water

⑩ smoothie

⑪ orangeade

⑫ cola

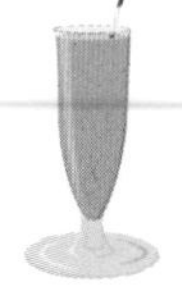
⑬ milkshake

⑭ sports drink / energy drink

⑮ red wine

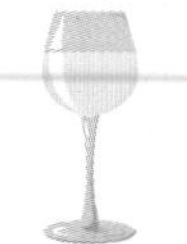
⑯ white wine

⑰ rosé wine

⑱ beer

52.2 CONTAINERS

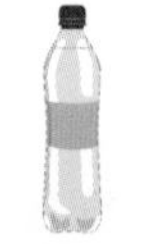
① bottle

② glass

③ carton

④ jar

⑤ bag

⑥ package (US) packet (UK)

⑦ box

⑧ can (US) tin (UK)

⑨ thermal flask

⑩ bowl

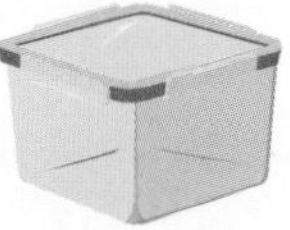
⑪ airtight container

⑫ Mason jar

See also:
27 Kitchen and tableware **28** Kitchenware
29 Cooking **52-72** Food

52.3 ADJECTIVES

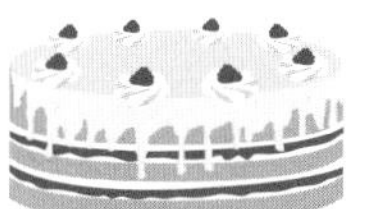
① sweet

② savory (US)
savoury (UK)

③ sour

④ salty

⑤ bitter

⑥ spicy / hot

⑦ fresh

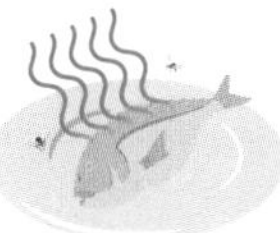
⑧ bad (US)
off (UK)

⑨ strong

⑩ iced / chilled

⑪ carbonated / sparkling

⑫ non-carbonated / still

⑬ rich

⑭ juicy

⑮ crunchy

⑯ delicious

⑰ disgusting

⑱ tasty

52.4 DRINKING AND EATING VERBS

① to eat

② to chew

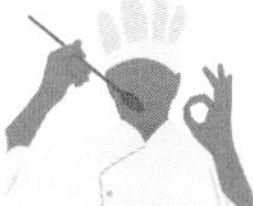
③ to taste

④ Cheers

⑤ to dine

⑥ to nibble

⑦ to bite

⑧ to swallow

⑨ to sip

⑩ to drink

⑪ to gulp

53 Meat

53.1 THE BUTCHER

① organic

② free-range

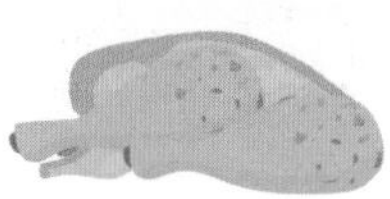
③ white meat

④ red meat

⑤ lean meat

⑥ ground meat (US) mince (UK)

⑦ salami
⑧ chorizo
⑨ ham
⑩ liver
⑪ chop
⑫ meat hook
⑬ rump roast (US) rump steak (UK)
⑭ butcher
⑮ rabbit
⑯ sausages
⑰ game
⑱ bacon (US) streaky bacon (UK)
⑲ back bacon
⑳ sirloin steak

See also:
29 Cooking **52** Drinking and eating **54** Fish and seafood
69 At the restaurant **72** Lunch and dinner **165** Farm animals

53.2 TYPES OF MEAT

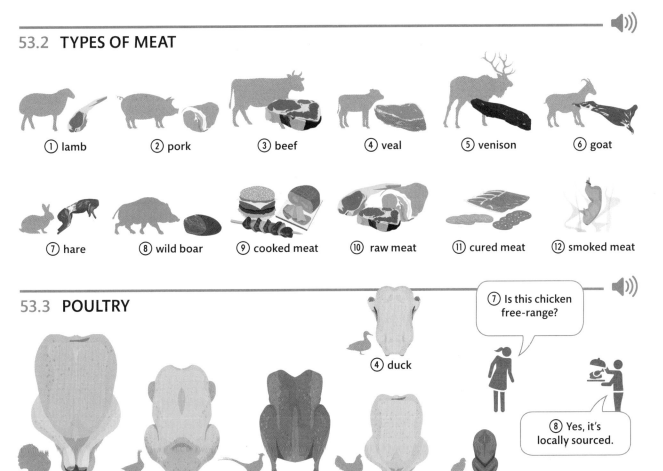

① lamb
② pork
③ beef
④ veal
⑤ venison
⑥ goat
⑦ hare
⑧ wild boar
⑨ cooked meat
⑩ raw meat
⑪ cured meat
⑫ smoked meat

53.3 POULTRY

① turkey
② goose
③ pheasant
④ duck
⑤ chicken
⑥ quail

⑦ Is this chicken free-range?

⑧ Yes, it's locally sourced.

53.4 CUTS OF MEAT

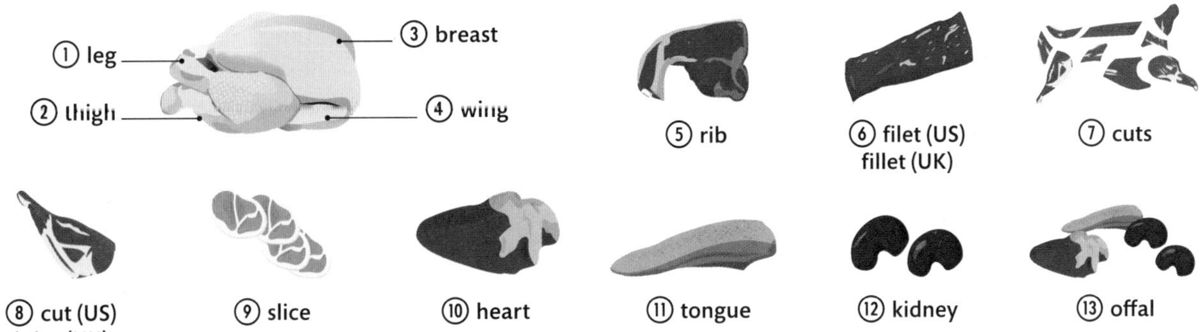
① leg
② thigh
③ breast
④ wing
⑤ rib
⑥ filet (US)
fillet (UK)
⑦ cuts
⑧ cut (US)
joint (UK)
⑨ slice
⑩ heart
⑪ tongue
⑫ kidney
⑬ offal

54 Fish and seafood

54.1 FISH

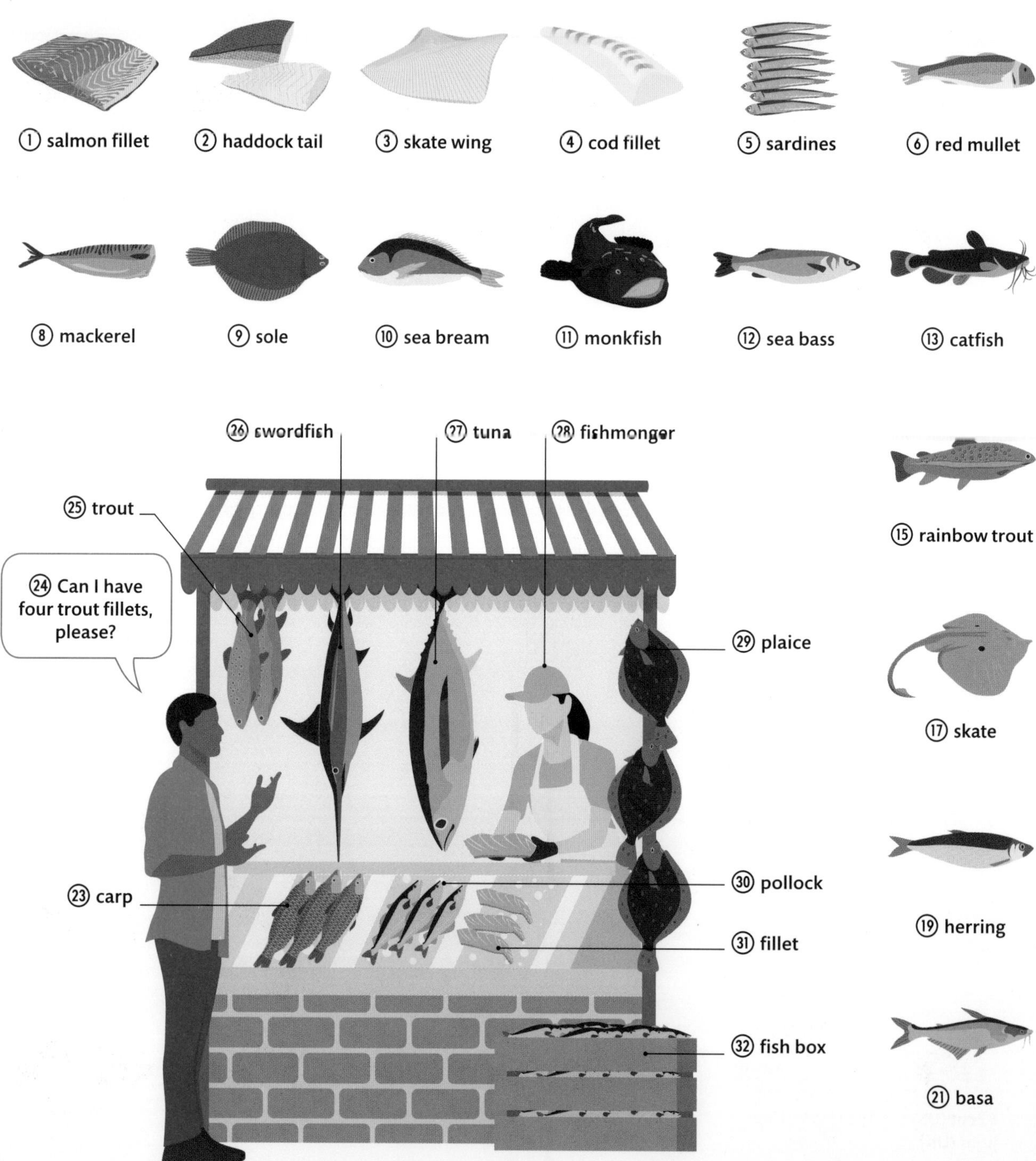

① salmon fillet
② haddock tail
③ skate wing
④ cod fillet
⑤ sardines
⑥ red mullet
⑧ mackerel
⑨ sole
⑩ sea bream
⑪ monkfish
⑫ sea bass
⑬ catfish
㉖ swordfish
㉗ tuna
㉘ fishmonger
㉕ trout
㉔ Can I have four trout fillets, please?
㉙ plaice
㉓ carp
㉚ pollock
㉛ fillet
㉜ fish box
⑮ rainbow trout
⑰ skate
⑲ herring
㉑ basa

See also:
29 Cooking **52** Drinking and eating **55-56** Vegetables
69 At the restaurant **72** Lunch and dinner **166** Ocean life

⑦ whiting

⑭ halibut

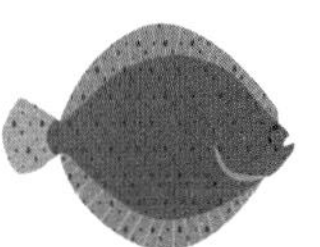
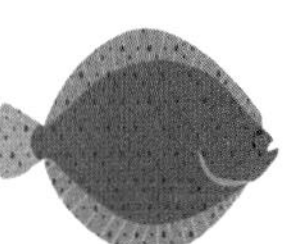
⑯ turbot

⑱ eel

⑳ perch

㉒ pike perch

54.2 SEAFOOD

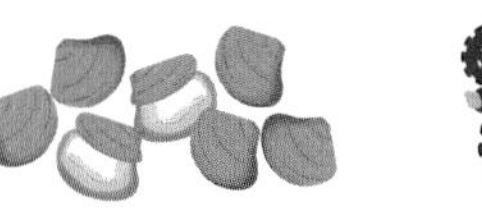
① clam

② octopus

③ lobster

④ scallop

⑤ crayfish

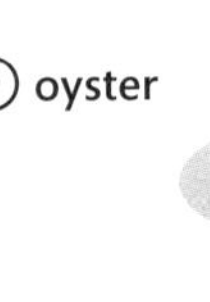

⑥ unpeeled shrimp (US) unpeeled prawn (UK)
⑦ peeled shrimp (US) peeled prawn (UK)
⑧ squid
⑨ oyster
⑩ mussel
⑫ crab
⑪ seafood platter

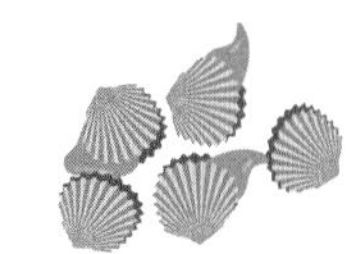
⑬ cockle

⑭ razor-shell

⑮ calamari

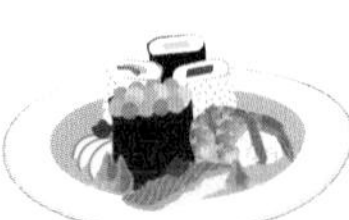
⑯ sushi

54.3 PREPARATION

① scale
③ tail
② fresh

④ frozen

⑤ smoked

⑥ salted

⑦ descaled

⑧ cleaned

⑨ boned

⑩ loin

55 Vegetables

55.1 VEGETABLES

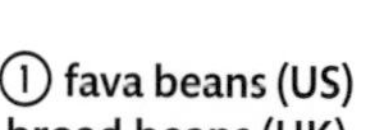

① fava beans (US)
broad beans (UK)

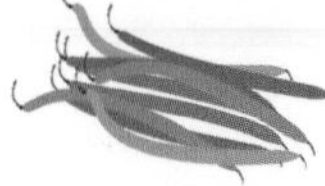

② runner beans

③ green beans /
French beans (UK)

④ dried beans

⑤ celery

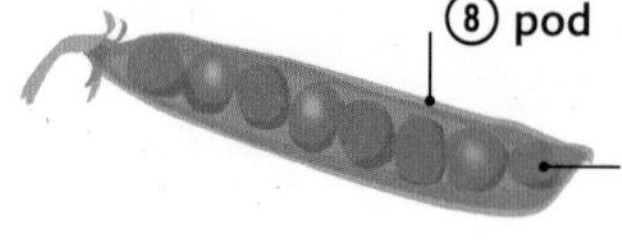
⑧ pod
⑨ pea

⑦ garden peas

⑩ snow peas (US)
mangetout (UK)

⑪ okra

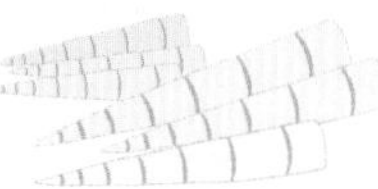

⑫ bamboo

⑬ bean sprouts

⑮ chicory

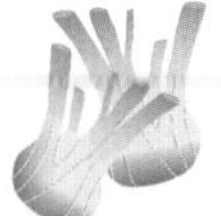

⑯ fennel

⑰ palm hearts

⑱ baby corn (US)
baby sweetcorn (UK)

⑲ kernel

⑳ corn /
sweetcorn (UK)

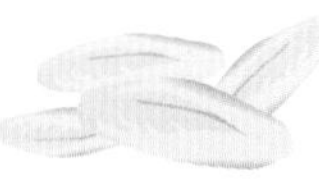

㉓ endive

㉔ dandelion

㉕ Swiss chard

㉖ kale

㉗ sorrel

㉘ spinach

㉛ bok choi (US)
pak-choi (UK)

㉜ kohlrabi

㉝ Brussels sprouts

㉞ spring greens

㊲ floret
㊳ leaf
㊱ stalk

㉟ broccoli

See also:
29 Cooking 52 Drinking and eating 56 Vegetables (continued) 57 Fruit
58 Fruit and nuts 59 Herbs and spices 69 At the restaurant 72 Lunch and dinner

⑥ collards

⑭ savoy cabbage

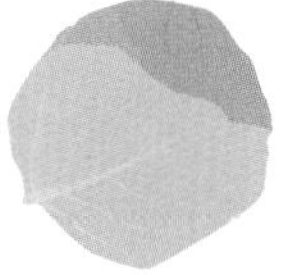

㉑ cabbage

㉒ red cabbage

㉙ cavolo nero

㉚ beet greens (US) beet leaves (UK)

㊵ pesticides

㊴ organic vegetables

55.2 SALAD VEGETABLES

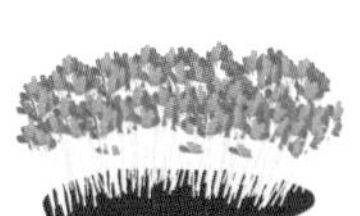

① cress

② arugula (US) rocket (UK)

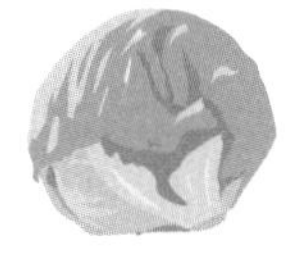

③ iceberg lettuce

④ romaine lettuce

⑤ little gem

⑥ spring onion

⑦ cherry tomatoes

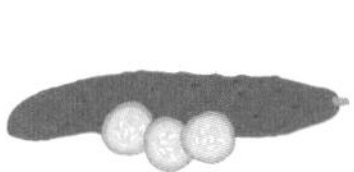

⑧ cucumber

⑨ frisée

⑩ watercress

⑪ radicchio

⑫ lettuce

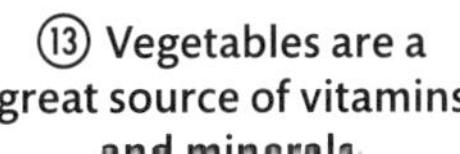

⑬ Vegetables are a great source of vitamins and minerals.
⑭ salad

56 Vegetables continued

56.1 AT THE GROCERY STORE (US) / GREENGROCERS (UK)

① turnip

② radish

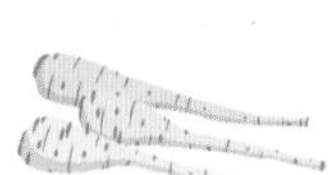
③ parsnip

④ celeriac

⑤ cassava

⑥ potato

⑦ water chestnut

⑧ yam

⑨ beet (US) beetroot (UK)

⑩ rutabaga (US) swede (UK)

⑪ Jerusalem artichoke

⑫ taro root

⑬ horseradish

⑭ breadfruit

⑮ shallot

⑯ chili (US) chilli (UK)

⑰ plum tomato

⑱ asparagus tip

⑲ artichoke heart

⑳ oyster mushroom

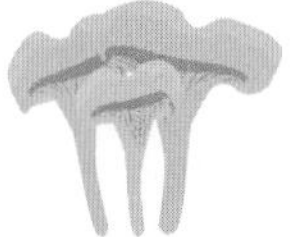
㉑ chanterelle

㉒ shiitake mushroom

㉓ truffle

㉔ enoki mushroom

㉕ marrow

㉖ butternut squash

㉗ acorn squash (US) button acorn squash (UK)

㉘ pumpkin

㉙ buttercup squash

㉚ patty pan

㉛ fresh

㉜ frozen

㉝ canned (US) tinned (UK)

㉞ raw

㉟ cooked

㊱ hot / spicy

See also:
29 Cooking **52** Drinking and eating **57** Fruit
58 Fruit and nuts **69** At the restaurant **72** Lunch and dinner

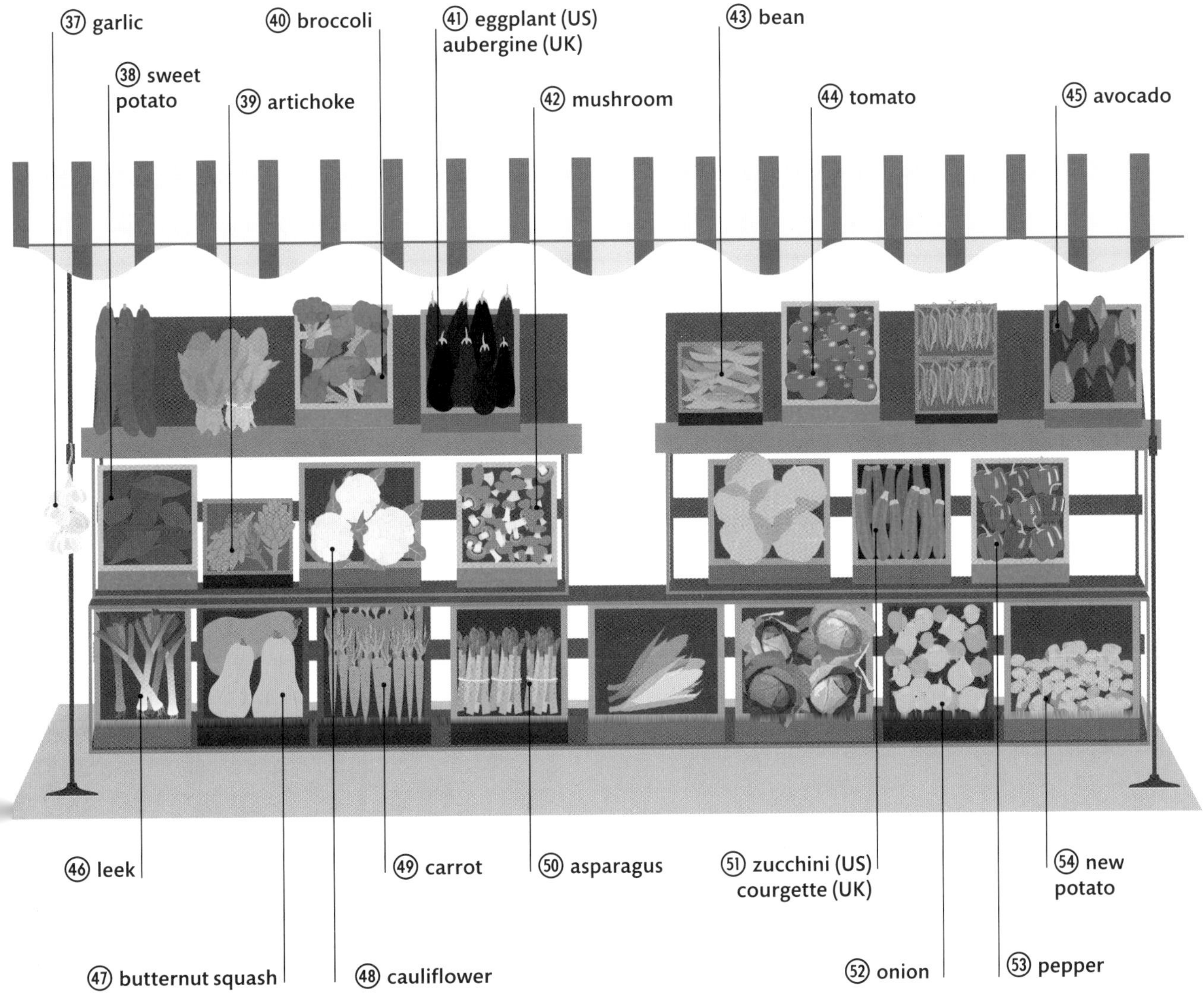

37 garlic
38 sweet potato
39 artichoke
40 broccoli
41 eggplant (US) aubergine (UK)
42 mushroom
43 bean
44 tomato
45 avocado
46 leek
47 butternut squash
48 cauliflower
49 carrot
50 asparagus
51 zucchini (US) courgette (UK)
52 onion
53 pepper
54 new potato

55 sweet

56 crunchy

57 bitter

58 leafy

57 Fruit

57.1 CITRUS FRUIT

57.2 DESCRIBING FRUIT

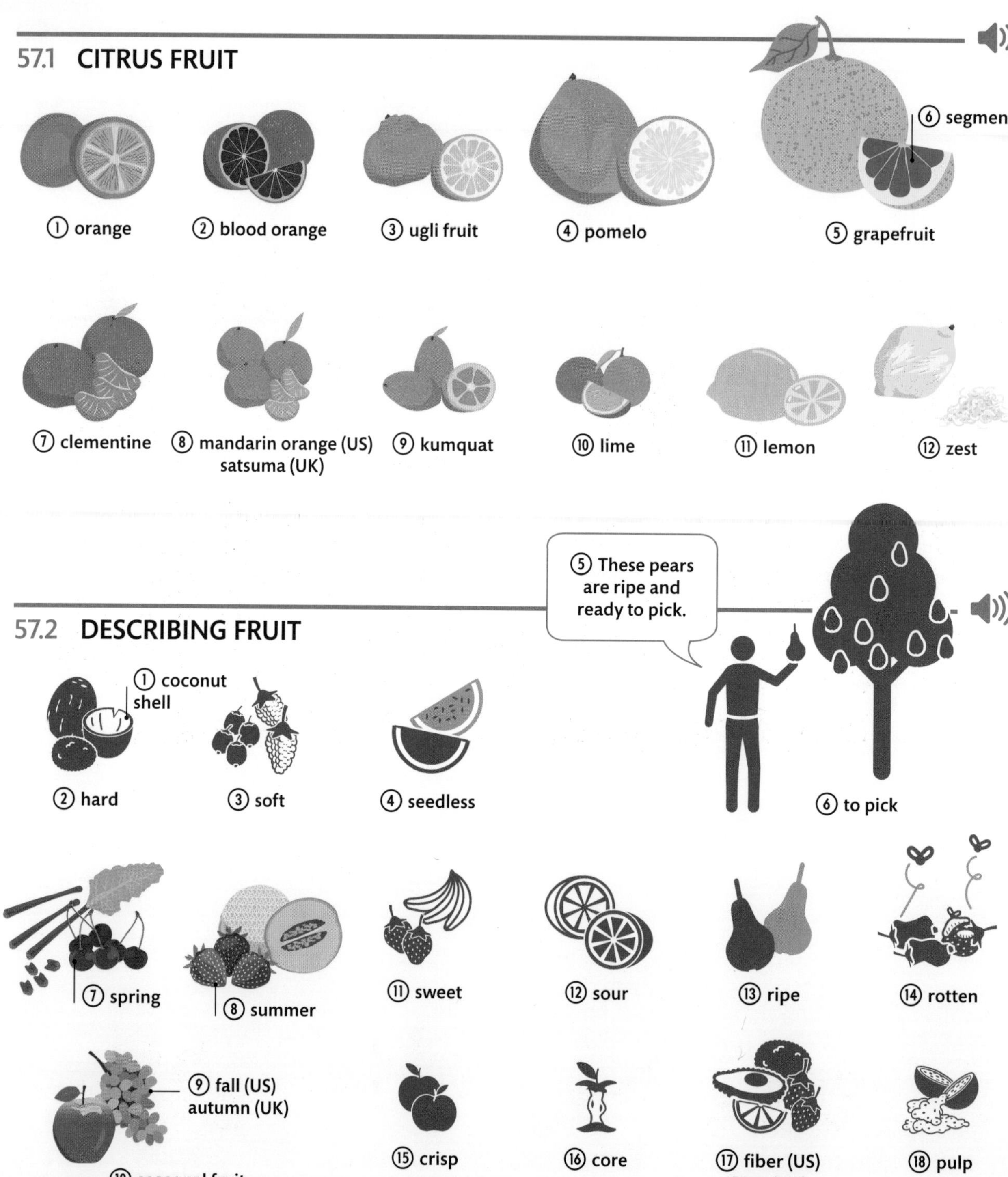

⑥ segment
① orange
② blood orange
③ ugli fruit
④ pomelo
⑤ grapefruit
⑦ clementine
⑧ mandarin orange (US)
satsuma (UK)
⑨ kumquat
⑩ lime
⑪ lemon
⑫ zest
⑤ These pears are ripe and ready to pick.
① coconut shell
② hard
③ soft
④ seedless
⑥ to pick
⑦ spring
⑧ summer
⑪ sweet
⑫ sour
⑬ ripe
⑭ rotten
⑨ fall (US)
autumn (UK)
⑩ seasonal fruit
⑮ crisp
⑯ core
⑰ fiber (US)
fibre (UK)
⑱ pulp

See also:
29 Cooking 52 Drinking and eating 55-56 Vegetables 58 Fruit and nuts
65-66 At the café 69 At the restaurant 71 Breakfast 72 Lunch and dinner

57.3 BERRIES AND STONE FRUIT

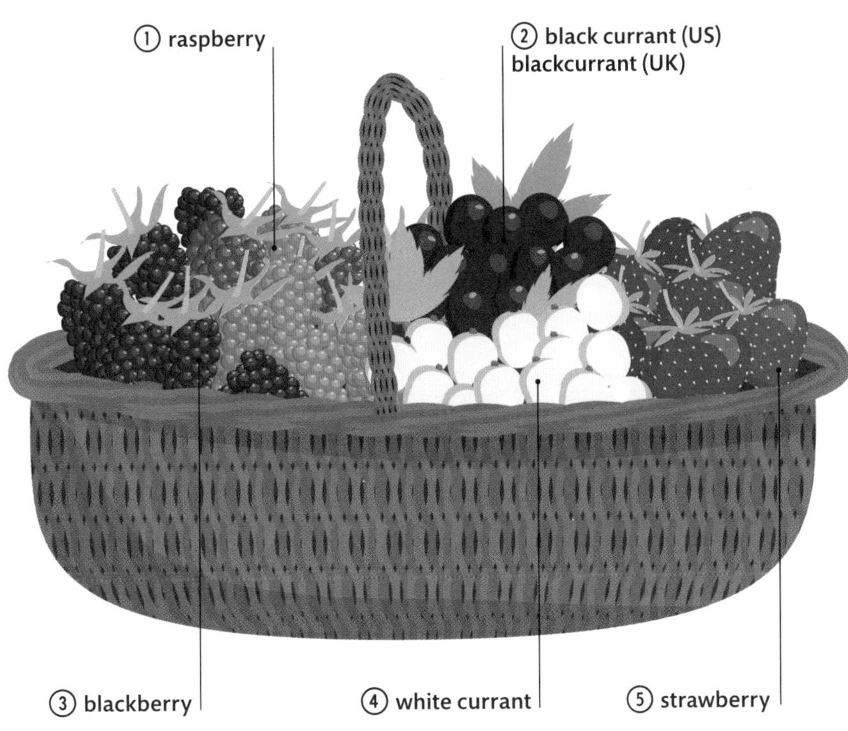
① raspberry
② black currant (US)
blackcurrant (UK)
③ blackberry
④ white currant
⑤ strawberry
⑥ basket of fruit

⑦ cranberry

⑧ blueberry

⑨ loganberry

⑩ cape gooseberry

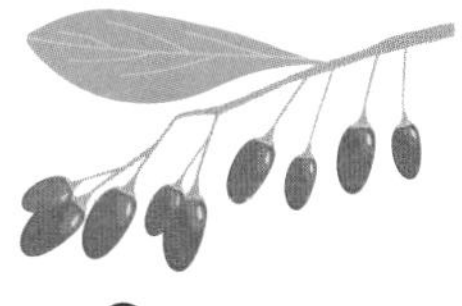
⑪ goji berry

⑫ gooseberry

⑬ red currant (US)
redcurrant (UK)

⑭ bilberry

⑮ elderberry

⑯ grapes

⑰ mulberry

⑱ peach

⑲ nectarine

⑳ apricot

㉑ mango

㉒ plum

㉓ cherry

㉔ date

㉕ lychee

58 Fruit and nuts

58.1 MELONS

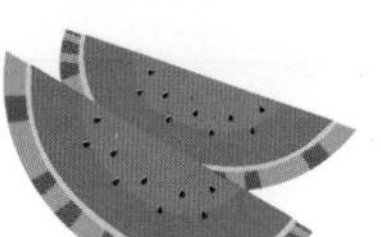
① watermelon

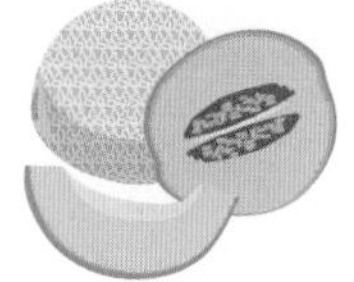
② cantaloupe

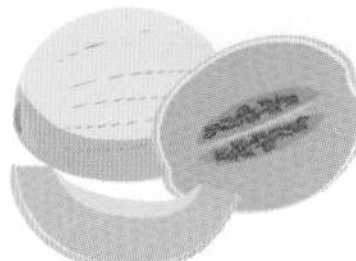
③ honeydew melon

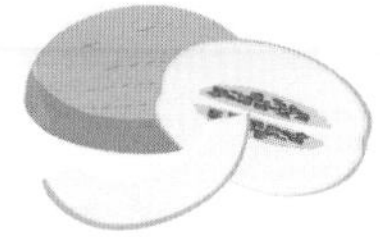
④ Canary melon

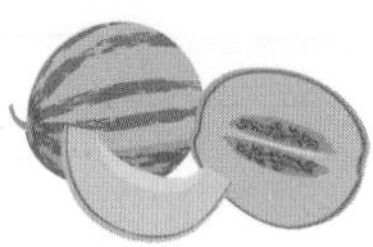
⑤ charentais

⑥ galia

58.2 OTHER FRUIT

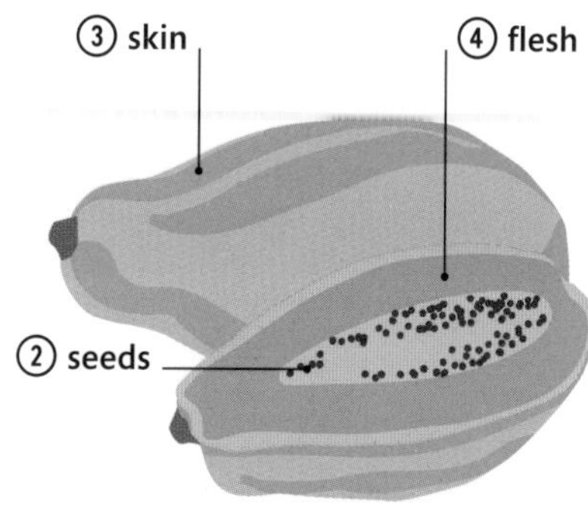
③ skin
④ flesh
② seeds
① papaya

⑤ quince

⑥ passion fruit

⑦ guava

⑩ feijoa

⑪ pineapple

⑧ starfruit

⑨ persimmon

⑫ prickly pear

⑬ tamarillo

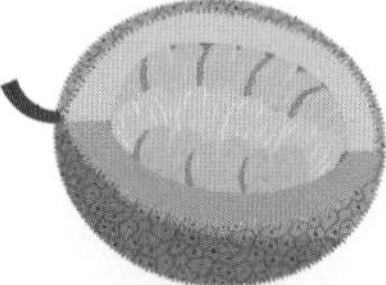
⑭ jackfruit

⑮ mangosteen

⑯ pomegranate

⑰ banana

⑱ kiwi
kiwi fruit (UK)

⑲ apple

⑳ crab apples

㉑ pear

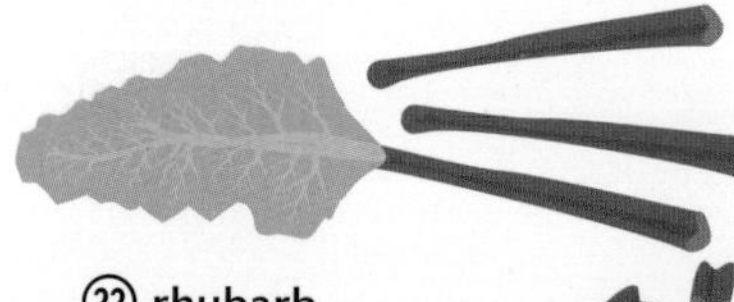
㉒ rhubarb

See also:
29 Cooking **52** Drinking and eating **55-56** Vegetables **57** Fruit
65-66 At the café **69** At the restaurant **71** Breakfast **72** Lunch and dinner

58.3 NUTS AND DRIED FRUIT

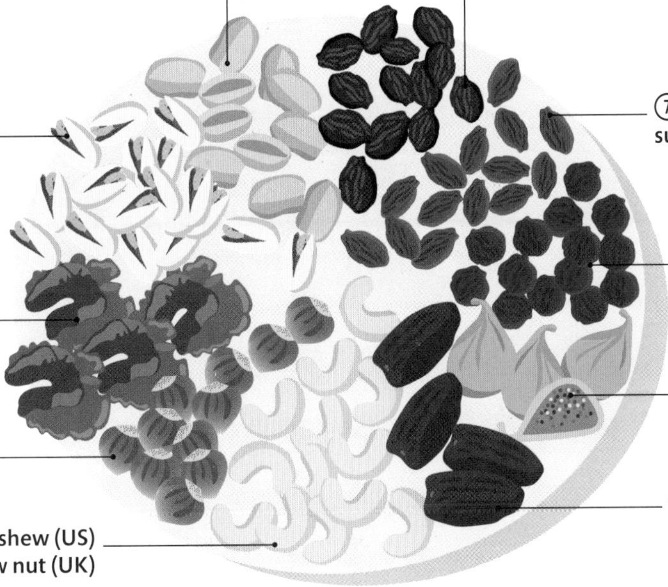

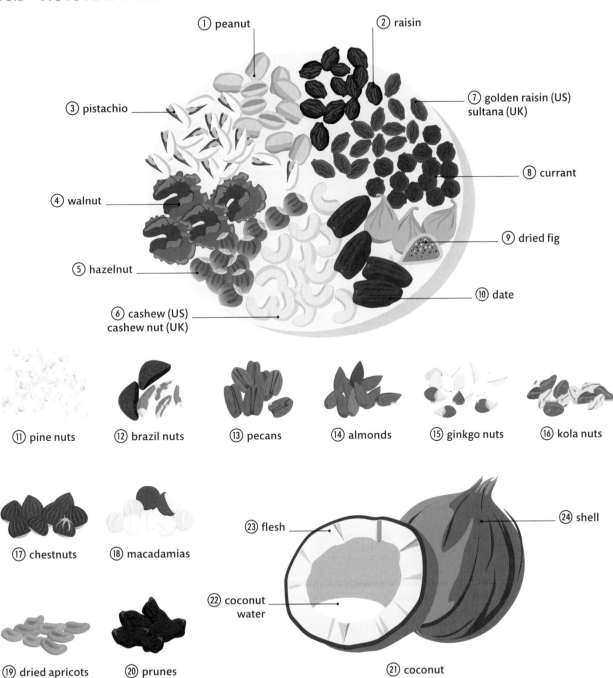

① peanut
② raisin
③ pistachio
④ walnut
⑤ hazelnut
⑥ cashew (US)
cashew nut (UK)
⑦ golden raisin (US)
sultana (UK)
⑧ currant
⑨ dried fig
⑩ date

⑪ pine nuts
⑫ brazil nuts 
⑬ pecans 
⑭ almonds 
⑮ ginkgo nuts 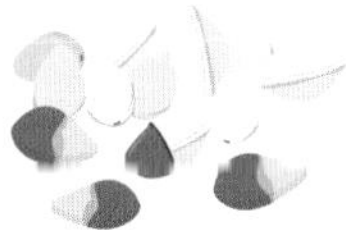
⑯ kola nuts 
⑰ chestnuts 
⑱ macadamias 
⑲ dried apricots 
⑳ prunes 
㉑ coconut 
㉒ coconut water
㉓ flesh
㉔ shell

59 Herbs and spices

59.1 SPICES

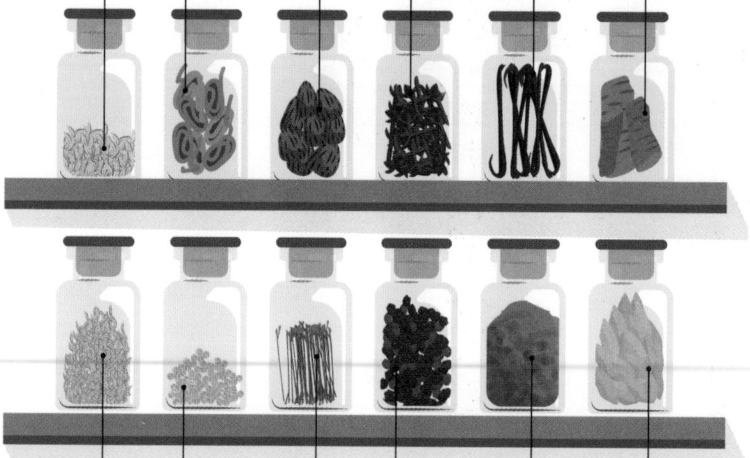

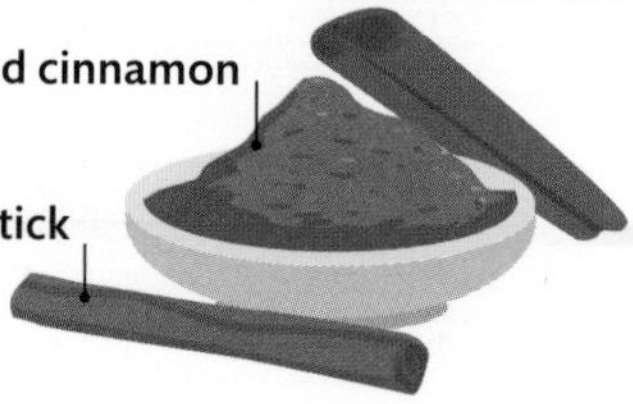

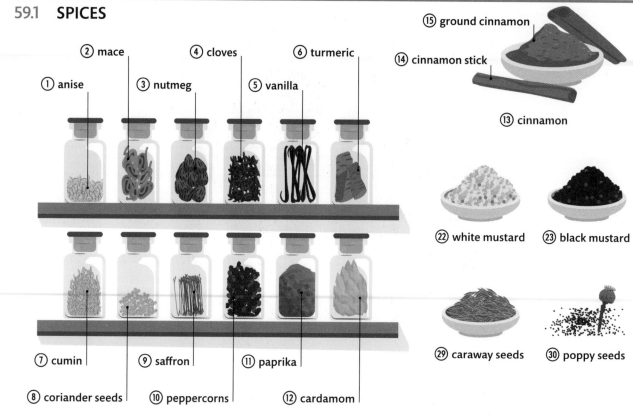

① anise
② mace
③ nutmeg
④ cloves
⑤ vanilla
⑥ turmeric
⑦ cumin
⑧ coriander seeds
⑨ saffron
⑩ peppercorns
⑪ paprika
⑫ cardamom
⑬ cinnamon
⑭ cinnamon stick
⑮ ground cinnamon 
㉒ white mustard 
㉓ black mustard 
㉙ caraway seeds 
㉚ poppy seeds

59.2 HERBS

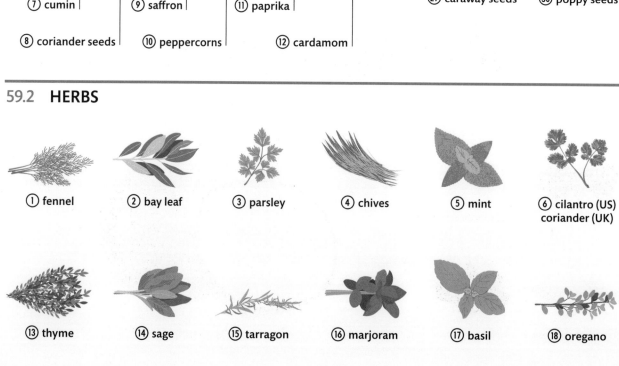

① fennel
② bay leaf 
③ parsley 
④ chives 
⑤ mint 
⑥ cilantro (US) coriander (UK) 
⑬ thyme 
⑭ sage 
⑮ tarragon 
⑯ marjoram 
⑰ basil 
⑱ oregano

See also:
29 Cooking **52** Drinking and eating **53** Meat
55-56 Vegetables **60** In the pantry

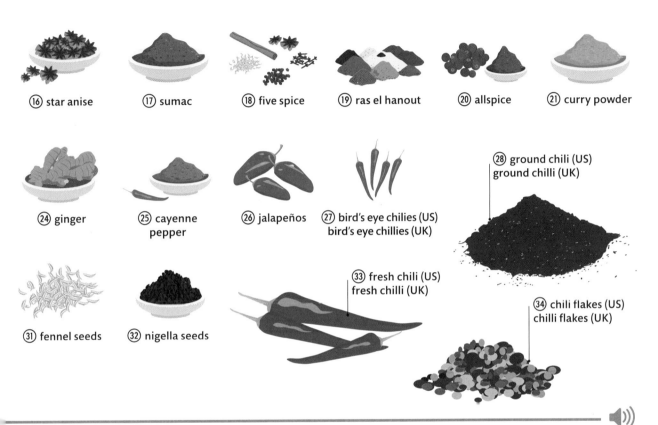

(16) star anise

(17) sumac

(18) five spice

(19) ras el hanout

(20) allspice

(21) curry powder

(24) ginger

(25) cayenne pepper

(26) jalapeños

(27) bird's eye chilies (US)
bird's eye chillies (UK)

(28) ground chili (US)
ground chilli (UK)

(31) fennel seeds

(32) nigella seeds

(33) fresh chili (US)
fresh chilli (UK)

(34) chili flakes (US)
chilli flakes (UK)

(7) hyssop

(8) dill

(9) rosemary

(10) chervil

(11) lovage

(12) sorrel

(19) lemongrass

(20) lemon balm

(21) borage

(22) fenugreek leaves

(23) bouquet garni

60 In the pantry

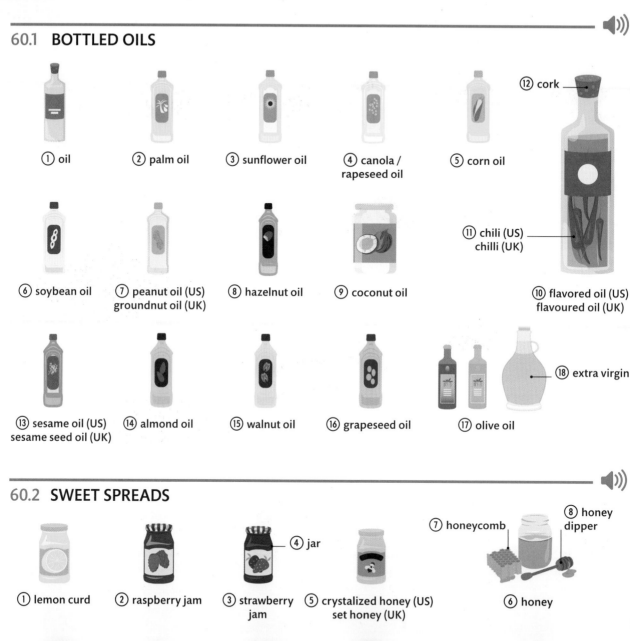

60.1 BOTTLED OILS

① oil
② palm oil
③ sunflower oil
④ canola / rapeseed oil
⑤ corn oil
⑥ soybean oil
⑦ peanut oil (US) groundnut oil (UK)
⑧ hazelnut oil
⑨ coconut oil
⑩ flavored oil (US) flavoured oil (UK)
⑪ chili (US) chilli (UK)
⑫ cork
⑬ sesame oil (US) sesame seed oil (UK)
⑭ almond oil
⑮ walnut oil
⑯ grapeseed oil
⑰ olive oil
⑱ extra virgin

60.2 SWEET SPREADS

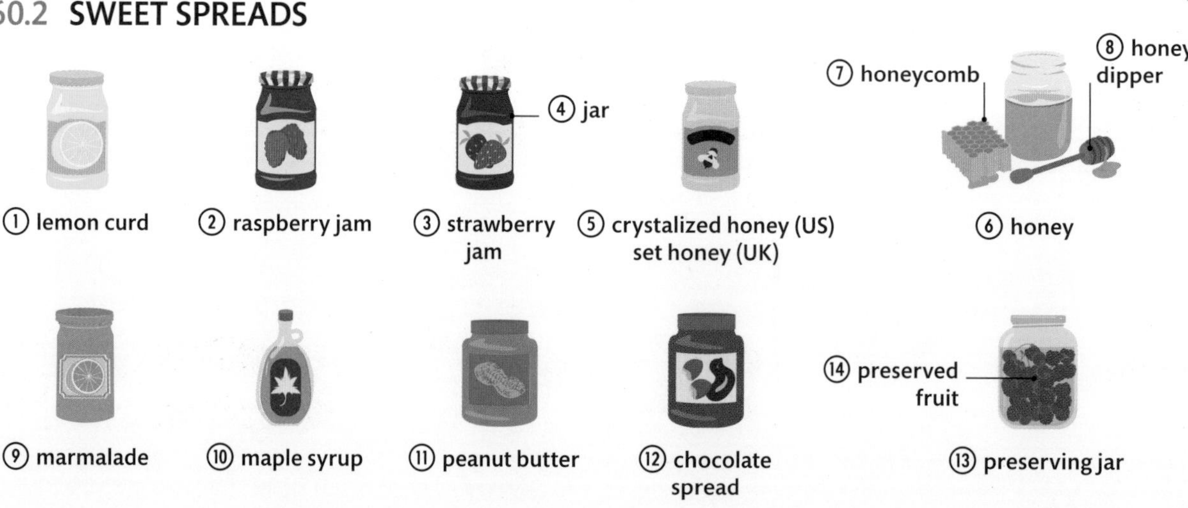
① lemon curd
② raspberry jam
③ strawberry jam
④ jar
⑤ crystalized honey (US) set honey (UK)
⑥ honey
⑦ honeycomb
⑧ honey dipper
⑨ marmalade
⑩ maple syrup
⑪ peanut butter
⑫ chocolate spread
⑬ preserving jar
⑭ preserved fruit

See also:
27 Kitchen and tableware 29 Cooking 52 Drinking and eating
53 Meat 55-56 Vegetables 65-66 At the café 69 At the restaurant

60.3 SAUCES AND CONDIMENTS

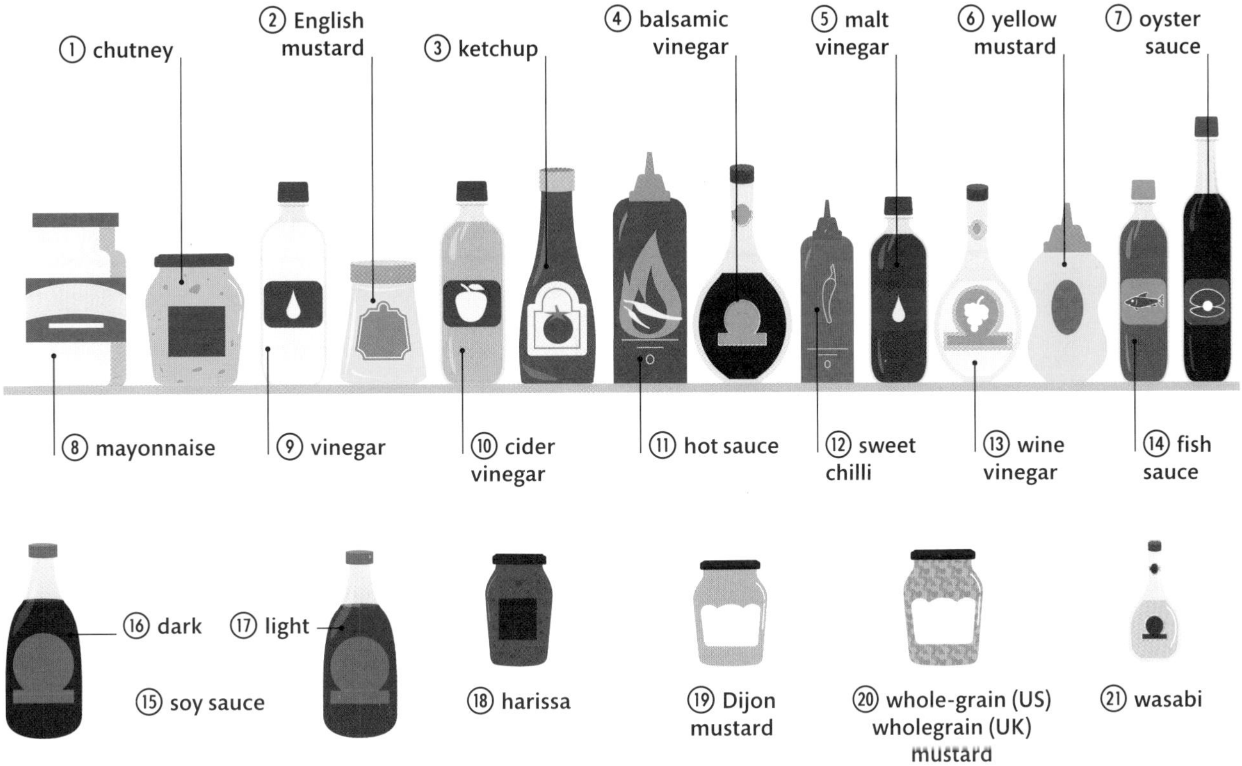

1. chutney
2. English mustard
3. ketchup
4. balsamic vinegar
5. malt vinegar
6. yellow mustard
7. oyster sauce
8. mayonnaise
9. vinegar
10. cider vinegar
11. hot sauce
12. sweet chilli
13. wine vinegar
14. fish sauce
15. soy sauce
16. dark
17. light
18. harissa
19. Dijon mustard
20. whole-grain (US) wholegrain (UK) mustard
21. wasabi

60.4 PICKLES

① dill
② gherkin
③ mustard seeds
④ sauerkraut
⑤ kimchi
⑥ lime pickle
⑦ pickled onions
⑧ pickled beets (US) beetroot (UK)
⑨ sandwich pickle
⑩ piccalilli
⑪ cornichons

61 Dairy produce

61.1 CHEESE

① hard cheese

② semi-hard cheese

③ semi-soft cheese

④ soft cheese

⑤ sheep's milk cheese

⑥ goat's cheese

⑦ blue cheese

⑧ rind

⑨ grated cheese

⑩ fresh cheese

⑪ cottage cheese

⑫ cream cheese

61.2 EGGS

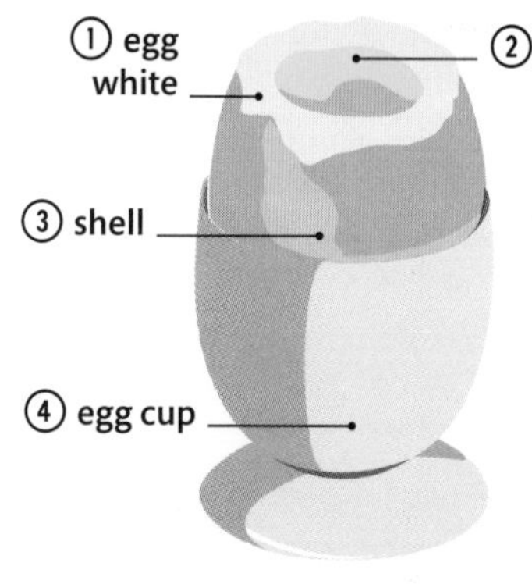
① egg white
② yolk
③ shell
④ egg cup
⑤ boiled egg

⑥ fried egg

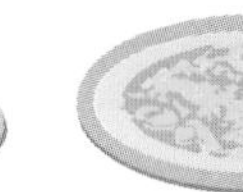
⑦ scrambled eggs

⑧ poached egg

⑨ omelet (US) omelette (UK)

⑩ goose egg

⑪ duck egg

⑫ chicken egg (US) hen's egg (UK)

⑬ quail egg

61.3 MILK

① pasteurized

② unpasteurized

③ lactose free

④ homogenized

0%
⑤ fat free

⑥ powdered milk

See also:
29 Cooking 52 Drinking and eating
65-66 At the café 69 At the restaurant 71 Breakfast

61.4 MILK PRODUCTS

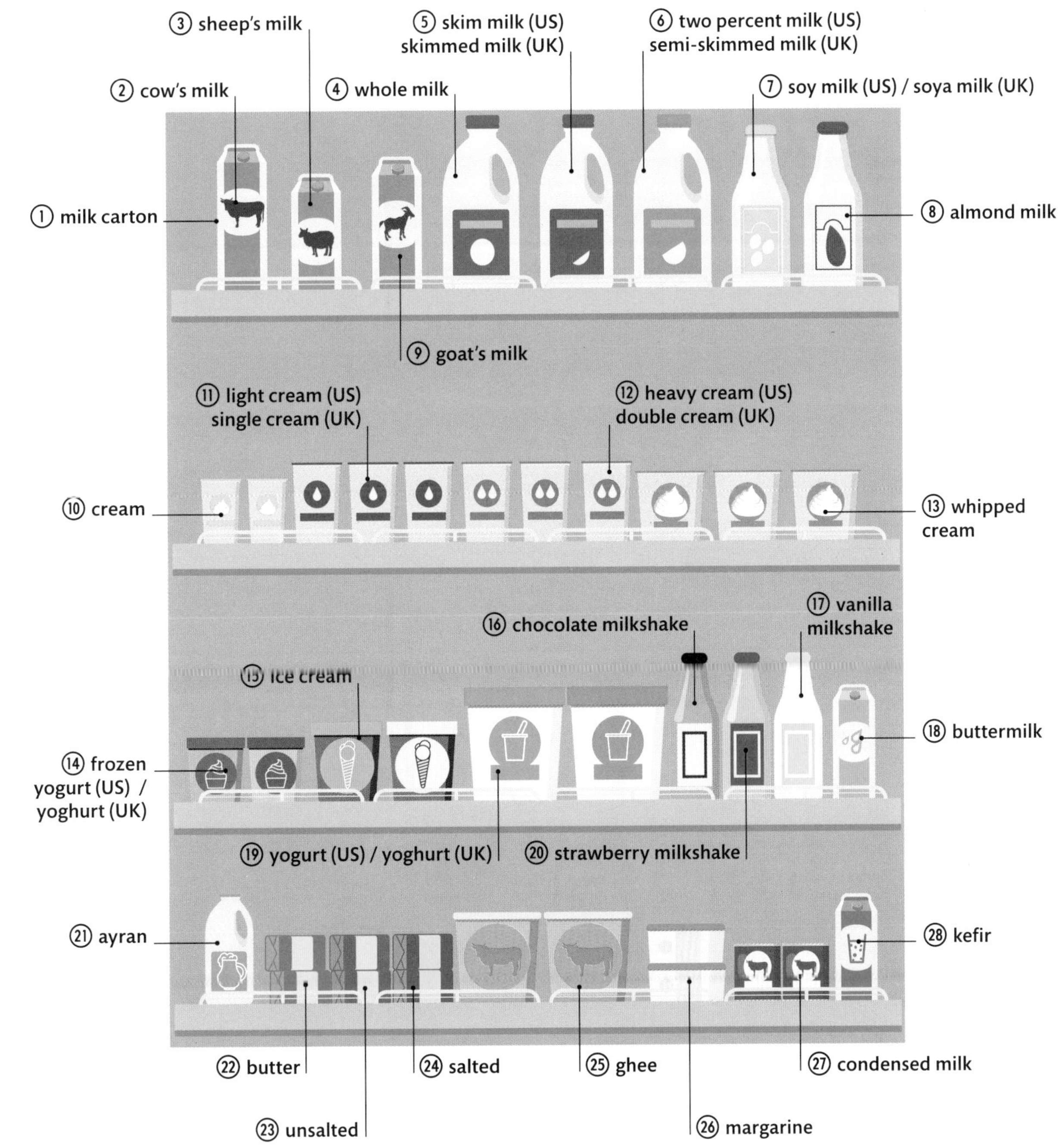

1. milk carton
2. cow's milk
3. sheep's milk
4. whole milk
5. skim milk (US) skimmed milk (UK)
6. two percent milk (US) semi-skimmed milk (UK)
7. soy milk (US) / soya milk (UK)
8. almond milk
9. goat's milk
10. cream
11. light cream (US) single cream (UK)
12. heavy cream (US) double cream (UK)
13. whipped cream
14. frozen yogurt (US) / yoghurt (UK)
15. ice cream
16. chocolate milkshake
17. vanilla milkshake
18. buttermilk
19. yogurt (US) / yoghurt (UK)
20. strawberry milkshake
21. ayran
22. butter
23. unsalted
24. salted
25. ghee
26. margarine
27. condensed milk
28. kefir

62 The bakery

62.1 BREADS AND FLOURS

① bakery
② matzo
③ shaobing
④ pretzel
⑤ pain au chocolat
⑥ baker
⑭ bagel
⑮ challah
⑯ injera
⑰ brioche
⑱ fruit bread
㉔ pita (US) / pitta bread (UK)
㉕ chapati
㉖ croissant
㉗ tortilla
㉘ slicer

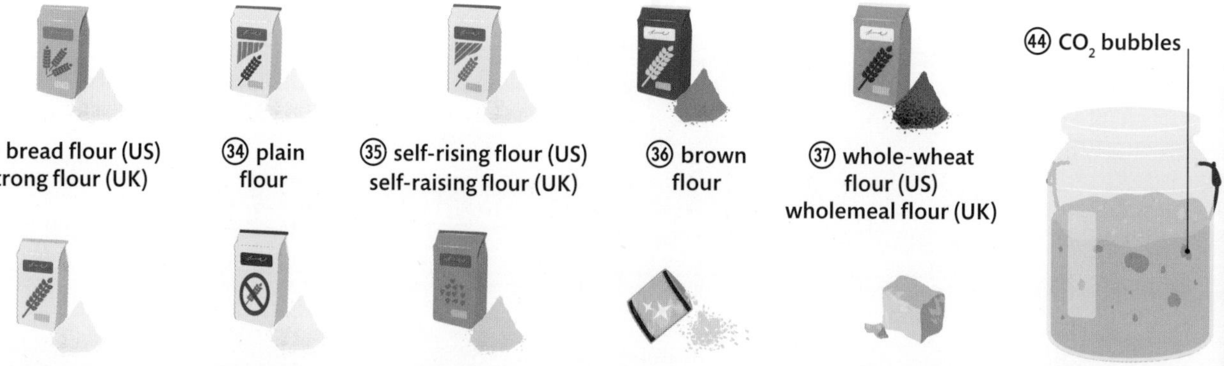

㉝ bread flour (US)
strong flour (UK)

㉞ plain flour

㉟ self-rising flour (US)
self-raising flour (UK)

㊱ brown flour

㊲ whole-wheat flour (US)
wholemeal flour (UK)

㊳ white flour

㊴ gluten-free flour

㊵ buckwheat flour

㊶ dried yeast

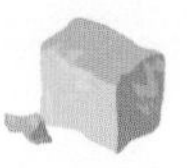

㊷ fresh yeast

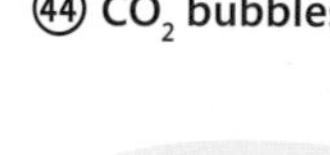

㊹ CO_2 bubbles

㊸ sourdough starter

See also:
29 Cooking 52 Drinking and eating 63 The bakery (continued)
65-66 At the café 69 At the restaurant 71 Breakfast

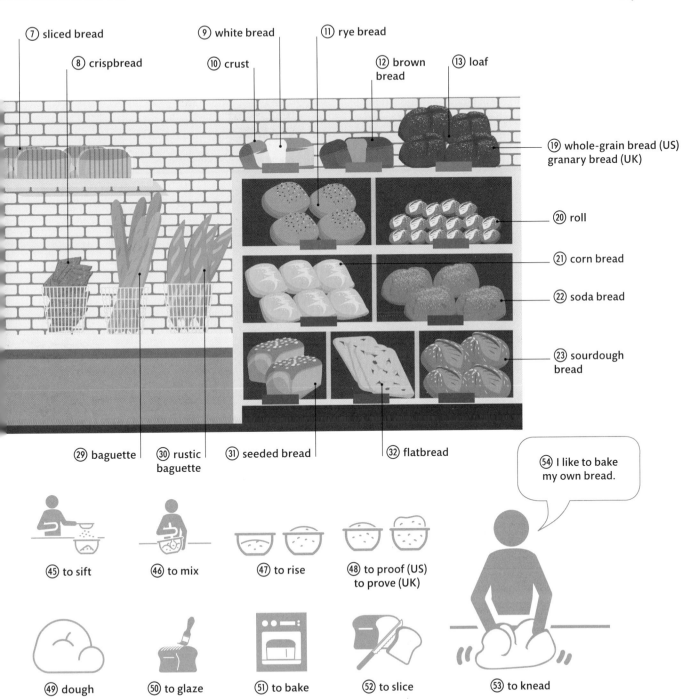

7 sliced bread
8 crispbread
9 white bread
10 crust
11 rye bread
12 brown bread
13 loaf
19 whole-grain bread (US) granary bread (UK)
20 roll
21 corn bread
22 soda bread
23 sourdough bread
29 baguette
30 rustic baguette
31 seeded bread
32 flatbread

54 I like to bake my own bread.

45 to sift
46 to mix
47 to rise
48 to proof (US) to prove (UK)
49 dough
50 to glaze
51 to bake
52 to slice
53 to knead

63 The bakery continued

63.1 CAKES AND DESSERTS

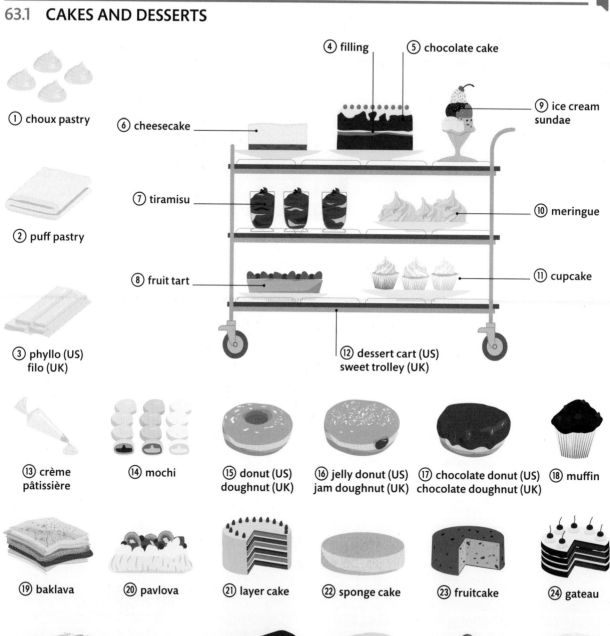

① choux pastry

② puff pastry

③ phyllo (US)
filo (UK)

④ filling

⑤ chocolate cake

⑥ cheesecake

⑦ tiramisu

⑧ fruit tart

⑨ ice cream sundae

⑩ meringue

⑪ cupcake

⑫ dessert cart (US)
sweet trolley (UK)

⑬ crème pâtissière

⑭ mochi

⑮ donut (US)
doughnut (UK)

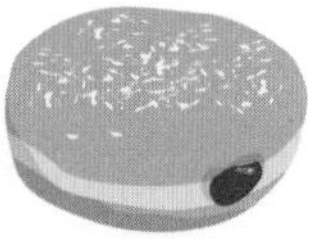

⑯ jelly donut (US)
jam doughnut (UK)

⑰ chocolate donut (US)
chocolate doughnut (UK)

⑱ muffin

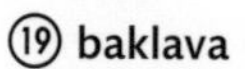

⑲ baklava

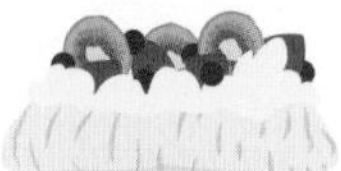

⑳ pavlova

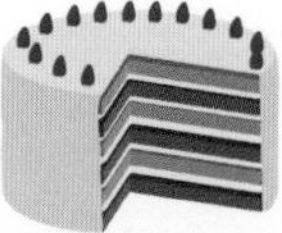

㉑ layer cake

㉒ sponge cake

㉓ fruitcake

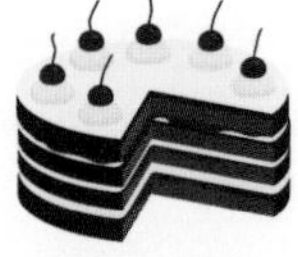

㉔ gateau

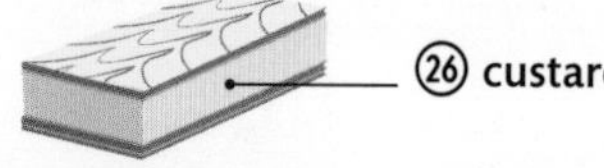

㉖ custard

㉕ Napoleon (US)
custard slice (UK)

㉗ éclair

㉘ iced bun

㉙ pastry

㉚ rice pudding

See also:
29 Cooking **52** Drinking and eating
67 Candy / Sweets **71** Breakfast

63.2 COOKIES AND BISCUITS

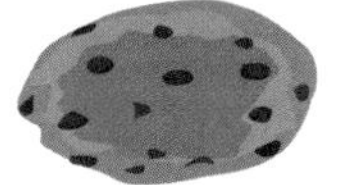

① chocolate chip cookie

② Florentine

③ shortbread

④ macaron

⑤ gingerbread man

⑥ fortune cookies

63.3 CELEBRATION CAKES

① Would you like a piece of cake?
② Yes, it looks absolutely delicious.
③ top tier
④ decoration
⑤ icing
⑥ cake topper
⑦ marzipan
⑧ ribbon

⑨ wedding cake

⑩ to glaze

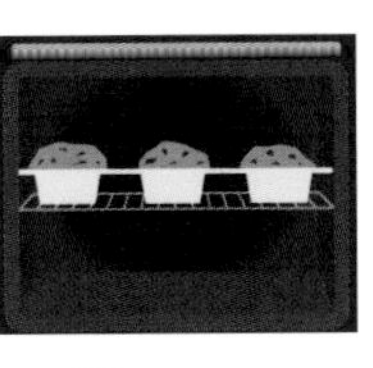

⑪ to bake

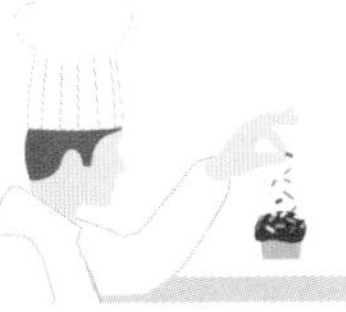

⑫ to decorate

⑮ to blow out
⑭ birthday candles
⑬ birthday cake

64 The delicatessen

64.1 DELICATESSEN

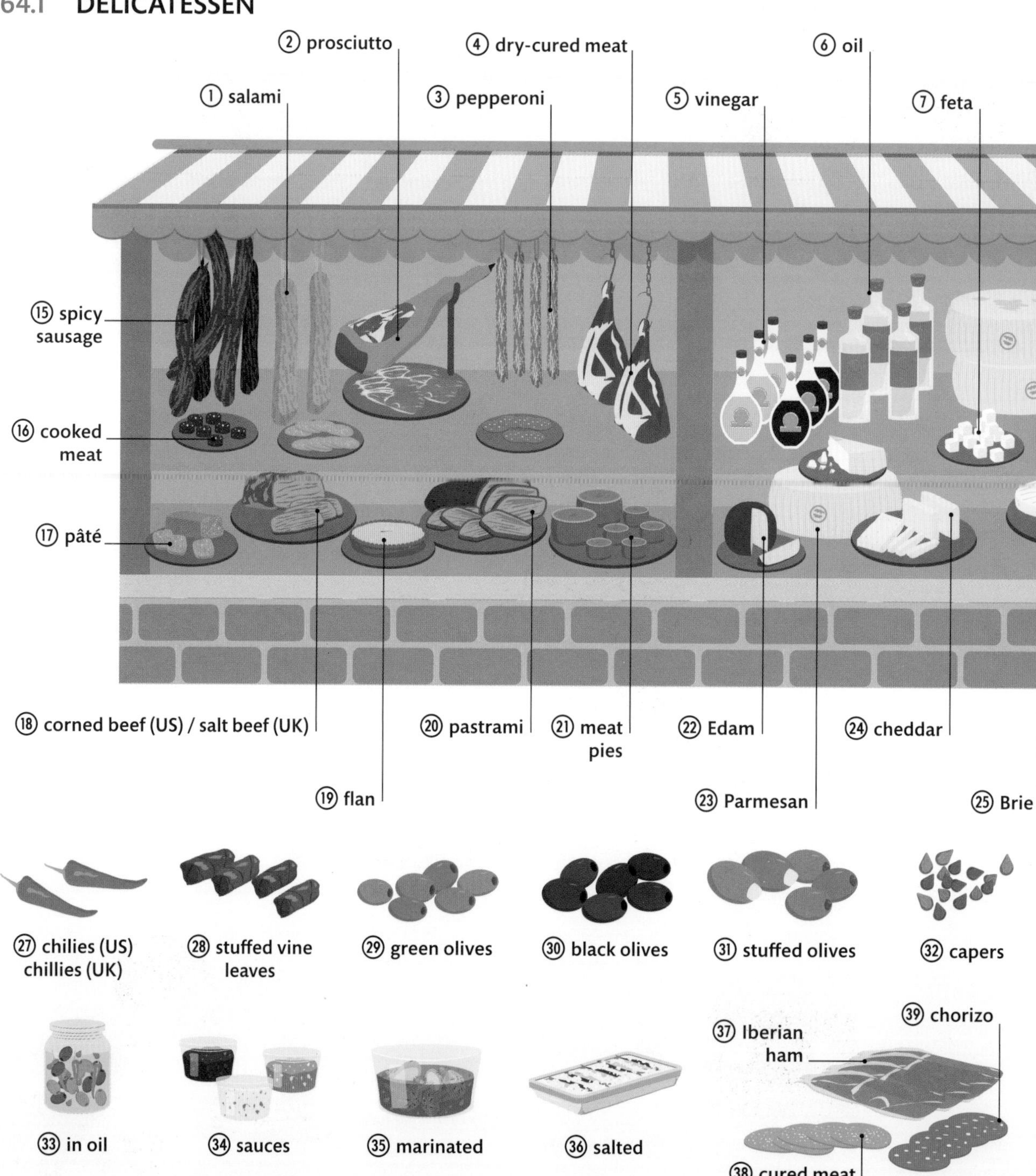

① salami
② prosciutto
③ pepperoni
④ dry-cured meat
⑤ vinegar
⑥ oil
⑦ feta
⑮ spicy sausage
⑯ cooked meat
⑰ pâté
⑱ corned beef (US) / salt beef (UK)
⑲ flan
⑳ pastrami
㉑ meat pies
㉒ Edam
㉓ Parmesan
㉔ cheddar
㉕ Brie
㉗ chilies (US) chillies (UK)
㉘ stuffed vine leaves
㉙ green olives
㉚ black olives
㉛ stuffed olives
㉜ capers
㉝ in oil
㉞ sauces
㉟ marinated
㊱ salted
㊲ Iberian ham
㊳ cured meat
㊴ chorizo

See also:
29 Cooking 52 Drinking and eating 53 Meat 60 In the pantry 61 Dairy produce
65-66 At the café 69 At the restaurant 71 Breakfast 72 Lunch and dinner

(8) rind
(9) Try these different types of cheese!
(10) paneer
(11) halloumi
(12) mozzarella
(13) manchego
(14) cheeses
(26) Camembert
(40) smoked salmon
(42) smoked haddock
(41) smoked mackerel
(43) smoked fish
(46) sardines
(45) anchovies
(44) in brine
(47) marinated fish

64.2 PASTA AND NOODLES

(1) lasagne
(2) conchiglie / shells
(3) fusilli
(4) macaroni
(5) gnocchi
(6) penne
(7) cannelloni
(8) tortellini
(9) noodles
(10) rice noodles
(11) ramen
(12) udon

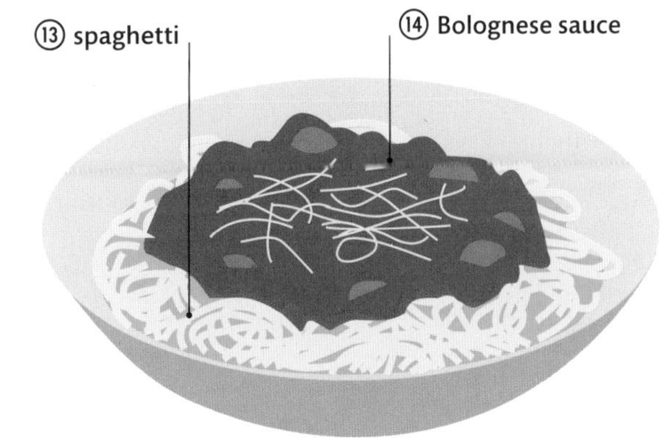
(13) spaghetti
(14) Bolognese sauce

65 At the café

65.1 CAFÉ

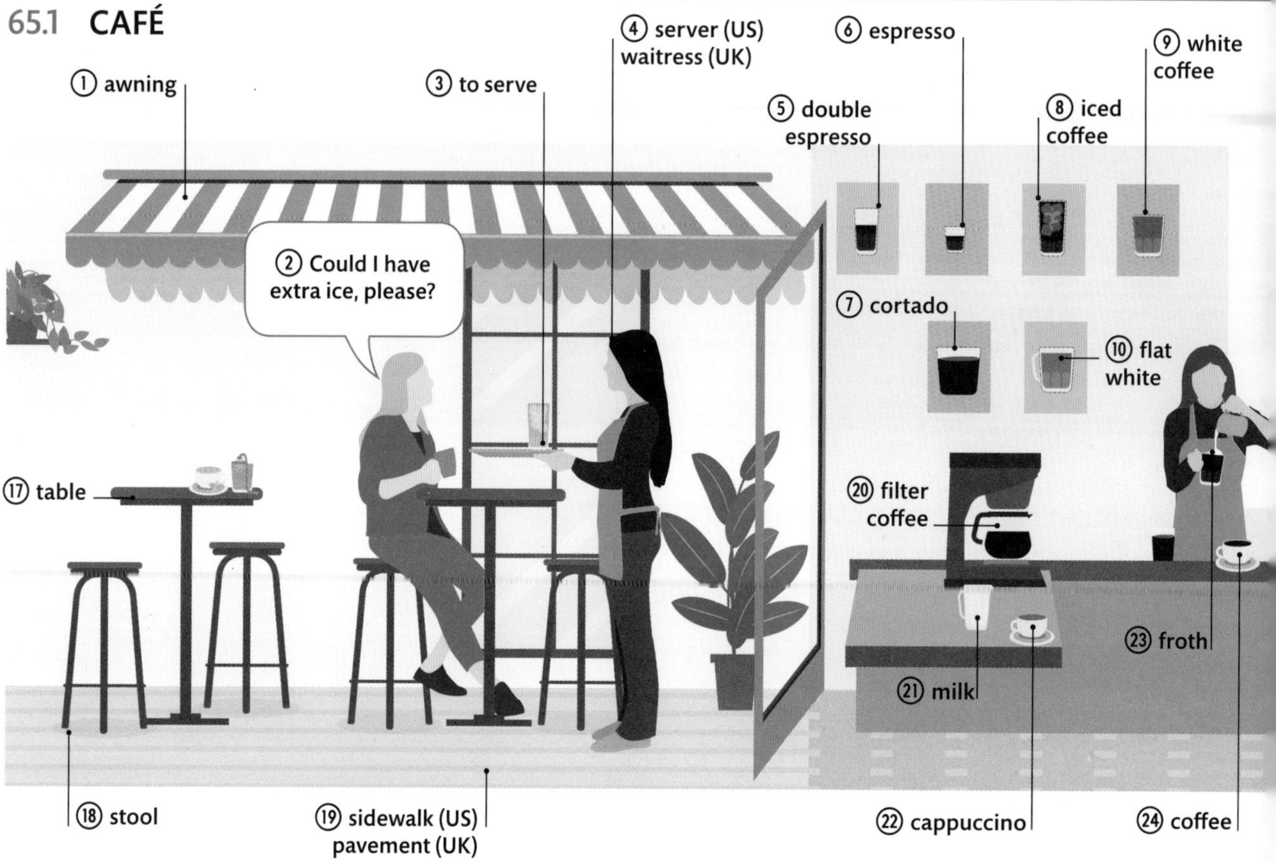

1. awning
2. Could I have extra ice, please?
3. to serve
4. server (US) waitress (UK)
5. double espresso
6. espresso
7. cortado
8. iced coffee
9. white coffee
10. flat white
17. table
18. stool
19. sidewalk (US) pavement (UK)
20. filter coffee
21. milk
22. cappuccino
23. froth
24. coffee

65.2 JUICES AND MILKSHAKES

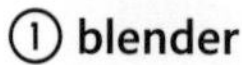
① blender

② coconut water

③ orange juice with pulp

④ smooth orange juice

⑤ apple juice

⑥ pineapple juice

⑦ tomato juice

⑧ mango juice

⑨ cranberry juice

⑩ strawberry smoothie

⑪ chocolate milkshake

⑫ strawberry milkshake

See also:
27 Kitchen and tableware 52 Drinking and eating
66 At the café (continued) 70 Fast food 72 Lunch and dinner

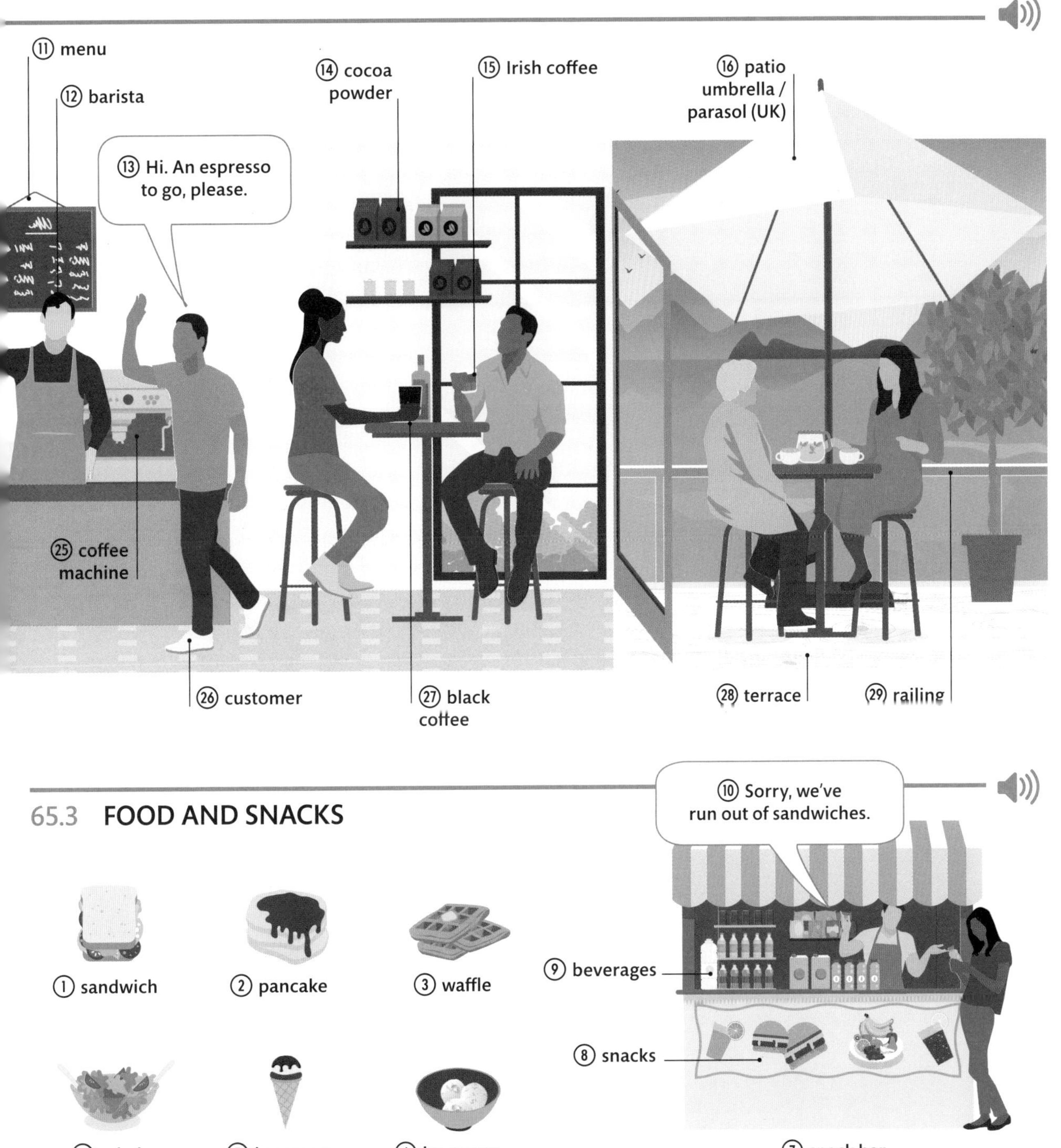
⑪ menu
⑫ barista
⑬ Hi. An espresso to go, please.
⑭ cocoa powder
⑮ Irish coffee
⑯ patio umbrella / parasol (UK)
㉕ coffee machine
㉖ customer
㉗ black coffee
㉘ terrace
㉙ railing

65.3 FOOD AND SNACKS

⑩ Sorry, we've run out of sandwiches.
① sandwich
② pancake
③ waffle
④ salad
⑤ ice cream cone
⑥ ice cream scoop
⑦ snack bar
⑧ snacks
⑨ beverages

66 At the café continued

See also:
27 Kitchen and tableware
52 Drinking and eating 72 Lunch and dinner

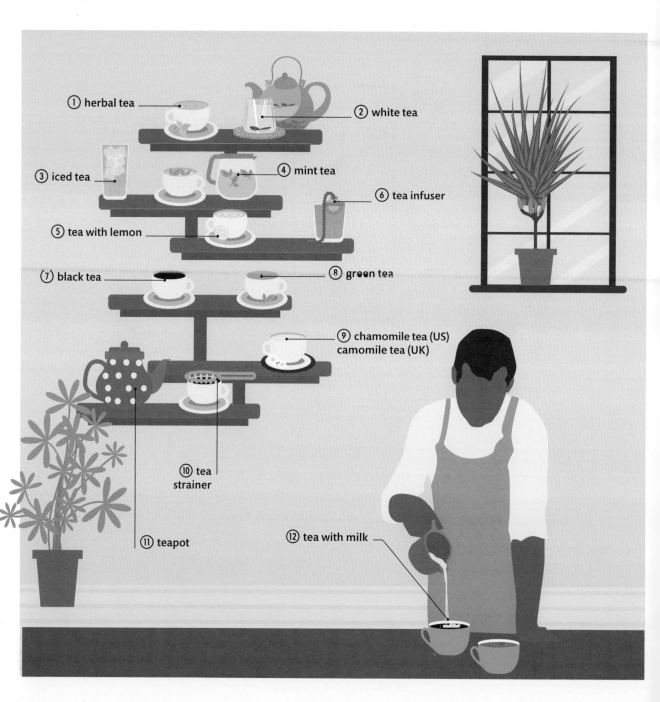

66.1 TEA

① herbal tea
② white tea
③ iced tea
④ mint tea
⑤ tea with lemon
⑥ tea infuser
⑦ black tea
⑧ green tea
⑨ chamomile tea (US) camomile tea (UK)
⑩ tea strainer
⑪ teapot
⑫ tea with milk

67 Candy (US) / Sweets (UK)

See also:
48 The supermarket
63 The bakery

67.1 CANDY STORE (US) / SWEET SHOP (UK)

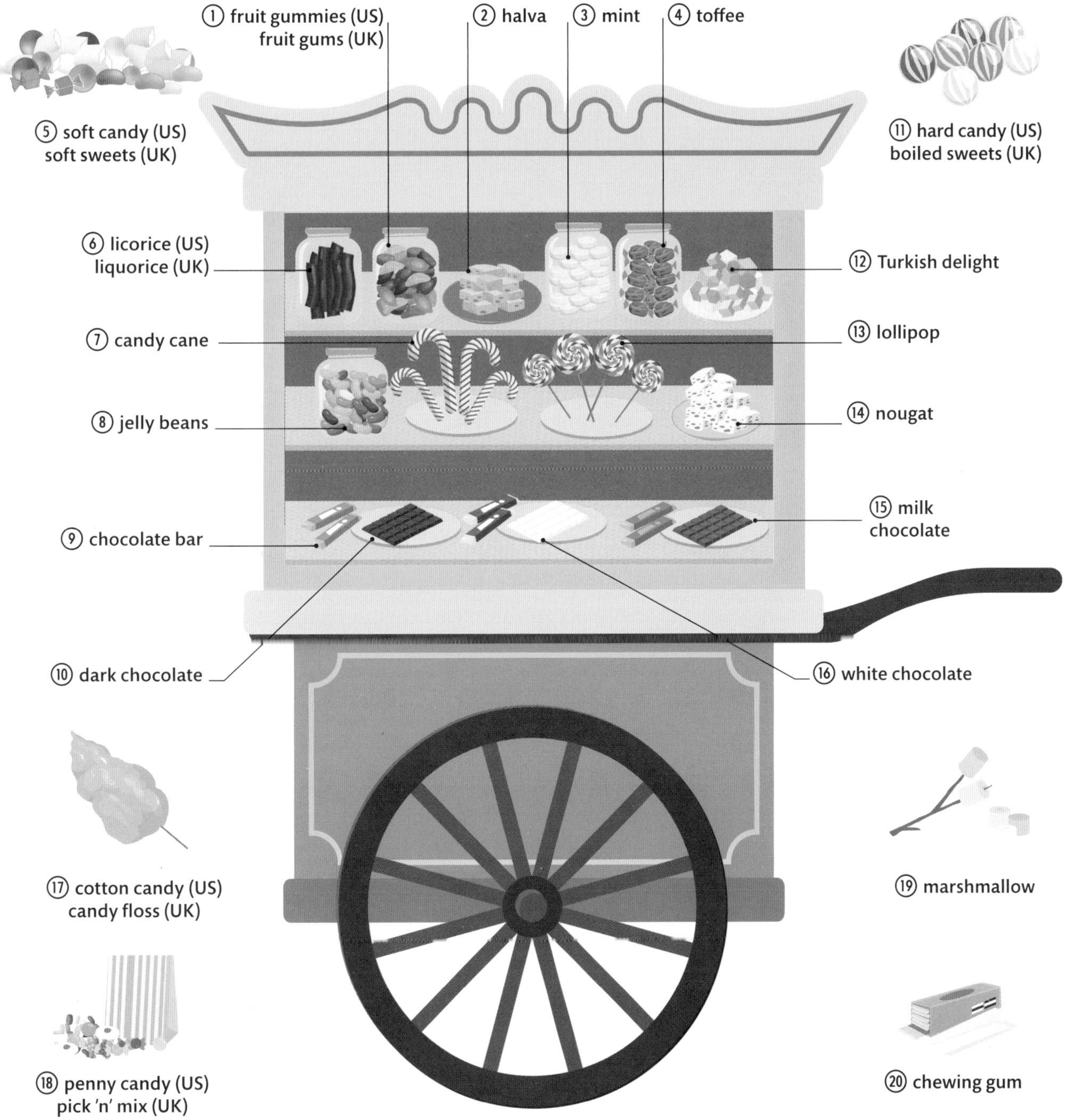

1. fruit gummies (US) / fruit gums (UK)
2. halva
3. mint
4. toffee
5. soft candy (US) / soft sweets (UK)
6. licorice (US) / liquorice (UK)
7. candy cane
8. jelly beans
9. chocolate bar
10. dark chocolate
11. hard candy (US) / boiled sweets (UK)
12. Turkish delight
13. lollipop
14. nougat
15. milk chocolate
16. white chocolate
17. cotton candy (US) / candy floss (UK)
18. penny candy (US) / pick 'n' mix (UK)
19. marshmallow
20. chewing gum

68 At the bar

68.1 BAR

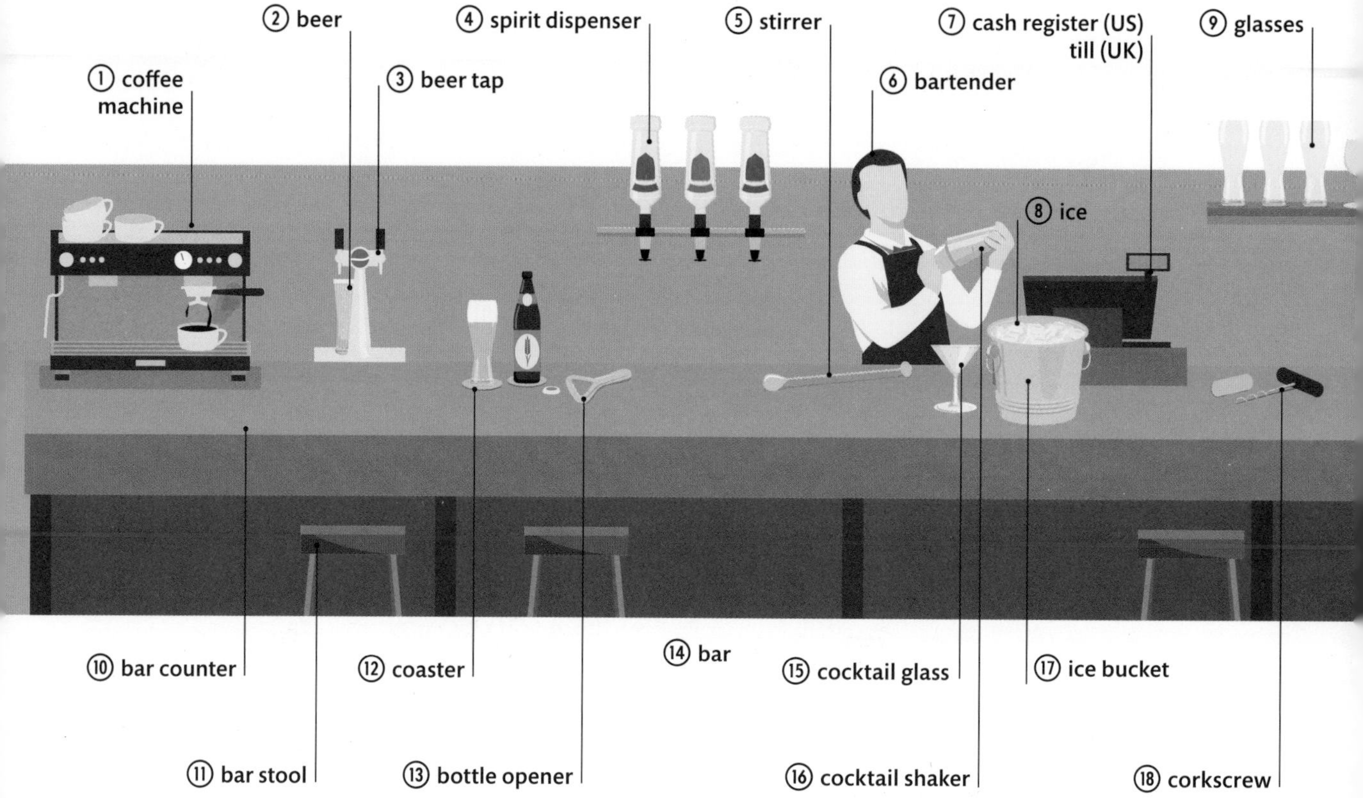

1. coffee machine
2. beer
3. beer tap
4. spirit dispenser
5. stirrer
6. bartender
7. cash register (US) till (UK)
8. ice
9. glasses
10. bar counter
11. bar stool
12. coaster
13. bottle opener
14. bar
15. cocktail glass
16. cocktail shaker
17. ice bucket
18. corkscrew

68.2 BEER AND WINE

1. lager
2. Pilsner
3. wheat beer
4. Indian pale ale (IPA)
5. ale
6. stout

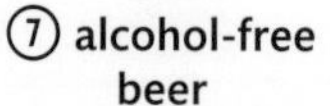

7. alcohol-free beer

8. red wine

9. white wine

10. rosé

11. sparkling wine

12. Champagne

See also:
52 Drinking and eating
69 At the restaurant 72 Lunch and dinner

68.3 DRINKS

① mineral water

② cider

③ rum

④ rum and cola

⑤ vodka

⑥ vodka and orange

⑦ gin and tonic

⑧ Martini

⑨ cocktail

⑩ mocktail

⑪ sherry

⑫ port

⑬ whiskey (US) whisky (UK)

⑭ Scotch and water

⑮ brandy

⑯ liqueur

⑰ with ice

⑱ without ice

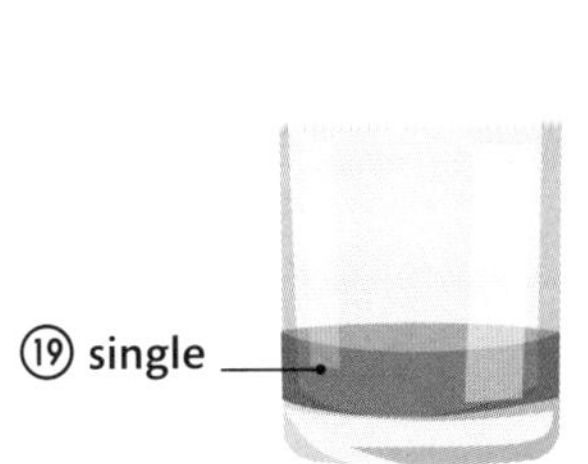
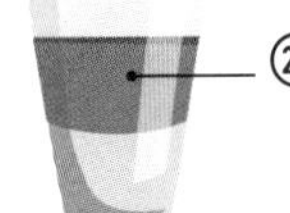
⑳ double
⑲ single
㉑ shot
㉒ measure

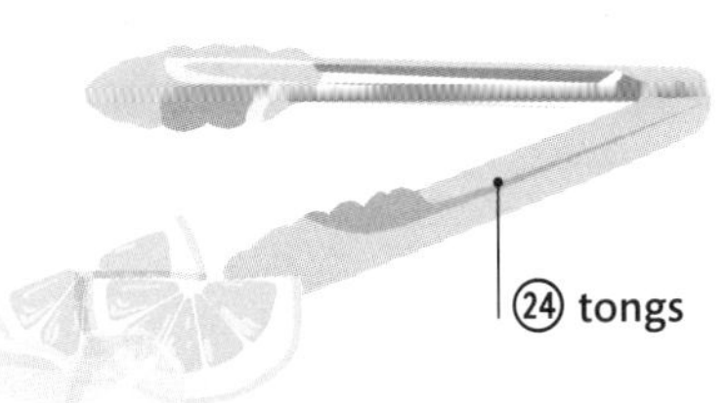
㉔ tongs
㉓ ice and lemon

68.4 BAR SNACKS

① chips (US) crisps (UK)

② nuts

③ almonds

④ cashews (US) cashew nuts (UK)

⑤ peanuts

⑥ olives

69 At the restaurant

69.1 RESTAURANT

① What are today's specials?

② wine list

③ bartender

④ customers

⑪ server (US) / waitress

⑫ restaurant manager

⑬ table setting

⑭ May we have a table for two, please?

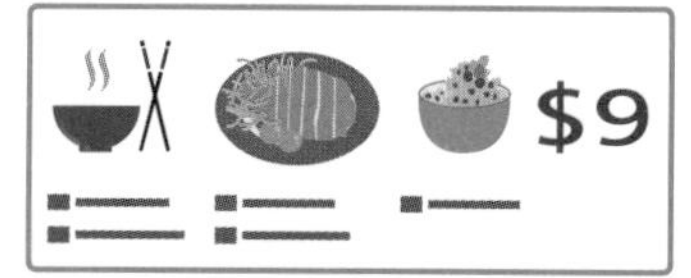
$9
⑱ fixed menu (US) / set menu (UK)

⑲ brunch

⑳ lunch menu

㉑ à la carte menu

㉒ specials

㉓ kids meal (US) child's meal (UK)

㉔ buffet

㉕ three-course meal

㉖ soup

㉗ appetizer (US) starter (UK)

㉘ entrée (US) main course (UK)

㉙ side / side order

㉚ cheese platter

㉛ dessert / pudding (UK)

㉜ beverage

㉝ coffee

㉞ digestif

See also:
27 Kitchen and tableware **52** Drinking and eating **53** Meat
54 Fish and seafood **55-56** Vegetables **72** Lunch and dinner

⑤ price

⑥ tray

⑦ Enjoy your meal!

⑧ kitchen

⑨ chef

⑩ commis chef

⑮ dinner menu (US)
evening menu (UK)

⑯ server (US)
waiter

⑰ dessert cart (US)
sweet trolley (UK)

㉟ sommelier

㊱ to eat out

㊲ to make a reservation

㊳ to cancel

㊴ to order

㊵ check (US)
bill (UK)

㊶ to pay separately

㊷ to split the check (US)
to split the bill (UK)

㊸ service charge

㊹ service included

㊺ service not included

㊻ tip

㊼ receipt

㊽ bistro

70 Fast food

70.1 IN A FAST-FOOD RESTAURANT

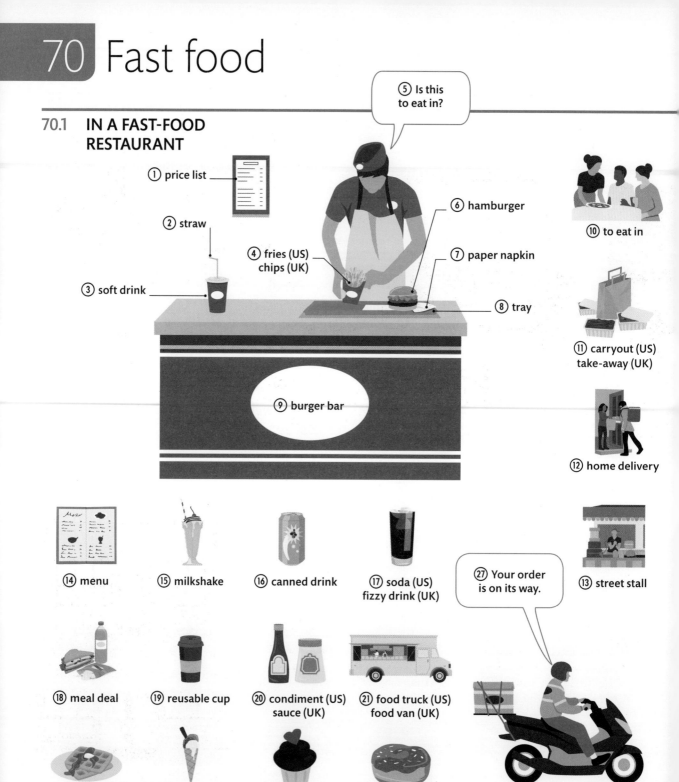

⑤ Is this to eat in?

① price list

② straw

③ soft drink

④ fries (US) chips (UK)

⑥ hamburger

⑦ paper napkin

⑧ tray

⑨ burger bar

⑩ to eat in

⑪ carryout (US) take-away (UK)

⑫ home delivery

⑬ street stall

⑭ menu

⑮ milkshake

⑯ canned drink

⑰ soda (US) fizzy drink (UK)

㉗ Your order is on its way.

⑱ meal deal

⑲ reusable cup

⑳ condiment (US) sauce (UK)

㉑ food truck (US) food van (UK)

㉒ waffle

㉓ ice cream

㉔ muffin

㉕ donut (US) doughnut (UK)

㉖ food delivery driver

See also:
52 Drinking and eating 60 In the pantry
65 At the café 67 Candy / Sweets

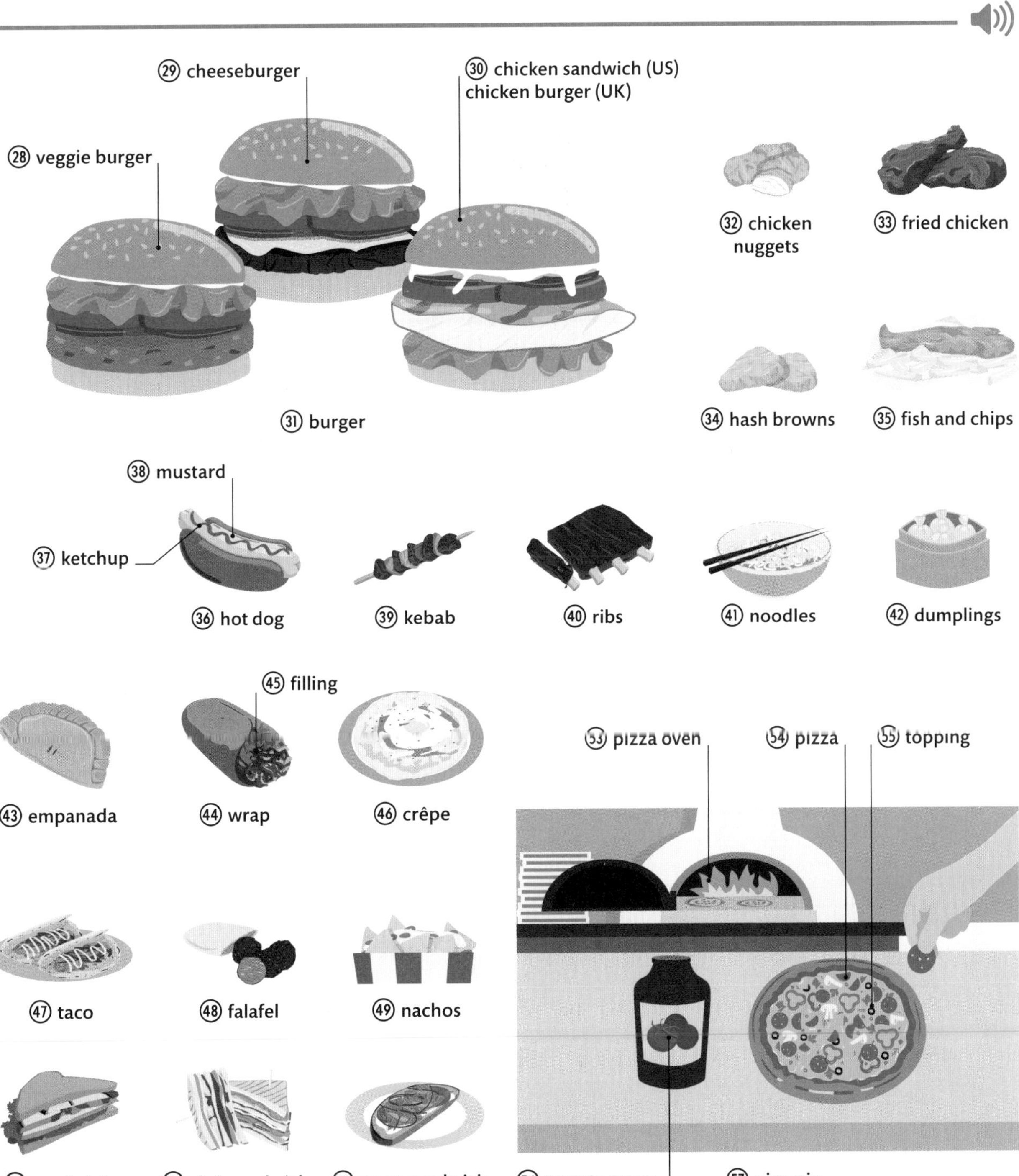
29 cheeseburger
30 chicken sandwich (US)
chicken burger (UK)
28 veggie burger
32 chicken nuggets
33 fried chicken
31 burger
34 hash browns
35 fish and chips
38 mustard
37 ketchup
36 hot dog
39 kebab
40 ribs
41 noodles
42 dumplings
45 filling
43 empanada
44 wrap
46 crêpe
53 pizza oven
54 pizza
55 topping
47 taco
48 falafel
49 nachos
50 sandwich
51 club sandwich
52 open sandwich
56 tomato sauce
57 pizzeria

71 Breakfast

71.1 BREAKFAST BUFFET

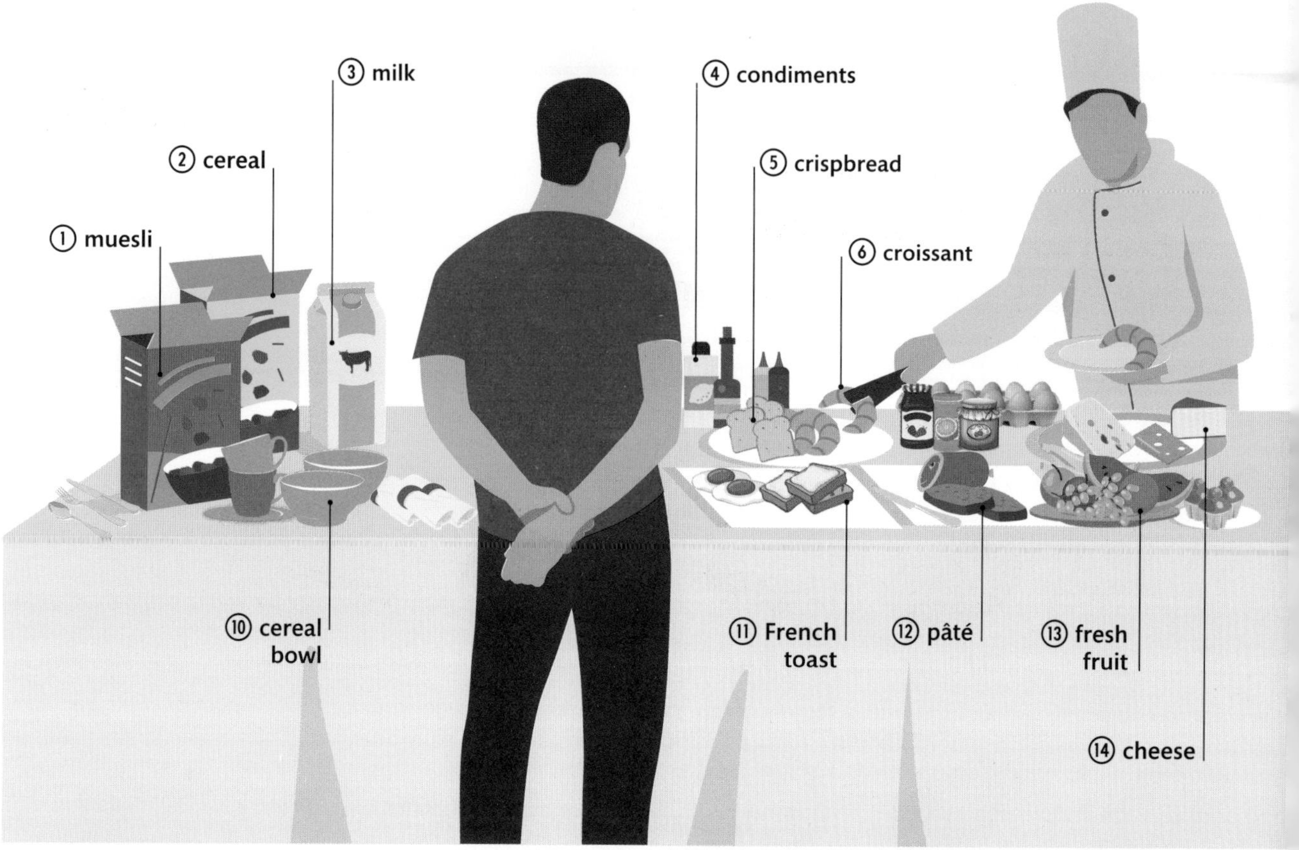

① muesli

② cereal

③ milk

④ condiments

⑤ crispbread

⑥ croissant

⑩ cereal bowl

⑪ French toast

⑫ pâté

⑬ fresh fruit

⑭ cheese

⑰ ham

⑱ toasted sandwich

⑲ omelet (US) omelette (UK)

⑳ avocado toast

㉑ bagel

㉒ cinnamon rolls

㉕ jam

㉖ marmalade

㉗ honey

㉘ tea

㉙ coffee

㉚ fruit juice

See also:
29 Cooking 52 Drinking and eating 53 Meat 57 Fruit
57 Fruit and nuts 61 Dairy produce 64 The delicatessen 65-66 At the café

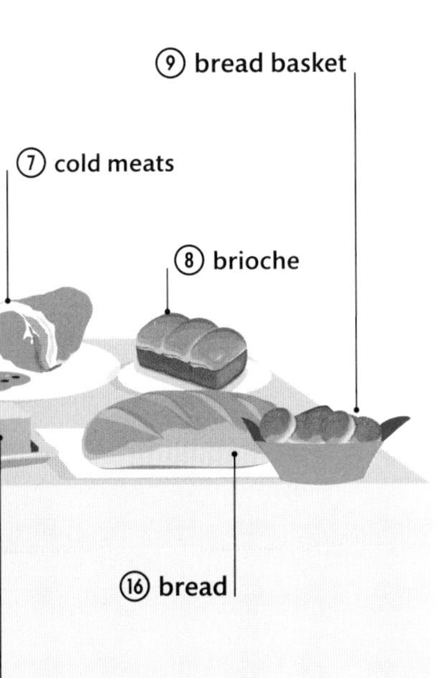
⑨ bread basket
⑦ cold meats
⑧ brioche
⑯ bread
⑮ butter

㉓ waffles

㉔ cream

㉛ dried fruit

㉜ fruit yogurt (US) fruit yoghurt (UK)

71.2 COOKED BREAKFAST

① sausage

② sausage patties

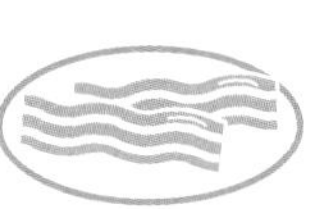
③ bacon

④ kippers

⑤ smoked salmon

⑥ smoked mackerel

⑦ black pudding / blood sausage (UK)

⑧ kidneys

⑨ scrambled eggs

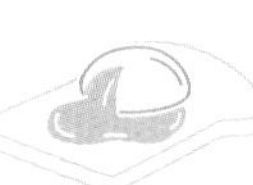
⑩ poached egg

⑪ boiled egg

⑫ egg white

⑬ yolk

⑭ fried egg

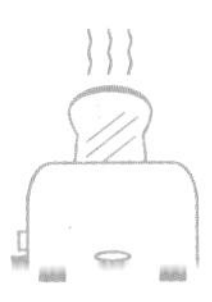
⑮ toast

⑯ fried mushrooms

⑰ hash browns

⑱ grilled tomato

⑲ canned tomato (US) tinned tomato (UK)

⑳ baked beans

㉑ breakfast roll

㉒ breakfast burrito

㉓ potato cakes

㉔ pancakes

㉕ oatmeal (US) porridge (UK)

72 Lunch and dinner

72.1 MEALS AND DISHES

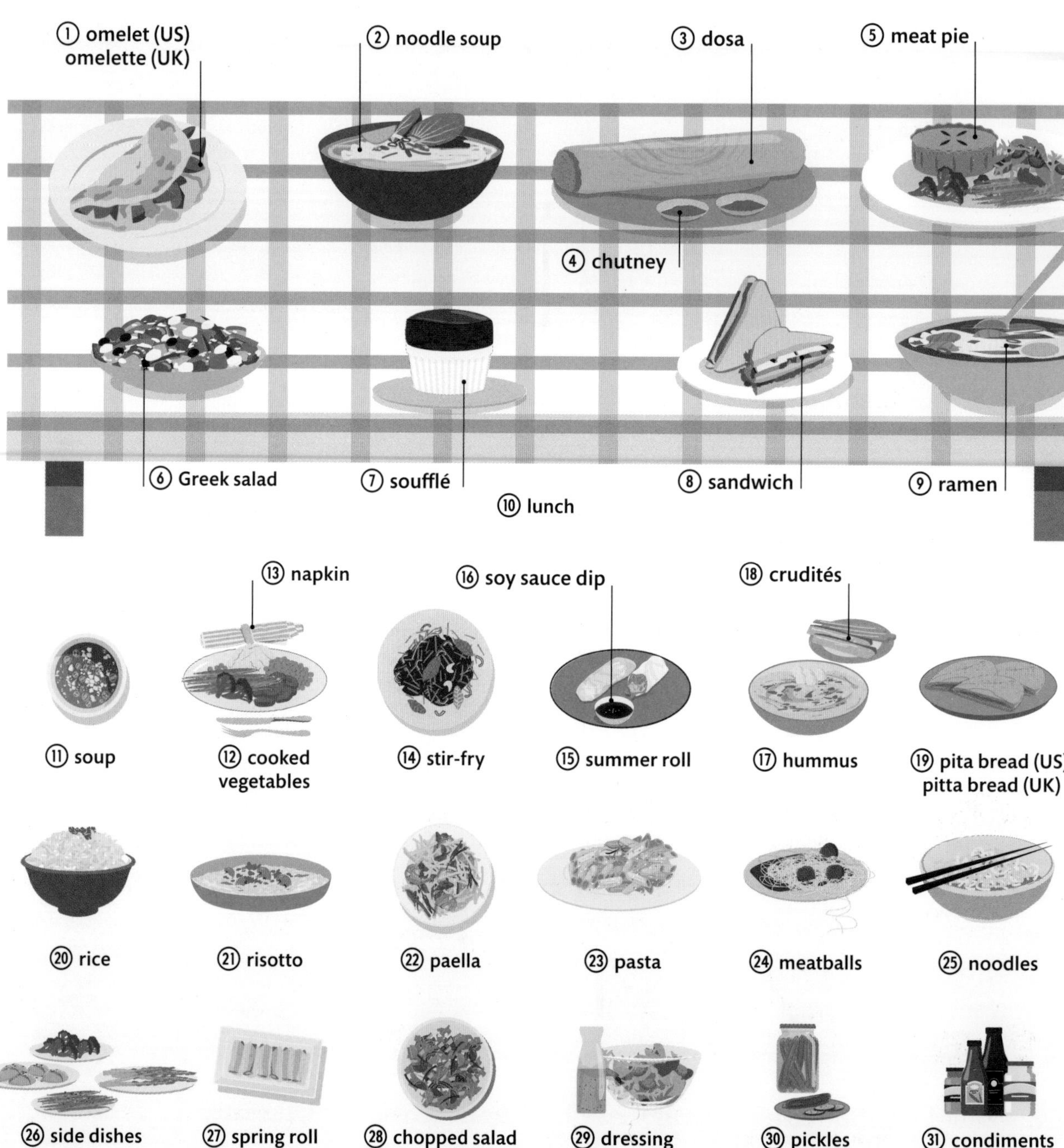

① omelet (US)
omelette (UK)
② noodle soup
③ dosa
④ chutney
⑤ meat pie
⑥ Greek salad
⑦ soufflé
⑧ sandwich
⑨ ramen
⑩ lunch
⑪ soup
⑫ cooked vegetables
⑬ napkin
⑭ stir-fry
⑮ summer roll
⑯ soy sauce dip
⑰ hummus
⑱ crudités
⑲ pita bread (US)
pitta bread (UK)
⑳ rice
㉑ risotto
㉒ paella
㉓ pasta
㉔ meatballs
㉕ noodles
㉖ side dishes
㉗ spring roll
㉘ chopped salad
㉙ dressing
㉚ pickles
㉛ condiments

See also:
27 Kitchen and tableware **29** Cooking **52** Drinking and eating **53** Meat
55-56 Vegetables **65-66** At the café **69** At the restaurant

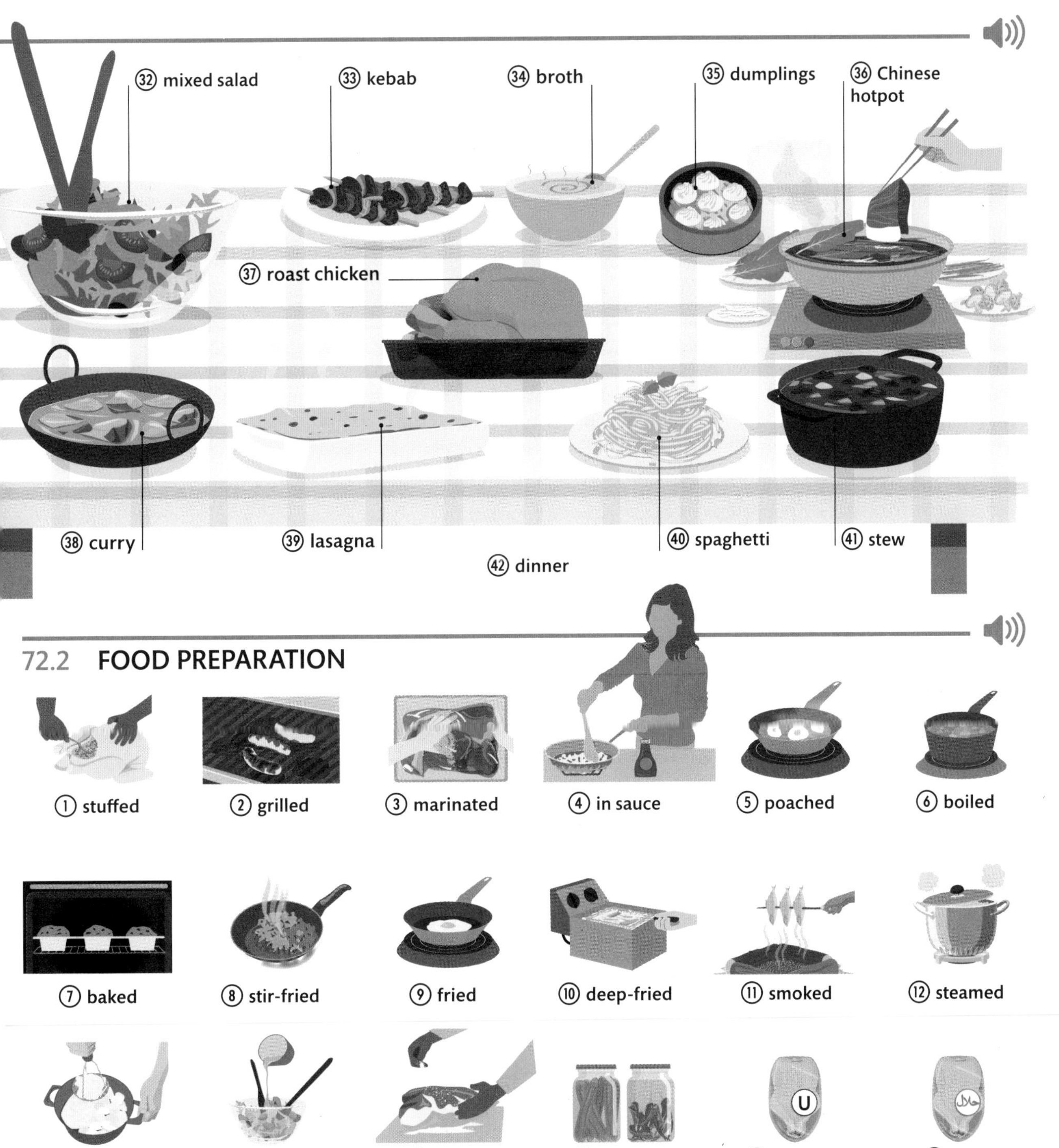
32 mixed salad
33 kebab
34 broth
35 dumplings
36 Chinese hotpot
37 roast chicken
38 curry
39 lasagna
40 spaghetti
41 stew
42 dinner
72.2 FOOD PREPARATION
1 stuffed
2 grilled
3 marinated
4 in sauce
5 poached
6 boiled
7 baked
8 stir-fried
9 fried
10 deep-fried
11 smoked
12 steamed
13 mashed
14 dressed
15 cured
16 pickled
17 kosher
18 halal

73 At school

73.1 SCHOOL AND STUDY

① school

② classroom

③ class

④ teacher
⑤ whiteboard
⑥ pupil

⑦ desk

⑧ school students

⑨ school bag

⑩ literature

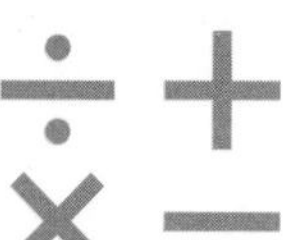
⑪ math (US)
maths (UK)

⑫ geography

⑬ history

⑭ science

⑮ chemistry

⑯ physics

⑰ biology

HELLO
⑱ English

Bonjour!
Hallo!
¡Hola!
⑲ languages

⑳ design and technology

@
㉑ information technology

㉒ art

㉓ music

㉔ drama

㉕ physical education

㉖ principal / head teacher (UK)

㉗ homework

㉘ lesson

㉙ exam

㉚ essay

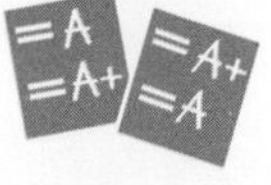
=A
=A+
=A+
=A
㉛ grade

㉜ encyclopedia

A
Z
㉝ dictionary

㉞ atlas

㉟ test

See also:
74 Mathematics 75 Physics 76 Chemistry 77 Biology
79 History 80 At college 83 Computers and technology

73.2 SCHOOL VERBS

① to read

② to write

③ to question

④ to take a test (US)
to take an exam (UK)

⑤ to learn

⑥ to draw

⑦ to answer

CAT

⑧ to spell

⑨ to review (US)
to revise (UK)

⑩ to retake (US)
to resit (UK)

⑪ to take notes

⑫ to discuss

⑬ to fail

⑭ to pass

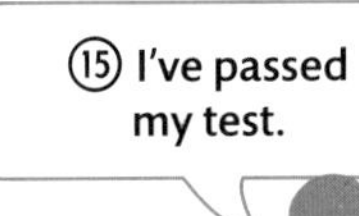

⑮ I've passed my test.

10
10

73.3 EQUIPMENT

① pencil

② pencil sharpener

③ pen

④ nib

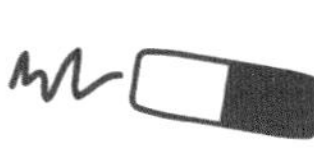

⑤ eraser (US)
rubber (UK)

⑥ colored pencils (US)
coloured pencils (UK)

⑦ pencil case

⑧ ruler

⑨ triangle (US)
set square (UK)

⑩ protractor

⑪ calculator

⑫ compass

⑬ textbook

⑭ notebook / exercise book

⑮ digital projector

⑯ highlighter

⑰ paper clip

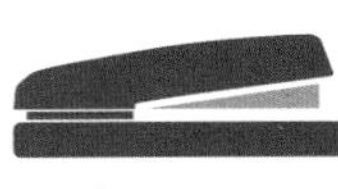

⑱ stapler

74 Mathematics

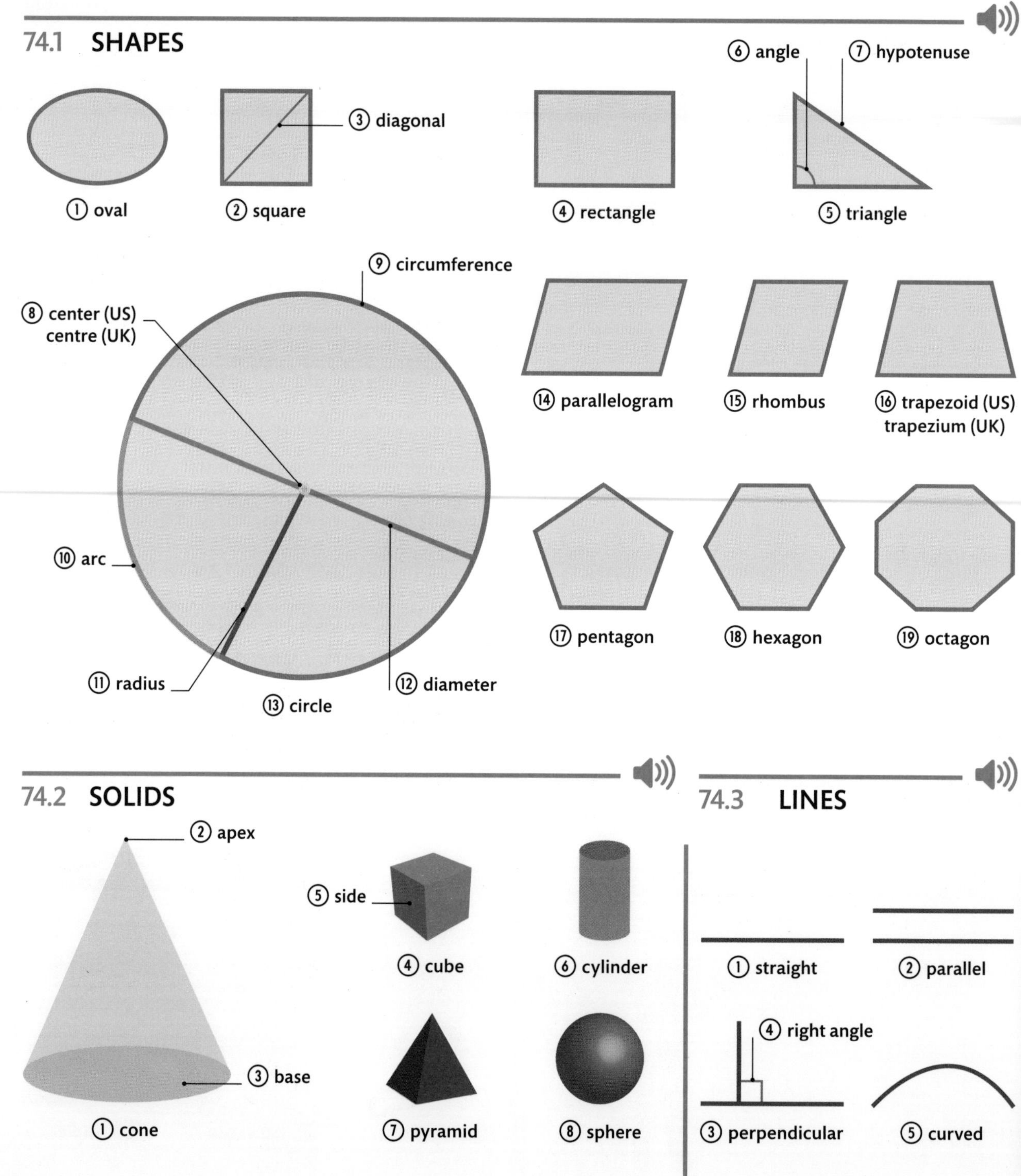

74.1 SHAPES
① oval
② square
③ diagonal
④ rectangle
⑤ triangle
⑥ angle
⑦ hypotenuse
⑧ center (US)
centre (UK)
⑨ circumference
⑩ arc
⑪ radius
⑫ diameter
⑬ circle
⑭ parallelogram
⑮ rhombus
⑯ trapezoid (US)
trapezium (UK)
⑰ pentagon
⑱ hexagon
⑲ octagon
74.2 SOLIDS
① cone
② apex
③ base
④ cube
⑤ side
⑥ cylinder
⑦ pyramid
⑧ sphere
74.3 LINES
① straight
② parallel
③ perpendicular
④ right angle
⑤ curved

See also:
73 At school 94 Money and finance
173 Numbers 174 Weights and measures

74.4 MEASUREMENTS

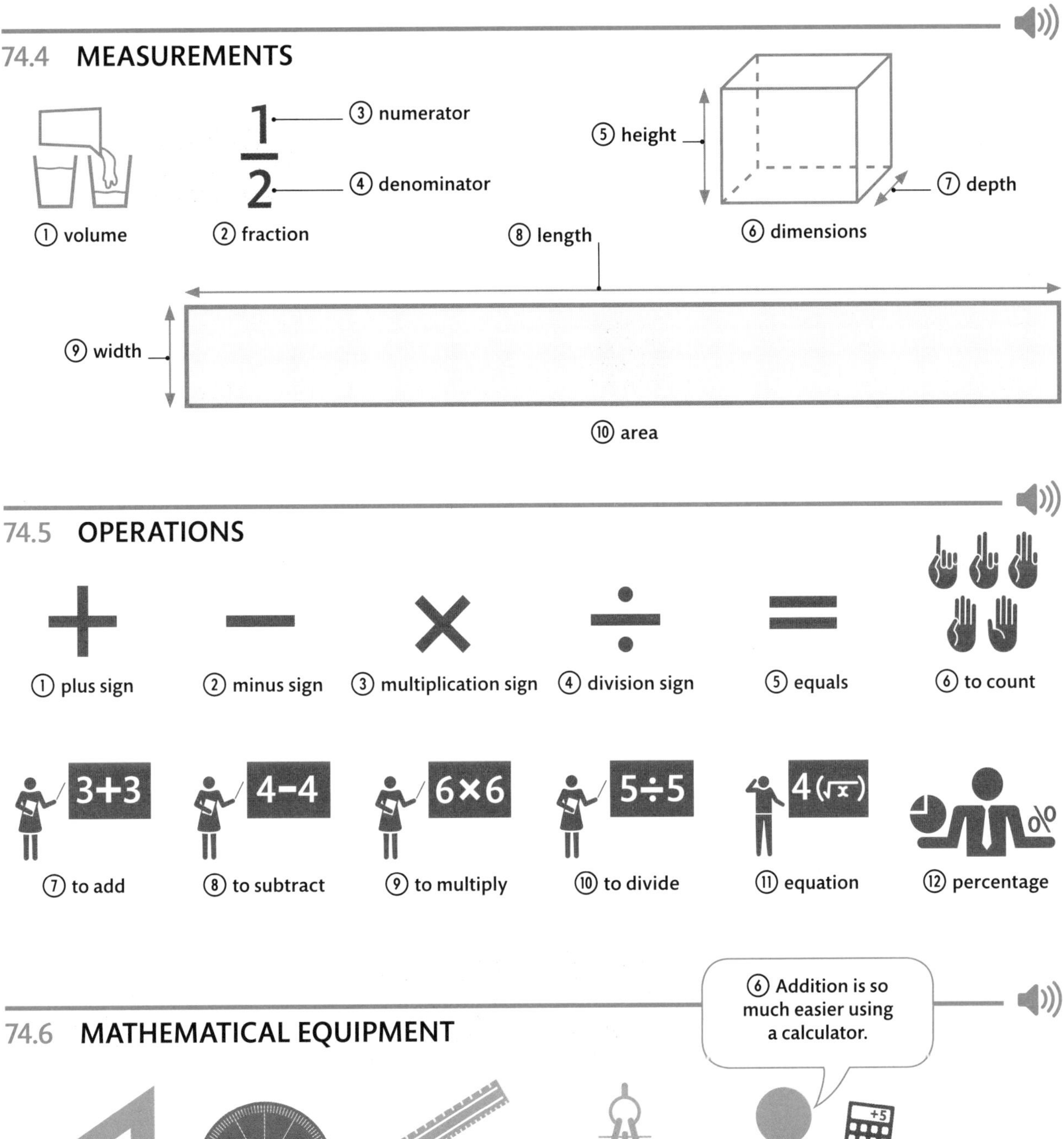
1
2
③ numerator
④ denominator
⑤ height
⑦ depth
⑧ length
⑨ width
3+3
4−4
6×6
5÷5
4(√x)
+5

① volume
② fraction
③ numerator
④ denominator
⑤ height
⑥ dimensions
⑦ depth
⑧ length
⑨ width
⑩ area

74.5 OPERATIONS

① plus sign
② minus sign
③ multiplication sign
④ division sign
⑤ equals
⑥ to count
⑦ to add
⑧ to subtract
⑨ to multiply
⑩ to divide
⑪ equation
⑫ percentage

74.6 MATHEMATICAL EQUIPMENT

⑥ Addition is so much easier using a calculator.

① triangle (US) set square (UK)
② protractor
③ ruler
④ compass
⑤ calculator

75 Physics

75.1 PHYSICS

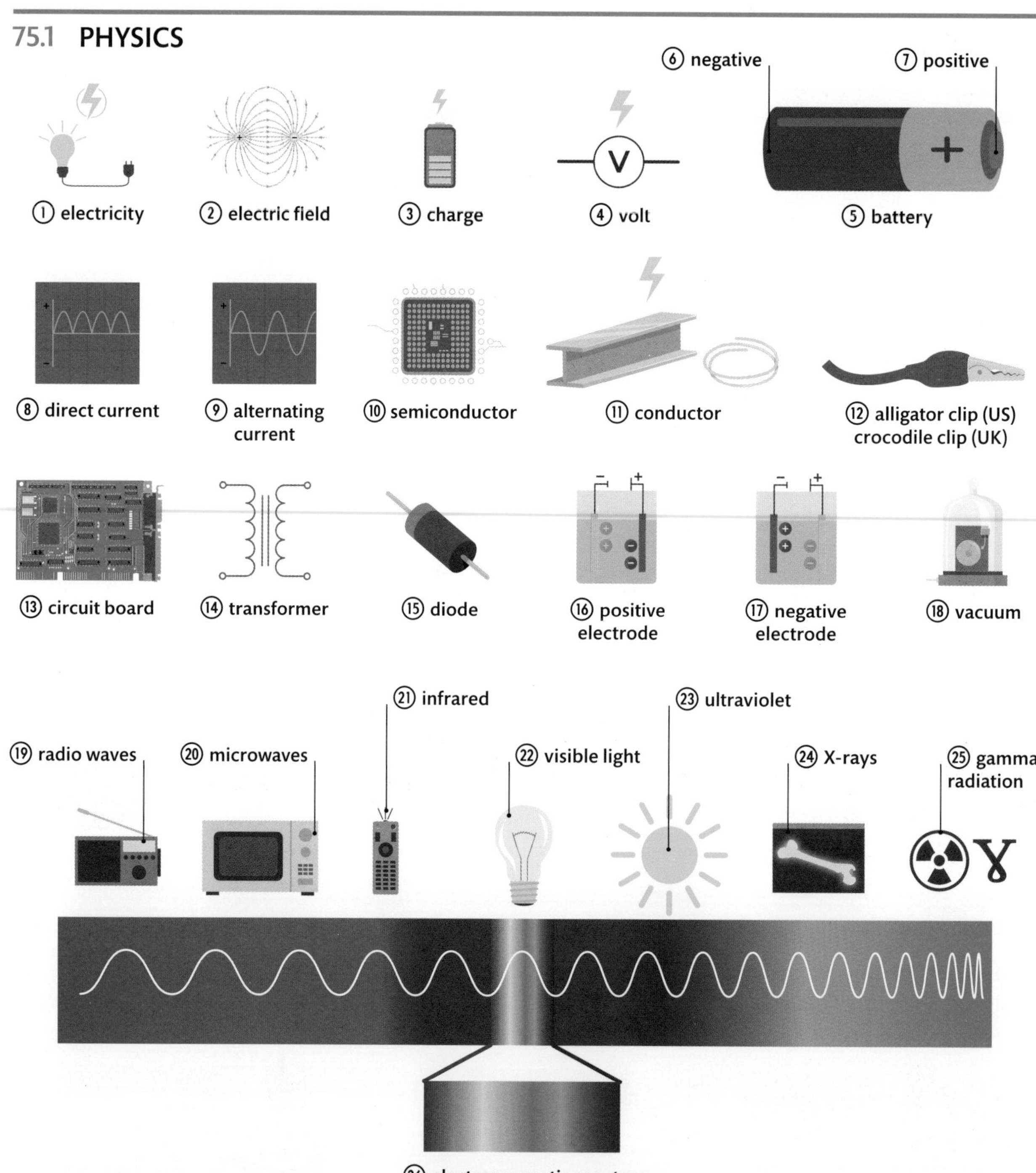

⑥ negative
⑦ positive
① electricity
② electric field
③ charge
V
④ volt
+
⑤ battery
⑧ direct current
⑨ alternating current
⑩ semiconductor
⑪ conductor
⑫ alligator clip (US) crocodile clip (UK)
⑬ circuit board
⑭ transformer
⑮ diode
⑯ positive electrode
⑰ negative electrode
⑱ vacuum
㉑ infrared
㉓ ultraviolet
⑲ radio waves
⑳ microwaves
㉒ visible light
㉔ X-rays
㉕ gamma radiation
γ
㉖ electromagnetic spectrum

See also:
73 At school **74** Mathematics **76** Chemistry
77 Biology **78** The periodic table

(27) north pole

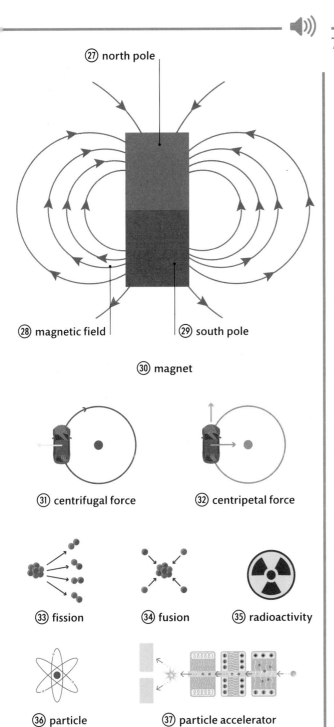

(28) magnetic field

(29) south pole

(30) magnet

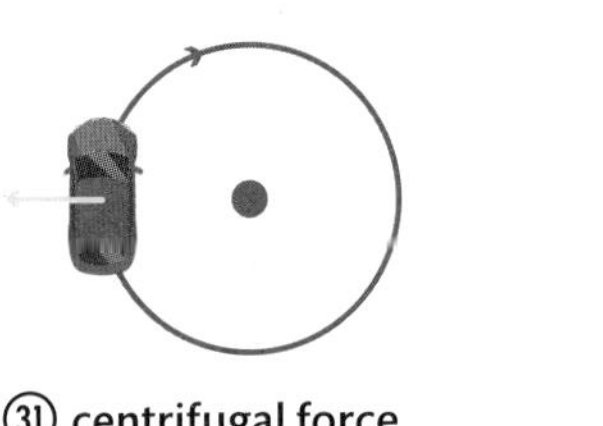

(31) centrifugal force

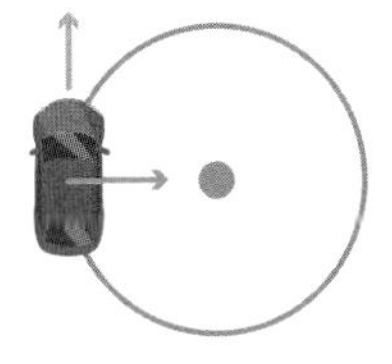

(32) centripetal force

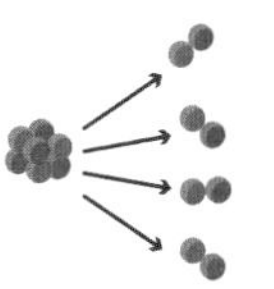

(33) fission

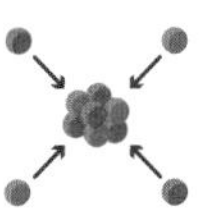

(34) fusion

(35) radioactivity

(36) particle

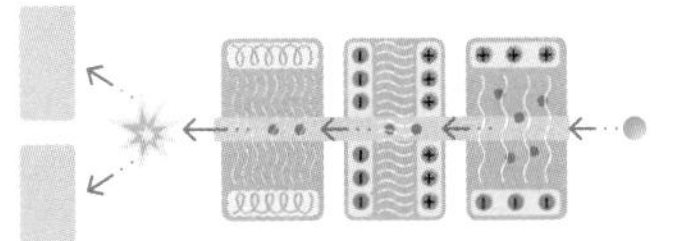

(37) particle accelerator

75.2 OPTICS

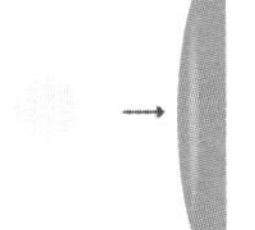

(1) lens

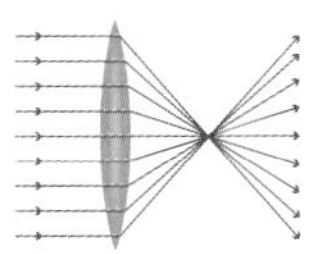

(2) convex lens

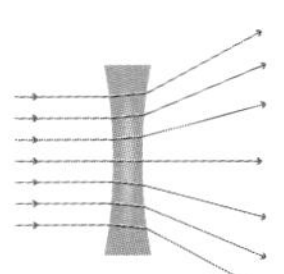

(3) concave lens

(4) laser

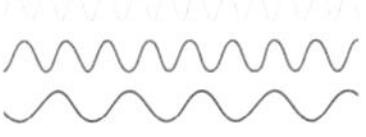

(5) wave

(6) wavelength

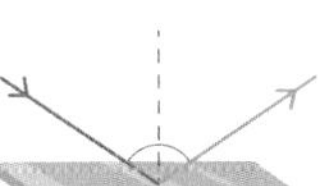

(7) reflection

(8) refraction

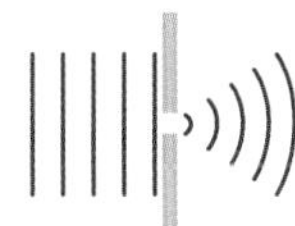

(9) diffraction

(10) prism
(12) I'm studying the dispersion of light.

(11) dispersion

76 Chemistry

76.1 IN THE LABORATORY

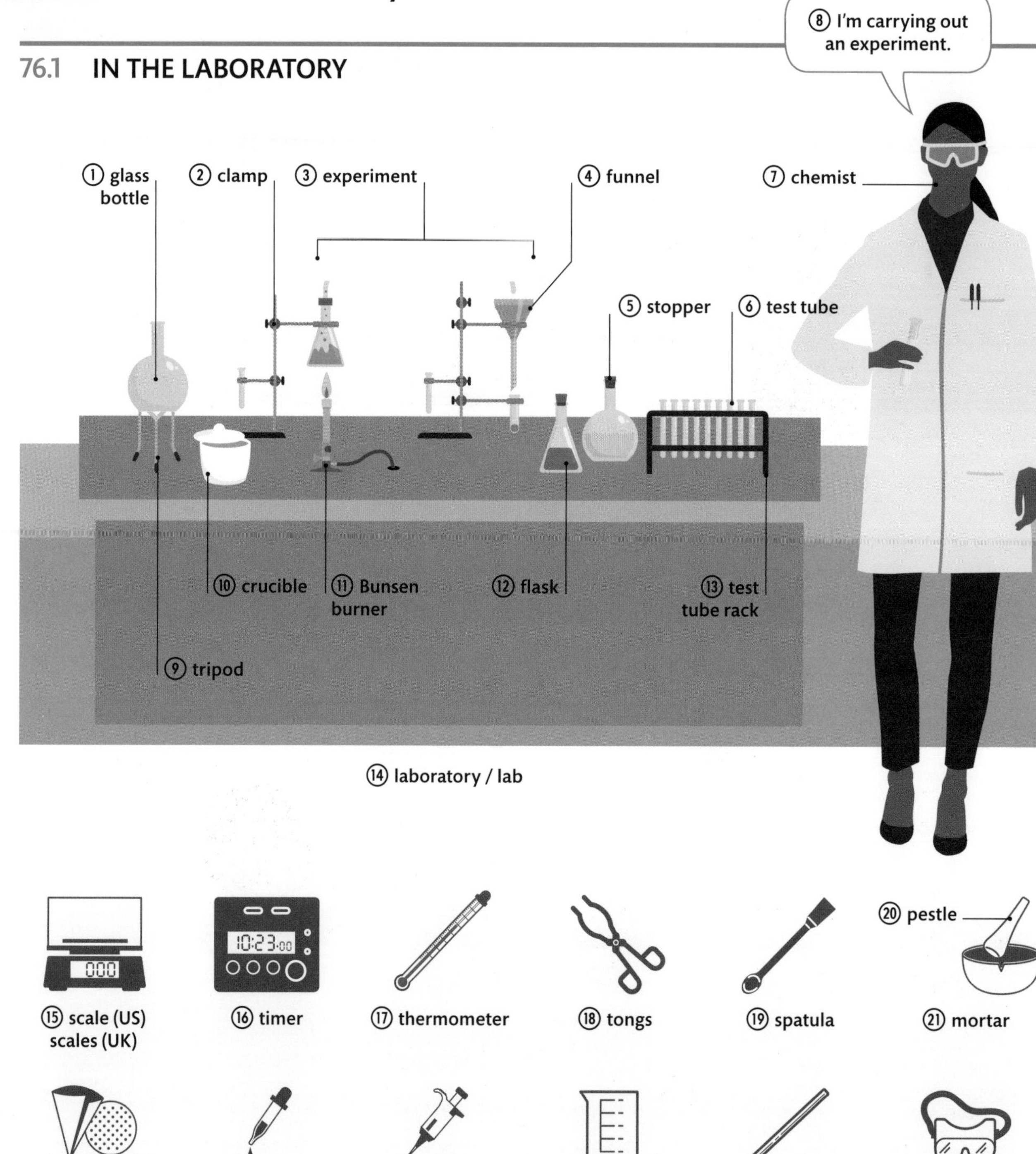

① glass bottle
② clamp
③ experiment
④ funnel
⑤ stopper
⑥ test tube
⑦ chemist
⑧ I'm carrying out an experiment.
⑨ tripod
⑩ crucible
⑪ Bunsen burner
⑫ flask
⑬ test tube rack
⑭ laboratory / lab
10:23·00
000
⑮ scale (US) scales (UK)
⑯ timer
⑰ thermometer
⑱ tongs
⑲ spatula
⑳ pestle
㉑ mortar
㉒ filter paper
㉓ dropper
㉔ pipette
㉕ beaker
㉖ glass rod
㉗ safety goggles

See also:
73 At school 74 Mathematics 75 Physics
77 Biology 78 The periodic table

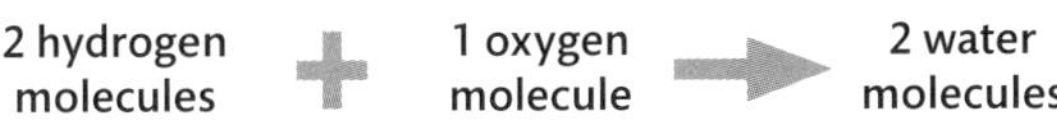
2 hydrogen molecules
1 oxygen molecule
2 water molecules

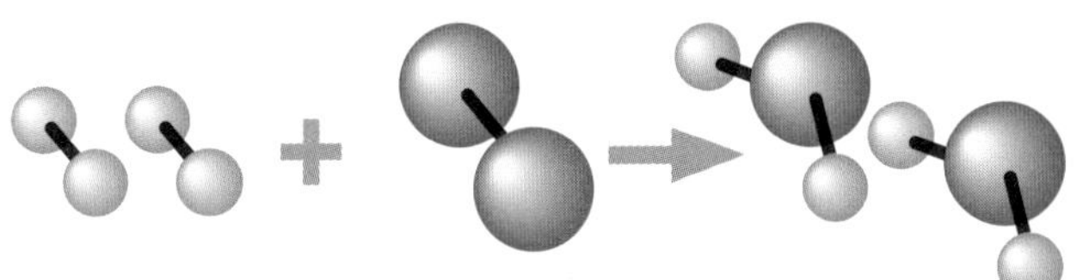

$$2H_2 + O_2 \rightarrow 2H_2O$$

㉙ chemical symbol

㉚ subscript

㉘ chemical equation

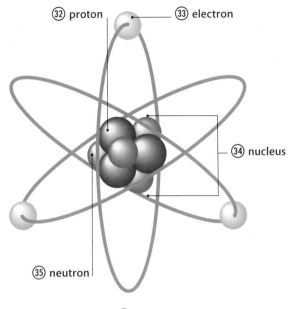

㉜ proton

㉝ electron

㉞ nucleus

㉟ neutron

㉛ atom

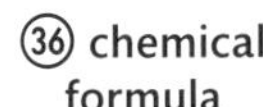

㊱ chemical formula

Na
Li
C

㊲ elements

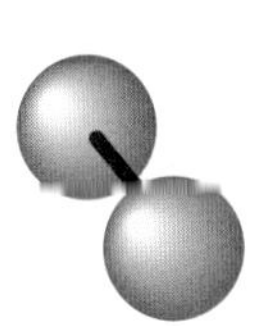

㊳ molecule

㊵ acid

1 2 3 5 6 7 8 9 10 11 13 14

㊶ alkali

㊴ pH level

㊷ reaction

Q<K

㊸ reaction direction

Q⇌K

㊹ reversible direction

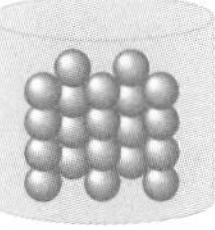
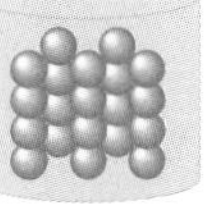

㊺ solid

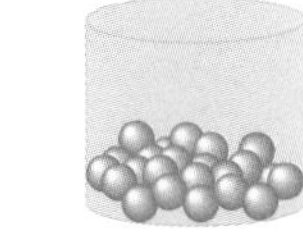

㊻ liquid

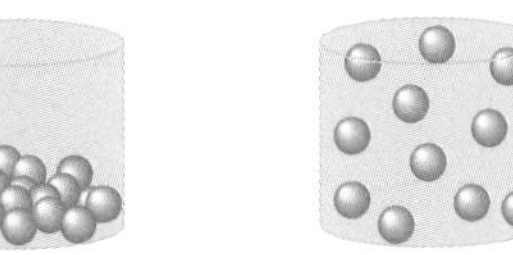

㊼ gas

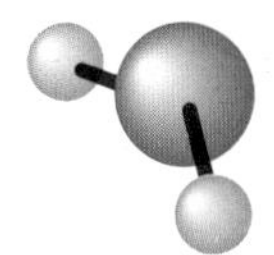

㊽ compound

㊾ base

㊿ diffusion

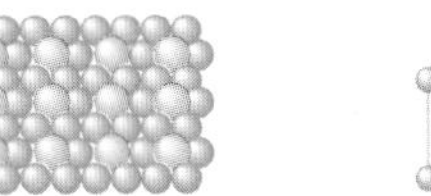

51 alloy

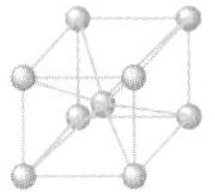

52 crystal

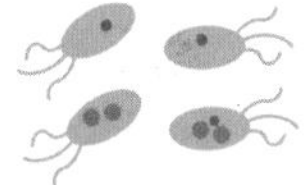

53 biochemistry

77 Biology

77.1 BIOLOGY

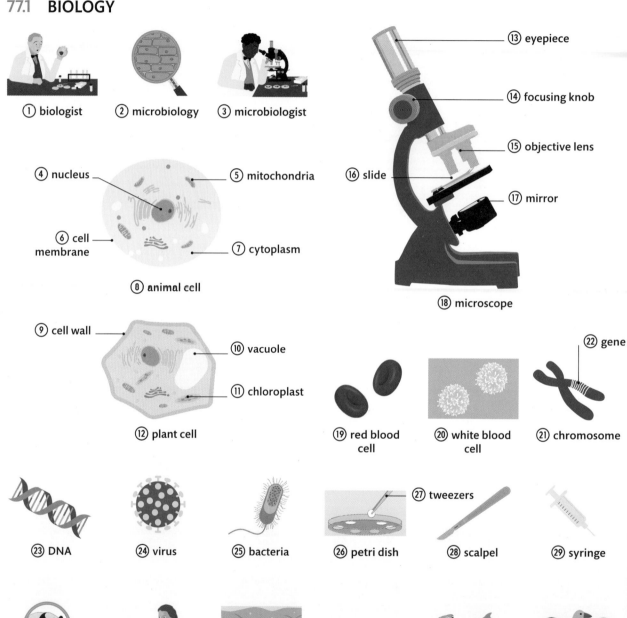

① biologist
② microbiology
③ microbiologist

④ nucleus
⑤ mitochondria
⑥ cell membrane
⑦ cytoplasm
⑧ animal cell

⑨ cell wall
⑩ vacuole
⑪ chloroplast
⑫ plant cell

⑬ eyepiece
⑭ focusing knob
⑮ objective lens
⑯ slide
⑰ mirror
⑱ microscope

⑲ red blood cell
⑳ white blood cell
㉑ chromosome
㉒ gene

㉓ DNA
㉔ virus
㉕ bacteria
㉖ petri dish
㉗ tweezers
㉘ scalpel
㉙ syringe

㉚ zoology

㉛ zoologist

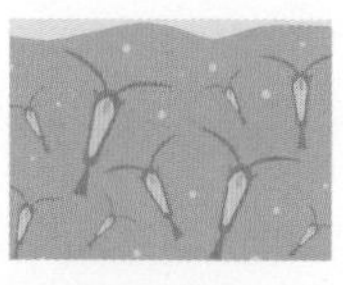
㉜ plankton

㉝ invertebrate

㉞ vertebrate

㉟ species

See also:
157 Natural history 158-159 Mammals 160-161 Birds 162 Insects and bugs
163 Reptiles and amphibians 166 Ocean life 167-169 Plants and trees 170 Fungi

㊱ ecosystem

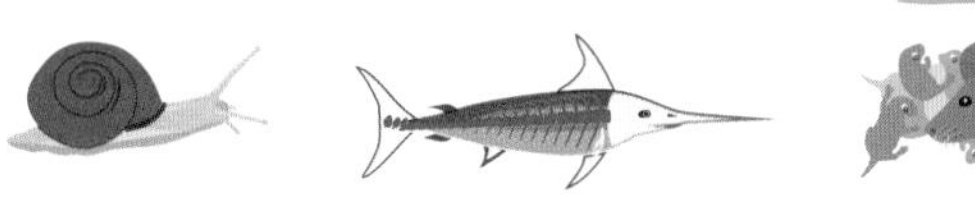

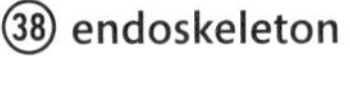

㊲ exoskeleton ㊳ endoskeleton ㊴ reproduction

㊵ hibernation ㊶ botany ㊷ botanist

㊸ plant ㊹ fungi ㊺ photosynthesis

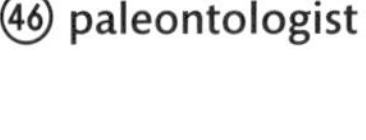

㊻ paleontologist ㊼ fossil

㊽ evolution

77.2 METAMORPHOSIS

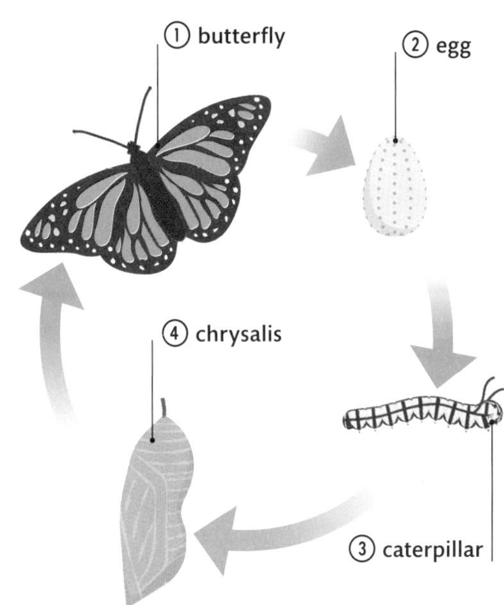
① butterfly
② egg
③ caterpillar
④ chrysalis

⑤ life cycle of a butterfly

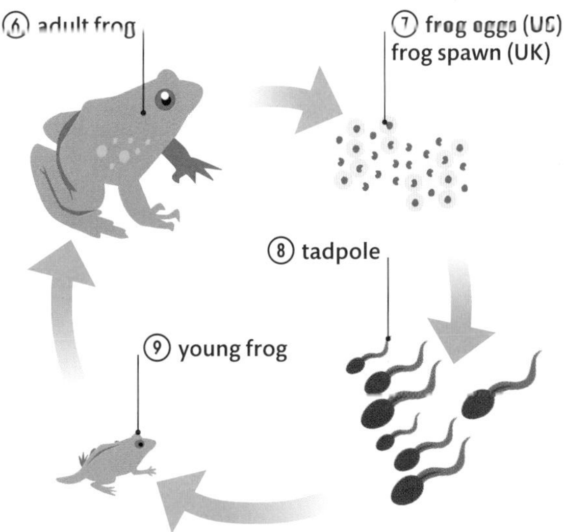
⑥ adult frog
⑦ frog eggs (US)
frog spawn (UK)
⑧ tadpole
⑨ young frog

⑩ life cycle of a frog

78 The periodic table

78.1 THE PERIODIC TABLE

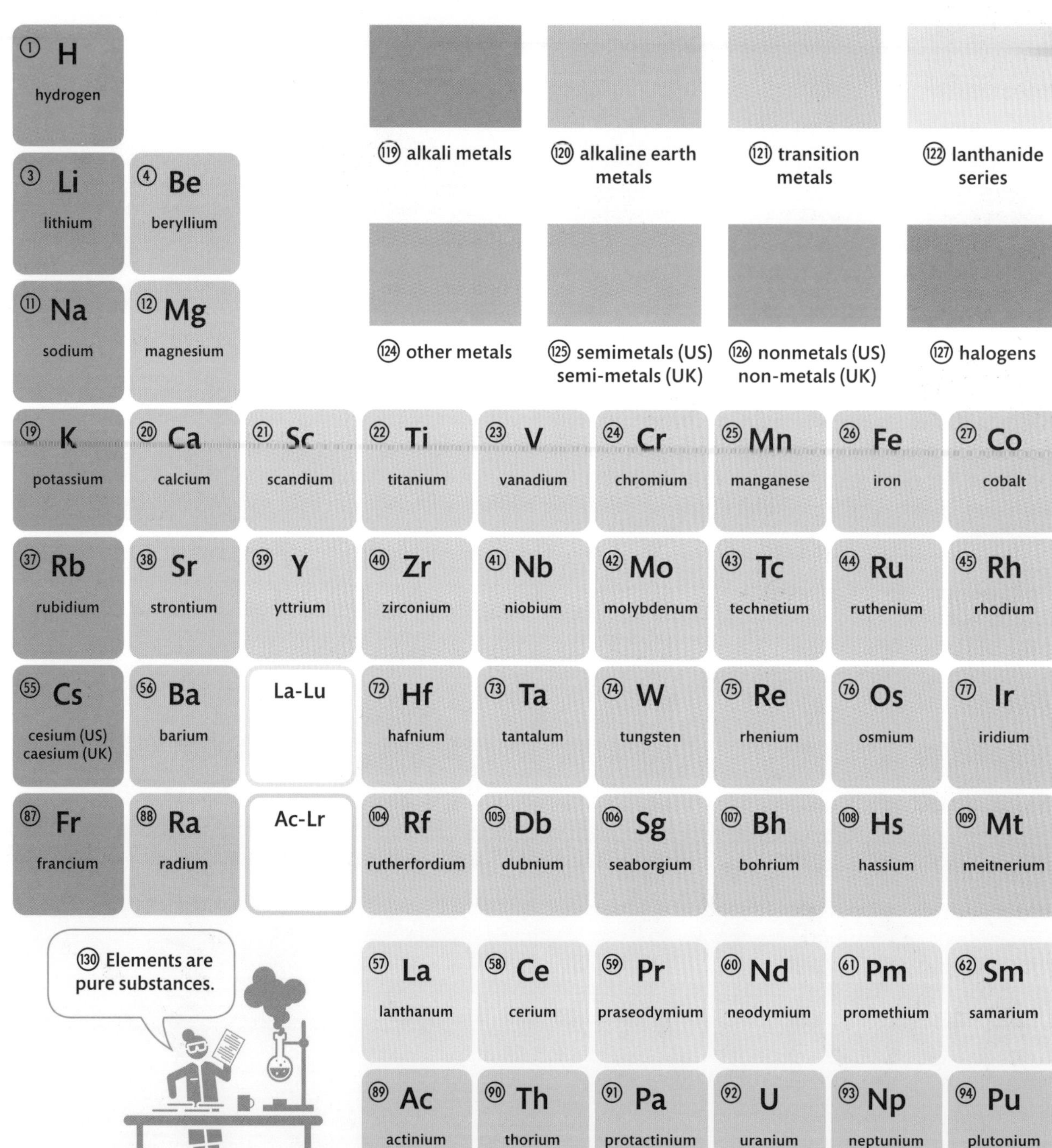

① H hydrogen
③ Li lithium
④ Be beryllium
⑪ Na sodium
⑫ Mg magnesium
⑲ K potassium
⑳ Ca calcium
㉑ Sc scandium
㉒ Ti titanium
㉓ V vanadium
㉔ Cr chromium
㉕ Mn manganese
㉖ Fe iron
㉗ Co cobalt
㊲ Rb rubidium
㊳ Sr strontium
㊴ Y yttrium
㊵ Zr zirconium
㊶ Nb niobium
㊷ Mo molybdenum
㊸ Tc technetium
㊹ Ru ruthenium
㊺ Rh rhodium
55 Cs cesium (US) caesium (UK)
56 Ba barium
La-Lu
72 Hf hafnium
73 Ta tantalum
74 W tungsten
75 Re rhenium
76 Os osmium
77 Ir iridium
87 Fr francium
88 Ra radium
Ac-Lr
104 Rf rutherfordium
105 Db dubnium
106 Sg seaborgium
107 Bh bohrium
108 Hs hassium
109 Mt meitnerium
57 La lanthanum
58 Ce cerium
59 Pr praseodymium
60 Nd neodymium
61 Pm promethium
62 Sm samarium
89 Ac actinium
90 Th thorium
91 Pa protactinium
92 U uranium
93 Np neptunium
94 Pu plutonium
119 alkali metals
120 alkaline earth metals
121 transition metals
122 lanthanide series
124 other metals
125 semimetals (US) semi-metals (UK)
126 nonmetals (US) non-metals (UK)
127 halogens
130 Elements are pure substances.

See also:
73 At school 75 Physics
76 Chemistry 156 Rocks and minerals

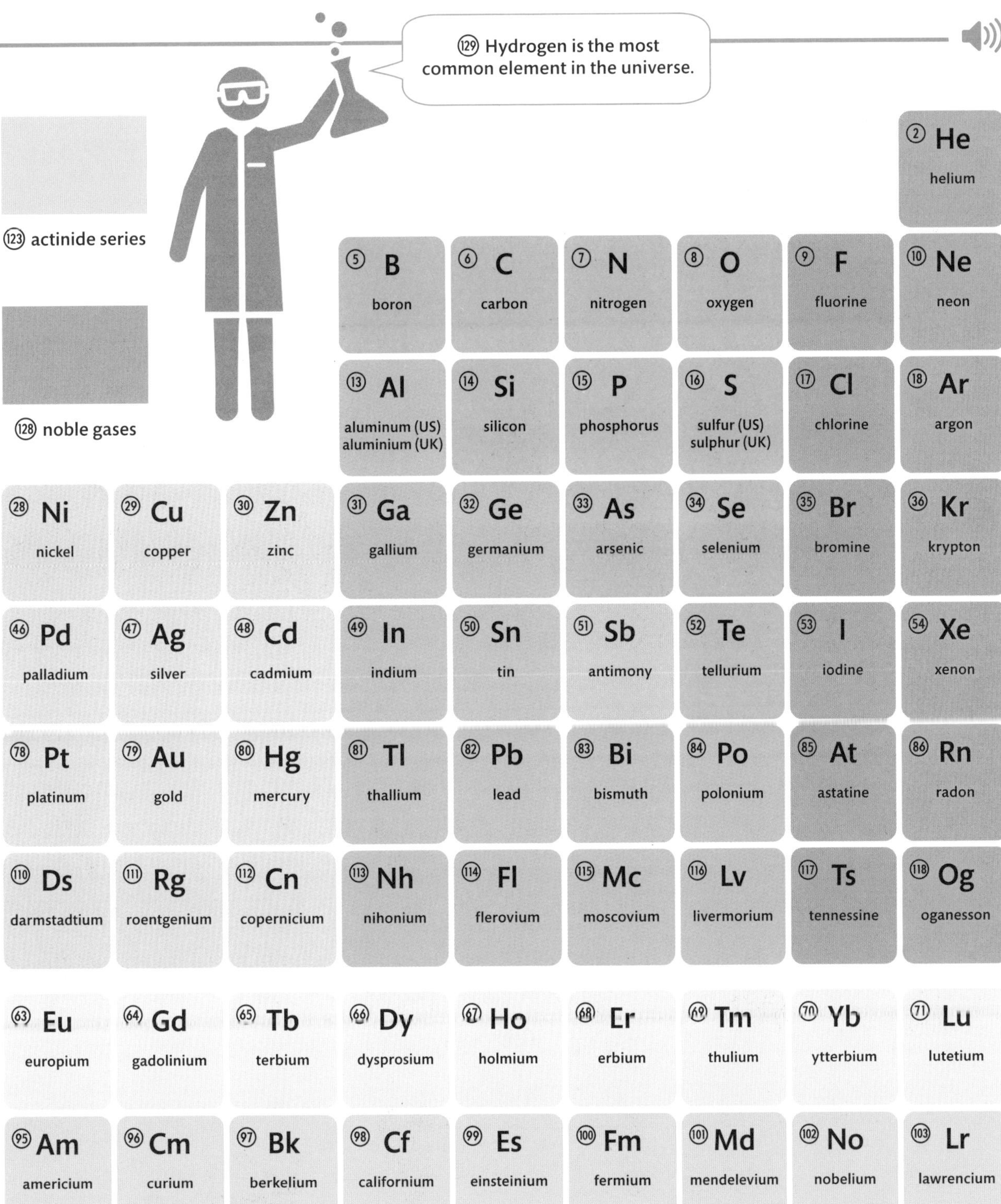
129 Hydrogen is the most common element in the universe.
123 actinide series
128 noble gases
2 He helium
5 B boron
6 C carbon
7 N nitrogen
8 O oxygen
9 F fluorine
10 Ne neon
13 Al aluminum (US) aluminium (UK)
14 Si silicon
15 P phosphorus
16 S sulfur (US) sulphur (UK)
17 Cl chlorine
18 Ar argon
28 Ni nickel
29 Cu copper
30 Zn zinc
31 Ga gallium
32 Ge germanium
33 As arsenic
34 Se selenium
35 Br bromine
36 Kr krypton
46 Pd palladium
47 Ag silver
48 Cd cadmium
49 In indium
50 Sn tin
51 Sb antimony
52 Te tellurium
53 I iodine
54 Xe xenon
78 Pt platinum
79 Au gold
80 Hg mercury
81 Tl thallium
82 Pb lead
83 Bi bismuth
84 Po polonium
85 At astatine
86 Rn radon
110 Ds darmstadtium
111 Rg roentgenium
112 Cn copernicium
113 Nh nihonium
114 Fl flerovium
115 Mc moscovium
116 Lv livermorium
117 Ts tennessine
118 Og oganesson
63 Eu europium
64 Gd gadolinium
65 Tb terbium
66 Dy dysprosium
67 Ho holmium
68 Er erbium
69 Tm thulium
70 Yb ytterbium
71 Lu lutetium
95 Am americium
96 Cm curium
97 Bk berkelium
98 Cf californium
99 Es einsteinium
100 Fm fermium
101 Md mendelevium
102 No nobelium
103 Lr lawrencium

79 History

79.1 WAR AND WEAPONS

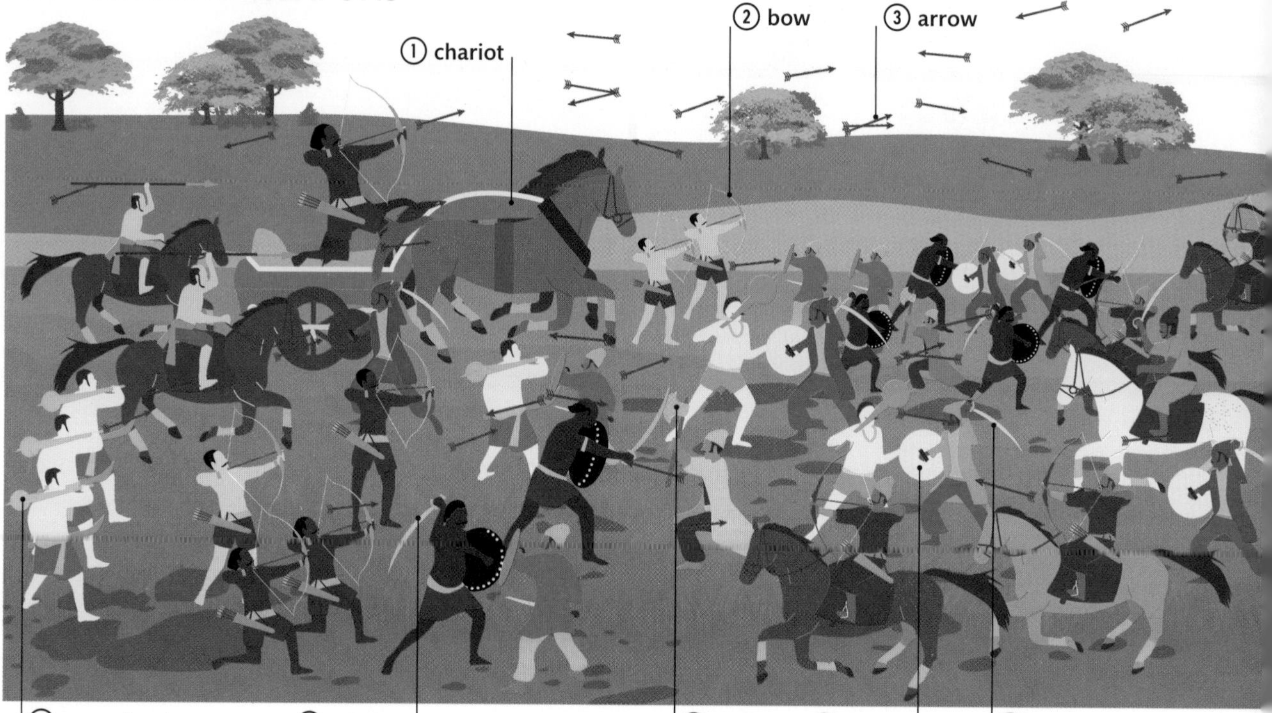

① chariot
② bow
③ arrow
⑤ mace / gada
⑥ scimitar
⑦ warfare
⑧ ax (US) axe (UK)
⑨ shield
⑩ sword

79.2 PEOPLE THROUGH TIME

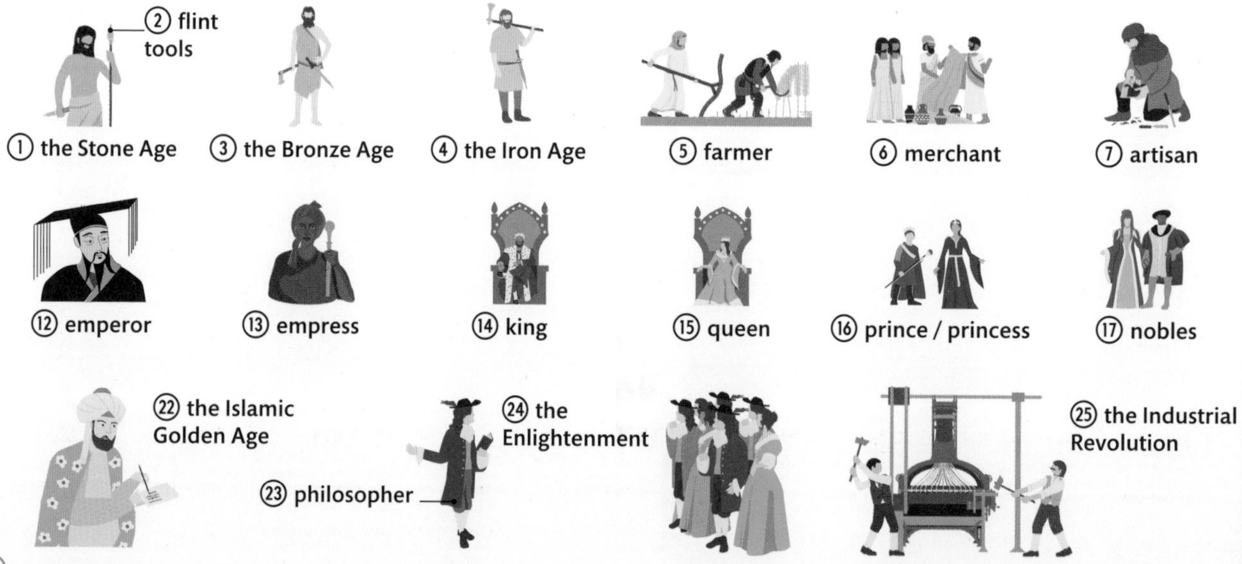

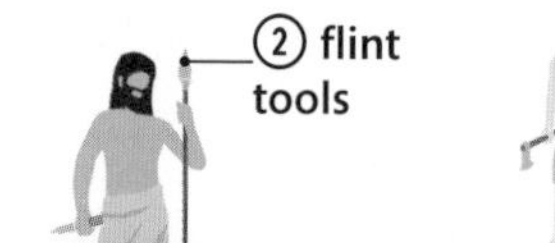
② flint tools

① the Stone Age

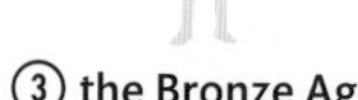
③ the Bronze Age

④ the Iron Age

⑤ farmer

⑥ merchant

⑦ artisan

⑫ emperor

⑬ empress

⑭ king

⑮ queen

⑯ prince / princess

⑰ nobles

㉒ the Islamic Golden Age

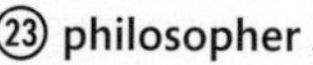

㉓ philosopher

㉔ the Enlightenment

㉕ the Industrial Revolution

See also:
44 Buildings and architecture
73 At school 80 At college 88 Military

④ spear

⑪ warhorse ⑫ war elephant

⑬ battle

⑭ cannon

⑮ catapult

⑯ battering ram

⑰ knight

⑱ armor (US) armour (UK)

⑲ warrior

⑧ blacksmith

⑨ peasants

⑩ kingdom

⑪ empire

⑱ lord / lady

⑲ minstrel

⑳ jester

㉑ scribe

㉖ the Technological Revolution

㉗ the Information Age

79.3 STUDYING THE PAST

① historian

② archive

③ sources

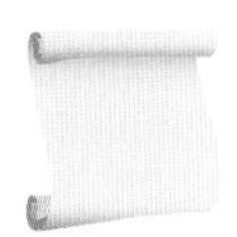
④ scroll

⑤ document

⑥ archeology (US) archaeology (UK)

⑦ archeologist (US) archaeologist (UK)

⑧ dig / excavation

⑩ peat bog
⑨ remains

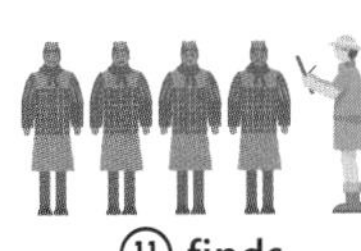
⑪ finds

⑫ tomb

⑬ historical site

80 At college

80.1 COLLEGE (US) / UNIVERSITY (UK)

① campus

③ lecturer

② auditorium (US)
lecture theatre (UK)

④ sports field

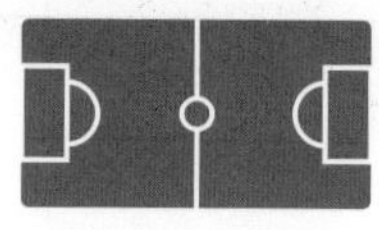

⑤ dining hall (US)
refectory (UK)

⑥ dorms (US)
halls of residence (UK)

⑦ scholarship

⑧ admissions

⑨ undergraduate

⑩ diploma

⑪ dissertation

⑫ degree

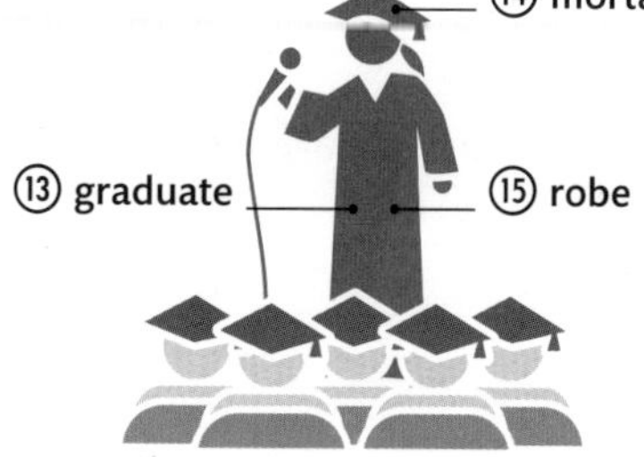

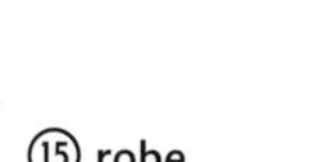

⑬ graduate

⑭ mortarboard

⑮ robe

⑯ graduation ceremony

⑰ postgraduate

⑱ thesis

⑲ master's degree

⑳ doctorate

80.2 DEPARTMENTS AND SCHOOLS

① humanities

② politics

③ literature

④ languages

%

⑤ economics

⑥ philosophy

⑦ history

⑧ social sciences

⑨ sociology

⑩ law

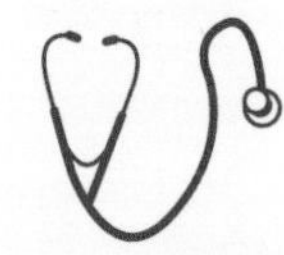

⑪ medicine

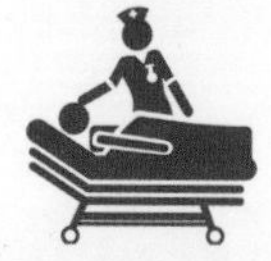

⑫ nursing

See also:
73 At school 74 Mathematics 75 Physics 76 Chemistry
77 Biology 79 History 85 Law 138 Books and reading

80.3 LIBRARY

① reading room

② reading list

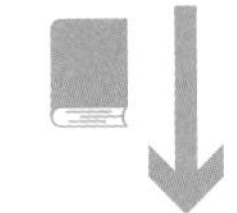
③ to borrow

④ to renew

⑤ to return

⑥ to reserve

⑦ aisle
⑧ bookshelf
⑨ librarian
⑩ library card
⑪ periodical / journal
⑫ book
⑭ circulation desk (US) / loans desk (UK)
⑬ library

⑭ I received a grant to do scientific research.

⑬ sciences

⑮ chemistry

⑯ physics

⑰ biology

⑱ engineering

⑲ zoology

⑳ music school

㉑ dance school

㉒ art college / school

81 At work

81.1 OFFICE WORK

① company

② branch

③ employment

④ to earn

⑤ permanent

⑥ temporary

⑩ nine-to-five job

⑪ to work part-time

⑫ to work shifts

⑬ vacation (US) annual leave (UK)

⑭ to have a day off

⑮ to go on maternity leave

⑲ to call in sick

⑳ to hand in your notice

㉑ to get fired

㉒ to be laid off

㉓ to be unemployed

㉔ unemployment benefit

㉙ headquarters
㉚ receptionist
㉝ CEO (chief executive officer)
㉞ businessman
㊳ apprentice
㊴ manager
㊵ PA (personal assistant)
㊶ leader
㉛ waiting area
㉟ business deal
㊱ businesswoman
㊷ clients
㉘ office reception
㉜ CEO's office
㊲ meeting

See also:
82 In the office 89-90 Jobs 91 Industries and departments
92 Applying for a job 93 Workplace skills 95 Meeting and presenting

⑦ flextime (US) flexitime (UK)

⑧ to work from home

⑨ to work full-time

⑯ to be promoted

⑰ to resign

⑱ to retire

㉕ business trip

㉖ appointment

㉗ business lunch

81.2 PAY

① hourly rate

② overtime

③ salary

④ wages

⑤ pay slip

⑥ bonus

⑦ benefits

25%
⑧ raise

25%
⑨ pay cut

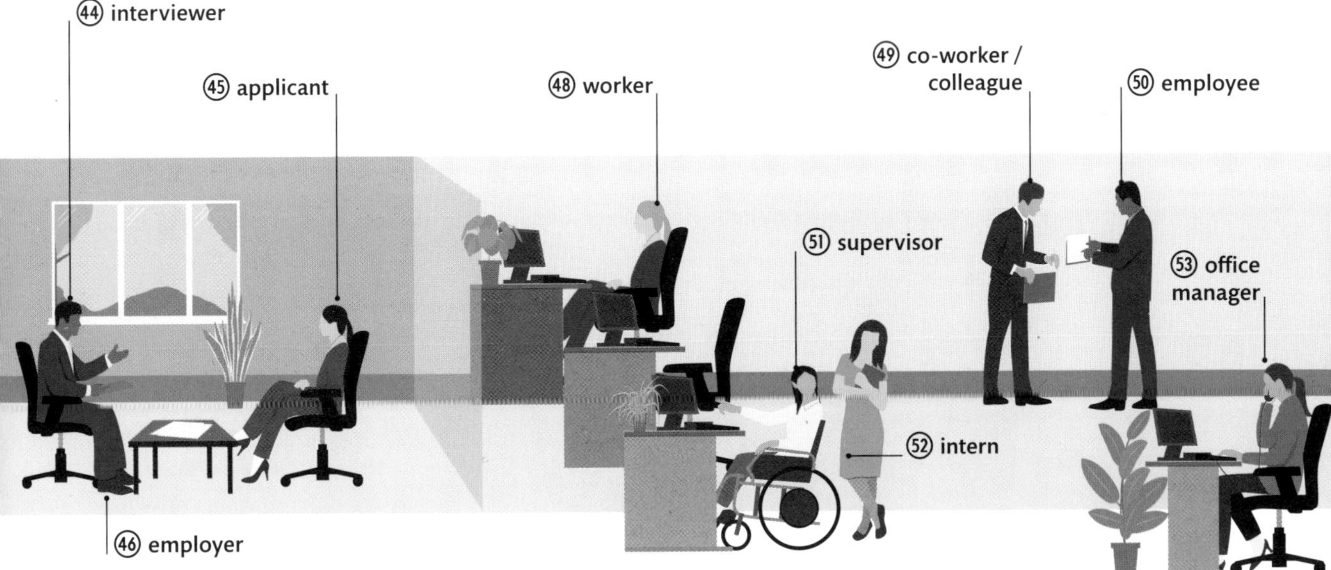
㊹ interviewer
㊺ applicant
㊻ employer
㊸ interview
㊽ worker
㊾ co-worker / colleague
㊿ employee
(51) supervisor
(52) intern
(53) office manager
㊼ staff

82 In the office

82.1 OFFICE

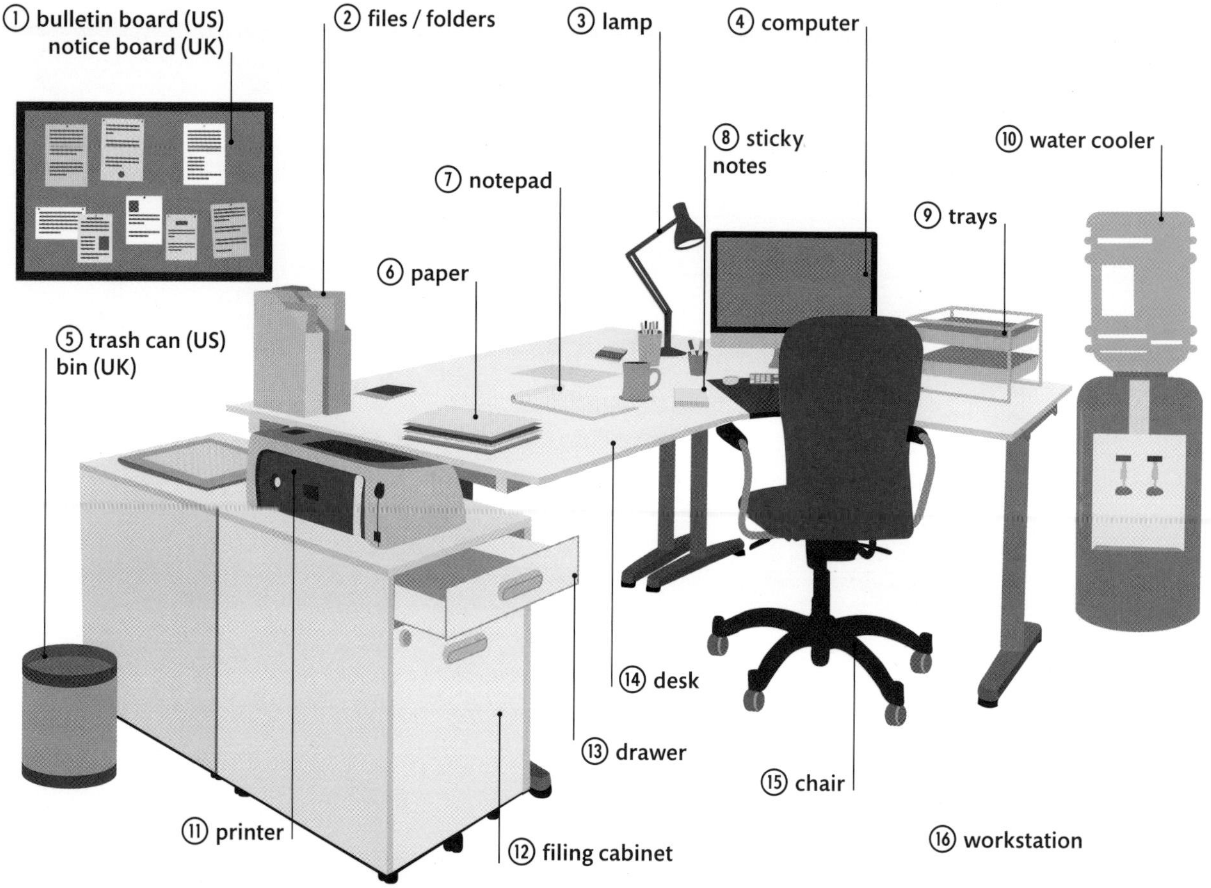

① bulletin board (US)
notice board (UK)

② files / folders

③ lamp

④ computer

⑤ trash can (US)
bin (UK)

⑥ paper

⑦ notepad

⑧ sticky notes

⑨ trays

⑩ water cooler

⑪ printer

⑫ filing cabinet

⑬ drawer

⑭ desk

⑮ chair

⑯ workstation

82.2 MEETING-ROOM EQUIPMENT

① presentation
② proposal
③ report
④ digital projector
⑤ meeting
⑥ flip chart
⑦ easel

See also:
81 At work 83 Computers and technology 91 Industries and departments
92 Applying for a job 93 Workplace skills 95 Meeting and presenting

82.3 OFFICE EQUIPMENT

① photocopier

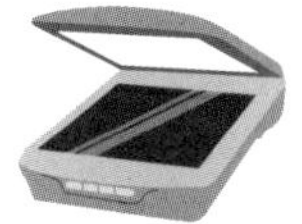
② scanner

③ telephone / phone

④ laptop

⑤ projector

⑥ headset

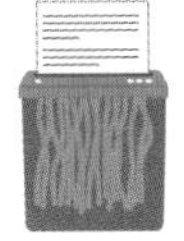
⑦ shredder

⑧ cell phone (US) mobile phone (UK)

⑨ footrest

⑩ kneeling chair

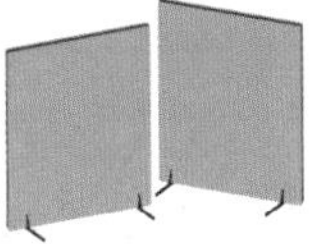
⑪ movable panel

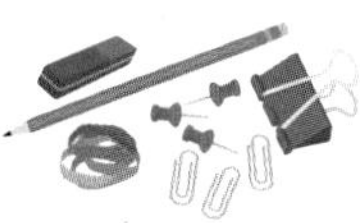
⑫ stationery

⑬ letter

⑭ envelope

JUNE
⑮ calendar

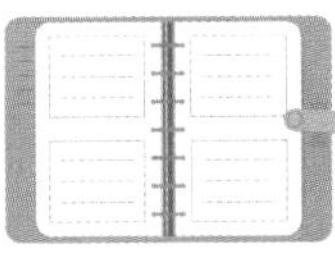
⑯ planner (US) diary (UK)

⑰ clipboard

⑱ hole punch

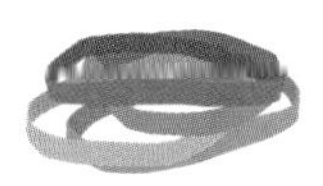
⑲ rubber bands

⑳ binder clip

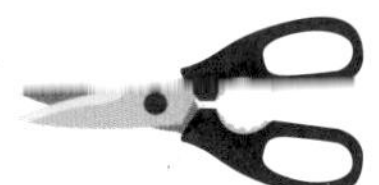
㉑ scissors

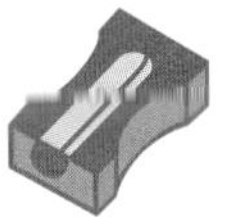
㉒ pencil sharpener

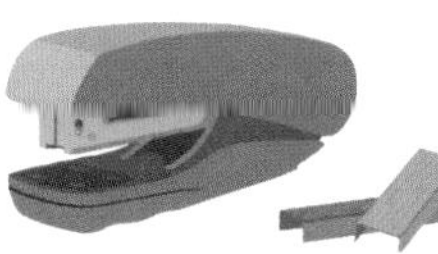
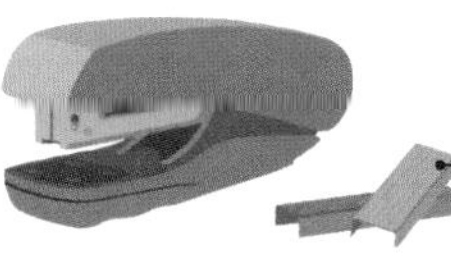
㉔ staples

㉓ stapler

㉕ correction fluid

MINUTES
㉖ minutes

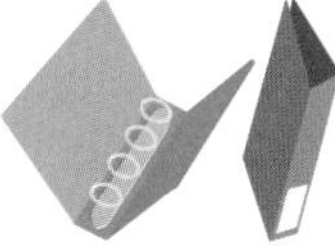
㉗ ring binder

㉘ highlighter

㉙ glue

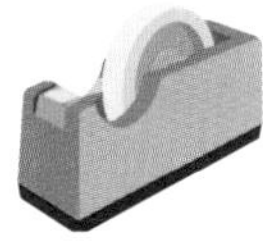
㉚ tape

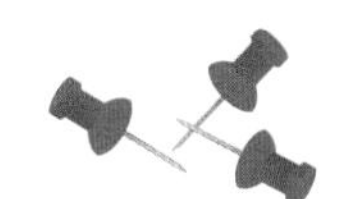
㉛ thumbtack (US) drawing pin (UK)

㉜ pencil

㉝ pen

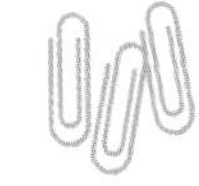
㉞ paper clips

㉟ eraser (US) rubber (UK)

㊱ ruler

83 Computers and technology

83.1 GADGETS AND TECHNOLOGY

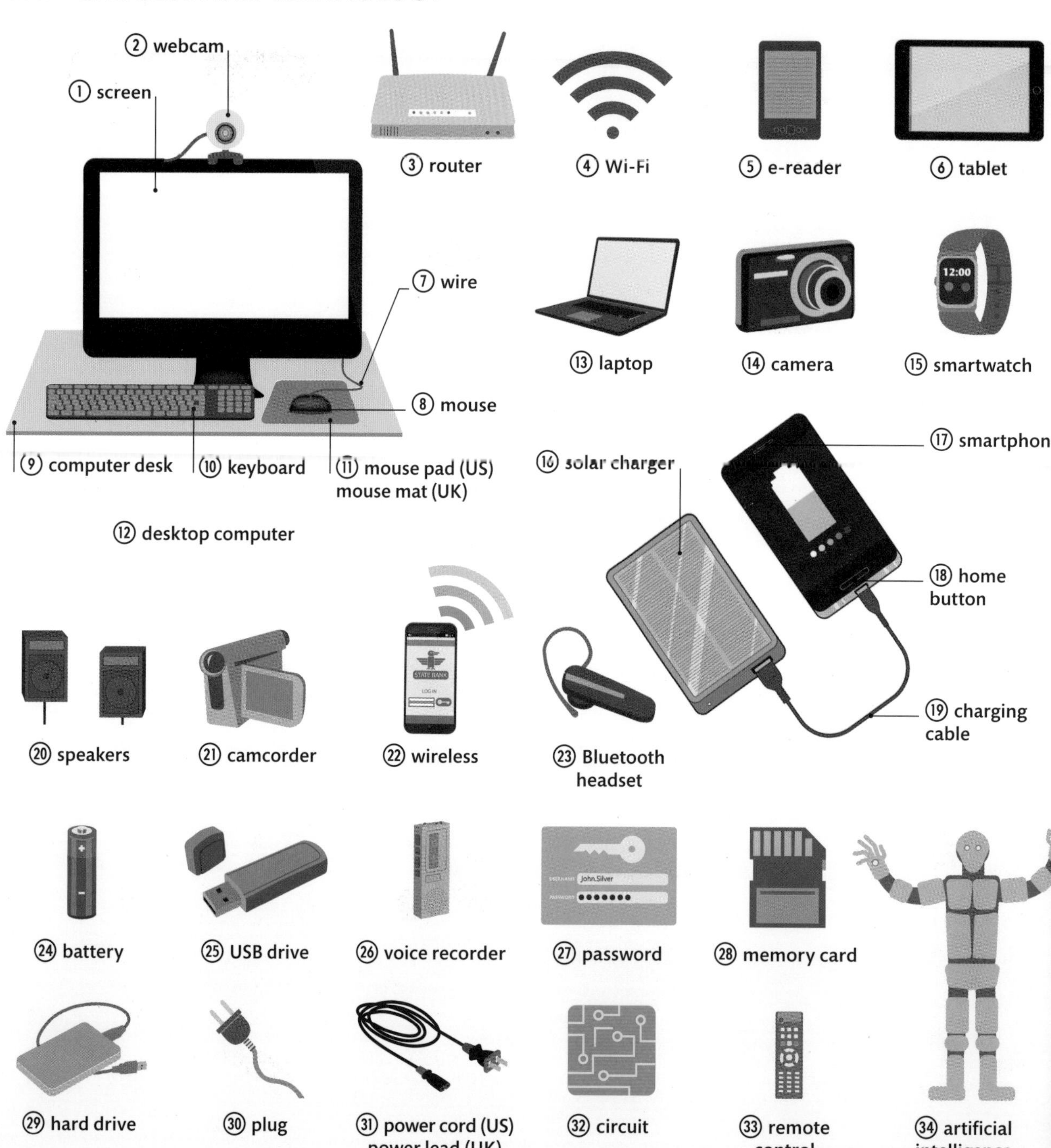

① screen
② webcam
③ router
④ Wi-Fi
⑤ e-reader
⑥ tablet
⑦ wire
⑧ mouse
⑨ computer desk
⑩ keyboard
⑪ mouse pad (US)
mouse mat (UK)
⑫ desktop computer
⑬ laptop
⑭ camera
12:00
⑮ smartwatch
⑯ solar charger
⑰ smartphone
⑱ home button
⑲ charging cable
⑳ speakers
㉑ camcorder
STATE BANK
LOG IN
㉒ wireless
㉓ Bluetooth headset
㉔ battery
㉕ USB drive
㉖ voice recorder
John.Silver
●●●●●●●
㉗ password
㉘ memory card
㉙ hard drive
㉚ plug
㉛ power cord (US)
power lead (UK)
㉜ circuit
㉝ remote control
㉞ artificial intelligence

See also:
73 At school 80 At college 81 At work
82 In the office 95 Meeting and presenting 140 Games

83.2 ONLINE COMMUNICATION

① to turn on

② to turn off

③ to log in

④ to log out

⑤ to download

⑥ to upload

⑦ to back up

⑧ to click

⑨ to plug in

⑩ to delete

⑪ to print

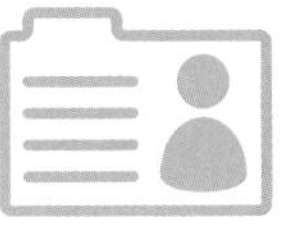
⑫ contact

⑬ email

⑭ to reply

⑮ to reply to all

⑯ to send

⑰ to forward

⑱ draft

⑲ inbox

⑳ outbox

Message
From
To
Subject
㉑ subject

㉒ junk mail / spam

㉓ trash

㉔ attachment

㉕ chat

㉖ video chat

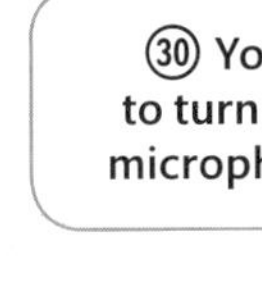
㉚ You need to turn on your microphone, Liz.

㉛ video conference

㉗ signature

㉘ hashtag

㉙ at sign / at symbol

84 Media

84.1 TELEVISION STUDIO

① light

② sound boom

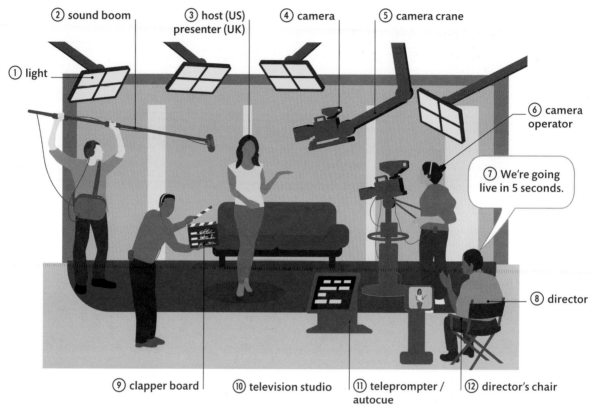

③ host (US) presenter (UK)

④ camera

⑤ camera crane

⑥ camera operator

⑦ We're going live in 5 seconds.

⑧ director

⑨ clapper board

⑩ television studio

⑪ teleprompter / autocue

⑫ director's chair

84.2 RADIO

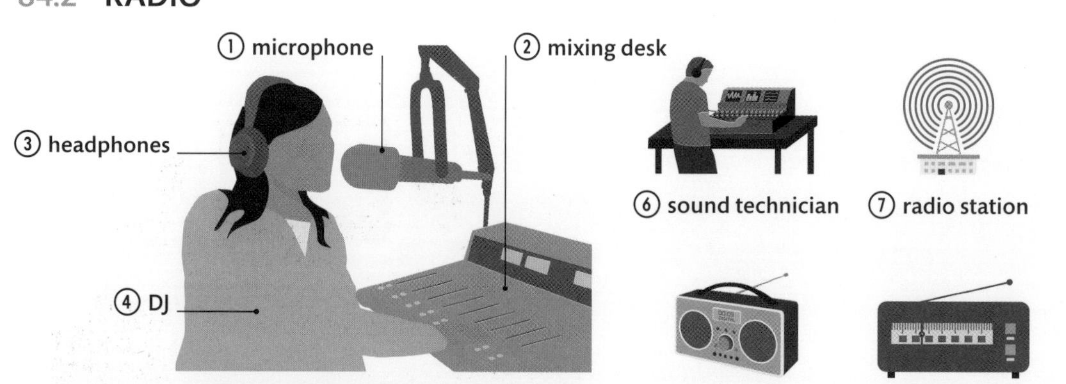
① microphone
② mixing desk
③ headphones
④ DJ
⑤ recording studio
⑥ sound technician
⑦ radio station
⑧ to broadcast
⑨ digital
⑩ FM
⑪ frequency

See also:
83 Computers and technology 128-129 Music
136 Home entertainment 137 Television

84.3 SOCIAL AND ONLINE MEDIA

① to follow

② to like

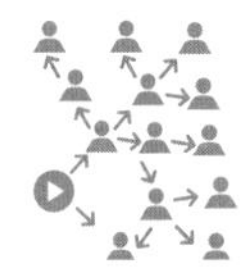
③ to go viral

④ to trend

⑨ My blog has over 500 followers.

⑤ avatar

⑥ vlog

⑦ vlogger

⑧ blog

⑩ blogger

⑪ to share

⑫ to block

⑬ to post

⑭ to DM someone

⑮ influencer

⑯ follower

⑰ podcast

⑱ emoji

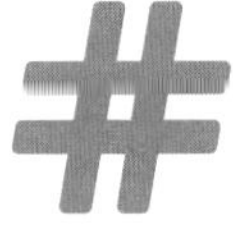
⑲ hashtag

⑳ thread

㉑ newsfeed

㉒ status update

㉓ CMS (content management system)

㉔ platform

㉕ cookie

㉖ pop-up

㉗ news website

㉘ magazine website

㉙ community website

㉚ trolling

85 Law

85.1 THE LEGAL SYSTEM

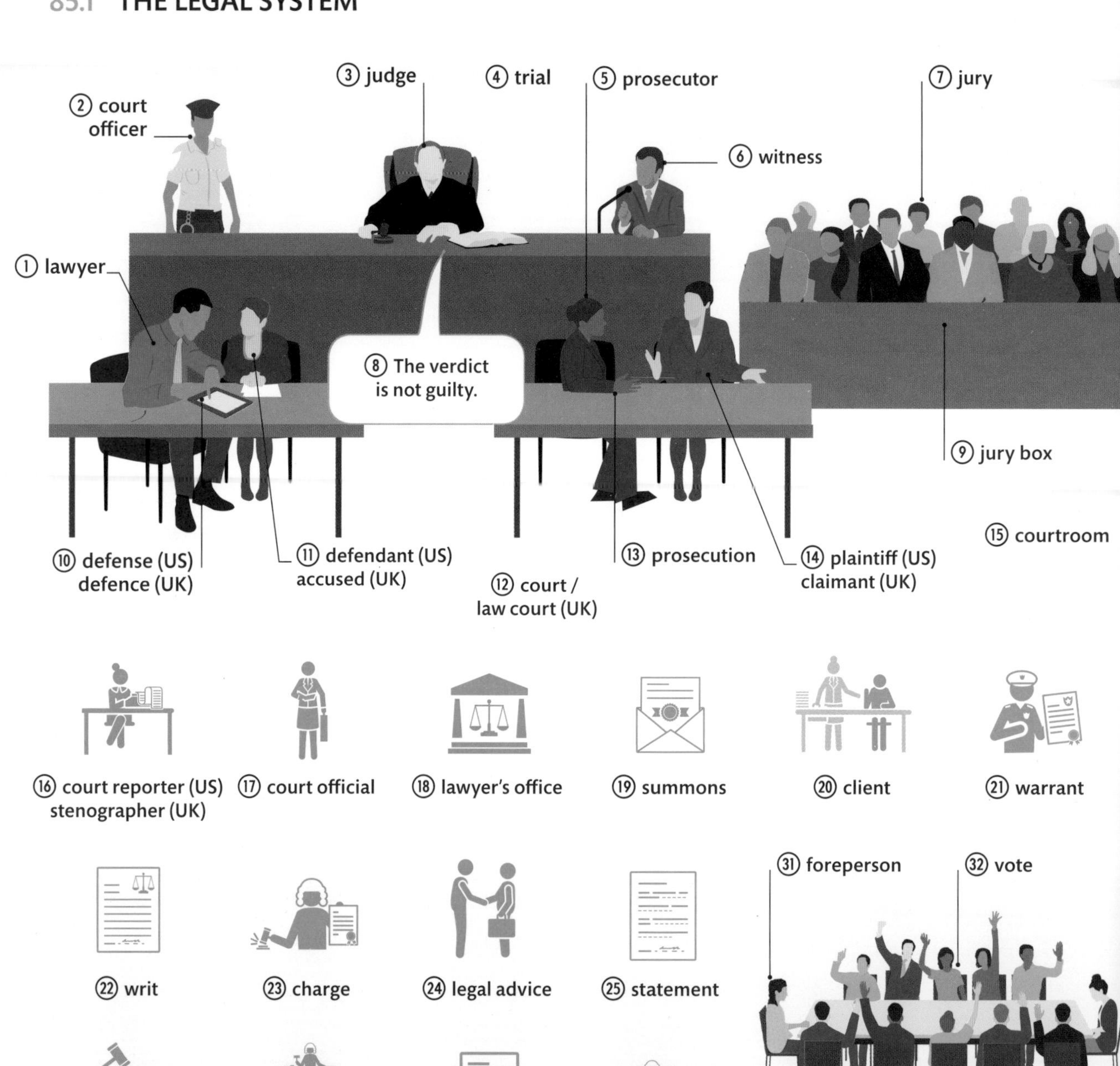

① lawyer
② court officer
③ judge
④ trial
⑤ prosecutor
⑥ witness
⑦ jury
⑧ The verdict is not guilty.
⑨ jury box
⑩ defense (US) defence (UK)
⑪ defendant (US) accused (UK)
⑫ court / law court (UK)
⑬ prosecution
⑭ plaintiff (US) claimant (UK)
⑮ courtroom
⑯ court reporter (US) stenographer (UK)
⑰ court official
⑱ lawyer's office
⑲ summons
⑳ client
㉑ warrant
㉒ writ
㉓ charge
㉔ legal advice
㉕ statement
㉖ court date
㉗ court case
㉘ verdict
㉙ to sentence
㉚ jury deliberation
㉛ foreperson
㉜ vote

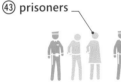

See also:
50 Emergency services
91 Industries and departments

33 composite (US) photofit (UK)

34 evidence

35 suspect

36 criminal record

37 criminal

38 accused

39 to plead

40 innocent

41 guilty

42 to appeal

43 prisoners

44 prison guards

45 prison

46 cell

47 bail

48 parole

49 fine

50 to be acquitted

85.2 CRIME

1 robbery / burglary

2 mugging

3 car theft

4 hooliganism

5 vandalism

6 smuggling

7 fraud

8 hacking

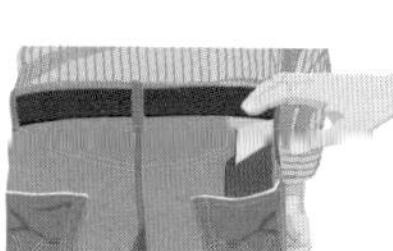
9 pickpocketing

10 bribery

11 speeding

12 drug dealing

13 graffiti

14 shoplifting

86 Farming

86.1 ON THE FARM

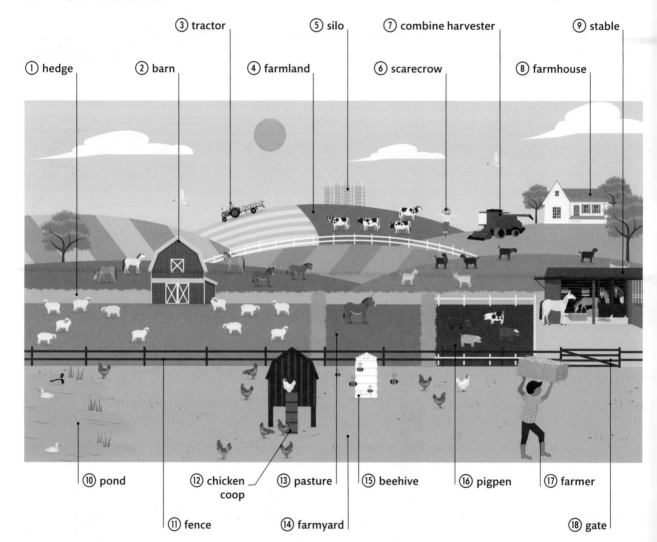

1. hedge
2. barn
3. tractor
4. farmland
5. silo
6. scarecrow
7. combine harvester
8. farmhouse
9. stable
10. pond
11. fence
12. chicken coop
13. pasture
14. farmyard
15. beehive
16. pigpen
17. farmer
18. gate

86.2 FARMING VERBS

① to plow (US)
to plough (UK)

② to sow

③ to milk

④ to feed

⑤ to plant

⑥ to harvest

See also:
53 Meat **55-56** Vegetables **57** Fruit
58 Fruit and nuts **61** Dairy produce **165** Farm animals

86.3 FARMING TERMS

① crop farm (US)
arable farm (UK)

② dairy farm

③ sheep farm

④ poultry farm

⑤ pig farm

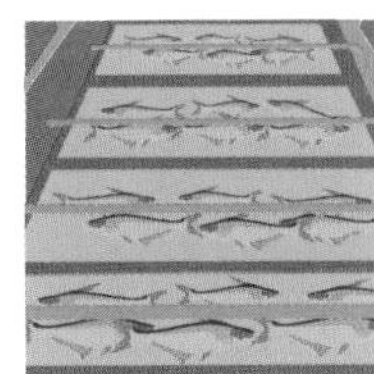
⑥ fish farm

⑦ herd

⑧ fruit farm

⑨ vineyard

⑩ vegetable garden / vegetable plot (UK)

⑪ herbicide

⑫ pesticide

86.4 CROPS

① wheat

② corn / maize (UK)

③ barley

④ rapeseed

⑤ sunflowers

⑥ hay

⑦ alfalfa

⑧ tobacco

⑨ rice

⑩ tea

⑪ coffee

⑫ sugar cane

⑬ flax

⑭ cotton

⑮ potatoes

⑯ yams

⑰ millet

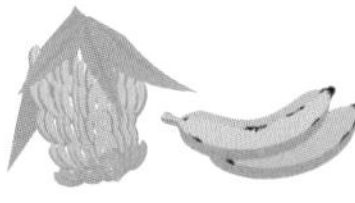
⑱ plantains

87 Construction

87.1 CONSTRUCTION SITE (US) / BUILDING SITE (UK)

① chimney
② rafter
③ ridge beam
④ brick
⑤ lintel
⑥ hard hat
⑦ construction worker (US) builder (UK)
⑧ window
⑨ wall
⑩ ladder
⑪ construction site (US) / building site (UK)
⑫ pallet
⑬ lumber (US) timber (UK)

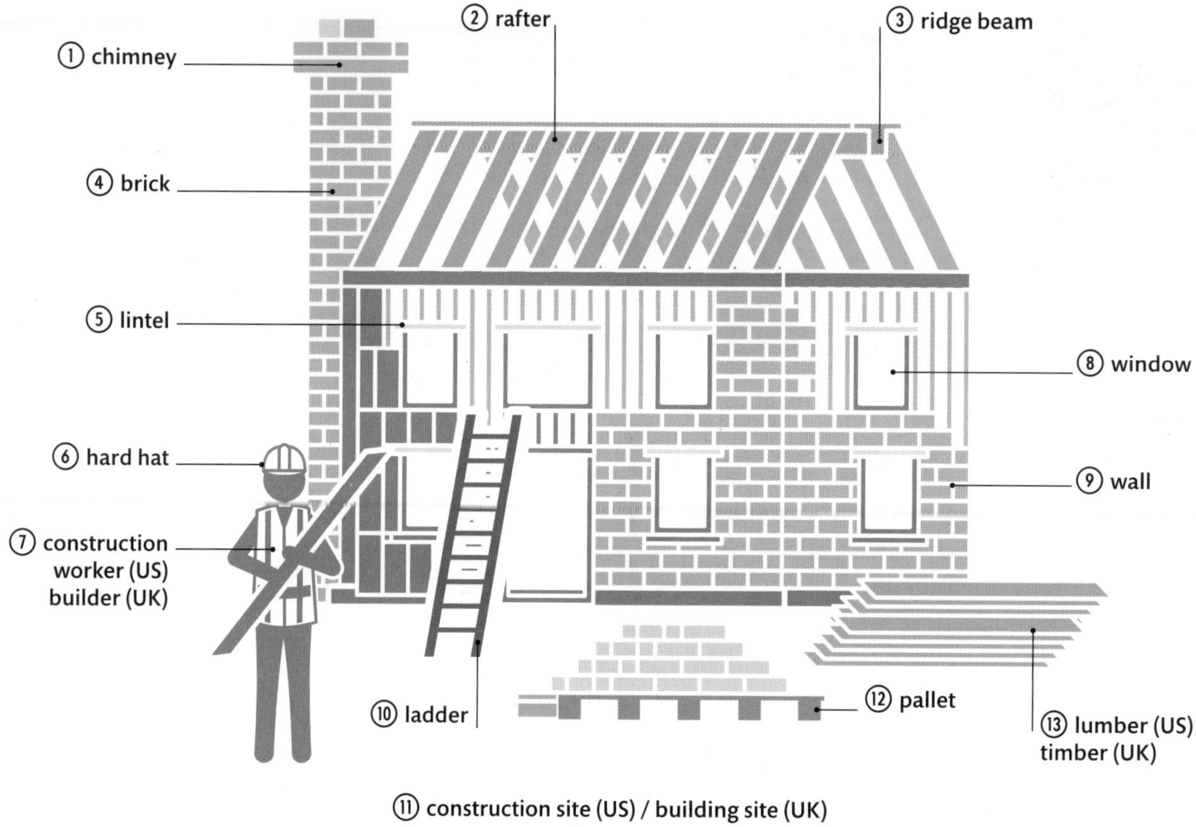

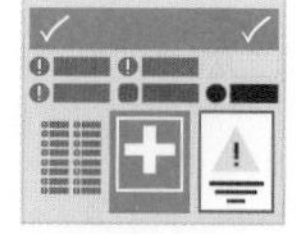
⑭ safety notice board

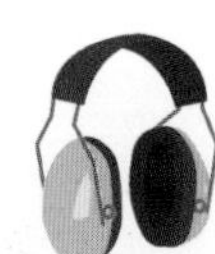
⑮ ear protectors ear muffs (UK)

⑯ high-visibility vest

⑰ safety gloves

⑱ safety glasses

⑲ tool belt

⑳ girder

㉑ pipe

㉒ cement / mortar

㉓ cinder block (US) breeze block (UK)

㉔ shingles (US) roof tiles (UK)

㉕ to build

See also:
25 A place to live 32 House and home 33 Electrics and plumbing
35 Home improvements 36 Tools 37 Decorating

87.2 MACHINERY

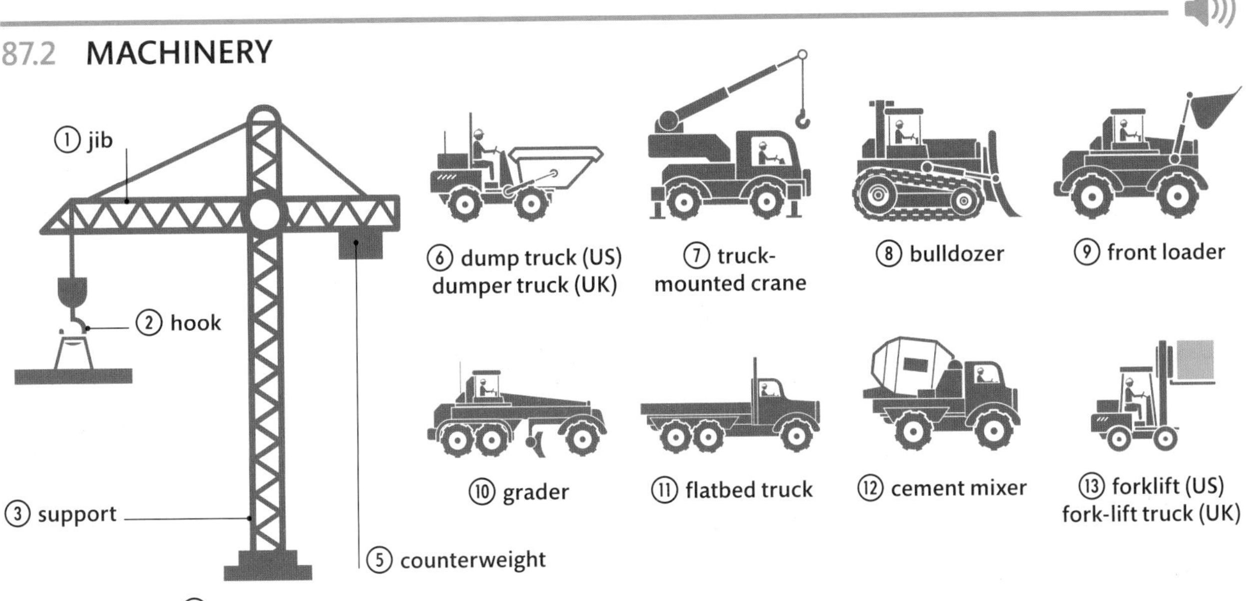
① jib
② hook
③ support
④ tower crane
⑤ counterweight
⑥ dump truck (US)
dumper truck (UK)
⑦ truck-
mounted crane
⑧ bulldozer
⑨ front loader
⑩ grader
⑪ flatbed truck
⑫ cement mixer
⑬ forklift (US)
fork-lift truck (UK)

87.3 TOOLS AND ROADWORKS

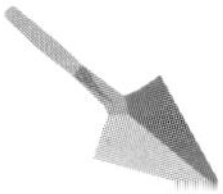

① trowel

② level (US)
spirit level (UK)

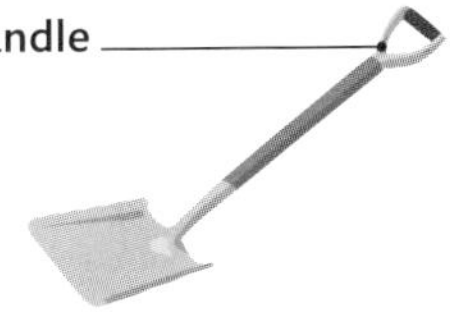

③ handle

④ shovel

⑤ pickax (US)
pickaxe (UK)

⑥ sledgehammer

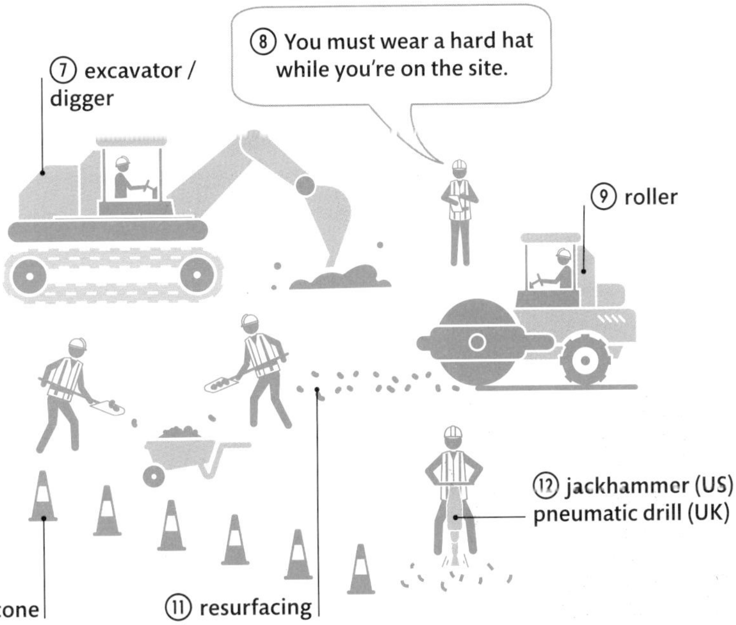

⑦ excavator /
digger

⑧ You must wear a hard hat while you're on the site.

⑨ roller

⑩ cone

⑪ resurfacing

⑫ jackhammer (US)
pneumatic drill (UK)

⑬ road construction (US) / roadworks (UK)

88 Military

88.1 ARMED FORCES

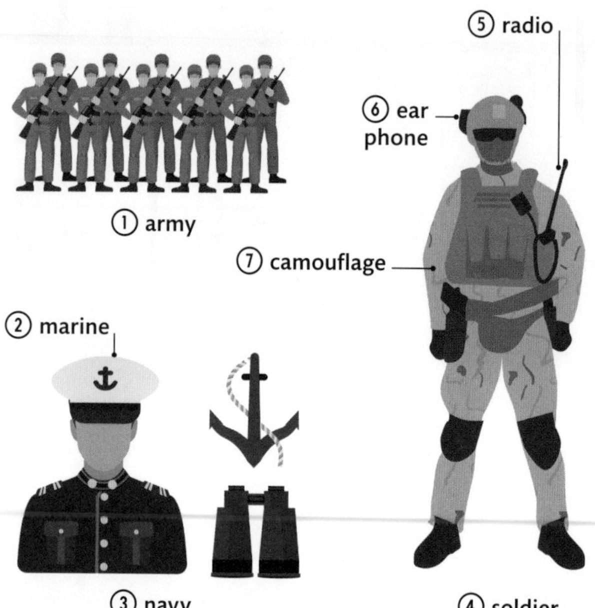

1 army
2 marine
3 navy
4 soldier
5 radio
6 ear phone
7 camouflage

8 sailors

9 general

10 admiral

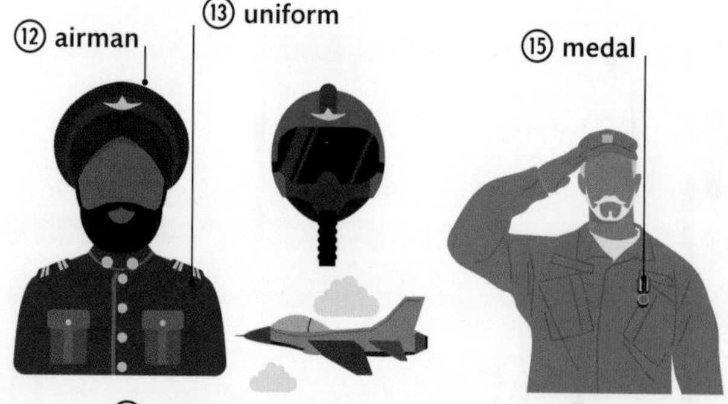

11 airforce
12 airman
13 uniform
14 veteran
15 medal

88.2 MILITARY VEHICLES

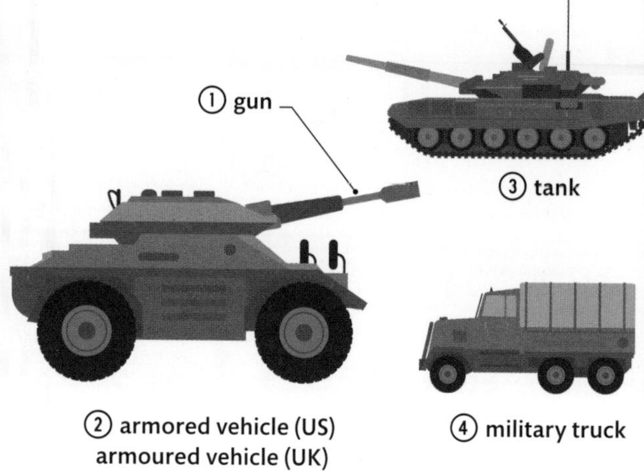

1 gun
2 armored vehicle (US)
armoured vehicle (UK)
3 tank
4 military truck

5 amphibious vehicle

6 military ambulance

7 reconnaissance vehicle

88.3 NAVY VESSELS

2 island

1 aircraft carrier

3 destroyer

4 cruiser

5 frigate

6 submarine

See also:
79 History 148 Maps and directions
149-151 Countries

88.4 COMBAT AIRCRAFT

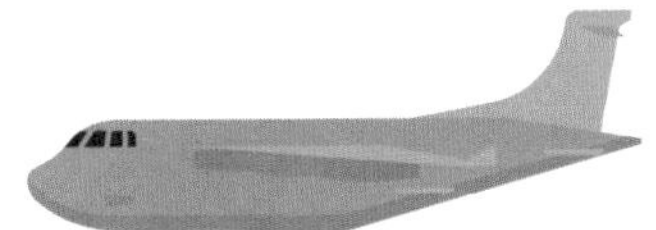
① military transport aircraft

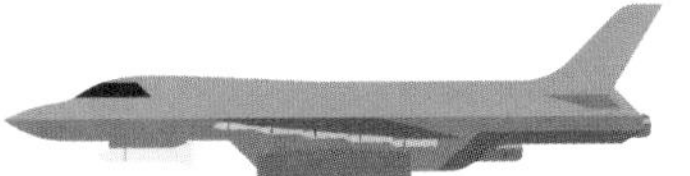
② bomber

③ attack helicopter

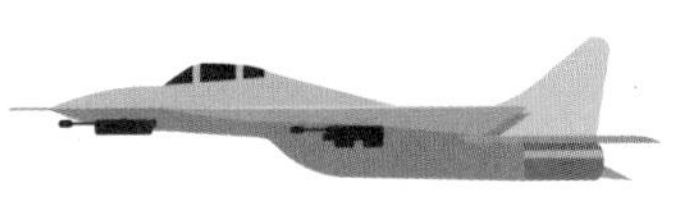
④ fighter

⑤ reconnaissance aircraft

⑥ transport helicopter

88.5 WAR AND WEAPONS

① battle

② front

③ gunfire

④ casualty

⑤ field hospital

⑥ mess

⑦ guns

⑧ machine gun

⑨ pistol

⑩ shotgun

⑪ rifle

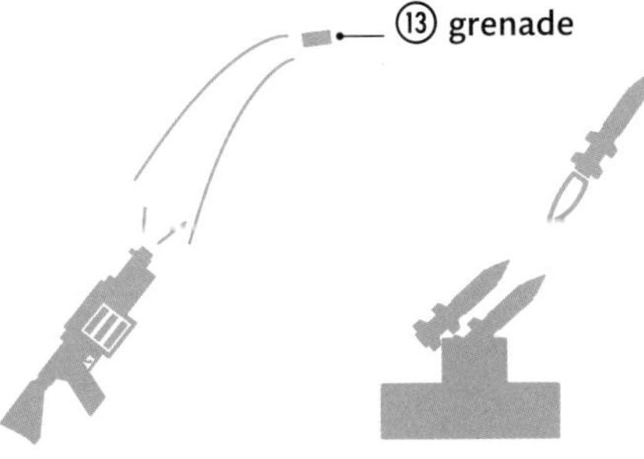
⑬ grenade
⑫ grenade launcher
⑭ surface-to-air missile

⑮ ballistic missile

⑯ shoulder-launched missile

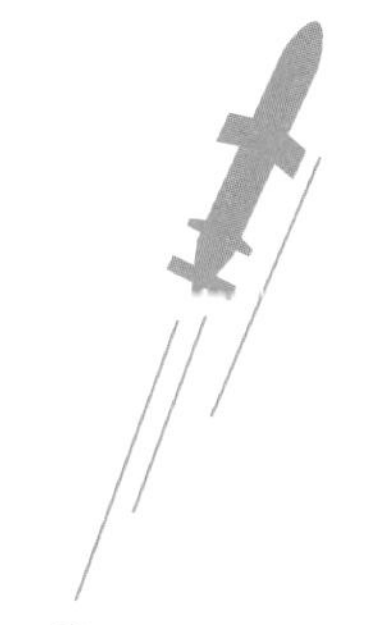
⑰ cruise missile

⑱ armed drone

89 Jobs

89.1 OCCUPATIONS

① actor

② sociologist

③ barber

④ editor

⑩ This pipe has sprung a leak.

⑨ plumber

⑤ bartender

⑥ fisherman

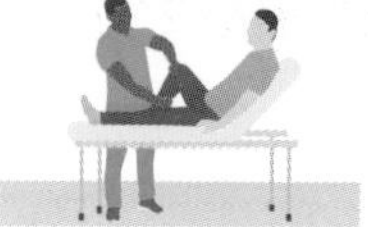

⑦ physical therapist/ physiotherapist

⑧ optician

⑪ carpenter

⑫ ship's captain

⑬ lecturer

⑭ comedian

⑮ dancer

⑯ clown

⑰ cleaner

⑱ doctor

⑲ driving instructor

⑳ painter

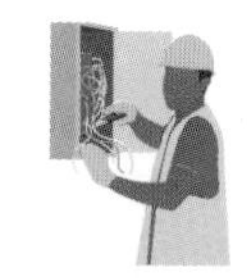

㉑ electrician

㉒ designer

㉓ barista

㉔ firefighter

㉕ app developer

㉖ spy

㉗ florist

㉘ ground maintenance

㉙ gardener

㉚ grocer (US) greengrocer (UK)

㉛ miner

㉜ IT manager

㉝ jeweler (US) jeweller (UK)

㉞ dentist

See also:
81 At work **82** In the office **90** Jobs (continued) **91** Industries and departments
92 Applying for a job **93** Workplace skills **95** Meeting and presenting

35 maid / housekeeper

36 hairdresser / stylist

37 mechanic

38 interpreter

39 museum curator

40 private investigator

41 site manager

42 orthodontist

43 broadcaster (US) newsreader (UK)

44 pharmacist

45 butcher

46 photographer

47 police officer

48 nurse

49 sailor

50 sales assistant

51 server (US) waitress

52 server (US) waiter

53 sculptor

54 security guard

55 tailor

56 ski instructor

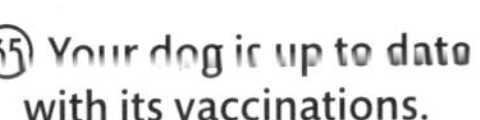
65 Your dog is up to date with its vaccinations.

57 soldier

58 farmer

59 sportsperson

60 fishmonger

64 vet

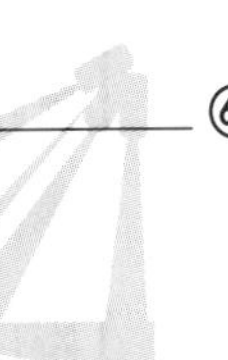

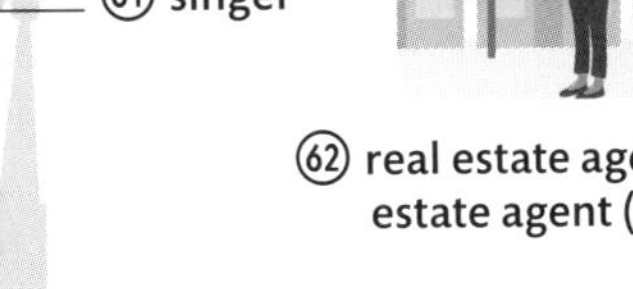
61 singer

62 real estate agent (US) estate agent (UK)

63 market researcher

90 Jobs continued

90.1 OCCUPATIONS

① security guard

② window cleaner

③ artist

④ bodyguard

⑤ psychologist

⑥ businessman

⑦ businesswoman

⑧ accountant

⑨ chef

⑩ construction worker (US) / builder (UK)

⑪ radio DJ

⑫ engineer

⑬ fashion designer

⑭ rock star

⑮ flight instructor

⑯ janitor

⑰ tour guide

⑱ mail carrier (US) postman / postwoman (UK)

⑲ personal assistant (PA)

⑳ librarian

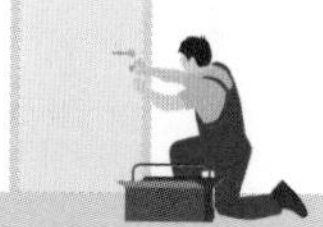
㉑ locksmith

㉒ paramedic

㉓ music teacher

㉔ childcare provider

㉕ kitchen installer / kitchen fitter (UK)

㉖ taxi driver

㉗ zookeeper

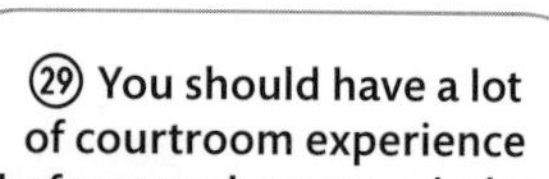
㉙ You should have a lot of courtroom experience before you become a judge.

㉘ judge

See also:
81 At work **82** In the office **91** Industries and departments
92 Applying for a job **93** Workplace skills **95** Meeting and presenting

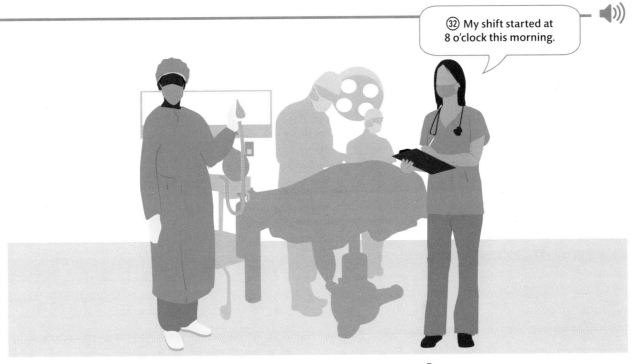

(32) My shift started at 8 o'clock this morning.

(30) anesthesiologist (US) / anaesthetist (UK)

(31) surgeon

(33) driver

(34) secretary

(35) receptionist

(36) flight attendant

(37) scientist

(38) bus driver

(39) musician

(40) surveyor

(41) lawyer

(42) teacher

(43) journalist

(44) train driver

(45) travel agent

(46) truck driver (US) lorry driver (UK)

(47) architect

(48) writer

(49) yoga teacher

(50) pilot

91 Industries and departments

91.1 INDUSTRIES

① advertising

② personal services

③ agriculture / farming

④ military

⑤ real estate (US) property (UK)

⑥ automotive industry

⑩ banking

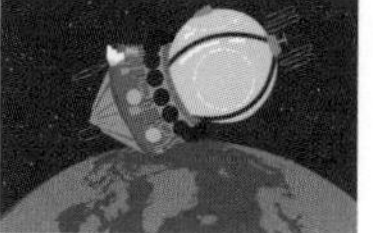
⑪ aerospace

⑫ petroleum engineering

⑬ chemical industry

⑭ arts

⑮ education

⑲ gaming

⑳ energy

㉑ research

㉒ fashion

㉓ recycling

㉔ entertainment

㉘ shipping

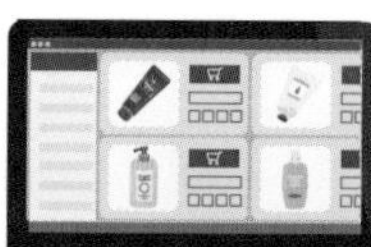
㉙ online retail

㉚ journalism

㉛ textiles

㉜ media

㉝ hospitality

㊲ online delivery

㊳ water

㊴ performing arts

㊵ biotechnology

㊷ Our stocks have fallen dramatically.
㊶ finance

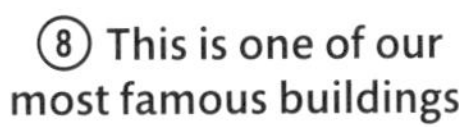

⑧ This is one of our most famous buildings.

⑦ tourism

⑨ pet services

⑯ catering / food

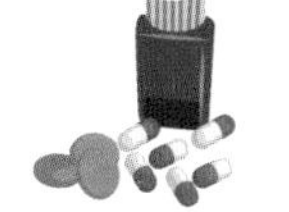

⑰ pharmaceuticals

⑱ construction

㉕ fishing

㉖ electronics

㉗ retail

㉞ healthcare

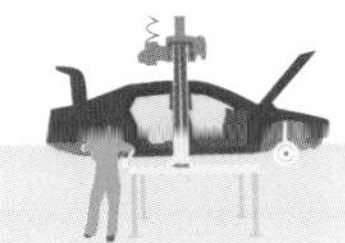

㉟ manufacturing

㊱ mining

㊸ transportation (US) / transport (UK)

See also:
81 At work **82** In the office **89-90** Jobs
92 Applying for a job **93** Workplace skills

91.2 DEPARTMENTS

① accounts / finance

② production

CONTRACT

③ legal

④ marketing

⑤ information technology (IT)

⑥ facilities / office services

⑦ sales

⑧ administration

⑨ public relations (PR)

⑩ purchasing

⑪ human resources (HR)

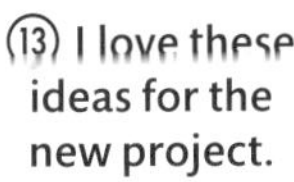

⑬ I love these ideas for the new project.

⑫ research and development (R&D)

92 Applying for a job

92.1 JOB APPLICATIONS

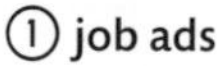

① job ads

② application form

③ cover letter

⑧ What kind of work are you looking for?
⑦ to fill out a form

⑥ recruiter (US)
recruitment agency (UK)

④ portfolio

⑤ résumé (US)
CV (UK)

92.2 APPLYING FOR A JOB

② vacancies

① to apply for a job

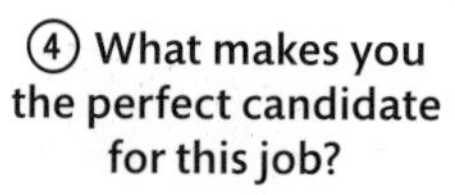
④ What makes you the perfect candidate for this job?

⑤ I'm hardworking and I'm a team player.

③ to have an interview

See also:
81 At work 89-90 Jobs 91 Industries and departments
93 Workplace skills 95 Meeting and presenting

92.3 TEAMWORK

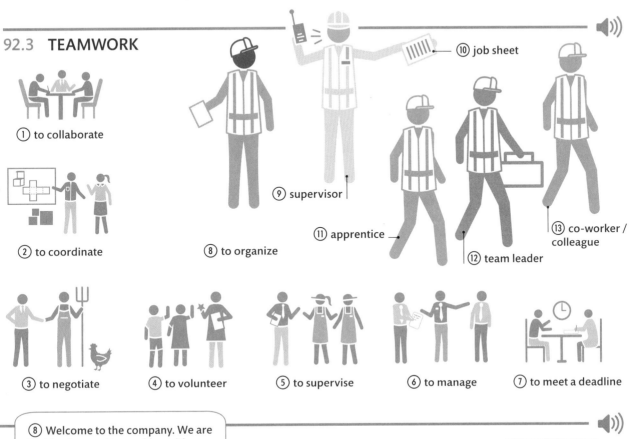

① to collaborate

② to coordinate

⑧ to organize

⑨ supervisor

⑩ job sheet

⑪ apprentice

⑫ team leader

⑬ co-worker / colleague

③ to negotiate

④ to volunteer

⑤ to supervise

⑥ to manage

⑦ to meet a deadline

⑧ Welcome to the company. We are looking forward to working with you.
⑦ to shake hands
⑪ I can't wait to get started.
⑩ contract

⑥ to get the job

⑨ to sign a contract

93 Workplace skills

93.1 PROFESSIONAL ATTRIBUTES

① organized

② patient

③ creative

④ honest

⑤ practical

⑥ professional

⑦ adaptable

⑧ ambitious

⑨ calm

⑩ confident

⑪ punctual

⑫ reliable

⑬ customer-focused

⑭ independent

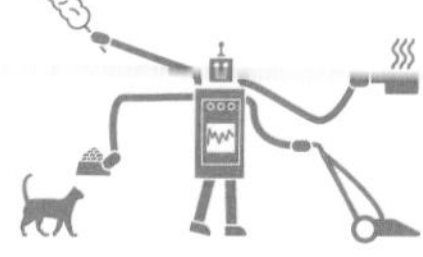

⑮ efficient

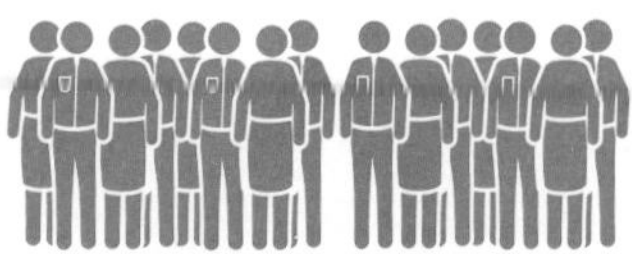

⑯ team player

⑰ responsible

⑱ innovative

⑲ motivated

⑳ determined

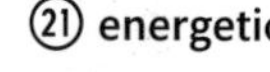

㉑ energetic

㉓ Carlo is the hardest-working chef I've ever met.

㉒ hard-working

㉔ competitive

㉕ assertive

㉖ imaginative

㉗ curious

㉘ original

㉙ accurate

㉚ good listener

㉛ flexible

See also:
10 Personality traits **11** Abilities and actions
81 At work **82** In the office

93.2 PROFESSIONAL EXPERTISE

① organization

② computer literacy

③ computing

④ problem-solving

⑤ analytics

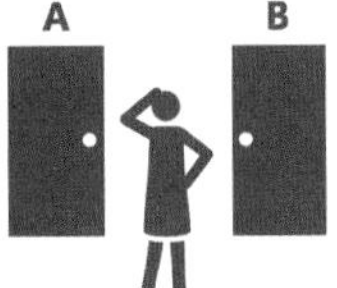
A
B
⑥ decision-making

⑦ teamwork

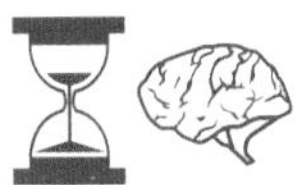
⑧ being a fast learner

⑨ paying attention to detail

⑩ customer service

⑪ leadership

⑫ research

⑬ fluent in languages

⑭ technology literate

⑮ public speaking

⑯ negotiating

⑰ written communication

⑱ initiative

⑲ telephone manner

⑳ working well under pressure

㉑ numeracy

㉒ ability to drive

㉓ well-qualified

㉔ self management

㉕ service focused

㉖ influencer

㉗ businesslike attitude

㉘ interpersonal skills

㉙ project management

㉚ administration

㉜ You must improve your time management! This report is late.
㉛ time management

94 Money and finance

94.1 MONEY

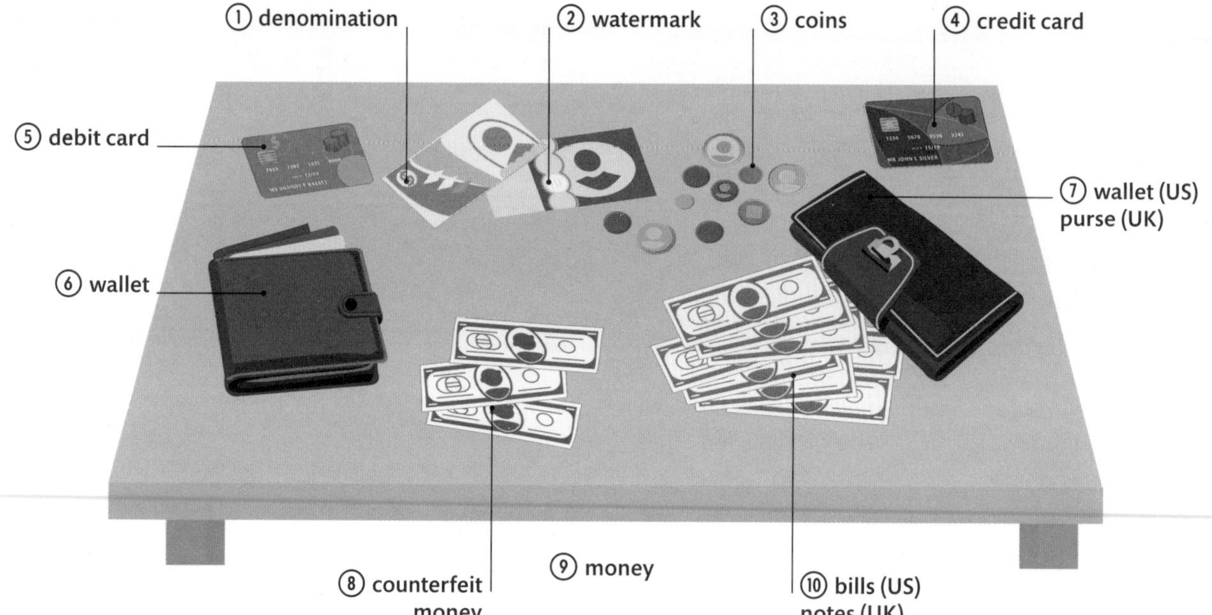
① denomination
② watermark
③ coins
④ credit card
⑤ debit card
⑥ wallet
⑦ wallet (US) purse (UK)
⑧ counterfeit money
⑨ money
⑩ bills (US) notes (UK)

⑪ digital wallet

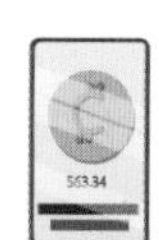
⑫ digital currency

⑬ bank

⑭ online banking

⑮ mobile banking

⑯ telephone banking

⑰ receipt

⑱ currency

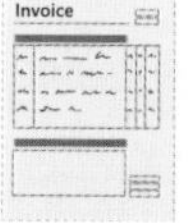
⑲ invoice

㉔ Do you accept cash here?
㉓ to pay with cash

⑳ check (US) cheque (UK)

㉑ cash register (US) till (UK)

㉒ to pay by card

See also:
45 The bank and post office
91 Industries and departments

94.2 FINANCE

① stockbroker

② stock exchange

③ shares

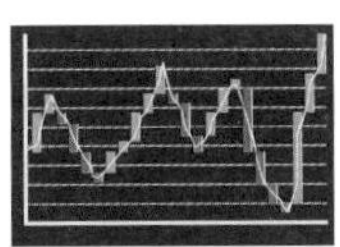

④ share price

⑤ dividends

5%

⑥ commission

VIDEO STORE

⑦ equity

⑧ investment

⑨ portfolio

⑩ stocks

£ → €
$ → ¥

⑪ exchange rate

⑫ income

$
Q1 Q2 Q3 Q4

⑬ budget

⑭ to get into debt

⑮ to make a profit

⑯ to take a loss (US) to make a loss (UK)

⑰ to break even

⑱ to go out of business

㉔ I can advise you where to invest your money.

㉓ financial advisor

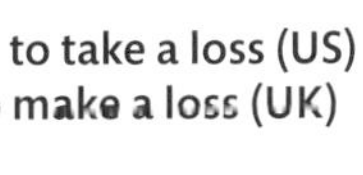

STATEMENT
BALANCE
-600.50
OVERDRAFT LIMIT
500

⑲ overdraft

⑳ expenditure / outlay

㉑ economic downturn

㉒ accountant

95 Meeting and presenting

95.1 MEETING

② What's on the agenda today, Maria?

③ We're discussing the presentations for next week.

① to attend a meeting

④ to have a conference call

⑤ to take minutes

⑥ to take questions

⑦ to be absent

⑧ to interrupt

⑨ to reach a consensus

⑩ unanimous vote

⑪ action points

⑫ show of hands

⑬ any other business

⑭ boardroom

⑮ board of directors

⑯ to reach an agreement

⑰ annual general meeting (AGM)

⑱ to wrap up the meeting

⑲ whiteboard

⑳ notebook

AGENDA

㉑ agenda

See also:
81 At work 82 In the office
83 Computers and technology 84 Media

95.2 PRESENTING

① to commence

② to sum up

③ to run out of time

④ slide

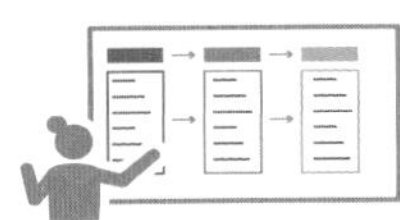

⑤ roadmap

⑥ to give a presentation

⑦ projector

⑧ timer

⑨ HDMI cable

⑩ portable speakers

⑪ handouts

⑫ notes

⑬ smartpen

⑭ microphone

⑮ headphones

⑯ flip chart

⑰ to share your screen

⑱ presenter remote

⑲ conference

⑳ guest speaker

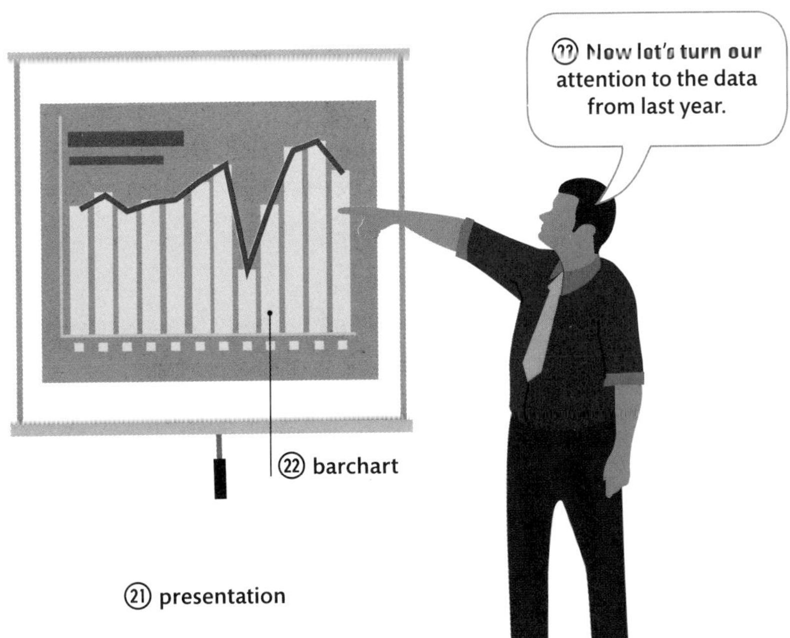
㉓ Now let's turn our attention to the data from last year.
㉒ barchart
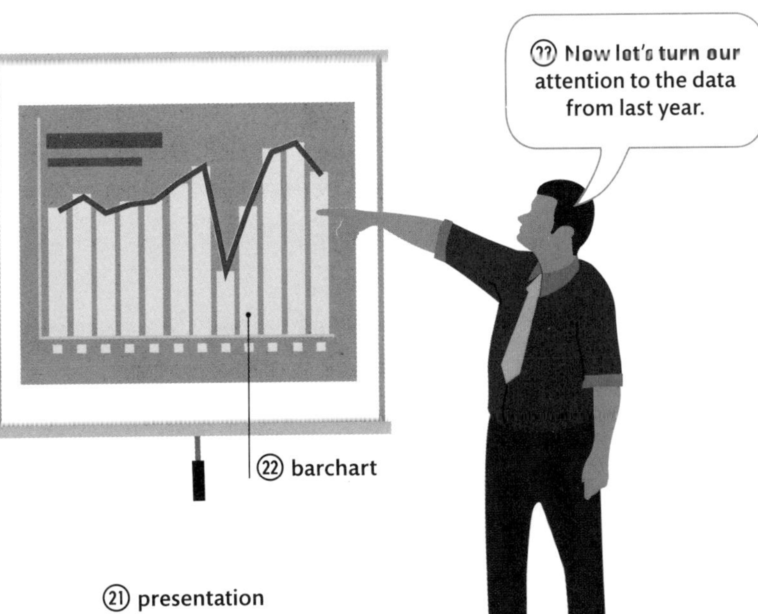

㉑ presentation

96 Roads

96.1 ON THE ROAD

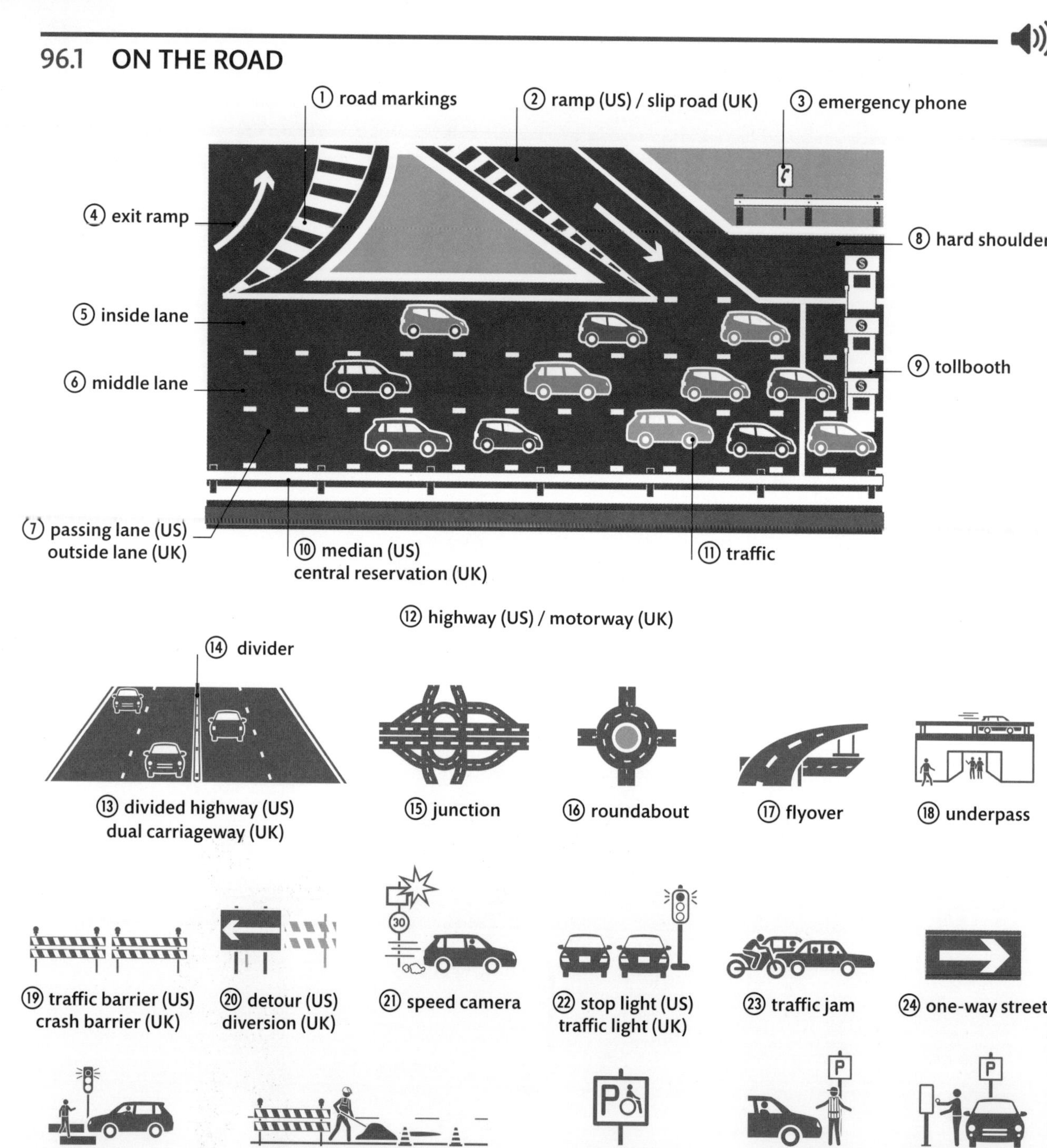

① road markings
② ramp (US) / slip road (UK)
③ emergency phone
④ exit ramp
⑤ inside lane
⑥ middle lane
⑦ passing lane (US)
outside lane (UK)
⑧ hard shoulder
⑨ tollbooth
⑩ median (US)
central reservation (UK)
⑪ traffic
⑫ highway (US) / motorway (UK)
⑭ divider
⑬ divided highway (US)
dual carriageway (UK)
⑮ junction
⑯ roundabout
⑰ flyover
⑱ underpass
30
P
⑲ traffic barrier (US)
crash barrier (UK)
⑳ detour (US)
diversion (UK)
㉑ speed camera
㉒ stop light (US)
traffic light (UK)
㉓ traffic jam
㉔ one-way street
㉕ pedestrian
crossing
㉖ road construction (US)
roadworks (UK)
㉗ disabled
parking
㉘ parking
attendant
㉙ parking meter

See also:
42-43 In town 97-98 Cars 99 Cars and buses 100 Motorcycles
101 Cycling 123 Motorsports 148 Maps and directions

96.2 ROAD SIGNS

① no entry

30
② speed limit

③ hazard

④ no right turn

⑤ no U-turn

⑥ right bend

⑦ yield (US)
give way (UK)

⑧ right of way (US)
priority traffic (UK)

⑨ no passing (US)
no overtaking (UK)

⑩ school zone

⑪ bumps

⑫ deer crossing

⑬ direction to
follow

⑭ construction ahead (US)
roadworks ahead (UK)

⑮ stop light (US) /
traffic light (UK)
ahead

⑯ closed to
bicycles

⑰ closed to
pedestrians

96.3 VERBS FOR DRIVING

① to drive

② to reverse

③ to stop

⑤ parking enforcement officer (US)
traffic warden (UK)

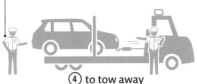

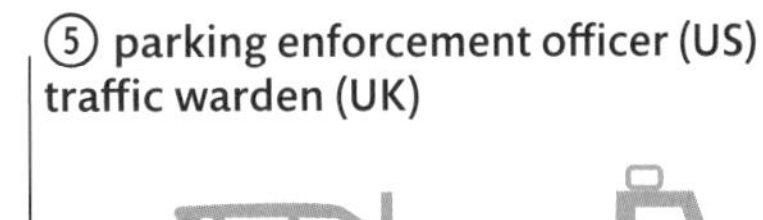
④ to tow away

⑥ to turn left

⑦ to turn right

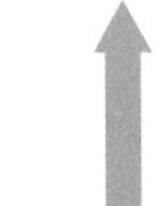
⑧ to go straight ahead /
to go straight on (UK)

⑨ to take the
first left

⑩ to take the
second right

97 Cars

97.1 CAR EXTERIOR

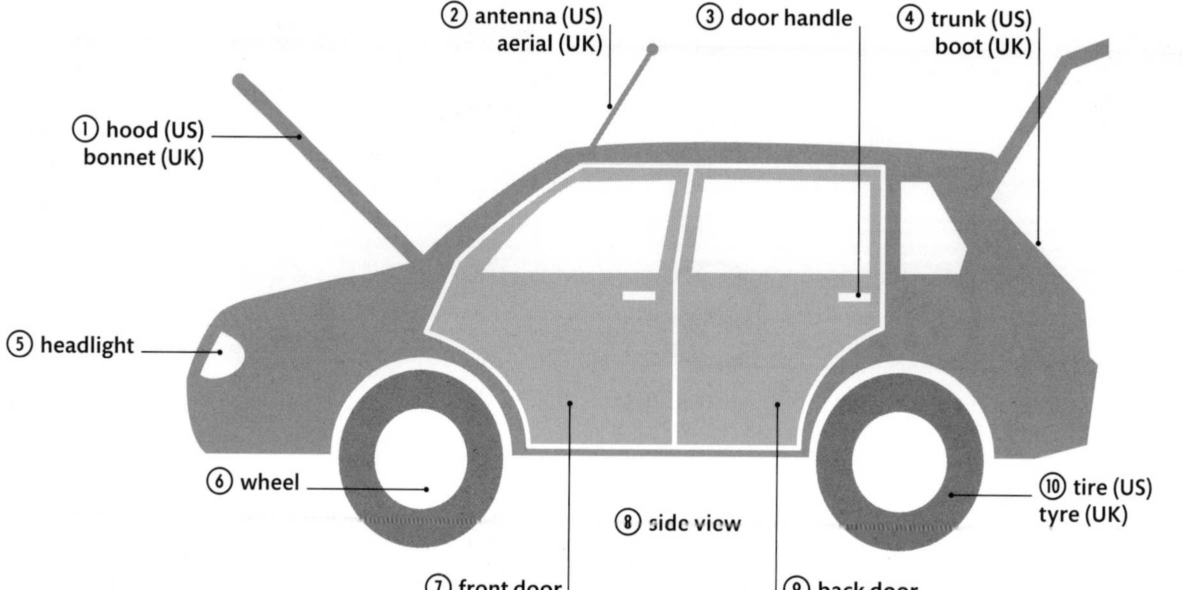

① hood (US)
bonnet (UK)
② antenna (US)
aerial (UK)
③ door handle
④ trunk (US)
boot (UK)
⑤ headlight
⑥ wheel
⑦ front door
⑧ side view
⑨ back door
⑩ tire (US)
tyre (UK)

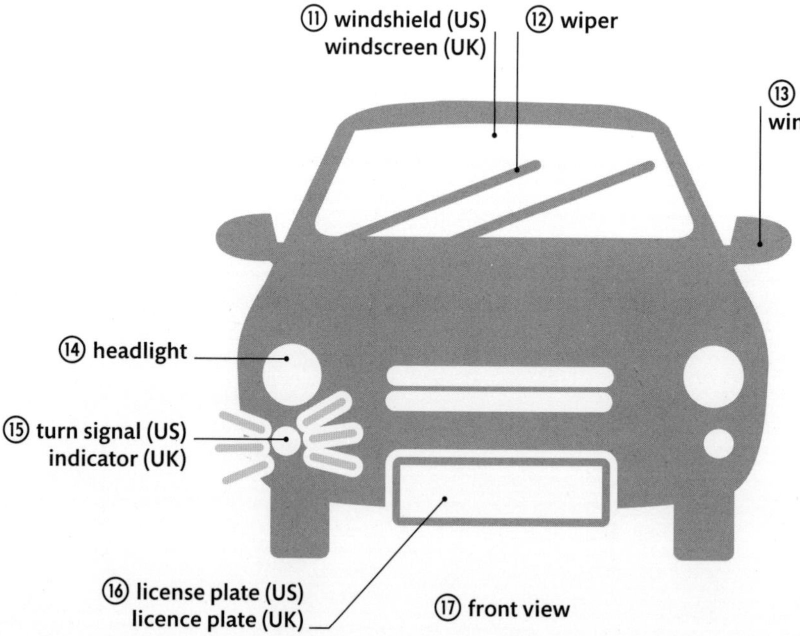

⑪ windshield (US)
windscreen (UK)

⑫ wiper

⑬ side-view mirror (US)
wing mirror (UK)

⑭ headlight

⑮ turn signal (US)
indicator (UK)

⑯ license plate (US)
licence plate (UK)

⑰ front view

⑱ bumper

⑲ snow tires (US)
snow tyres (UK)

⑳ roof rack

㉑ tailgate

See also:
42-43 In town 96 Roads 98 Cars (continued)
99 Cars and buses 100 Motorcycles 123 Motorsports

97.2 TYPES OF CARS

① electric car

② hybrid

③ plug-in hybrid

④ hatchback

⑤ sedan (US)
saloon (UK)

⑥ station wagon (US)
estate (UK)

⑦ four-wheel drive

⑧ minivan (US)
people carrier (UK)

⑨ limousine

⑪ spoiler
⑩ sports car

⑫ convertible

⑬ vintage

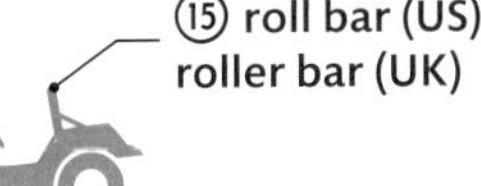
⑮ roll bar (US)
roller bar (UK)
⑭ dune buggy (US)
beach buggy (UK)

⑱ rear wing
⑰ front wing
⑯ race car (US)
racing car (UK)

97.3 GAS STATION (US) / PETROL STATION (UK)

① gas pump (US)
petrol pump (UK)

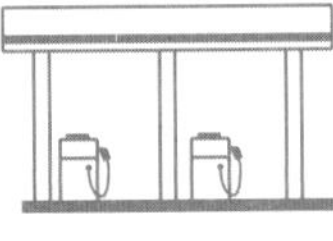
② canopy (US)
forecourt (UK)

③ EV charging station (US)
electric charge point (UK)

④ washer fluid (US)
screen wash (UK)

⑤ antifreeze

⑥ gasoline (US)
petrol (UK)

⑦ unleaded

Pb
⑧ leaded

D
⑨ diesel

⑩ oil

⑪ car wash

98 Cars continued

98.1 BREAKDOWN ASSISTANCE

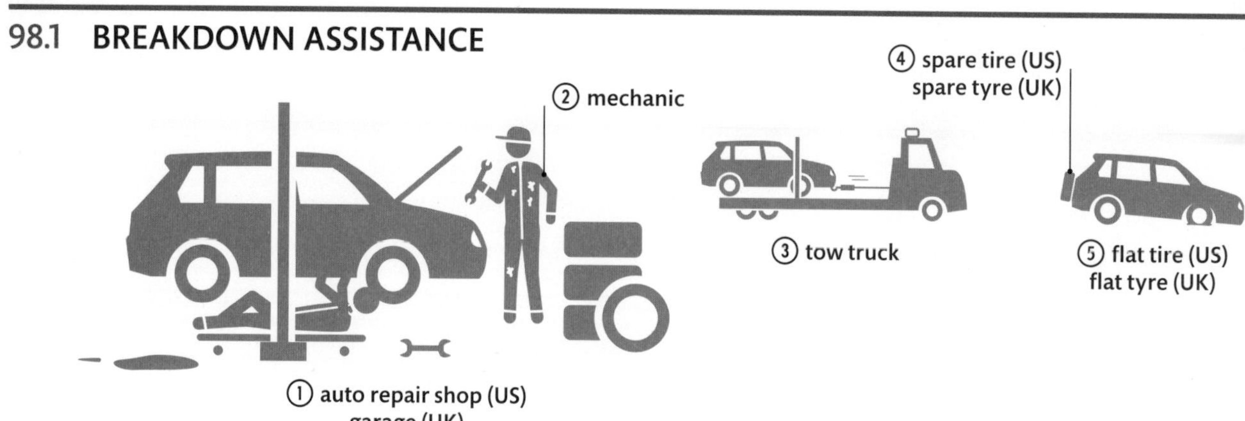

① auto repair shop (US)
garage (UK)
② mechanic
③ tow truck
④ spare tire (US)
spare tyre (UK)
⑤ flat tire (US)
flat tyre (UK)

98.2 MECHANICS

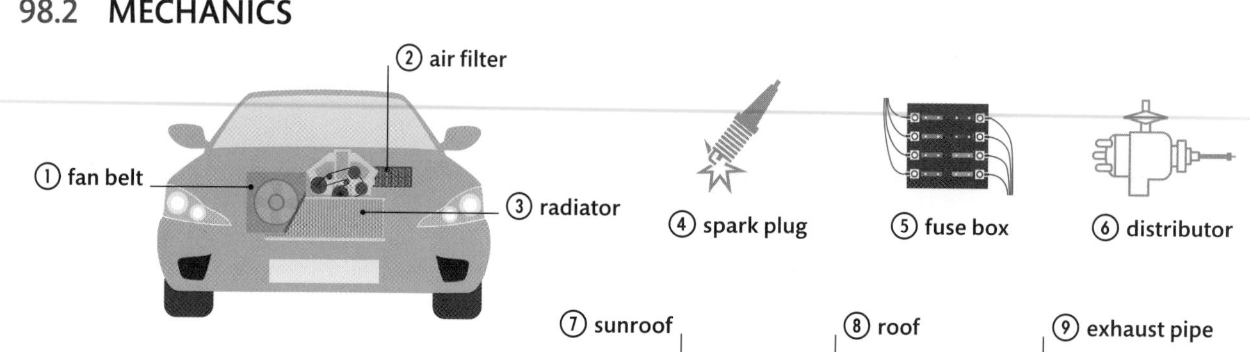

① fan belt
② air filter
③ radiator
④ spark plug
⑤ fuse box
⑥ distributor
⑦ sunroof 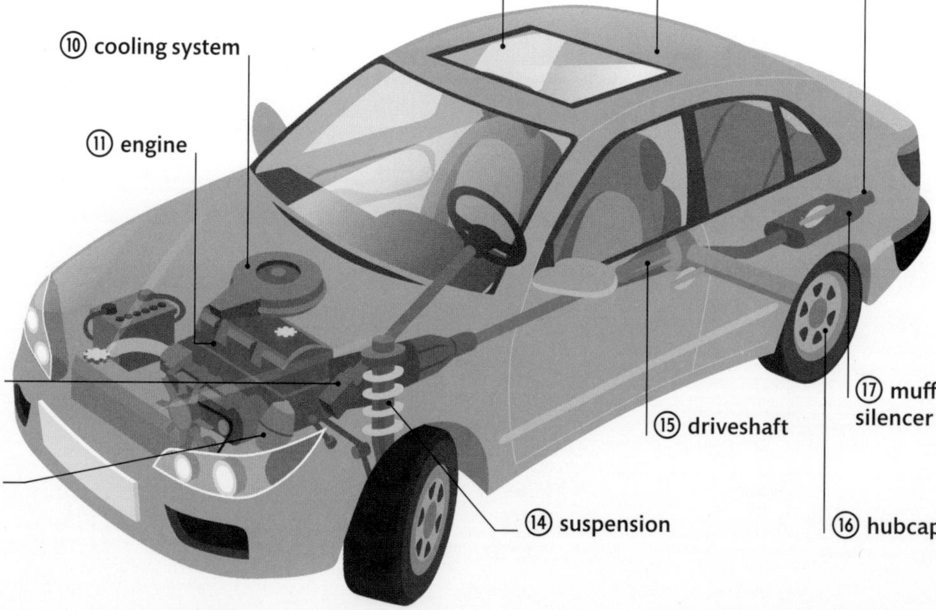
⑧ roof
⑨ exhaust pipe
⑩ cooling system
⑪ engine
⑫ gearbox
⑬ transmission
⑭ suspension
⑮ driveshaft
⑯ hubcap
⑰ muffler (US)
silencer (UK)

See also:
42-43 In town **96** Roads **99** Cars and buses
100 Motorcycles **123** Motorsports

⑥ wrench

⑦ lug nuts (US)
wheel nuts (UK)

⑧ jack

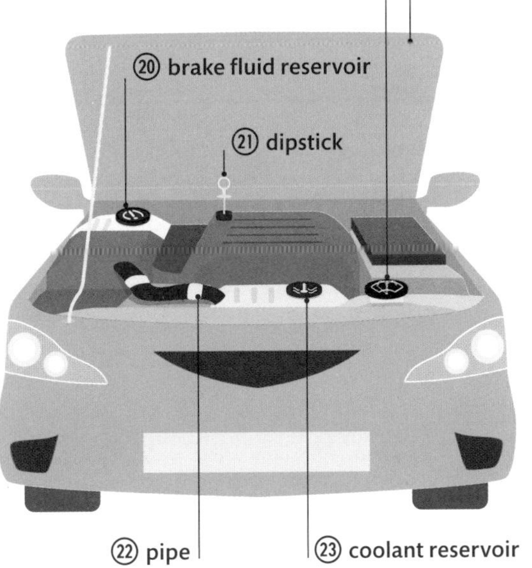
⑱ washer fluid reservoir (US)
screen wash reservoir (UK)
⑲ hood (US)
bonnet (UK)
⑳ brake fluid reservoir
㉑ dipstick
㉒ pipe
㉓ coolant reservoir

㉔ battery

㉕ bodywork

㉖ cylinder head

98.3 VERBS FOR DRIVING

① to fill up

② to check the oil

③ to check the tires (US) / to check the tyres (UK)

④ to service the car

P
⑤ to park

P
⑥ to take off (US)
to set off (UK)

⑦ to signal (US)
to indicate (UK)

⑧ to brake

40
30
⑨ to slow down

⑩ to speed up

⑪ to pick someone up

⑫ to drop someone off

⑬ to have a car accident

⑭ to break down

⑮ to pass (US)
to overtake (UK)

99 Cars and buses

99.1 CAR INTERIOR

99.2 DASHBOARD AND CONTROLS

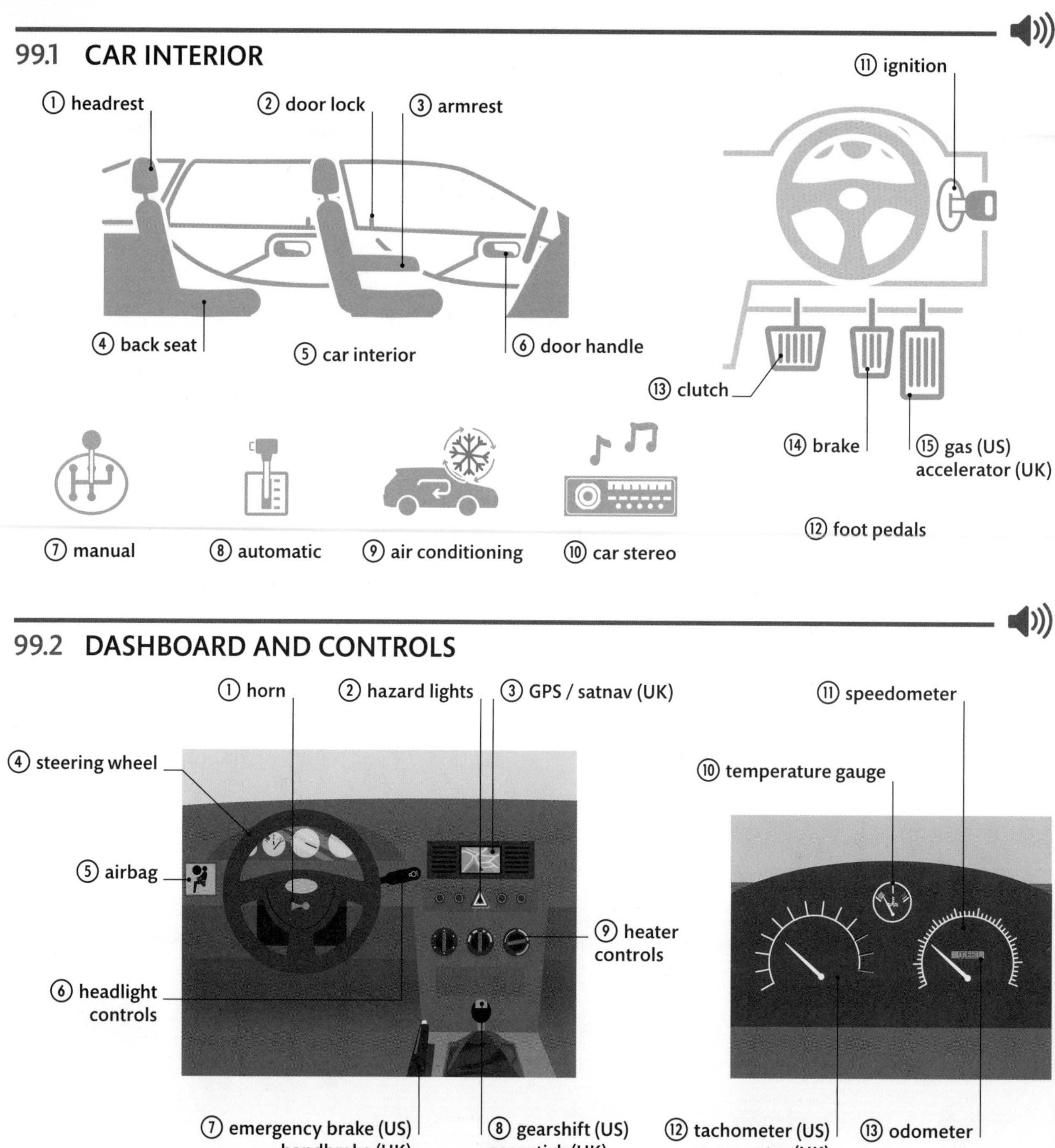

1 headrest
2 door lock
3 armrest
4 back seat
5 car interior
6 door handle
7 manual
8 automatic
9 air conditioning
10 car stereo
11 ignition
12 foot pedals
13 clutch
14 brake
15 gas (US) accelerator (UK)
1 horn
2 hazard lights
3 GPS / satnav (UK)
4 steering wheel
5 airbag
6 headlight controls
7 emergency brake (US) handbrake (UK)
8 gearshift (US) gear stick (UK)
9 heater controls
10 temperature gauge
11 speedometer
12 tachometer (US) rev counter (UK)
13 odometer

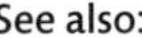

See also:
42-43 In town 96 Roads 97-98 Cars
100 Motorcycles 123 Motorsports

99.3 BUS

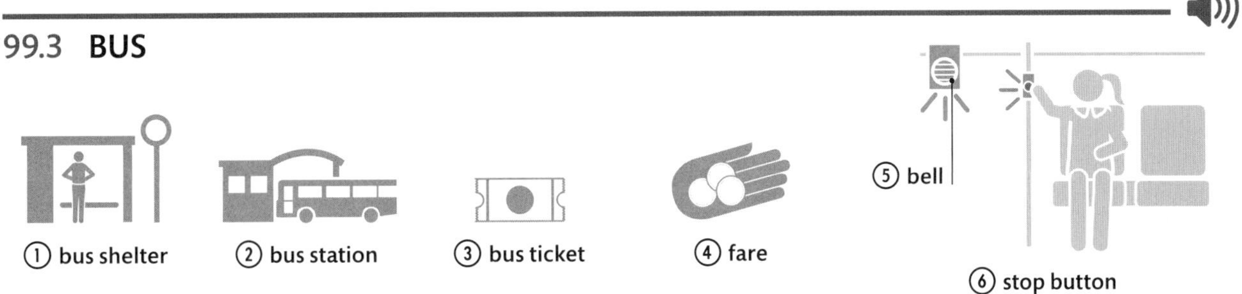
① bus shelter
② bus station
③ bus ticket
④ fare
⑤ bell
⑥ stop button

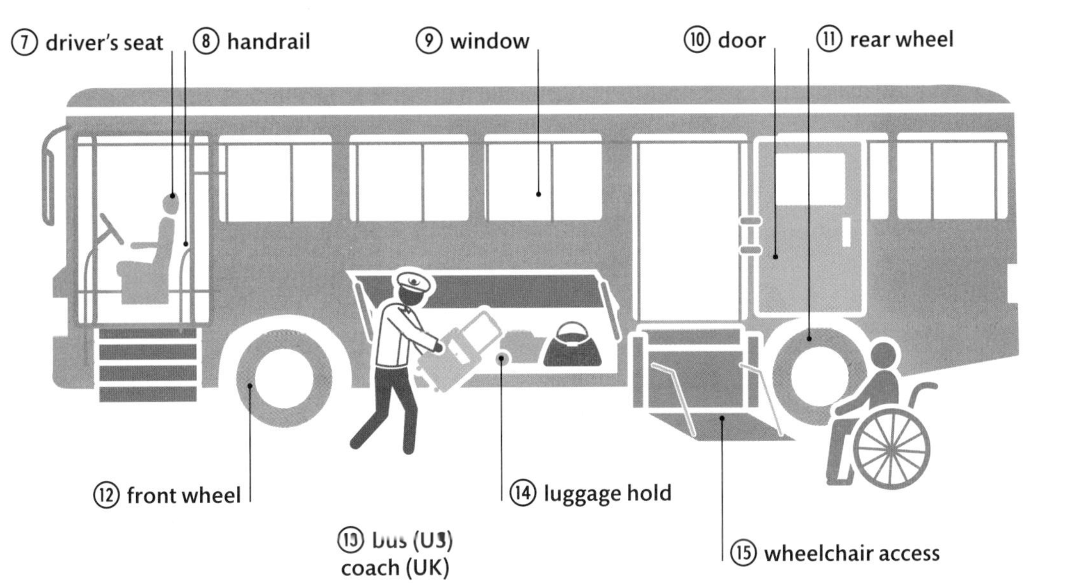
⑦ driver's seat
⑧ handrail
⑨ window
⑩ door
⑪ rear wheel
⑫ front wheel
⑭ luggage hold
⑬ bus (US)
coach (UK)
⑮ wheelchair access

99.4 TYPES OF BUSES

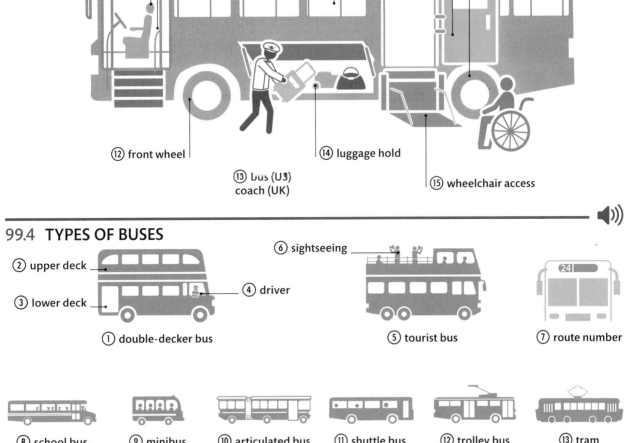

② upper deck
③ lower deck 
④ driver
① double-decker bus

⑥ sightseeing 
⑤ tourist bus

24
⑦ route number

⑧ school bus
⑨ minibus 
⑩ articulated bus 
⑪ shuttle bus 
⑫ trolley bus 
⑬ tram

100 Motorcycles

100.1 MOTORCYCLE (US) / MOTORBIKE (UK)

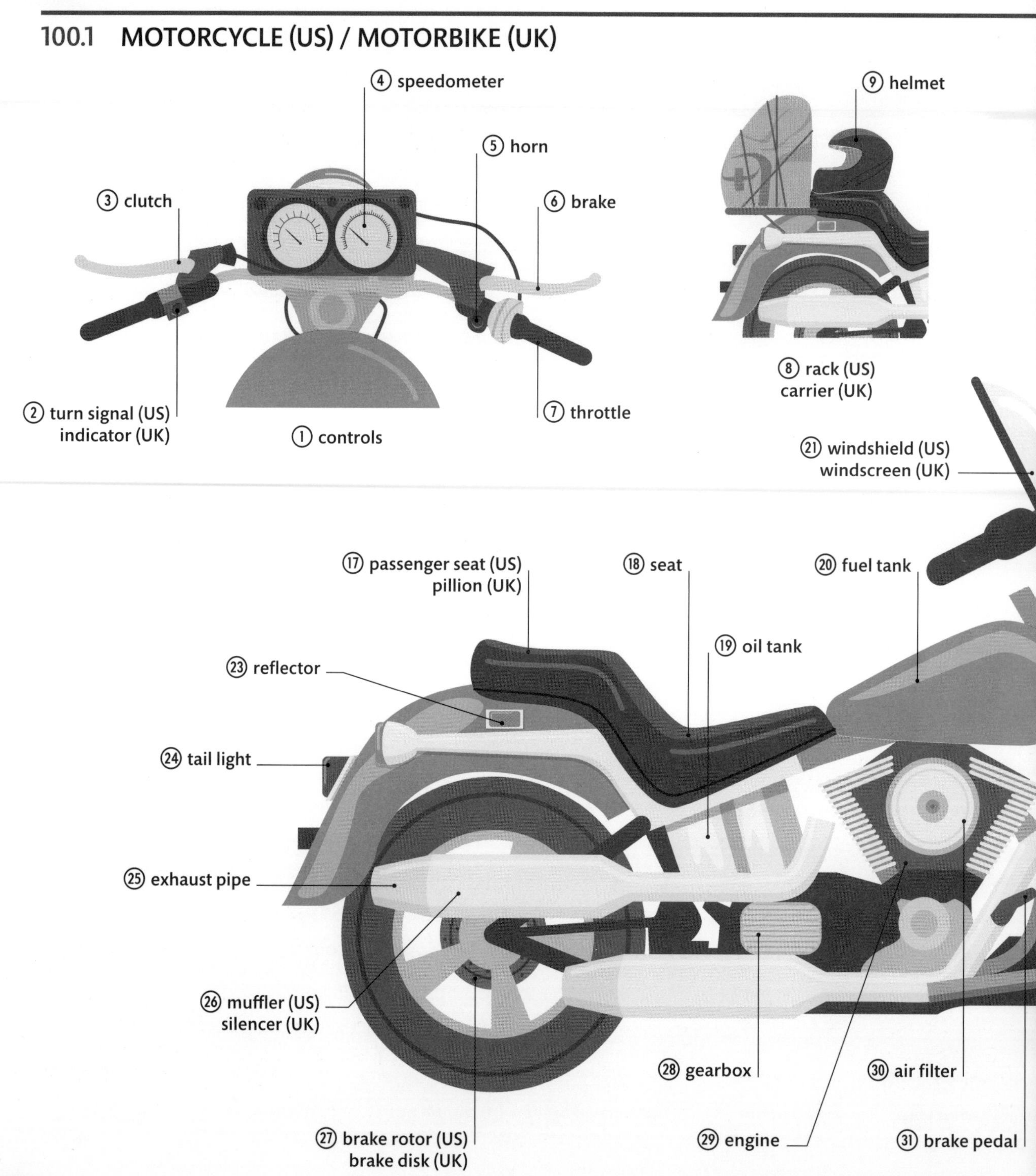

④ speedometer
⑨ helmet
⑤ horn
③ clutch
⑥ brake
⑧ rack (US)
carrier (UK)
② turn signal (US)
indicator (UK)
① controls
⑦ throttle
㉑ windshield (US)
windscreen (UK)
⑰ passenger seat (US)
pillion (UK)
⑱ seat
⑳ fuel tank
⑲ oil tank
㉓ reflector
㉔ tail light
㉕ exhaust pipe
㉖ muffler (US)
silencer (UK)
㉘ gearbox
㉚ air filter
㉗ brake rotor (US)
brake disk (UK)
㉙ engine
㉛ brake pedal

See also:
42-43 In town 96 Roads
97-98 Cars 112 Motorsports

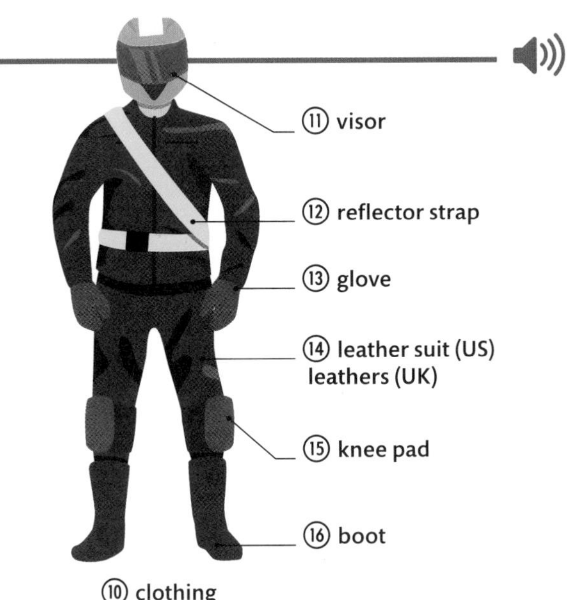
⑪ visor
⑫ reflector strap
⑬ glove
⑭ leather suit (US)
leathers (UK)
⑮ knee pad
⑯ boot
⑩ clothing
㉒ headlight

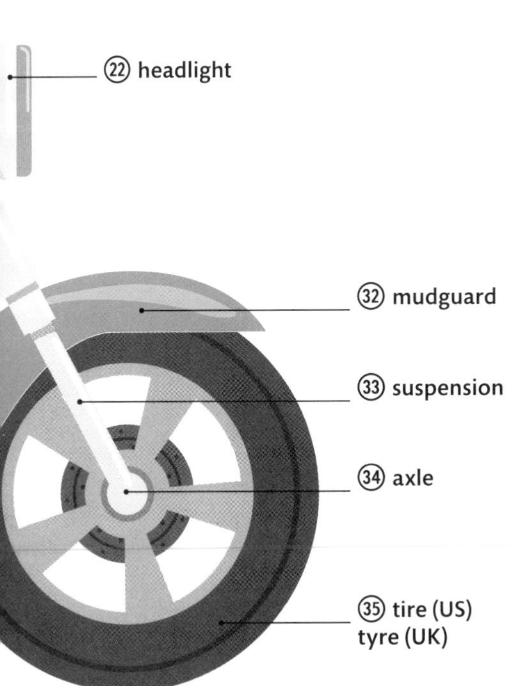
㉜ mudguard
㉝ suspension
㉞ axle
㉟ tire (US)
tyre (UK)

100.2 TYPES OF MOTORCYCLES

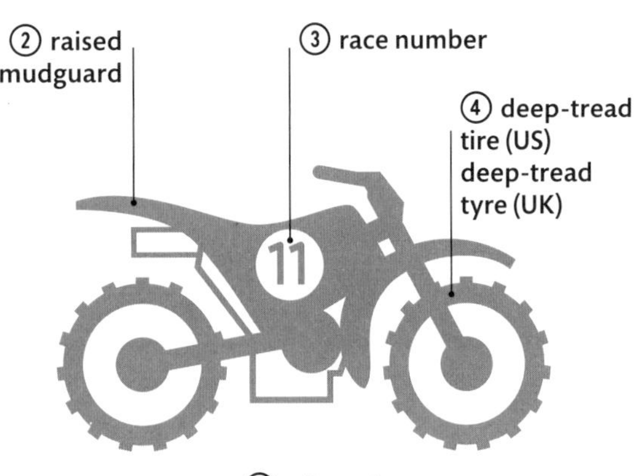
② raised mudguard
③ race number
④ deep-tread tire (US)
deep-tread tyre (UK)
11

① off-road motorcycle

⑤ racing bike

⑥ tourer

⑦ all-terrain vehicle / quad bike

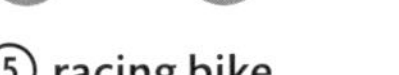

⑧ side car

⑨ electric motorcycle

⑩ electric scooter

⑪ three-wheeler

⑫ motor scooter

⑬ rider

⑭ to ride passenger (US)
to ride pillion (UK)

⑮ to get on / mount

⑯ to get off / dismount

101 Cycling

101.1 BICYCLE

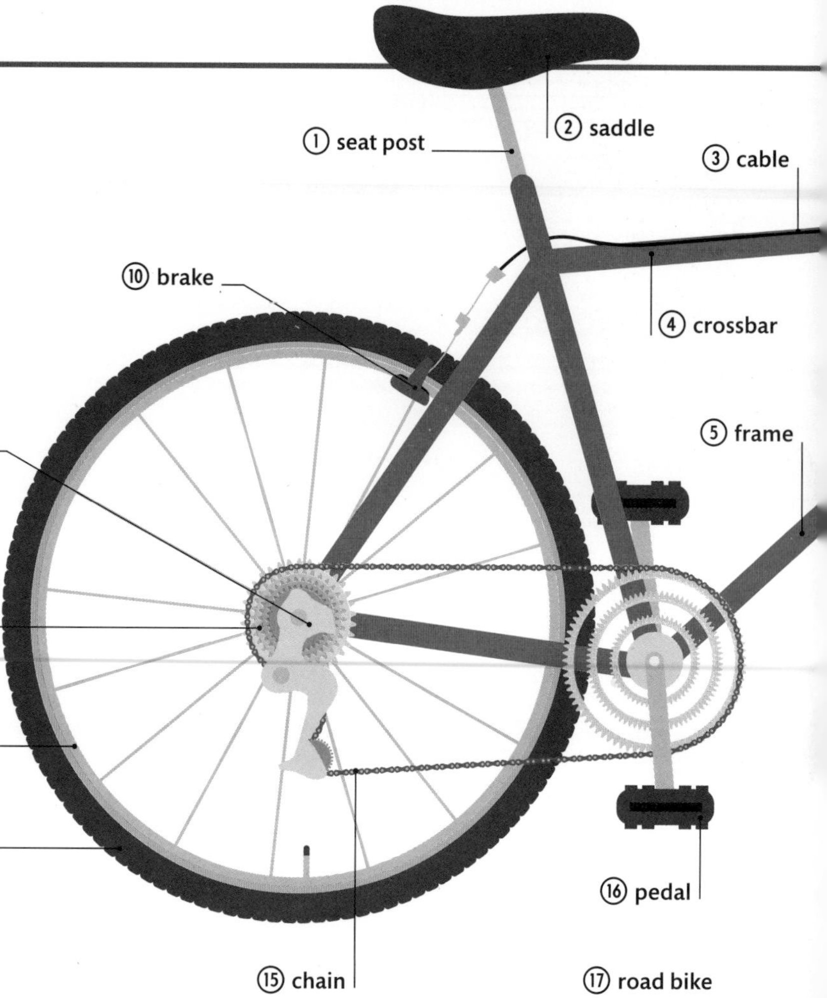

① seat post
② saddle
③ cable
④ crossbar
⑤ frame
⑩ brake
⑪ hub
⑫ gears
⑬ rim
⑭ tire (US)
tyre (UK)
⑮ chain
⑯ pedal
⑰ road bike

㉔ racing bike

㉕ touring bike

㉖ mountain bike

㉗ electric bike

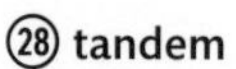
㉘ tandem

㉙ basket

㉚ child seat

㉛ kickstand

㉜ brake pad

㉝ training wheels (U
stabilizers (UK)

㉞ unicycle

㉟ toe clip

㊱ toe strap

㊲ lamp

㊳ rear light

㊴ inner tube

See also:
42-43 In town 96 Roads
100 Motorcycles 133 Outdoor activities

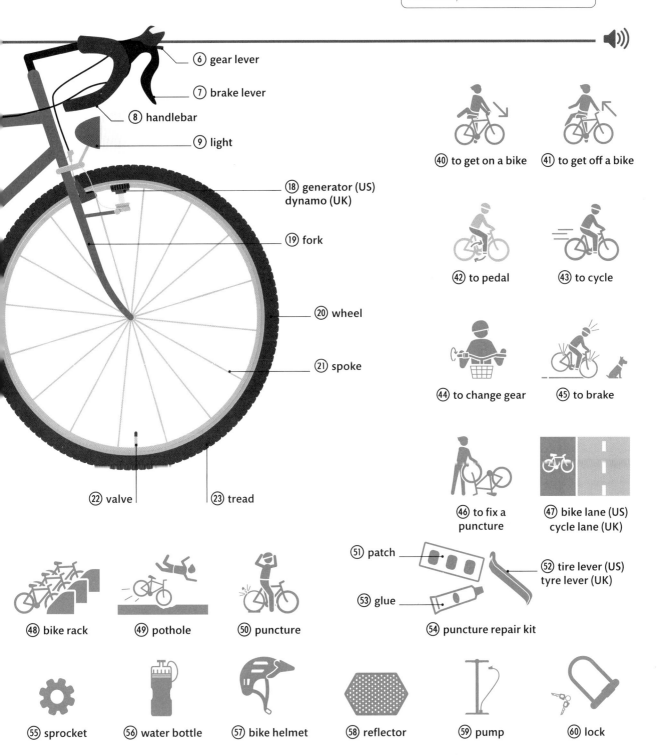

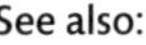

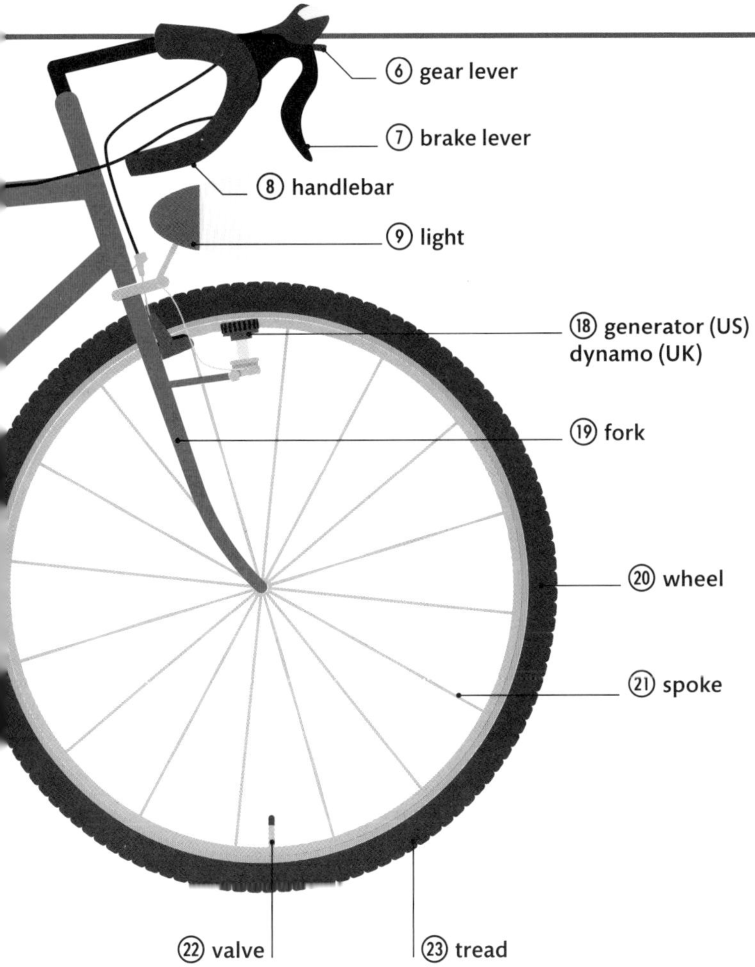

⑥ gear lever

⑦ brake lever

⑧ handlebar

⑨ light

⑱ generator (US) dynamo (UK)

⑲ fork

⑳ wheel

㉑ spoke

㉒ valve

㉓ tread

㊵ to get on a bike

㊶ to get off a bike

㊷ to pedal

㊸ to cycle

㊹ to change gear

㊺ to brake

㊻ to fix a puncture

㊼ bike lane (US) cycle lane (UK)

㊽ bike rack

㊾ pothole

㊿ puncture

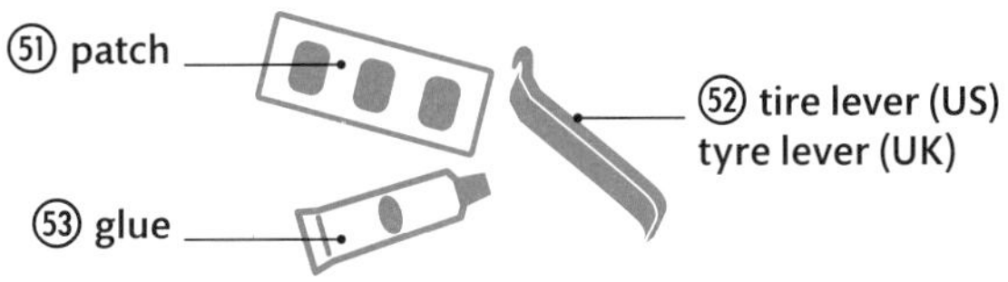

51 patch

52 tire lever (US) tyre lever (UK)

53 glue

54 puncture repair kit

55 sprocket

56 water bottle

57 bike helmet

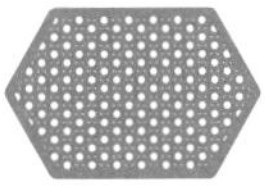

58 reflector

59 pump

60 lock

102 Trains

102.1 TRAIN STATION

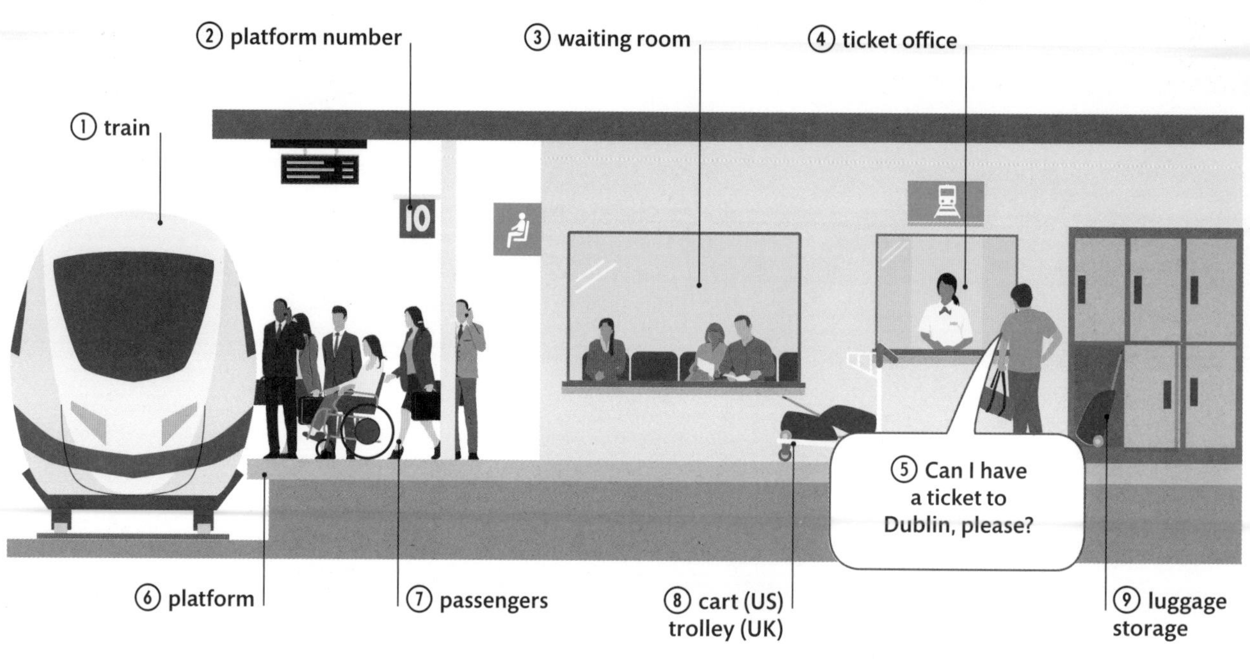

① train
② platform number
③ waiting room
④ ticket office
10
⑤ Can I have a ticket to Dublin, please?
⑥ platform
⑦ passengers
⑧ cart (US) trolley (UK)
⑨ luggage storage

⑩ lost property office

⑪ ticket

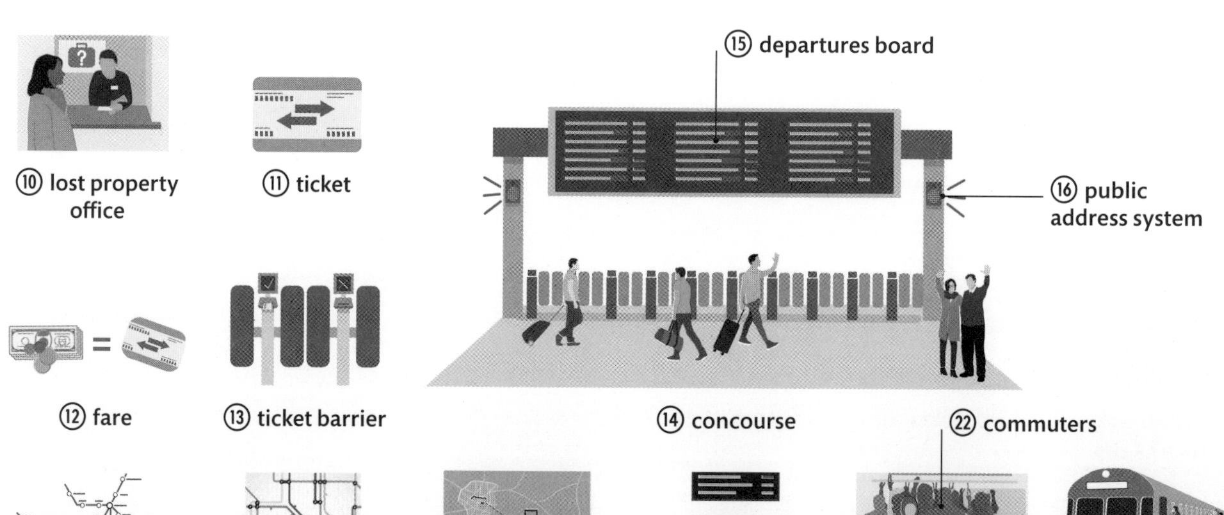

⑮ departures board
⑯ public address system

⑫ fare

⑬ ticket barrier

⑭ concourse

⑰ rail network

⑱ subway map (US) underground map (UK)

⑲ intercity train

⑳ delay

㉑ rush hour

㉒ commuters

㉓ to catch a train

See also:
42-43 In town
131 Travel and accommodation

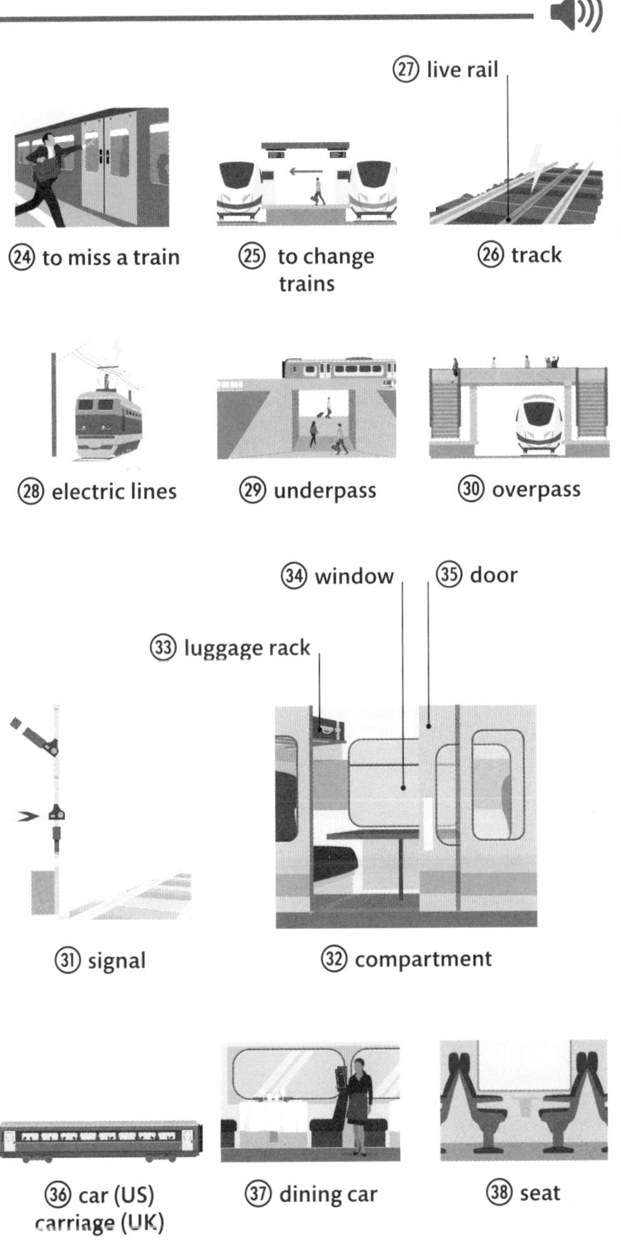
㉗ live rail
㉔ to miss a train
㉕ to change trains
㉖ track
㉘ electric lines
㉙ underpass
㉚ overpass
㉞ window
㉟ door
㉝ luggage rack
㉛ signal
㉜ compartment
㊱ car (US) carriage (UK)
㊲ dining car
㊳ seat
㊴ sleeping compartment
㊵ conductor (US) ticket inspector (UK)
㊶ emergency signal (US) emergency lever (UK)

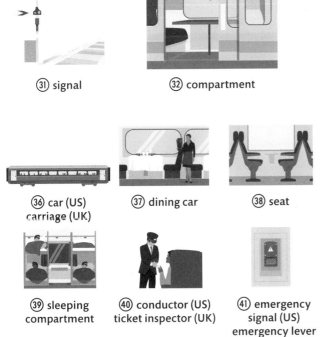

102.2 TYPES OF TRAINS

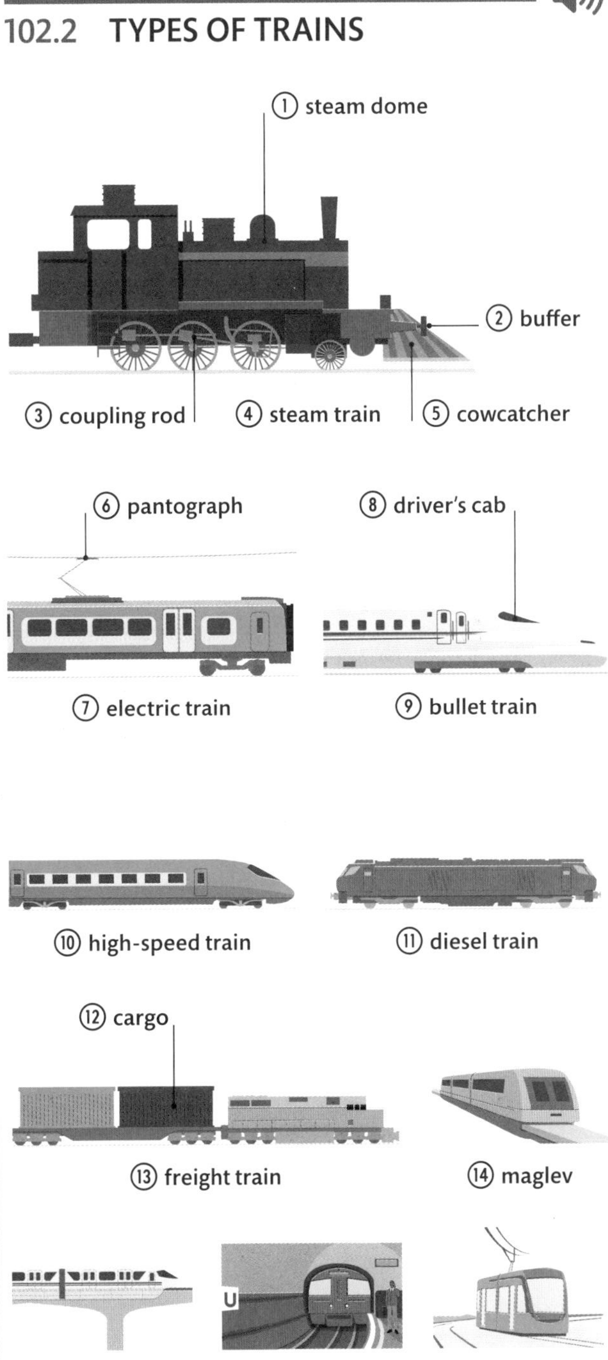
① steam dome
② buffer
③ coupling rod
④ steam train
⑤ cowcatcher
⑥ pantograph
⑧ driver's cab
⑦ electric train
⑨ bullet train
⑩ high-speed train
⑪ diesel train
⑫ cargo
⑬ freight train
⑭ maglev
⑮ monorail
⑯ subway train (US) underground train (UK)
⑰ tram

103 Aircraft

103.1 PASSENGER AIRPLANE (US) / AEROPLANE (UK)

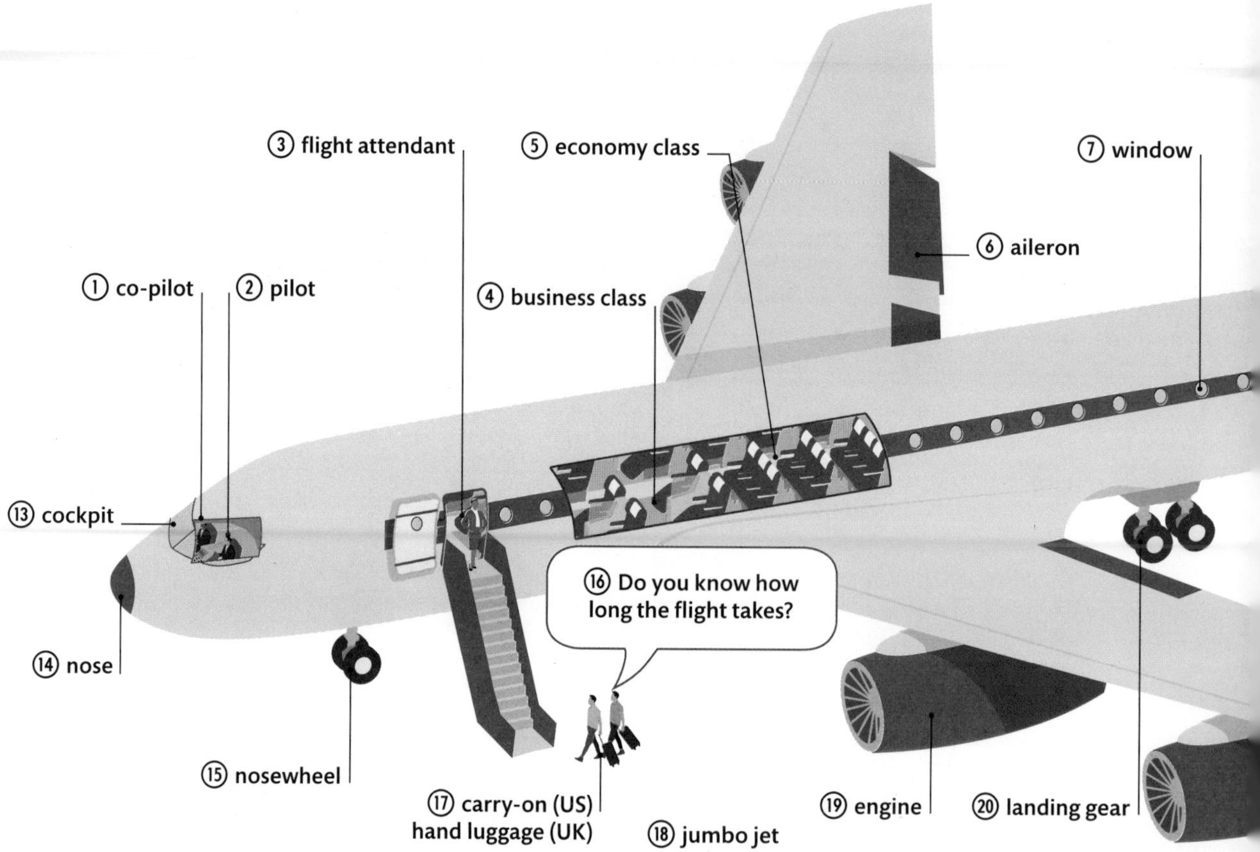

① co-pilot
② pilot
③ flight attendant
④ business class
⑤ economy class
⑥ aileron
⑦ window
⑬ cockpit
⑭ nose
⑮ nosewheel
⑯ Do you know how long the flight takes?
⑰ carry-on (US) hand luggage (UK)
⑱ jumbo jet
⑲ engine
⑳ landing gear

103.3 TYPES OF AIRCRAFT

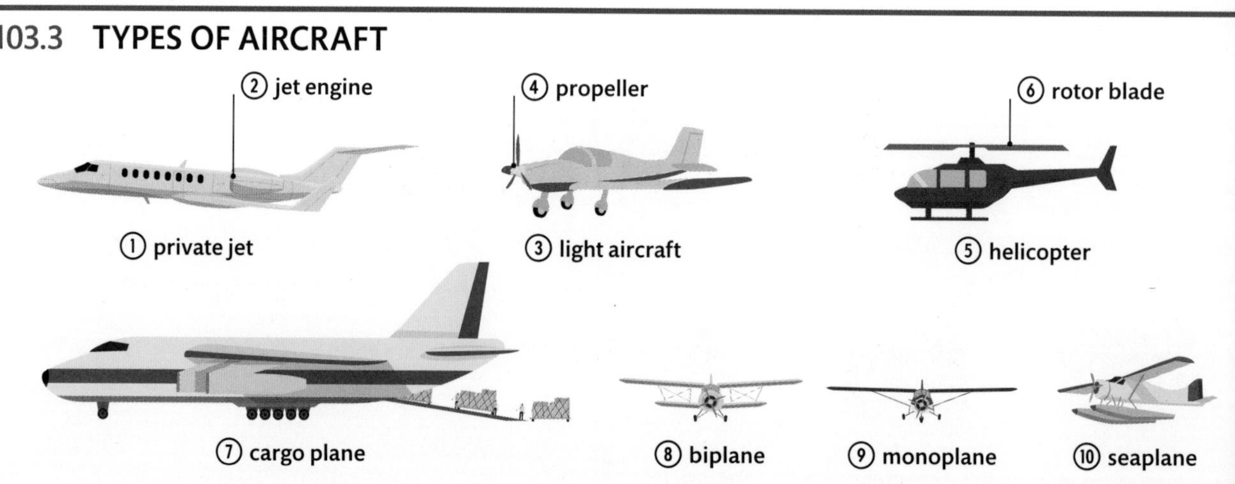

② jet engine
① private jet
④ propeller
③ light aircraft
⑥ rotor blade
⑤ helicopter
⑦ cargo plane
⑧ biplane
⑨ monoplane
⑩ seaplane

See also:
42-43 In town 104 At the airport
131 Travel and accommodation

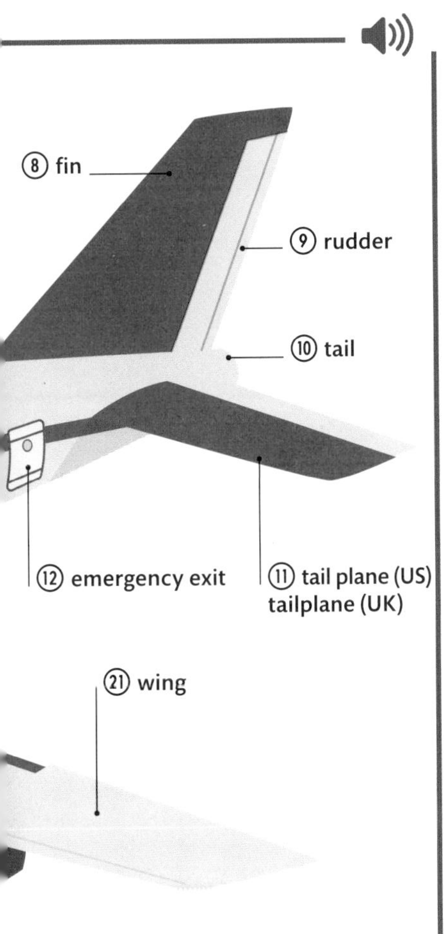
⑧ fin
⑨ rudder
⑩ tail
⑫ emergency exit
⑪ tail plane (US)
tailplane (UK)
㉑ wing

103.2 CABIN

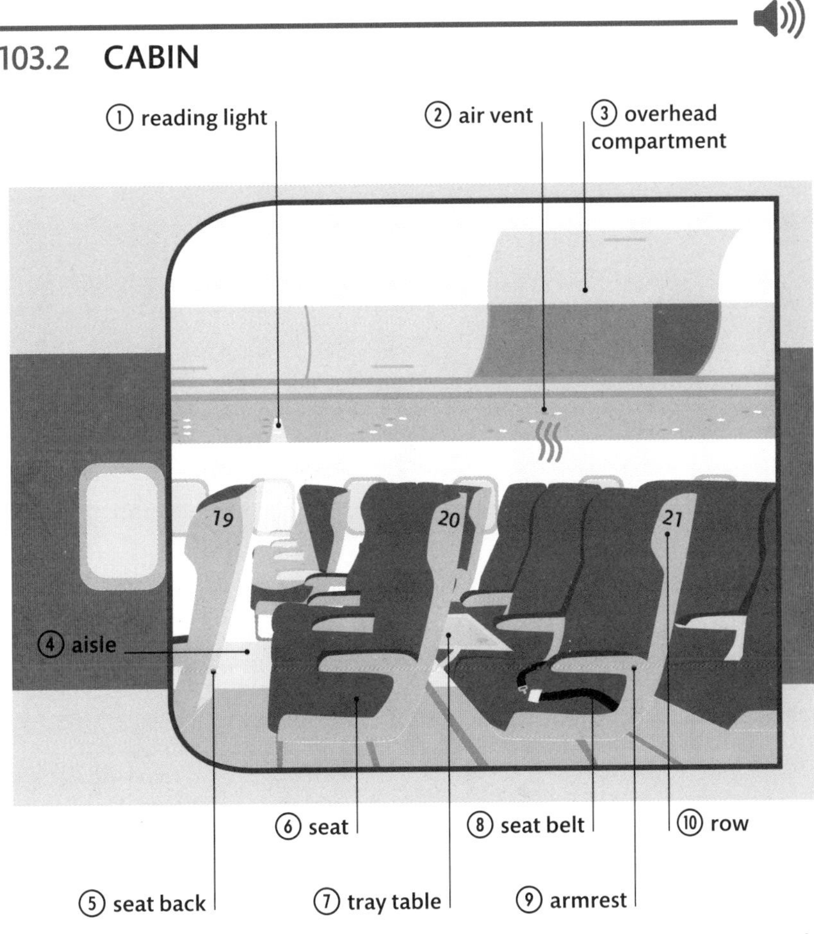
① reading light
② air vent
③ overhead compartment
④ aisle
19
20
21
⑤ seat back
⑥ seat
⑦ tray table
⑧ seat belt
⑨ armrest
⑩ row

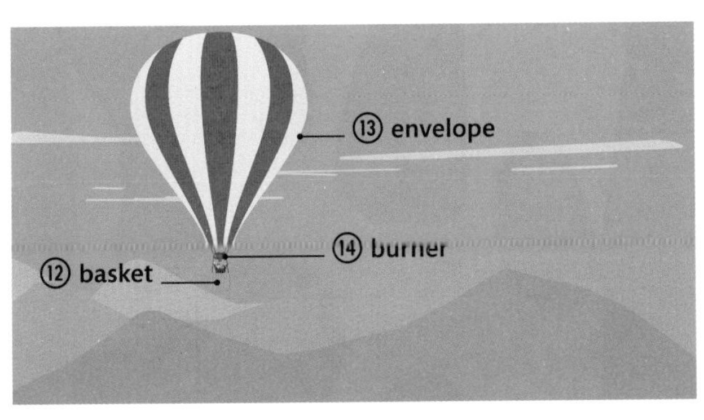
⑬ envelope
⑭ burner
⑫ basket

⑪ hot-air balloon

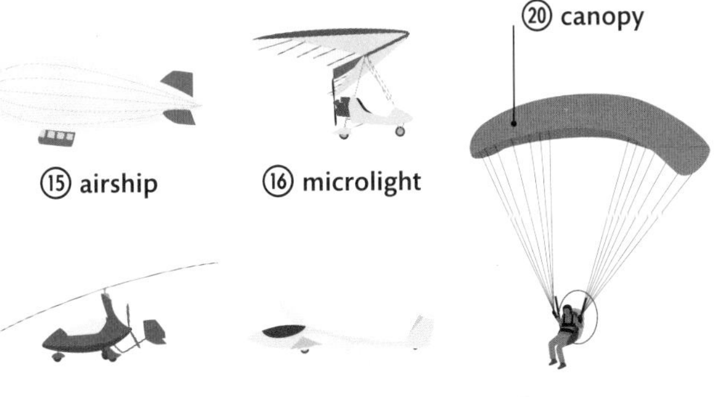
⑮ airship
⑯ microlight
⑳ canopy
⑰ gyrocopter
⑱ glider
⑲ paramotor

104 At the airport

104.1 AT THE TERMINAL

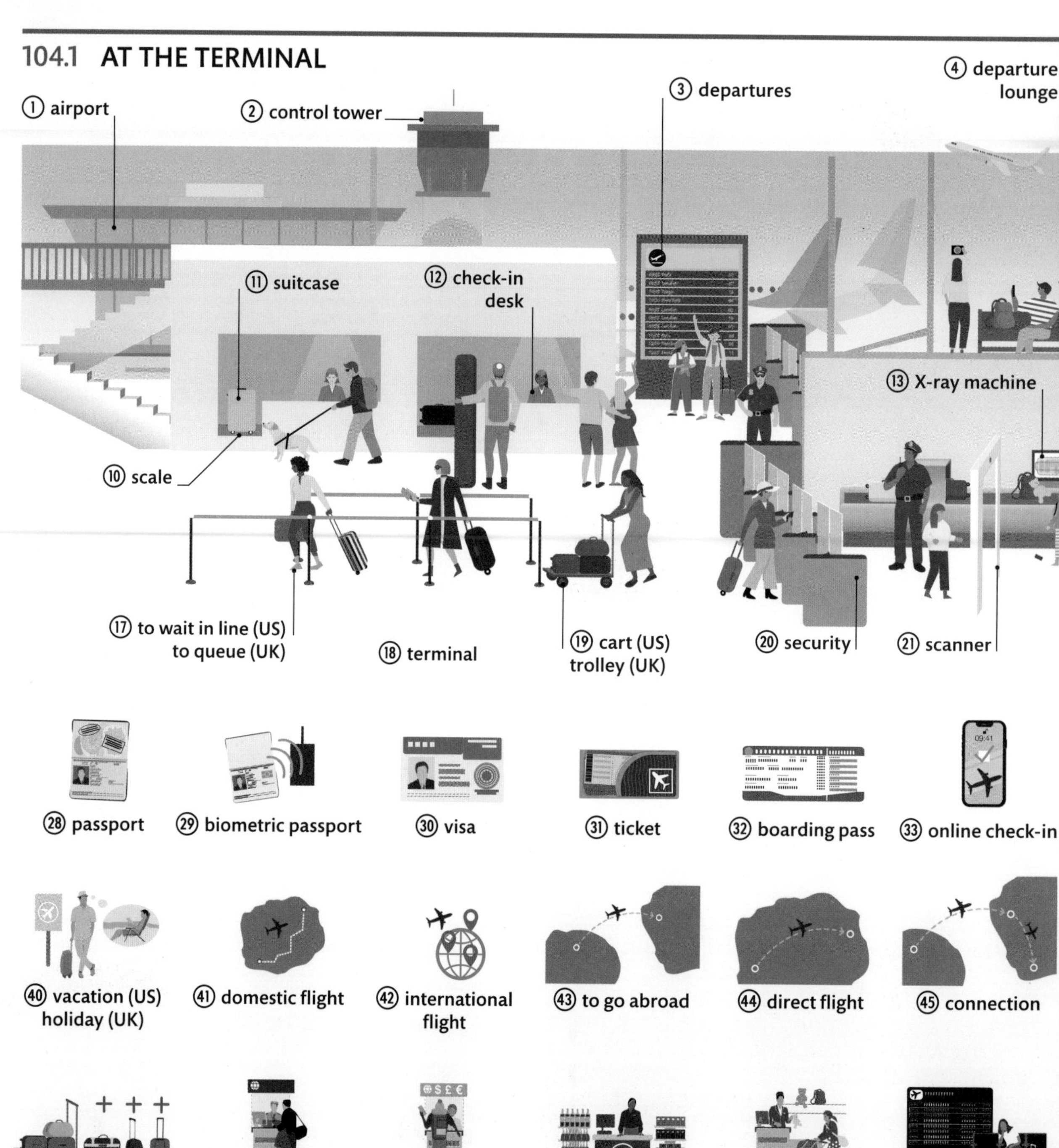

① airport
② control tower
③ departures
④ departure lounge
⑪ suitcase
⑫ check-in desk
⑬ X-ray machine
⑩ scale
⑰ to wait in line (US) to queue (UK)
⑱ terminal
⑲ cart (US) trolley (UK)
⑳ security
㉑ scanner
㉘ passport
㉙ biometric passport
㉚ visa
㉛ ticket
㉜ boarding pass
㉝ online check-in
㊵ vacation (US) holiday (UK)
㊶ domestic flight
㊷ international flight
㊸ to go abroad
㊹ direct flight
㊺ connection
51 excess baggage
52 passport control
53 currency exchange
54 duty-free shop
55 lost and found
56 to be delayed

See also:
103 Aircraft 131 Travel and accommodation
149-151 Countries

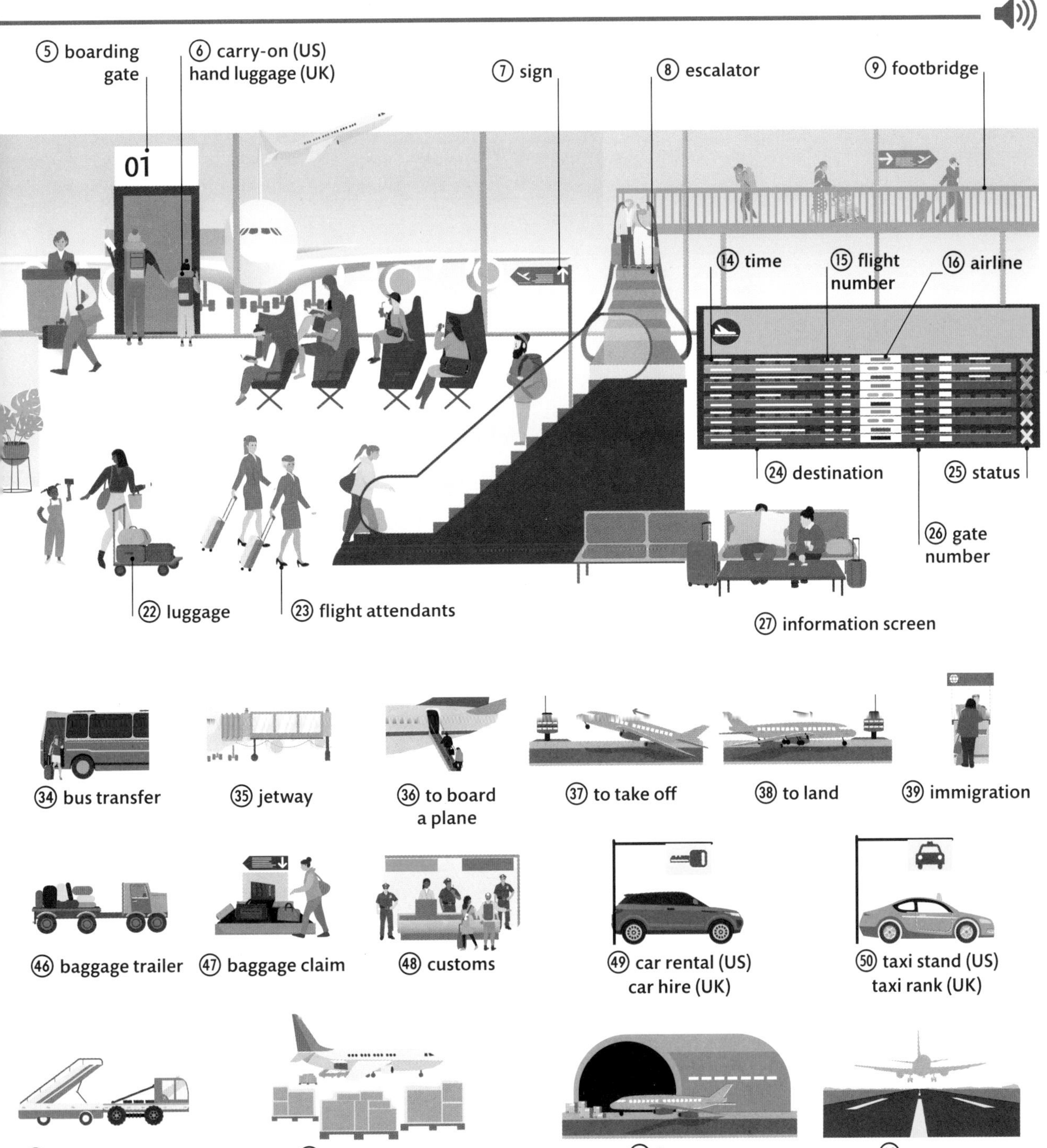
⑤ boarding gate
⑥ carry-on (US) hand luggage (UK)
⑦ sign
⑧ escalator
⑨ footbridge
01
⑭ time
⑮ flight number
⑯ airline
㉔ destination
㉕ status
㉖ gate number
㉒ luggage
㉓ flight attendants
㉗ information screen
㉞ bus transfer
㉟ jetway
㊱ to board a plane
㊲ to take off
㊳ to land
㊴ immigration
㊻ baggage trailer
㊼ baggage claim
㊽ customs
㊾ car rental (US) car hire (UK)
㊿ taxi stand (US) taxi rank (UK)
57 service vehicle
58 air cargo
59 hangar
60 runway

105 Sea vessels

105.1 SHIP

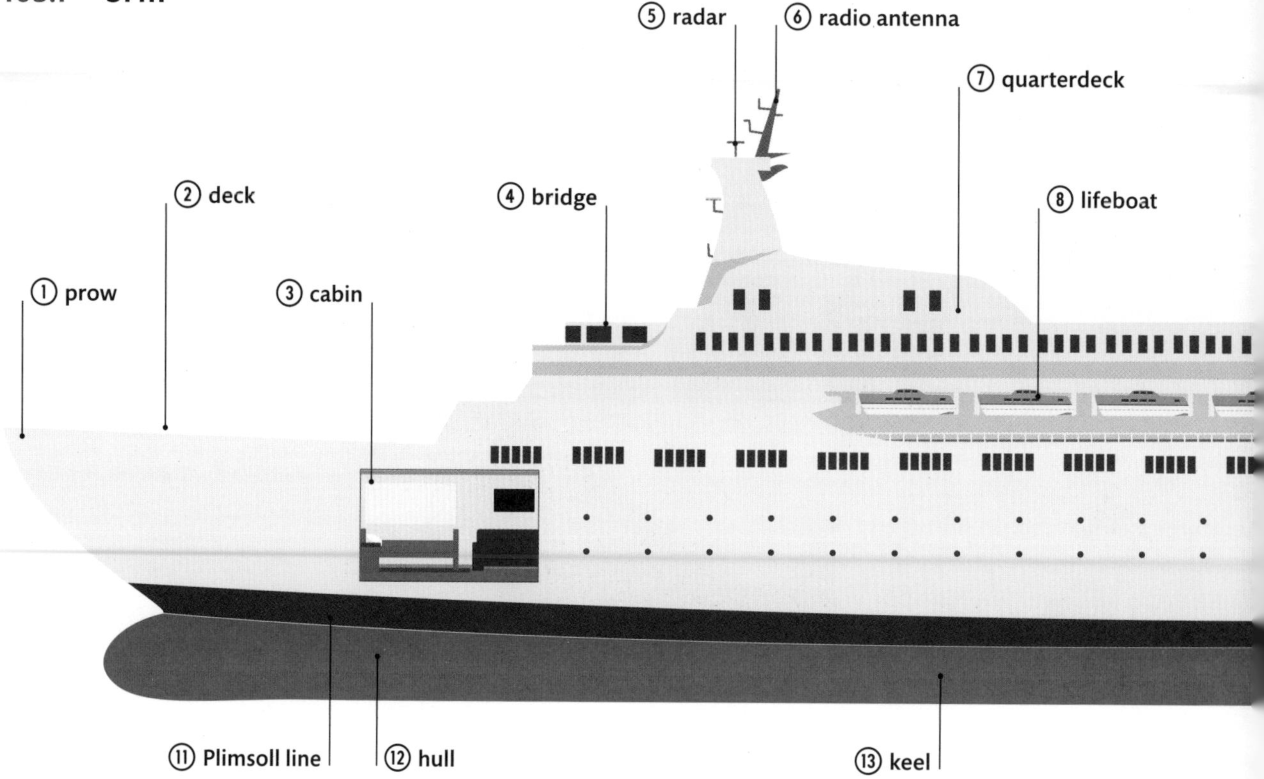

① prow
② deck
③ cabin
④ bridge
⑤ radar
⑥ radio antenna
⑦ quarterdeck
⑧ lifeboat
⑪ Plimsoll line
⑫ hull
⑬ keel

105.2 OTHER BOATS AND SHIPS

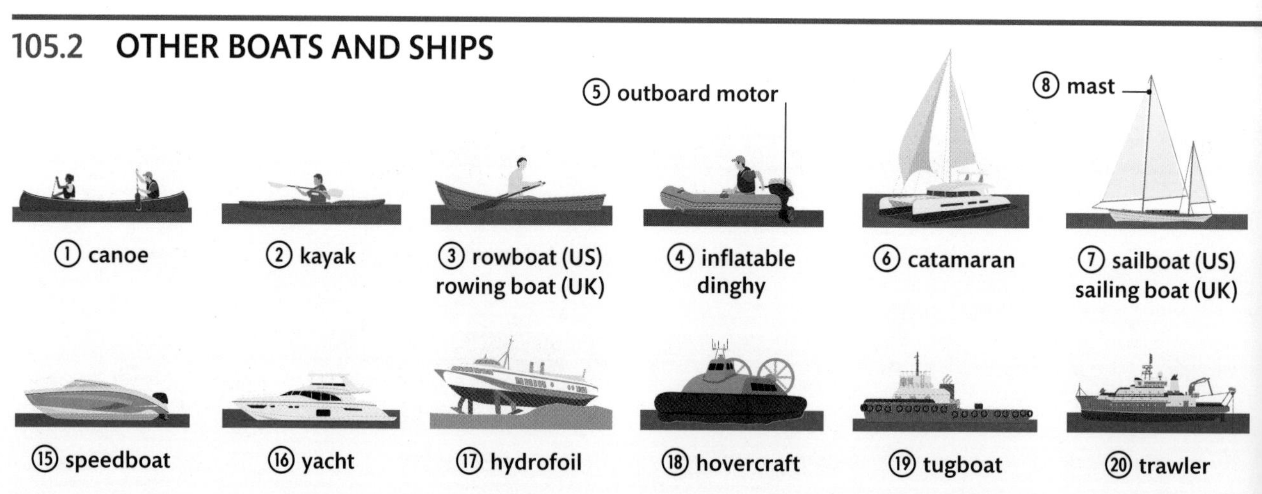

⑤ outboard motor
⑧ mast
① canoe
② kayak
③ rowboat (US) rowing boat (UK)
④ inflatable dinghy
⑥ catamaran
⑦ sailboat (US) sailing boat (UK)
⑮ speedboat
⑯ yacht
⑰ hydrofoil
⑱ hovercraft
⑲ tugboat
⑳ trawler

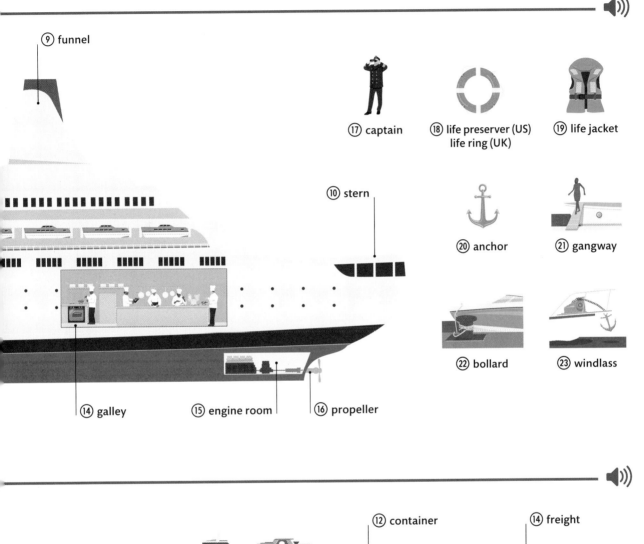

See also:
106 The port 119 Sailing and watersports
131 Travel and accommodation

⑨ funnel

⑰ captain

⑱ life preserver (US)
life ring (UK)

⑲ life jacket

⑩ stern

⑳ anchor

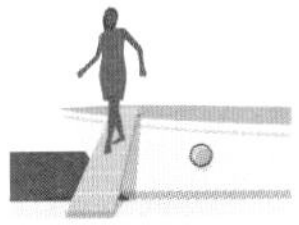

㉑ gangway

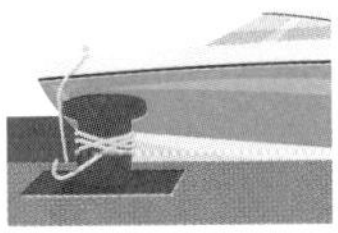

㉒ bollard

㉓ windlass

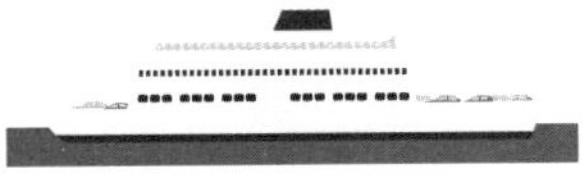

⑭ galley

⑮ engine room

⑯ propeller

⑫ container

⑭ freight

⑨ ferry

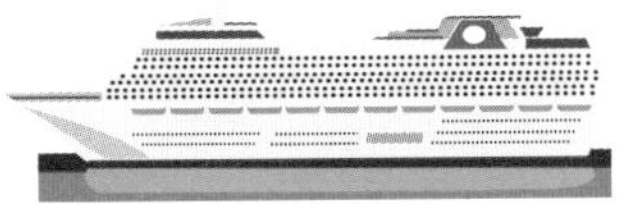

⑩ cruise ship

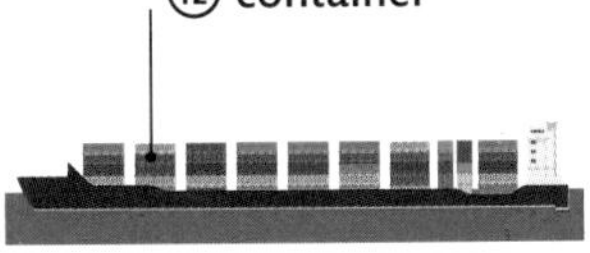

⑪ container ship

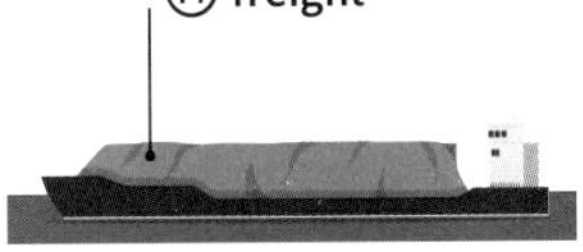

⑬ freighter

㉕ conning tower

㉑ oil tanker

㉒ aircraft carrier

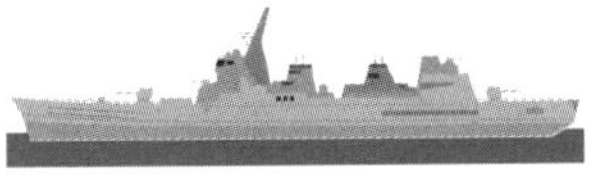

㉓ battleship

㉔ submarine

106 The port

106.1 AT THE DOCKS

① container ship

② crane

③ shipping container

④ warehouse

⑤ forklift (US)
fork-lift truck (UK)

⑥ access road

⑦ dock

⑧ customhouse (US)
customs house (UK)

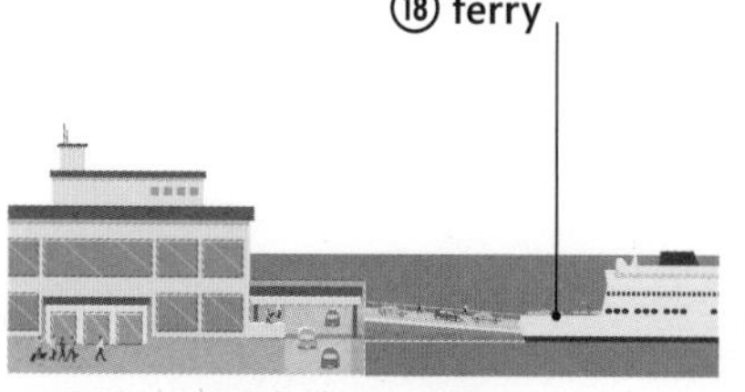
⑱ ferry

⑰ ferry terminal

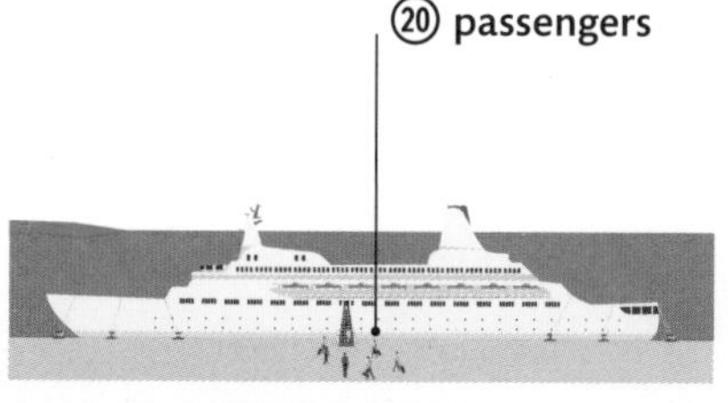
⑳ passengers

⑲ passenger port

㉑ fishing port

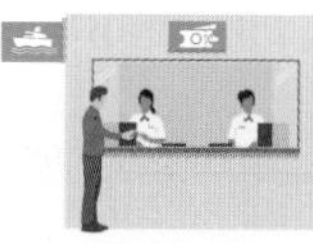

㉒ ticket office

㉗ mooring

㉘ harbor (US)
harbour (UK)

㉙ marina

㉚ pier

㉛ jetty

㉜ shipyard

See also:
96 Roads 102 Trains
105 Sea vessels

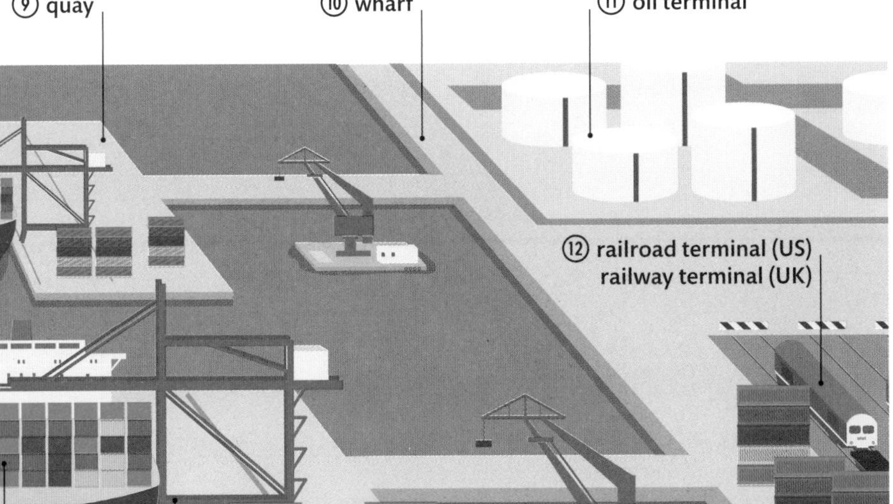
⑨ quay
⑩ wharf
⑪ oil terminal
⑫ railroad terminal (US)
railway terminal (UK)
⑬ cargo
⑭ bridge crane
⑮ port
⑯ floating crane

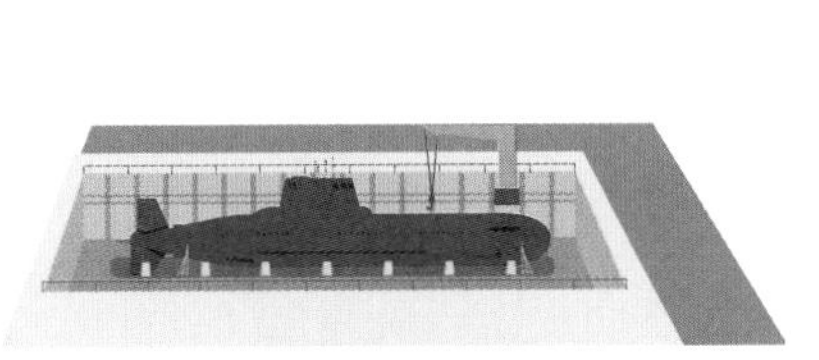

㉓ dry dock

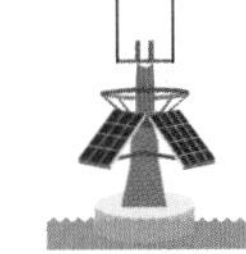

㉔ buoy

㉖ lamp

㉕ lighthouse

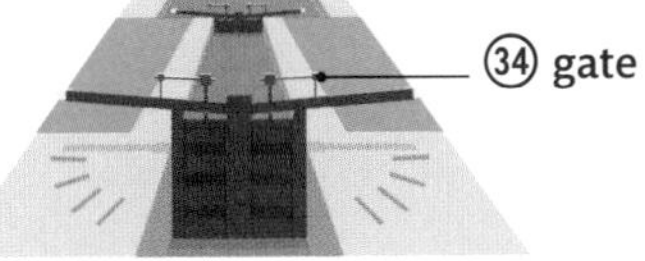
㉞ gate

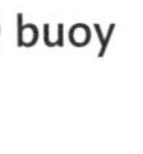

㉝ lock

㉟ coastguard

㊱ harbor master (US)
harbour master (UK)

106.2 VERBS

① to board

② to moor

③ to disembark

④ to drop anchor

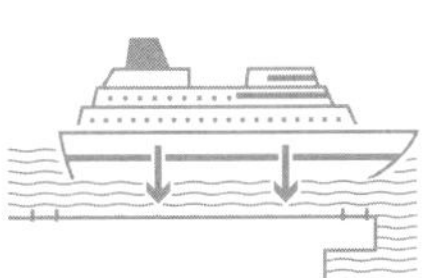

⑤ to dock

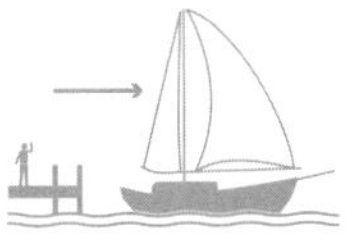

⑥ to set sail

107 American football

107.1 AMERICAN FOOTBALL

① left cornerback

② outside linebacker

③ left defensive end

④ left safety

⑤ left defensive tackle

⑥ middle linebacker

⑦ right defensive tackle

⑧ right safety

⑨ right defensive end

⑩ outside linebacker

⑪ right cornerback

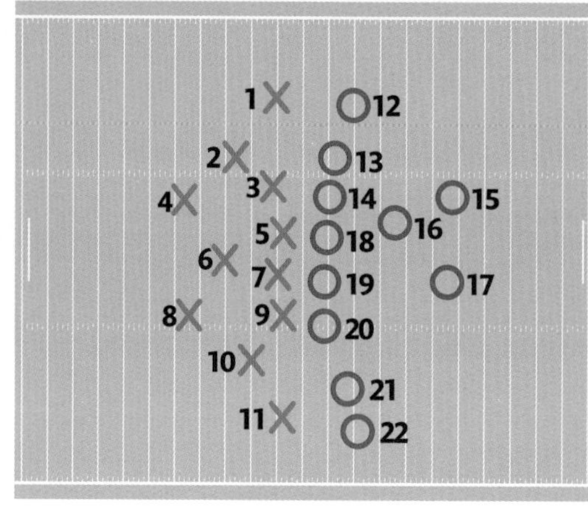
1
2
3
4
5
6
7
8
9
10
11
12
13
14
15
16
17
18
19
20
21
22

㉔ defense (US) defence (UK)

㉓ American football positions

㉕ offense (US) offence (UK)

⑫ wide receiver

⑬ right tackle

⑭ right guard

⑮ running back / halfback

⑯ fullback

⑰ quarterback

⑱ center (US) centre (UK)

⑲ left guard

⑳ left tackle

㉑ ㉒ wide receiver

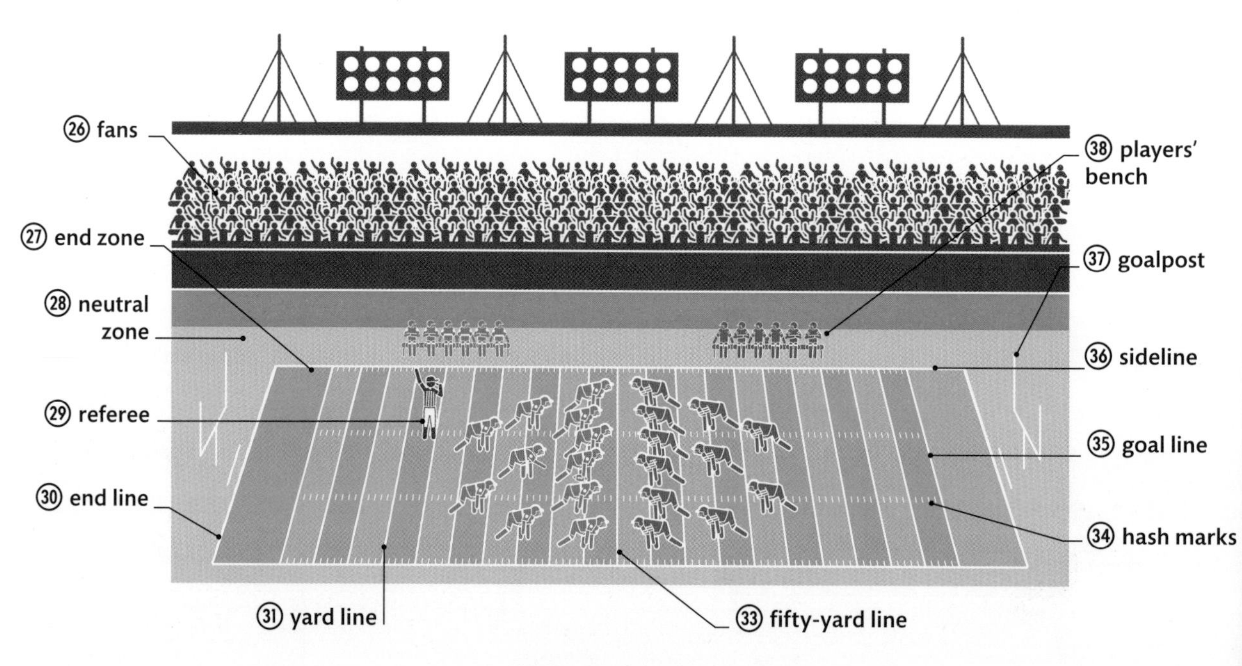

㉖ fans

㉗ end zone

㉘ neutral zone

㉙ referee

㉚ end line

㉛ yard line

㉜ field / pitch

㉝ fifty-yard line

㉞ hash marks

㉟ goal line

㊱ sideline

㊲ goalpost

㊳ players' bench

See also:
108 Rugby **109** Soccer / Football
110 Hockey and lacrosse

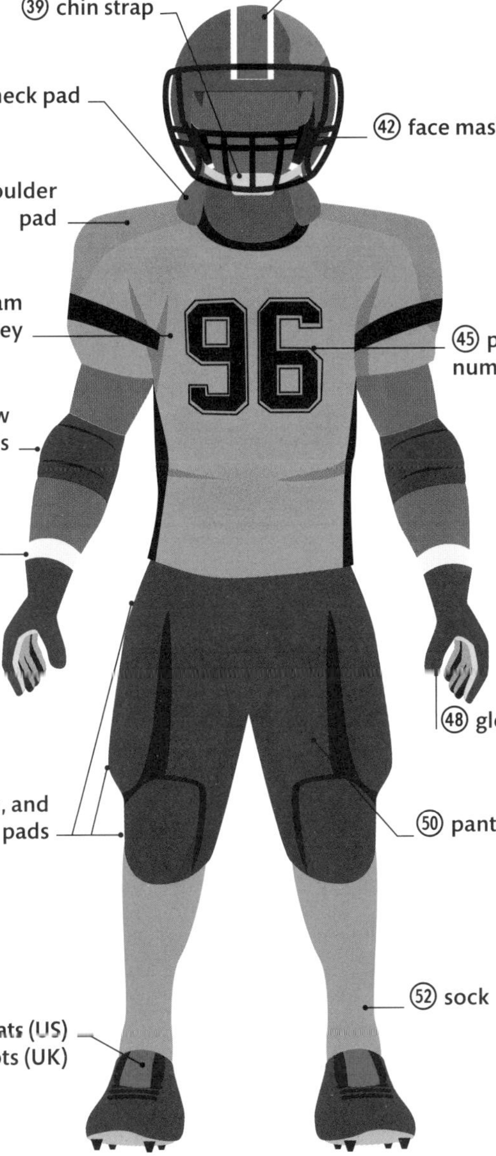

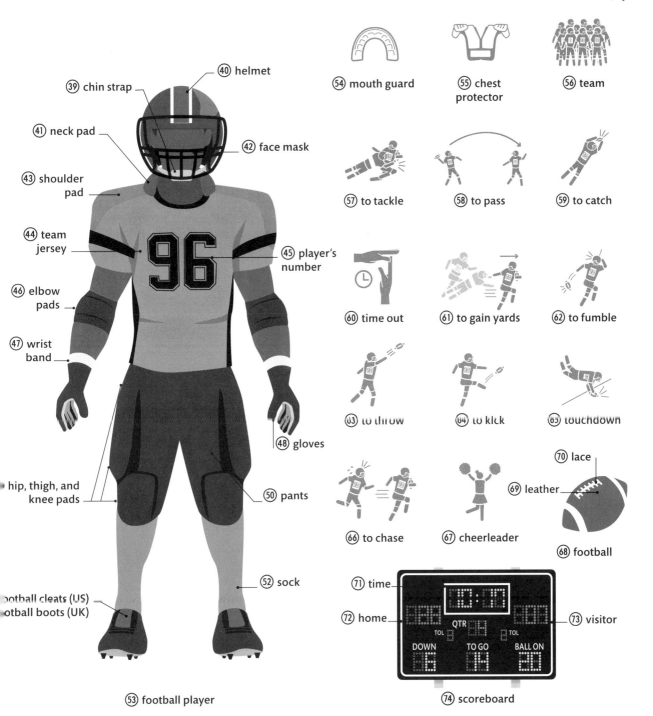

(39) chin strap
(40) helmet
(41) neck pad
(42) face mask
(43) shoulder pad
(44) team jersey
(45) player's number
(46) elbow pads
(47) wrist band
(48) gloves
hip, thigh, and knee pads
(50) pants
(52) sock
otball cleats (US)
otball boots (UK)
(53) football player

(54) mouth guard
(55) chest protector 
(56) team 
(57) to tackle 
(58) to pass 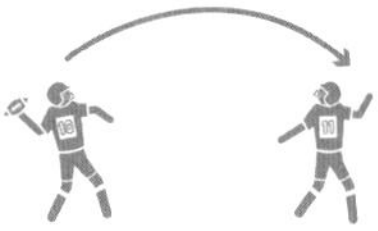
(59) to catch 
(60) time out 
(61) to gain yards 
(62) to fumble 
(63) to throw 
(64) to kick 
(65) touchdown 
(66) to chase 
(67) cheerleader 
(68) football  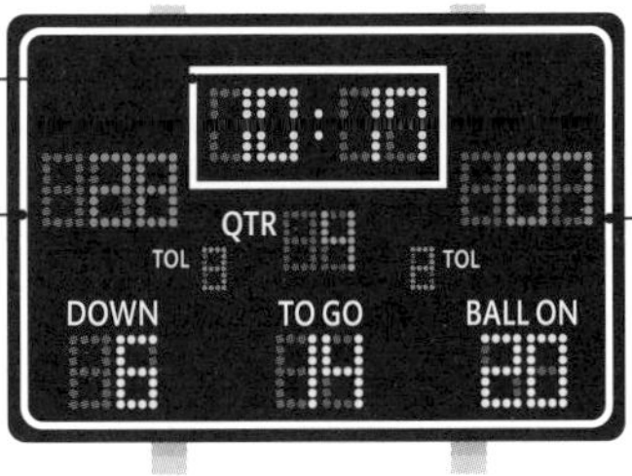
(69) leather
(70) lace
(71) time
(72) home
(73) visitor
(74) scoreboard

QTR
TOL
TOL
DOWN
TO GO
BALL ON

108 Rugby

108.1 RUGBY

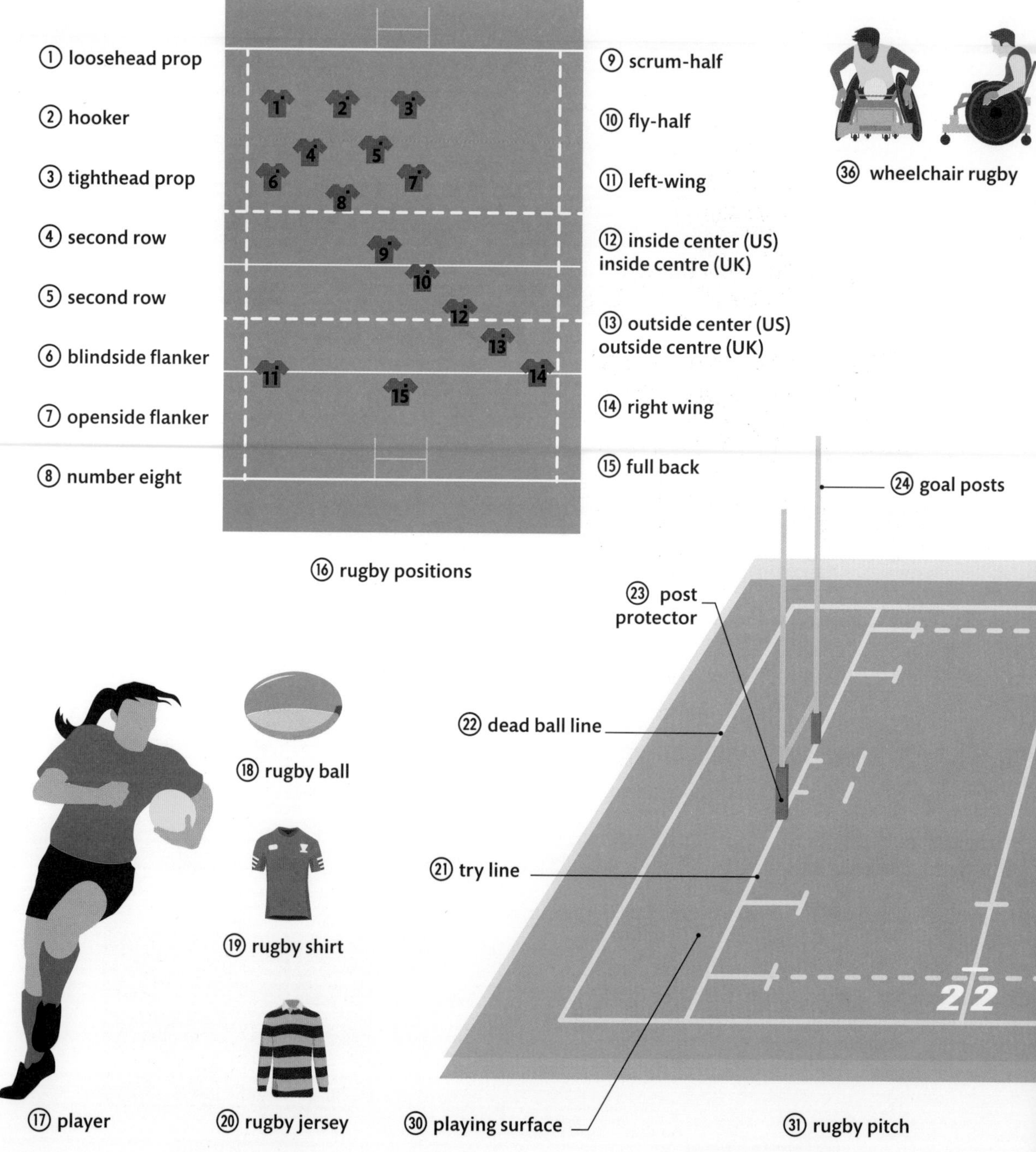

① loosehead prop
② hooker
③ tighthead prop
④ second row
⑤ second row
⑥ blindside flanker
⑦ openside flanker
⑧ number eight
⑨ scrum-half
⑩ fly-half
⑪ left-wing
⑫ inside center (US)
inside centre (UK)
⑬ outside center (US)
outside centre (UK)
⑭ right wing
⑮ full back
⑯ rugby positions
㊱ wheelchair rugby
㉔ goal posts
㉓ post protector
㉒ dead ball line
㉑ try line
⑰ player
⑱ rugby ball
⑲ rugby shirt
⑳ rugby jersey
㉚ playing surface
㉛ rugby pitch
22

See also:
107 American football **109** Soccer / Football
110 Hockey and lacrosse **112** Basketball and volleyball

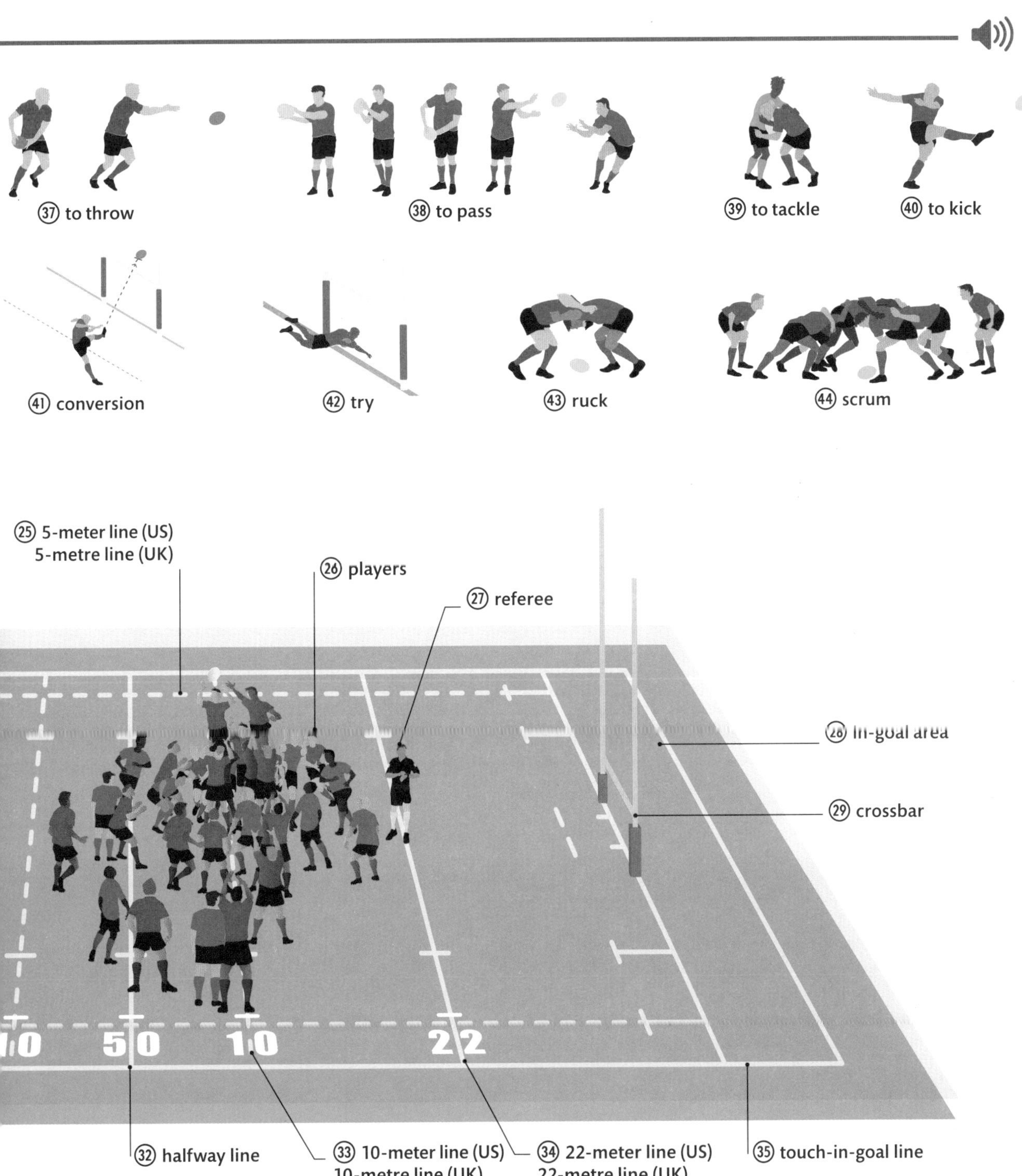
37 to throw
38 to pass
39 to tackle
40 to kick
41 conversion
42 try
43 ruck
44 scrum
25 5-meter line (US)
5-metre line (UK)
26 players
27 referee
28 in-goal area
29 crossbar
10
50
10
22
32 halfway line
33 10-meter line (US)
10-metre line (UK)
34 22-meter line (US)
22-metre line (UK)
35 touch-in-goal line

109 Soccer (US) / Football (UK)

109.1 SOCCER (US) / FOOTBALL (UK) GAME

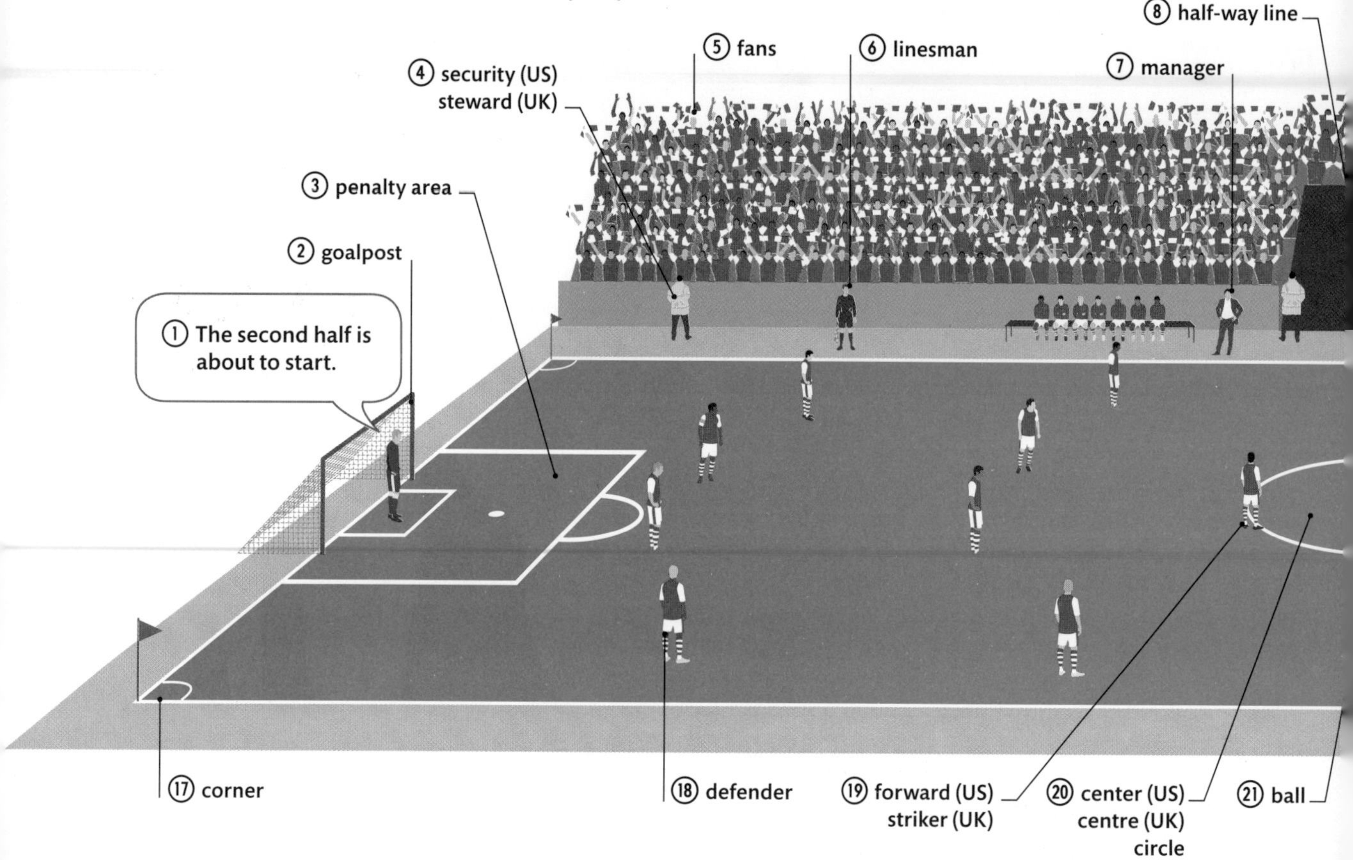

① The second half is about to start.

② goalpost

③ penalty area

④ security (US) steward (UK)

⑤ fans

⑥ linesman

⑦ manager

⑧ half-way line

⑰ corner

⑱ defender

⑲ forward (US) striker (UK)

⑳ center (US) centre (UK) circle

㉑ ball

109.2 TIMING AND RULES

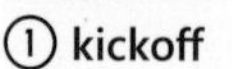
00:00
① kickoff

45:00
② half time

90:00
③ full time

④ throw-in

⑤ final whistle

⑥ stoppage time (US) injury time (UK)

⑨ corner kick

⑩ yellow card

⑪ red card

⑫ to be sent off

00
00
⑬ to tie (US) to draw (UK)

00
05
⑭ to lose

See also:
107 American football 108 Rugby
110 Hockey and lacrosse 112 Basketball and volleyball

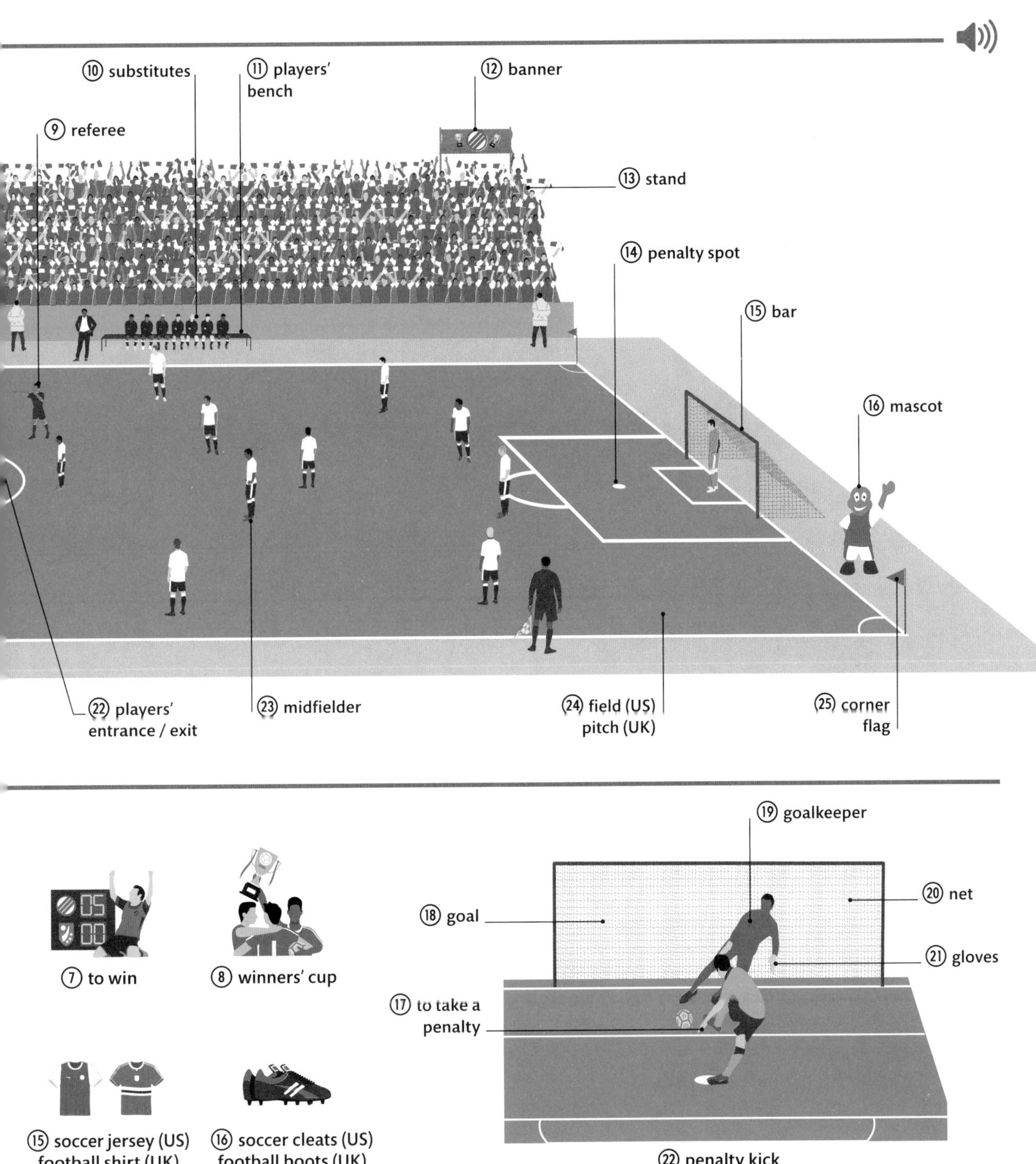
9 referee
10 substitutes
11 players' bench
12 banner
13 stand
14 penalty spot
15 bar
16 mascot
22 players' entrance / exit
23 midfielder
24 field (US) pitch (UK)
25 corner flag
7 to win
8 winners' cup
15 soccer jersey (US) football shirt (UK)
16 soccer cleats (US) football boots (UK)
18 goal
19 goalkeeper
20 net
21 gloves
17 to take a penalty
22 penalty kick

110 Hockey and lacrosse

110.1 ICE HOCKEY

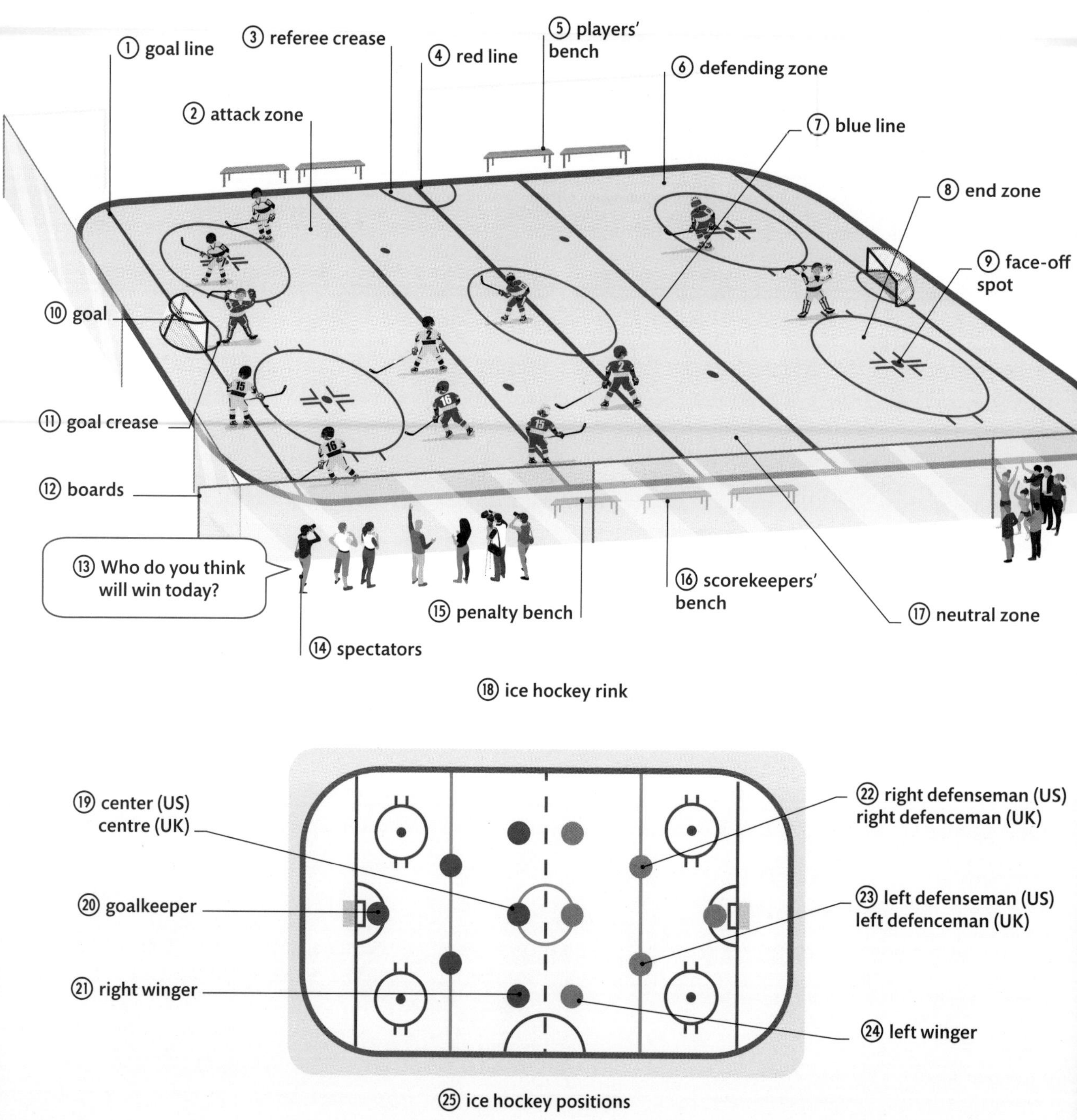

① goal line
② attack zone
③ referee crease
④ red line
⑤ players' bench
⑥ defending zone
⑦ blue line
⑧ end zone
⑨ face-off spot
⑩ goal
⑪ goal crease
⑫ boards
⑬ Who do you think will win today?
⑭ spectators
⑮ penalty bench
⑯ scorekeepers' bench
⑰ neutral zone
⑱ ice hockey rink
⑲ center (US) centre (UK)
⑳ goalkeeper
㉑ right winger
㉒ right defenseman (US) right defenceman (UK)
㉓ left defenseman (US) left defenceman (UK)
㉔ left winger
㉕ ice hockey positions

See also:
107 American football 111 Cricket
`112 Basketball and volleyball 113 Baseball 114 Tennis

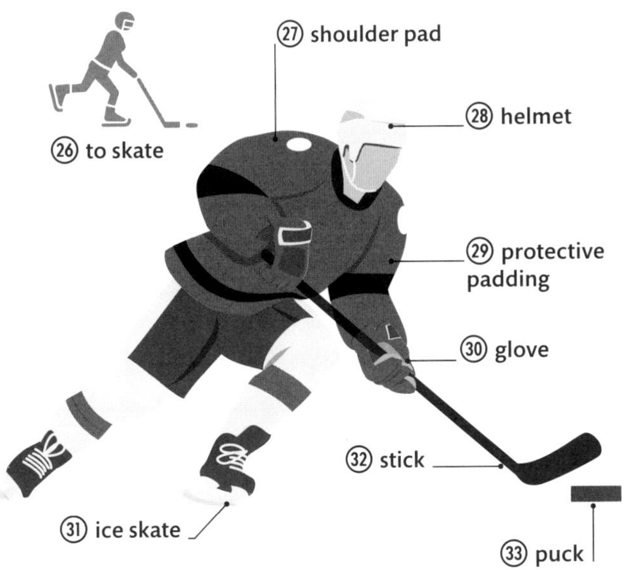
26 to skate
27 shoulder pad
28 helmet
29 protective padding
30 glove
31 ice skate
32 stick
33 puck

34 ice hockey player

35 blocking glove
36 face mask
37 catcher glove (US) catching glove (UK)
38 leg guard
39 goalie stick

40 goalkeeper

110.2 FIELD HOCKEY

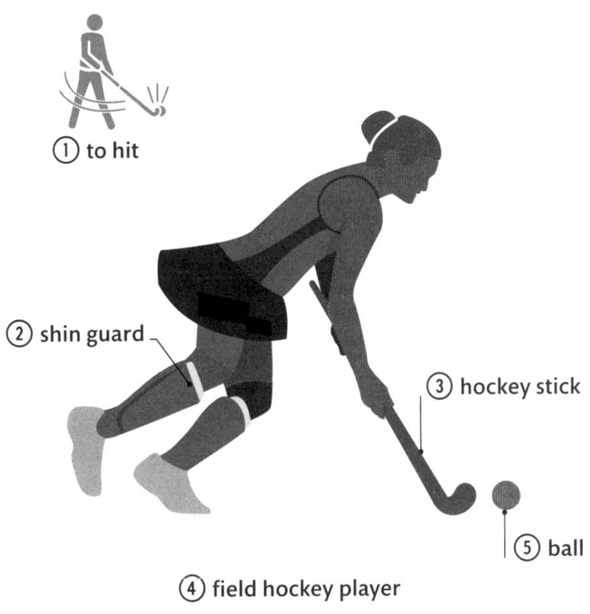
1 to hit
2 shin guard
3 hockey stick
5 ball

4 field hockey player

110.3 LACROSSE

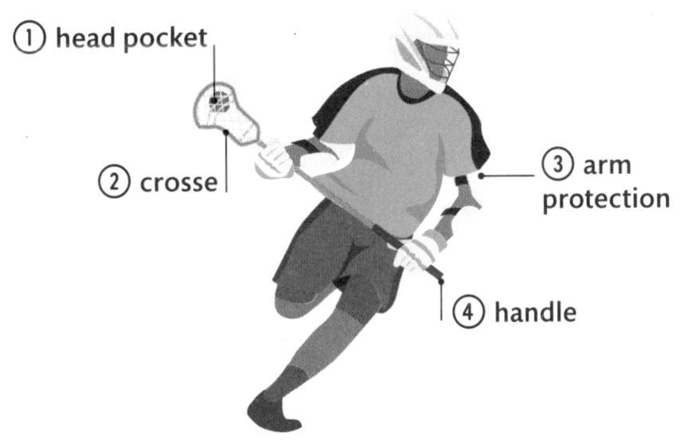
1 head pocket
2 crosse
3 arm protection
4 handle

5 lacrosse player

6 to pass

7 to scoop

8 face-off

111 Cricket

111.1 CRICKET PITCH AND POSITIONS

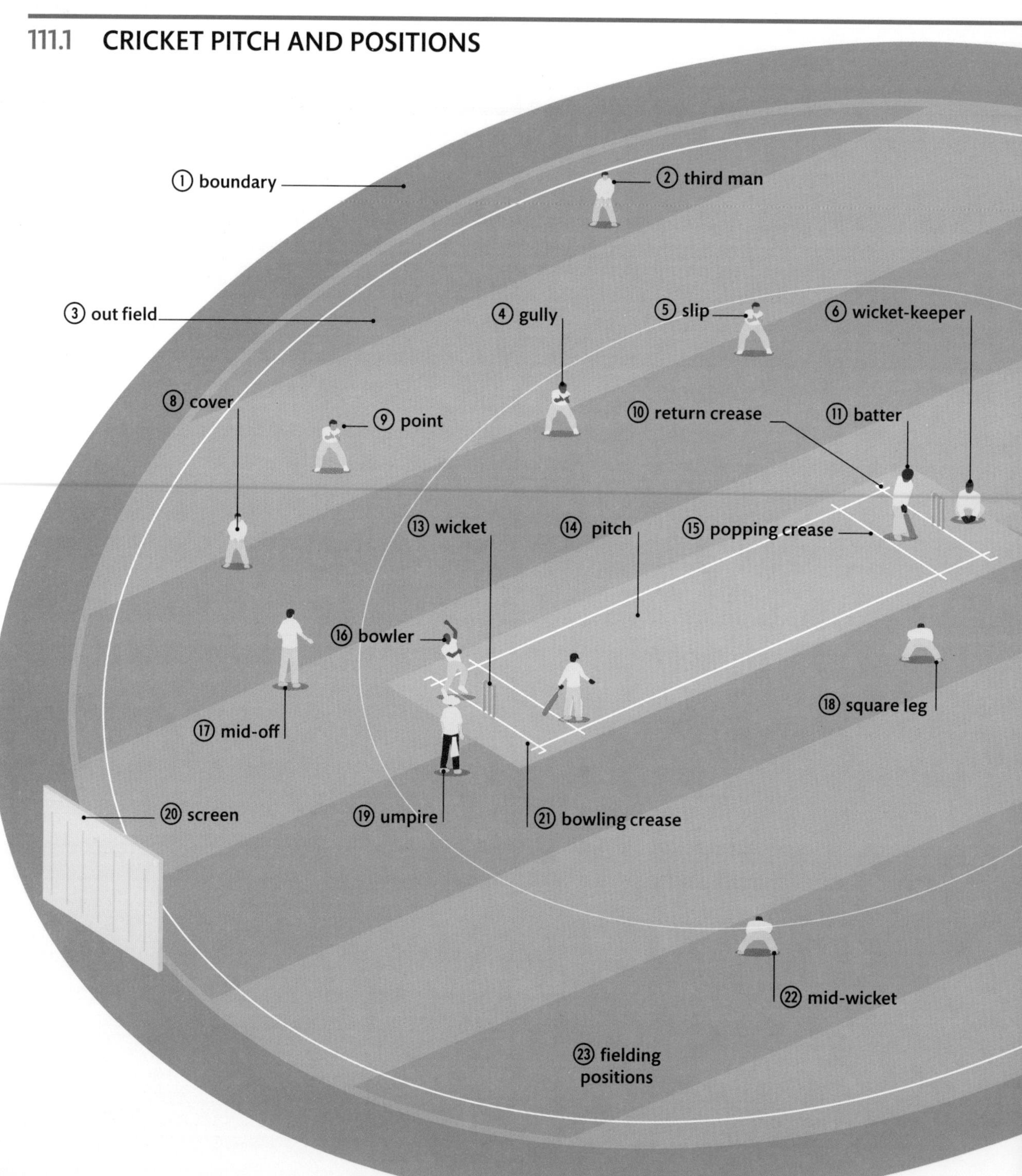

① boundary
② third man
③ out field
④ gully
⑤ slip
⑥ wicket-keeper
⑧ cover
⑨ point
⑩ return crease
⑪ batter
⑬ wicket
⑭ pitch
⑮ popping crease
⑯ bowler
⑰ mid-off
⑱ square leg
⑲ umpire
⑳ screen
㉑ bowling crease
㉒ mid-wicket
㉓ fielding positions

See also:
109 Soccer / Football 110 Hockey and lacrosse
113 Baseball 115 Golf

111.2 CRICKET EQUIPMENT

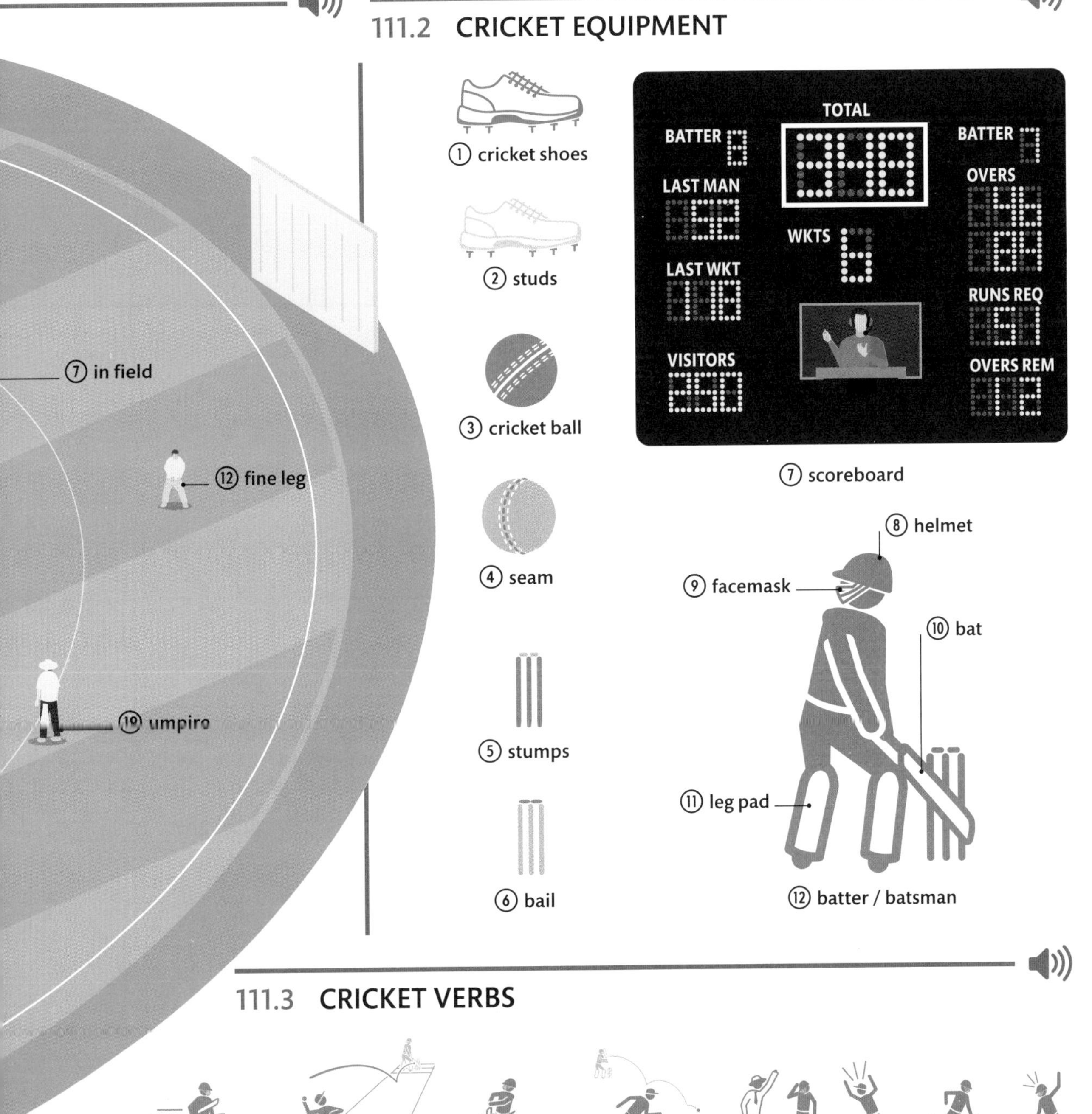
7 in field
12 fine leg
19 umpire
1 cricket shoes
2 studs
3 cricket ball
4 seam
5 stumps
6 bail
TOTAL
BATTER
LAST MAN
LAST WKT
VISITORS
WKTS
OVERS
RUNS REQ
OVERS REM
7 scoreboard
8 helmet
9 facemask
10 bat
11 leg pad
12 batter / batsman

111.3 CRICKET VERBS

1 to run
2 to bowl
3 to bat
4 to field
5 to strike out
6 to stump

112 Basketball and volleyball

112.1 BASKETBALL

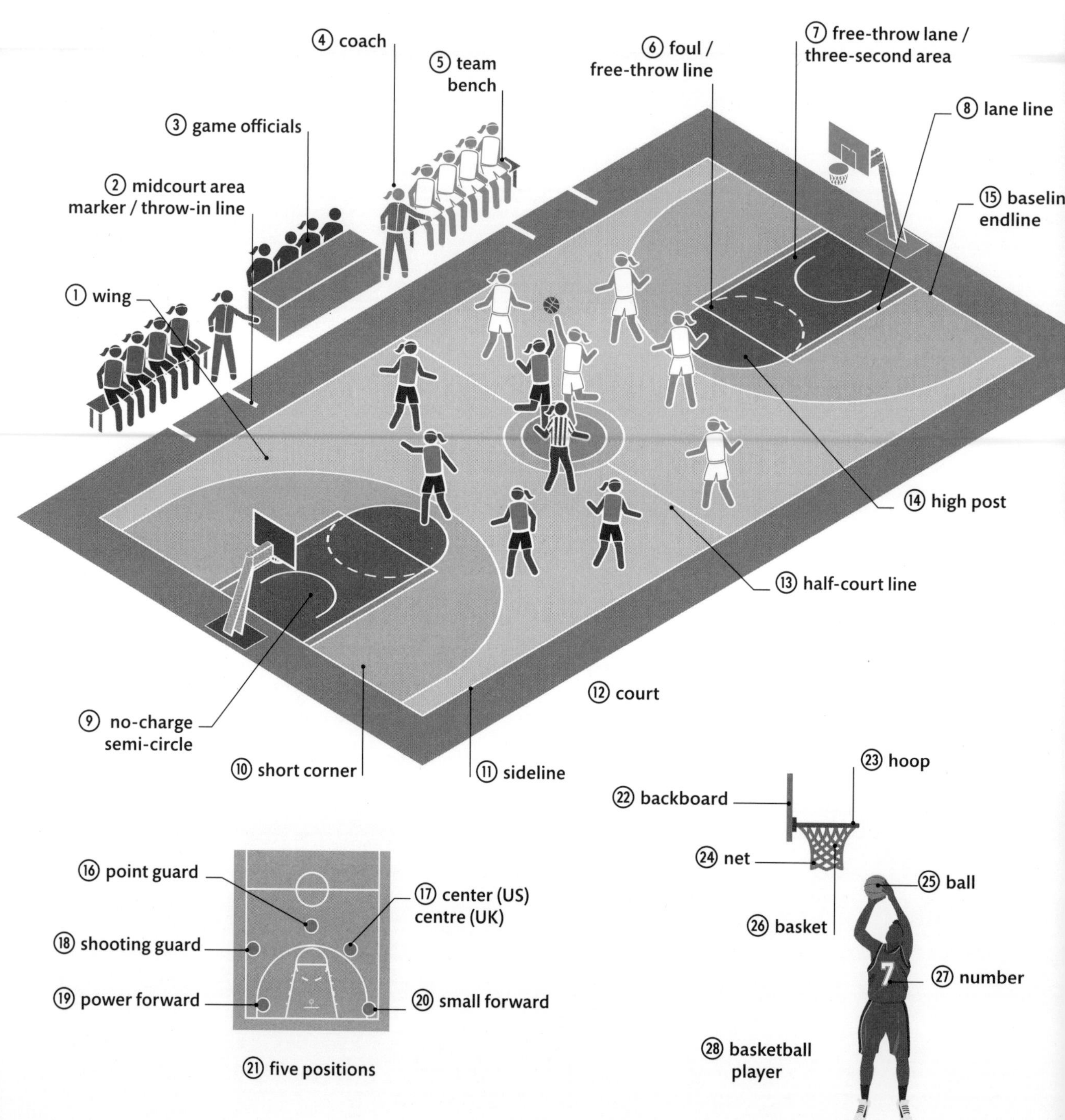

① wing
② midcourt area marker / throw-in line
③ game officials
④ coach
⑤ team bench
⑥ foul / free-throw line
⑦ free-throw lane / three-second area
⑧ lane line
⑨ no-charge semi-circle
⑩ short corner
⑪ sideline
⑫ court
⑬ half-court line
⑭ high post
⑮ baseline endline
⑯ point guard
⑰ center (US) centre (UK)
⑱ shooting guard
⑲ power forward
⑳ small forward
㉑ five positions
㉒ backboard
㉓ hoop
㉔ net
㉕ ball
㉖ basket
㉗ number
㉘ basketball player

See also:
107 American football 108 Rugby
109 Soccer / Football 124 At the gym 125 Other sports

29 pass
30 out of bounds
31 throw-in
32 rebound
33 airball
34 jump ball
35 foul
36 to mark
37 to bounce
38 to dunk
39 to shoot
40 to block

112.2 VOLLEYBALL

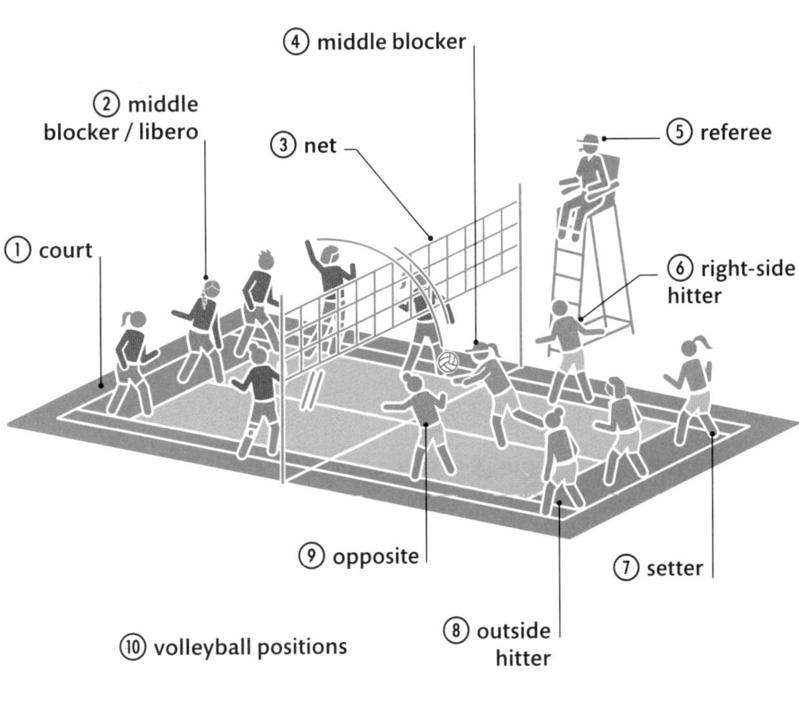
1 court
2 middle blocker / libero
3 net
4 middle blocker
5 referee
6 right-side hitter
7 setter
8 outside hitter
9 opposite

10 volleyball positions

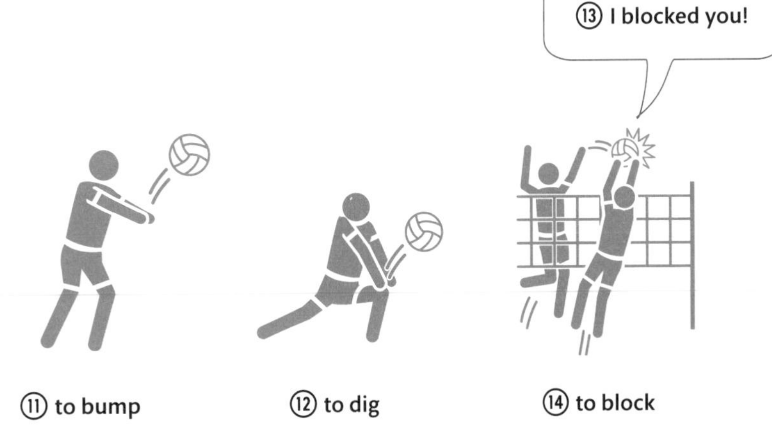
13 I blocked you!
11 to bump
12 to dig
14 to block

113 Baseball

113.1 BASEBALL GAME

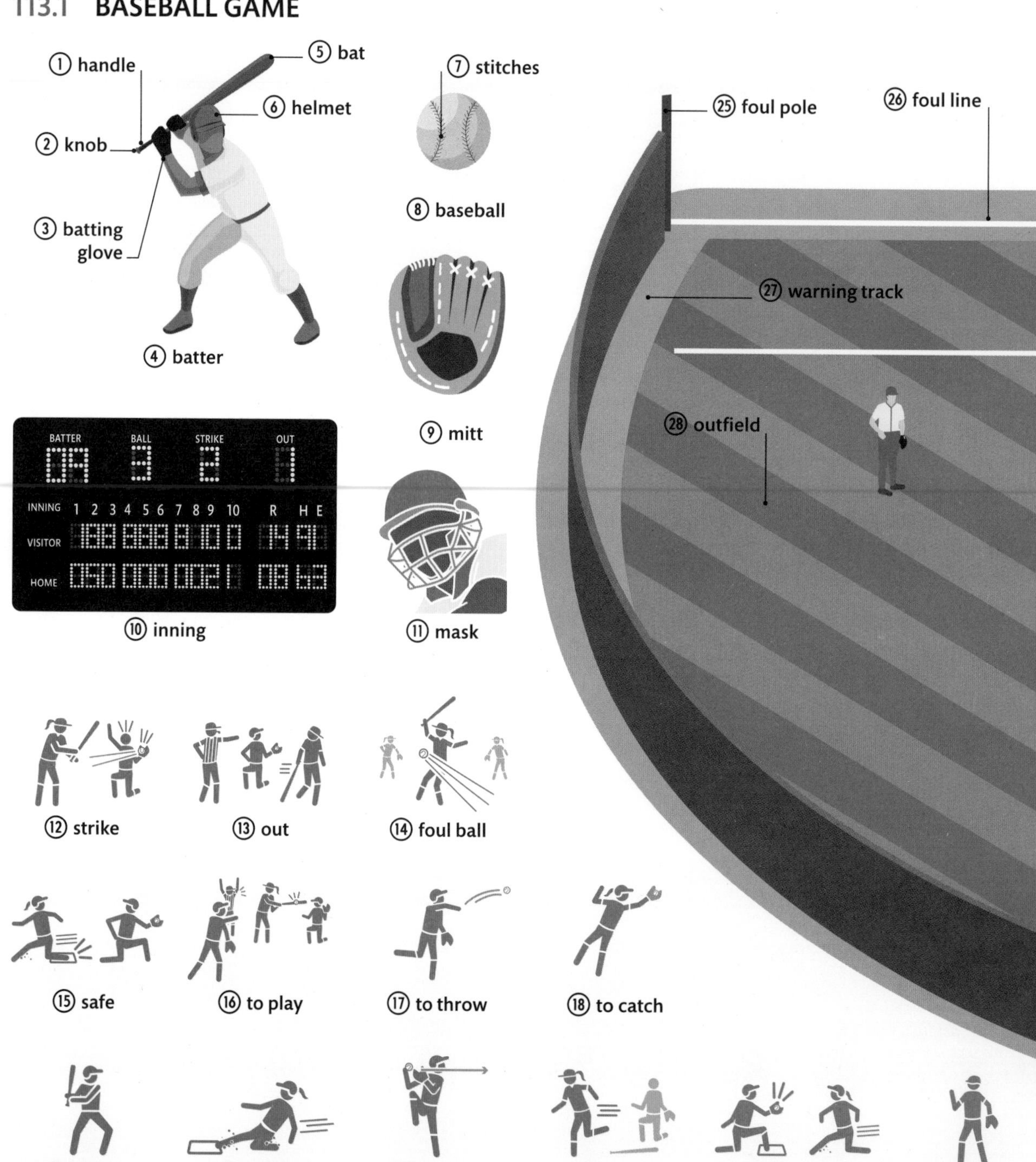
① handle
② knob
③ batting glove
④ batter
⑤ bat
⑥ helmet
⑦ stitches
⑧ baseball
⑨ mitt
BATTER
BALL
STRIKE
OUT
INNING 1 2 3 4 5 6 7 8 9 10 R H E
VISITOR
HOME
⑩ inning
⑪ mask
⑫ strike
⑬ out
⑭ foul ball
⑮ safe
⑯ to play
⑰ to throw
⑱ to catch
⑲ to bat
⑳ to slide
㉑ to pitch
㉒ to run
㉓ to tag
㉔ to field
㉕ foul pole
㉖ foul line
㉗ warning track
㉘ outfield

See also:
107 American football 110 Hockey and lacrosse
111 Cricket 112 Basketball and volleyball

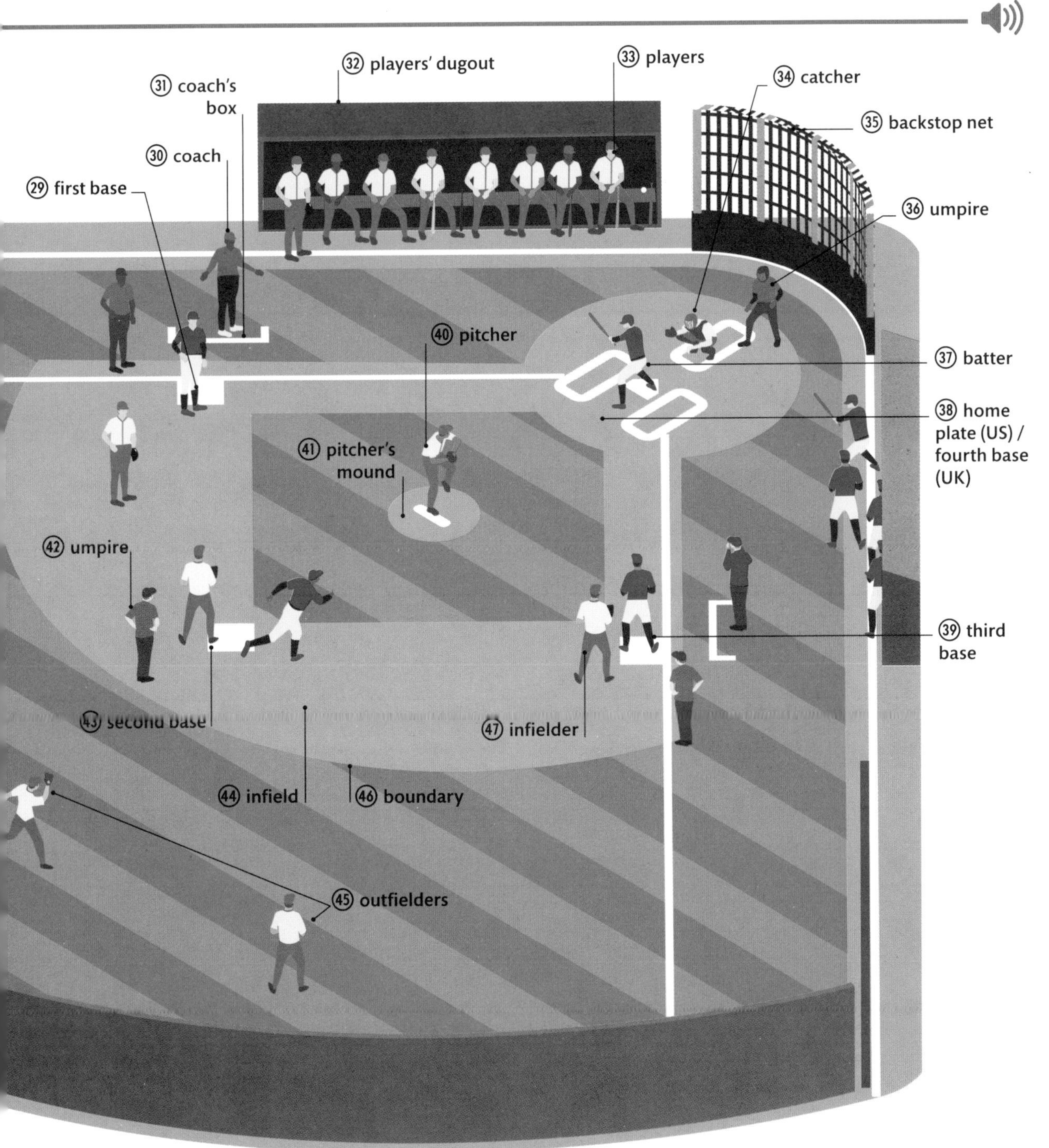

31 coach's box
32 players' dugout
33 players
34 catcher
35 backstop net
30 coach
29 first base
36 umpire
40 pitcher
37 batter
38 home plate (US) / fourth base (UK)
41 pitcher's mound
42 umpire
39 third base
43 second base
47 infielder
44 infield
46 boundary
45 outfielders

48 baseball field

114 Tennis

114.1 TENNIS MATCH

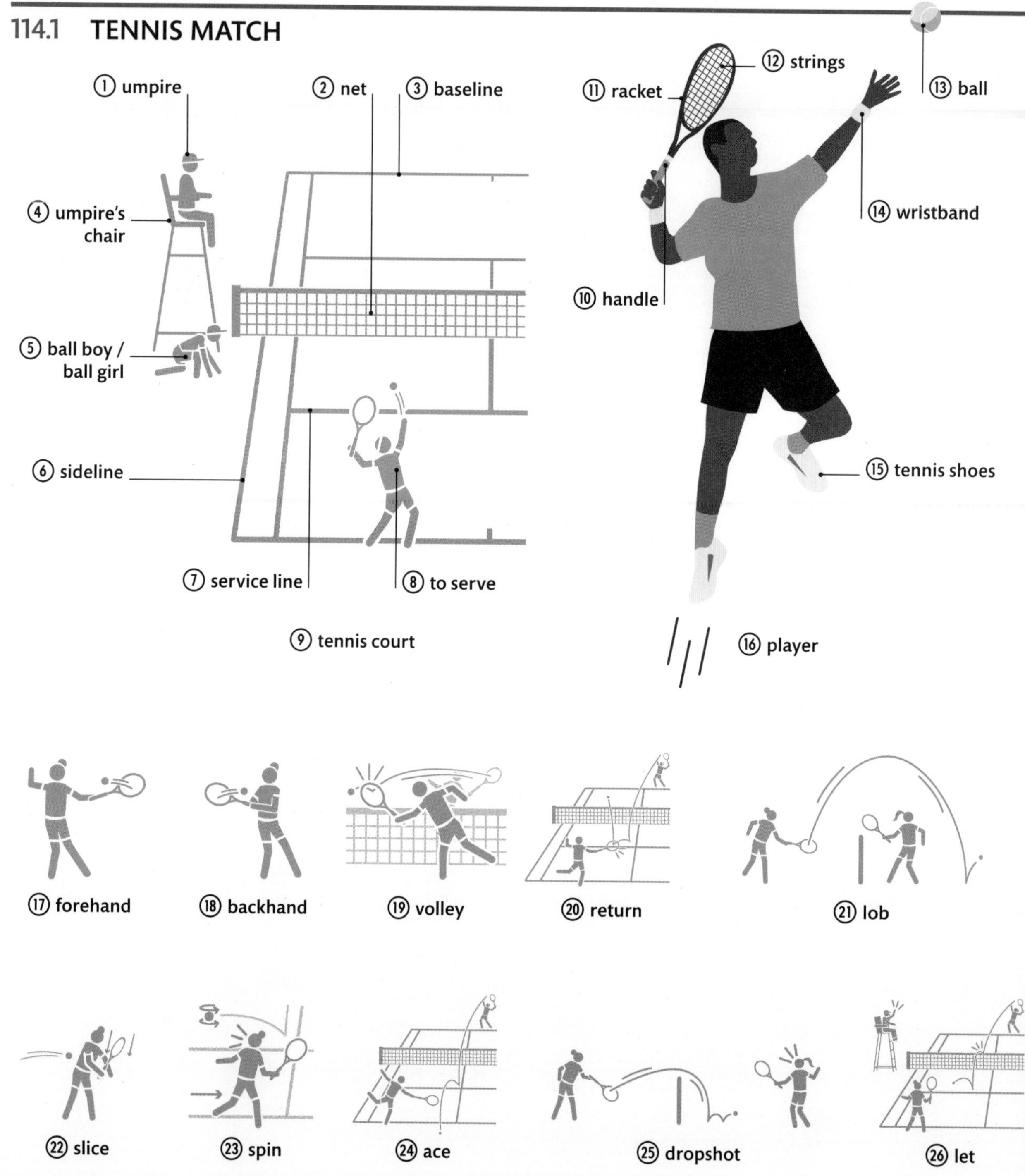

① umpire
② net
③ baseline
④ umpire's chair
⑤ ball boy / ball girl
⑥ sideline
⑦ service line
⑧ to serve
⑨ tennis court
⑩ handle
⑪ racket
⑫ strings
⑬ ball
⑭ wristband
⑮ tennis shoes
⑯ player
⑰ forehand
⑱ backhand
⑲ volley
⑳ return
㉑ lob
㉒ slice
㉓ spin
㉔ ace
㉕ dropshot
㉖ let

See also:
111 Cricket 113 Baseball
115 Golf 116 Athletics

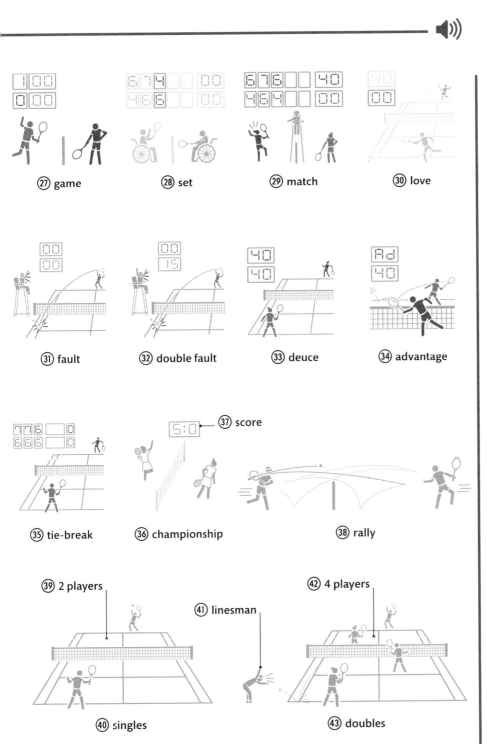

(27) game

(28) set

(29) match

(30) love

(31) fault

(32) double fault

(33) deuce

(34) advantage

(35) tie-break

(36) championship

(37) score

(38) rally

(39) 2 players

(40) singles

(41) linesman

(42) 4 players

(43) doubles

114.2 RACKET GAMES

(1) squash

(2) racquetball

(3) ping pong / table tennis

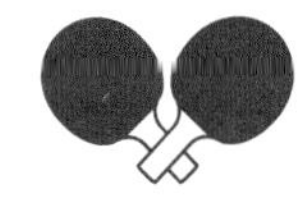

(4) paddle (US) / bat (UK)

(5) badminton

(6) shuttlecock

115 Golf

115.1 ON THE GOLF COURSE

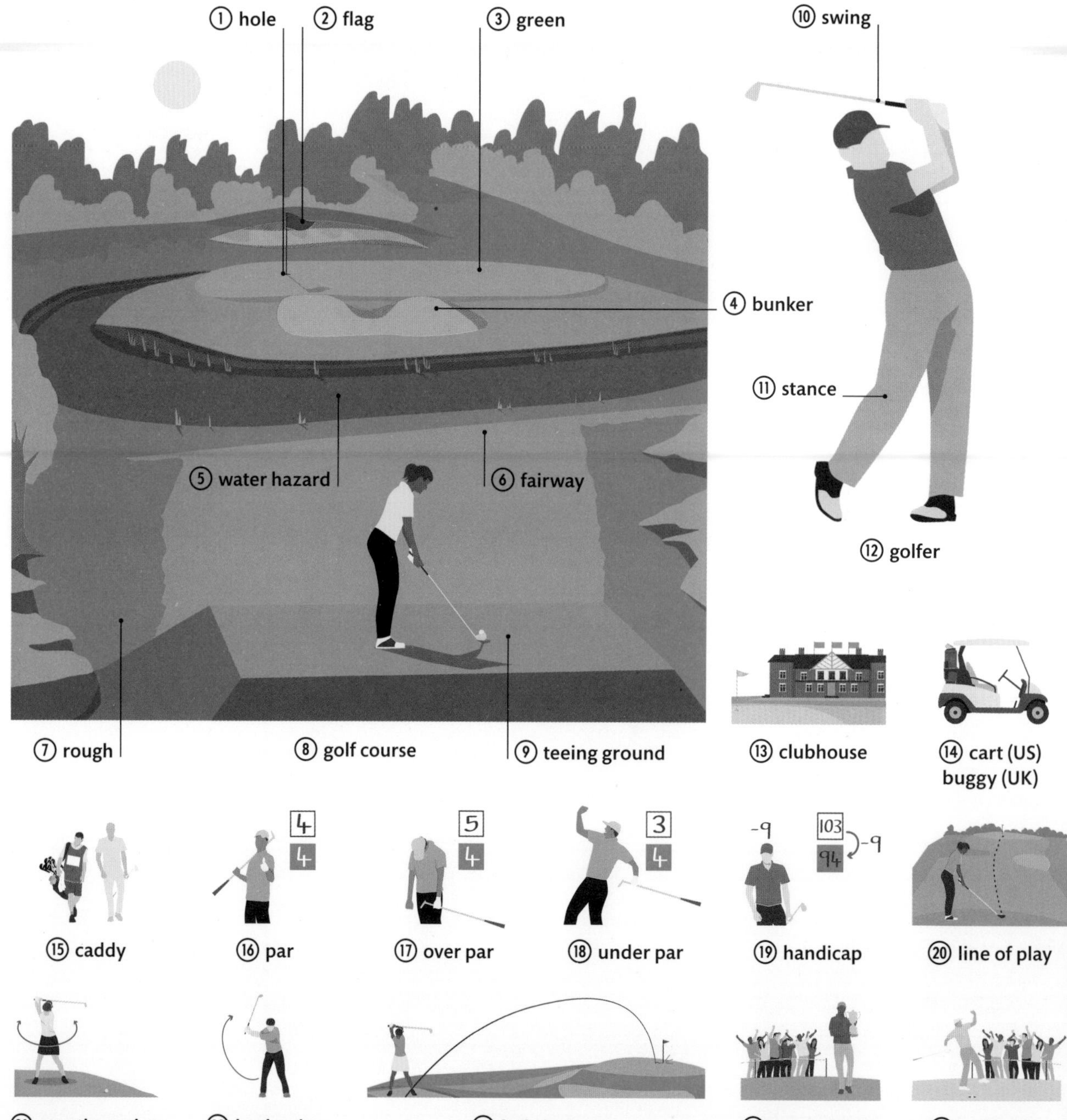

① hole
② flag
③ green
④ bunker
⑤ water hazard
⑥ fairway
⑦ rough
⑧ golf course
⑨ teeing ground
⑩ swing
⑪ stance
⑫ golfer
⑬ clubhouse
⑭ cart (US) buggy (UK)
4
4
⑮ caddy
⑯ par
5
4
⑰ over par
3
4
⑱ under par
-9
103
-9
94
⑲ handicap
⑳ line of play
㉑ practice swing
㉒ backswing
㉓ hole in one
㉔ tournament
㉕ spectators

See also:
111 Cricket
113 Baseball 114 Tennis

115.2 GOLF EQUIPMENT

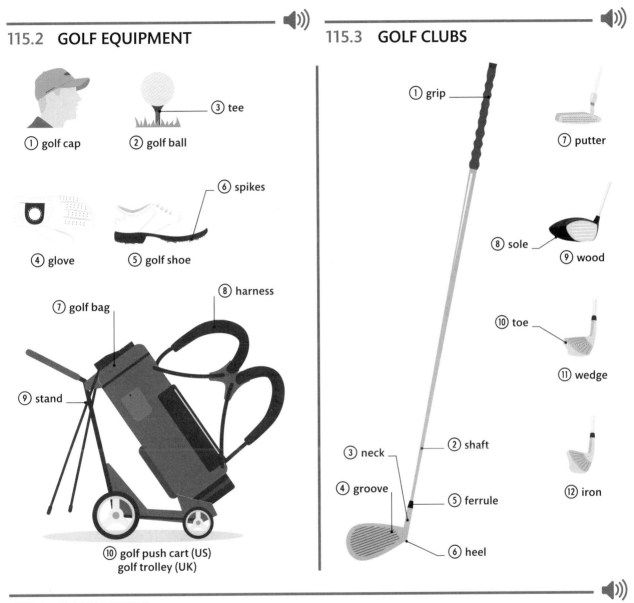

① golf cap
② golf ball
③ tee
④ glove
⑤ golf shoe
⑥ spikes
⑦ golf bag
⑧ harness
⑨ stand
⑩ golf push cart (US)
golf trolley (UK)

115.3 GOLF CLUBS

① grip
② shaft
③ neck
④ groove
⑤ ferrule
⑥ heel
⑦ putter
⑧ sole
⑨ wood
⑩ toe
⑪ wedge
⑫ iron

115.4 GOLF VERBS

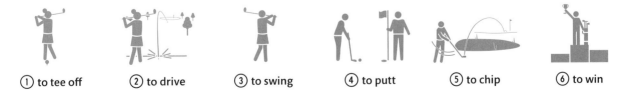

① to tee off
② to drive
③ to swing
④ to putt
⑤ to chip
⑥ to win

116 Athletics

116.1 ATHLETICS TRACK

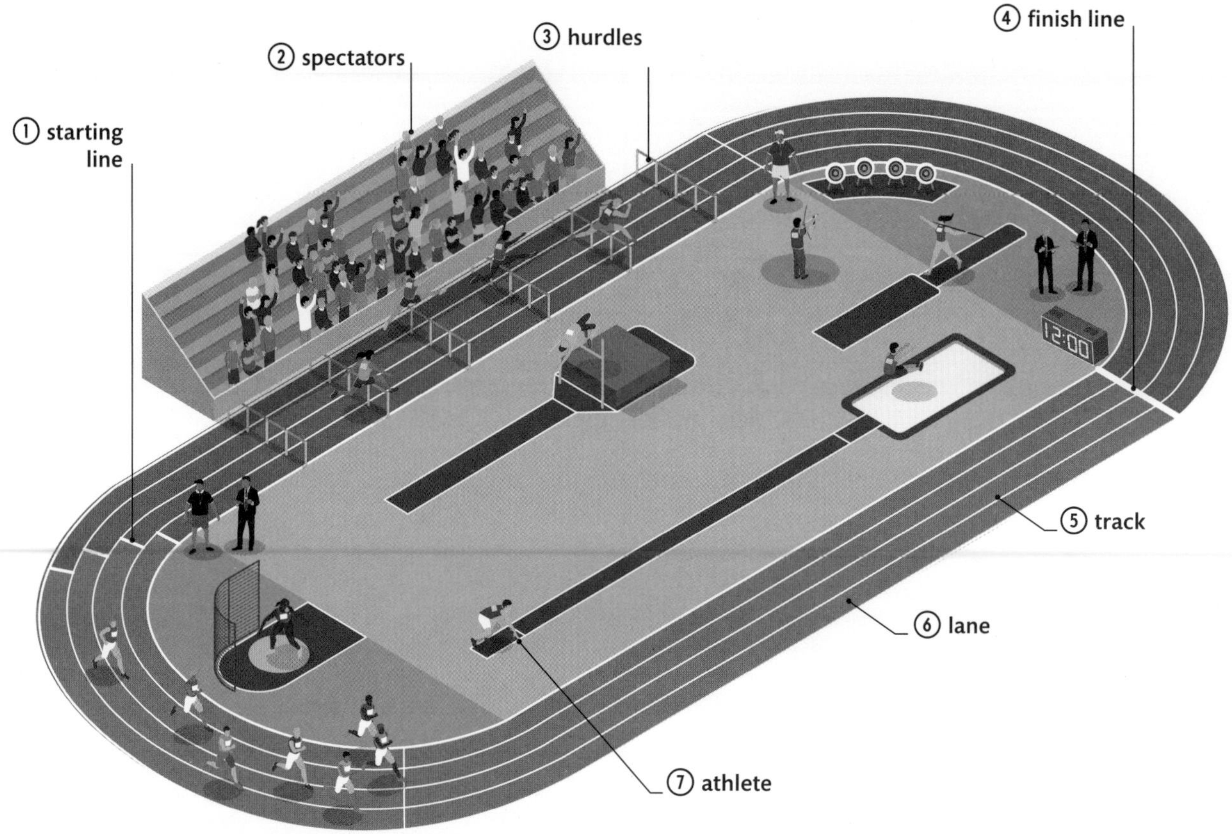

① starting line
② spectators
③ hurdles
④ finish line
⑤ track
⑥ lane
⑦ athlete

116.2 RACING EVENTS

① race

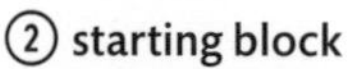
② starting block

③ sprinter

④ T11 (visual impairment) race

⑤ wheelchair race

⑥ relay race

⑦ baton

⑧ marathon

⑨ photo finish

See also:
117 Combat sports **118** Swimming **119** Sailing and watersports
120 Horse riding **122** Winter sports **124** At the gym **125** Other sports

116.3 FIELD EVENTS

① discus

② shot put

③ hammer

④ javelin

⑤ pole vault

⑥ long jump

⑦ high jump

⑧ triple jump

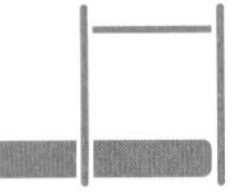
⑨ crossbar

⑩ laser run

⑪ fencing

116.4 ON THE PODIUM

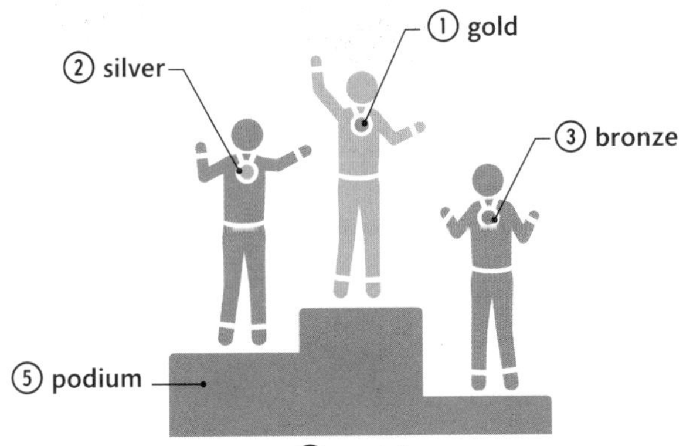
① gold
② silver
③ bronze
④ medals
⑤ podium

116.5 COMBINED EVENTS

① triathlon

② modern pentathlon

③ women's heptathlon

④ men's decathlon

117 Combat sports

117.1 MARTIAL ARTS

① groin protector
② glove
③ belt
④ head guard
⑤ chest protection
⑥ taekwondo

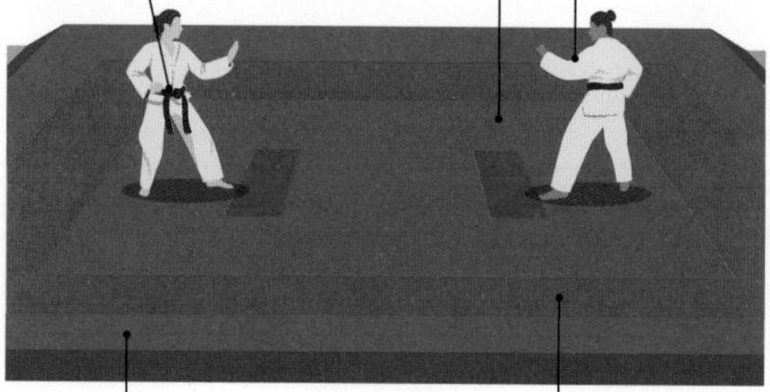

⑦ black belt
⑧ karate mat
⑨ opponent
⑩ safety area
⑪ karate
⑫ danger area

⑬ judo 
⑭ aikido 
⑮ hakama
⑯ kung fu 
⑰ jujitsu 
⑱ capoeira

⑲ kickboxing 
⑳ tai chi 
㉑ wrestling 
㉒ sumo wrestling

㉓ mask
㉔ sword
㉕ kendo

117.2 ACTIONS

① to fall

② to hold

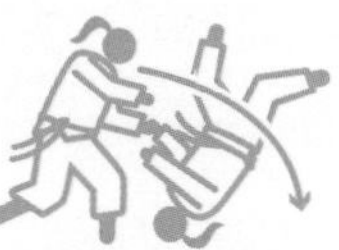
③ to throw

④ to pin

⑤ front kick

⑥ flying kick

See also:
116 Athletics 124 At the gym
125 Other sports

117.3 BOXING

117.4 FENCING

① boxing ring
② ropes
③ boxing match
④ round
⑤ knock out
⑥ boxing gloves
⑦ mouth guard
⑧ punching bag (US)
punchbag (UK)
① to lunge
② to parry
③ hilt
④ foil
⑤ blade
⑥ épée
⑦ saber (US)
sabre (UK)

⑦ to punch

⑧ to strike

⑨ to block

⑩ to jump

⑪ to chop

118 Swimming

118.1 SWIMMING

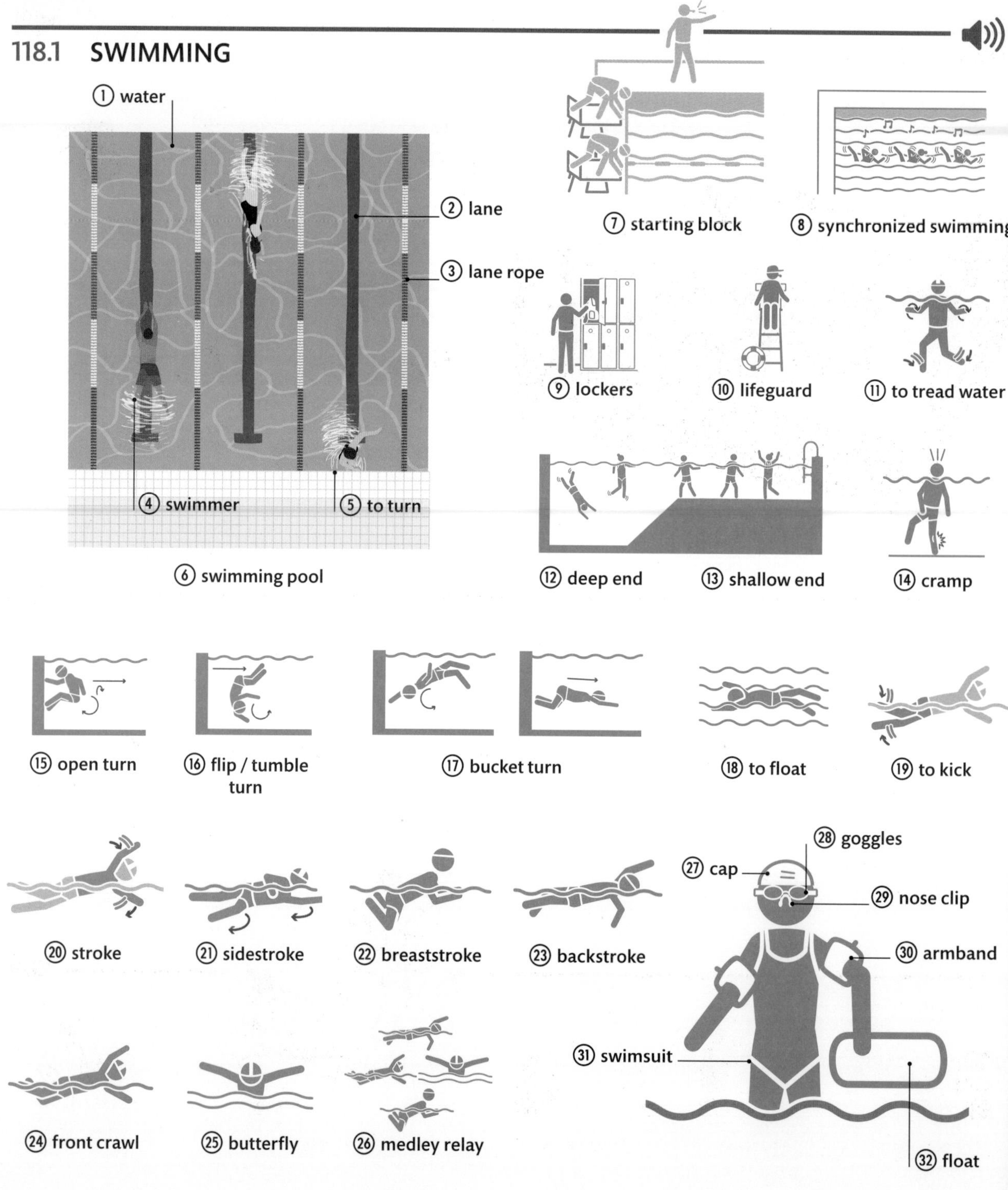

① water
② lane
③ lane rope
④ swimmer
⑤ to turn
⑥ swimming pool
⑦ starting block
⑧ synchronized swimming
⑨ lockers
⑩ lifeguard
⑪ to tread water
⑫ deep end
⑬ shallow end
⑭ cramp
⑮ open turn
⑯ flip / tumble turn
⑰ bucket turn
⑱ to float
⑲ to kick
⑳ stroke
㉑ sidestroke
㉒ breaststroke
㉓ backstroke
㉗ cap
㉘ goggles
㉙ nose clip
㉚ armband
㉛ swimsuit
㉜ float
㉔ front crawl
㉕ butterfly
㉖ medley relay

See also:
119 Sailing and watersports
134 On the beach **166** Ocean life

118.2 DIVING

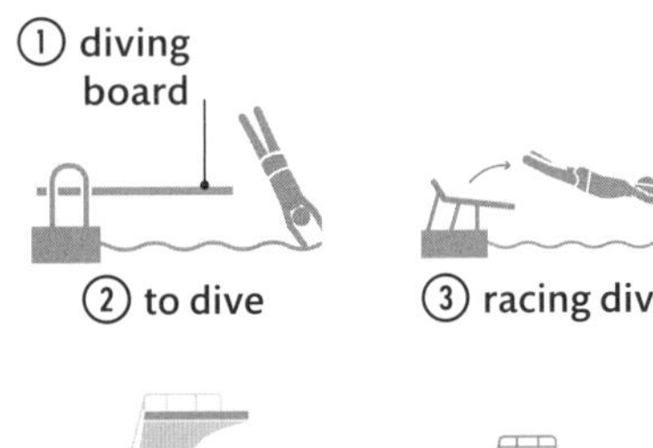
① diving board
② to dive
③ racing dive

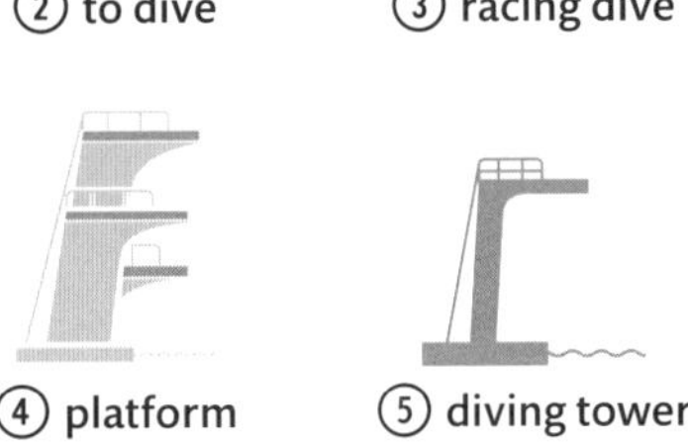
④ platform
⑤ diving tower

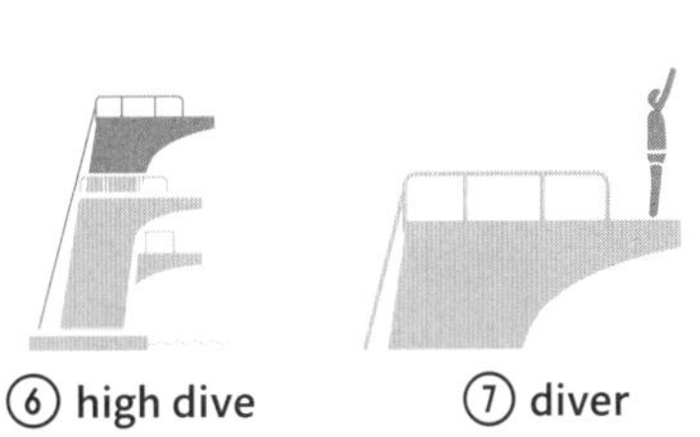
⑥ high dive
⑦ diver

⑧ front-flip
⑨ back-flip

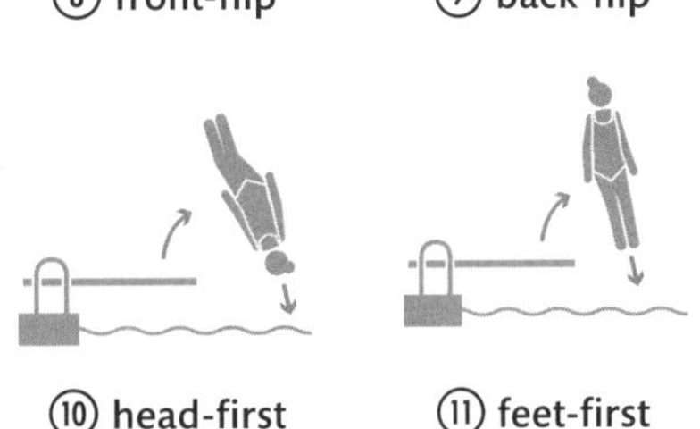
⑩ head-first
⑪ feet-first

⑫ springboard

118.3 UNDERWATER DIVING

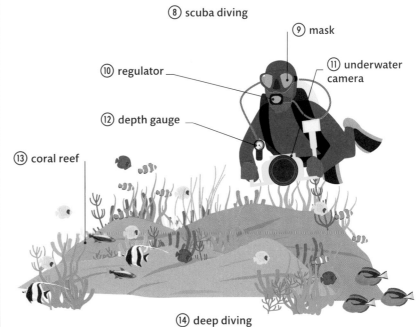

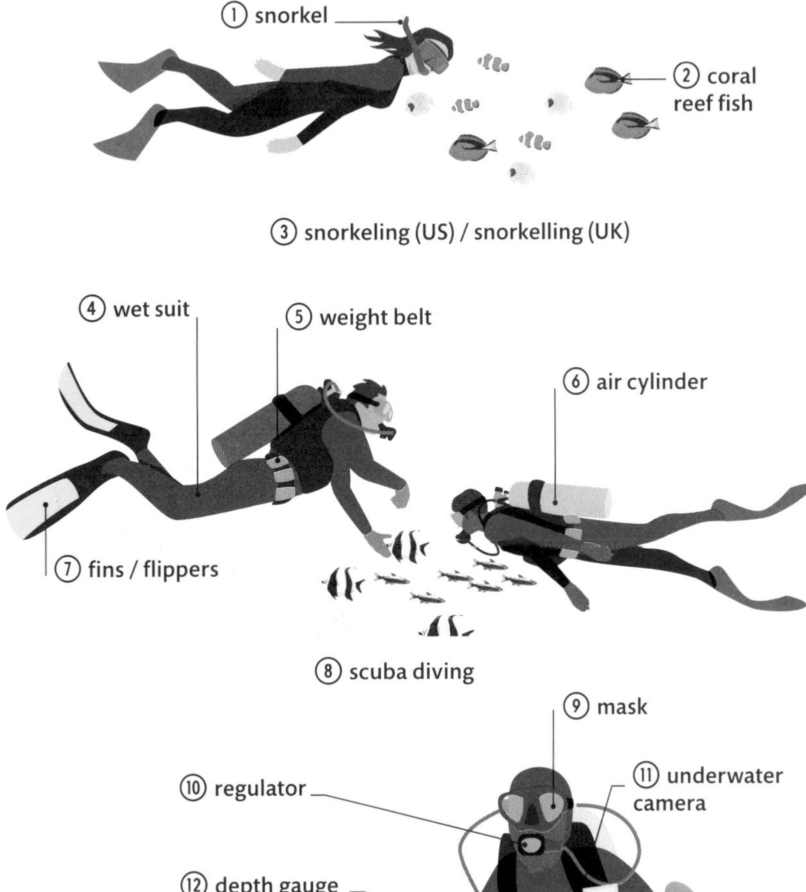
① snorkel
② coral reef fish
③ snorkeling (US) / snorkelling (UK)
④ wet suit
⑤ weight belt
⑥ air cylinder
⑦ fins / flippers
⑧ scuba diving
⑨ mask
⑩ regulator
⑪ underwater camera
⑫ depth gauge
⑬ coral reef
⑭ deep diving

119 Sailing and watersports

119.1 SAILING

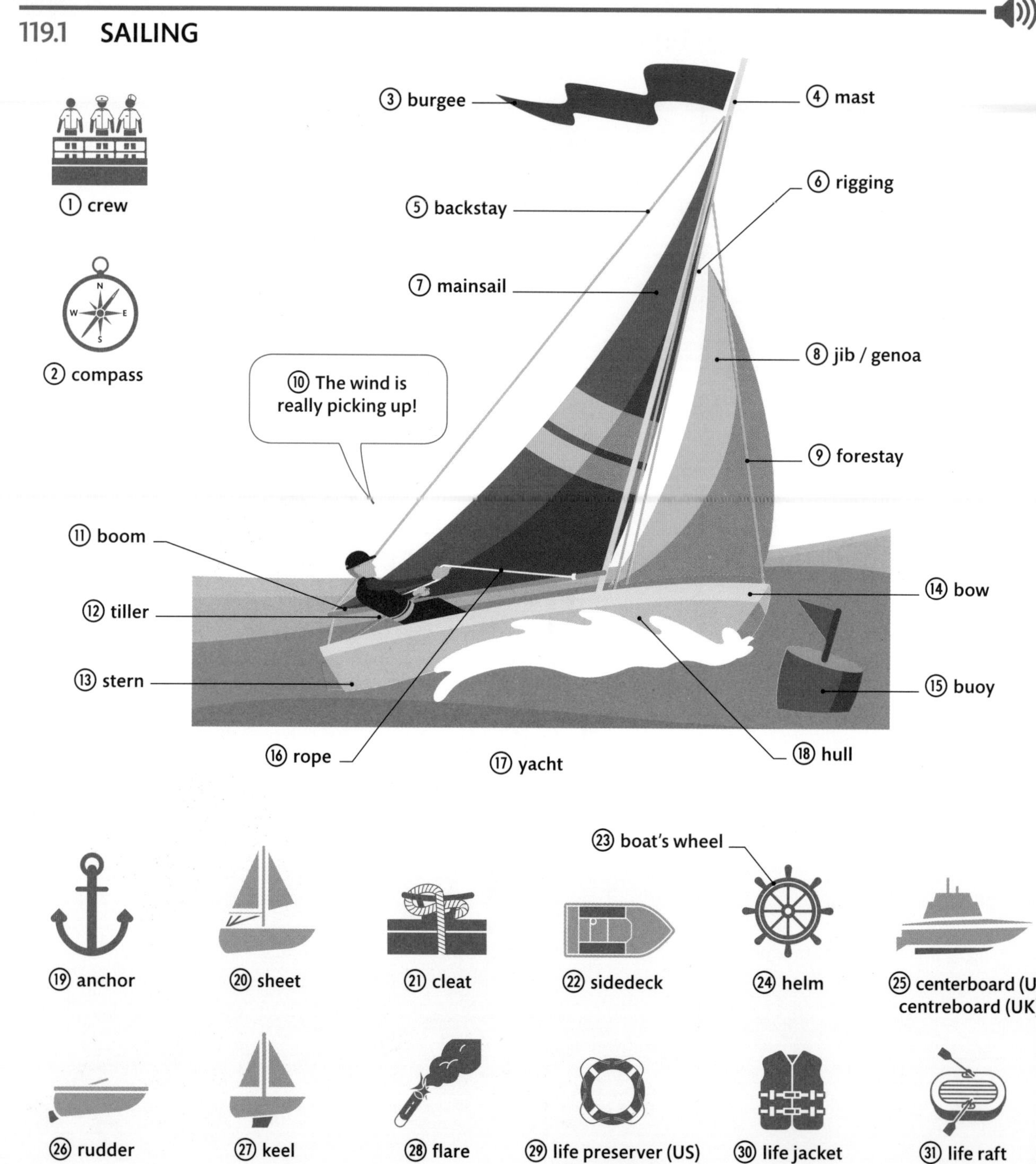

① crew
② compass
③ burgee
④ mast
⑤ backstay
⑥ rigging
⑦ mainsail
⑧ jib / genoa
⑨ forestay
⑩ The wind is really picking up!
⑪ boom
⑫ tiller
⑬ stern
⑭ bow
⑮ buoy
⑯ rope
⑰ yacht
⑱ hull
⑲ anchor
⑳ sheet
㉑ cleat
㉒ sidedeck
㉓ boat's wheel
㉔ helm
㉕ centerboard (US)
centreboard (UK)
㉖ rudder
㉗ keel
㉘ flare
㉙ life preserver (US)
life ring (UK)
㉚ life jacket
㉛ life raft

See also:
105 Sea vessels 106 The port 118 Swimming
121 Fishing 134 On the beach

119.2 WATERSPORTS

① rower
③ oar
② rowing
④ kayak
⑥ paddle
⑤ kayaking
⑨ surfboard
⑦ surfer
⑧ surfing
⑩ boogie board
⑪ bodyboarding
⑫ paddleboarding
⑬ parasailing
⑭ kite surfing
⑳ ski
㉑ water skier
⑮ speed boating
⑯ rafting
⑰ jet skiing
⑱ water polo
⑲ water skiing
㉒ to capsize
㉓ to navigate
㉔ to tack
㉚ windsurfer
㉛ sail
㉙ board
㉗ surf
㉖ rapids
㉝ boom
㉜ foot strap
㉕ wave
㉘ windsurfing

120 Horse riding

120.1 HORSEBACK RIDING (US) / HORSE RIDING (UK)

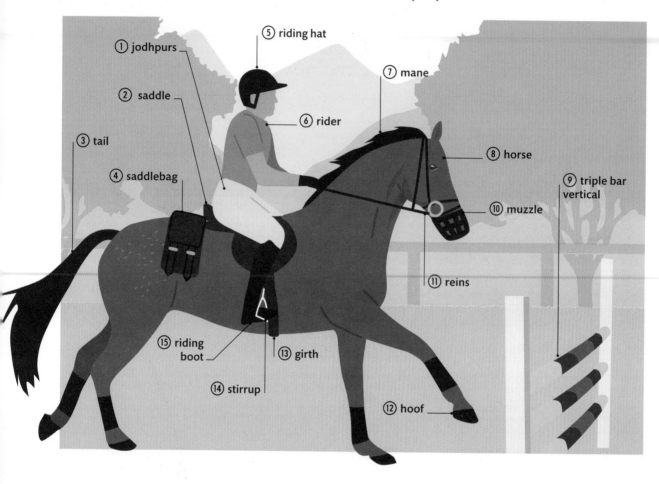

① jodhpurs
② saddle
③ tail
④ saddlebag
⑤ riding hat
⑥ rider
⑦ mane
⑧ horse
⑨ triple bar vertical
⑩ muzzle
⑪ reins
⑫ hoof
⑬ girth
⑭ stirrup
⑮ riding boot

⑯ horseshoe

⑰ halter

⑱ noseband

⑲ bit

⑳ browband

㉑ bridle

㉒ pommel

㉓ seat

㉔ riding crop

5
㉕ jockey

5
㉖ racehorse

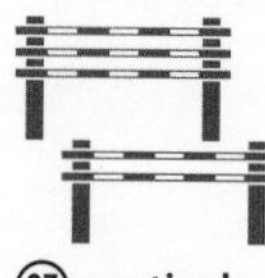
㉗ verticals

See also:
116 Athletics 125 Other sports
133 Outdoor activities

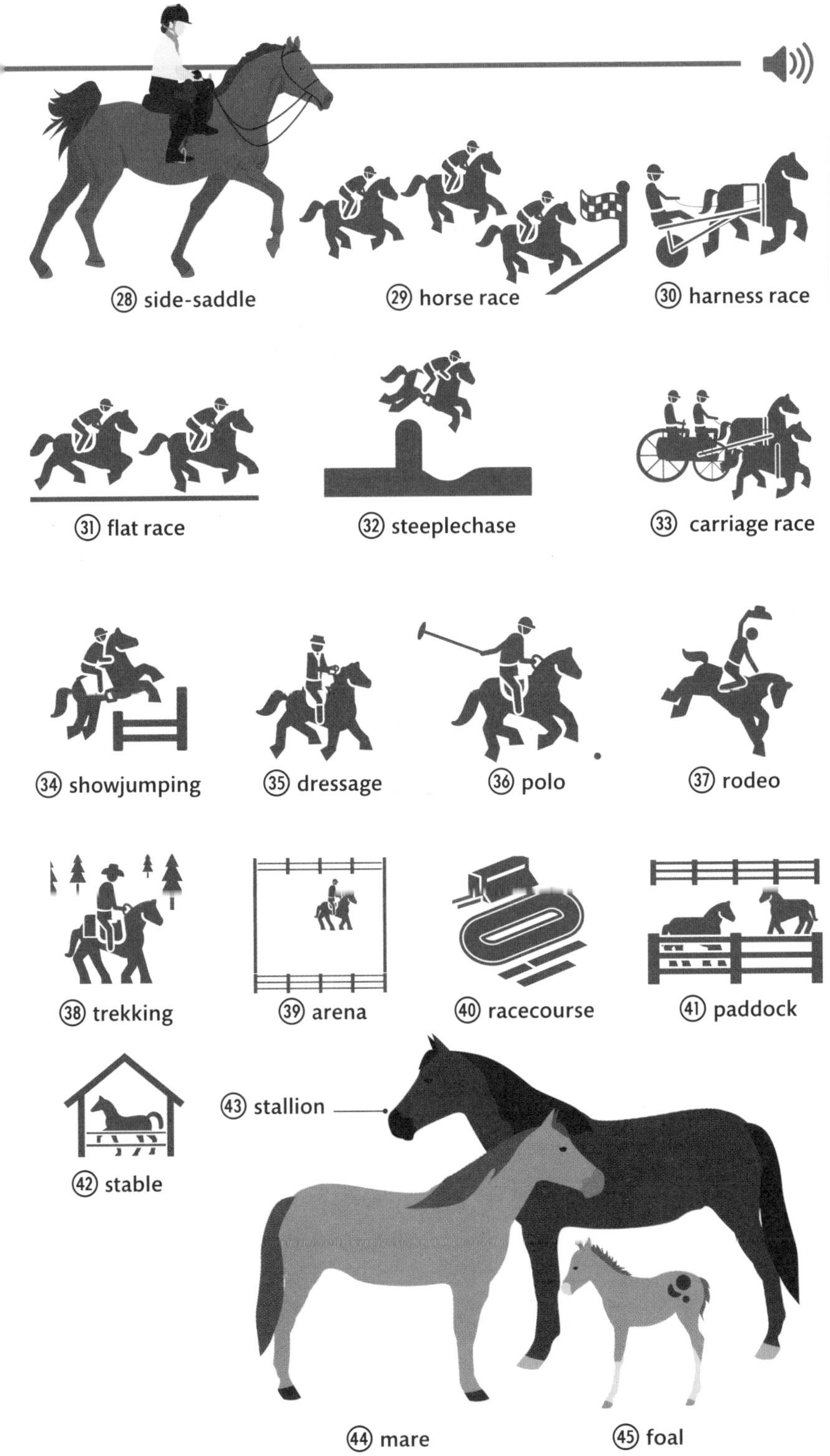

(28) side-saddle

(29) horse race

(30) harness race

(31) flat race

(32) steeplechase

(33) carriage race

(34) showjumping

(35) dressage

(36) polo

(37) rodeo

(38) trekking

(39) arena

(40) racecourse

(41) paddock

(42) stable

(43) stallion

(44) mare

(45) foal

120.2 VERBS

(1) to groom

(2) to walk

(3) to trot

(4) to canter

(5) to gallop

(6) to jump

(7) to breed

(8) to muck out

121 Fishing

121.1 ANGLER

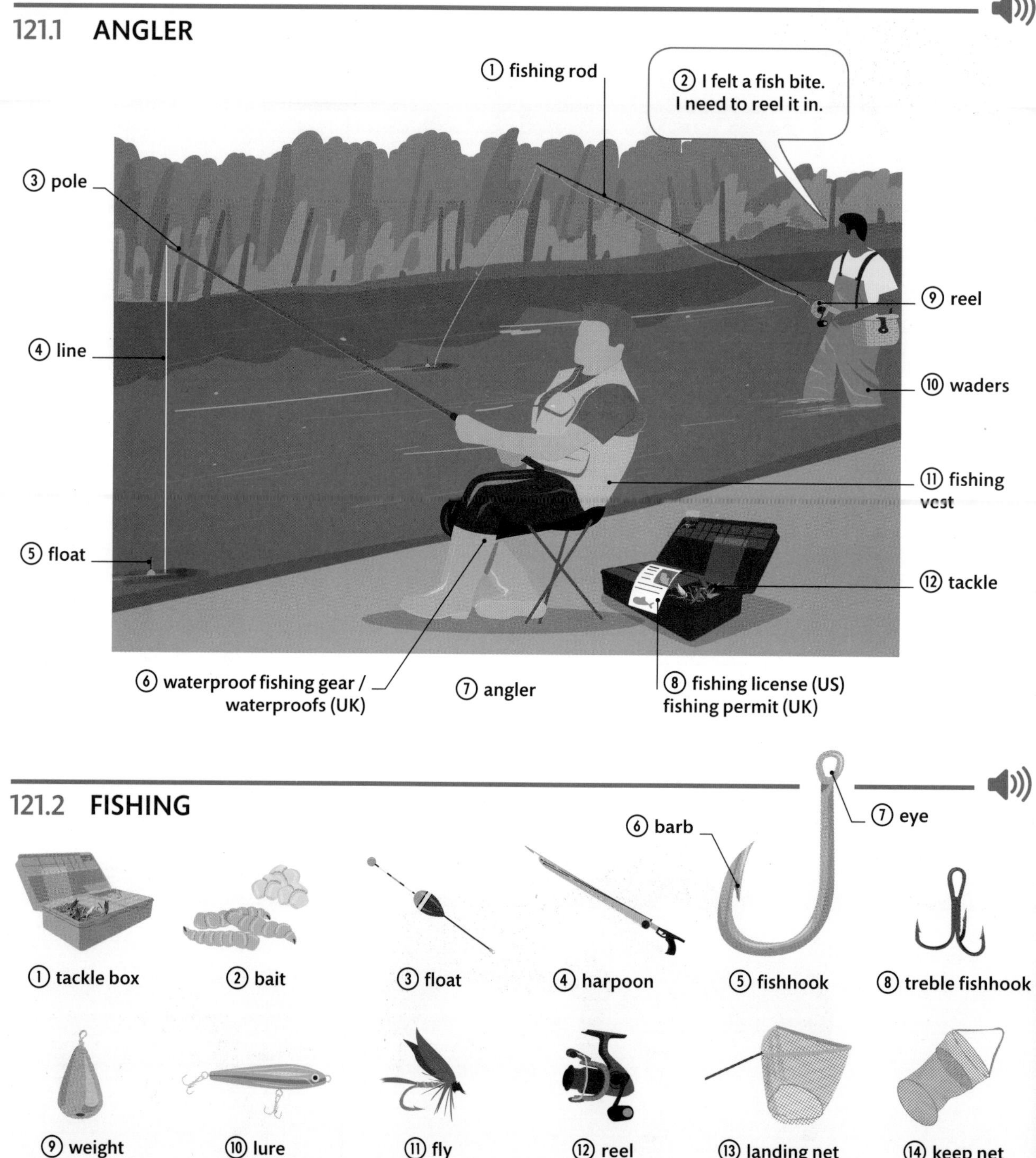

① fishing rod
② I felt a fish bite. I need to reel it in.
③ pole
④ line
⑤ float
⑥ waterproof fishing gear / waterproofs (UK)
⑦ angler
⑧ fishing license (US) fishing permit (UK)
⑨ reel
⑩ waders
⑪ fishing vest
⑫ tackle

121.2 FISHING

① tackle box
② bait
③ float
④ harpoon
⑤ fishhook
⑥ barb
⑦ eye
⑧ treble fishhook
⑨ weight
⑩ lure
⑪ fly
⑫ reel
⑬ landing net
⑭ keep net

See also:
54 Fish and seafood
119 Sailing and watersports **166** Ocean life

121.3 TYPES OF FISHING

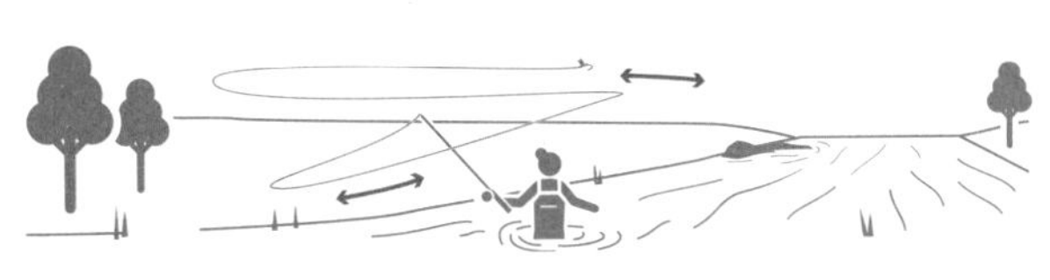

① fly fishing

② freshwater fishing

③ marine fishing

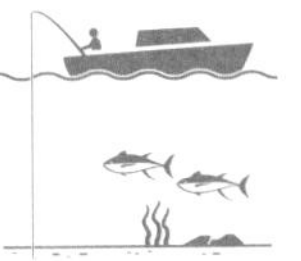

④ deep sea fishing

⑤ sport fishing

⑥ spearfishing

⑦ ice fishing

⑧ stand

⑨ surfcasting

121.4 FISHING VERBS

① to bait

② to cast

③ to bite

④ to catch

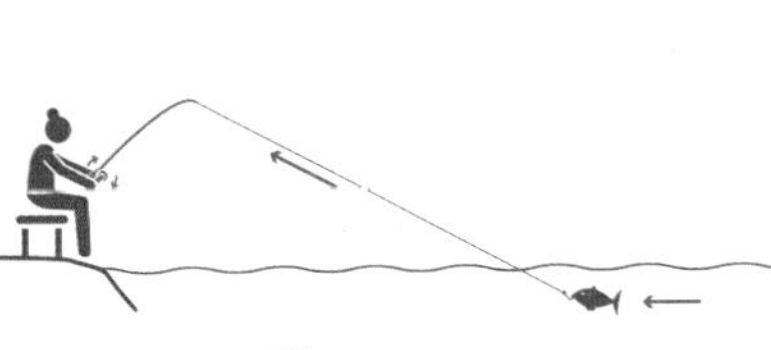

⑤ to reel in

⑥ to net

⑦ to release

121.5 KNOTS

① clinch knot

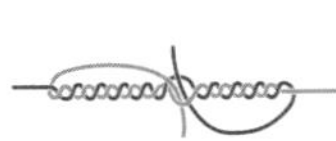

② blood knot

③ arbor knot

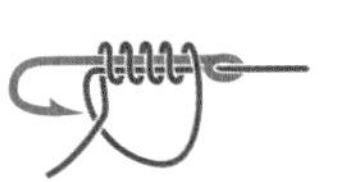

④ snell knot

⑤ turle knot

⑥ palomar knot

122 Winter sports

122.1 SKIING

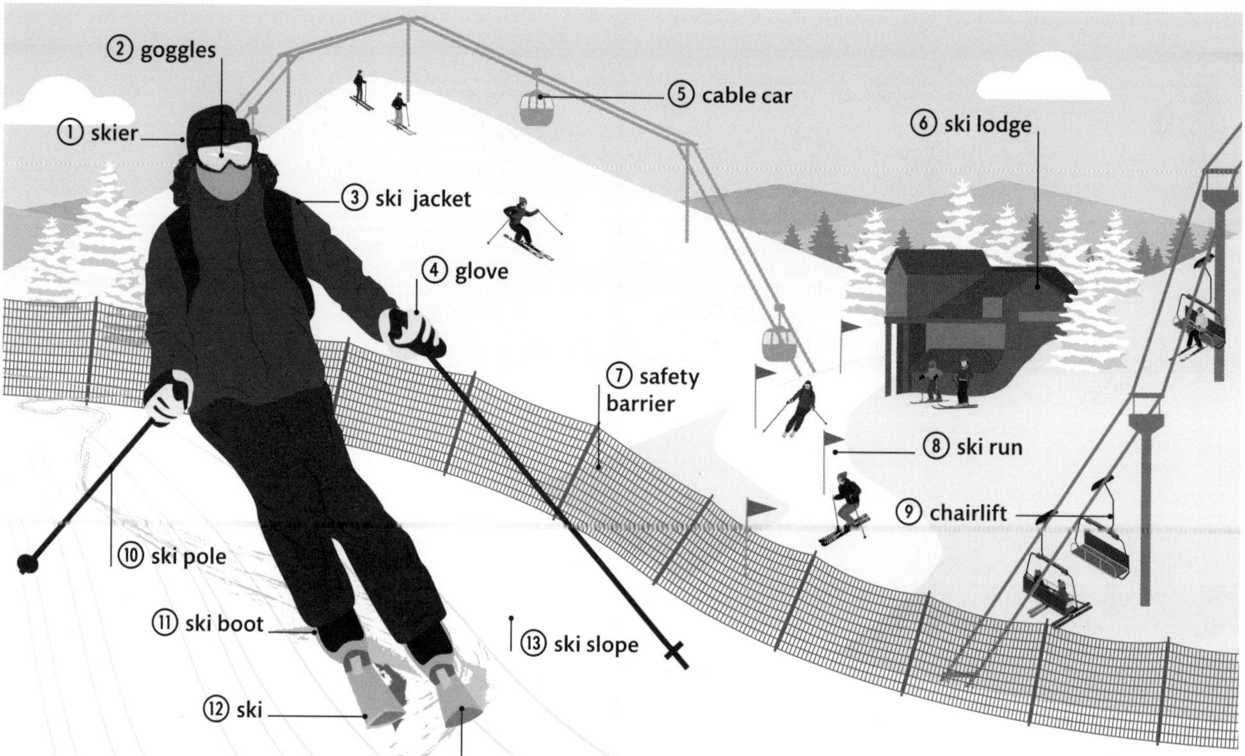

① skier
② goggles
③ ski jacket
④ glove
⑤ cable car
⑥ ski lodge
⑦ safety barrier
⑧ ski run
⑨ chairlift
⑩ ski pole
⑪ ski boot
⑫ ski
⑬ ski slope
⑭ tip
⑮ ski resort

⑯ to ski

⑰ downhill skiing

⑱ slalom

⑲ giant slalom

⑳ cross-country skiing

㉑ off-piste

㉒ biathlon

㉓ avalanche

㉔ landing hill

㉕ gate

㉖ ski jump

㉗ jumping ramp

See also:
116 Athletics **124** At the gym
125 Other sports

122.2 OTHER WINTER SPORTS

① winter sports

② skate

③ ice-skating

④ speed skating

⑤ figure skating

⑥ snowboarding

⑦ luge

⑧ skeleton

⑨ sledding (US)
sledging (UK)

⑪ runners
⑫ sled (US)
sleigh (UK)
⑩ bobsled (US) / bobsleigh (UK)

⑬ ice climbing

⑭ snowmobile

⑮ para ice hockey

⑯ wheelchair curling

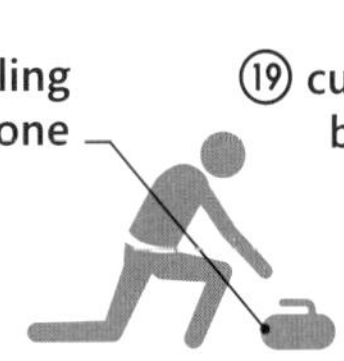
⑱ curling
stone
⑲ curling
brush
⑰ curling

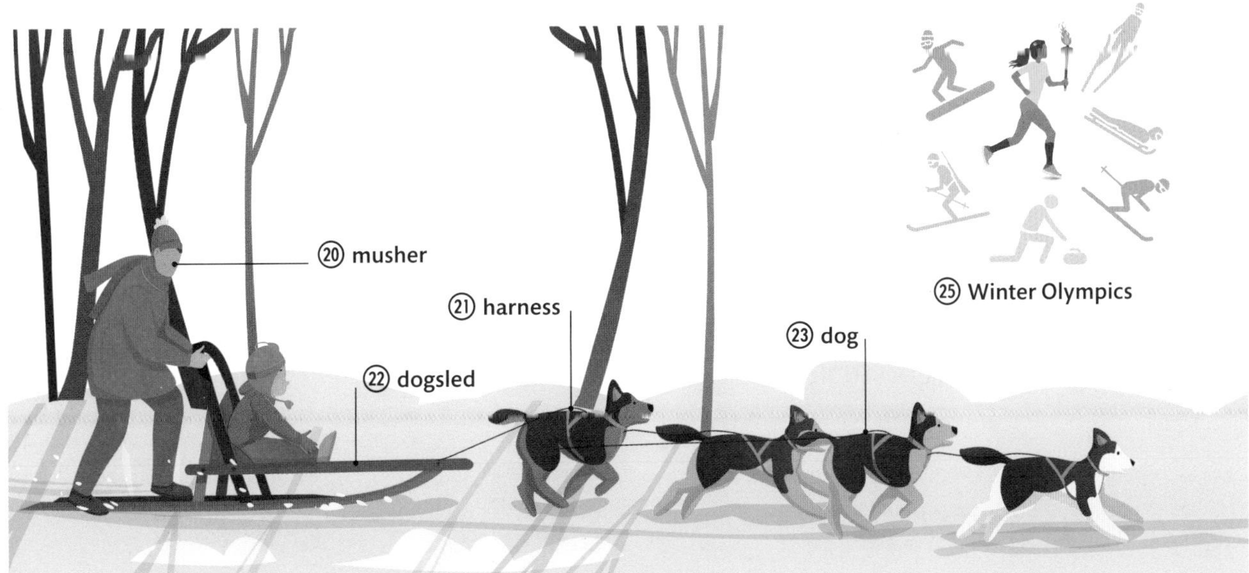
⑳ musher
㉑ harness
㉒ dogsled
㉓ dog
㉕ Winter Olympics
㉔ dog sledding

123 Motorsports

123.1 RACE CAR (US) / RACING CAR (UK)

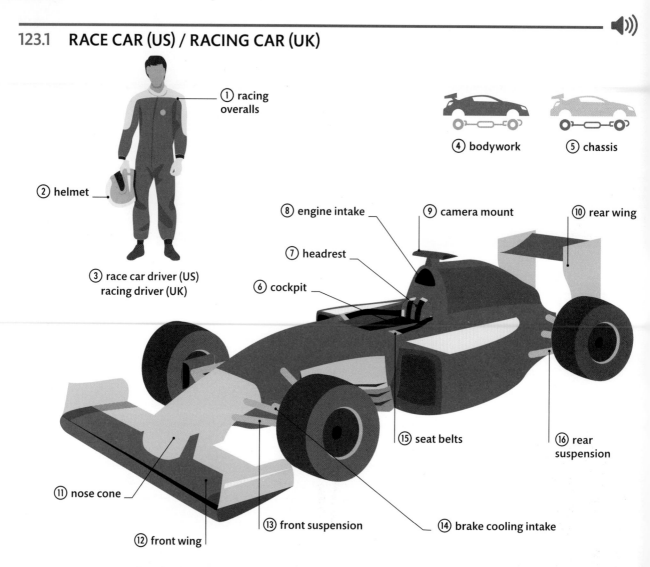

① racing overalls

② helmet

③ race car driver (US)
racing driver (UK)

④ bodywork

⑤ chassis

⑥ cockpit

⑦ headrest

⑧ engine intake

⑨ camera mount

⑩ rear wing

⑪ nose cone

⑫ front wing

⑬ front suspension

⑭ brake cooling intake

⑮ seat belts

⑯ rear suspension

123.2 TYPES OF MOTORSPORTS

① auto racing (US)
motor racing (UK)

② rally driving

③ drag racing

See also:
96 Roads 97-98 Cars
99 Cars and buses 100 Motorcycles

123.3 RACE TRACK

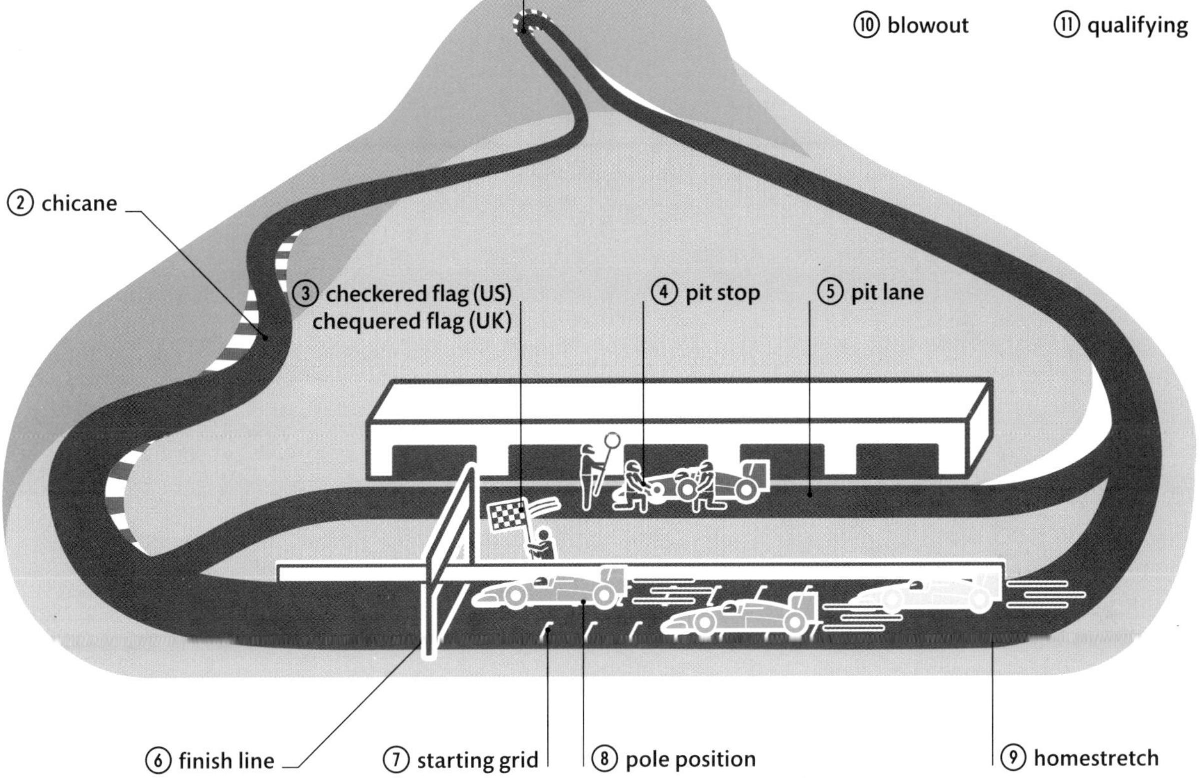

(1) hairpin turn

(2) chicane

(3) checkered flag (US)
chequered flag (UK)

(4) pit stop

(5) pit lane

(6) finish line

(7) starting grid

(8) pole position

(9) homestretch

(10) blowout

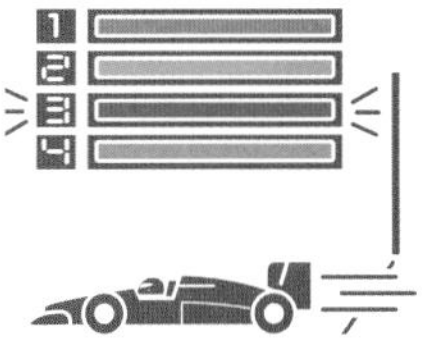

(11) qualifying

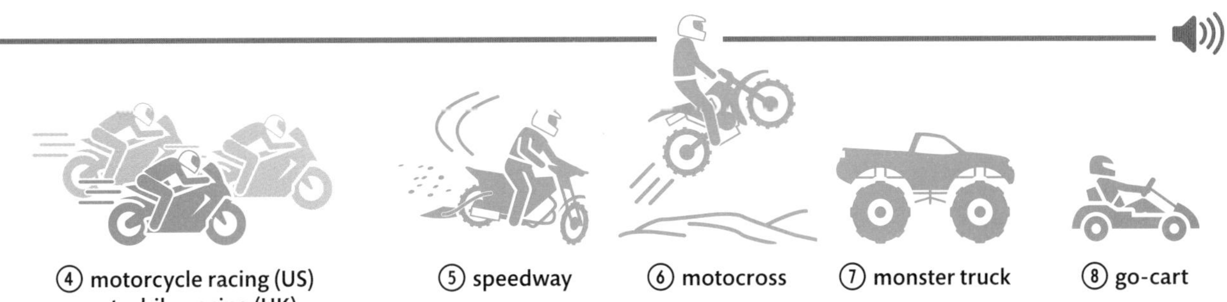

(4) motorcycle racing (US)
motorbike racing (UK)

(5) speedway

(6) motocross

(7) monster truck

(8) go-cart

124 At the gym

124.1 WORKING OUT

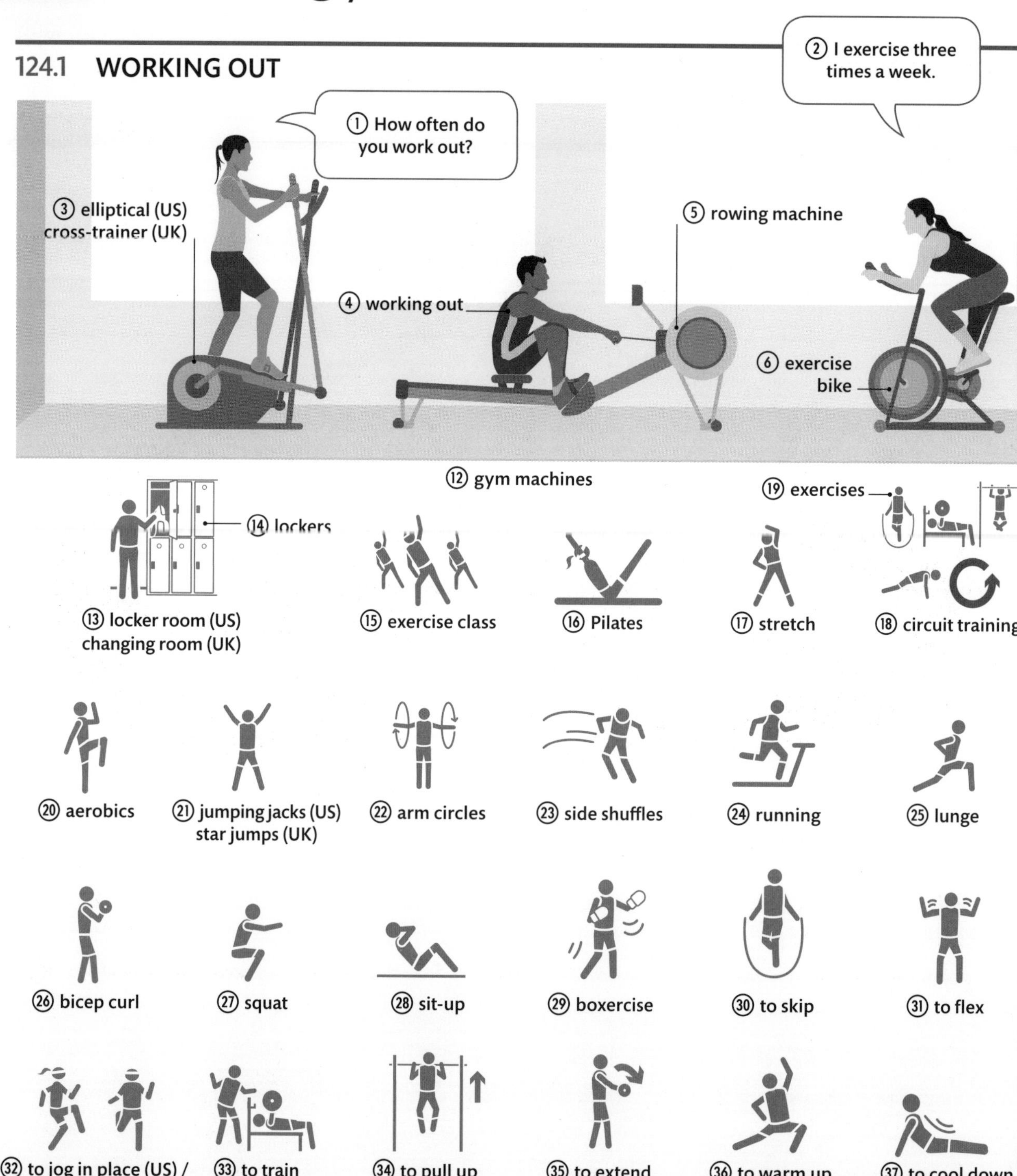

① How often do you work out?
② I exercise three times a week.
③ elliptical (US) cross-trainer (UK)
④ working out
⑤ rowing machine
⑥ exercise bike
⑫ gym machines
⑬ locker room (US) changing room (UK)
⑭ lockers
⑮ exercise class
⑯ Pilates
⑰ stretch
⑱ circuit training
⑲ exercises
⑳ aerobics
㉑ jumping jacks (US) star jumps (UK)
㉒ arm circles
㉓ side shuffles
㉔ running
㉕ lunge
㉖ bicep curl
㉗ squat
㉘ sit-up
㉙ boxercise
㉚ to skip
㉛ to flex
㉜ to jog in place (US) / on the spot (UK)
㉝ to train
㉞ to pull up
㉟ to extend
㊱ to warm up
㊲ to cool down

See also:
116 Athletics 117 Combat sports 118 Swimming
122 Winter sports 125 Other sports

7 weight training
8 free weights
9 exercise mat
10 push ups / press ups (UK)
11 treadmill

38 membership

39 gym equipment

40 aerobics step

41 dumbbell

42 hand grips

43 barbell / weight bar

44 bar

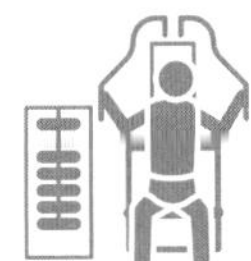
45 chest press

46 jump rope (US) skipping rope (UK)

47 exercise ball

48 twist bar

49 ankle weights / wrist weights

50 leg press

51 chest expander

52 ab wheel (US) wheel roller (UK)

53 running machine

54 bench

55 heart rate

56 sauna

57 hot tub

58 personal trainer

125 Other sports

125.1 GYMNASTICS

① floor mat
② hoop
③ ribbon
④ horizontal bar
⑤ vault
⑥ uneven bars
⑦ beam
⑧ pommel horse
⑨ rings
⑩ parallel bars
⑪ springboard

125.2 OTHER SPORTS

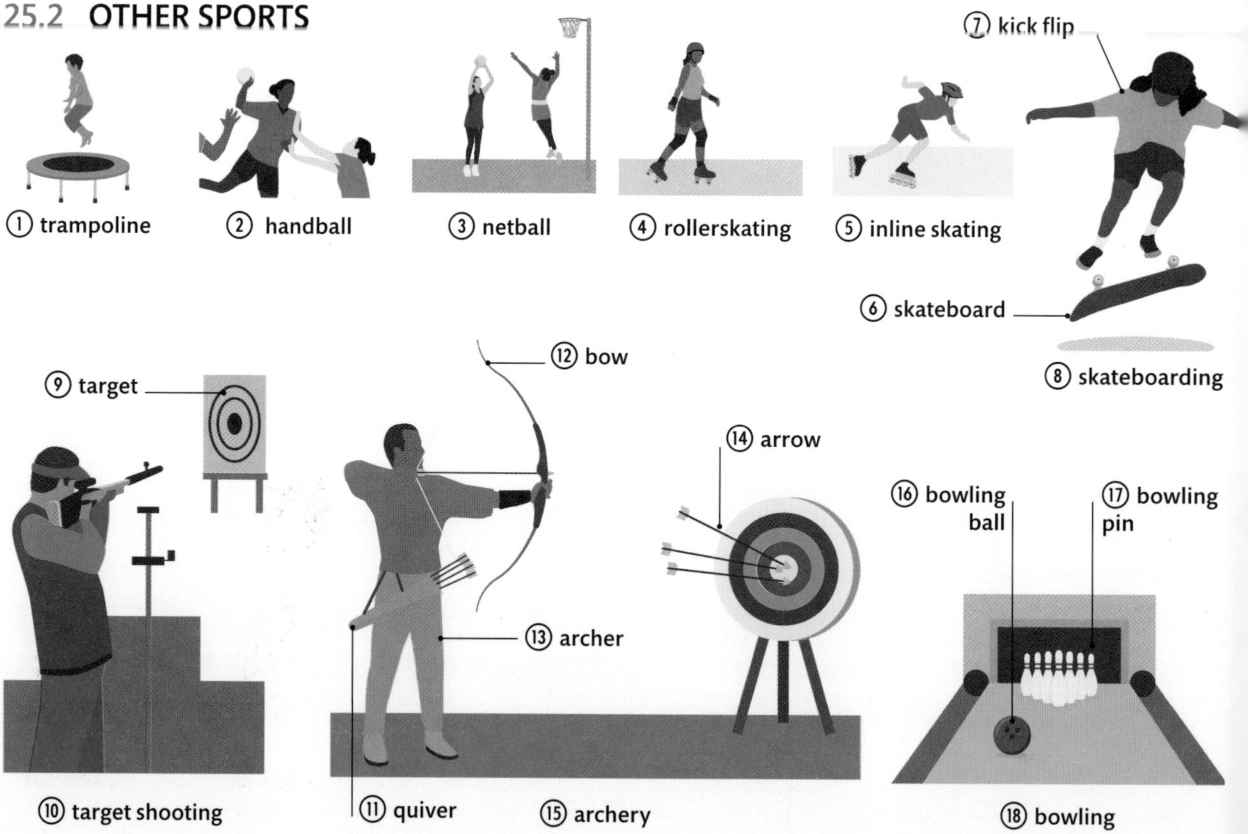

① trampoline
② handball
③ netball
④ rollerskating
⑤ inline skating
⑥ skateboard
⑦ kick flip
⑧ skateboarding
⑨ target
⑩ target shooting
⑪ quiver
⑫ bow
⑬ archer
⑭ arrow
⑮ archery
⑯ bowling ball
⑰ bowling pin
⑱ bowling

See also:
116 Athletics 117 Combat sports 118 Swimming
120 Horse riding 122 Winter sports 124 At the gym

125.3 PARASPORTS

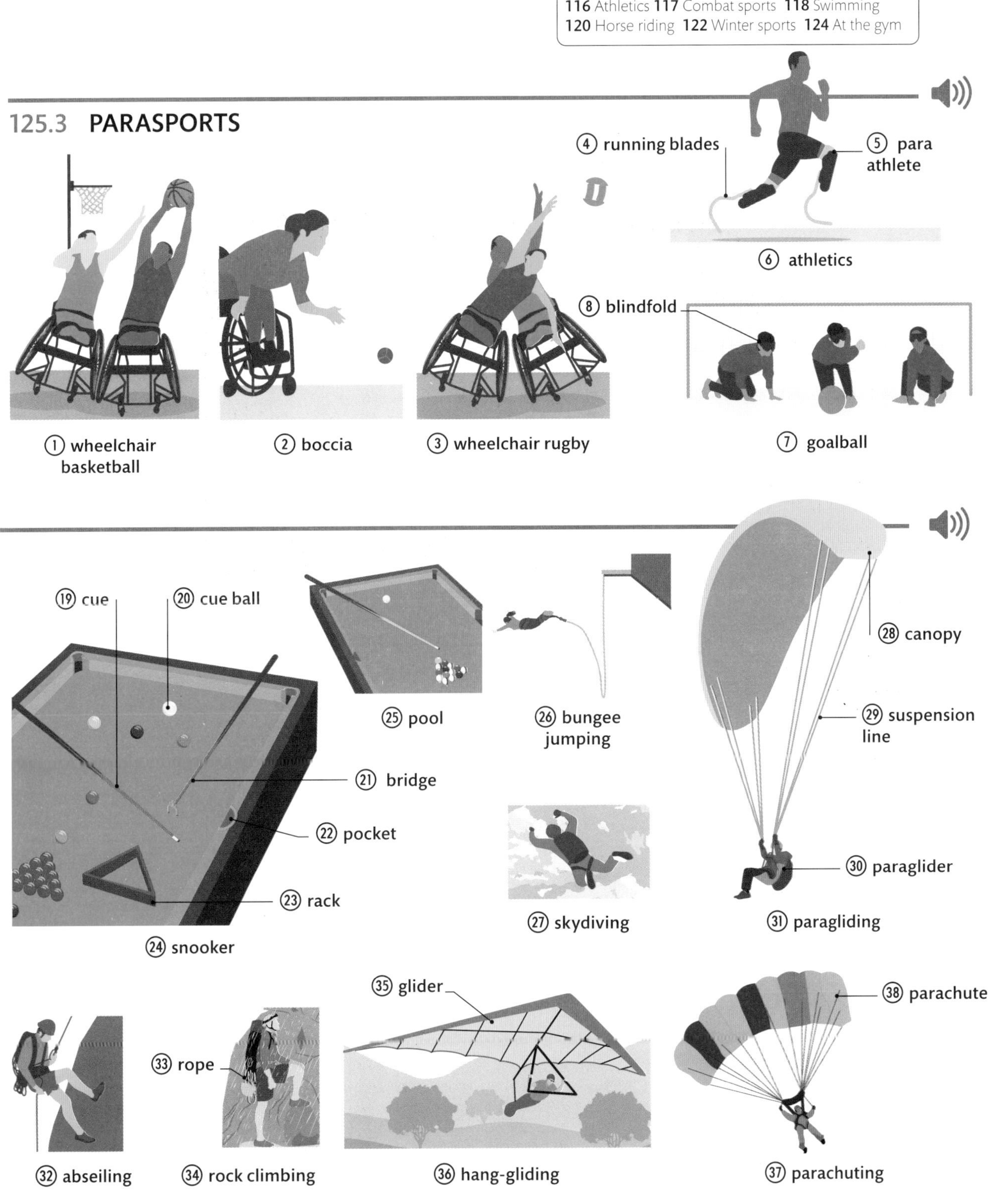
④ running blades
⑤ para athlete
⑥ athletics
⑧ blindfold
① wheelchair basketball
② boccia
③ wheelchair rugby
⑦ goalball
⑲ cue
⑳ cue ball
㉑ bridge
㉒ pocket
㉓ rack
㉔ snooker
㉕ pool
㉖ bungee jumping
㉗ skydiving
㉘ canopy
㉙ suspension line
㉚ paraglider
㉛ paragliding
㉜ abseiling
㉝ rope
㉞ rock climbing
㉟ glider
㊱ hang-gliding
㊲ parachuting
㊳ parachute

126 On stage

126.1 THEATER (US) / THEATRE (UK)

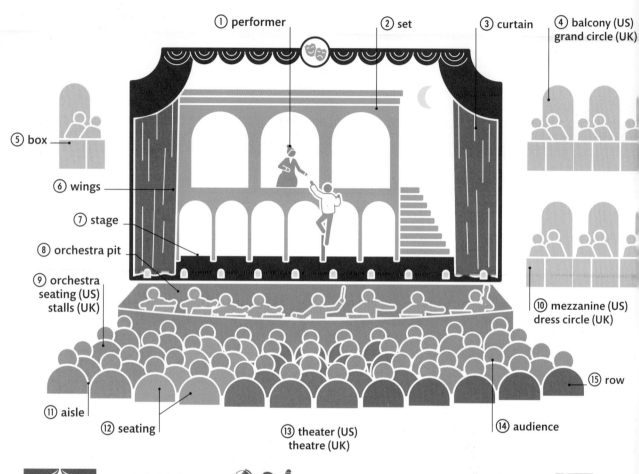

① performer
② set
③ curtain
④ balcony (US) grand circle (UK)
⑤ box
⑥ wings
⑦ stage
⑧ orchestra pit
⑨ orchestra seating (US) stalls (UK)
⑩ mezzanine (US) dress circle (UK)
⑪ aisle
⑫ seating
⑬ theater (US) theatre (UK)
⑭ audience
⑮ row

⑯ play

⑰ costumes

⑱ props

⑲ sets

⑳ backdrop

㉑ script

㉒ producer

㉓ director

㉔ actor

㉕ cast

㉖ opening night

㉗ intermission (US) interval (UK)

See also:
127 Movies / Films 128-129 Music
139 Fantasy and myth

126.2 BALLET

㉘ program (US) programme (UK)

㉙ usher

㉚ tragedy

㉛ comedy

㉜ musical

㉝ standing ovation

① arm
② knee
③ toe box
④ to pirouette / to turn

⑤ to plié / to bend

⑥ male ballet dancer

⑦ ballerina

⑧ tutu

⑨ ballet leotard

⑩ ballet slippers (US) ballet shoes (UK)

⑪ performance

⑫ encore

⑬ applause

126.3 OPERA

① bass

② baritone

③ tenor

④ opera house

⑤ alto

⑥ mezzo-soprano

⑦ soprano

⑧ prima donna

⑨ libretto

127 Movies (US) / Films (UK)

127.1 AT THE MOVIES (US) / CINEMA (UK)

① drama

② musical

③ science fiction

④ thriller

⑤ comedy

⑥ action movie

⑦ horror

⑧ animation

⑨ romantic comedy

⑩ crime drama

⑪ western

⑫ historical drama

⑬ fantasy

⑭ martial arts

⑮ special effects

⑯ box office

⑰ multiplex

⑱ popcorn

⑲ movie star (US) film star (UK)

⑳ screen

㉑ audience

㉒ movie theater (US) / cinema (UK)

㉓ main character

㉔ hero

㉕ villain

See also:
126 On stage 136 Home entertainment
137 Television

127.2 FILM STUDIO

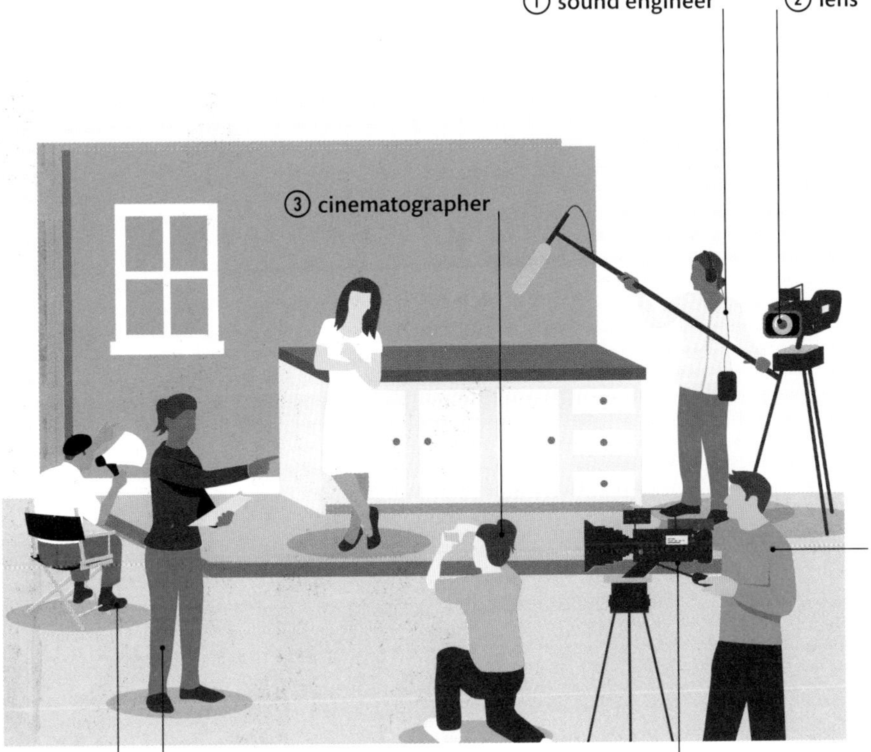

① sound engineer
② lens
③ cinematographer
④ camera operator
⑤ director
⑥ producer
⑦ movie camera
⑧ film set 
⑨ paparazzi
⑩ red carpet
⑪ celebrity
⑫ premiere
⑬ audition 
⑭ cast 
⑮ extras 
⑯ stunt 
⑰ props 
⑱ screenplay 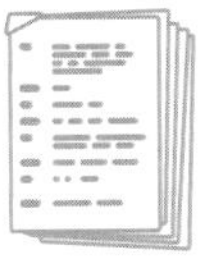
⑲ costumes 
⑳ soundtrack 
㉑ screenwriter

128 Music

128.1 ORCHESTRAL INSTRUMENTS

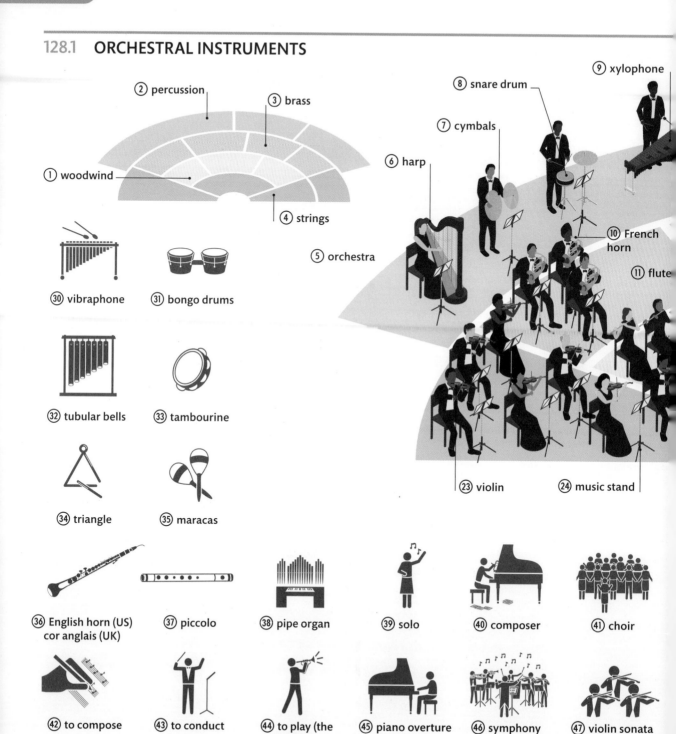

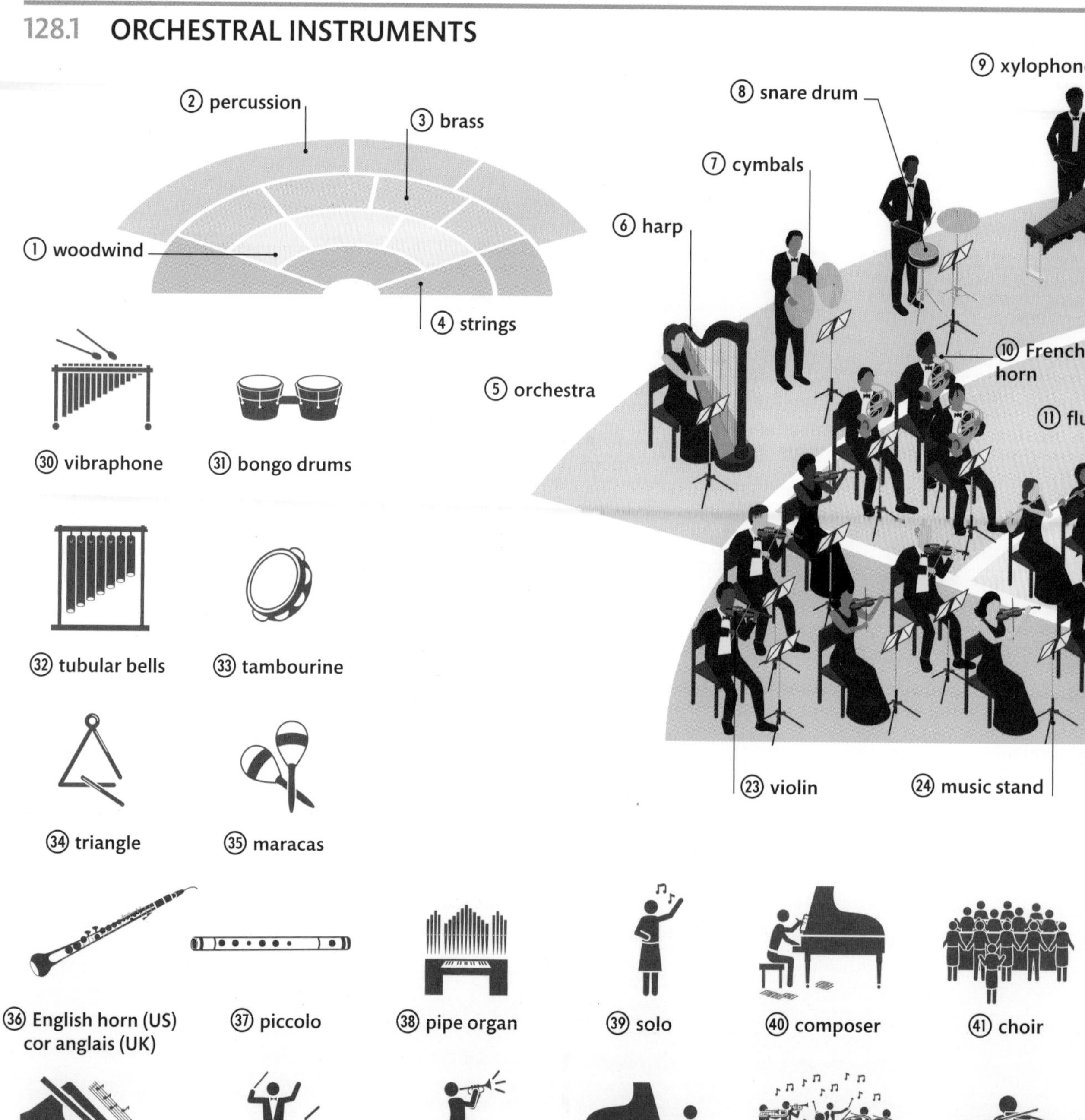
① woodwind
② percussion
③ brass
④ strings
⑤ orchestra
⑥ harp
⑦ cymbals
⑧ snare drum
⑨ xylophone
⑩ French horn
⑪ flute
㉓ violin
㉔ music stand
㉚ vibraphone
㉛ bongo drums
㉜ tubular bells
㉝ tambourine
㉞ triangle
㉟ maracas
㊱ English horn (US) cor anglais (UK)
㊲ piccolo
㊳ pipe organ
㊴ solo
㊵ composer
㊶ choir

㊷ to compose

㊸ to conduct

㊹ to play (the trumpet)

㊺ piano overture

㊻ symphony

㊼ violin sonata

See also:
126 On stage 127 Movies / Films
129 Music (continued) 136 Home entertainment

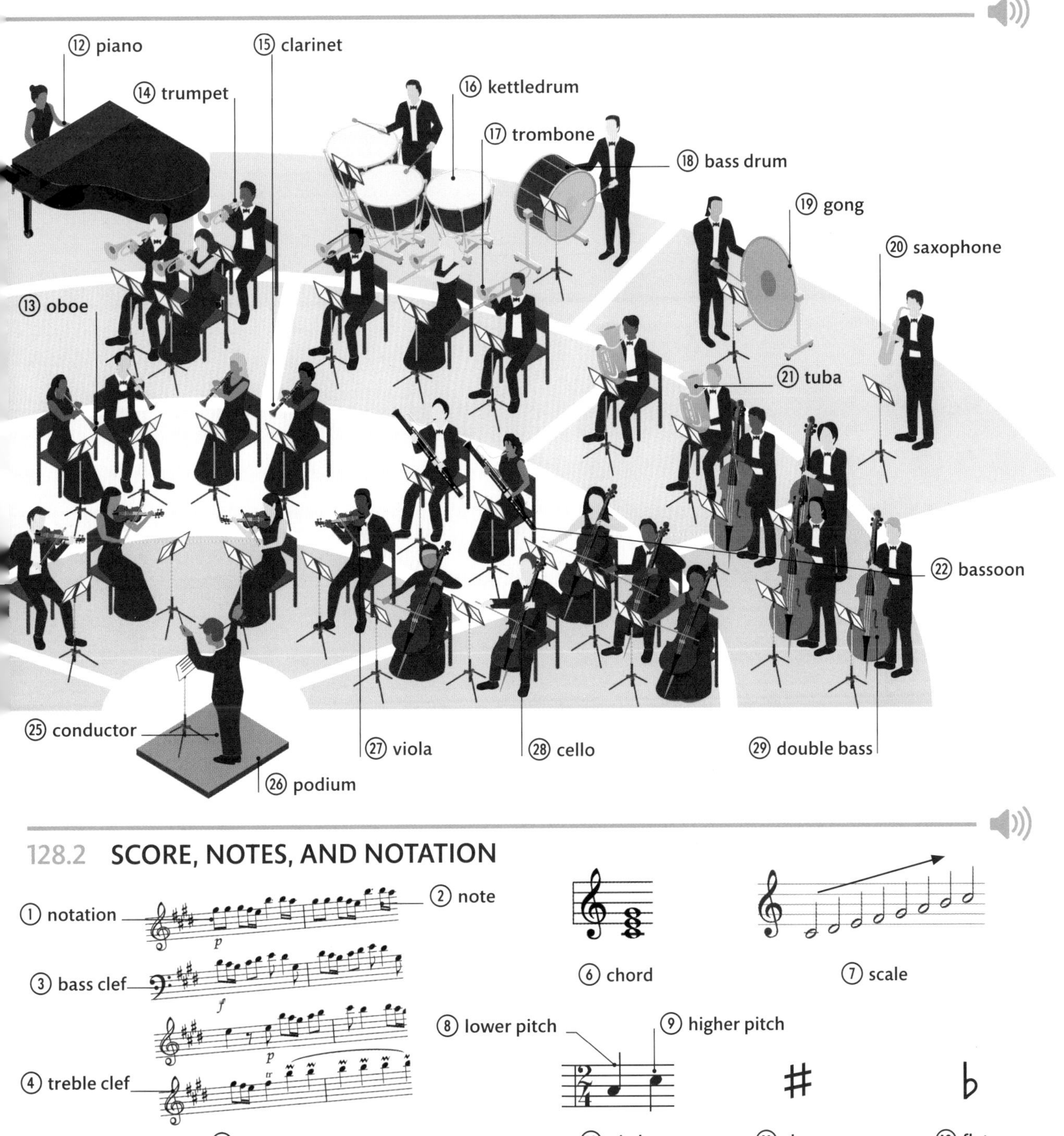
(12) piano
(15) clarinet
(14) trumpet
(16) kettledrum
(17) trombone
(18) bass drum
(19) gong
(20) saxophone
(13) oboe
(21) tuba
(22) bassoon
(25) conductor
(27) viola
(28) cello
(29) double bass
(26) podium

128.2 SCORE, NOTES, AND NOTATION

(1) notation
(2) note
(3) bass clef
(4) treble clef
(5) score
(6) chord
(7) scale
(8) lower pitch
(9) higher pitch
(10) pitch
(11) sharp
(12) flat

129 Music continued

129.1 POPULAR MUSIC

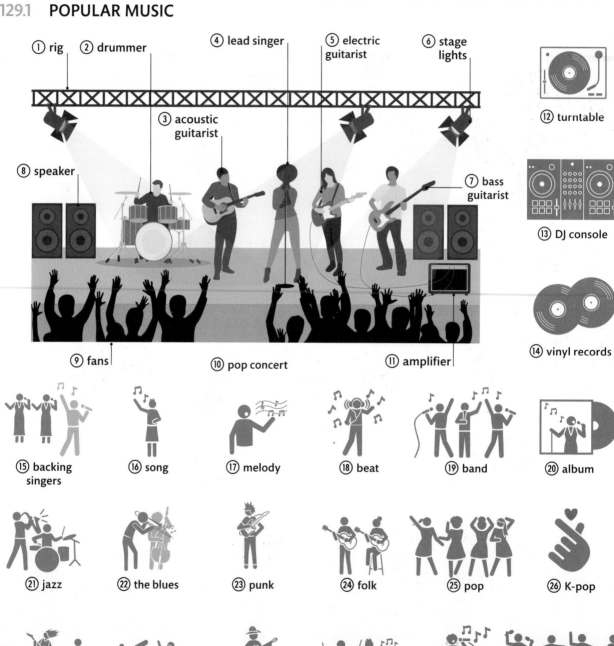

① rig
② drummer
③ acoustic guitarist
④ lead singer
⑤ electric guitarist
⑥ stage lights
⑦ bass guitarist
⑧ speaker
⑨ fans
⑩ pop concert 
⑪ amplifier
⑫ turntable
⑬ DJ console 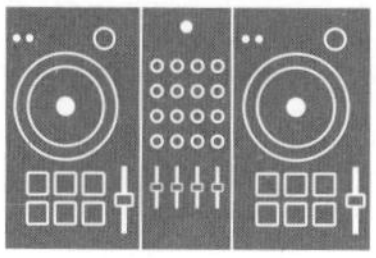
⑭ vinyl records 

⑮ backing singers
⑯ song 
⑰ melody 
⑱ beat 
⑲ band 
⑳ album 

㉑ jazz
㉒ the blues 
㉓ punk 
㉔ folk 
㉕ pop 
㉖ K-pop 

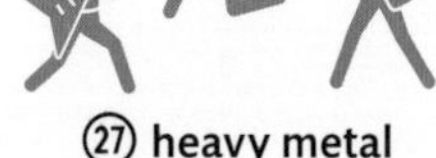
㉗ heavy metal

㉘ hip-hop

㉙ country

㉚ rock

㉛ soul

㉜ Latin

See also:
126 On stage 127 Movies / Films
136 Home entertainment

129.2 MORE INSTRUMENTS

33 dance
34 bhangra
35 reggae
36 opera
37 classical music
38 gospel
1 harmonica
2 panpipe
3 recorder
4 flute
5 didgeridoo
6 bagpipes
7 trumpet
8 saxophone
9 accordion
10 keyboard
11 piano
12 violin
13 oud
14 sitar
15 banjo
16 mandolin
17 ukulele
18 reverb
19 pick-up
20 body
21 neck
22 tuning peg
23 headstock
24 jack connector
25 electric guitar
26 tuner
27 waist
28 fret
29 nut
30 position markers
31 neck
32 string
33 sound hole
34 bridge
35 acoustic guitar

130 Museums and galleries

130.1 AT THE MUSEUM AND ART GALLERY

① gallery

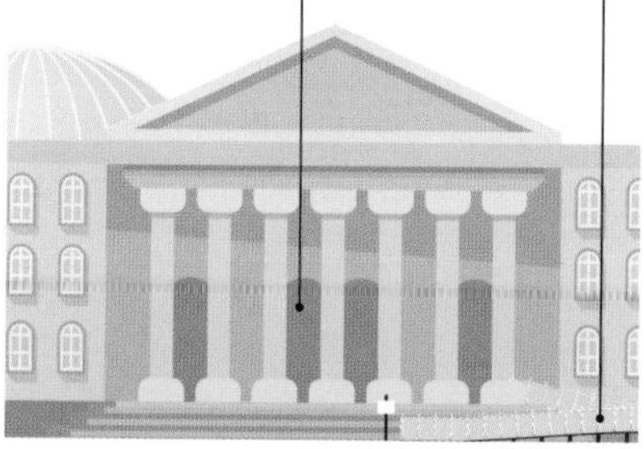

② entrance

③ wheelchair ramp

④ museum

⑤ restrooms (US) / toilets (UK)

⑥ cloakroom

⑦ admission fee

⑧ ticket

⑨ ticket office

⑩ donation

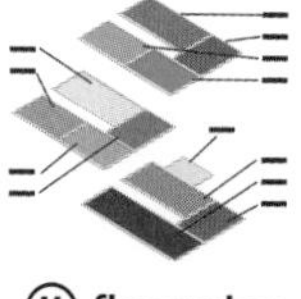

⑪ floor plan

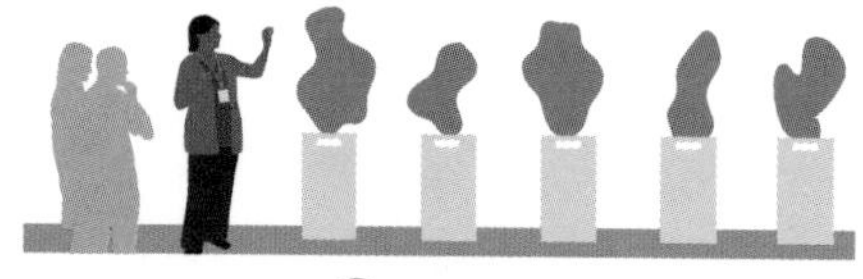

⑫ curator

⑭ exhibit

⑬ exhibition

⑮ permanent exhibition

⑰ installation

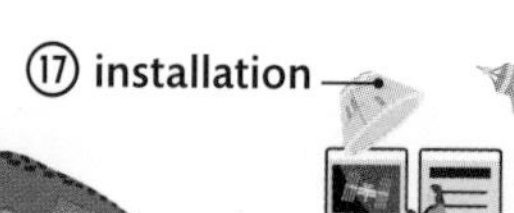

UNTIL
MAY 14

⑯ temporary exhibition

⑱ collection

⑲ conservation

⑳ tour guide

㉑ audio guide

㉒ no photography

㉓ gift shop

See also:
42-43 In town 132 Sightseeing
141-142 Arts and crafts

24 sculpture
25 surveillance camera
29 This masterpiece is priceless!
30 frame
26 label
27 masterpiece
28 security guard
31 painting

32 oil painting

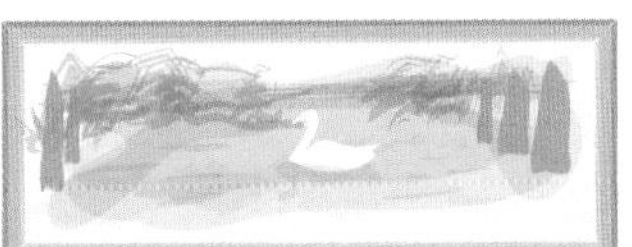
33 watercolor (US) / watercolour (UK)

34 Classicism

35 Impressionism

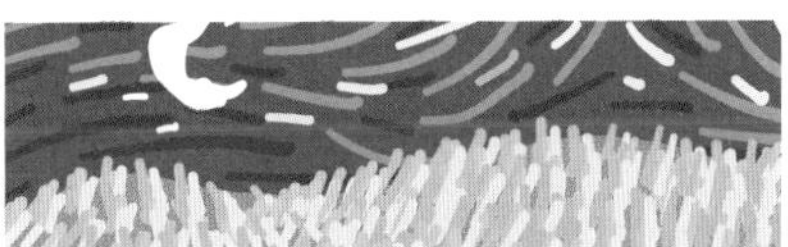
36 Post-Impressionism

41 Art Deco

42 Art Nouveau

37 Cubism

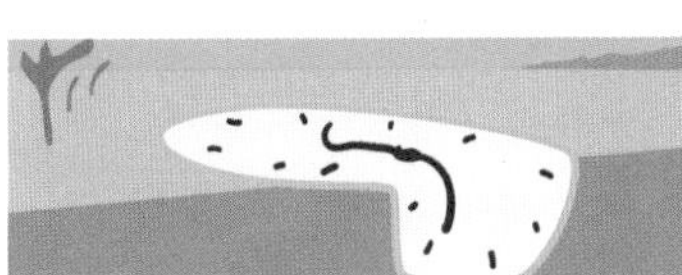
38 Surrealism

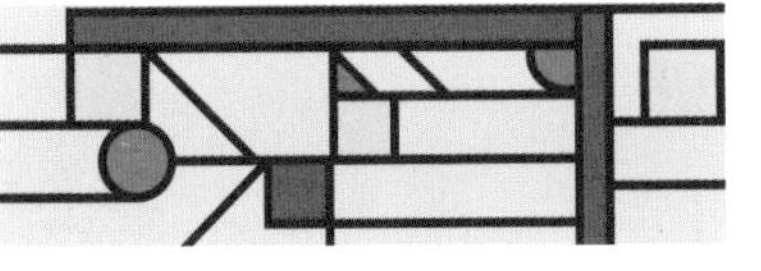
39 Bauhaus

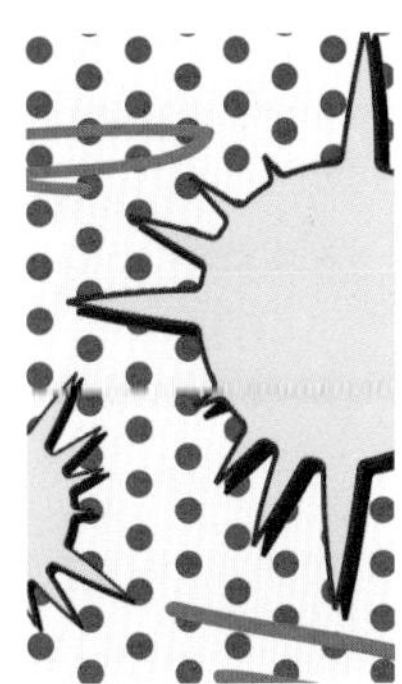
40 Pop Art

43 conceptual art

131 Travel and accommodation

131.1 TRAVEL

① guidebook

② phrasebook

③ one-way ticket

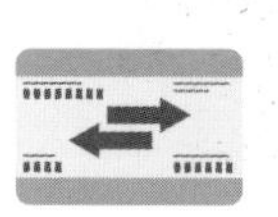
④ round-trip (US)
return ticket (UK)

⑤ to book a vacation (US)
to book a holiday (UK)

⑥ to pack
your bags

⑦ to go on a vacation (US)
to go on a holiday (UK)

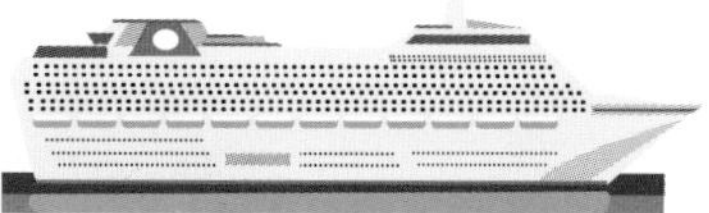
⑧ to go on a cruise

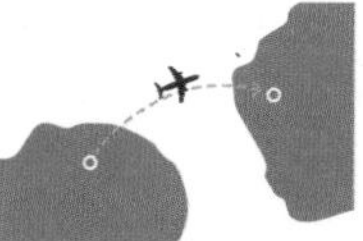
⑨ to go abroad

⑩ to make
a reservation

⑪ to rent
a cottage

⑫ to go
backpacking

⑬ to check in

⑭ to check out

⑮ to stay
in a hotel

131.2 ACCOMMODATION

① hotel

② apartment

③ hostel

B&B
⑨ guest house

⑩ bed and
breakfast

⑪ villa

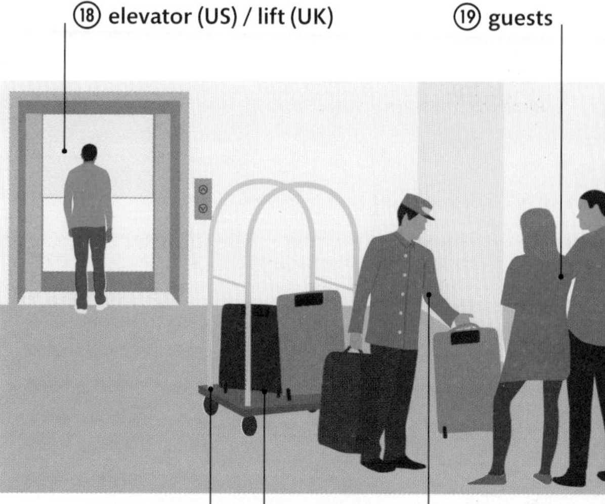
⑱ elevator (US) / lift (UK)
⑲ guests
㉔ trolley
㉕ luggage
㉖ porter

131.3 SERVICES

① restaurant

② gym

③ swimming
pool

See also:
104 At the airport 132 Sightseeing
133 Outdoor activities 134 On the beach

④ chalet

⑤ cabin

⑥ ecotourism

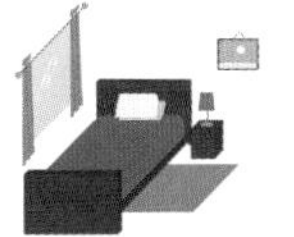
⑦ single room

⑧ twin room

⑫ double room

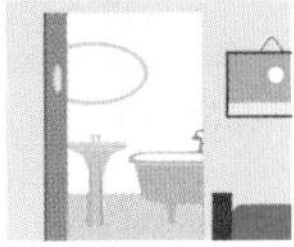
⑬ private bathroom / en suite (UK) bathroom

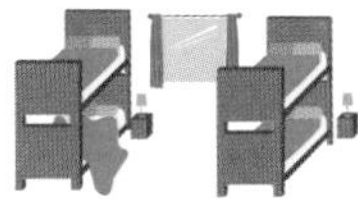
⑭ dorm

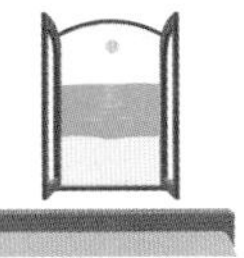
⑮ room with a view

1
2
3
4
5
6
7
8
9
⑯ vacancies

1
2
3
4
5
6
7
8
9
⑰ no vacancies

⑳ receptionist
㉑ front desk (US) reception (UK)
㉒ restrooms (US) toilets (UK)
㉓ emergency exit
㉗ counter
㉘ hotel lobby

⑤ breakfast tray
④ room service

⑥ laundry service

⑦ maid service

⑧ minibar

⑨ safe

132 Sightseeing

132.1 TOURIST ATTRACTION

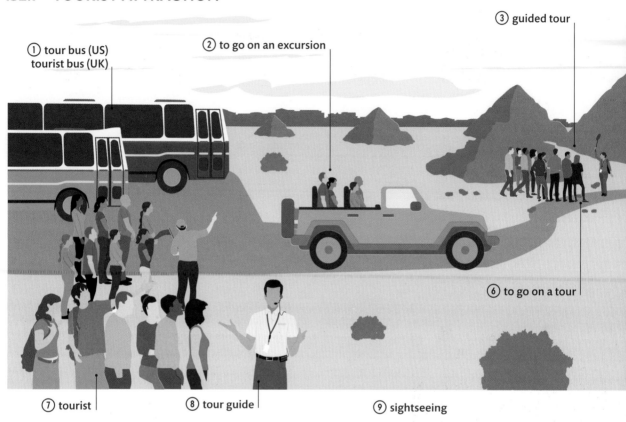

① tour bus (US)
tourist bus (UK)

② to go on an excursion

③ guided tour

⑥ to go on a tour

⑦ tourist

⑧ tour guide

⑨ sightseeing

132.2 ATTRACTIONS

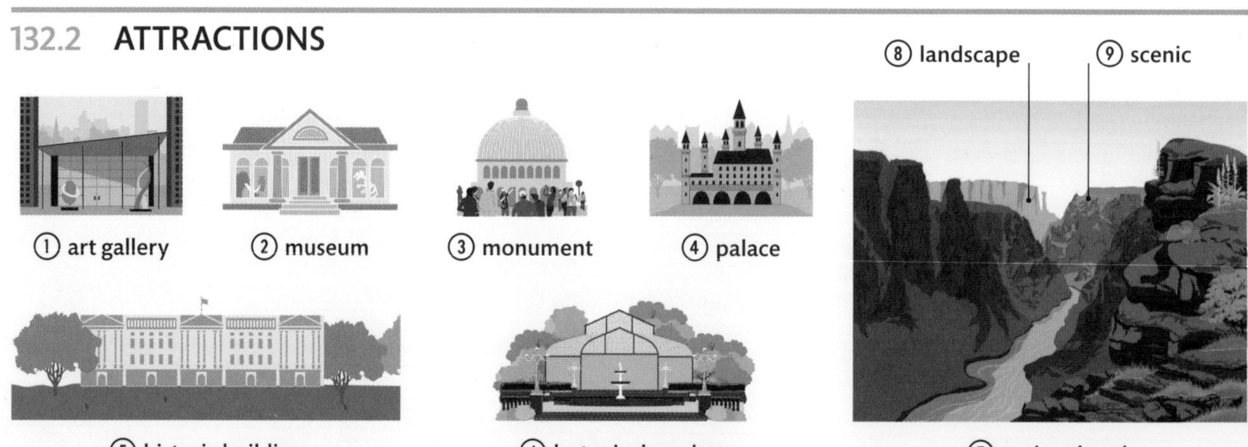

⑧ landscape
⑨ scenic
① art gallery
② museum
③ monument
④ palace
⑤ historic building
⑥ botanical gardens
⑦ national park

See also:
99 Cars and buses **130** Museums and galleries
131 Travel and accommodation **149-151** Countries

⑤ Do we have to pay an admission fee?

④ archeological site (US)
archaeological site (UK)

⑩ line (US)
queue (UK)

⑪ souvenir stall

ADMISSION

OPEN

CLOSED

⑫ entrance fee

⑬ open

⑭ closed

⑮ guidebook

⑯ postcard

⑰ souvenir

⑱ tourist map

⑲ directions

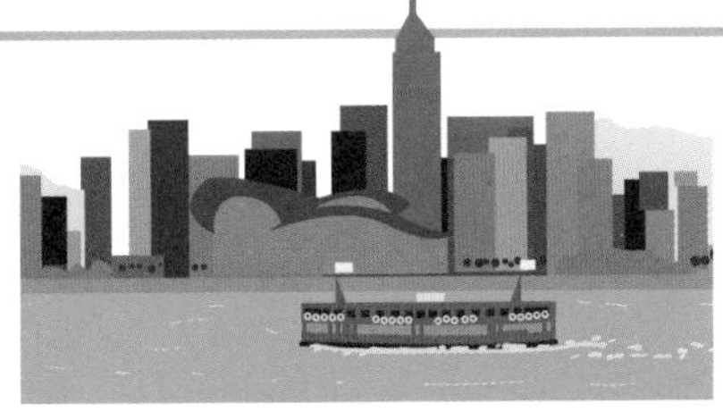

⑩ waterfront

⑪ craft market

⑬ Can I have some information on the local sights?
i

⑫ tourist office (US)
tourist information (UK)

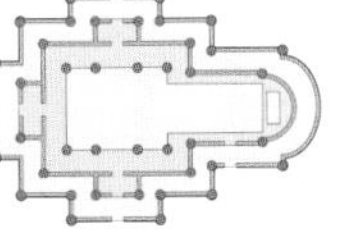

⑭ floor plan

⑮ map

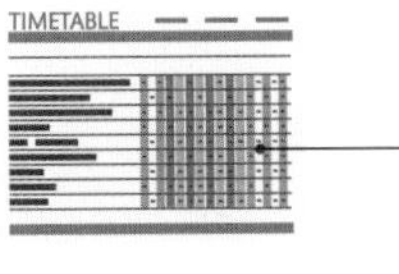
TIMETABLE

⑰ opening times

⑯ timetable

133 Outdoor activities

133.1 OPEN-AIR ACTIVITIES

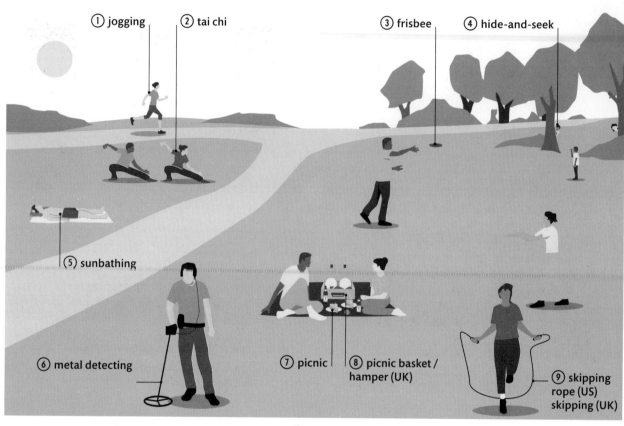

① jogging
② tai chi
③ frisbee
④ hide-and-seek
⑤ sunbathing
⑥ metal detecting
⑦ picnic
⑧ picnic basket / hamper (UK)
⑨ skipping rope (US) skipping (UK)
⑩ park

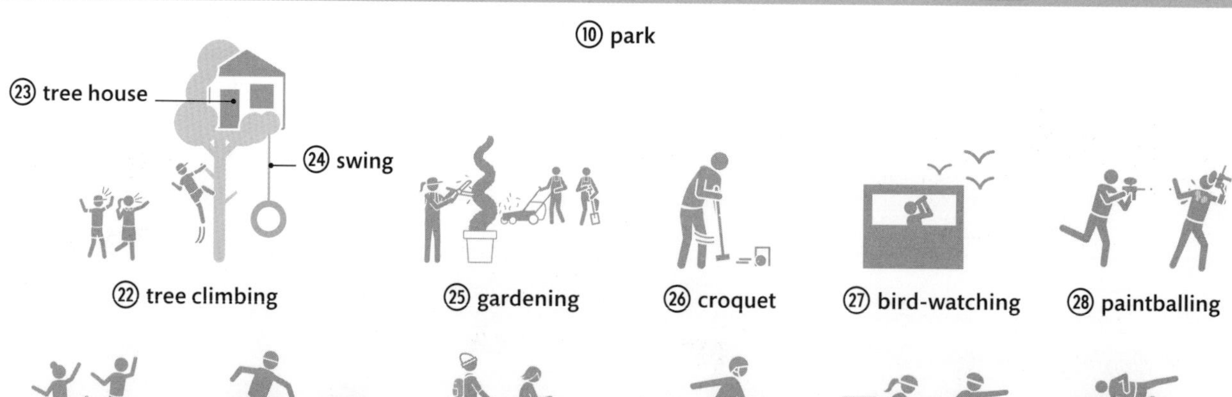

㉓ tree house
㉔ swing
㉒ tree climbing
㉕ gardening
㉖ croquet
㉗ bird-watching
㉘ paintballing

㉛ wading pool (US) paddling pool (UK)

㉜ skateboarding

㉝ scootering

㉞ rollerblading

㉟ bicycling (US) cycling (UK)

㊱ parkour

See also:
11 Abilities and actions **134** On the beach
135 Camping **148** Maps and directions

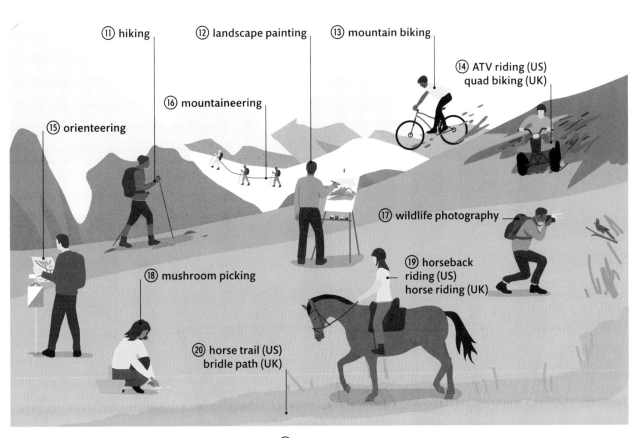

⑪ hiking
⑫ landscape painting
⑬ mountain biking
⑭ ATV riding (US)
quad biking (UK)
⑮ orienteering
⑯ mountaineering
⑰ wildlife photography
⑱ mushroom picking
⑲ horseback riding (US)
horse riding (UK)
⑳ horse trail (US)
bridle path (UK)
㉑ national park

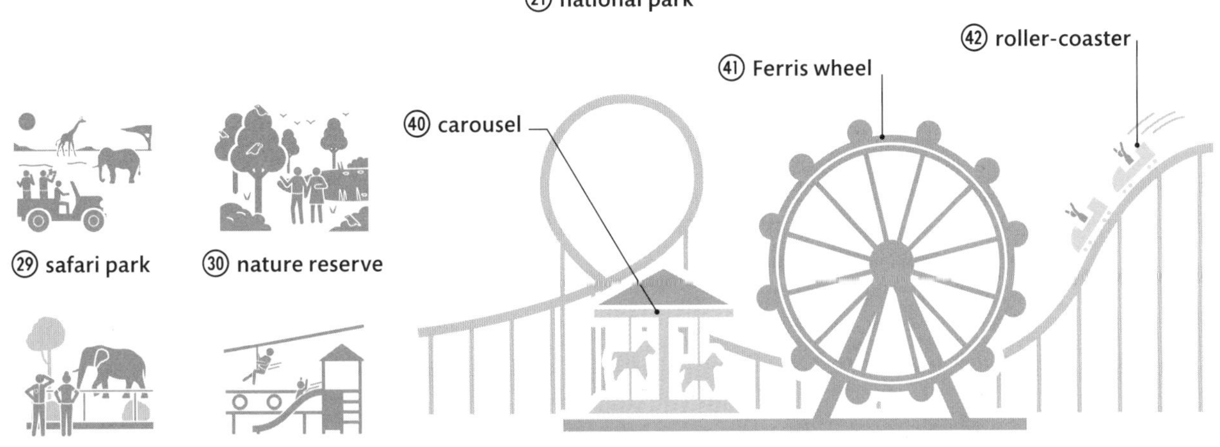
㉙ safari park
㉚ nature reserve
㊲ zoo
㊳ adventure playground
㊵ carousel
㊶ Ferris wheel
㊷ roller-coaster
㊴ theme park

134 On the beach

134.1 THE BEACH

① bodyboarding
② surfing
③ windbreak
④ wave
⑤ snorkel and mask
⑥ swimsuit
⑦ Jet Ski
⑪ ocean (US) sea (UK)
⑫ picnic basket / hamper (UK)
⑬ life preserver (US) life ring (UK)
⑭ sand
⑮ beach ball
㉑ inflatable boat
㉒ deck chair
㉓ fins / flippers

㉕ sail
㉖ yacht
㉗ boardwalk 
㉘ promenade 
㉙ beach hut

See also:
105 Sea vessels 118 Swimming 119 Sailing and watersports
121 Fishing 133 Outdoor activities 166 Ocean life

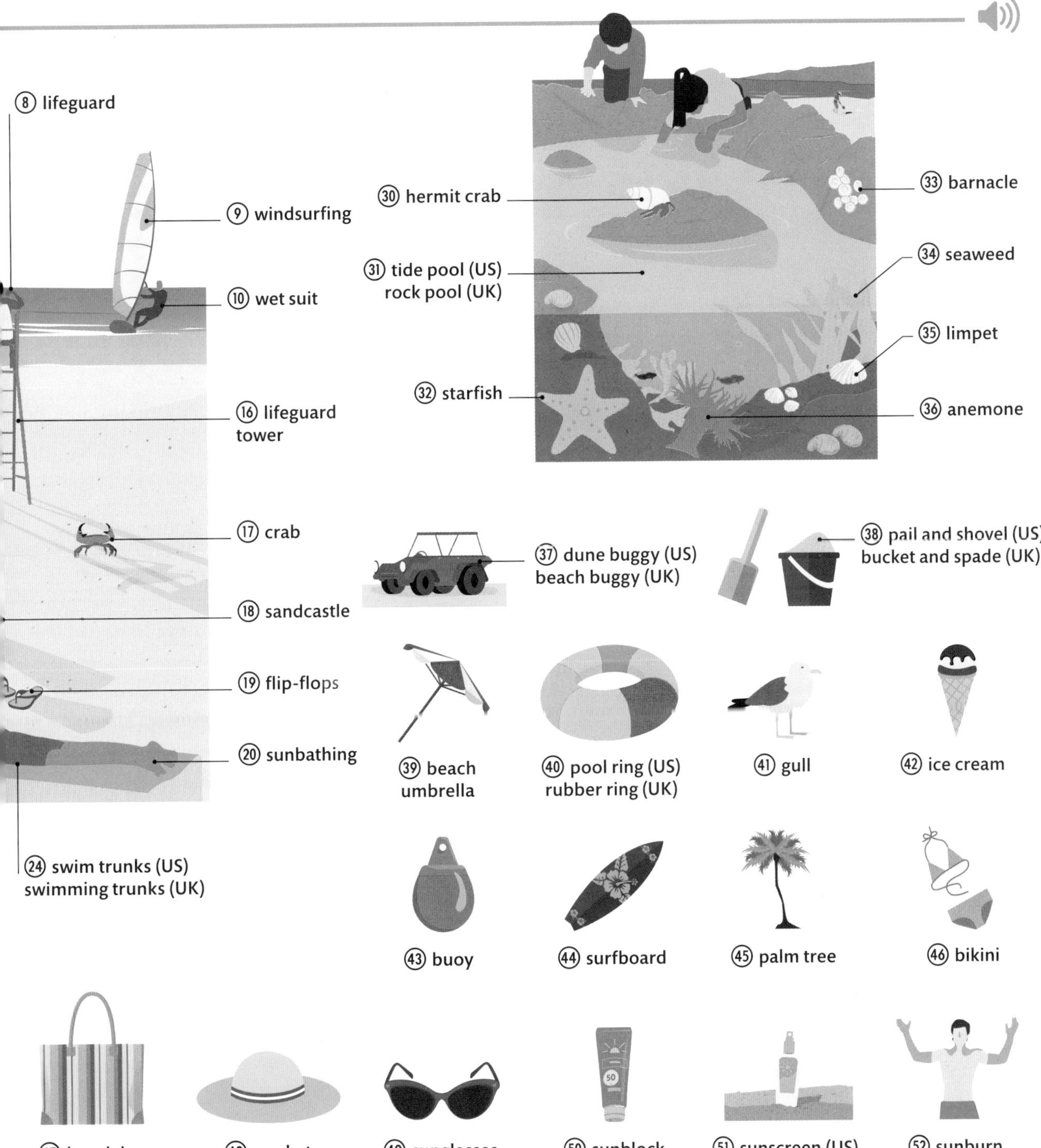
⑧ lifeguard
⑨ windsurfing
⑩ wet suit
⑯ lifeguard tower
⑰ crab
⑱ sandcastle
⑲ flip-flops
⑳ sunbathing
㉔ swim trunks (US) swimming trunks (UK)
㉚ hermit crab
㉛ tide pool (US) rock pool (UK)
㉜ starfish
㉝ barnacle
㉞ seaweed
㉟ limpet
㊱ anemone
㊲ dune buggy (US) beach buggy (UK)
㊳ pail and shovel (US) bucket and spade (UK)
㊴ beach umbrella
㊵ pool ring (US) rubber ring (UK)
㊶ gull
㊷ ice cream
㊸ buoy
㊹ surfboard
㊺ palm tree
㊻ bikini
㊼ beach bag
㊽ sun hat
㊾ sunglasses
㊿ sunblock
51 sunscreen (US) sun cream (UK)
52 sunburn
50

135 Camping

135.1 CAMPING EQUIPMENT AND FACILITIES

① to camp

② to pitch a tent

③ two-person tent

5
④ site (US) pitch (UK)

⑤ sites available (US) pitches available (UK)

⑥ full

⑧ electric hook-up

⑨ trailer

⑩ motor home (US) camper van (UK)

⑪ hammock

⑫ campfire

⑬ to light a fire

⑮ charcoal

⑯ barbecue

⑰ single-burner camping stove

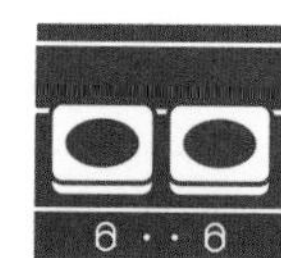
⑱ double burner camping stove

⑲ folding grill

⑳ picnic bench

M
M
㉒ shower block

W
W
㉓ toilet block

㉔ waste disposal

㉕ site manager's office

㉖ backpack / rucksack (UK)

㉗ flashlight (US) torch (UK)

N
W
E
S
㉙ compass

㉚ thermals

㉛ walking boots

㉜ rain gear (US) waterproofs (UK)

㉝ multi-purpose knife

㉞ insect repellent

㊱ sleeping bag

㊲ sleeping mat

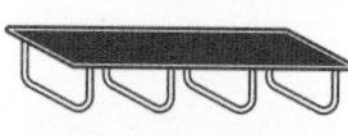
㊳ camp bed

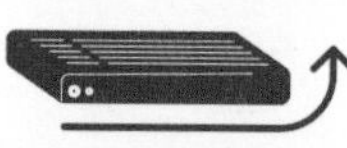
㊴ self-inflating mattress

㊵ air bed / air mattress

㊶ air pump

See also:
131 Travel and accommodation
133 Outdoor activities 146-147 Geography

135.2 CAMPGROUND (US) / CAMPSITE (UK)

⑦ camper (US)
caravan (UK)

⑭ firestarter (US)
firelighter (UK)

㉑ water bottles

㉘ headlamp

㉟ mosquito net

㊷ electric pump

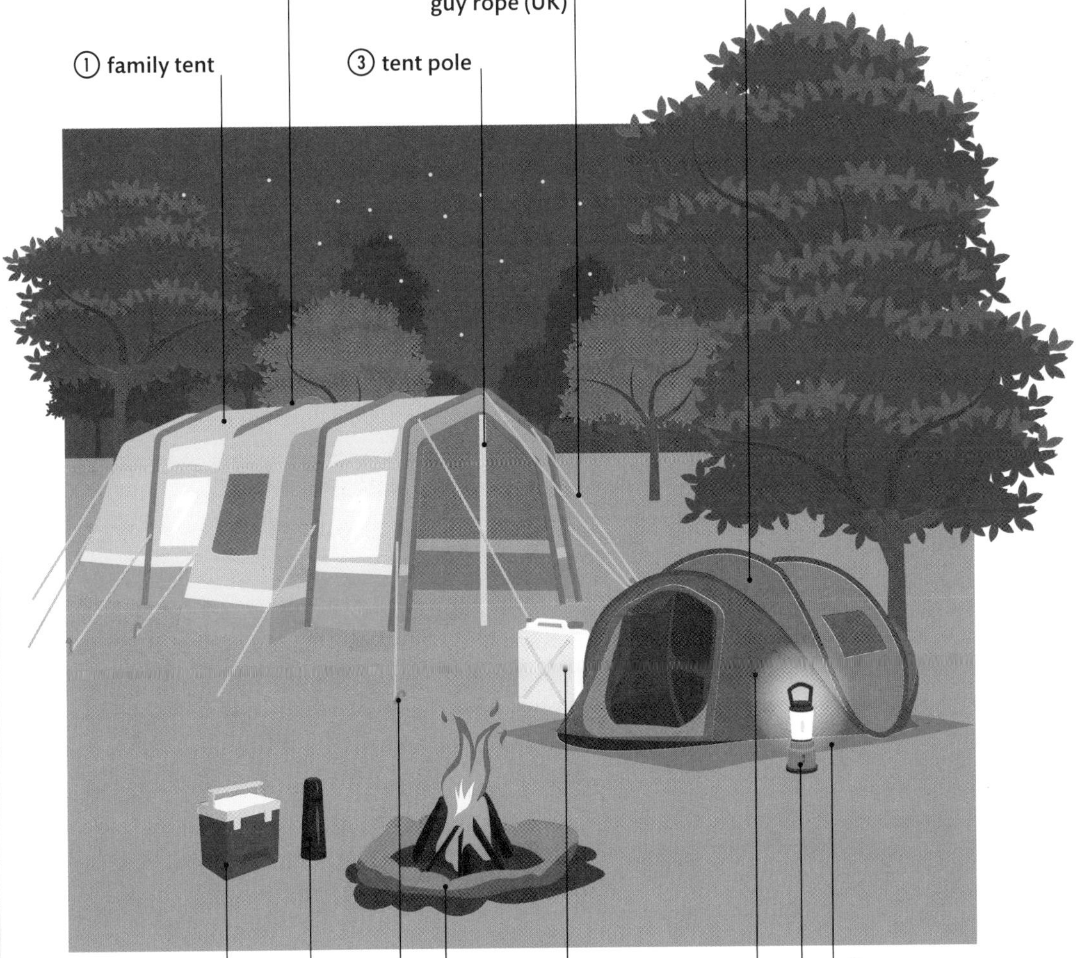

① family tent
② frame
③ tent pole
④ guy line (US)
guy rope (UK)
⑤ pop-up tent
⑥ cooler
⑦ thermal flask
⑧ tent peg
⑨ firepit
⑩ water carrier
⑪ rainfly (US)
flysheet (UK)
⑫ lamp / lantern
⑬ groundsheet

136 Home entertainment

136.1 TELEVISION AND AUDIO

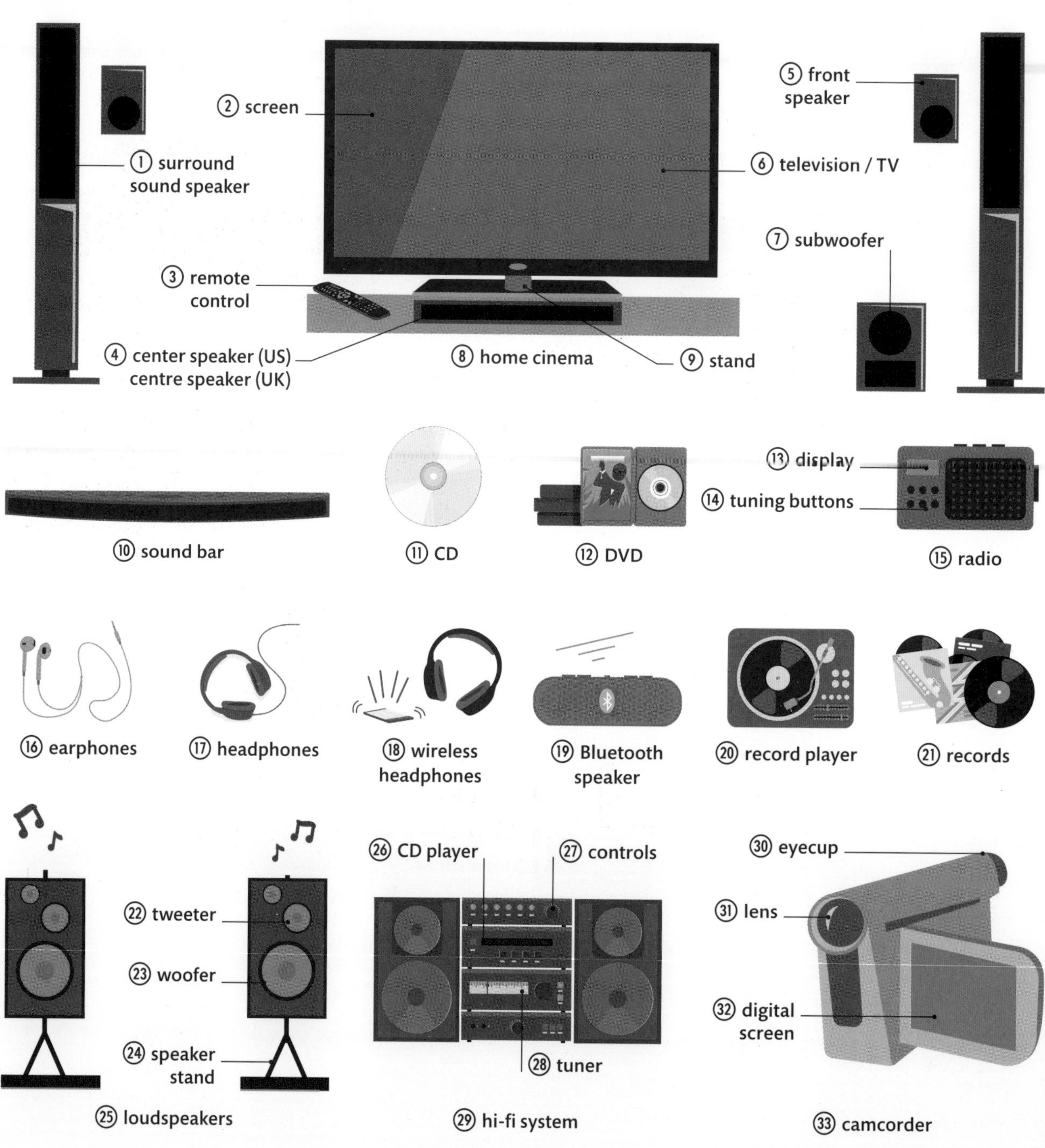

① surround sound speaker
② screen
③ remote control
④ center speaker (US) centre speaker (UK)
⑤ front speaker
⑥ television / TV
⑦ subwoofer
⑧ home cinema
⑨ stand
⑩ sound bar
⑪ CD
⑫ DVD
⑬ display
⑭ tuning buttons
⑮ radio
⑯ earphones
⑰ headphones
⑱ wireless headphones
⑲ Bluetooth speaker
⑳ record player
㉑ records
㉒ tweeter
㉓ woofer
㉔ speaker stand
㉕ loudspeakers
㉖ CD player
㉗ controls
㉘ tuner
㉙ hi-fi system
㉚ eyecup
㉛ lens
㉜ digital screen
㉝ camcorder

See also:
127 Movies / Films 128-129 Music
137 Television 140 Games

(34) stereo

(35) mono

(36) to tune in

(37) volume

(38) to turn up

(39) to turn down

(40) satellite dish

(41) digital box

(42) microphone

(43) karaoke

136.2 VIDEO GAMES

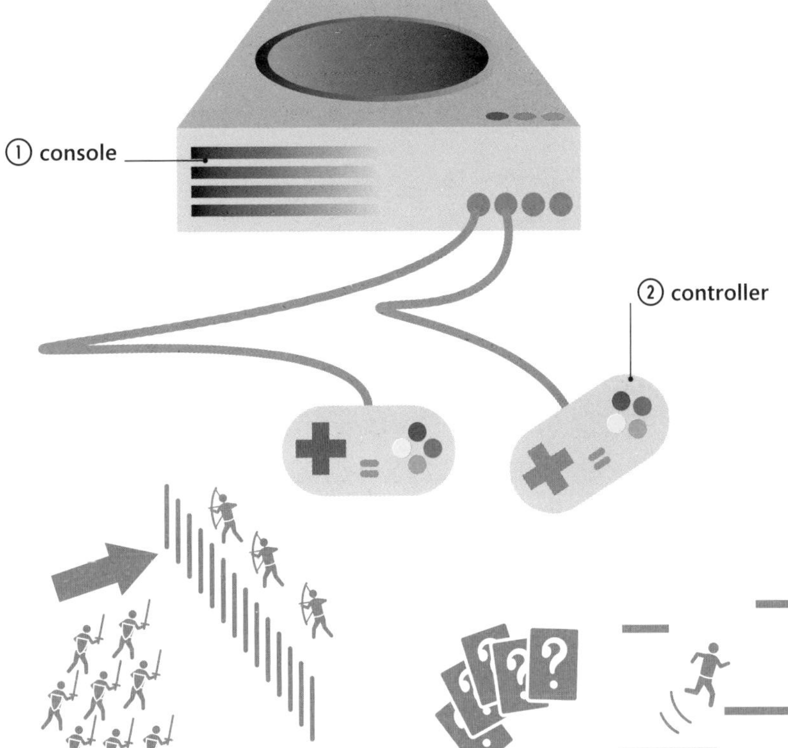

(1) console

(2) controller

(3) strategy game

(4) trivia game

(5) platform game

(6) adventure game

(7) role-playing game

(8) action game

(9) multiplayer game

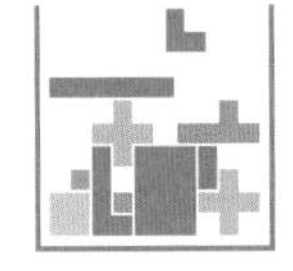

(10) simulation game

(11) sports game

(12) puzzle game

(13) logic game

137 Television

137.1 WATCHING TELEVISION

① screen

② TV set

③ remote control

④ high-definition

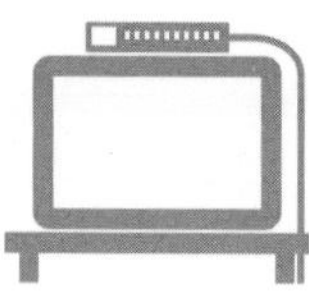

⑤ cable TV

⑥ satellite TV

⑦ video on demand

3

⑧ channel

$

⑨ pay-per-view channel

⑩ episode

⑪ season (US) series (UK)

⑫ show (US) programme (UK)

⑬ subtitles

⑭ interview

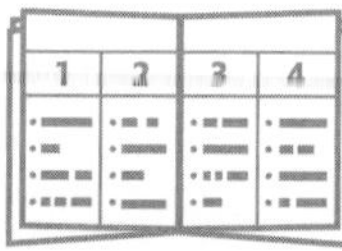
1
2
3
4

⑮ TV guide / schedule

⑯ preview

⑰ reporter

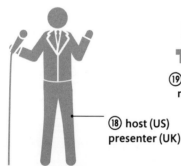

⑱ host (US) presenter (UK)

⑲ news anchor (US) newsreader (UK)

⑳ commercial break (US) adverts (UK)

㉑ weather forecaster

㉒ couch potato

137.2 TELEVISION VERBS

① to turn on

② to turn off

③ to turn up the volume

④ to turn down the volume

1
3

⑤ to change the channel

⑥ to stream

See also:
26 Living room and dining room 84 Media
127 Movies / Films 136 Home entertainment

137.3 TV SHOWS AND CHANNELS

① cooking show

② talk show (US)
chat show (UK)

③ sports

④ documentary

⑤ nature documentary

⑥ period drama / costume drama

⑦ sitcom

⑧ quiz show

⑨ current affairs

⑩ news

⑪ weather

⑫ soap opera

⑬ game show

⑭ comedy

⑮ cartoon

⑯ crime

⑰ thriller

⑱ satire

⑲ children's show (US)
children's TV (UK)

⑳ morning show (US)
breakfast TV (UK)

㉑ reality TV

㉒ catch-up TV

㉓ shopping channel

㉔ music channel

⑦ to play

⑧ to stop

⑨ to pause

⑩ to rewind

⑪ to fast forward

•REC
⑫ to record

138 Books and reading

138.1 BOOKS

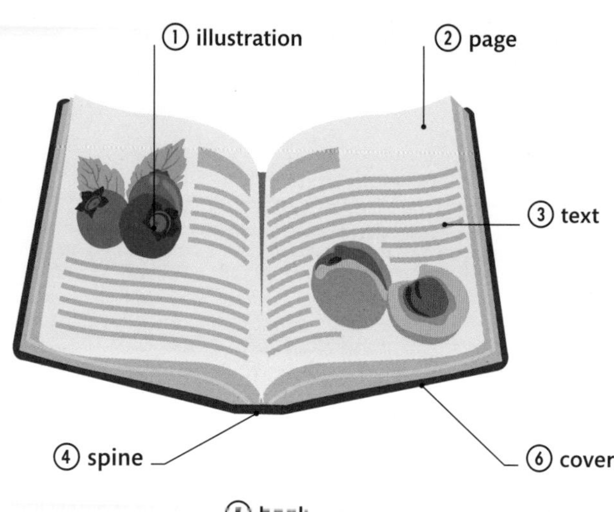
① illustration
② page
③ text
④ spine
⑤ book
⑥ cover

⑦ author

⑧ paperback

⑨ hardback

⑬ review

⑭ contents

⑮ chapter

138.2 READING AND GENRES

① nonfiction (US) non-fiction (UK)

② dictionary

③ encyclopedia

④ gardening book

⑤ TV guide

⑥ self-help

⑦ autobiography

⑧ biography

⑨ cookbook

⑩ guidebook

⑪ nature writing

⑫ textbook / course book

⑬ fiction

Great Adventure Stories
⑭ novel

⑮ science fiction

⑯ fantasy

⑰ comic

⑱ travel writing

See also:
127 Movies / Films 136 Home entertainment
139 Fantasy and myth 175 Writing

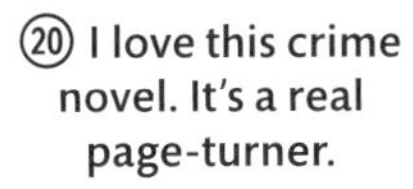
⑳ I love this crime novel. It's a real page-turner.

㉑ I hate this fantasy novel. The plot is ridiculous.

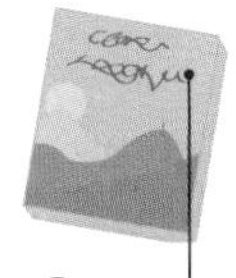
⑩ title

⑪ to flip through

⑫ e-reader

Bibliography
⑯ bibliography

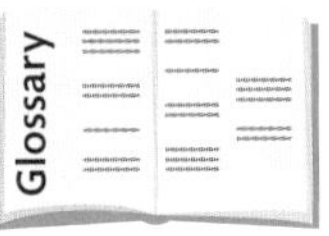
Glossary
⑰ glossary

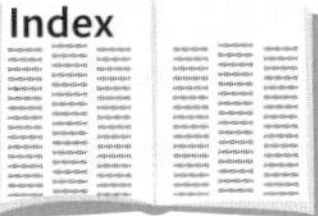
Index
⑱ index

⑲ reading

Jane Austen
Charles Dickens
Chinua Achebe
SHAKESPEARE
Virginia Woolf
MARY SHELLEY
Gabriel Garcia Marquez
G. FLAUBERT
⑲ literary fiction

㉑ character

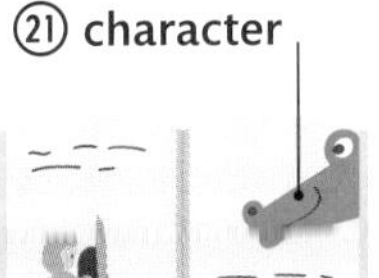
⑳ children's book

㉒ coloring book (US)
colouring book (UK)

㉓ fairy tale

㉔ romance

㉕ crime fiction

㉖ humor (US)
humour (UK)

MON
WED
TUES
THUR
㉗ planner (US)
diary (UK)

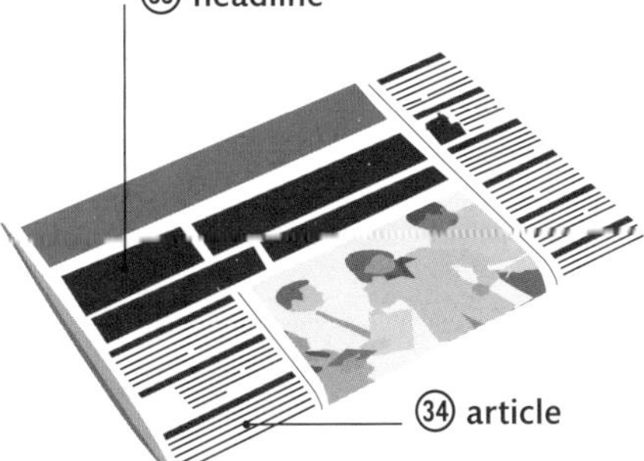
㉝ headline

㉞ article

㉜ newspaper

#1
㉘ bestseller

㉙ horoscope

㉚ gossip
magazine

㉛ puzzles

139 Fantasy and myth

139.1 MYTHS, STORIES, AND FANTASTIC CREATURES

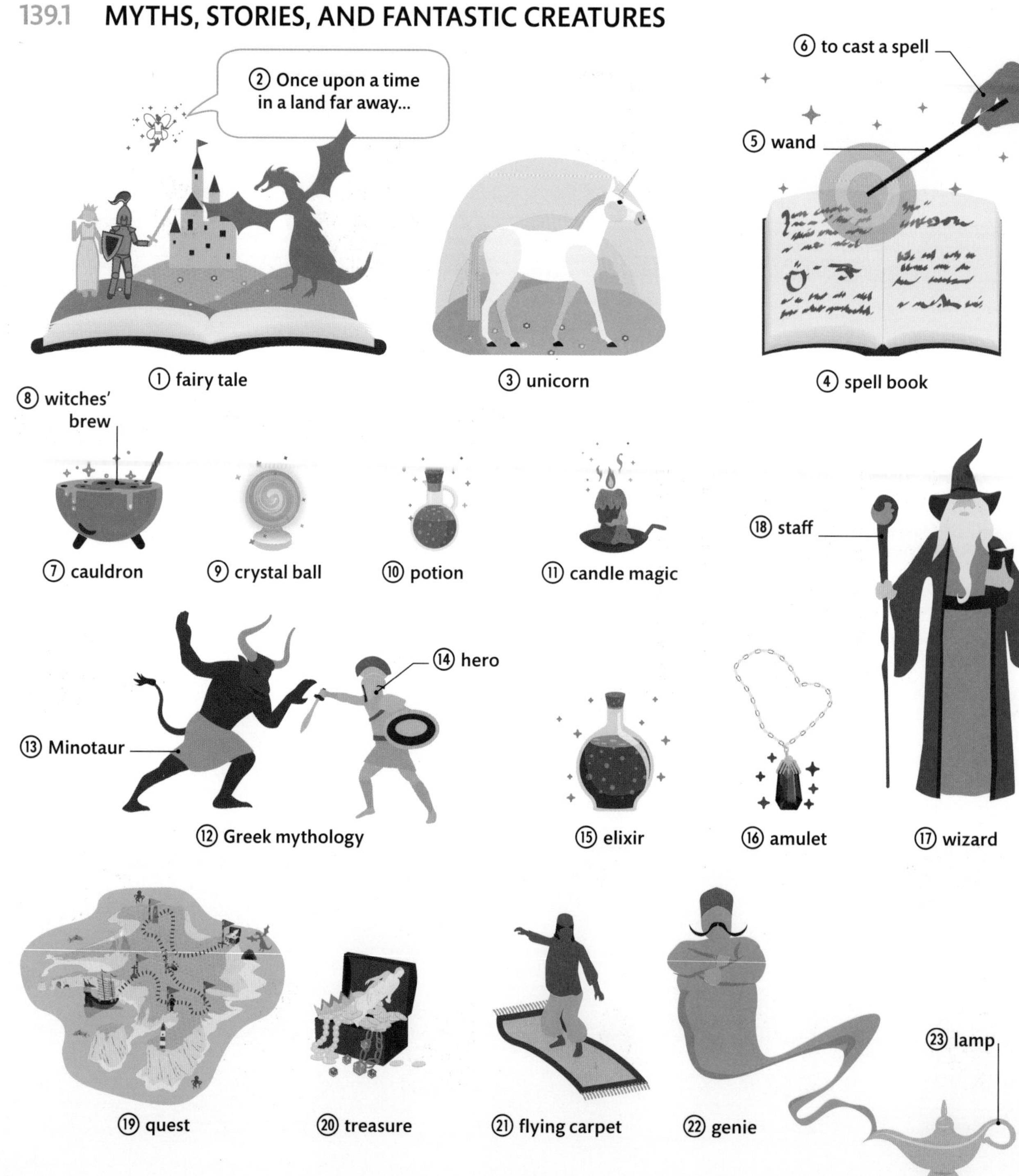

② Once upon a time in a land far away...
⑥ to cast a spell
⑤ wand
① fairy tale
③ unicorn
④ spell book
⑧ witches' brew
⑦ cauldron
⑨ crystal ball
⑩ potion
⑪ candle magic
⑱ staff
⑭ hero
⑬ Minotaur
⑫ Greek mythology
⑮ elixir
⑯ amulet
⑰ wizard
㉓ lamp
⑲ quest
⑳ treasure
㉑ flying carpet
㉒ genie

See also:
127 Movies / Films
137 Television **138** Books and reading

(24) sea serpent

(25) Hugin and Munin

(26) the Disir

(27) monster

(28) zombie

(29) werewolf

(30) vampire

(31) ghost

(32) jack-o'-lantern

(33) dragon

(34) knight

(36) broomstick

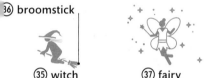

(35) witch

(37) fairy

(38) pixie

(39) faun

(40) gnome

(41) leprechaun

(42) gremlin

(43) goblin

(44) troll

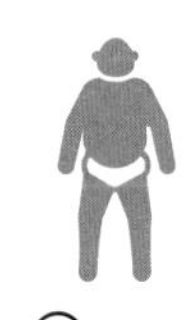
(45) ogre

(46) orc

(47) giant

(48) elf

(49) dwarf

(50) mermaid

(51) merman

(52) phoenix

(53) griffin

(54) hydra

(55) centaur

(56) sphinx

(57) Cerberus

(58) bad robot

(59) alien

140 Games

140.1 CHESS

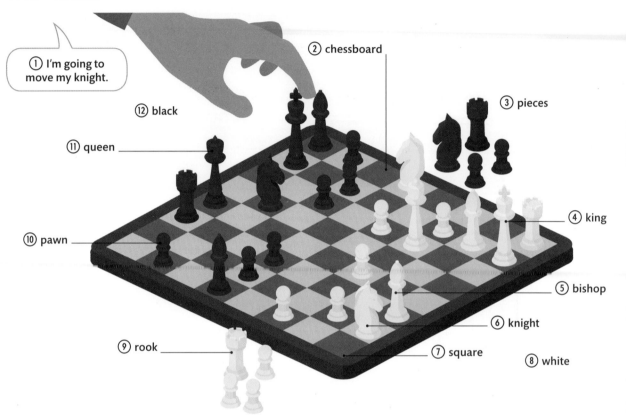

① I'm going to move my knight.

② chessboard

③ pieces

④ king

⑤ bishop

⑥ knight

⑦ square

⑧ white

⑨ rook

⑩ pawn

⑪ queen

⑫ black

140.3 GAMES

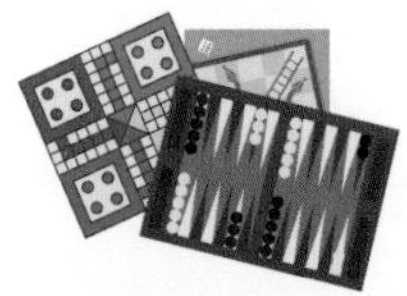

① board games

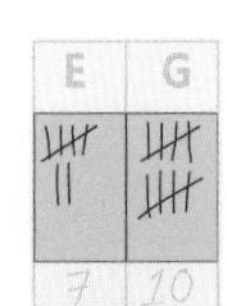
E G
7 10

② points

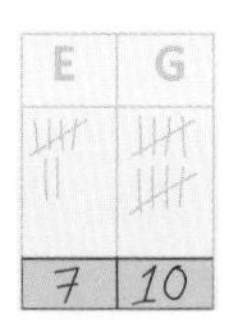
E G
7 10

③ score

④ tic-tac-toe (US)
noughts and crosses (UK)

⑤ dice

⑥ solitaire

⑦ pieces

⑧ jigsaw puzzle

⑨ dominoes

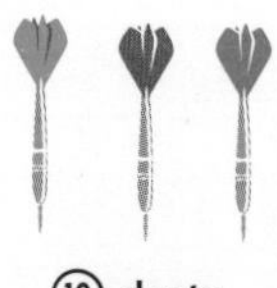

⑩ darts

⑪ dartboard

⑫ bull's-eye (US)
bullseye (UK)

See also:
136 Home entertainment **138** Books and reading
141-142 Arts and crafts

140.2 PLAYING CARDS

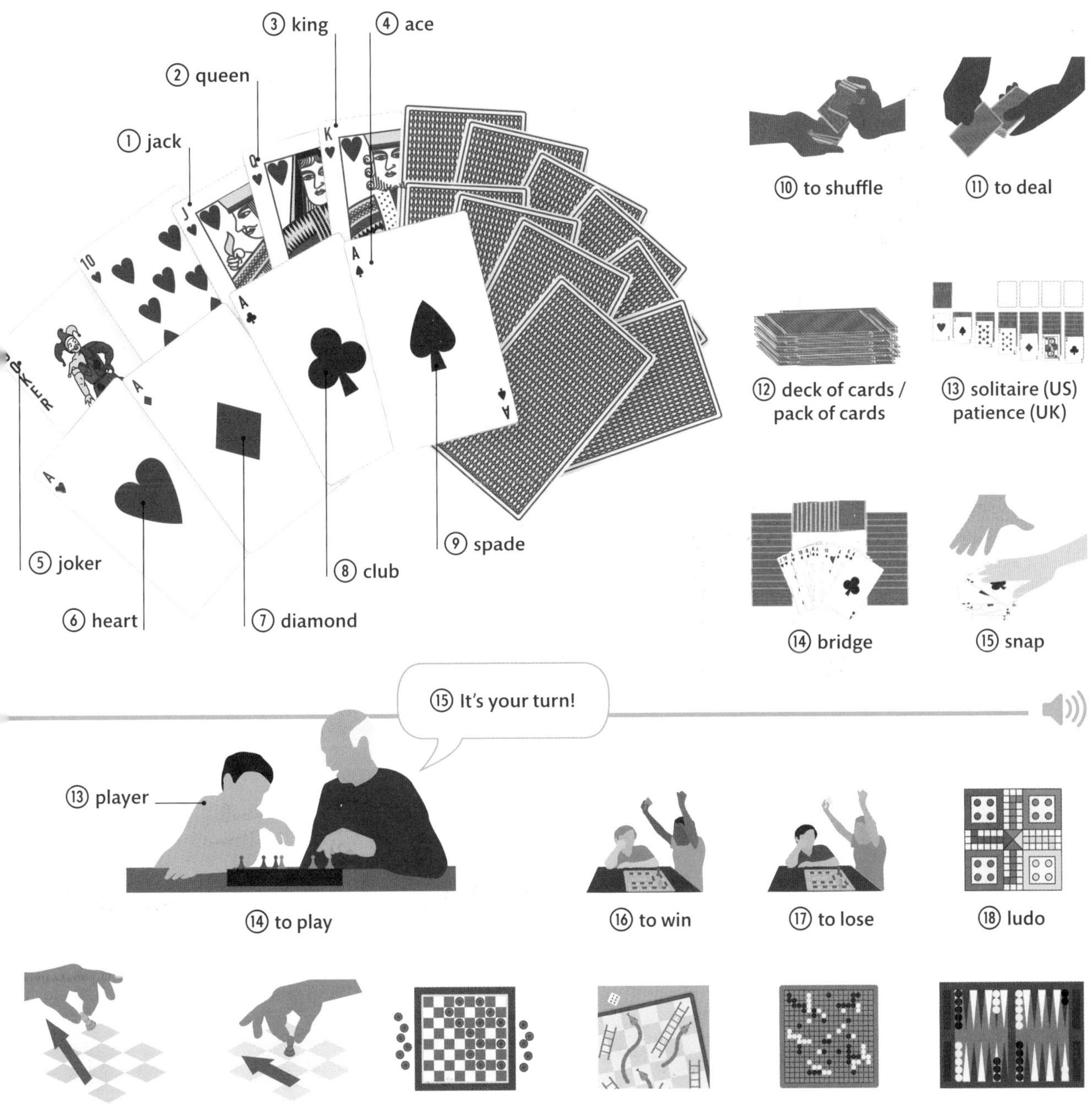
① jack
② queen
③ king
④ ace
⑤ joker
⑥ heart
⑦ diamond
⑧ club
⑨ spade
⑩ to shuffle
⑪ to deal
⑫ deck of cards / pack of cards
⑬ solitaire (US) patience (UK)
⑭ bridge
⑮ snap
⑮ It's your turn!
⑬ player
⑭ to play
⑯ to win
⑰ to lose
⑱ ludo

⑲ to take

⑳ to move

㉑ checkers (US) draughts (UK)

㉒ chutes and ladders (US) snakes and ladders (UK)

㉓ go

㉔ backgammon

141 Arts and crafts

141.1 PAINTING

① brush
② painting
③ canvas
④ artist
⑤ palette
⑥ paint tube
⑦ palette knife
⑧ easel

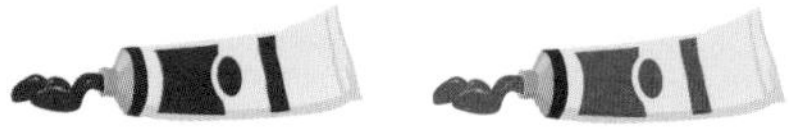

⑨ red
⑩ scarlet 
⑪ blue
⑫ turquoise
⑬ navy blue
⑭ yellow 
⑮ green
⑯ orange

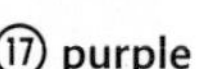
⑰ purple

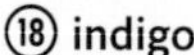
⑱ indigo

⑲ pink

⑳ brown

㉑ gray (US)
grey (UK)

㉒ black

㉓ white

㉔ oil paints

㉕ watercolors (US)
watercolour paints (UK)

㉖ pastels

㉗ acrylic paints

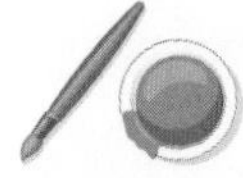
㉘ poster paint

See also:
37 Decorating **130** Museums and galleries
142 Arts and crafts (continued)

141.2 OTHER ARTS AND CRAFTS

① sculpture
② chisel
③ mallet
④ stone
⑤ sculpting
⑥ drawing 
⑦ sketch 
⑧ charcoal 
⑨ pencil 
⑩ sketch pad 
⑪ printing 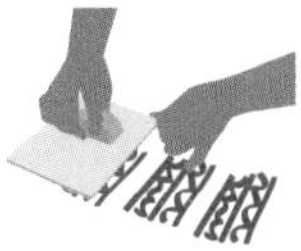
⑫ ink 
⑬ engraving  
⑭ woodworking 
⑮ wood
⑯ cardboard (US) card (UK)
⑰ collage 
⑱ glue 
⑲ origami 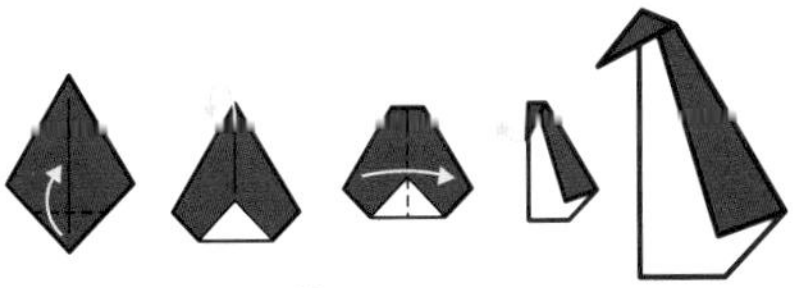
⑳ model making 
㉑ papier-mâché 
㉒ modeling tool (US) / modelling tool (UK) 
㉓ making jewelry (US) jewellery (UK) 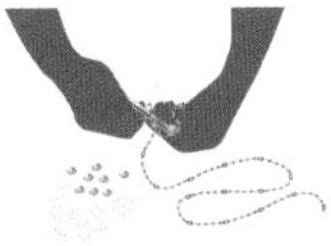
㉔ potter
㉕ clay
㉖ potter's wheel
㉗ pottery
㉘ I make pots in my spare time.

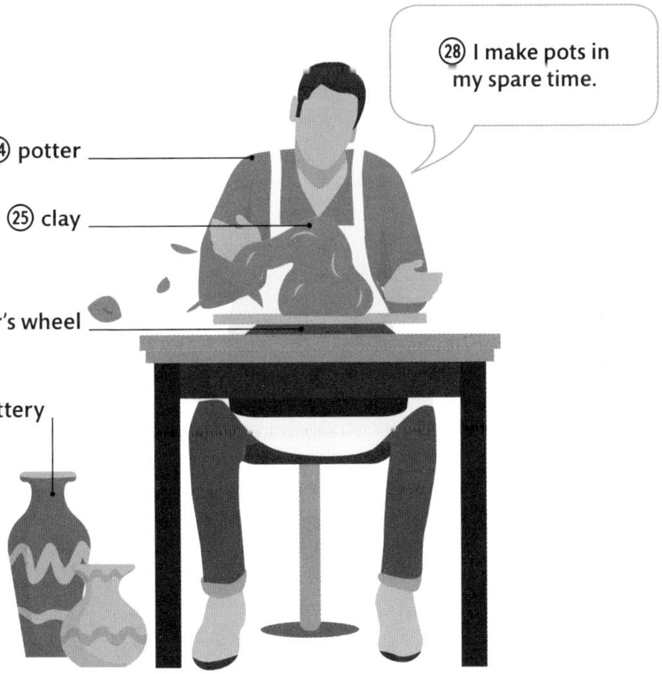

142 Arts and crafts continued

142.1 SEWING

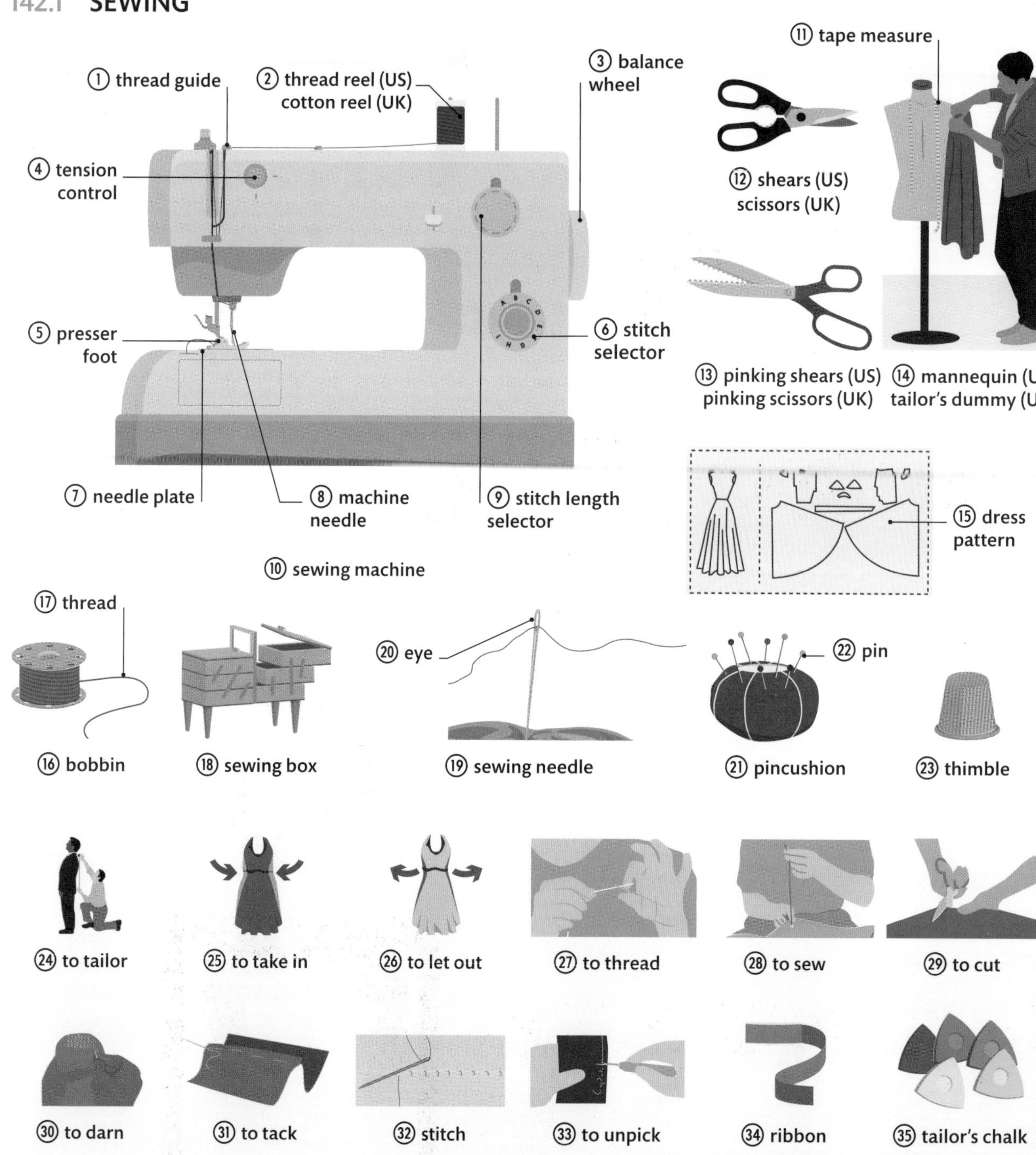

① thread guide
② thread reel (US) cotton reel (UK)
③ balance wheel
④ tension control
⑤ presser foot
⑥ stitch selector
⑦ needle plate
⑧ machine needle
⑨ stitch length selector
⑩ sewing machine
⑪ tape measure
⑫ shears (US) scissors (UK)
⑬ pinking shears (US) pinking scissors (UK)
⑭ mannequin (US) tailor's dummy (UK)
⑮ dress pattern
⑯ bobbin
⑰ thread
⑱ sewing box
⑲ sewing needle
⑳ eye
㉑ pincushion
㉒ pin
㉓ thimble
㉔ to tailor
㉕ to take in
㉖ to let out
㉗ to thread
㉘ to sew
㉙ to cut
㉚ to darn
㉛ to tack
㉜ stitch
㉝ to unpick
㉞ ribbon
㉟ tailor's chalk

See also:
11 Abilities and actions 13-15 Clothes
37 Decorating 39 Practical gardening

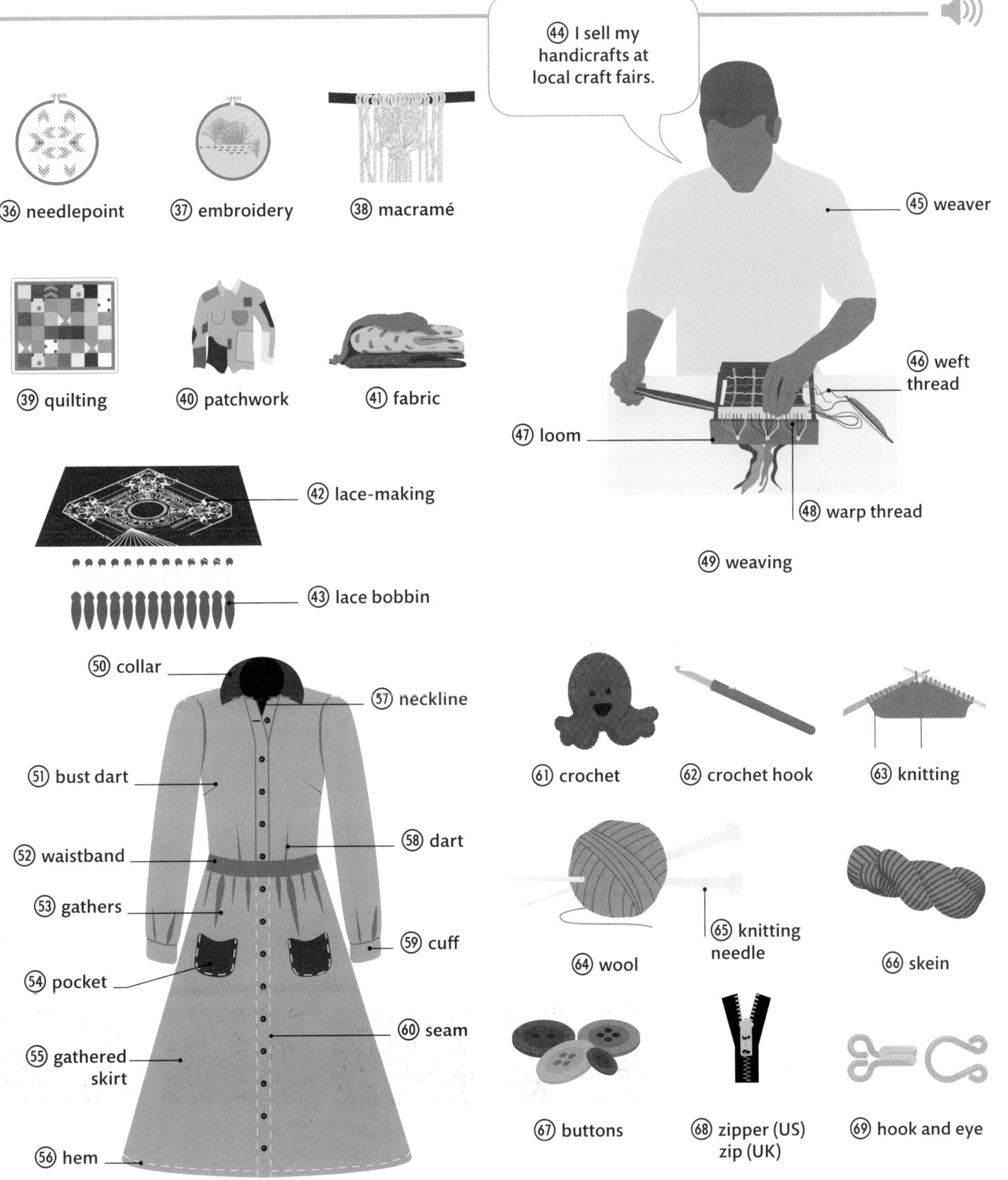
44 I sell my handicrafts at local craft fairs.
36 needlepoint
37 embroidery
38 macramé
45 weaver
39 quilting
40 patchwork
41 fabric
46 weft thread
47 loom
42 lace-making
48 warp thread
49 weaving
43 lace bobbin
50 collar
57 neckline
61 crochet
62 crochet hook
63 knitting
51 bust dart
52 waistband
58 dart
53 gathers
59 cuff
64 wool
65 knitting needle
66 skein
54 pocket
60 seam
55 gathered skirt
56 hem
67 buttons
68 zipper (US) zip (UK)
69 hook and eye

143 Space

143.1 THE SOLAR SYSTEM

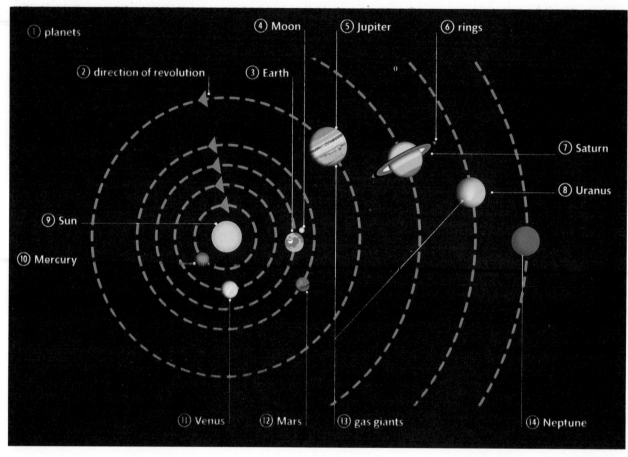

① planets
② direction of revolution
③ Earth
④ Moon
⑤ Jupiter
⑥ rings
⑦ Saturn
⑧ Uranus
⑨ Sun
⑩ Mercury
⑪ Venus
⑫ Mars
⑬ gas giants
⑭ Neptune

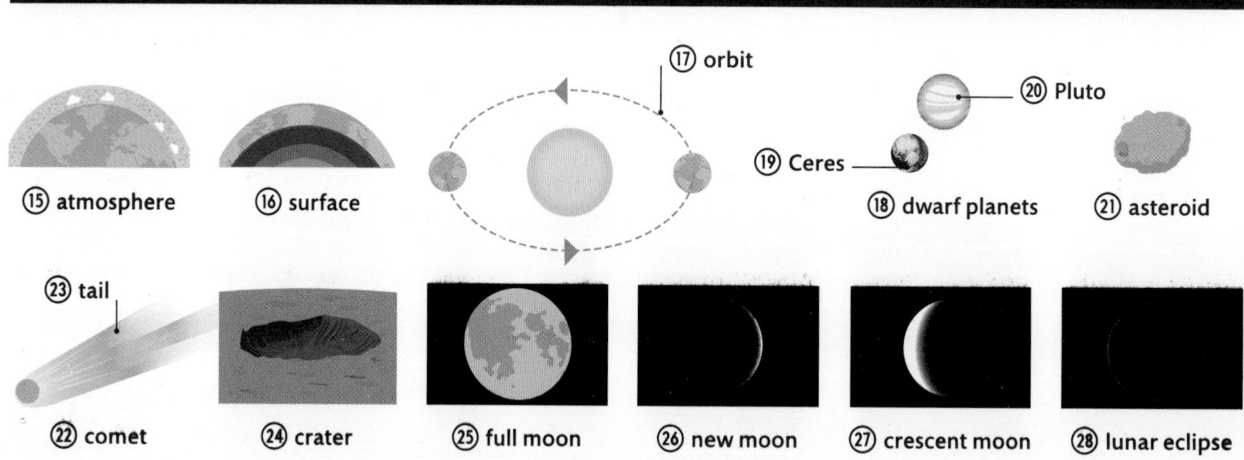
⑰ orbit
⑳ Pluto
⑲ Ceres
⑮ atmosphere
⑯ surface
⑱ dwarf planets
㉑ asteroid
㉓ tail
㉒ comet
㉔ crater
㉕ full moon
㉖ new moon
㉗ crescent moon
㉘ lunar eclipse

See also:
74 Mathematics **75** Physics **83** Computers and technology
144 Space (continued) **145** Planet Earth **156** Rocks and minerals

143.2 SPACE EXPLORATION

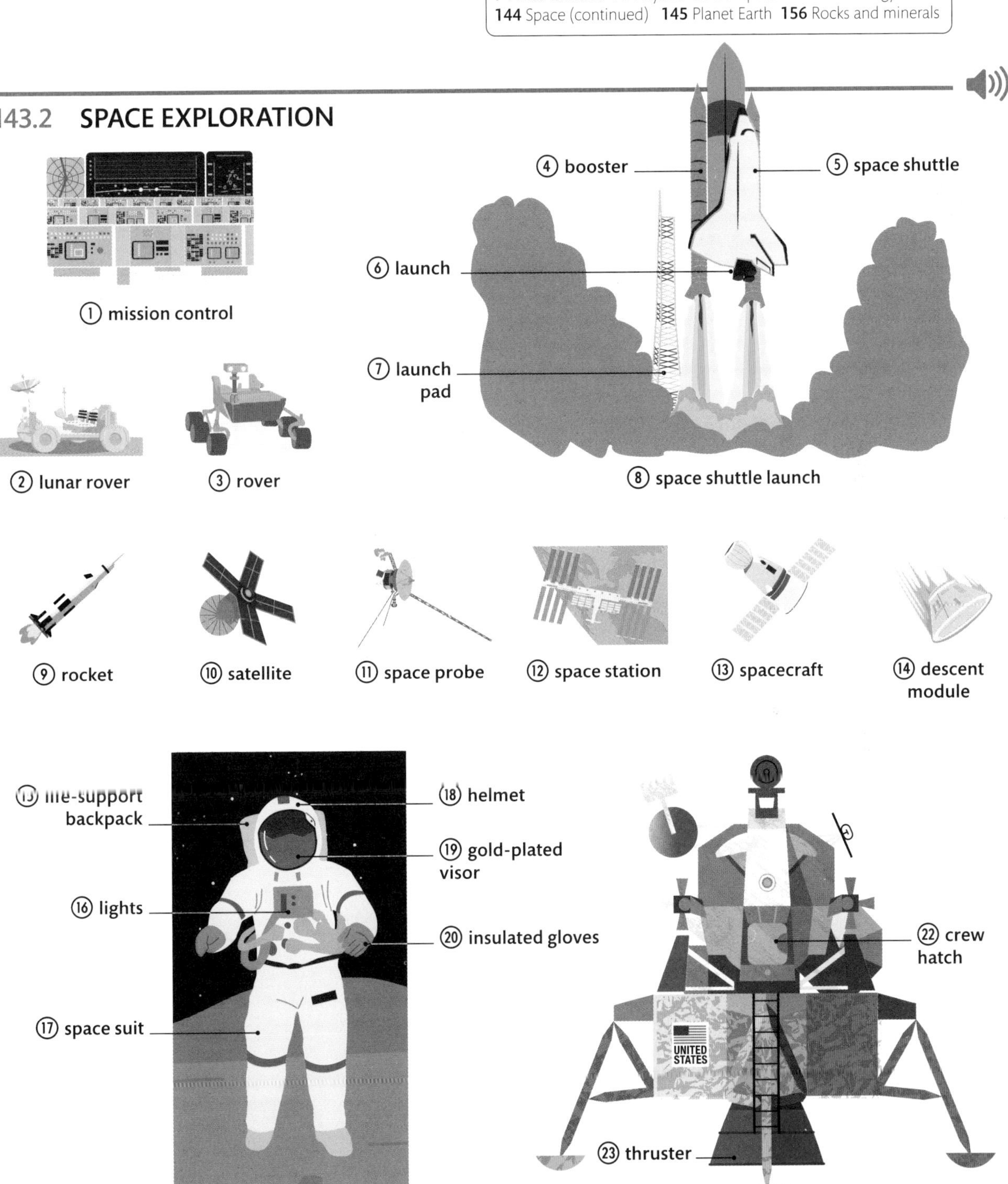
1 mission control
2 lunar rover
3 rover
4 booster
5 space shuttle
6 launch
7 launch pad
8 space shuttle launch
9 rocket
10 satellite
11 space probe
12 space station
13 spacecraft
14 descent module
15 life-support backpack
16 lights
17 space suit
18 helmet
19 gold-plated visor
20 insulated gloves
21 astronaut
22 crew hatch
23 thruster
24 lunar module
UNITED STATES

144 Space continued

144.1 ASTRONOMY

① binoculars

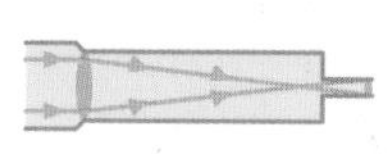
② refractor telescope

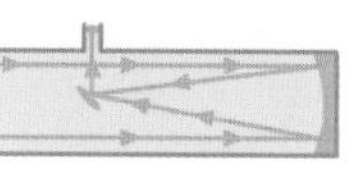
③ reflector telescope

④ radio telescope

⑤ observatory

⑥ space telescope

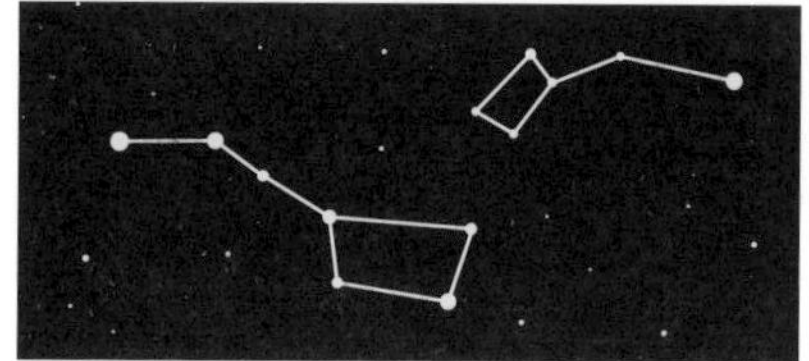
⑦ constellation

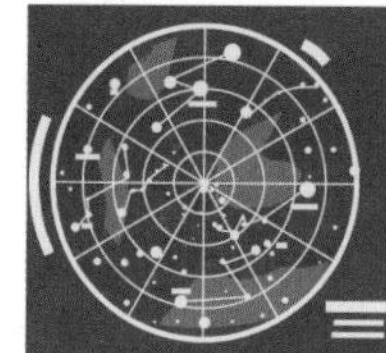
⑧ star chart

⑨ I've just spotted a comet.
⑩ eyepiece
⑪ finderscope
⑫ comet
⑬ tripod
⑭ focusing knob
⑮ telescope

144.2 STARS AND CONSTELLATIONS

① gravity

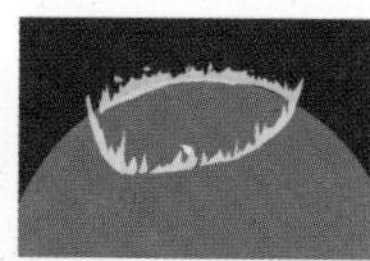
② aurora

③ star

④ flare

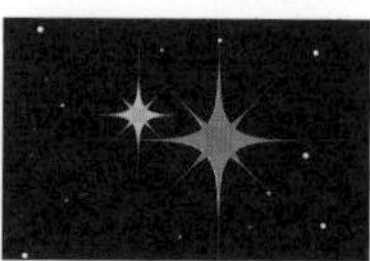
⑤ double star

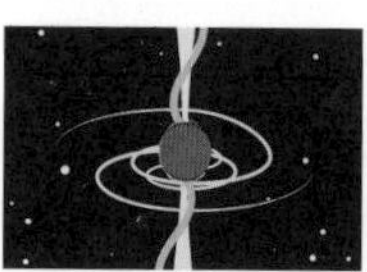
⑥ neutron star

⑬ the Pole Star / Polaris

⑭ the Big Dipper (US) the Plough (UK)

⑮ the Southern Cross

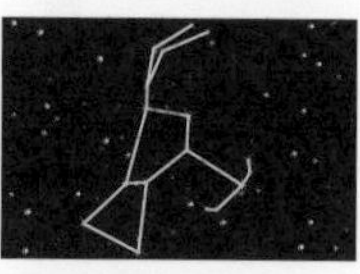
⑯ Orion

⑰ red giant

⑱ white dwarf

See also:
74 Mathematics **75** Physics **83** Computers and technology
145 Planet Earth **156** Rocks and minerals

144.3 THE ZODIAC

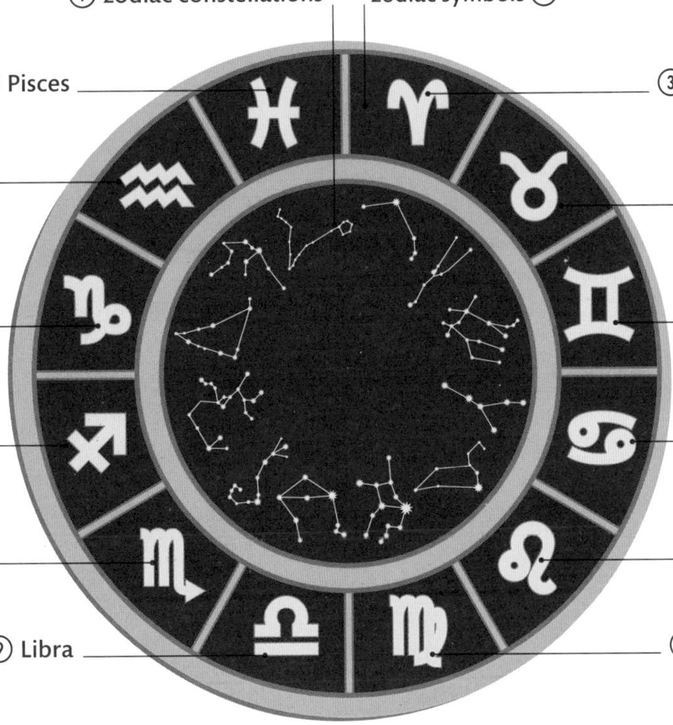

① zodiac constellations
zodiac symbols ②
③ Aries
④ Taurus
⑤ Gemini
⑥ Cancer
⑦ Leo
⑧ Virgo
⑨ Libra
⑩ Scorpio
⑪ Sagittarius
⑫ Capricorn
⑬ Aquarius
⑭ Pisces

⑦ supernova

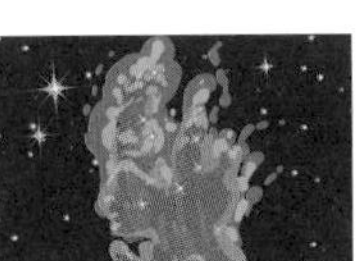

⑧ nebula

⑨ the Big Bang

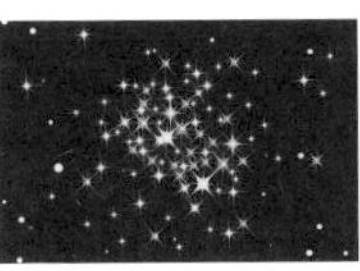

⑩ star cluster

⑪ elliptical galaxy

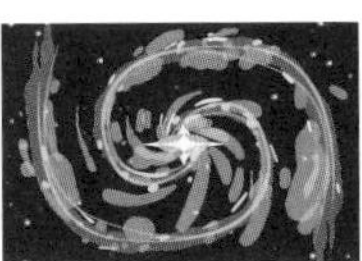

⑫ spiral galaxy

⑲ black hole

⑳ meteor

㉑ meteor shower

㉒ the Milky Way

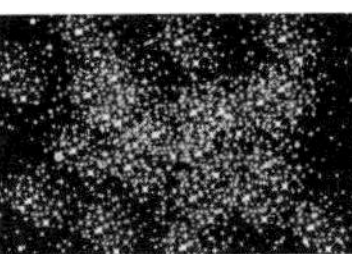

㉓ the universe

145 Planet Earth

145.1 THE EARTH

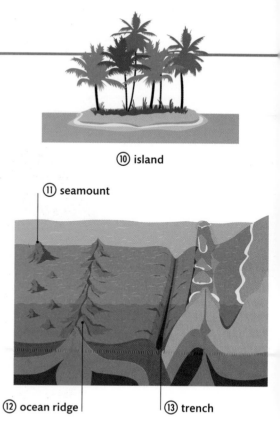

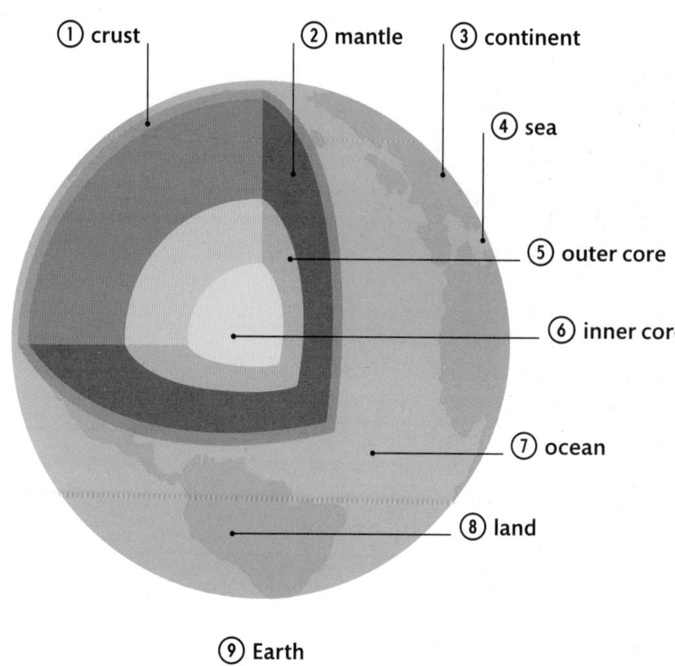

1 crust
2 mantle
3 continent
4 sea
5 outer core
6 inner core
7 ocean
8 land

9 Earth

10 island

11 seamount

12 ocean ridge

13 trench

14 undersea features

145.2 PLATE TECTONICS

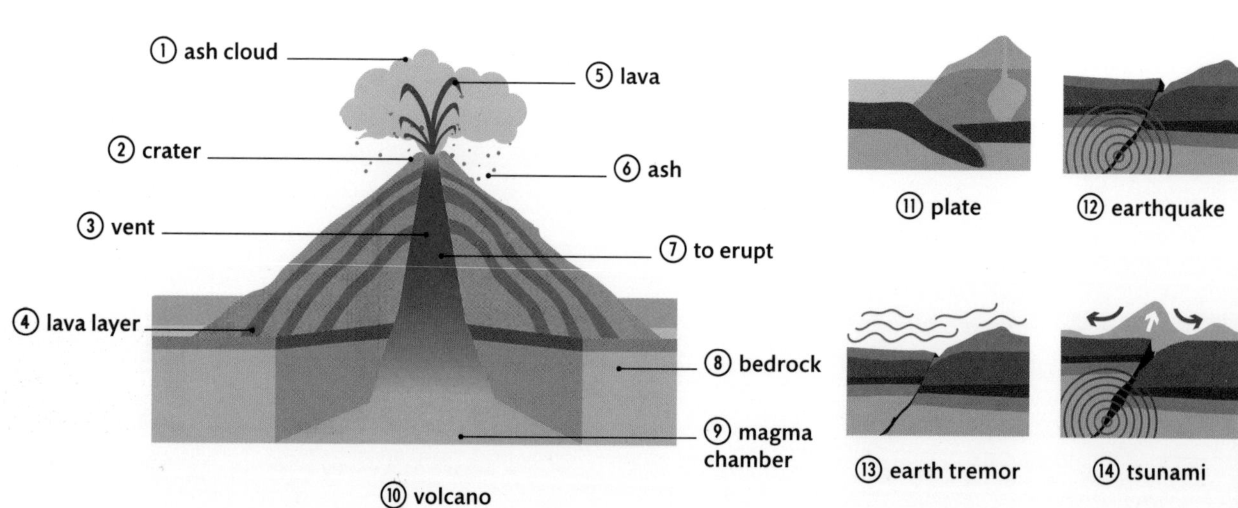

1 ash cloud
2 crater
3 vent
4 lava layer
5 lava
6 ash
7 to erupt
8 bedrock
9 magma chamber
10 volcano
11 plate
12 earthquake
13 earth tremor
14 tsunami

See also:
143-144 Space **146-147** Geography
148 Maps and directions **149-151** Countries

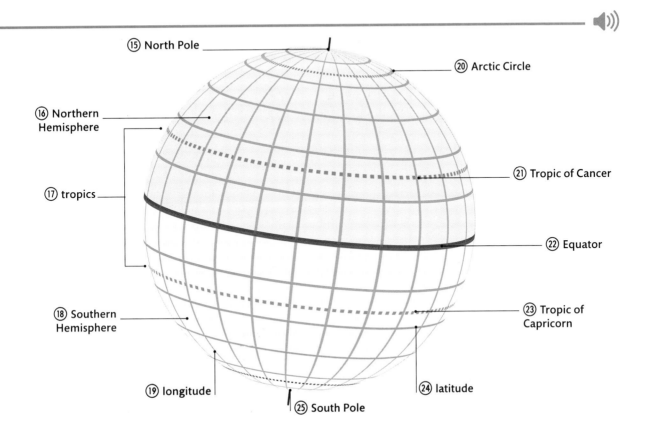

⑮ North Pole

⑳ Arctic Circle

⑯ Northern Hemisphere

㉑ Tropic of Cancer

⑰ tropics

㉒ Equator

㉓ Tropic of Capricorn

⑱ Southern Hemisphere

⑲ longitude

㉔ latitude

㉕ South Pole

145.3 WATER FEATURES AND PHENOMENA

① Victoria Falls

② Hang Son Doong

③ the Amazon

④ the Dead Sea

⑤ Caño Cristales

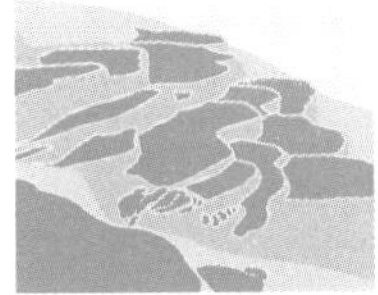

⑥ Pamukkale

⑦ the Barrier Reef

⑧ the Ganges

⑨ Angel Falls

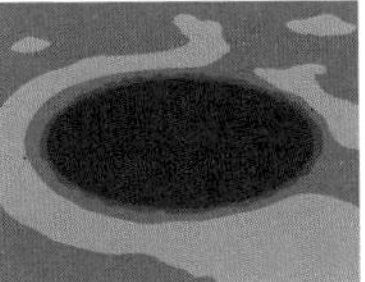

⑩ the Great Blue Hole

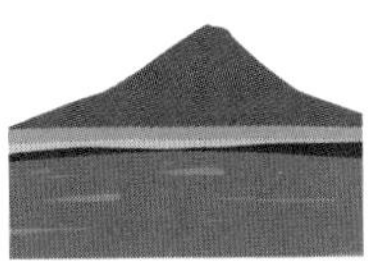

⑪ Lake Natron

⑫ Spotted Lake

146 Geography

146.1 GEOGRAPHICAL FEATURES AND LANDSCAPE

① woods (US) wood (UK)

② rain forest

③ coniferous forest

④ deciduous forest

⑨ waterfall

⑤ rapids

⑥ countryside

⑦ lake

⑧ swamp

⑩ field

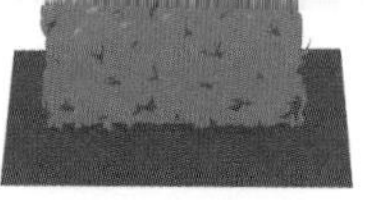
⑪ hedge

⑫ valley

⑬ farmland

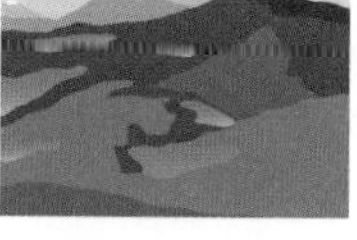
⑭ wetlands

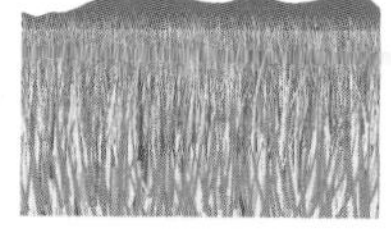
⑮ grassland

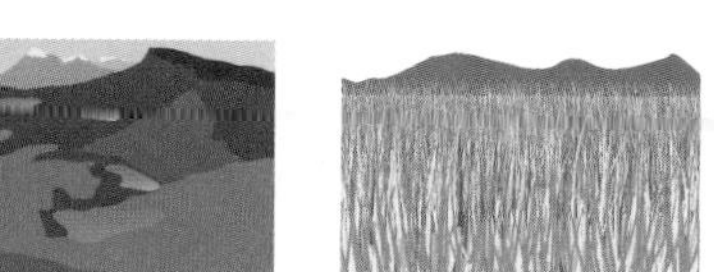

⑯ prairie

⑰ steppe

⑱ mesa

⑲ highland

⑳ ridge

㉑ mountain range

㉒ savannah

㉓ mountain chain

㉔ geyser

㉕ plain

㉖ oasis

㉗ desert

㉘ sand dune

See also:
133 Outdoor activites 145 Planet Earth 147 Geography (continued)
148 Maps and directions 149-151 Countries

(29) canyon

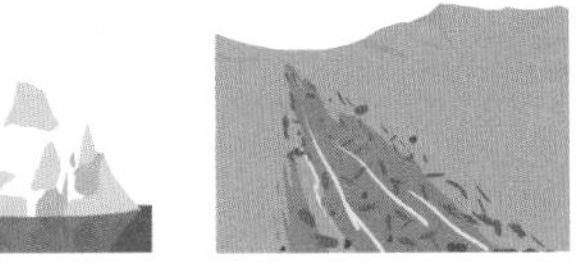
(30) iceberg

(31) mudslide

(32) landslide

(36) glacier

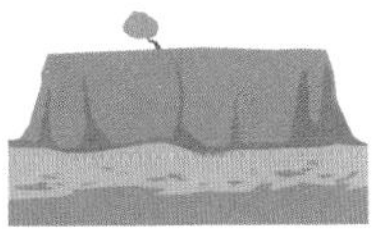
(33) plateau

(34) polar region

(35) tundra

146.2 CAVES AND CAVING

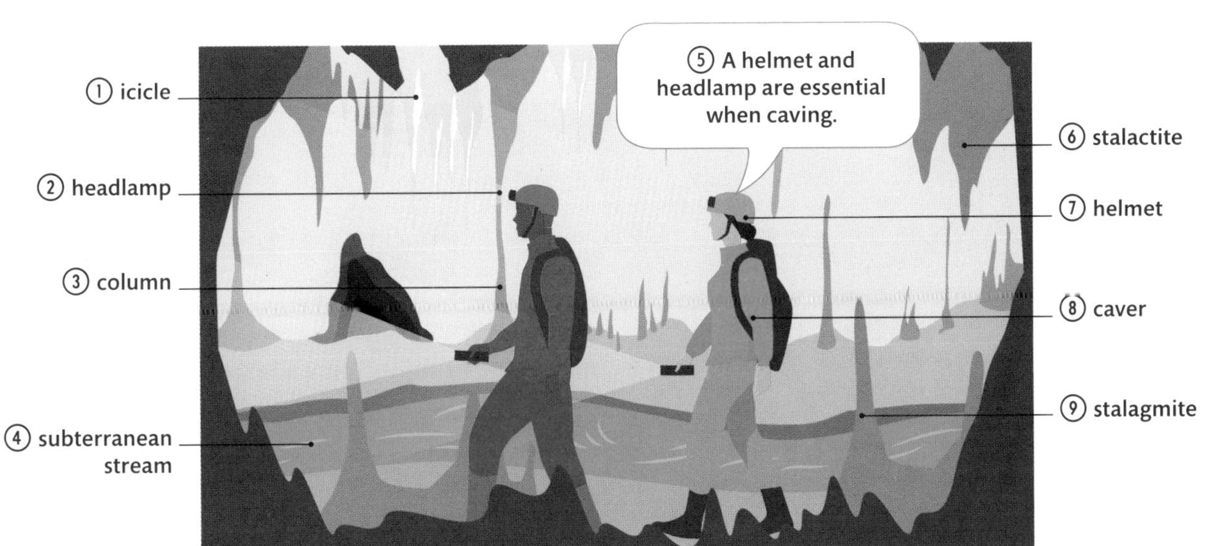
(1) icicle
(2) headlamp
(3) column
(4) subterranean stream
(5) A helmet and headlamp are essential when caving.
(6) stalactite
(7) helmet
(8) caver
(9) stalagmite

147 Geography continued

147.1 COASTAL FEATURES

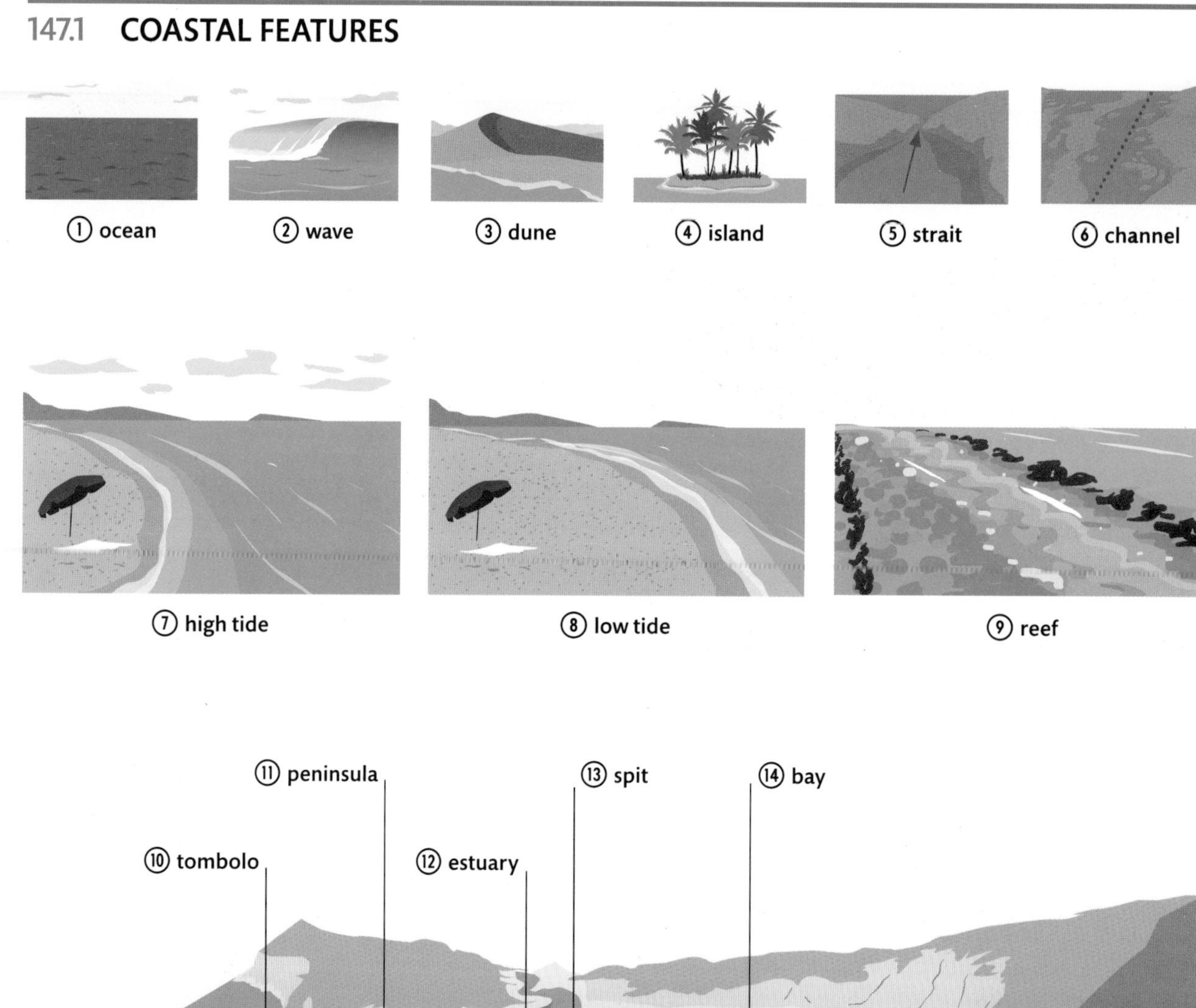

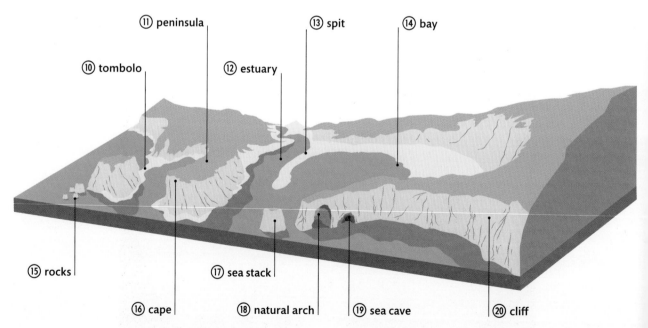

① ocean
② wave
③ dune
④ island
⑤ strait
⑥ channel
⑦ high tide
⑧ low tide
⑨ reef
⑪ peninsula
⑬ spit
⑭ bay
⑩ tombolo
⑫ estuary
⑮ rocks
⑰ sea stack
⑯ cape
⑱ natural arch
⑲ sea cave
⑳ cliff

See also:
133 Outdoor activities **145** Planet Earth
148 Maps and directions **149-151** Countries

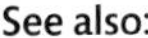

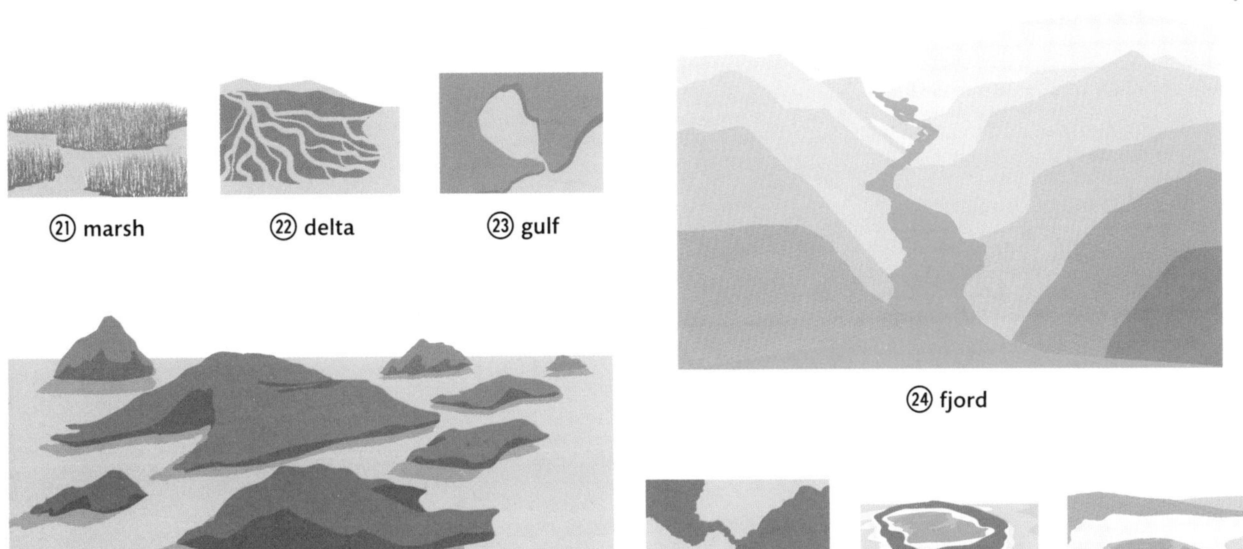

㉑ **marsh**

㉒ **delta**

㉓ **gulf**

㉔ **fjord**

㉕ **archipelago**

㉖ **isthmus**

㉗ **atoll**

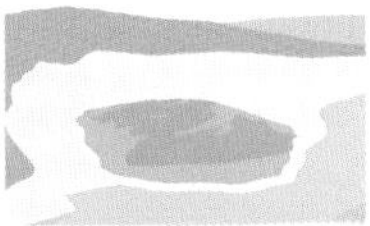

㉘ **lagoon**

147.2 RIVER FEATURES

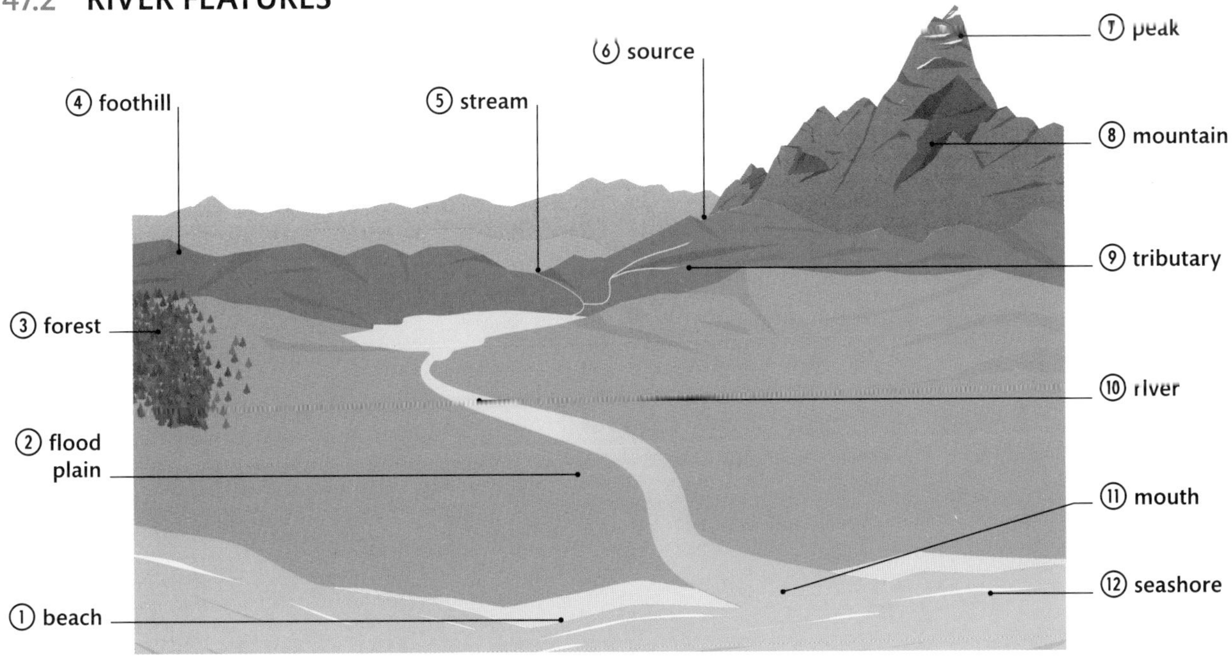

① beach

② flood plain

③ forest

④ foothill

⑤ stream

⑥ source

⑦ peak

⑧ mountain

⑨ tributary

⑩ river

⑪ mouth

⑫ seashore

148 Maps and directions

148.1 READING A MAP

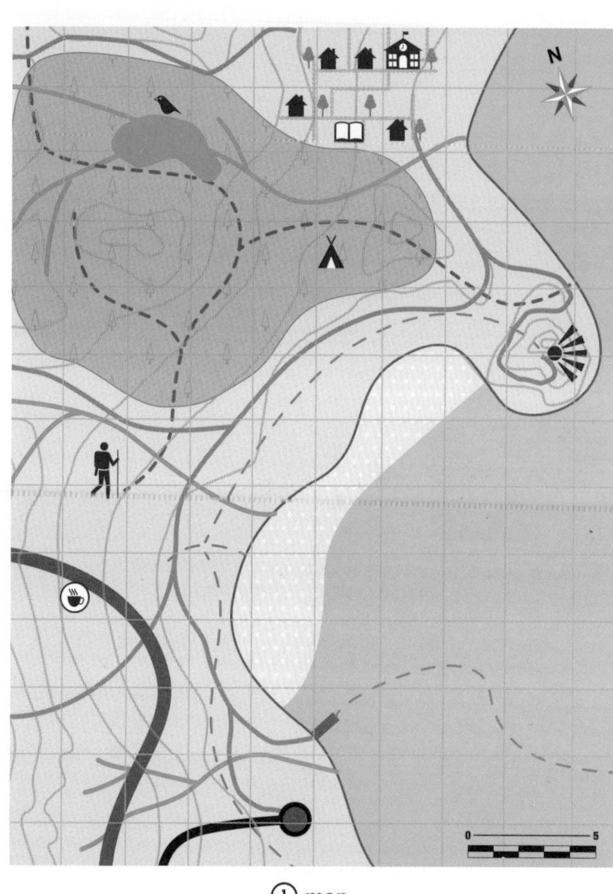
N
0
5

① map

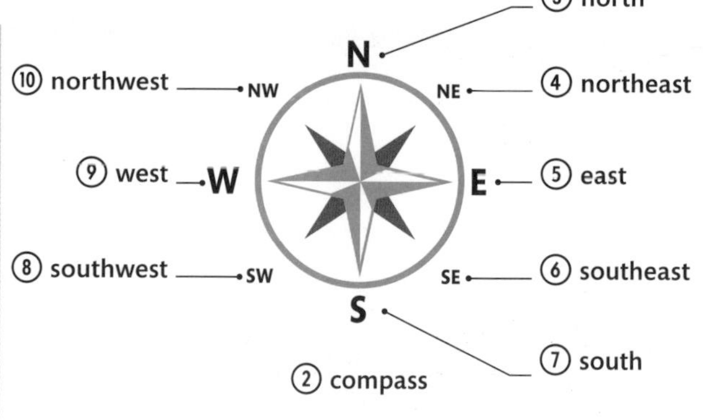
③ north
④ northeast
⑤ east
⑥ southeast
⑦ south
⑧ southwest
⑨ west
⑩ northwest
N
NE
E
SE
S
SW
W
NW

② compass

⑪ main road

⑫ secondary road

⑬ public footpath

⑭ railroad (US) railway (UK)

⑮ train station

⑯ campground (US) campsite (UK)

⑰ rest stop (US) service station (UK)

⑱ grid lines

⑲ nature reserve

⑳ viewpoint

㉑ walking trail

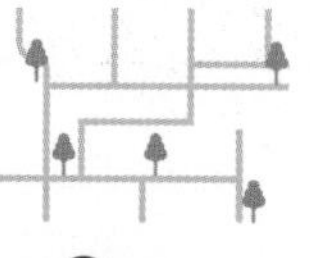

㉒ town

㉓ house / building

㉔ school

㉕ library

㉖ ferry route

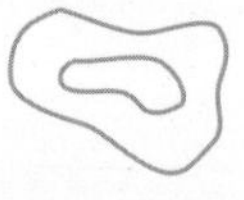

㉗ contours

㉘ river

㉙ lake

㉚ forest

㉛ beach

See also:
96 Roads 133 Outdoor activities 145 Planet Earth
146-147 Geography 150-153 Countries

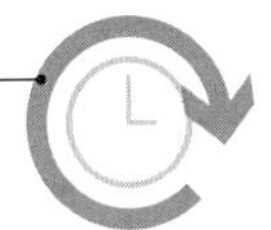

(32) clockwise

(33) counterclockwise (US)
anticlockwise (UK)

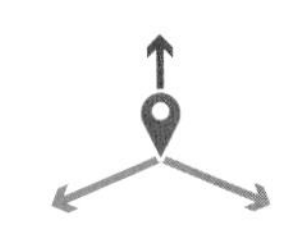

(34) coordinates

(35) orienteering

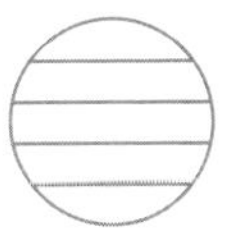

(36) latitude

(37) longitude

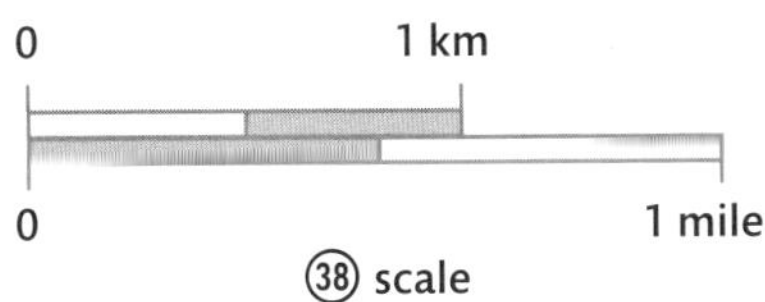
0
1 km
0
1 mile

(38) scale

(39) cartographer

(40) online map

(41) trail map (US)
hiking map (UK)

(42) roadmap (US)
streetmap (UK)

148.2 PREPOSITIONS OF PLACE

(1) next to / beside

(2) across from (US)
opposite (UK)

(3) between

(4) on the corner

(5) in front of

(6) behind

(7) on the left

(8) on the right

148.3 DIRECTION VERBS

(1) to go left / to turn left

(2) to go right / to turn right

(3) to go straight ahead / on (UK)

(4) to go back

(5) to go past (the restaurant)

(6) to take the first left

(7) to take the second right

(8) to stop at (the hotel)

(9) to plan your route

(10) to lose your way

(11) to read a map

(12) to ask directions

149 Countries

149.1 AFRICA

① Morocco

② Mauritania

③ Cape Verde

④ Senegal

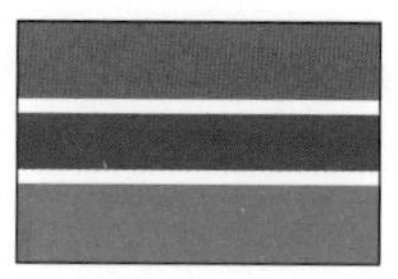
⑤ Gambia

⑥ Guinea-Bissau

⑦ Guinea

⑧ Sierra Leone

⑨ Liberia

⑩ Ivory Coast

⑪ Burkina Faso

⑫ Mali

⑬ Algeria

⑭ Tunisia

⑮ Libya

⑯ Niger

⑰ Ghana

⑱ Togo

⑲ Benin

⑳ Nigeria

㉑ São Tomé and Príncipe

㉒ Equatorial Guinea

㉓ Gabon

㉔ Cameroon

㉕ Chad

㉖ Rwanda

㉗ Burundi

㉘ Tanzania

㉙ Mozambique

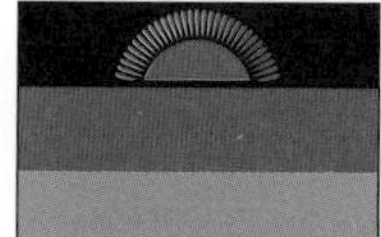
㉚ Malawi

㉛ Republic of the Congo

㉜ Democratic Republic of the Congo

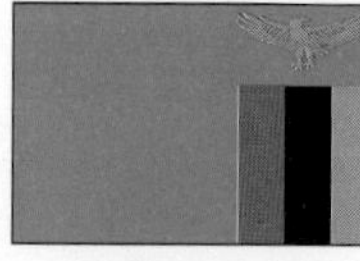
㉝ Zambia

㉞ Angola

㉟ Namibia

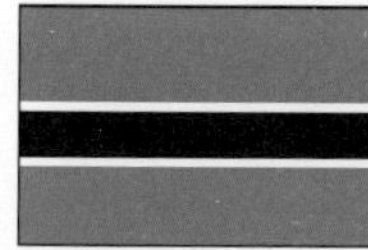
㊱ Botswana

See also:
145 Planet Earth 146-147 Geography 148 Maps and directions
150-151 Countries (continued) 152-153 Nationalities

㊲ Zimbabwe

㊳ South Africa

㊴ Lesotho

㊵ Comoros

㊶ Madagascar

㊷ Egypt

㊸ Sudan

㊹ South Sudan

㊺ Ethiopia

㊻ Eritrea

㊼ Somalia

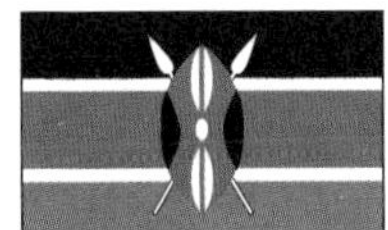
㊽ Kenya

㊾ Uganda

㊿ Djibouti

(51) Seychelles

(52) Mauritius

(53) Central African Republic

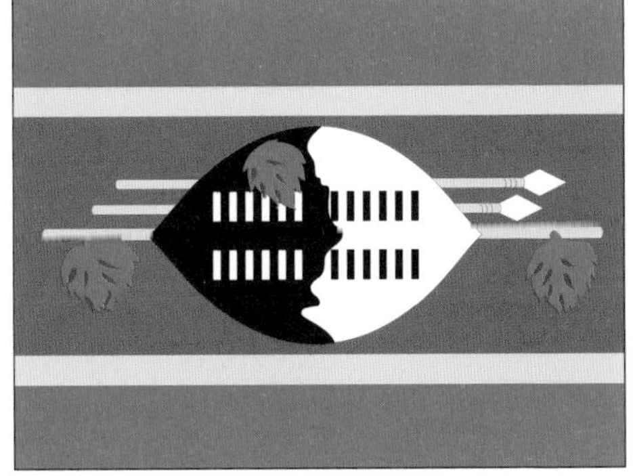
(54) Eswatini

149.2 SOUTH AMERICA

① Venezuela

② Colombia

③ Brazil

④ Bolivia

⑤ Ecuador

⑥ Peru

⑦ Chile

⑧ Argentina

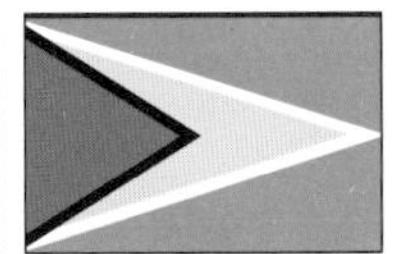
⑨ Guyana

⑩ Suriname

⑪ Paraguay

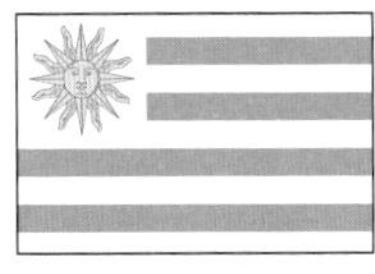
⑫ Uruguay

150 Countries continued

150.1 NORTH AND CENTRAL AMERICA AND THE CARIBBEAN

(1) Canada

(2) United States of America

(3) Mexico

(4) Guatemala

(5) Belize

(6) El Salvador

(8) Honduras

(9) Nicaragua

(10) Costa Rica

(11) Panama

(12) Cuba

(13) Bahamas

(15) Jamaica

(16) Haiti

(17) Dominican Republic

(18) Barbados

(19) Trinidad and Tobago

(20) St. Kitts and Nevis

(22) Dominica

(23) Antigua and Barbuda

150.2 OCEANIA

(1) Papua New Guinea

(2) Australia

(3) New Zealand

(4) Marshall Islands

(5) Palau

(6) Micronesia

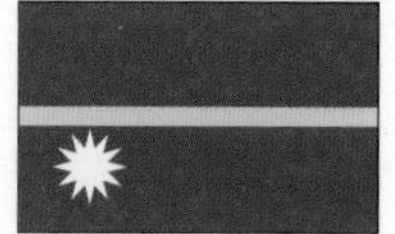
(8) Nauru

(9) Kiribati

(10) Tuvalu

(11) Samoa

(12) Tonga

(13) Vanuatu

See also:
145 Planet Earth **146-147** Geography **148** Maps and directions
151 Countries (continued) **152-153** Nationalities

⑦ Grenada

⑭ St. Lucia

㉑ St. Vincent and The Grenadines

⑦ Solomon Islands

⑭ Fiji

150.3 ASIA

① Türkiye

② Russian Federation

③ Georgia

④ Armenia

⑤ Azerbaijan

الله اكبر
⑥ Iraq

⑦ Syria

⑧ Lebanon

⑨ Israel

⑩ Jordan

⑪ Pakistan

⑫ India

⑬ Maldives

⑭ Sri Lanka

⑮ China

⑯ Mongolia

⑰ North Korea

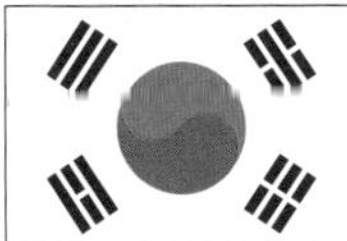
⑱ South Korea

⑲ Japan

⑳ Bangladesh

㉑ Bhutan

㉒ Myanmar (Burma)

㉓ Thailand

㉔ Laos

㉕ Vietnam

㉖ Cambodia

㉗ Nepal

151.1 ASIA CONTINUED

① Singapore

② Indonesia

③ Brunei

④ Philippines

⑤ East Timor

⑥ Malaysia

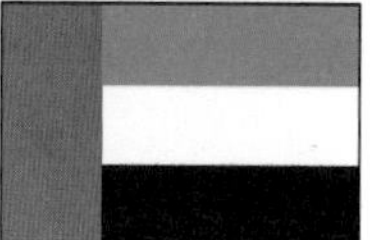
⑦ United Arab Emirates

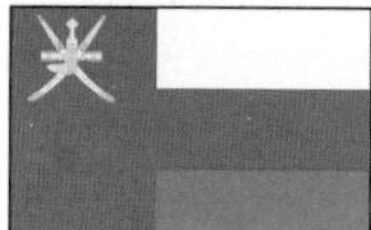
⑧ Oman

⑨ Bahrain

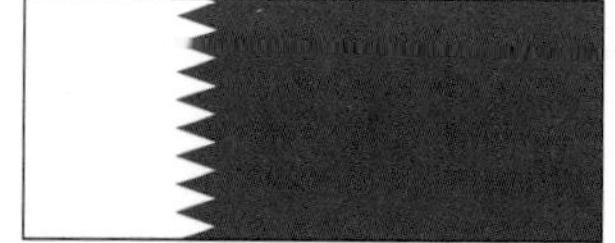
⑩ Qatar

⑪ Kuwait

⑫ Iran

⑬ Yemen

⑭ Saudi Arabia

⑮ Uzbekistan

⑯ Turkmenistan

⑰ Afghanistan

⑱ Tajikistan

⑲ Kyrgyzstan

⑳ Kazakhstan

151.2 EUROPE

① Ireland

② United Kingdom

⑨ Belgium

⑩ Netherlands

⑰ Portugal

⑱ Spain

㉕ Luxembourg

㉖ Germany

㉝ Andorra

㉞ France

㊶ Denmark

㊷ Norway

See also:
145 Planet Earth **146-147** Geography
148 Maps and directions **152-153** Nationalities

3 Sweden

4 Finland

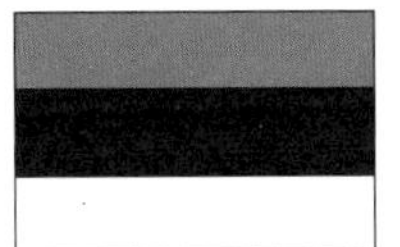
5 Estonia

6 Latvia

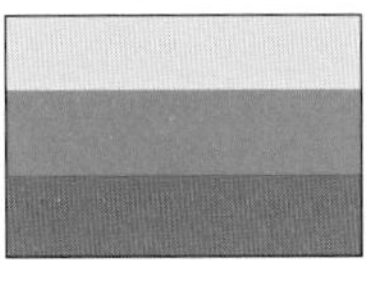
7 Lithuania

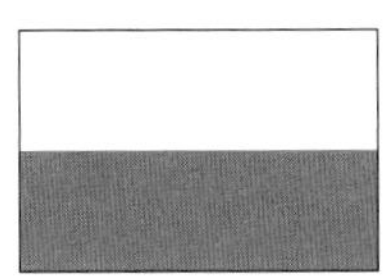
8 Poland

11 Czech Republic

12 Austria

13 Liechtenstein

14 Italy

15 Monaco

16 San Marino

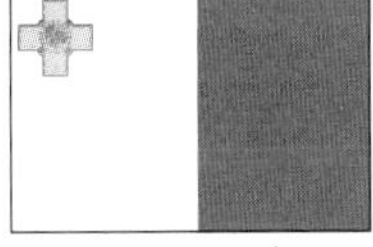
19 Malta

20 Slovenia

21 Croatia

22 Hungary

23 Slovakia

24 Ukraine

27 Belarus

28 Moldova

29 Romania

30 Serbia

31 Bulgaria

32 Albania

35 Greece

36 Iceland

37 Cyprus

38 Montenegro

39 Vatican City

40 Türkiye

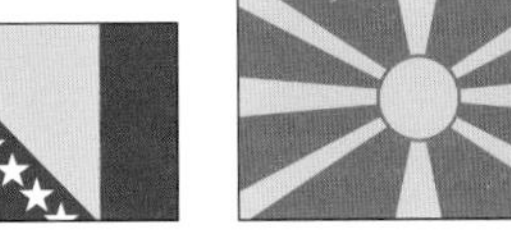
43 Bosnia and Herzegovina

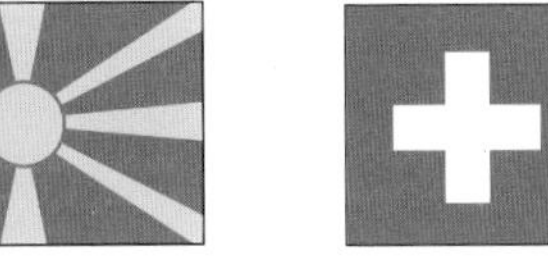
44 North Macedonia

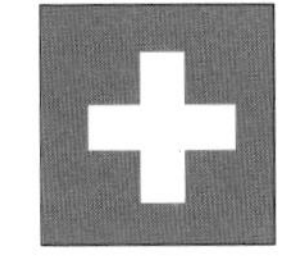
45 Switzerland

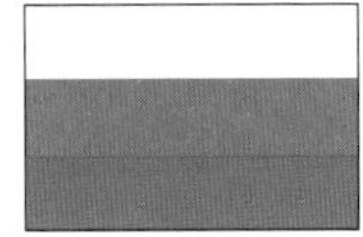
46 Russian Federation

152 Nationalities

152.1 AFRICA

Country	Adjective	Demonym (noun)
① Africa	African	Africans
② Morocco	Moroccan	Moroccans
③ Mauritania	Mauritanian	Mauritanians
④ Cape Verde	Cape Verdean	Cape Verdeans
⑤ Senegal	Senegalese	Senegalese people
⑥ Gambia	Gambian	Gambians
⑦ Guinea-Bissau	Bissau-Guinean	Bissau-Guineans
⑧ Guinea	Guinean	Guineans
⑨ Sierra Leone	Sierra Leonean	Sierra Leoneans
⑩ Liberia	Liberian	Liberians
⑪ Ivory Coast	Ivorian	Ivorians
⑫ Burkina Faso	Burkinabe	Burkinabes
⑬ Mali	Malian	Malians
⑭ Algeria	Algerian	Algerians
⑮ Tunisia	Tunisian	Tunisians
⑯ Libya	Libyan	Libyans
⑰ Niger	Nigerien	Nigeriens
⑱ Ghana	Ghanaian	Ghanaians
⑲ Togo	Togolese	Togolese people
⑳ Benin	Beninese	Beninese people
㉑ Nigeria	Nigerian	Nigerians
㉒ São Tomé and Príncipe	São Toméan	São Toméans
㉓ Equatorial Guinea	Equatorial Guinean	Equatorial Guineans
㉔ Cameroon	Cameroonian	Cameroonians
㉕ Chad	Chadian	Chadians
㉖ Egypt	Egyptian	Egyptians
㉗ Sudan	Sudanese	Sudanese people
㉘ South Sudan	South Sudanese	South Sudanese people
㉙ Eritrea	Eritrean	Eritreans

Country	Adjective	Demonym (noun)
㉚ Djibouti	Djiboutian	Djiboutians
㉛ Ethiopia	Ethiopian	Ethiopians
㉜ Somalia	Somalian	Somalians
㉝ Kenya	Kenyan	Kenyans
㉞ Uganda	Ugandan	Ugandans
㉟ Central African Republic	Central African	Central Africans
㊱ Gabon	Gabonese	Gabonese people
㊲ Republic of the Congo	Congolese	Congolese people
㊳ Democratic Republic of the Congo	Congolese	Congolese people
㊴ Rwanda	Rwandan	Rwandans
㊵ Burundi	Burundian	Burundians
㊶ Tanzania	Tanzanian	Tanzanians
㊷ Mozambique	Mozambican	Mozambicans
㊸ Malawi	Malawian	Malawians
㊹ Zambia	Zambian	Zambians
㊺ Angola	Angolan	Angolans
㊻ Namibia	Namibian	Namibians
㊼ Botswana	Botswanan	Botswanans
㊽ Zimbabwe	Zimbabwean	Zimbabweans
㊾ South Africa	South African	South Africans
㊿ Lesotho	Basotho	Basothos
(51) Eswatini	Swazi	Swazis
(52) Comoros	Comoran	Comorans
(53) Madagascar	Madagascan	Madagascans
(54) Seychelles	Seychellois	Seychellois
(55) Mauritius	Mauritian	Mauritians

See also:
145 Planet Earth 146-147 Geography 148 Maps and directions
149-151 Countries 153 Nationalities (continued)

152.2 SOUTH AMERICA

Country	Adjective	Demonym (noun)	Country	Adjective	Demonym (noun)
① South America	South American	South Americans	⑧ Brazil	Brazilian	Brazilians
② Venezuela	Venezuelan	Venezuelans	⑨ Bolivia	Bolivian	Bolivians
③ Colombia	Colombian	Colombians	⑩ Chile	Chilean	Chileans
④ Ecuador	Ecuadorian	Ecuadorians	⑪ Argentina	Argentinian	Argentinians
⑤ Peru	Peruvian	Peruvians	⑫ Paraguay	Paraguayan	Paraguayans
⑥ Guyana	Guyanese	Guyanese people	⑬ Uruguay	Uruguayan	Uruguayans
⑦ Suriname	Surinamese	Surinamese people			

152.3 NORTH AND CENTRAL AMERICA AND THE CARIBBEAN

Country	Adjective	Demonym (noun)	Country	Adjective	Demonym (noun)
① North and Central America and the Caribbean	North American Central American Caribbean	North Americans Central Americans Caribbean people	⑭ Jamaica	Jamaican	Jamaicans
			⑮ Haiti	Haitian	Haitians
② Canada	Canadian	Canadians	⑯ Dominican Republic	Dominican	Dominicans
③ United States of America	American	Americans	⑰ Barbados	Barbadian	Barbadians
④ Mexico	Mexican	Mexicans	⑱ Trinidad and Tobago	Trinidadian or Tobagonian	Trinidadians or Tobagonians
⑤ Guatemala	Guatemalan	Guatemalans	⑲ St. Kitts and Nevis	Kittitian or Nevisian	Kittitians or Nevisians
⑥ Belize	Belizean	Belizeans	⑳ Antigua and Barbuda	Antiguan or Barbudan	Antiguans or Barbudans
⑦ El Salvador	Salvadoran	Salvadorans	㉑ Dominica	Dominican	Dominicans
⑧ Honduras	Honduran	Hondurans	㉒ St. Lucia	St. Lucian	St. Lucians
⑨ Nicaragua	Nicaraguan	Nicaraguans	㉓ St. Vincent and The Grenadines	Vincentian	Vincentians
⑩ Costa Rica	Costa Rican	Costa Ricans	㉔ Grenada	Grenadian	Grenadians
⑪ Panama	Panamanian	Panamanians			
⑫ Cuba	Cuban	Cubans			
⑬ Bahamas	Bahamian	Bahamians			

153 Nationalities continued

153.1 OCEANIA

Country	Adjective	Demonym
① Oceania	Oceanian	Oceanians
② Papua New Guinea	Papua New Guinean	Papua New Guineans
③ Australia	Australian	Australians
④ New Zealand	New Zealand	New Zealanders
⑤ Marshall Islands	Marshallese	Marshallese people
⑥ Palau	Palauan	Palauans
⑦ Micronesia	Micronesian	Micronesians
⑧ Nauru	Nauruan	Nauruans
⑨ Kiribati	Kiribati	Kiribati people
⑩ Tuvalu	Tuvaluan	Tuvaluans
⑪ Samoa	Samoan	Samoans
⑫ Tonga	Tongan	Tongans
⑬ Vanuatu	Vanuatuan	Vanuatuans
⑭ Solomon Islands	Solomon Island	Solomon Islanders
⑮ Fiji	Fijian	Fijians

153.2 ASIA

Country	Adjective	Demonym
① Asia	Asian	Asians
② Turkey	Turkish	Turks
③ Russian Federation	Russian	Russians
④ Georgia	Georgian	Georgians
⑤ Armenia	Armenian	Armenians
⑥ Azerbaijan	Azerbaijani	Azerbaijanis
⑦ Iran	Iranian	Iranians
⑧ Iraq	Iraqi	Iraqis
⑨ Syria	Syrian	Syrians
⑩ Lebanon	Lebanese	Lebanese people
⑪ Israel	Israeli	Israelis
⑫ Jordan	Jordanian	Jordanians
⑬ Saudi Arabia	Saudi	Saudis
⑭ Kuwait	Kuwaiti	Kuwaitis
⑮ Bahrain	Bahraini	Bahrainis
⑯ Qatar	Qatari	Qataris
⑰ United Arab Emirates	Emirati	Emiratis
⑱ Oman	Omani	Omanis
⑲ Yemen	Yemeni	Yemenis
⑳ Kazakhstan	Kazakh	Kazakhs
㉑ Uzbekistan	Uzbek	Uzbeks
㉒ Turkmenistan	Turkmen	Turkmens
㉓ Afghanistan	Afghan	Afghans
㉔ Tajikistan	Tajikistani	Tajiks
㉕ Kyrgyzstan	Kyrgyz	Kyrgyz people
㉖ Pakistan	Pakistani	Pakistanis
㉗ India	Indian	Indians
㉘ Maldives	Maldivian	Maldivians
㉙ Sri Lanka	Sri Lankan	Sri Lankans
㉚ China	Chinese	Chinese people
㉛ Mongolia	Mongolian	Mongolians
㉜ North Korea	North Korean	North Koreans
㉝ South Korea	South Korean	South Koreans
㉞ Japan	Japanese	Japanese people
㉟ Nepal	Nepalese	Nepalese people
㊱ Bhutan	Bhutanese	Bhutanese people
㊲ Bangladesh	Bangladeshi	Bangladeshis
㊳ Myanmar (Burma)	Burmese	Burmese people
㊴ Thailand	Thai	Thais

See also:
145 Planet Earth 146-147 Geography
148 Maps and directions 149-151 Countries

153.2 ASIA CONTINUED

Country	Adjective	Demonym	Country	Adjective	Demonym
(40) Laos	Laotian	Laotians	(44) Singapore	Singaporean	Singaporeans
(41) Vietnam	Vietnamese	Vietnamese people	(45) Indonesia	Indonesian	Indonesians
(42) Cambodia	Cambodian	Cambodians	(46) Brunei	Bruneian	Bruneians
(43) Malaysia	Malaysian	Malaysians	(47) Philippines	Filipino	Filipinos
			(48) East Timor	Timorese	Timorese people

153.3 EUROPE

Country	Adjective	Demonym
(1) Europe	European	Europeans
(2) Ireland	Irish	Irish people
(3) United Kingdom	British	British
(4) Portugal	Portuguese	Portuguese people
(5) Spain	Spanish	Spaniards
(6) Andorra	Andorran	Andorrans
(7) France	French	French people
(8) Belgium	Belgian	Belgians
(9) Netherlands	Dutch	Dutch people
(10) Luxembourg	Luxembourg	Luxembourgers
(11) Germany	German	Germans
(12) Denmark	Danish	Danes
(13) Norway	Norwegian	Norwegians
(14) Sweden	Swedish	Swedes
(15) Finland	Finnish	Finns
(16) Estonia	Estonian	Estonians
(17) Latvia	Latvian	Latvians
(18) Lithuania	Lithuanian	Lithuanians
(19) Poland	Polish	Poles
(20) Czech Republic	Czech	Czechs
(21) Austria	Austrian	Austrians
(22) Liechtenstein	Liechtensteiner	Liechtensteiners
(23) Switzerland	Swiss	Swiss people
(24) Italy	Italian	Italians
(25) Monaco	Monacan	Monégasques
(26) San Marino	Sammarinese	Sammarinese people
(27) Malta	Maltese	Maltese people
(28) Slovenia	Slovenian	Slovenians
(29) Croatia	Croatian	Croats
(30) Hungary	Hungarian	Hungarians
(31) Slovakia	Slovakian	Slovaks
(32) Ukraine	Ukrainian	Ukrainians
(33) Belarus	Belarusian	Belarusians
(34) Moldova	Moldovan	Moldovans
(35) Romania	Romanian	Romanians
(36) Serbia	Serbian	Serbs
(37) Bosnia and Herzegovina	Bosnian or Herzegovinian	Bosnians or Herzegovinians
(38) Albania	Albanian	Albanians
(39) North Macedonia	North Macedonian	North Macedonians
(40) Bulgaria	Bulgarian	Bulgarians
(41) Greece	Greek	Greeks
(42) Montenegro	Montenegrin	Montenegrins
(43) Iceland	Icelandic	Icelanders
(44) Cyprus	Cypriot	Cypriots
(45) Türkiye	Turkish	Turkish people
(46) Russian Federation	Russian	Russians

154 Weather

154.1 WEATHER

① humidity

② heat wave (US)
heatwave (UK)

③ drought

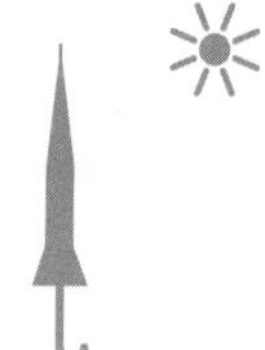

④ dry

⑤ wet

⑥ overcast

⑦ smog

⑧ raindrop

⑨ light shower

⑩ drizzle

⑪ downpour

⑫ flood

⑬ sandstorm

⑭ gale

⑮ storm

⑯ thunder

⑰ lightning

⑱ rainbow

⑲ sleet

⑳ snowflake

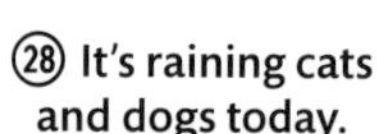

㉘ It's raining cats
and dogs today.

㉑ snowdrift

㉒ blizzard

㉓ snowstorm

㉔ hailstone

㉕ hurricane

㉖ tornado

㉗ puddle

See also:
145 Planet Earth **146-147** Geography
155 Climate and the environment

154.2 TEMPERATURE

① freezing

② cold

③ chilly

④ warm

⑤ hot

⑥ stifling

⑦ freezing point

⑧ boiling point

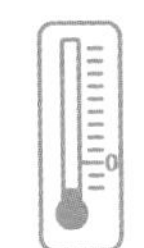
⑨ minus 10

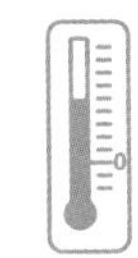
⑩ 25 degrees

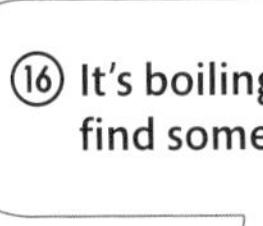
⑯ It's boiling! I need to find some shade.

⑪ Celsius

⑫ Fahrenheit

⑬ cool

⑭ mild

⑮ boiling

154.3 WEATHER ADJECTIVES

① sun → sunny

② cloud → cloudy

③ fog → foggy

④ rain → rainy

⑤ snow → snowy

⑥ ice → icy

⑦ frost → frosty

⑧ wind → windy

⑨ storm → stormy

⑩ thunder → thundery

⑪ mist → misty

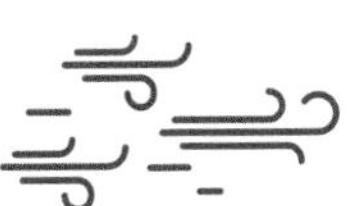
⑫ breeze → breezy

155 Climate and the environment

155.1 ATMOSPHERE

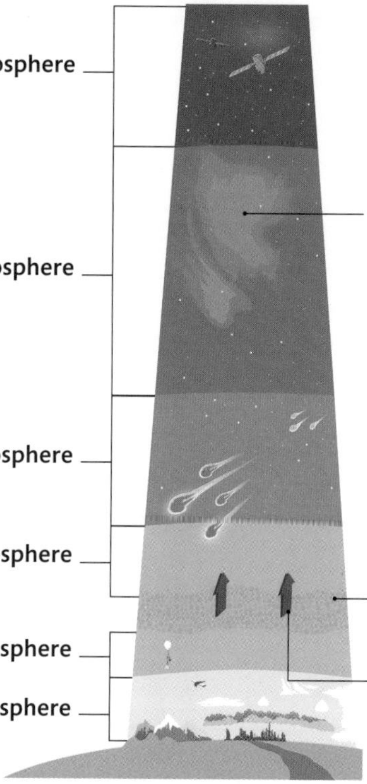

① exosphere
② thermosphere
③ ionosphere
④ mesosphere
⑤ stratosphere
⑥ troposphere
⑦ aurora
⑧ ozone layer
⑨ ultraviolet rays
⑩ atmosphere

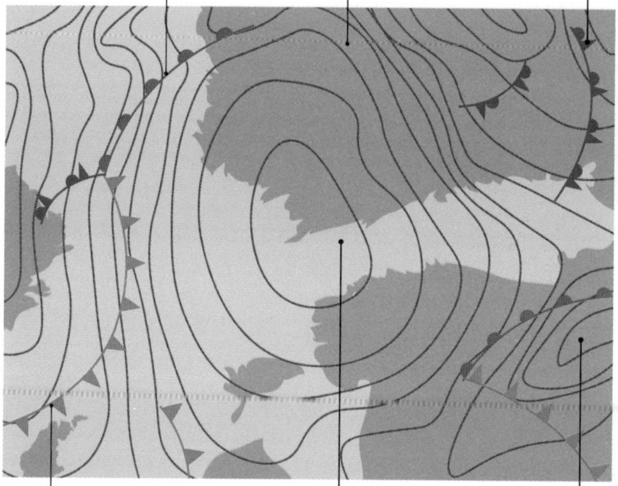

⑪ warm front
⑫ isobar
⑬ occluded front
⑭ cold front
⑮ high pressure
⑯ low pressure
⑰ weather map

155.2 ENVIRONMENTAL ISSUES

① deforestation

② habitat loss

③ endangered species

④ plastic waste

⑤ overfishing

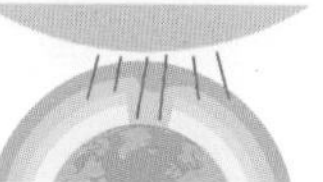
⑥ ozone depletion

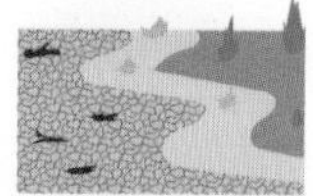
⑦ desertification

⑧ oil slick

⑨ acid rain

See also:
145 Planet Earth **146-147** Geography
154 Weather

155.3 CLIMATE CHANGE

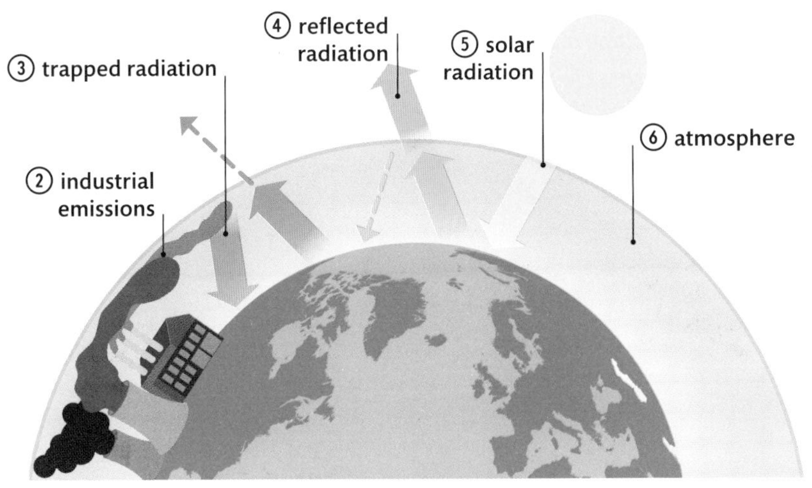
④ reflected radiation
③ trapped radiation
⑤ solar radiation
⑥ atmosphere
② industrial emissions

① greenhouse effect

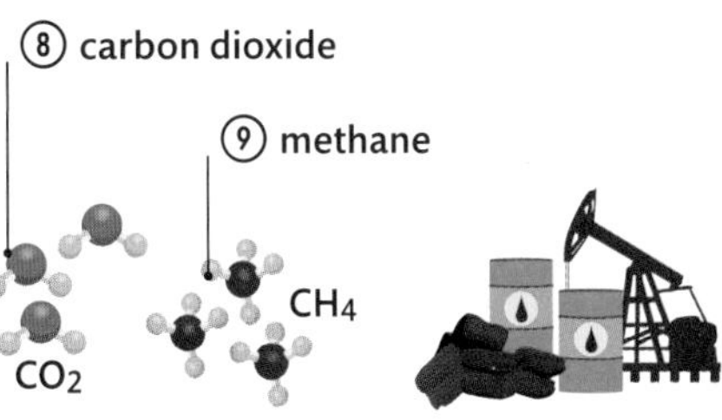
⑧ carbon dioxide
⑨ methane
CH_4
CO_2

⑦ greenhouse gases

⑩ fossil fuels

⑪ emissions

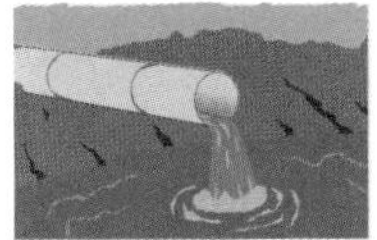

⑫ pollution

⑬ ecosystem

CO_2

⑭ zero carbon

⑮ shrinking glaciers

⑯ melting ice caps

155.4 WASTE AND RECYCLING

② I try to recycle plastic and paper as much as possible.

① to sort your trash (US)
to sort your rubbish (UK)

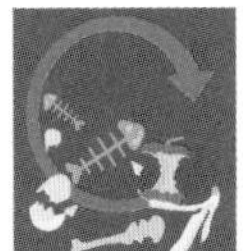

③ food waste

④ paper

⑤ plastic

⑥ glass

⑦ metal

⑧ compostable bags

⑨ landfill

156 Rocks and minerals

156.1 ROCKS

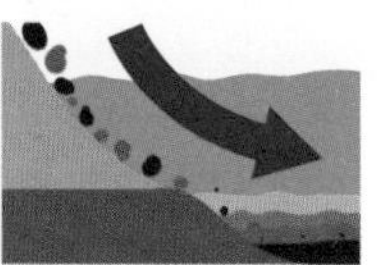
① sedimentary

② sandstone

③ limestone

④ chalk

⑤ flint

⑥ conglomerate

⑦ metamorphic

⑧ slate

⑨ schist

⑩ gneiss

⑪ marble

⑫ quartzite

⑬ igneous

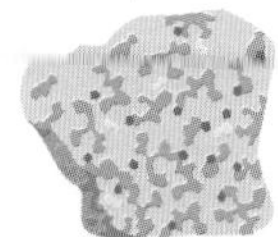
⑭ granite

⑮ obsidian

⑯ basalt

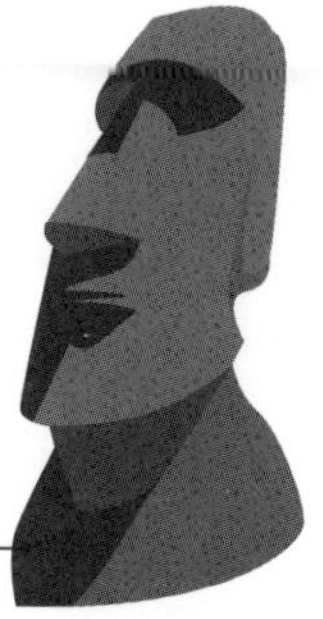
⑰ tuff

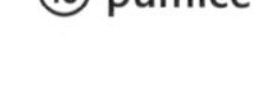
⑱ pumice

156.2 MINERALS

① quartz

② mica

③ agate

④ hematite

⑤ calcite

⑥ malachite

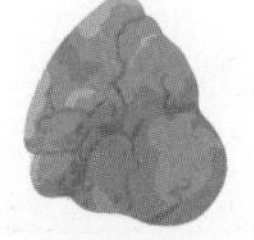
⑦ turquoise

⑧ onyx

⑨ sulfur (US)
sulphur (UK)

⑩ graphite

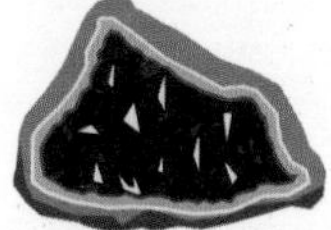
⑪ geode

⑫ sand rose

See also:
76 Chemistry **78** The periodic table
145 Planet Earth **146-147** Geography

156.3 GEMS

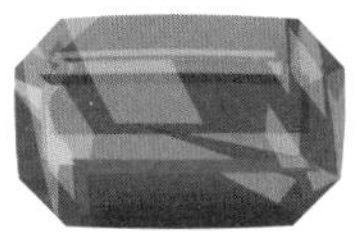

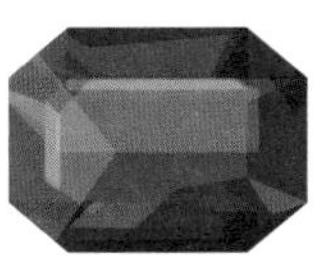

① diamond ② sapphire ③ emerald ④ ruby ⑤ amethyst ⑥ topaz

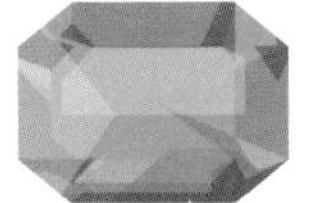

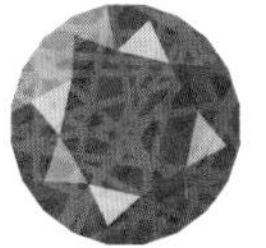

⑦ aquamarine ⑧ moonstone ⑨ opal ⑩ tourmaline ⑪ garnet ⑫ citrine

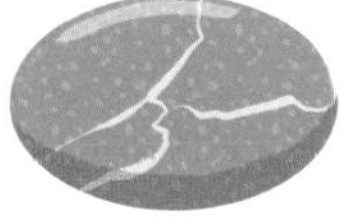

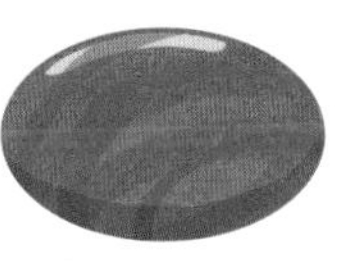

⑬ jade ⑭ jet ⑮ lapis lazuli ⑯ jasper ⑰ tiger's eye ⑱ carnelian

156.4 METALS

① gold ② silver ③ platinum ④ magnesium ⑤ iron ⑥ copper

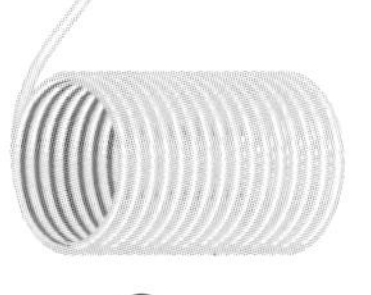

⑦ tin ⑧ aluminum (US) aluminium (UK) ⑨ mercury ⑩ nickel ⑪ zinc ⑫ chromium

157 Natural history

157.1 GEOLOGICAL PERIODS

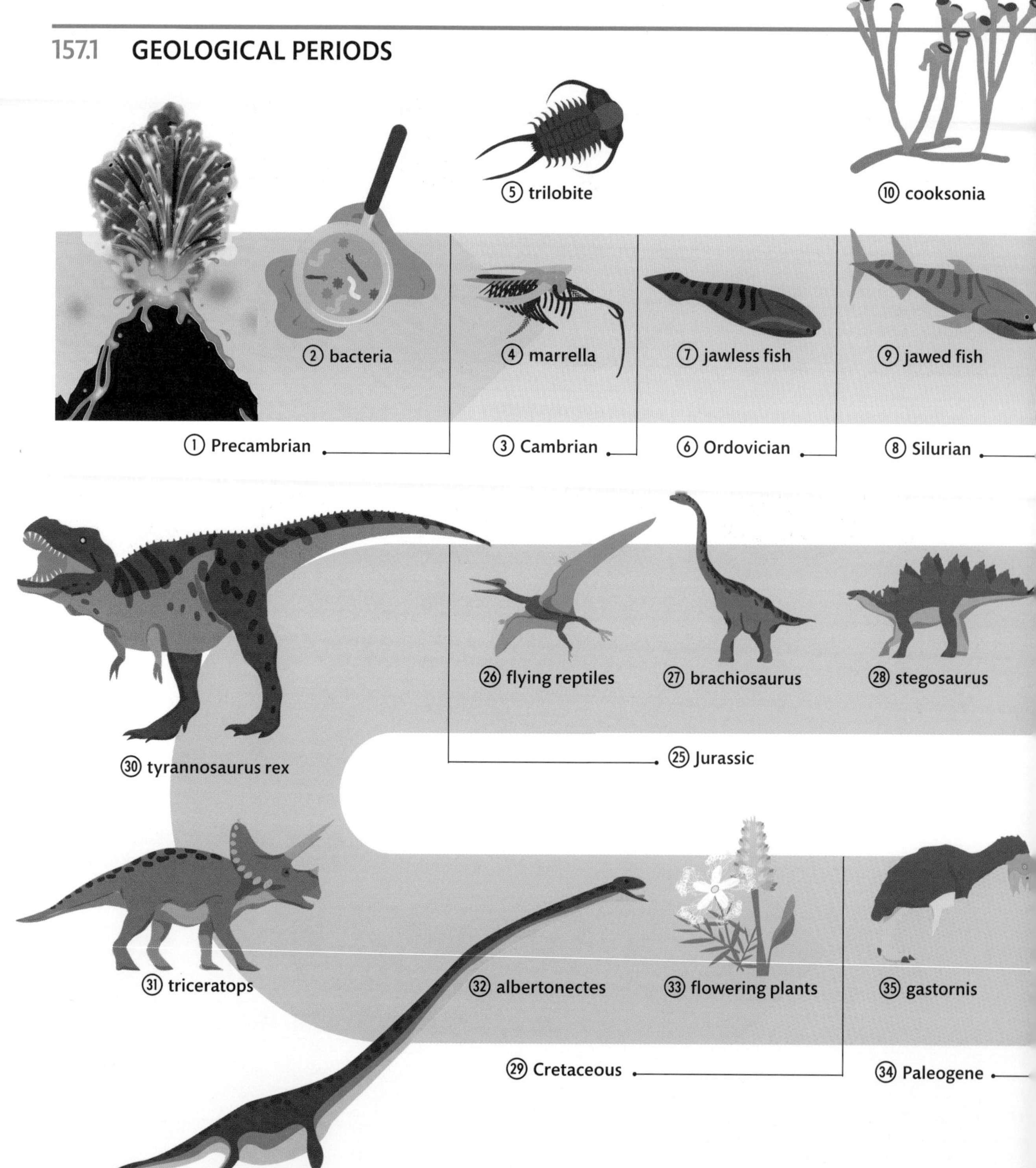

⑤ trilobite
⑩ cooksonia
② bacteria
④ marrella
⑦ jawless fish
⑨ jawed fish
① Precambrian
③ Cambrian
⑥ Ordovician
⑧ Silurian
㉖ flying reptiles
㉗ brachiosaurus
㉘ stegosaurus
㉚ tyrannosaurus rex
㉕ Jurassic
㉛ triceratops
㉜ albertonectes
㉝ flowering plants
㉟ gastornis
㉙ Cretaceous
㉞ Paleogene

See also:
145 Planet Earth 158-159 Mammals 160-161 Birds 162 Insects and bugs
163 Amphibians and reptiles 166 Ocean life 167-169 Plants and trees

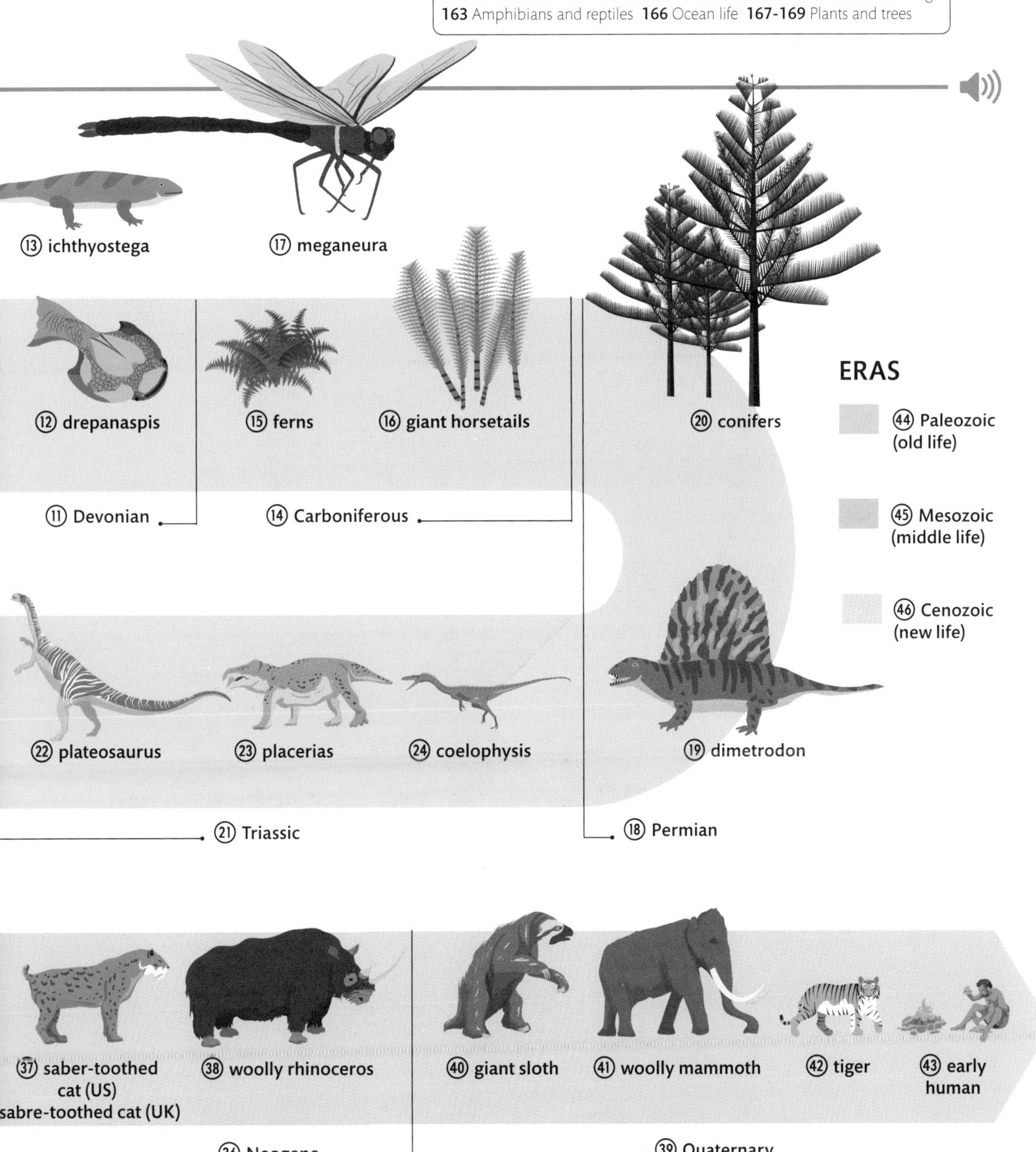
⑬ ichthyostega
⑰ meganeura
⑫ drepanaspis
⑮ ferns
⑯ giant horsetails
⑳ conifers
⑪ Devonian
⑭ Carboniferous
㉒ plateosaurus
㉓ placerias
㉔ coelophysis
⑲ dimetrodon
㉑ Triassic
⑱ Permian
㊲ saber-toothed cat (US)
sabre-toothed cat (UK)
㊳ woolly rhinoceros
㊵ giant sloth
㊶ woolly mammoth
㊷ tiger
㊸ early human
㊱ Neogene
㊴ Quaternary

ERAS

㊹ Paleozoic (old life)

㊺ Mesozoic (middle life)

㊻ Cenozoic (new life)

158 Mammals

158.1 SPECIES OF MAMMALS

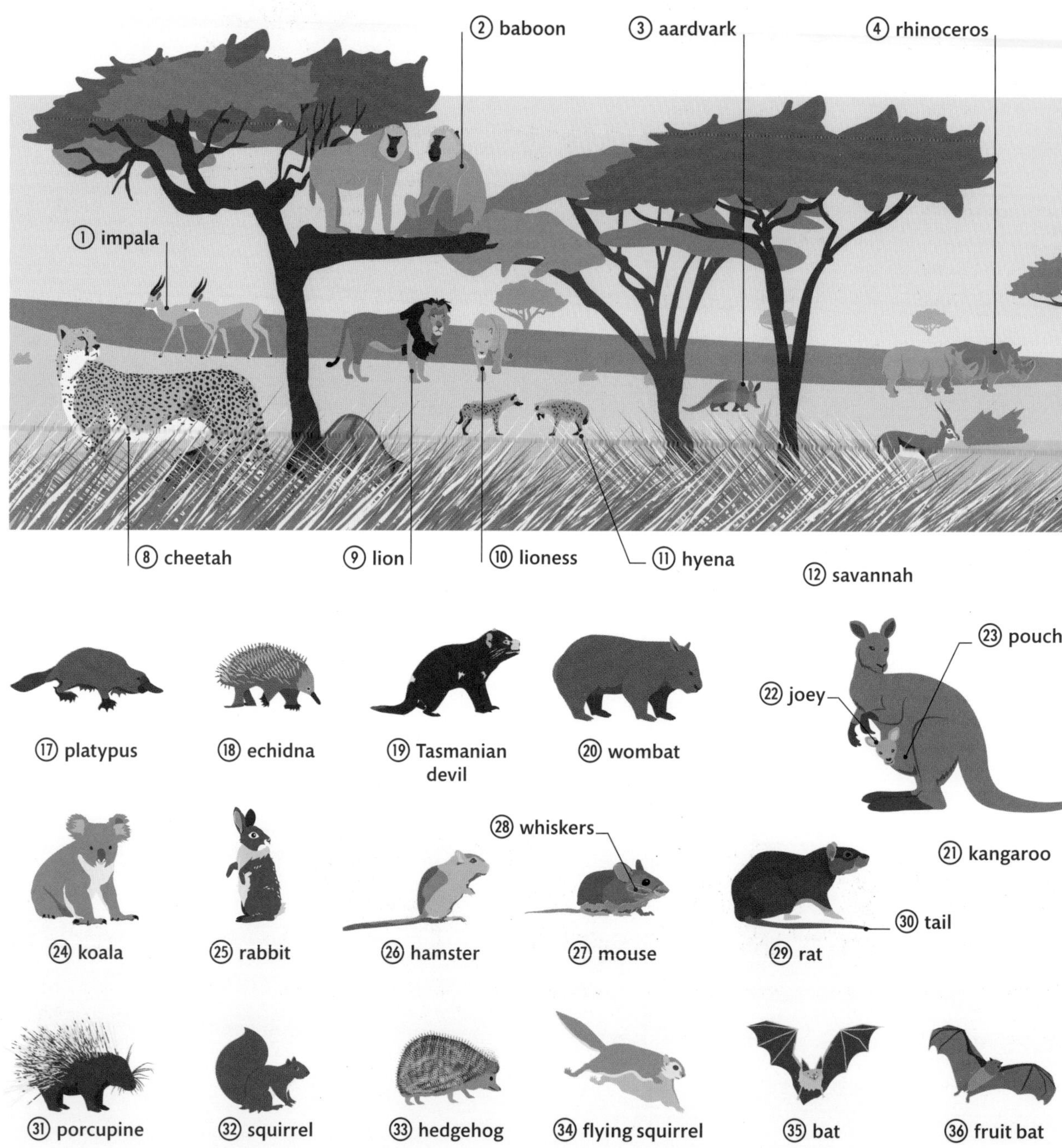

① impala
② baboon
③ aardvark
④ rhinoceros
⑧ cheetah
⑨ lion
⑩ lioness
⑪ hyena
⑫ savannah
⑰ platypus
⑱ echidna
⑲ Tasmanian devil
⑳ wombat
㉑ kangaroo
㉒ joey
㉓ pouch
㉔ koala
㉕ rabbit
㉖ hamster
㉗ mouse
㉘ whiskers
㉙ rat
㉚ tail
㉛ porcupine
㉜ squirrel
㉝ hedgehog
㉞ flying squirrel
㉟ bat
㊱ fruit bat

See also:
157 Natural history 159 Mammals (continued)
164 Pets 165 Farm animals 166 Ocean life

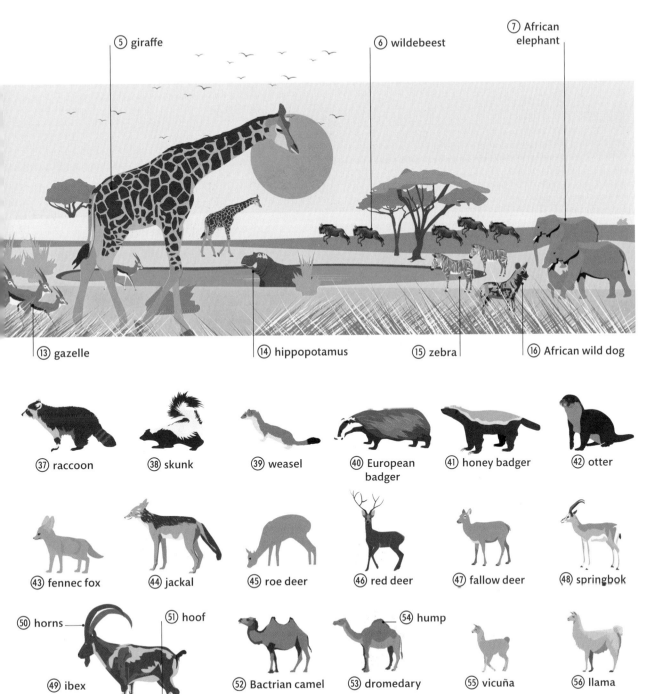

⑤ giraffe
⑥ wildebeest
⑦ African elephant
⑬ gazelle
⑭ hippopotamus
⑮ zebra
⑯ African wild dog

㊲ raccoon
㊳ skunk
㊴ weasel
㊵ European badger
㊶ honey badger
㊷ otter

㊸ fennec fox
㊹ jackal
㊺ roe deer
㊻ red deer
㊼ fallow deer
㊽ springbok

㊾ ibex
㊿ horns
(51) hoof
(52) Bactrian camel
(53) dromedary
(54) hump
(55) vicuña
(56) llama

159 Mammals continued

159.1 SPECIES OF MAMMALS

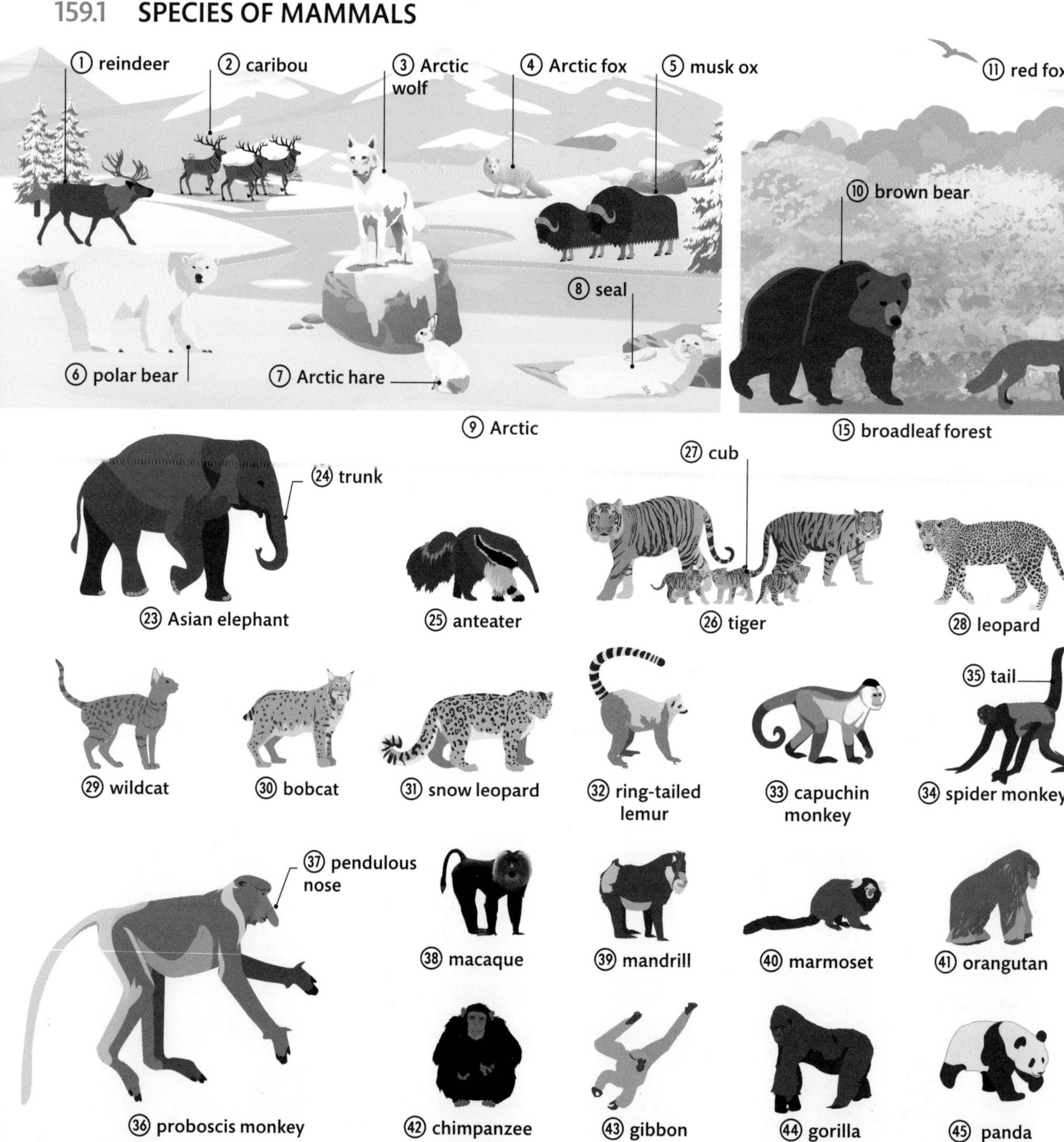

① reindeer
② caribou
③ Arctic wolf
④ Arctic fox
⑤ musk ox
⑪ red fox
⑩ brown bear
⑧ seal
⑥ polar bear
⑦ Arctic hare
⑨ Arctic
⑮ broadleaf forest
㉗ cub
㉔ trunk
㉓ Asian elephant
㉕ anteater
㉖ tiger
㉘ leopard
㉟ tail
㉙ wildcat
㉚ bobcat
㉛ snow leopard
㉜ ring-tailed lemur
㉝ capuchin monkey
㉞ spider monkey
㊲ pendulous nose
㊳ macaque
㊴ mandrill
㊵ marmoset
㊶ orangutan
㊱ proboscis monkey
㊷ chimpanzee
㊸ gibbon
㊹ gorilla
㊺ panda

See also:
157 Natural history 164 Pets
165 Farm animals 166 Ocean life

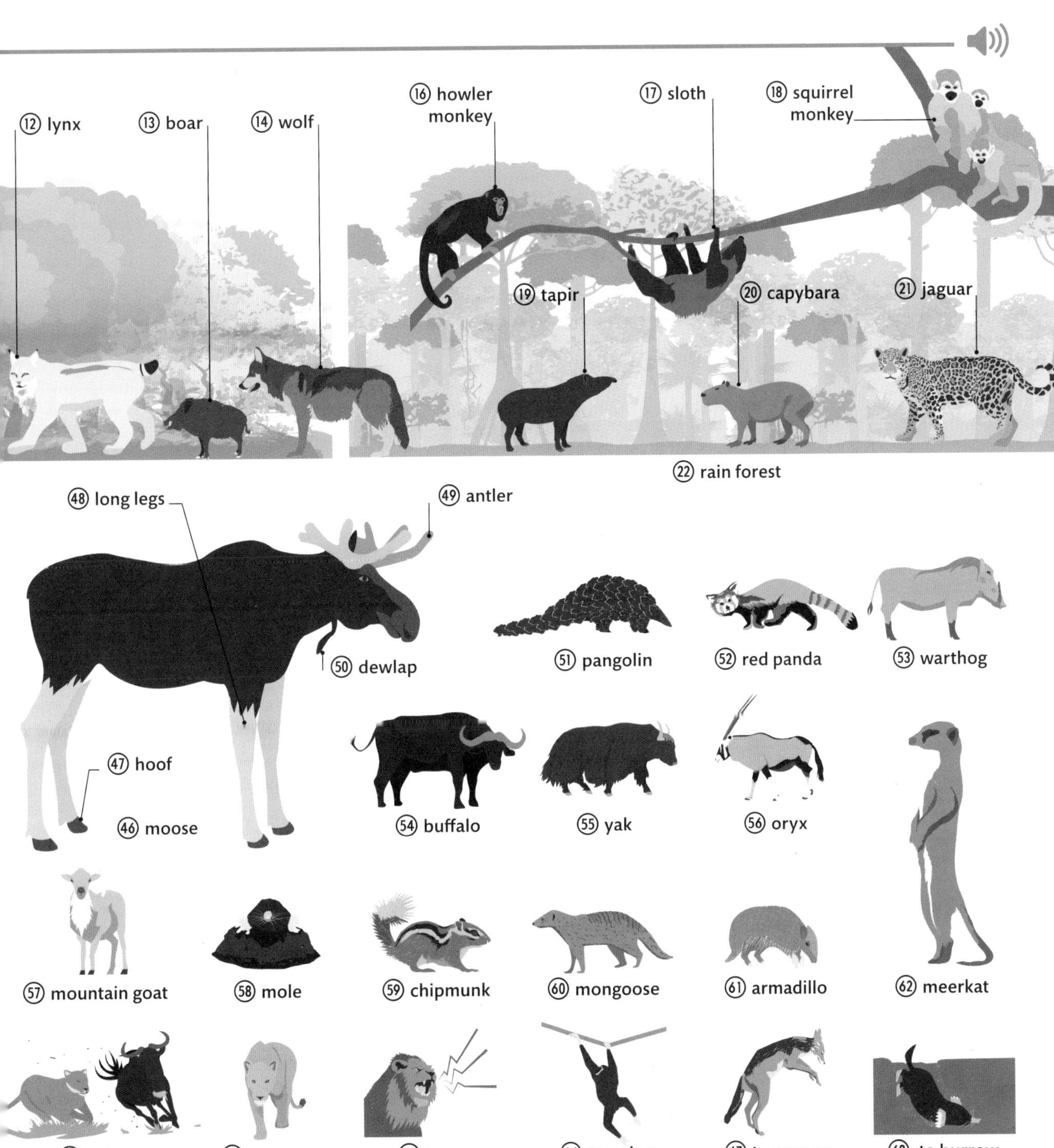
⑫ lynx
⑬ boar
⑭ wolf
⑯ howler monkey
⑰ sloth
⑱ squirrel monkey
⑲ tapir
⑳ capybara
㉑ jaguar
㉒ rain forest
㊽ long legs
㊾ antler
㊿ dewlap
㊼ hoof
㊻ moose
51 pangolin
52 red panda
53 warthog
54 buffalo
55 yak
56 oryx
57 mountain goat
58 mole
59 chipmunk
60 mongoose
61 armadillo
62 meerkat
63 to hunt
64 to prowl
65 to roar
66 to swing
67 to pounce
68 to burrow

160 Birds

160.1 SPECIES OF BIRDS

① green woodpecker
② black woodpecker
③ hummingbird
④ house martin
⑤ seagull
⑥ swift
⑦ sand martin
⑧ Arctic tern
⑨ pileated woodpecker
⑩ greater spotted woodpecker
⑪ tail
⑫ swallow
⑬ canary
⑭ budgerigar
⑮ starling
⑯ nightingale
⑰ weaverbird
⑱ vermilion flycatcher
⑲ albatross
⑳ frigate
㉑ golden eagle
㉒ bald eagle
㉓ osprey
㉔ cormorant
㉕ gannet
㉖ Andean condor
㉗ peregrine falcon
㉘ vulture
㉙ harpy eagle
㉚ guillemot
㉛ Atlantic puffin

See also:
157 Natural history 161 Birds (continued)
165 Farm animals

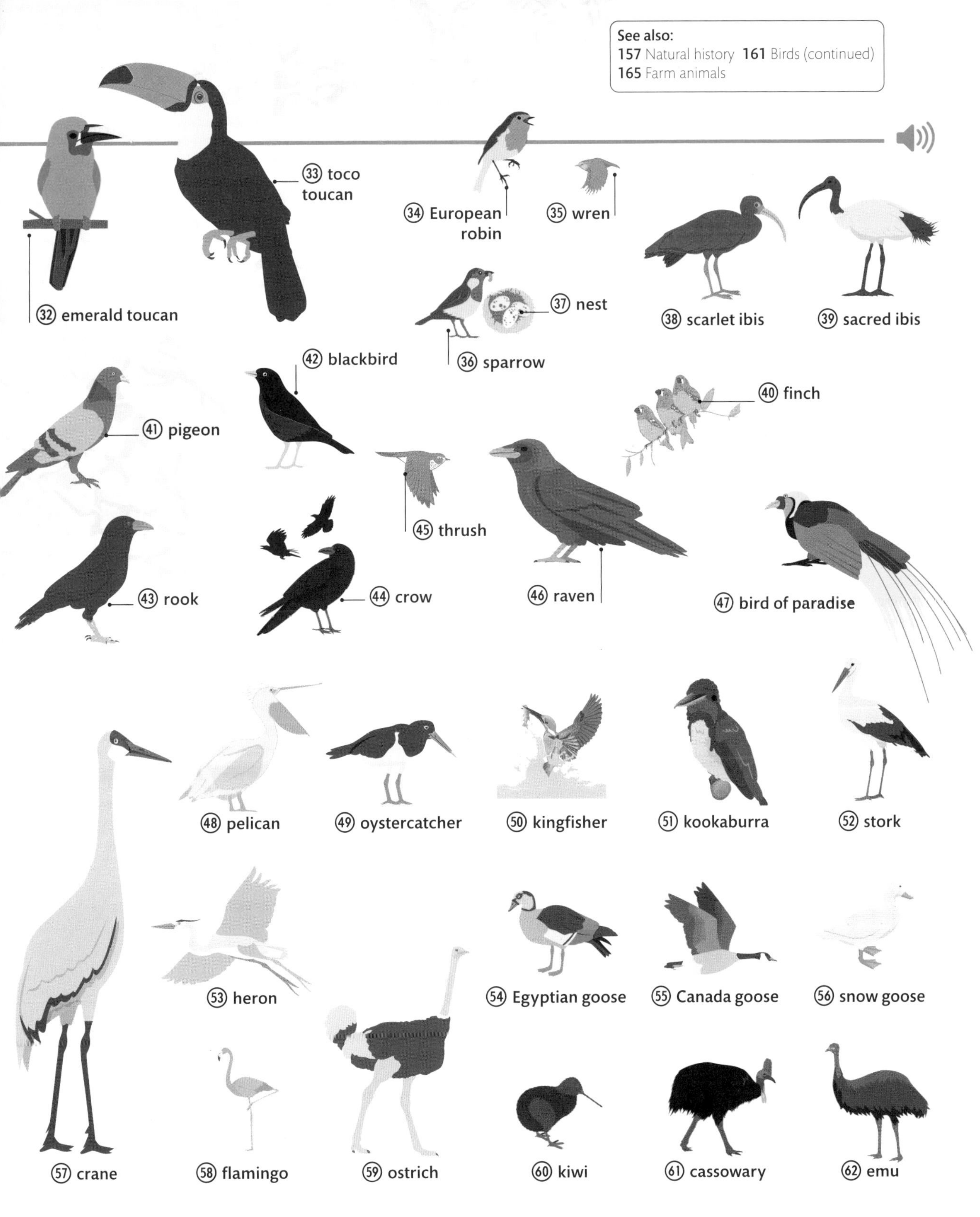
32 emerald toucan
33 toco toucan
34 European robin
35 wren
36 sparrow
37 nest
38 scarlet ibis
39 sacred ibis
40 finch
41 pigeon
42 blackbird
43 rook
44 crow
45 thrush
46 raven
47 bird of paradise
48 pelican
49 oystercatcher
50 kingfisher
51 kookaburra
52 stork
53 heron
54 Egyptian goose
55 Canada goose
56 snow goose
57 crane
58 flamingo
59 ostrich
60 kiwi
61 cassowary
62 emu

161 Birds continued

161.1 SPECIES OF BIRDS

① galah

② eclectus parrot

③ rose-ringed parakeet

④ scarlet macaw

⑤ lorikeet

⑩ snowy owl

⑪ eagle owl

⑫ great gray owl (US)
great grey owl (UK)

⑬ crested owl

⑮ to hoot
⑭ barn owl

㉒ mute swan

㉓ black swan

㉔ whooper swan

㉕ coot

㉖ mallard

㉗ mandarin duck

㉘ grebe

㉙ wood duck

㉚ water rail

㉛ curlew

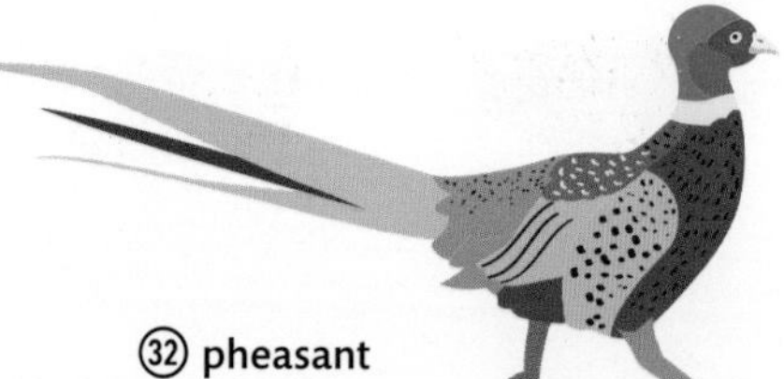
㉜ pheasant

㉝ turkey

㉟ feathers displayed
㊱ neck

㉞ peacock

See also:
157 Natural history
165 Farm animals

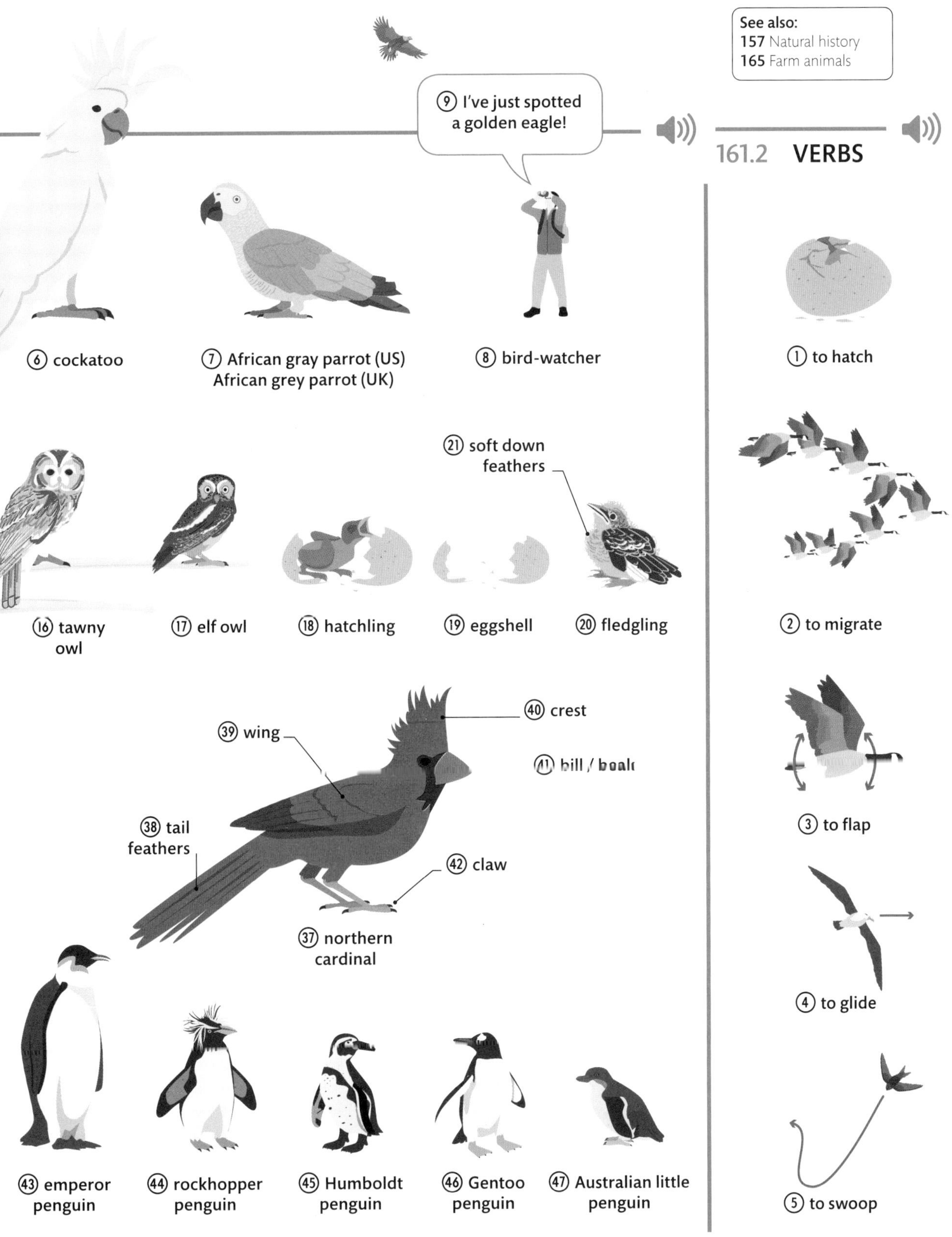
9 I've just spotted a golden eagle!
6 cockatoo
7 African gray parrot (US)
African grey parrot (UK)
8 bird-watcher
16 tawny owl
17 elf owl
18 hatchling
19 eggshell
20 fledgling
21 soft down feathers
37 northern cardinal
38 tail feathers
39 wing
40 crest
41 bill / beak
42 claw
43 emperor penguin
44 rockhopper penguin
45 Humboldt penguin
46 Gentoo penguin
47 Australian little penguin

161.2 VERBS

1 to hatch
2 to migrate
3 to flap
4 to glide
5 to swoop

162 Insects and bugs

162.1 BUTTERFLIES AND MOTHS

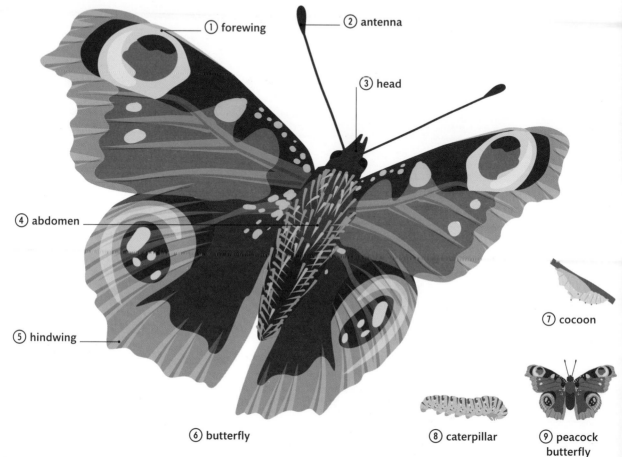

① forewing

② antenna

③ head

④ abdomen

⑤ hindwing

⑥ butterfly

⑦ cocoon

⑧ caterpillar

⑨ peacock butterfly

⑩ monarch butterfly

⑪ painted lady butterfly

⑫ swallowtail butterfly

⑬ glasswing butterfly

⑭ cabbage white butterfly

⑮ peppered moth

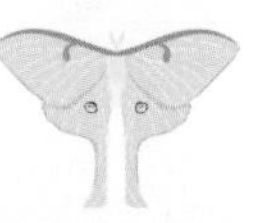

⑯ luna moth

⑰ hummingbird hawksmoth

⑱ emperor moth

⑲ atlas moth

⑳ clothes moth

㉑ hawk moth

See also:
157 Natural history 158-159 Mammals
160-161 Birds 163 Amphibians and reptiles

162.2 OTHER BUGS AND INVERTEBRATES

① rhinoceros beetle

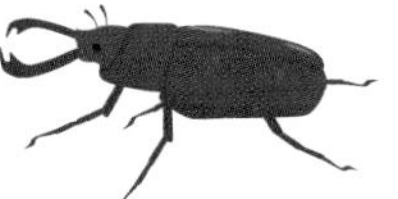
② stag beetle

③ weevil

④ cockroach

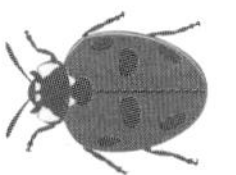
⑤ ladybug (US) ladybird (UK)

⑥ fly

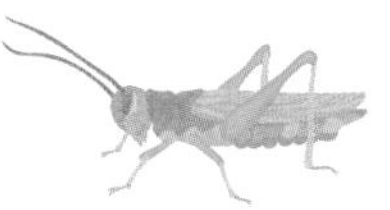
⑦ grasshopper

⑧ locust

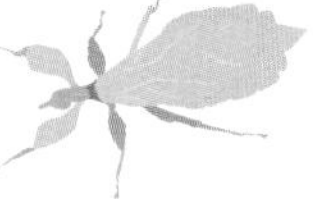
⑨ leaf insect

⑩ praying mantis

⑫ sting

⑪ scorpion

⑬ cricket

⑭ centipede

⑮ millipede

⑯ dragonfly

⑰ mosquito

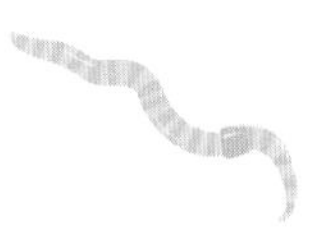
⑱ worm

⑲ tarantula

⑳ black widow spider

㉑ jumping spider

㉒ orb weaver

㉓ slug

㉔ snail

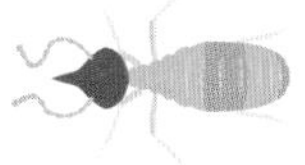
㉕ termite

㉖ ant

㉗ bumble bee

㉘ wasp

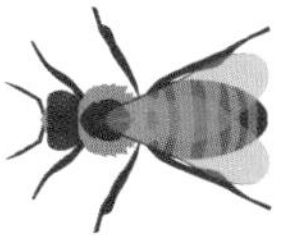
㉙ honey bee

㉚ to sting

㉛ to fly

㉜ to buzz

㉝ wasp nest

㉞ beehive

㉟ swarm

163 Amphibians and reptiles

163.1 AMPHIBIANS

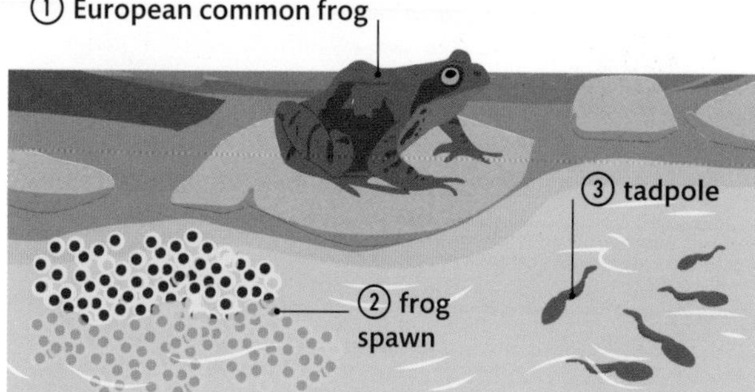

① European common frog
③ tadpole
② frog spawn

④ Wallace's flying frog

⑤ poison dart frog

⑥ Darwin's frog

⑦ red-eyed tree frog

⑧ common toad

⑨ African bullfrog

⑩ Oriental fire-bellied toad

⑪ Great Plains toad

⑫ fire salamander

⑬ olm

⑭ Mexican axolotl

⑮ great crested newt

⑯ red salamander

163.2 REPTILES

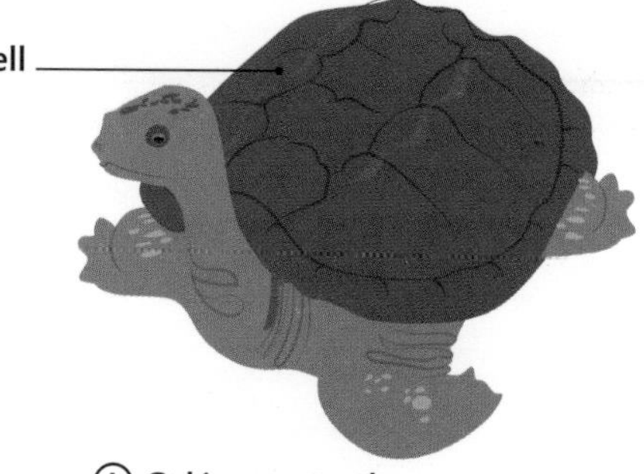

② shell

① Galápagos turtle

③ radiated tortoise

④ matamata

⑤ diamond back terrapin

⑥ common snake-necked turtle

⑦ green sea turtle

⑧ leatherback sea turtle

⑨ parson's chameleon

⑩ panther chameleon

⑪ Jackson's chameleon

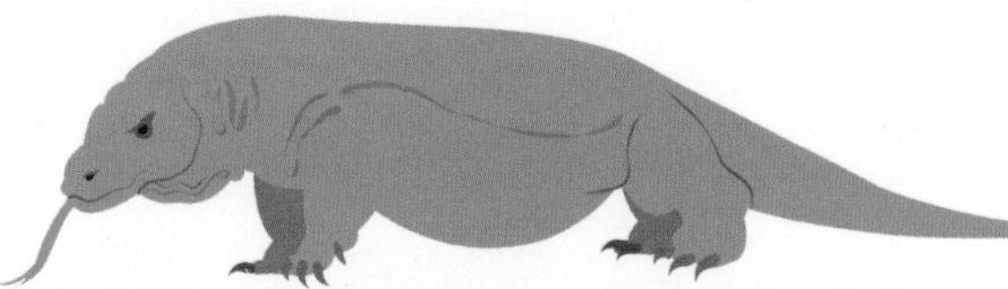
⑫ Komodo dragon

See also:
77 Biology 157 Natural history 158-159 Mammals
160-161 Birds 162 Bugs and insects

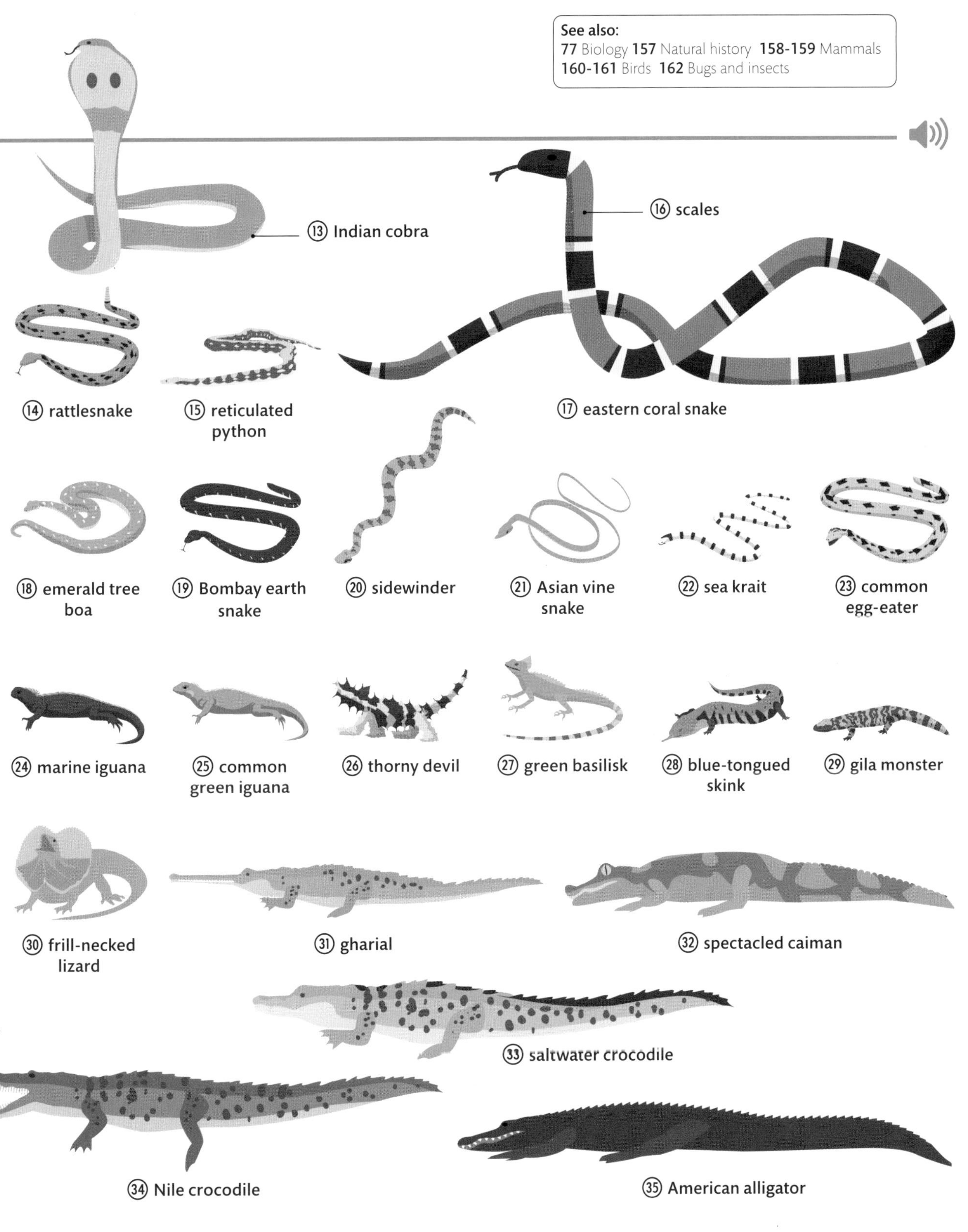
⑬ Indian cobra
⑯ scales
⑭ rattlesnake
⑮ reticulated python
⑰ eastern coral snake
⑱ emerald tree boa
⑲ Bombay earth snake
⑳ sidewinder
㉑ Asian vine snake
㉒ sea krait
㉓ common egg-eater
㉔ marine iguana
㉕ common green iguana
㉖ thorny devil
㉗ green basilisk
㉘ blue-tongued skink
㉙ gila monster
㉚ frill-necked lizard
㉛ gharial
㉜ spectacled caiman
㉝ saltwater crocodile
㉞ Nile crocodile
㉟ American alligator

164 Pets

164.1 CAT BREEDS

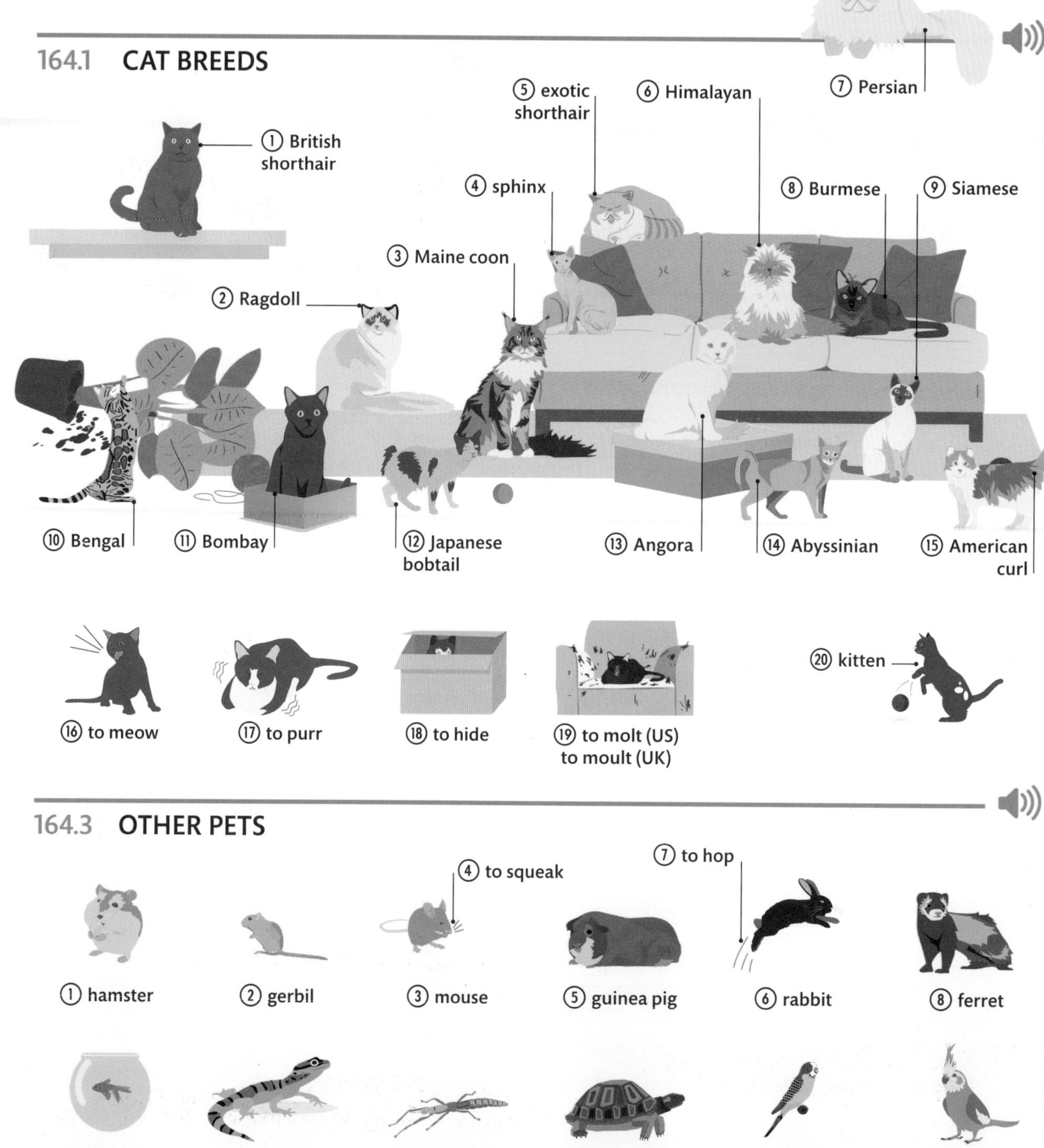

① British shorthair
② Ragdoll
③ Maine coon
④ sphinx
⑤ exotic shorthair
⑥ Himalayan
⑦ Persian
⑧ Burmese
⑨ Siamese
⑩ Bengal
⑪ Bombay
⑫ Japanese bobtail
⑬ Angora
⑭ Abyssinian
⑮ American curl
⑯ to meow
⑰ to purr
⑱ to hide
⑲ to molt (US) to moult (UK)
⑳ kitten

164.3 OTHER PETS

① hamster
② gerbil
③ mouse
④ to squeak
⑤ guinea pig
⑥ rabbit
⑦ to hop
⑧ ferret
⑨ fish
⑩ lizard
⑪ stick insect
⑫ tortoise
⑬ budgerigar / budgie
⑭ cockatiel

See also:
158-159 Mammals 160-161 Birds
162 Insects and bugs 163 Amphibians and reptiles

164.2 DOG BREEDS

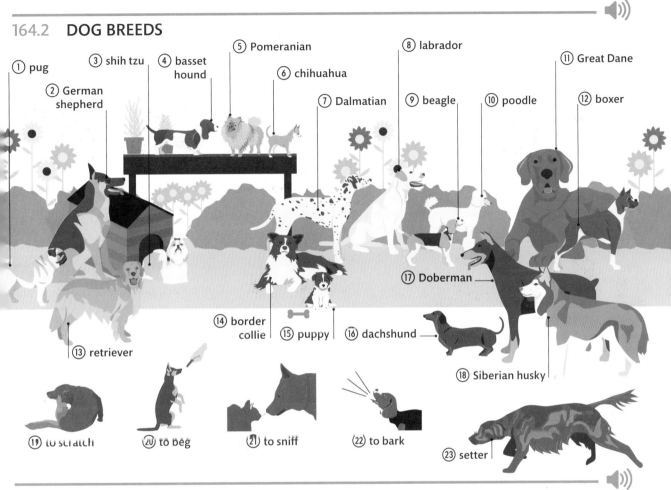

1. pug
2. German shepherd
3. shih tzu
4. basset hound
5. Pomeranian
6. chihuahua
7. Dalmatian
8. labrador
9. beagle
10. poodle
11. Great Dane
12. boxer
13. retriever
14. border collie
15. puppy
16. dachshund
17. Doberman
18. Siberian husky
19. to scratch
20. to beg
21. to sniff
22. to bark
23. setter

164.4 PET SUPPLIES

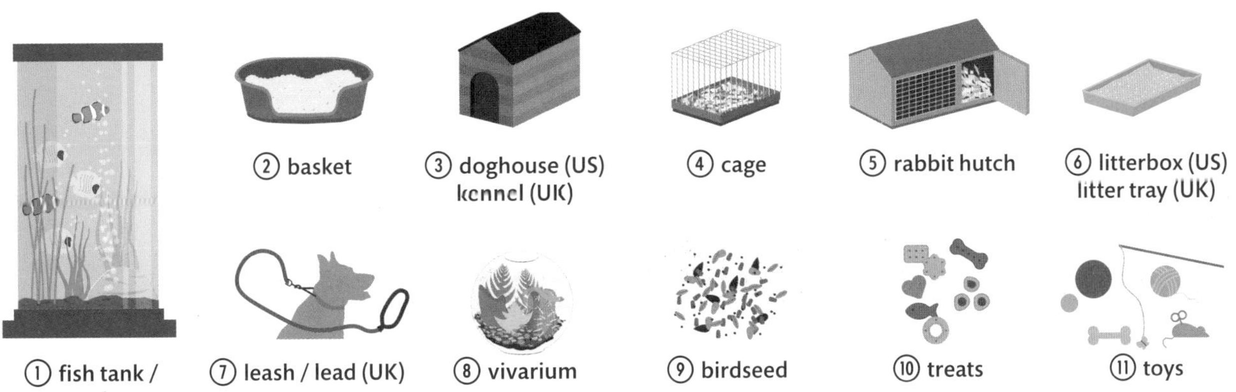
① fish tank / aquarium
② basket
③ doghouse (US) kennel (UK)
④ cage
⑤ rabbit hutch
⑥ litterbox (US) litter tray (UK)
⑦ leash / lead (UK)
⑧ vivarium
⑨ birdseed
⑩ treats
⑪ toys

165 Farm animals

165.1 ON THE FARM

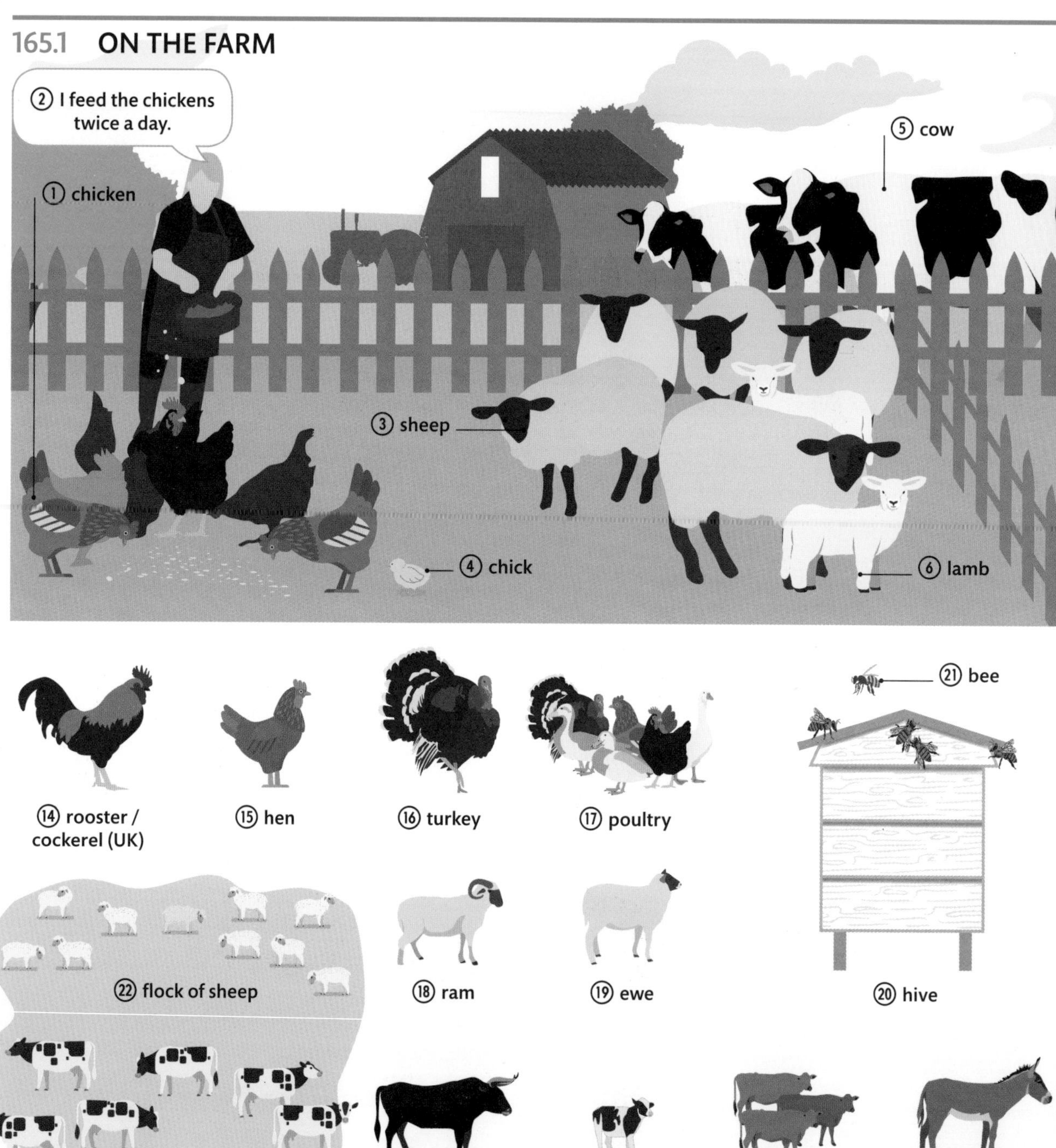
② I feed the chickens twice a day.
① chicken
③ sheep
④ chick
⑤ cow
⑥ lamb
⑭ rooster / cockerel (UK)
⑮ hen
⑯ turkey
⑰ poultry
㉑ bee
⑳ hive
㉒ flock of sheep
⑱ ram
⑲ ewe
㉓ herd of cows
㉔ bull
㉕ calf
㉖ cattle
㉗ donkey

See also:
53 Meat 86 Farming
158-159 Mammals 164 Pets

⑦ horse
⑧ goose
⑨ gosling
⑩ pig
⑪ piglet
⑫ duck
⑬ duckling
㉘ stallion
㉙ mare
㉚ foal
㉛ goat
㉜ kid
㉝ ostrich
㉞ llama
㉟ alpaca
㊱ to shear
㊲ to trot
㊳ to gallop
㊴ to charge
㊵ to crow
㊶ to bleat
㊷ to snort
㊸ to grunt
㊹ to bray
㊺ to quack

166 Ocean life

166.1 MARINE SPECIES

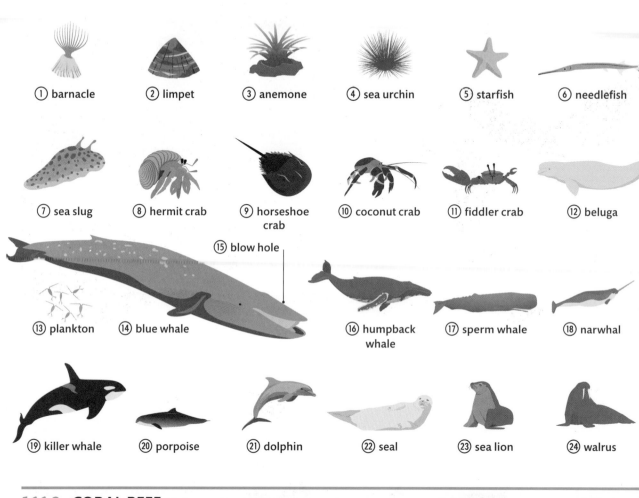

① barnacle
② limpet
③ anemone
④ sea urchin
⑤ starfish
⑥ needlefish
⑦ sea slug
⑧ hermit crab
⑨ horseshoe crab
⑩ coconut crab
⑪ fiddler crab
⑫ beluga
⑬ plankton
⑭ blue whale
⑮ blow hole
⑯ humpback whale
⑰ sperm whale
⑱ narwhal
⑲ killer whale
⑳ porpoise
㉑ dolphin
㉒ seal
㉓ sea lion
㉔ walrus

166.2 CORAL REEF

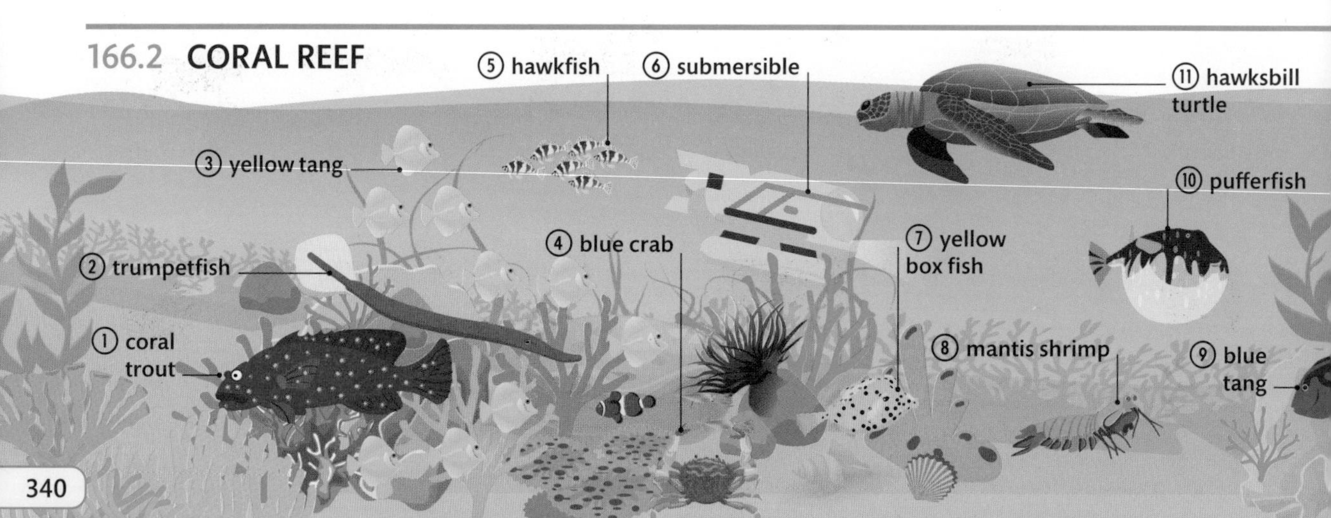
⑤ hawkfish
⑥ submersible
⑪ hawksbill turtle
③ yellow tang
⑩ pufferfish
④ blue crab
⑦ yellow box fish
② trumpetfish
① coral trout
⑧ mantis shrimp
⑨ blue tang

See also:
54 Fish and seafood 121 Fishing 134 On the beach
146-147 Geography 157 Natural history

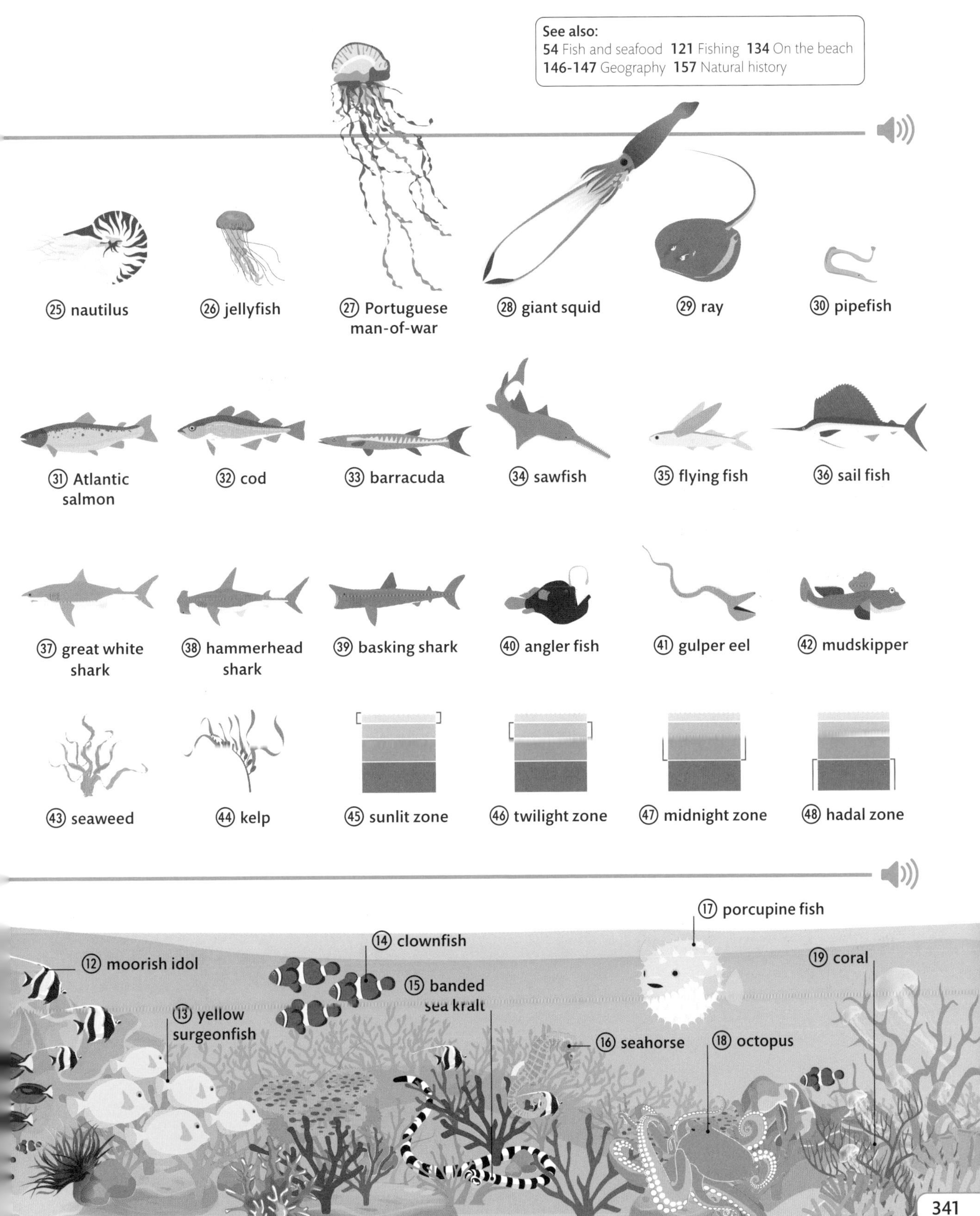
㉕ nautilus
㉖ jellyfish
㉗ Portuguese man-of-war
㉘ giant squid
㉙ ray
㉚ pipefish
㉛ Atlantic salmon
㉜ cod
㉝ barracuda
㉞ sawfish
㉟ flying fish
㊱ sail fish
㊲ great white shark
㊳ hammerhead shark
㊴ basking shark
㊵ angler fish
㊶ gulper eel
㊷ mudskipper
㊸ seaweed
㊹ kelp
㊺ sunlit zone
㊻ twilight zone
㊼ midnight zone
㊽ hadal zone
⑫ moorish idol
⑬ yellow surgeonfish
⑭ clownfish
⑮ banded sea krait
⑯ seahorse
⑰ porcupine fish
⑱ octopus
⑲ coral

167 Plants and trees

167.1 PLANTS AND TREES

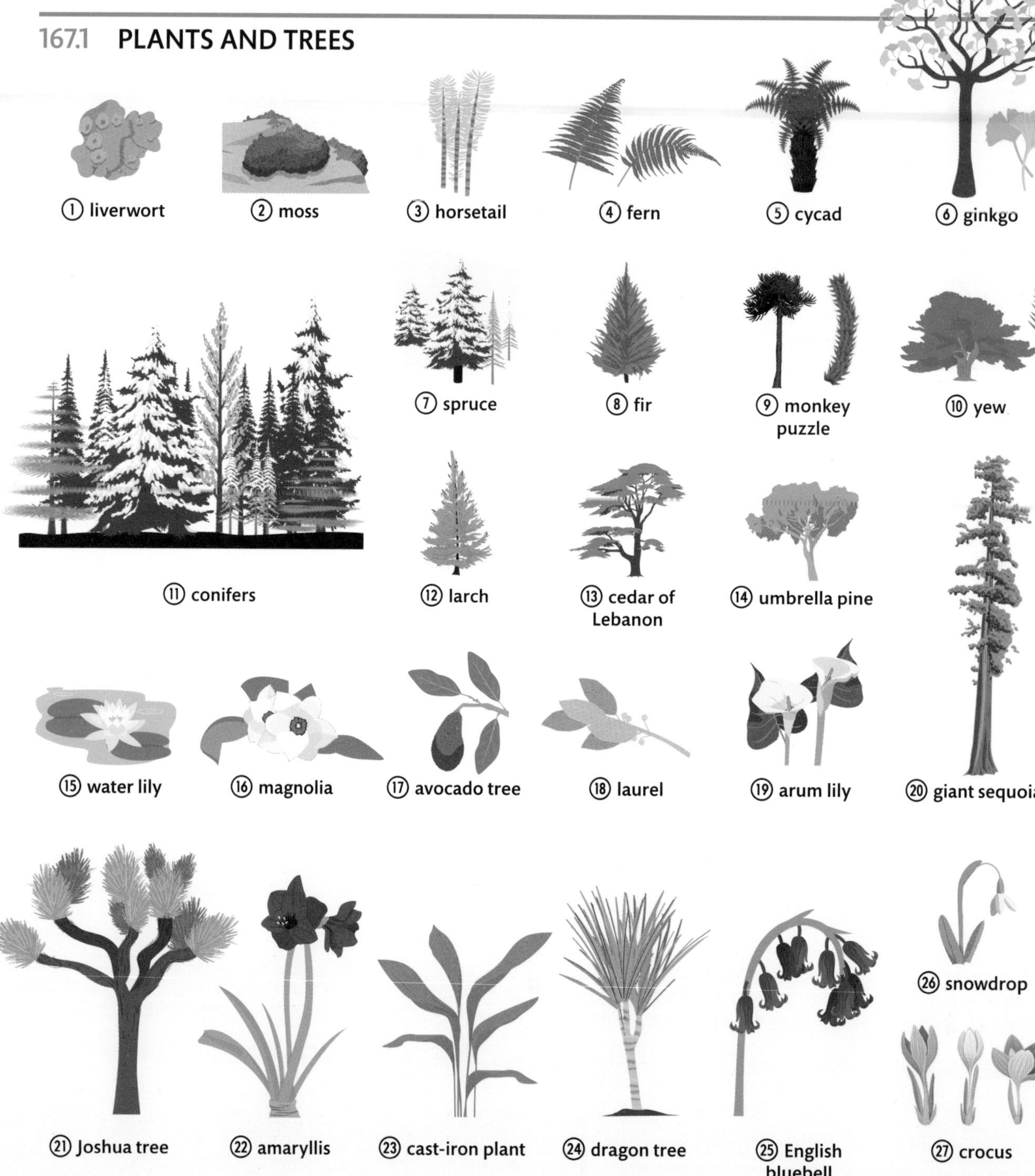

① liverwort
② moss
③ horsetail
④ fern
⑤ cycad
⑥ ginkgo
⑦ spruce
⑧ fir
⑨ monkey puzzle
⑩ yew
⑪ conifers
⑫ larch
⑬ cedar of Lebanon
⑭ umbrella pine
⑮ water lily
⑯ magnolia
⑰ avocado tree
⑱ laurel
⑲ arum lily
⑳ giant sequoia
㉑ Joshua tree
㉒ amaryllis
㉓ cast-iron plant
㉔ dragon tree
㉕ English bluebell
㉖ snowdrop
㉗ crocus

See also:
38 Garden plants and houseplants **57** Fruit **58** Fruit and nuts
157 Natural history **168-169** Plants and trees (continued) **170** Fungi

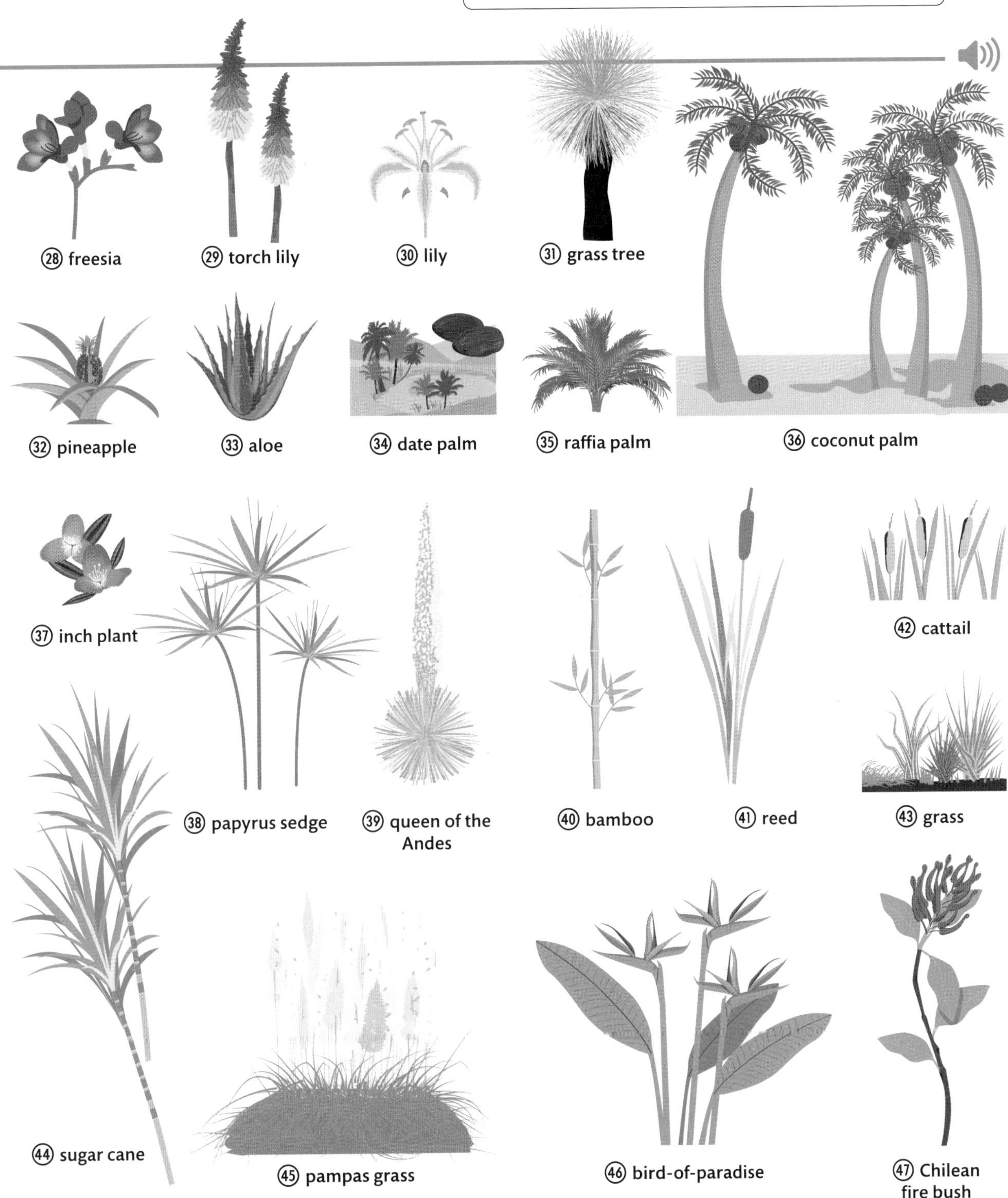
28 freesia
29 torch lily
30 lily
31 grass tree
32 pineapple
33 aloe
34 date palm
35 raffia palm
36 coconut palm
37 inch plant
38 papyrus sedge
39 queen of the Andes
40 bamboo
41 reed
42 cattail
43 grass
44 sugar cane
45 pampas grass
46 bird-of-paradise
47 Chilean fire bush

168.1 PLANTS AND TREES

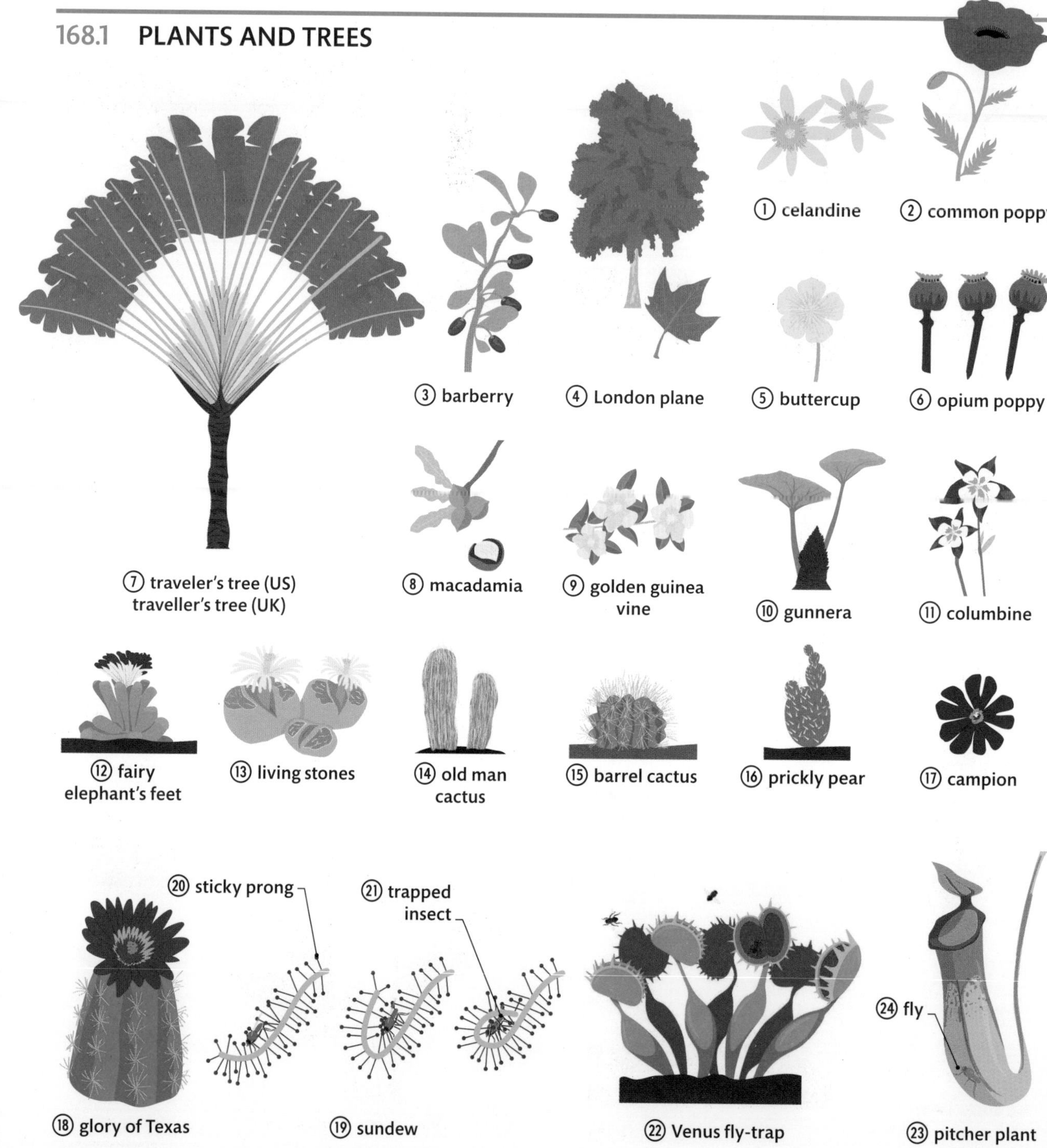
① celandine
② common poppy
③ barberry
④ London plane
⑤ buttercup
⑥ opium poppy
⑦ traveler's tree (US)
traveller's tree (UK)
⑧ macadamia
⑨ golden guinea vine
⑩ gunnera
⑪ columbine
⑫ fairy elephant's feet
⑬ living stones
⑭ old man cactus
⑮ barrel cactus
⑯ prickly pear
⑰ campion
⑳ sticky prong
㉑ trapped insect
⑱ glory of Texas
⑲ sundew
㉒ Venus fly-trap
㉔ fly
㉓ pitcher plant

See also:
38 Garden plants and houseplants 57 Fruit 58 Fruit and nuts
157 Natural history 169 Plants and trees (continued) 170 Fungi

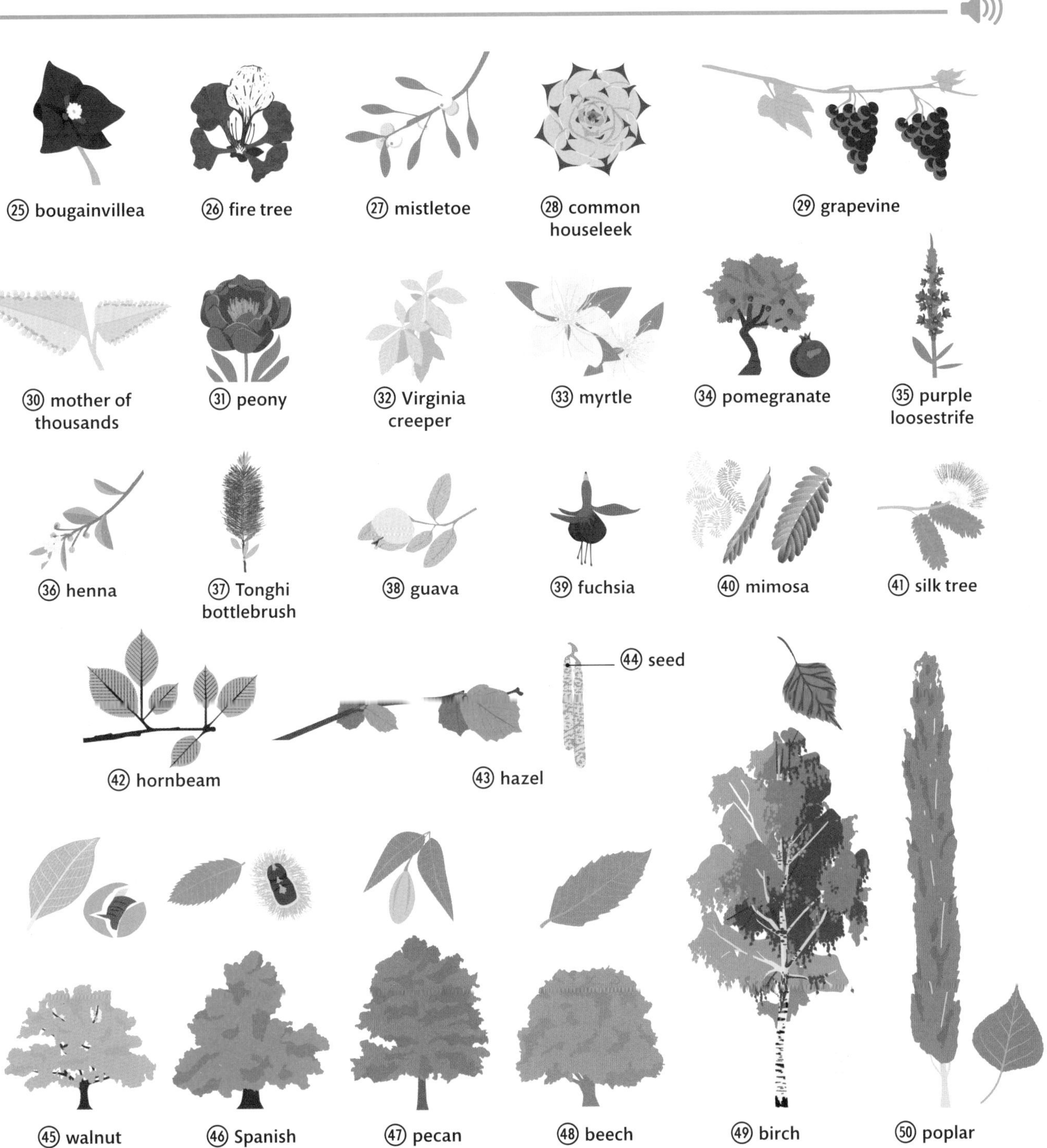
25 bougainvillea
26 fire tree
27 mistletoe
28 common houseleek
29 grapevine
30 mother of thousands
31 peony
32 Virginia creeper
33 myrtle
34 pomegranate
35 purple loosestrife
36 henna
37 Tonghi bottlebrush
38 guava
39 fuchsia
40 mimosa
41 silk tree
42 hornbeam
43 hazel
44 seed
45 walnut
46 Spanish chestnut
47 pecan
48 beech
49 birch
50 poplar

169 Plants and trees continued

169.1 PLANTS AND TREES

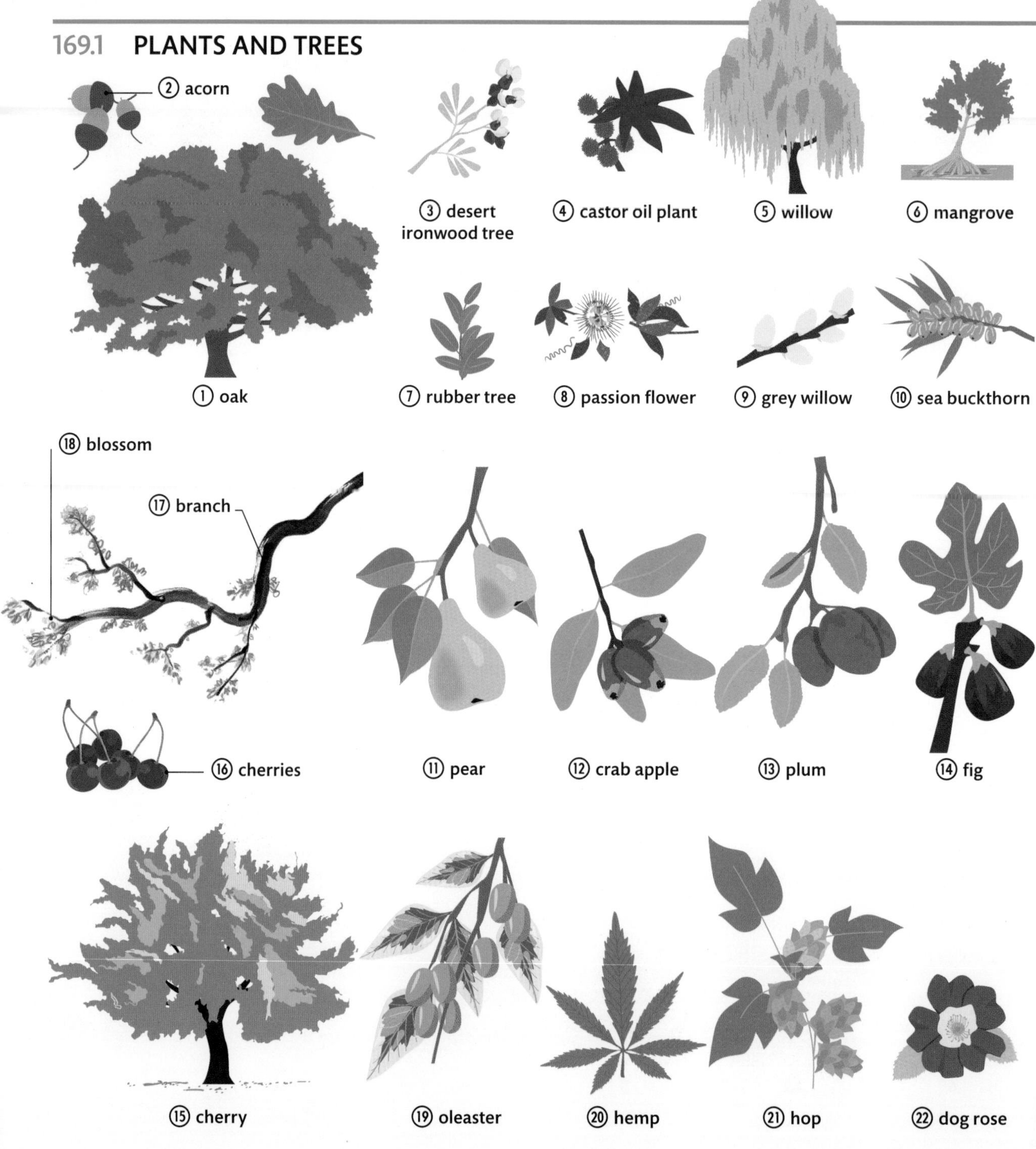

② acorn
③ desert ironwood tree
④ castor oil plant
⑤ willow
⑥ mangrove
① oak
⑦ rubber tree
⑧ passion flower
⑨ grey willow
⑩ sea buckthorn
⑱ blossom
⑰ branch
⑯ cherries
⑪ pear
⑫ crab apple
⑬ plum
⑭ fig
⑮ cherry
⑲ oleaster
⑳ hemp
㉑ hop
㉒ dog rose

See also:
38 Garden plants and houseplants 57 Fruit
58 Fruit and nuts 157 Natural history 170 Fungi

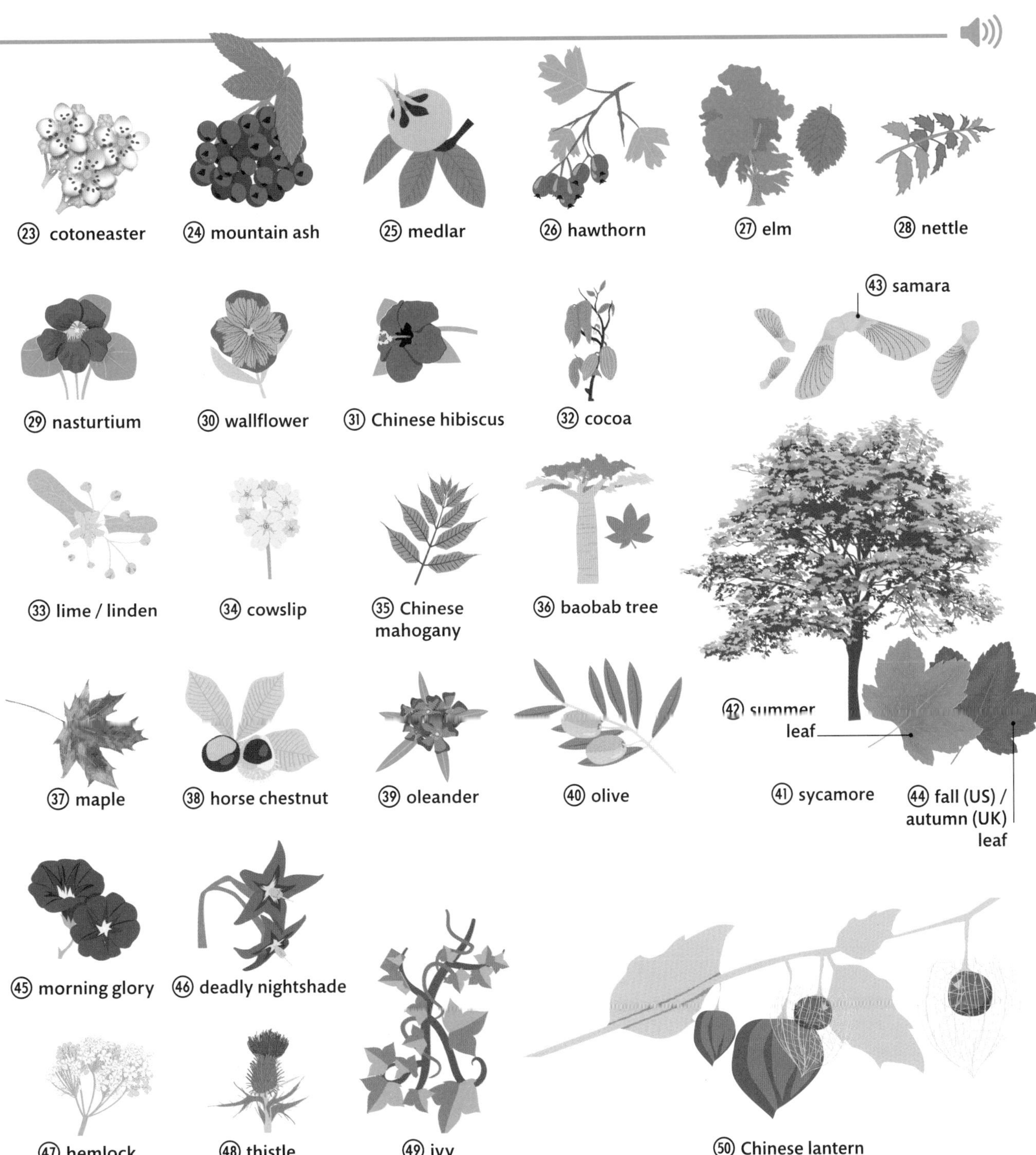
23 cotoneaster
24 mountain ash
25 medlar
26 hawthorn
27 elm
28 nettle
29 nasturtium
30 wallflower
31 Chinese hibiscus
32 cocoa
43 samara
33 lime / linden
34 cowslip
35 Chinese mahogany
36 baobab tree
42 summer leaf
37 maple
38 horse chestnut
39 oleander
40 olive
41 sycamore
44 fall (US) / autumn (UK) leaf
45 morning glory
46 deadly nightshade
47 hemlock
48 thistle
49 ivy
50 Chinese lantern

170 Fungi

170.1 SPECIES OF FUNGI

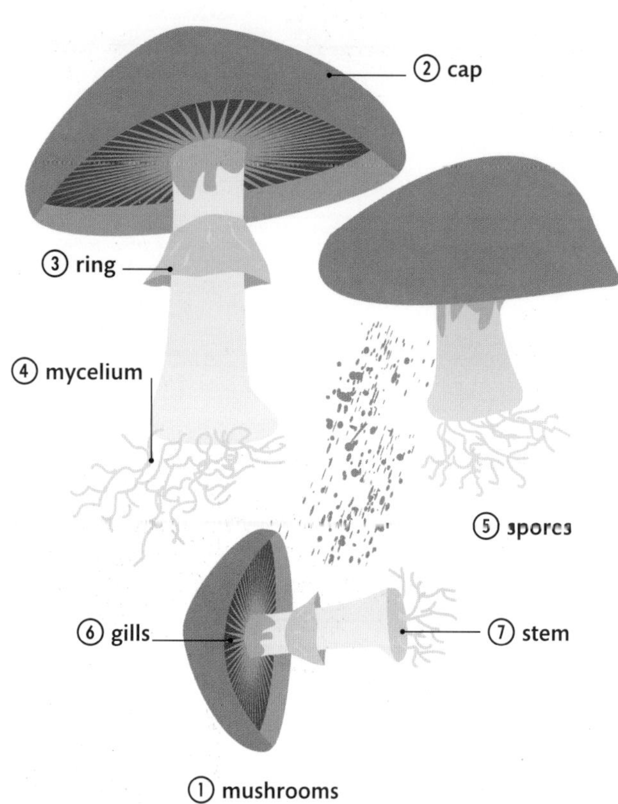

② cap
③ ring
④ mycelium
⑤ spores
⑥ gills
⑦ stem
① mushrooms

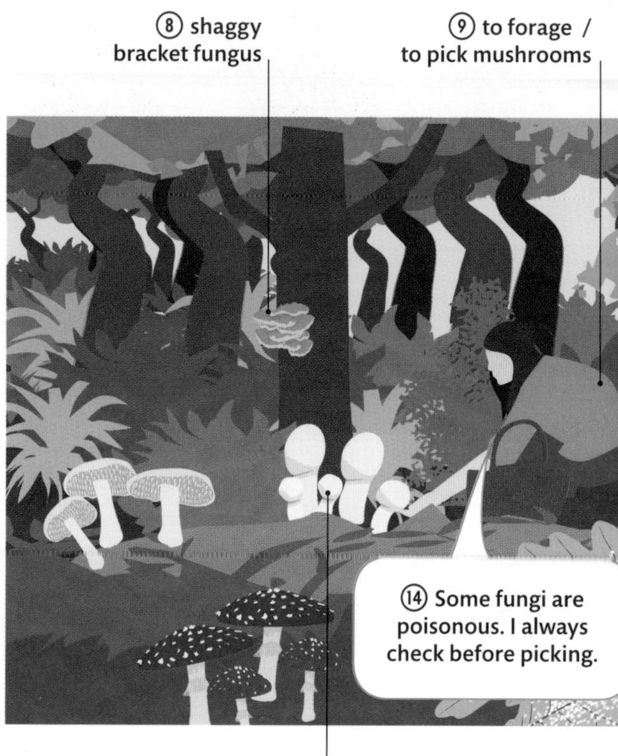

⑧ shaggy bracket fungus
⑨ to forage / to pick mushrooms
⑭ Some fungi are poisonous. I always check before picking.
⑬ common puffball

㉑ cultivated mushrooms

㉒ toadstools

㉓ fairy ring

㉔ oyster mushroom

㉕ orange-cap boletus

㉖ chicken of the woods

㉗ hedgehog mushroom

㉘ bear's head tooth

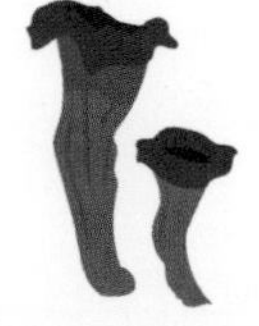
㉙ black trumpet

㉚ shaggy mane mushroom

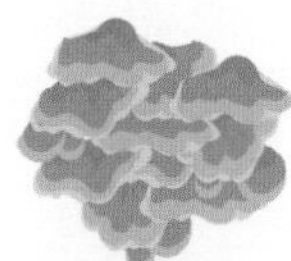
㉛ hen of the wood

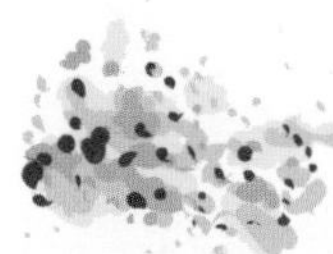
㉜ mold

See also:
55-56 Vegetables 133 Outdoor activities
167-169 Plants and trees

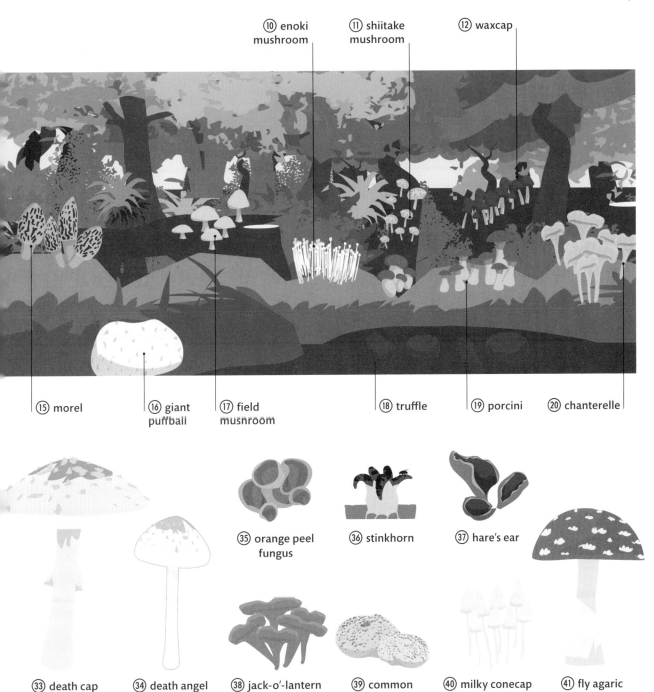

(10) enoki mushroom
(11) shiitake mushroom
(12) waxcap
(15) morel
(16) giant puffball
(17) field mushroom
(18) truffle
(19) porcini
(20) chanterelle
(35) orange peel fungus
(36) stinkhorn
(37) hare's ear
(33) death cap
(34) death angel
(38) jack-o'-lantern
(39) common earthball
(40) milky conecap
(41) fly agaric

171 Time

171.1 TELLING THE TIME

① What time is it?

② It's three o'clock.

③ one o'clock

④ five past one

⑤ ten past one

⑥ quarter past one

⑦ twenty past one

⑧ twenty-five past one

⑨ one thirty / half past one

⑩ twenty-five to two

⑪ twenty to two

⑫ quarter to two

⑬ ten to two

⑭ five to two

⑮ two o'clock

⑯ second

⑰ minute

⑱ quarter of an hour

171.2 PARTS OF THE DAY

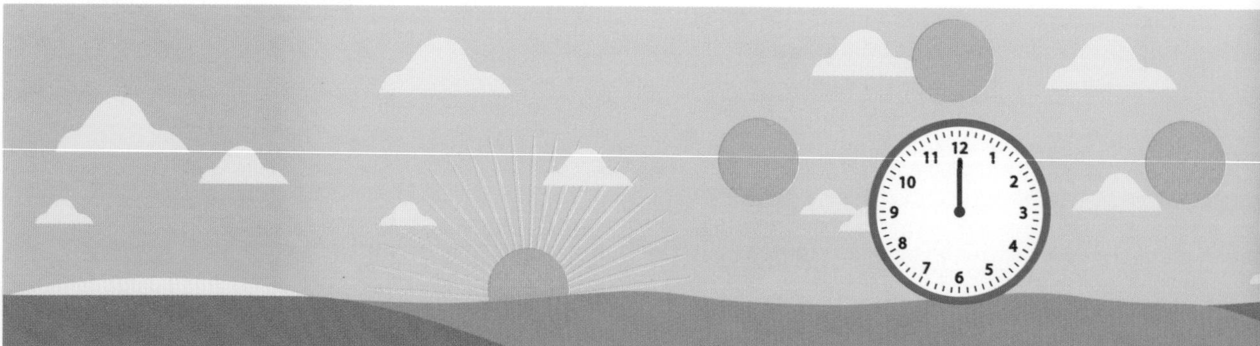

① dawn ② sunrise ③ morning ④ midday ⑤ afternoon

See also:
172 The calendar 173 Numbers
174 Weights and measures

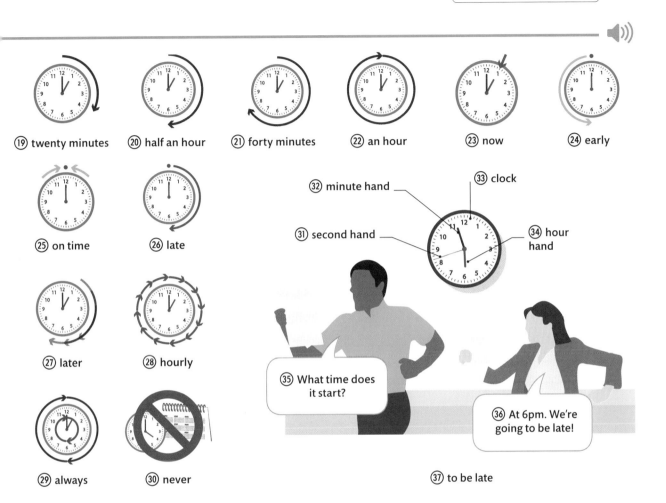

⑲ twenty minutes ⑳ half an hour ㉑ forty minutes ㉒ an hour ㉓ now ㉔ early

㉕ on time ㉖ late

㉗ later ㉘ hourly

㉙ always ㉚ never

㉜ minute hand ㉝ clock ㉛ second hand ㉞ hour hand

㉟ What time does it start?

㊱ At 6pm. We're going to be late!

㊲ to be late

⑥ evening ⑦ sunset ⑧ dusk ⑨ midnight ⑩ night ⑪ day

172 The calendar

172.1 CALENDAR AND SEASONS

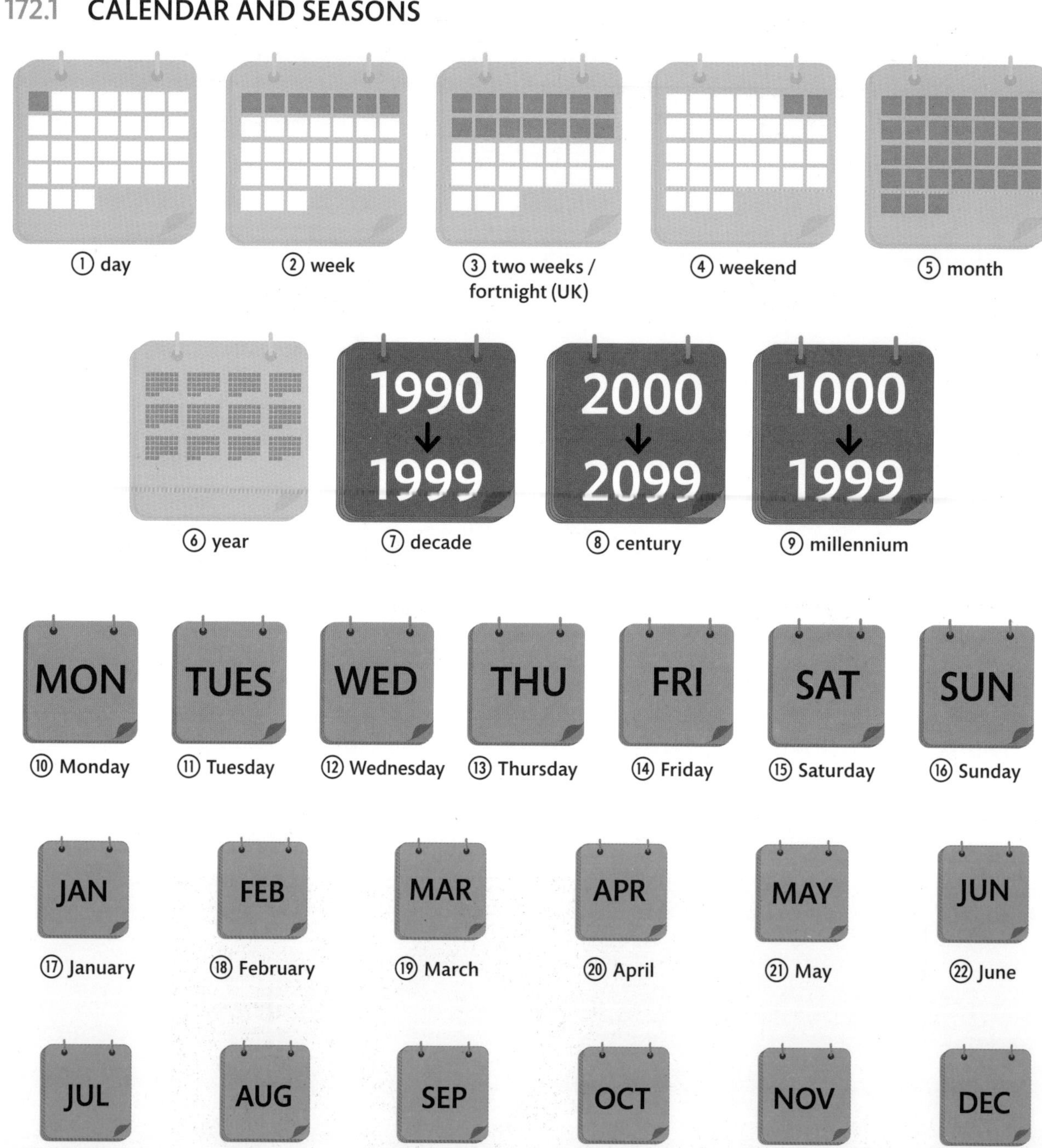

1990
1999
2000
2099
1000
1999
MON
TUES
WED
THU
FRI
SAT
SUN
JAN
FEB
MAR
APR
MAY
JUN
JUL
AUG
SEP
OCT
NOV
DEC

① day ② week ③ two weeks / fortnight (UK) ④ weekend ⑤ month

⑥ year ⑦ decade ⑧ century ⑨ millennium

⑩ Monday ⑪ Tuesday ⑫ Wednesday ⑬ Thursday ⑭ Friday ⑮ Saturday ⑯ Sunday

⑰ January ⑱ February ⑲ March ⑳ April ㉑ May ㉒ June

㉓ July ㉔ August ㉕ September ㉖ October ㉗ November ㉘ December

See also:
171 Time
173 Numbers

1900
(29) nineteen hundred

1901
(30) nineteen-oh-one

1910
(31) nineteen ten

2000
(32) two thousand

2001
(33) two thousand and one

2033
(34) twenty thirty-three

(35) once a week

(36) twice a week

(37) three times a week

(38) every day

(39) every other day

(40) only weekends

(41) hourly

(42) daily

(43) weekly

(44) monthly

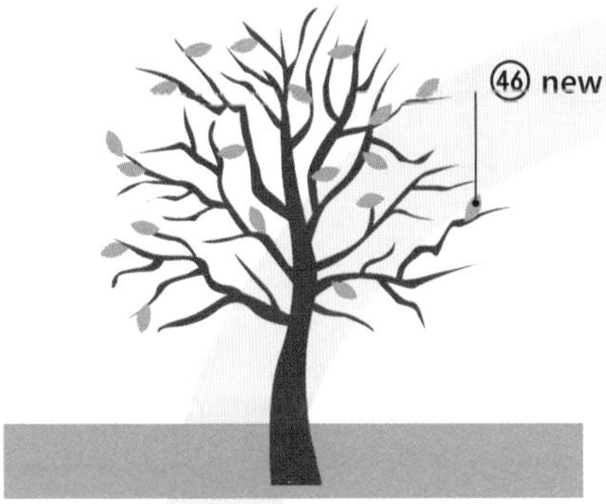

(45) spring

(46) new leaves

(47) summer

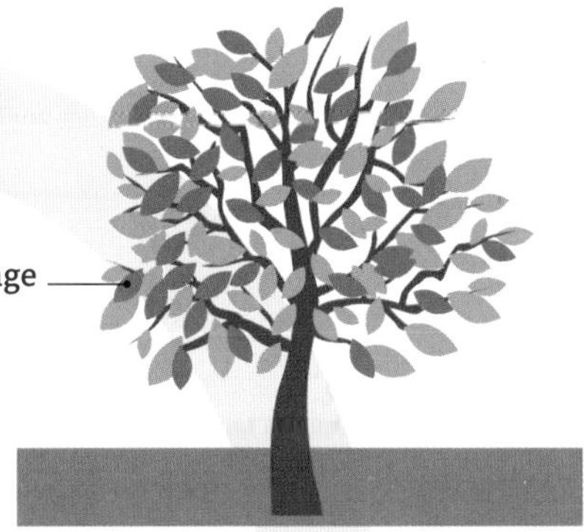

(48) green foliage

(49) seasons

(50) fall (US) autumn (UK)

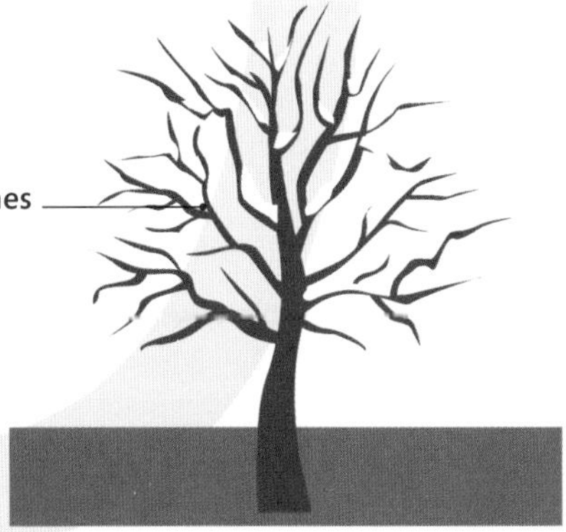

(51) leaf fall

(52) winter

(53) bare branches

173 Numbers

173.1 CARDINAL NUMBERS

1 ① one	2 ② two	3 ③ three	4 ④ four	5 ⑤ five	6 ⑥ six
7 ⑦ seven	8 ⑧ eight	9 ⑨ nine	10 ⑩ ten	11 ⑪ eleven	12 ⑫ twelve
13 ⑬ thirteen	14 ⑭ fourteen	15 ⑮ fifteen	16 ⑯ sixteen	17 ⑰ seventeen	18 ⑱ eighteen
19 ⑲ nineteen	20 ⑳ twenty	21 ㉑ twenty-one	22 ㉒ twenty-two	30 ㉓ thirty	40 ㉔ forty

50 ㉕ fifty	60 ㉖ sixty	70 ㉗ seventy	80 ㉘ eighty	90 ㉙ ninety	100 ㉚ one hundred	0 ㉛ zero

173.2 ORDINAL NUMBERS

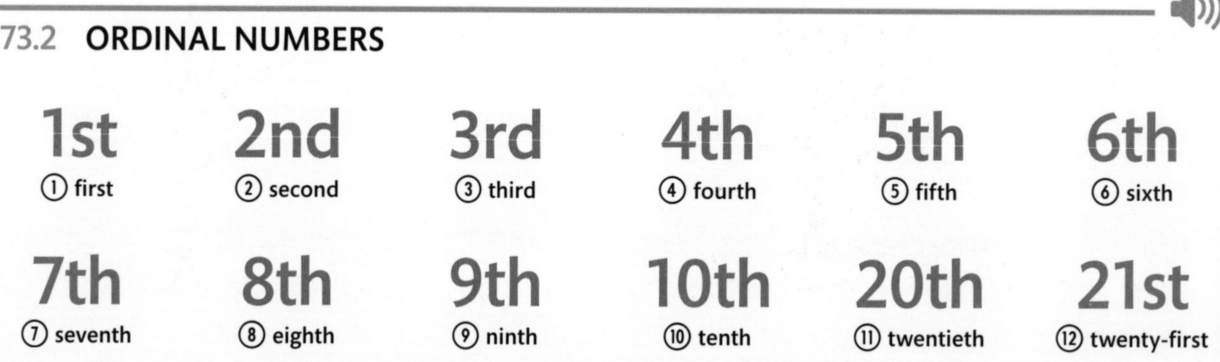
1st
① first
2nd
② second
3rd
③ third
4th
④ fourth
5th
⑤ fifth
6th
⑥ sixth
7th
⑦ seventh
8th
⑧ eighth
9th
⑨ ninth
10th
⑩ tenth
20th
⑪ twentieth
21st
⑫ twenty-first

See also:
74 Mathematics 171 Time 172 The calendar
174 Weights and measures

173.3 LARGE NUMBERS

200
① two hundred

250
② two hundred and fifty

500
③ five hundred

750
④ seven hundred and fifty

1,000
⑤ one thousand

1,200
⑥ one thousand two hundred

10,000
⑦ ten thousand

100,000
⑧ one hundred thousand

1,000,000
⑨ one million

5,000,000
⑩ five million

500,000,000
⑪ five hundred million / half a billion

1,000,000,000
⑫ one billion

3,846
⑬ three thousand, eight hundred and forty-six

82,043
⑭ eighty-two thousand and forty-three

⑮ I've lost count!

234,407
⑯ two hundred and thirty-four thousand, four hundred and seven

3,089,342
⑰ three million, eighty-nine thousand, three hundred and forty-two

173.4 FRACTIONS, DECIMALS, AND PERCENTAGES

1/8
① an eighth

1/4
② a quarter

1/3
③ a third

1/2
④ a half

3/5
⑤ three-fifths

7/8
⑥ seven-eighths

0.5

⑦ zero (US) / nought (UK) point five

1.7
⑧ one point seven

3.97
⑨ three point nine seven

1%
⑩ one percent

99%
⑪ ninety-nine percent

100%
⑫ one hundred percent

174 Weights and measures

174.1 WEIGHT

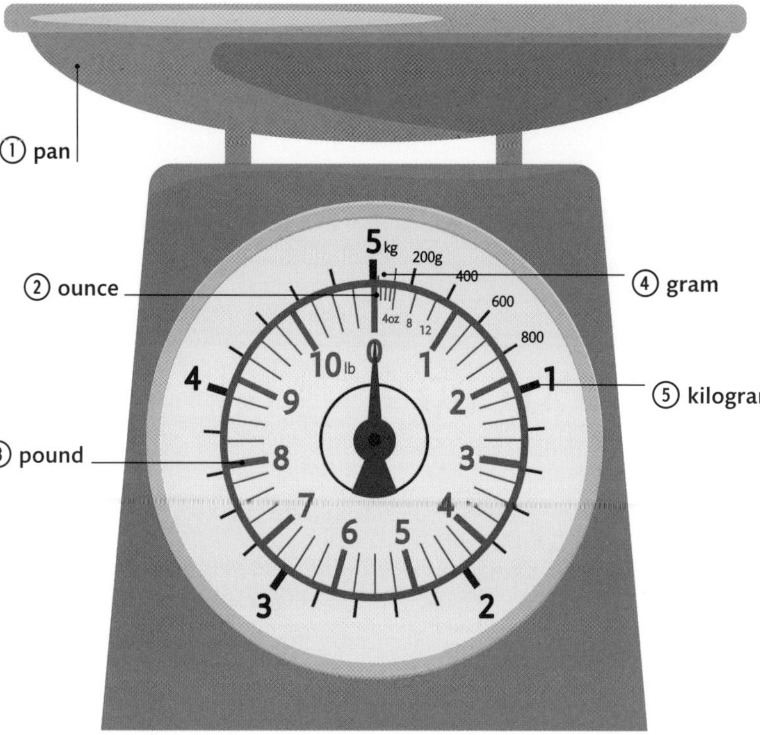

① pan

② ounce

③ pound

④ gram

⑤ kilogram

⑥ scales

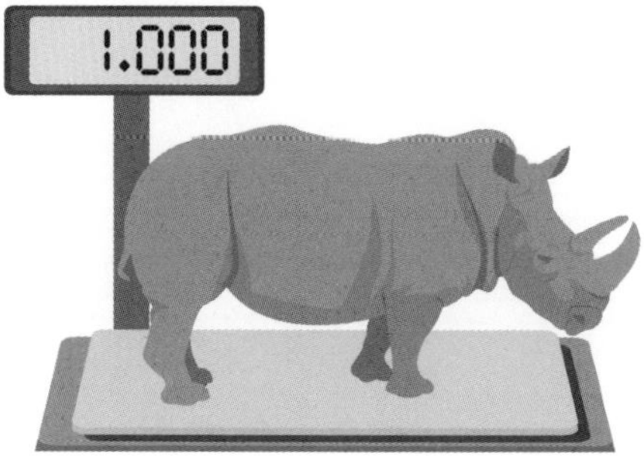

⑦ tonne / ton

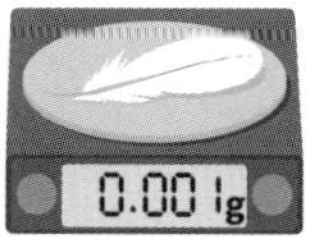

⑧ milligram

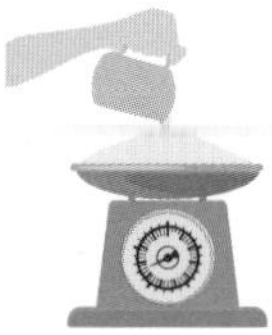

⑨ to weigh

174.2 DISTANCE , AREA, AND LENGTH

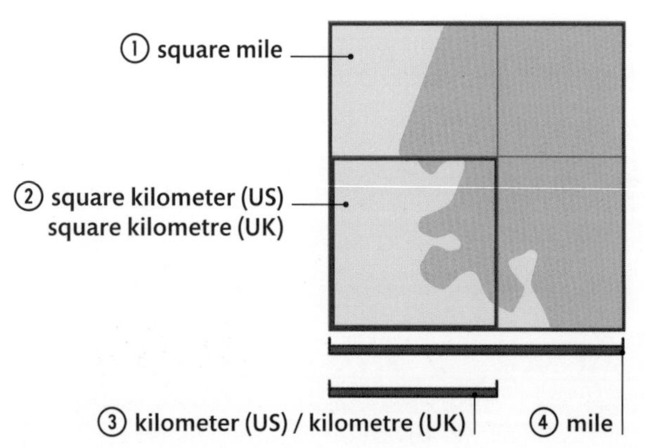
① square mile
② square kilometer (US)
square kilometre (UK)
③ kilometer (US) / kilometre (UK)
④ mile

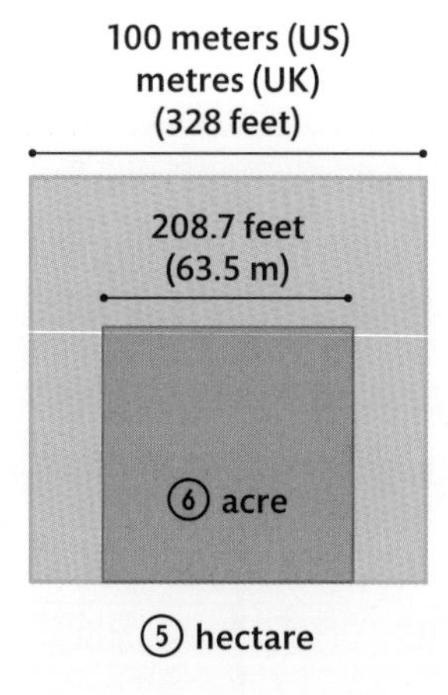
100 meters (US)
metres (UK)
(328 feet)
208.7 feet
(63.5 m)
⑥ acre
⑤ hectare

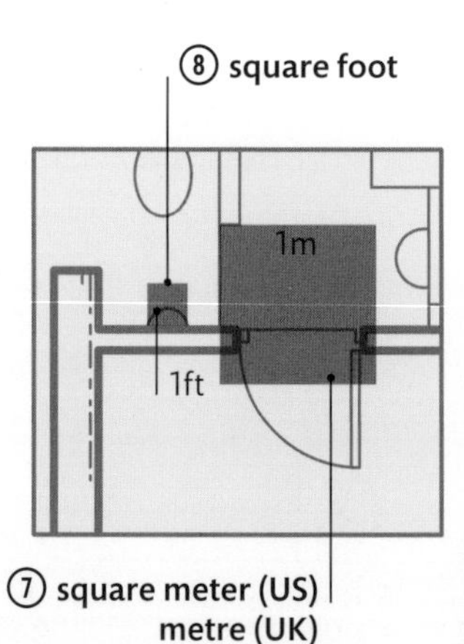
⑧ square foot
1m
1ft
⑦ square meter (US)
metre (UK)

See also:
29 Cooking 35 Home improvements
74 Mathematics 173 Numbers

174.3 LIQUID MEASUREMENTS / VOLUME

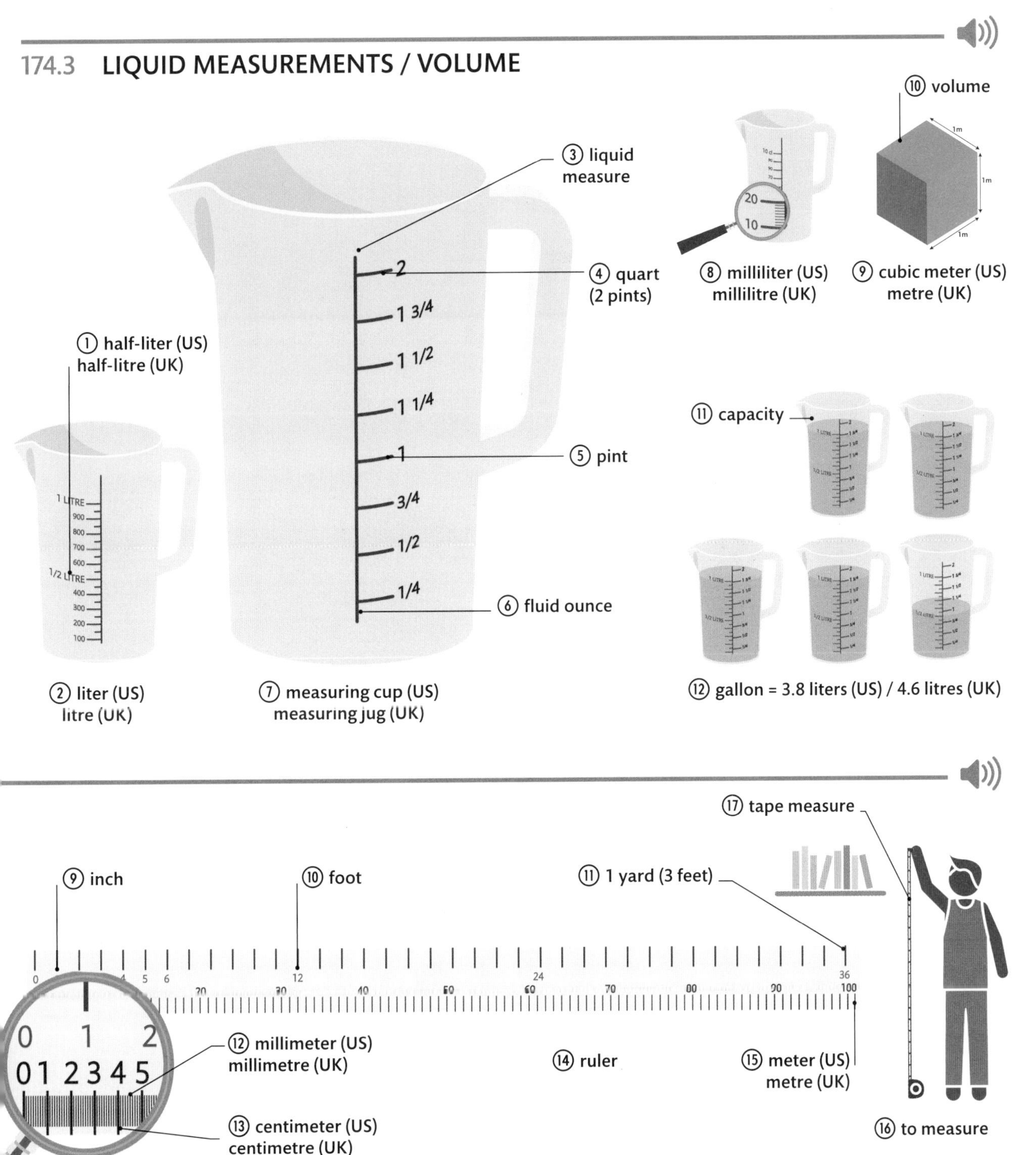
① half-liter (US)
half-litre (UK)
② liter (US)
litre (UK)
③ liquid measure
④ quart (2 pints)
⑤ pint
⑥ fluid ounce
⑦ measuring cup (US)
measuring jug (UK)
⑧ milliliter (US)
millilitre (UK)
⑨ cubic meter (US)
metre (UK)
⑩ volume
⑪ capacity
⑫ gallon = 3.8 liters (US) / 4.6 litres (UK)
2
1 3/4
1 1/2
1 1/4
1
3/4
1/2
1/4
1 LITRE
900
800
700
600
1/2 LITRE
400
300
200
100
20
10
1m
⑨ inch
⑩ foot
⑪ 1 yard (3 feet)
⑫ millimeter (US)
millimetre (UK)
⑬ centimeter (US)
centimetre (UK)
⑭ ruler
⑮ meter (US)
metre (UK)
⑯ to measure
⑰ tape measure
0 1 2
0 1 2 3 4 5
12
24
36
100

175 Writing

175.1 WRITING AND WRITING EQUIPMENT

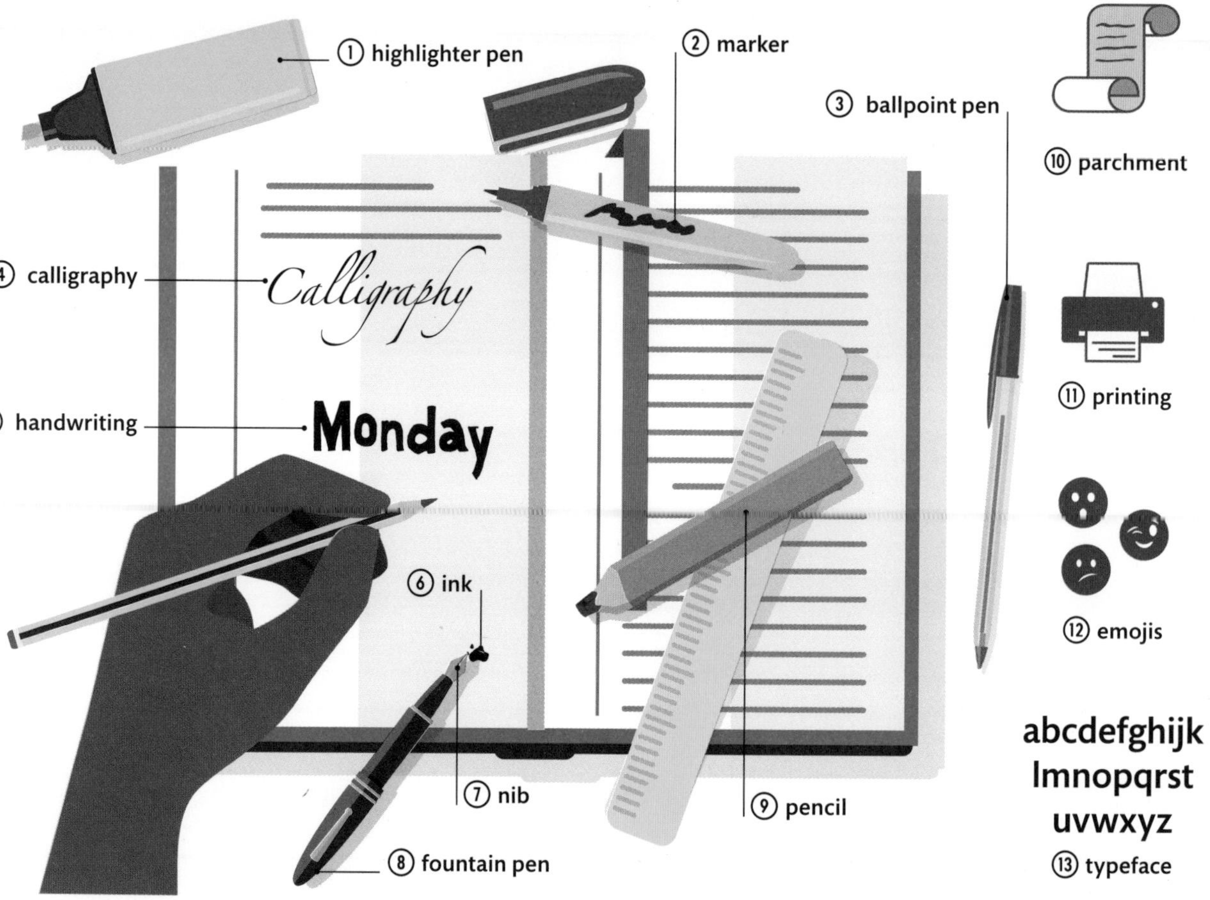

① highlighter pen
② marker
③ ballpoint pen
④ calligraphy

Calligraphy

⑤ handwriting

Monday

⑥ ink
⑦ nib
⑧ fountain pen
⑨ pencil
⑩ parchment
⑪ printing
⑫ emojis

abcdefghijk
lmnopqrst
uvwxyz

⑬ typeface

Aa	ABC	abc	**abc**	*abc*	123
⑭ letters	⑮ uppercase / capital letters	⑯ lowercase	⑰ bold	⑱ italic	⑲ numerals

ft	.	-	—	_	,
⑳ ligature	㉑ period (US) full stop (UK)	㉒ hyphen	㉓ dash	㉔ underscore	㉕ comma

See also:
73 At school
138 Books and reading

;
(26) semicolon

:
(27) colon

...
(28) ellipsis

!
(29) exclamation mark

?
(30) question mark

’
(31) apostrophe

‘
(32) single quotation mark

“
(33) double quotation mark

*
(34) asterisk

@
(35) at sign / at symbol

&
(36) ampersand

ũ
(37) tilde

é
(38) acute accent

è
(39) grave accent

ü
(40) umlaut

ĉ
(41) circumflex

ç
(42) cedilla

©
(43) copyright

®
(44) registered trademark

()
(45) brackets

#
(46) hashtag

cat
(47) Latin alphabet

Γάτα
(48) Greek alphabet

кошка
(49) Cyrillic alphabet

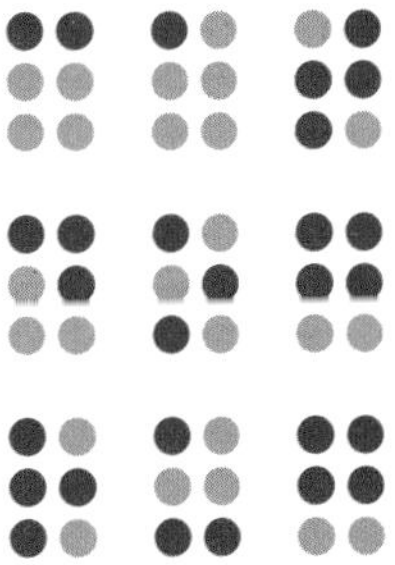

(50) Braille

قط
شجرة
ماء
(51) Arabic script

市
車両
道
(52) Japanese characters

桃
橘子
柠檬
(53) Chinese characters

खेत
घोड़ा
नदी
(54) Devanagari script

(55) Ancient Egyptian hieroglyphs

176 Describing things

176.1 MATERIALS

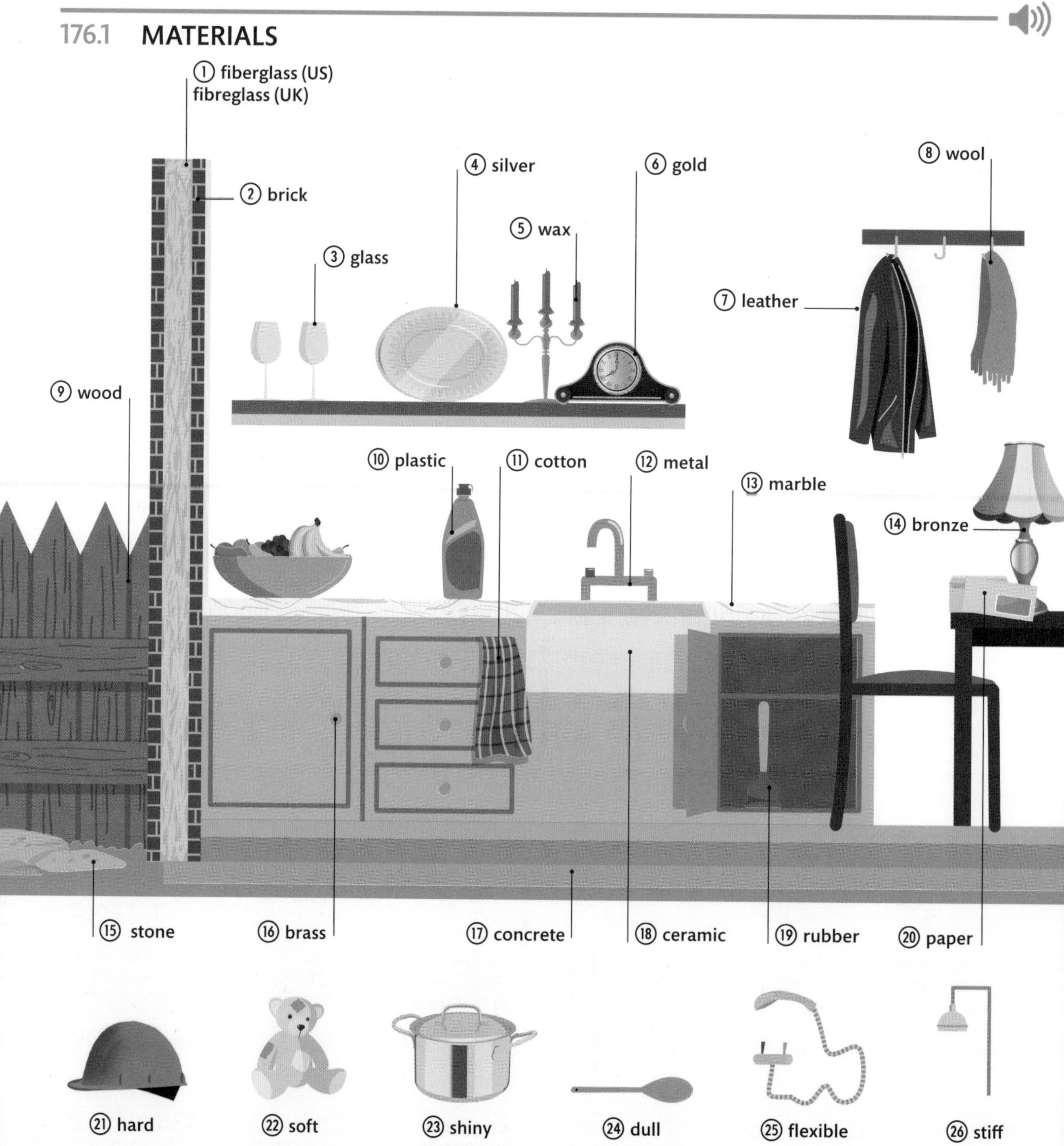

① fiberglass (US)
fibreglass (UK)
② brick
③ glass
④ silver
⑤ wax
⑥ gold
⑦ leather
⑧ wool
⑨ wood
⑩ plastic
⑪ cotton
⑫ metal
⑬ marble
⑭ bronze
⑮ stone
⑯ brass
⑰ concrete
⑱ ceramic
⑲ rubber
⑳ paper
㉑ hard
㉒ soft
㉓ shiny
㉔ dull
㉕ flexible
㉖ stiff

See also:
32 House and home 35 Home improvements 37 Decorating
87 Construction 177 Describing things (continued)

176.2 ADJECTIVES

① big / large

② small / little

③ wide

④ narrow

⑤ deep

⑥ shallow

⑦ high

⑧ low

⑨ heavy

⑩ light

⑪ clean

⑫ dirty

⑬ hot

⑭ cold

⑮ long

⑯ short

⑰ loose

⑱ tight

⑲ thin

⑳ thick

㉑ near

㉒ far

㉓ slow

㉔ fast

㉕ new

㉖ old

㉗ empty

㉘ full

㉙ noisy

㉚ quiet

㉛ correct

㉜ incorrect

㉝ light

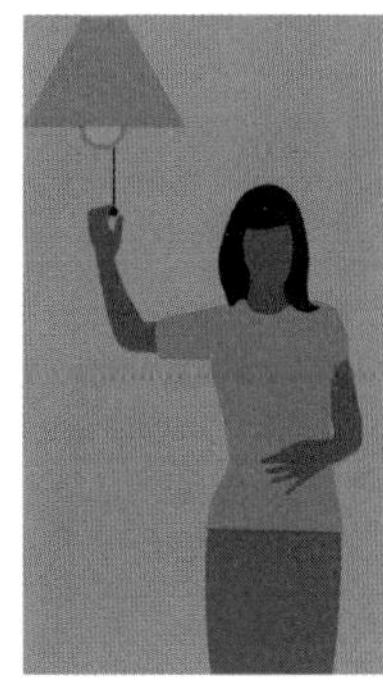
㉞ dark

177.1 OPINIONS

② The view here is absolutely breathtaking.

① breathtaking

③ exciting

④ beautiful

⑤ thrilling

⑥ fun

⑦ romantic

⑧ stunning

⑨ great

⑩ incredible

⑪ important

⑫ cute

⑬ respectful

⑭ special

⑮ graceful

⑯ remarkable

⑰ outstanding

⑱ hilarious

⑲ funny

⑳ extraordinary

㉑ wonderful

㉒ harmless

㉓ old-fashioned

See also:
06 Feelings and moods 10 Personality traits
11 Abilities and actions 93 Workplace skills

24 good

25 bad

26 fantastic

27 terrible

28 pleasant

29 unpleasant

30 brilliant

31 dreadful

32 useful

33 useless

34 delicious

35 disgusting

36 pretty

37 ugly

38 interesting

39 boring

40 relaxing

41 exhausting

42 superb

43 awful

44 nice

45 nasty

46 amazing

47 mediocre

48 frightening

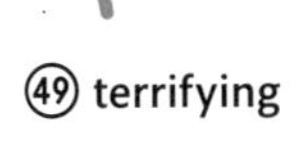
49 terrifying

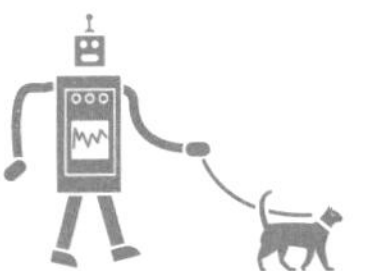

50 strange / odd

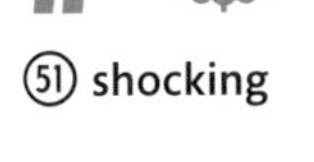
51 shocking

52 annoying

53 horrible

54 disastrous

55 confusing

56 tiring

57 irritating

58 dire

59 disappointing

178 Common phrasal verbs

178.1 VERBS FOR DAILY LIFE

① to calm down

② to chill out

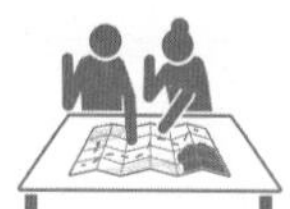
③ to look for

④ to grow up

⑤ to call up

⑥ to put on

⑦ to dress up

⑧ to show off

⑨ to pile up

⑩ to give back

⑪ to doze off

⑫ to sleep in

⑬ to get up

⑭ to go up

⑮ to go down

⑯ to catch up

⑰ to mess around

⑱ to hang up

⑲ to let in

⑳ to rip out

㉑ to run out (of)

㉒ to set off

㉓ to trip over

㉔ to measure (US)
to measure out (UK)

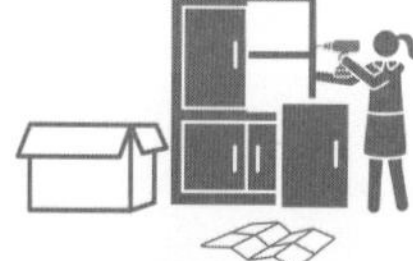
㉕ to put together

㉖ to fix up (US)
to do up (UK)

㉗ to put away

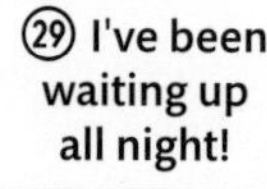
㉙ I've been waiting up all night!

㉘ to wait up

㉚ to fill out

㉛ to log in

㉜ to log out

See also:
09 Daily routines **11** Abilities and actions
179-180 Useful expressions

(33) to wake up

(34) to weigh (US)
to weigh out (UK)

(35) to turn on

(36) to turn off

(37) to turn up

(38) to turn down

(39) to break down

(40) to fill up

(41) to check in

(42) to check out

(43) to eat out

(44) to wait on

(45) to get on

(46) to get off

(47) to pour down

(48) to go away /
to get away

(49) to point out

(50) to care for (US)
to look after (UK)

(51) to look at

(52) to give away

(53) to give out

(54) to give up

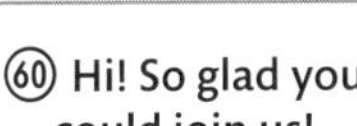
(60) Hi! So glad you could join us!

(59) to get together

(55) to break up

(56) to call off

(57) to make up

(58) to meet up

(61) to hand out

(62) to clean up

(63) to pick up

(64) to throw away

(65) to run away

(66) to take off

179 Useful expressions

179.1 GREETINGS

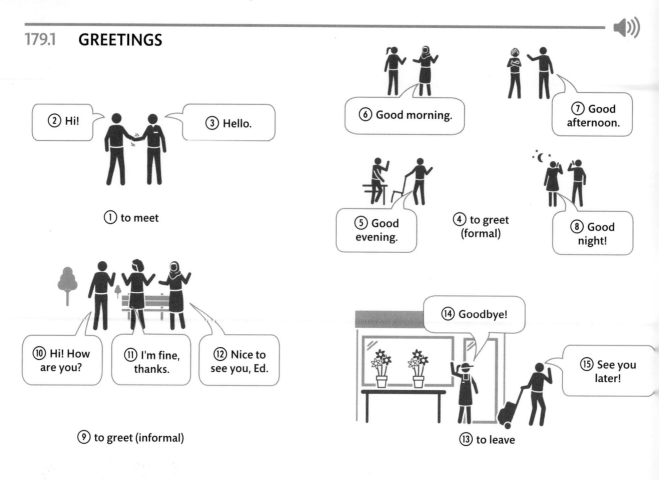

① to meet

② Hi!

③ Hello.

④ to greet (formal)

⑤ Good evening.

⑥ Good morning.

⑦ Good afternoon.

⑧ Good night!

⑨ to greet (informal)

⑩ Hi! How are you?

⑪ I'm fine, thanks.

⑫ Nice to see you, Ed.

⑬ to leave

⑭ Goodbye!

⑮ See you later!

179.2 GETTING TO KNOW SOMEONE

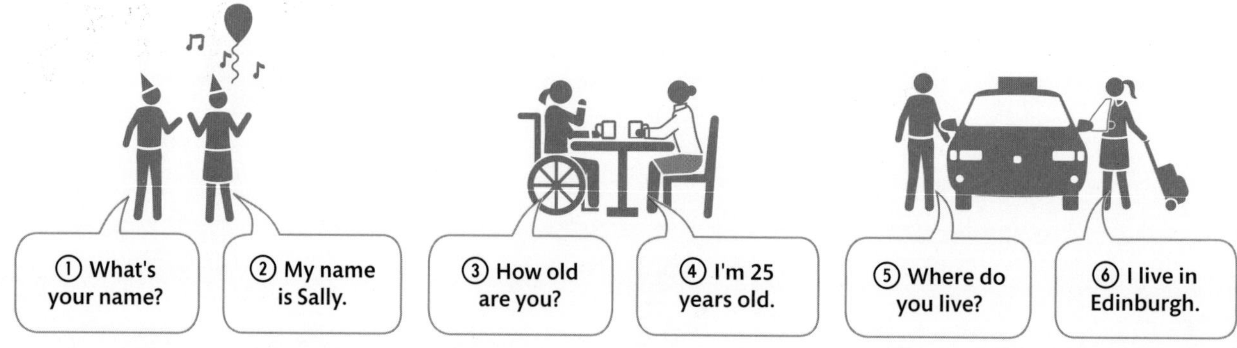
① What's your name?
② My name is Sally.
③ How old are you?
④ I'm 25 years old.
⑤ Where do you live?
⑥ I live in Edinburgh.

See also:
09 Daily routines **07** Life events **46** Shopping
180 Useful expressions (continued)

179.3 SHOPPING

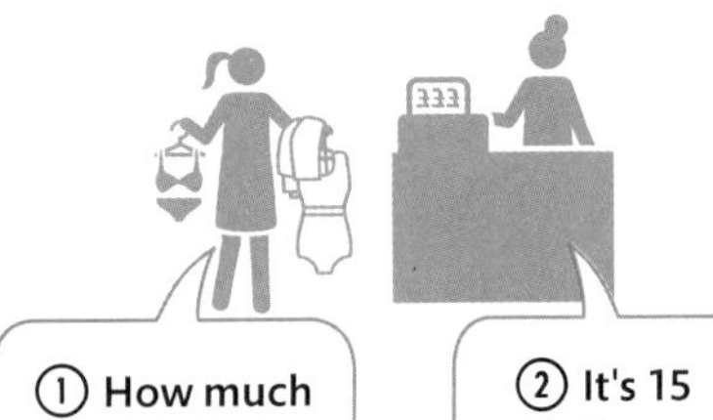
① How much is this?
② It's 15 dollars.

③ Can I pay here?

④ Could you get the red cup for me, please?

⑤ Can I help you?
⑥ I'm just browsing, thanks.

⑦ Do you sell umbrellas?

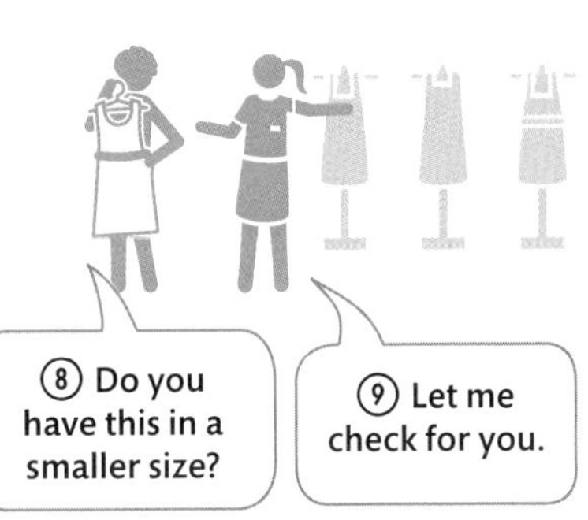
⑧ Do you have this in a smaller size?
⑨ Let me check for you.

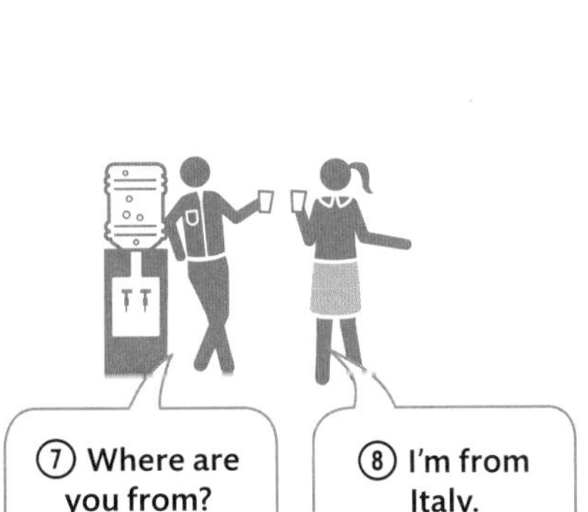
⑦ Where are you from?
⑧ I'm from Italy.

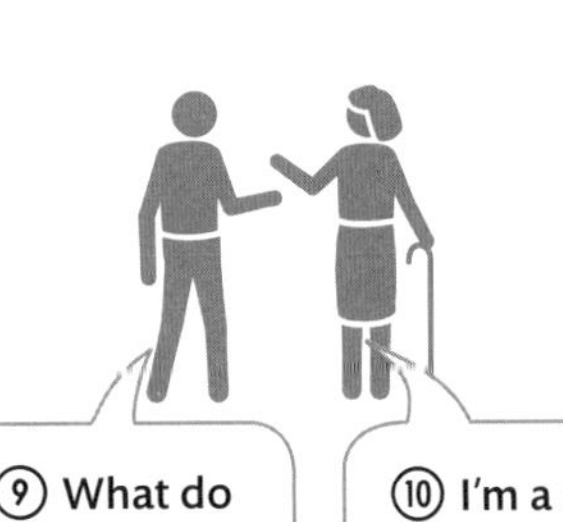
⑨ What do you do?
⑩ I'm a retired diplomat.

⑪ Do you speak English?
?
⑫ Only a little. Could you speak more slowly, please?

180 Useful expressions continued

180.1 DIRECTIONS

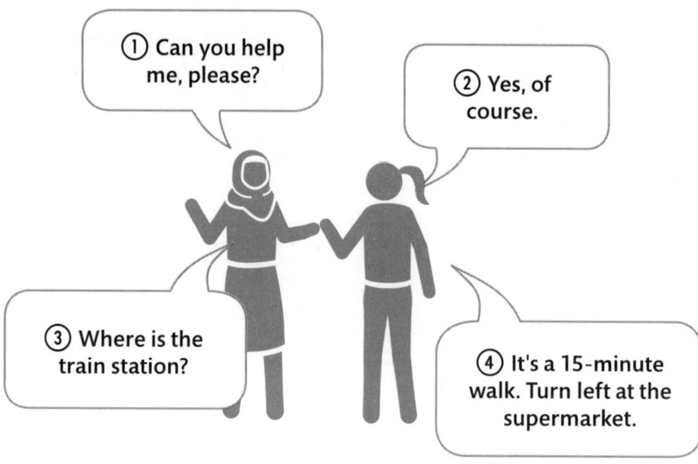
① Can you help me, please?
② Yes, of course.
③ Where is the train station?
④ It's a 15-minute walk. Turn left at the supermarket.

⑤ How far is it to the hotel?

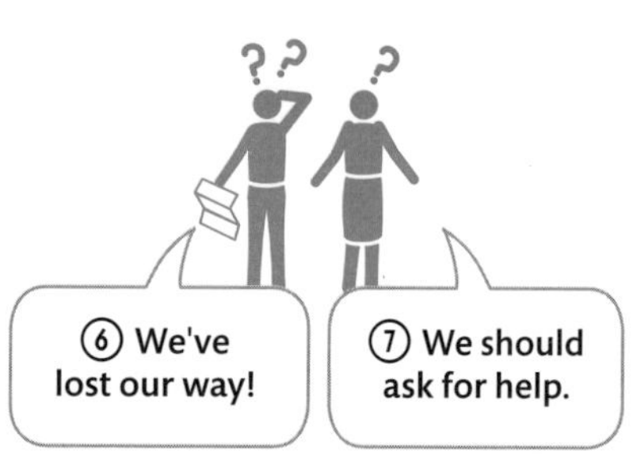
⑥ We've lost our way!
⑦ We should ask for help.

⑧ Can you show us the way to the lake?

⑨ How do we get to the beach?
⑩ It's straight ahead!

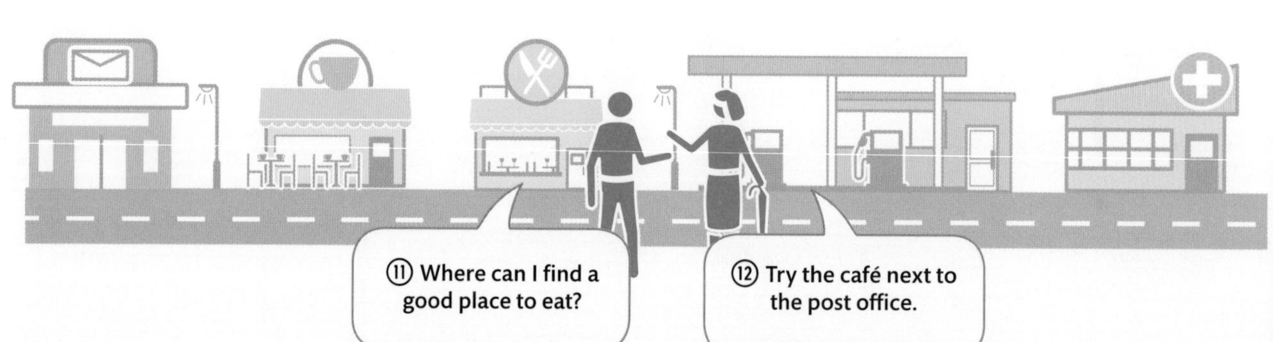
⑪ Where can I find a good place to eat?
⑫ Try the café next to the post office.

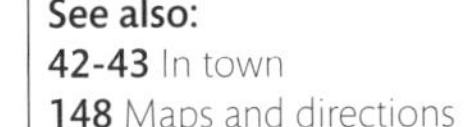
See also:
42-43 In town
148 Maps and directions

180.2 PREPOSITIONS

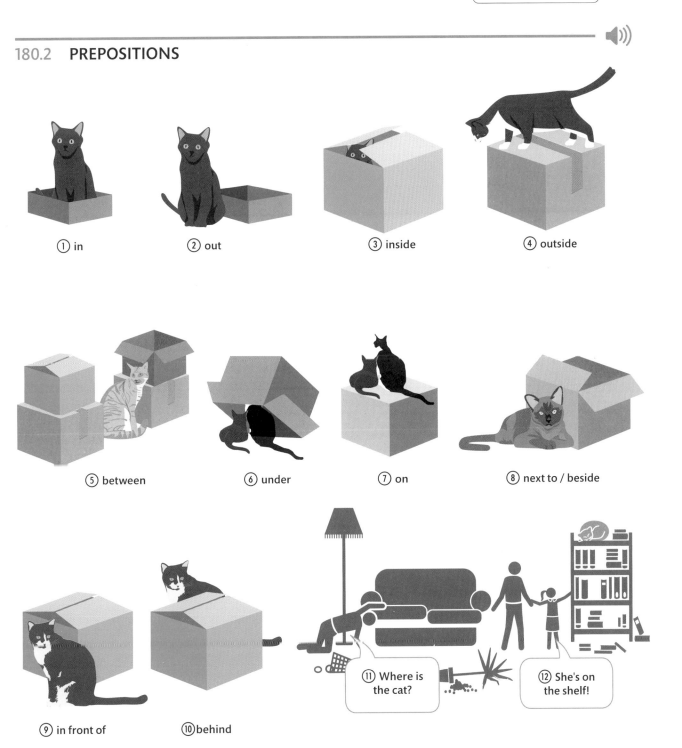

① in

② out

③ inside

④ outside

⑤ between

⑥ under

⑦ on

⑧ next to / beside

⑨ in front of

⑩ behind

⑪ Where is the cat?

⑫ She's on the shelf!

Word list

The numbers after each word or phrase refer to the units in which they can be found.

KEY
adj - adjective
adv - adverb
n - noun
num - number
phr - phrase
prep - preposition
v - verb

A

à la carte menu *n* 69
A&E (UK) *n* 21, 50
aardvark *n* 158
ab wheel (US) *n* 124
abandoned building (US) *n* 44
abdomen *n* 01, 162
abdominals *n* 03
abilities *n* 11
ability to drive *n* 93
abseiling *n* 125
Abyssinian *n* 164
acacia *n* 47
accelerator (UK) *n* 99
access road *n* 106
accessories *n* 16
accident *n* 19
accident and emergency *n* 50
accommodation *n* 131
accordion *n* 129
account number *n* 45
accountant *n* 90, 94
accounts *n* 91
accurate *adj* 93
accused (UK) *n* 85
ace *n* 114, 140
ache *v* 20
Achilles tendon *n* 03
acid *n* 76
acid rain *n* 51, 155
acorn *n* 169
acorn squash *n* 56
acoustic guitar *n* 129
acoustic guitarist *n* 129
acquaintance *n* 07
acquitted *adj* 85
acre *n* 174
across from (US) *prep* 148
acrylic paint *n* 141
act *v* 11
actinide series *n* 78
actinium *n* 78
action game *n* 136
action movie *n* 127
action points *n* 95
actions *n* 11
actor *n* 89, 126
acupressure *n* 24
acupuncture *n* 24
acute accent *n* 175
Adam's apple *n* 04
adaptable *adj* 93
add *v* 11, 29, 74
add to cart *v* 46
add to wishlist *v* 46
additives *n* 23
address *n* 45
adhesive bandage (US) *n* 20
adhesive tape *n* 20
administration *n* 91, 93
admiral *n* 88
admission fee *n* 130
admissions *n* 80
admit *v* 21
adrenal gland *n* 04
adult frog *n* 77
adult teeth *n* 03
adults *n* 05
advantage *n* 114
adventure game *n* 136
adventure playground *n* 133
adventurous *adj* 10
advertising *n* 91
adverts (UK) *n* 137
aerate *v* 39
aerial (UK) *n* 25, 97
aerobics *n* 124
aerobics step *n* 124
aerospace *n* 91
Afghan *adj* 153
Afghanistan *n* 151, 153
Afghans *n* 153
Africa *n* 149, 152
African *adj* 152
African bullfrog *n* 163
African daisy *n* 38
African elephant *n* 158
African gray parrot (US) *n* 161
African grey parrot (UK) *n* 161
African wild dog *n* 158
Africans *n* 152
Afro *n* 12
afternoon *n* 09, 171
aftershave *n* 18, 31
agate *n* 156
agbada *n* 15
agenda *n* 95
agriculture *n* 91
aikido *n* 117
aileron *n* 103
air ambulance *n* 50
air bed *n* 135
air cargo *n* 104
air conditioning *n* 33, 99
air control tower *n* 43
air cylinder *n* 118
air filter *n* 98, 100
air mattress *n* 135
air pump *n* 135
air vent *n* 103
airbag *n* 99
airball *n* 112
aircraft carrier *n* 88, 105
aircraft *n* 103
airforce *n* 88
airline *n* 104
airmail *n* 45
airman *n* 88
airport *n* 43, 104
airship *n* 103
airtight container *n* 52
aisle, aisles *n* 48, 80, 103, 126
alarm *n* 50
alarm clock *n* 30
alarm goes off *phr* 09
Albania *n* 151, 153
Albanian *adj* 153
Albanians *n* 153
albatross *n* 160
albertonectes *n* 157
album *n* 129
alcohol-free beer *n* 68
ale *n* 68
alfalfa *n* 86
Algeria *n* 149, 152
Algerian *adj* 152
Algerians *n* 152
Alice band (UK) *n* 16
alien *n* 139
alkali *n* 76
alkali metals *n* 78
alkaline earth metals *n* 78
all-terrain vehicle *n* 100
Allen keys (UK) *n* 36
allergic *adj* 23
allergy *n* 19
alley *n* 42
alligator clip (US) *n* 75
alloy *n* 76
allspice *n* 59
almond milk *n* 61
almond oil *n* 60
almonds *n* 58, 68
aloe *n* 167
alpaca *n* 165
alpine plants *n* 41
alternating current *n* 33, 75
alto *n* 126
aluminium (UK) *n* 78, 156
aluminum (US) *n* 78, 156
always *adj* 171
amaryllis *n* 167
amazed *adj* 06
amazing *adj* 177
Amazon *n* 145
ambitious *adj* 10, 93
ambulance *n* 21, 50
ambulance stretcher *n* 50
American *adj* 152
American alligator *n* 163
American curl *n* 164
American football field *n* 107
American football *n* 107
American football positions *n* 107
Americans *n* 152
americium *n* 78
amethyst *n* 156
amount *n* 45
amp *n* 33
ampersand *n* 175
amphibians *n* 163
amphibious vehicle *n* 88
amplifier *n* 129
amulet *n* 139
amused *adj* 06
anaesthetist (UK) *n* 90
analytics *n* 93
anchor *n* 105, 119
anchovies *n* 64
Ancient Egyptian hieroglyphs *n* 175
Ancient Greek temple *n* 44
ancient ruins *n* 44
Andean condor *n* 160
Andorra *n* 151, 153
Andorran *adj* 153
Andorrans *n* 153
anemone *n* 134, 166
anesthesiologist (US) *n* 90
Angel Falls *n* 145
angle *n* 74
angler *n* 121
angler fish *n* 166
Angola *n* 149, 152
Angolan *adj* 152
Angolans *n* 152
Angora *n* 164
angry *adj* 06
animal cell *n* 77
animation *n* 127
anise *n* 59
ankle *n* 01-02
ankle boots *n* 17
ankle strap heels *n* 17
ankle weights *n* 124
anklet *n* 16
anniversary *n* 07
annoyed *adj* 06
annoying *adj* 177
annual *n* 41
annual general meeting (AGM) *n* 95
annual leave (UK) *n* 81
anorak *n* 15
answer *v* 73
ant *n* 162
anteater *n* 159
antenna (US) *n* 25, 97
antenna *n* 162
anther *n* 38
anti-inflammatory *n* 49
antibiotics *n* 49
anticlockwise (UK) *adv* 148
antifreeze *n* 97
Antigua and Barbuda *n* 150, 152
Antiguan *adj* 152
Antiguans *n* 152
antimony *n* 78
antiques shop (UK) *n* 46
antiques store (US) *n* 46
antiseptic *n* 20
antiseptic wipes *n* 20
antler *n* 159
anxious *adj* 06
any other business *phr* 95
apartment (US) *n* 25
apartment *n* 131
apartment building (US) *n* 25, 43
apartment buzzer (US) *n* 25
apex *n* 74
apostrophe *n* 175
app developer *n* 89
appeal *n* 85
appearance *n* 12
appendicitis *n* 19
appendix *n* 04
appetizer (US) *n* 69
applause *n* 126
apple *n* 58
apple corer *n* 28
apple juice *n* 65
applicant *n* 81
application form *n* 92
apply for a job *v* 92
applying for a job *n* 92
appointment *n* 20, 81
appreciative *adj* 06
apprentice *n* 81, 92
approachable *adj* 10
apricot *n* 57
April *n* 172
apron *n* 13, 29
aquamarine *n* 156
aquarium *n* 164
Aquarius *n* 144
Arabic script *n* 175
arable farm *n* 86
arbor knot *n* 121
arc *n* 74, 112
arch *n* 02, 41, 44
arch window *n* 32
archaeological site (UK) *n* 132
archaeology (UK) *n* 79
archaeologist (UK) *n* 79
archeological site (US) *n* 132

archeologist (US) *n* 79
archeology (US) *n* 79
archer *n* 125
archery *n* 125
archipelago *n* 147
architect *n* 90
architecture *n* 44
archive *n* 79
Arctic *n* 159
Arctic Circle *n* 145
Arctic fox *n* 159
Arctic hare *n* 159
Arctic tern *n* 160
Arctic wolf *n* 159
area *n* 74, 174
arena *n* 120
Argentina *n* 149, 152
Argentinian *adj* 152
Argentinians *n* 152
argon *n* 78
Aries *n* 144
arm, arms *n* 01, 126
arm circles *n* 124
arm protection *n* 110
armadillo *n* 159
armband *n* 118
armchair *n* 26
armed drone *n* 88
armed forces *n* 88
Armenia *n* 150, 153
Armenian *adj* 153
Armenians *n* 153
armor (US) *n* 79
armored vehicle (US) *n* 88
armour (UK) *n* 79
armoured vehicle (UK) *n* 88
armpit *n* 01
armrest *n* 99, 103
army *n* 88
aromatherapy *n* 24
arrest *n* 50
arrival *n* 43
arrive *v* 09
arrive early *v* 09
arrive home *v* 09
arrive late *v* 09
arrive on time *v* 09
arrogant *adj* 10
arrow *n* 79, 125
arrow slit *n* 44
arsenic *n* 78
art, arts *n* 73, 91, 141–142
art college *n* 80
Art Deco *n* 130
art gallery *n* 43, 130, 132
Art Nouveau *n* 130
art school *n* 80
art shop (UK) *n* 46
art store (US) *n* 46
art therapy *n* 24
artery *n* 04
artichoke heart *n* 56
artichoke *n* 56
article *n* 138
articulated bus *n* 99
artificial intelligence *n* 83
artisan *n* 79
artist *n* 90, 141
arugula (US) *n* 55
arum lily *n* 167
ash *n* 145
ash cloud *n* 145
Asia *n* 150, 153
Asian *adj* 153
Asian elephant *n* 159
Asian vine snake *n* 163
Asians *n* 153
ask directions *v* 148
asparagus *n* 56
asparagus tip *n* 56
assertive *adj* 10, 93
astatine *n* 78
asterisk *n* 175
asteroid *n* 143
asthma *n* 19
astigmatism *n* 22
astronaut *n* 143
astronomy *n* 144
at sign *n* 83, 175
at symbol *n* 83, 175
athlete *n* 116
athletics *n* 116, 125
athletics track *n* 116
Atlantic puffin *n* 160
Atlantic salmon *n* 166
atlas moth *n* 162
atlas *n* 73
ATM *n* 45
ATV riding (US) *n* 133
atmosphere *n* 143, 155
atoll *n* 147
atom *n* 76
attachment *n* 83
attack helicopter *n* 88
attack zone *n* 110
attend a meeting *v* 95
attic *n* 25
attractions *n* 132
aubergine (UK) *n* 56
auburn hair *n* 12
audience *n* 126, 127
audio *n* 136
audio guide *n* 130
audition *n* 127
auditorium (US) *n* 80
August *n* 172
aunt *n* 05
aurora *n* 144, 155
Australia *n* 150, 153
Australian *adj* 153
Australian little penguin *n* 161
Australians *n* 153
Austria *n* 151, 153
Austrian *adj* 153
Austrians *n* 153
author *n* 138
auto racing (US) *n* 123
auto repair shop (US) *n* 98
autobiography *n* 138
autocue *n* 84
automatic *n* 99
automotive industry *n* 91
autumn (UK) *n* 57, 172
autumn leaf *n* 169
avalanche *n* 122
avatar *n* 84
avenue *n* 43
avocado *n* 56
avocado toast *n* 71
avocado tree *n* 167
awful *adj* 177
awning *n* 65
ax (US) *n* 36, 50, 79
axe (UK) *n* 36, 50, 79
axle *n* 100
ayran *n* 61
ayurveda *n* 24
azalea *n* 38
Azerbaijan *n* 150, 153
Azerbaijani *adj* 153
Azerbaijanis *n* 153

B

babies' clothes *n* 13
baboon *n* 158
baby *n* 05
baby bath *n* 08
baby carriage (US) *n* 08
baby changing facilities *n* 47
baby corn (US) *n* 55
baby formula *n* 08
baby monitor *n* 08, 30
baby products *n* 48
baby sweetcorn (UK) *n* 55
baby teeth (US) *n* 22
babygro (UK) *n* 13
back *adj* 03
back *n* 26
back bacon *n* 53
back brush *n* 31
back door *n* 97
back seat *n* 99
back up *v* 83
back-flip *n* 118
backache *n* 19
backboard *n* 112
backdrop *n* 126
backgammon *n* 140
backhand *n* 114
backing singers *n* 129
backpack *n* 16, 135
backpack sprayer *n* 40
backsplash (US) *n* 37
backstay *n* 119
backstop net *n* 113
backstroke *n* 118
backswing *n* 115
bacon *n* 53, 71
bacteria *n* 77, 157
Bactrian camel *n* 158
bad *adj* 52, 177
bad robot *n* 139
badge *n* 50
badge (UK) *n* 16
badminton *n* 114
bag, bags *n* 16, 52
bag store *n* 47
bagel *n* 62, 71
baggage claim *n* 104
baggage trailer *n* 104
bagpipes *n* 129
baguette *n* 62
baggy *adj* 13, 176
Bahamas *n* 150, 162
Bahamian *adj* 152
Bahamians *n* 152
Bahrain *n* 151, 153
Bahraini *adj* 153
Bahrainis *n* 153
bail *n* 85, 111
Baisakhi *n* 07
bait *n* 121
bait *v* 121
bake *v* 29, 62–63
baked *adj* 72
baked beans *n* 71
baker *n* 62
bakery *n* 46, 48, 62–63
baking *n* 29
baking pan (US) *n* 29
baking tray (UK) *n* 29
baklava *n* 63
balance wheel *n* 142
balanced diet *n* 23
balcony (US) *n* 126
balcony *n* 25
bald *adj* 12
bald eagle *n* 160
ball *n* 02, 08, 109–110, 112, 114
ball boy *n* 114
ball girl *n* 114
ballerina flats *n* 17
ballerina *n* 126
ballet *n* 126
ballet flats *n* 17
ballet leotard *n* 126
ballet shoes *n* 126
ballet slippers *n* 126
ballistic missile *n* 88
balloon *n* 08
ballpoint pen *n* 175
balsamic vinegar *n* 60
bamboo *n* 41, 55, 167
banana *n* 58
band *n* 129
bandage *n* 20, 49
banded sea krait *n* 166
Bangladesh *n* 150, 153
Bangladeshi *adj* 153
Bangladeshis *n* 153
bangle *n* 16
banister *n* 25–26
banjo *n* 129
bank *n* 45, 94
bank loan *n* 45
bank statement *n* 45
banking *n* 91
banner *n* 109
baobab tree *n* 169
baptism *n* 07
bar, bars *n* 30, 68, 109, 124
bar chart *n* 95
bar counter *n* 68
bar mitzvah *n* 07
bar snacks *n* 68
bar stool *n* 68
bar tender *n* 69
barb *n* 121
Barbadian *adj* 152
Barbadians *n* 152
Barbados *n* 150, 152
barbecue (UK) *n* 41
barbecue *n* 135
barbell *n* 124
barber *n* 89
barberry *n* 168
Barbudan *adj* 152
Barbudans *n* 152
barcode *n* 48
bare branches *n* 172
bargain *n* 48
barista *n* 65, 89
baritone *n* 126
barium *n* 78
bark *v* 164
barley *n* 86
barn *n* 86
barn owl *n* 161
barnacle *n* 134, 166
barracuda *n* 166
barrel cactus *n* 168
Barrier Reef *n* 145
bartender *n* 68, 89
basa *n* 54
basalt *n* 156
base *n* 74, 76
baseball *n* 113
baseball cap *n* 16
baseball cleats *n* 17
baseball game *n* 113
baseboard (US) *n* 30
baseline *n* 112, 114
basement *n* 25, 47
basil *n* 59
basin *n* 22, 33
basket *n* 48, 101, 103, 112, 164
basket of fruit *n* 57
basketball *n* 112
basketball player *n* 112
basking shark *n* 166
Basotho *adj* 152
Basothos *n* 152
basque (UK) *n* 14
bass *n* 126
bass clef *n* 128
bass drum *n* 128
bass guitarist *n* 129
basset hound *n* 164
bassoon *n* 128
bat *n* 111, 113–114, 158
bat *v* 111, 113
bat mitzvah *n* 07
bath towel *n* 31

bath toys *n* 31
bath tub *n* 31
bathmat *n* 31
bathrobe (US) *n* 14, 31
bathroom *n* 31
bathroom exhaust fan (US) *n* 31
bathroom extractor fan (UK) *n* 31
bathroom scale (US) scales (UK) *n* 31
baton (US) *n* 50
baton *n* 116
batsman *n* 111
Battenburg markings *n* 50
batter *n* 111, 113
battering ram *n* 79
battery *n* 75, 83, 98
battery pack *n* 35
batting glove *n* 113
battle *n* 79, 88
battlement *n* 44
battleship *n* 105
Bauhaus *n* 130
bay *n* 147
bay leaf *n* 59
bay tree *n* 38
bay window *n* 25
bayonet base *n* 33
be absent *v* 95
be born *v* 07
be delayed *v* 104
be laid off *v* 81
be late *v* 09, 171
be promoted *v* 81
be sent off *v* 109
be unemployed *v* 81
beach *n* 134, 147–148
beach bag *n* 134
beach ball *n* 134
beach buggy (UK) *n* 97, 134
beach hut *n* 134
beach umbrella *n* 134
bead maze *n* 08
beagle *n* 164
beak *n* 161
beaker *n* 27, 76
beam *n* 125
bean sprouts *n* 55
beanie *n* 16
bean *n* 56
bear's head tooth *n* 170
beard *n* 12
beat *n* 129
beat eggs *v* 29
beautiful *adj* 12, 177
beauty *n* 18, 47
beauty treatments *n* 18
bed *n* 30
bed and breakfast *n* 131
bed linen *n* 30
bedrock *n* 145
bedroom *n* 30
bedside lamp *n* 30
bedside table (UK) *n* 30
bedspring (UK) *n* 30
bee *n* 165
beech *n* 168
beef *n* 53
beehive *n* 86, 162
beer *n* 52, 68
beer tap *n* 68
beet greens (US) *n* 55
beet leaves (UK) *n* 55
beetroot (UK) *n* 56
beet (US) *n* 56
beg *v* 164
begonia *n* 38
behind *prep* 148, 180
being a fast learner *n* 93
Belarus *n* 151, 153
Belarusian *adj* 153
Belarusians *n* 153
Belgian *adj* 153
Belgians *n* 153
Belgium *n* 151, 153
Belize *n* 150, 152
Belizean *adj* 152
Belizeans *n* 152
bell *n* 99
bell tower *n* 44
belt *n* 15–16, 117
beluga *n* 166
bench *n* 124
bend *v* 126
benefits *n* 81
Bengal *n* 164
Benin *n* 149, 152
Beninese *adj* 152
Beninese people *n* 152
beret *n* 16
berkelium *n* 78
Bermuda shorts *n* 14
berries *n* 57
beryllium *n* 78
beside *prep* 180
best friend *n* 07
bestseller *n* 138
between *prep* 148, 180
beverage, beverages *n* 65, 69
bhangra *n* 129
Bhutan *n* 150, 153
Bhutanese *adj* 153
Bhutanese people *n* 153
biathlon *n* 122
bib *n* 13
bibliography *n* 138
bicep curl *n* 124
biceps *n* 03
bicuspids (US) *n* 03
bicycle *n* 101
bicycling *n* 133
bidet *n* 31
biennial *n* 41
bifocal *n* 22
big *adj* 176
Big Bang *n* 144
Big Ben *n* 44
Big Dipper (US) *n* 144
big toe *n* 02
bike helmet *n* 101
bike lane (US) *n* 101
bike parking (US) *n* 43
bike path (US) *n* 43
bike rack *n* 101
bikini *n* 134
bilberry *n* 57
bill *n* 161, 32
bill (UK) *n* 69
bill (US) *n* 45, 94
bin (UK) *n* 82
bin liner (UK) *n* 33, 34
binder clip *n* 82
binoculars *n* 144
biochemistry *n* 76
biodegradable waste *n* 33
biography *n* 138
biologist *n* 77
biology *n* 73, 77, 80
biomass energy *n* 51
biometric passport *n* 104
biotechnology *n* 91
biplane *n* 103
birch *n* 168
bird of paradise *n* 160
bird-of-paradise *n* 167
bird seed *n* 164
bird-watching *n* 133
bird's eye chili (US) *n* 59
bird's eye chillies (UK) *n* 59
birds *n* 160, 161
birdwatcher *n* 161
birth *n* 08
birth certificate *n* 07
birthday *n* 07
birthday cake *n* 63
birthday candles *n* 63
birthday card *n* 07
biscuits *n* 63
bishop *n* 140
bismuth *n* 78
Bissau-Guinean *adj* 152
Bissau-Guineans *n* 152
bistro *n* 69
bit *n* 120
bite *n* 19
bite *v* 52, 121
bitter *adj* 52, 56
black *adj* 140–141
black *n* 140–141
black belt *n* 117
black coffee *n* 65
black currant (US) *n* 57
black hair *n* 12
black hole *n* 144
black mustard *n* 59
black olives *n* 64
black pudding *n* 70
black swan *n* 161
black tea *n* 66
black trumpet *n* 170
black widow spider *n* 162
black woodpecker *n* 160
blackberry *n* 57
blackbird *n* 160
blackcurrant (UK) *n* 57
blacksmith *n* 79
blade *n* 33, 40, 51, 117
blanket *n* 30
bleach *n* 34
bleat *v* 165
bleed *v* 20
blender *n* 27, 65
blindfold *n* 125
blindside flanker *n* 108
blink *v* 02
blister *n* 19
blizzard *n* 154
block *v* 84, 112, 117
block of flats (UK) *n* 25, 43
blocker *n* 112
blocking glove *n* 110
blog *n* 84
blogger *n* 84
blond hair *n* 12
blonde hair *n* 12
blood knot *n* 121
blood orange *n* 57
blood pressure *n* 20
blood pressure monitor *n* 21
blood sausage *n* 71
blood test *n* 20–21
blossom *n* 169
blouse *n* 14
blow *v* 11
blow hole *n* 166
blow out *v* 03
blowout *n* 123
blue *adj* 01, 141
blue *n* 01, 141
blue cheese *n* 61
blue crab *n* 166
blue line *n* 110
blue tang *n* 166
blue whale *n* 166
blue-tongued skink *n* 163
blueberry *n* 57
blues *n* 129
Bluetooth headset *n* 83
Bluetooth speaker *n* 136
blush *v* 02
blush (US) *n* 18
blusher (UK) *n* 18
boar *n* 53, 159
board *n* 119
board *v* 106
board a plane *v* 104
board game *n* 08
board games *n* 140
board of directors *n* 95
boarding gate *n* 104
boarding pass *n* 104
boardroom *n* 95
boards *n* 110
boardwalk *n* 134
boat shoes *n* 17
boat's wheel *n* 119
boater *n* 16
boats *n* 105
bob *n* 12
bobbin *n* 142
bobble hat (UK) *n* 16
bobcat *n* 159
bobsled (US) *n* 122
bobsleigh (UK) *n* 122
boccia *n* 125
body *n* 129
body lotion *n* 31
body powder *n* 31
body systems *n* 04
bodyboarding *n* 119, 134
bodyguard *n* 90
bodysuit (US) *n* 13
bodywork *n* 98, 123
bohrium *n* 78
boil *v* 29
boiled *adj* 72
boiled egg *n* 61, 71
boiled sweets (UK) *n* 67
boiler (UK) *n* 33
boiling *adj* 154
boiling point *n* 154
bok choi (US) *n* 55
bold *adj* 175
bold *n* 175
Bolivia *n* 149, 152
Bolivian *adj* 152
Bolivians *n* 152
bollard, bollards *n* 43, 105
Bolognese sauce *n* 64
bolt *n* 25, 36
Bombay *n* 164
Bombay earth snake *n* 163
bomber *n* 88
bomber jacket *n* 15
bone *n* 03
bone meal *n* 39
boned *adj* 54
bongo drums *n* 128
bonnet (UK) *n* 97–98
bonsai tree *n* 38
bonus *n* 81
boogie board *n* 119
book, books *n* 26, 80, 138
book a holiday (UK) *v* 131
book a vacation (US) *v* 131
bookcase *n* 26
bookshelf *n* 80
bookshop (UK) *n* 46
bookstore (US) *n* 46
boom *n* 50, 119
booster *n* 143
boot (UK) *n* 97
boot, boots *n* 17, 100
boot shapers *n* 17
booties *n* 13
borage *n* 59
border collie *n* 164
bored *adj* 06
boring *adj* 177
boron *n* 78
borrow *v* 80
Bosnia and Herzegovina *n* 151, 153
Bosnian *adj* 153
Bosnians *n* 153
boss *n* 81
botanical gardens *n* 132

botanist *n* 77
botany *n* 77
Botswana *n* 149, 152
Botswanan *adj* 152
Botswanans *n* 152
bottle *n* 08, 52
bottle opener *n* 28, 68
bottled oils *n* 60
bougainvillea *n* 168
bounce *v* 112
bound ankle pose *n* 24
boundary *n* 111, 113
bouquet *n* 15, 47
bouquet garni *n* 59
boutique *n* 46
bow *n* 79, 119, 125
bow *v* 02
bow pose *n* 24
bow tie *n* 16
bowl *n* 27, 33, 52
bowl *v* 111
bowler *n* 111
bowling *n* 125
bowling ball *n* 125
bowling crease *n* 111
bowling pin *n* 125, 08
box, boxes *n* 32, 52, 126
box office *n* 127
box spring (US) *n* 30
boxer *n* 164
boxer shorts *n* 14
boxercise *n* 124
boxing *n* 117
boxing gloves *n* 117
boxing match *n* 117
boxing ring *n* 117
boy *n* 05
boyfriend *n* 05
bra *n* 14
brace *n* 35
bracelet *n* 16
braces *n* [illegible]
brachiosaurus *n* 157
brackets *n* 175
braids *n* 12
Braille *n* 175
brain *n* 04
brake *n* 99–101
brake cooling intake *n* 123
brake disk (UK) *n* 100
brake fluid reservoir *n* 98
brake lever *n* 101
brake pad *n* 101
brake pedal *n* 100
brake rotor (US) *n* 100
brake *v* 98, 101
branch *n* [illegible]
branch manager *n* 45
brandy *n* 68
brass *adj* 176
brass *n* 128, 176
brave *adj* 10
bray *v* 165
Brazil *n* 149, 152
brazil nuts *n* 58
Brazilian *adj* 152
Brazilians *n* 152
bread, breads *n* 62, 71
bread basket *n* 71
bread flour (US) *n* 62
bread knife *n* 28
breadfruit *n* 56
break down *v* 98, 178
break even *v* 94
break in *n* 50
break up *v* 178
breakdown assistance *n* 98
breaker (US) *n* 33
breakfast *n* 26, 71
breakfast buffet *n* 71
breakfast burrito *n* 71
breakfast cereals *n* 48
breakfast roll *n* 71
breakfast tray *n* 131
breakfast TV (UK) *n* 137
breast *n* 01, 53
breastbone *n* 03
breaststroke *n* 118
Breathalyzer *n* 50
breathe *v* 02
breathtaking *adj* 177
breed *v* 120
breeze *n* 154
breeze block (UK) *n* 87
breezy *adj* 154
bribery *n* 85
brick *adj* 176
brick, bricks *n* 35, 87, 176
bride *n* 07
bridesmaid's dress *n* 15
bridge crane *n* 106
bridge *n* 02, 43, 105, 125, 129, 140
bridge pose *n* 24
bridle *n* 120
bridle path (UK) *n* 133
Brie *n* 64
briefcase *n* 16
briefs (US) *n* 16
brilliant *adj* 177
bring *v* 11
brioche *n* 62, 71
British *adj* 153
British *n* 153
British shorthair *n* 164
broad beans (UK) *n* 55
broadcast *v* 84
broadcaster (US) *n* 89
broadleaf forest *n* 159
broccoli *n* 55–56
brogues *n* 17
broil (US) *v* 29
broken bone *n* 19
bromine *n* 78
bronze *adj* 176
bronze *n* 116, 176
Bronze age *n* 79
brooch *n* 16
broom *n* 34, 40
broomstick *n* 139
broth *n* 72
brother *n* 05
brother-in-law *n* 05
browband *n* 120
brown *adj* 01
brown *n* 01, 141
brown bear *n* 159
brown bread *n* 62
brown flour *n* 62
brown hair *n* 12
bruise *n* 19
brunch *n* 69
Brunei *n* 151, 153
Bruneian *adj* 153
Bruneians *n* 153
brush *n* 34, 141
brush *v* 22
brush your hair *v* 09
brush your teeth *v* 09
Brussels sprouts *n* 55
bubble bath *n* 18, 31
bucket *n* 34, 37, 40
bucket and spade (UK) *n* 134
bucket turn *n* 118
buckle *n* 16
buckled shoes *n* 17
buckwheat flour *n* 62
budgerigar *n* 160, 164
budget *n* 94
budgie *n* 160, 164
buffalo *n* 159
buffer *n* 102
buffet *n* 69
buggy (UK) *n* 00, 115
bugs *n* 162
build *v* 11, 87
builder (UK) *n* 87
building, buildings *n* 42–44, 148
building blocks/bricks *n* 08
building site (UK) *n* 87
built-in wardrobe (UK) *n* 30
bulb *n* 41
Bulgaria *n* 151, 153
Bulgarian *adj* 153
Bulgarians *n* 153
bull *n* 165
bull-nose pliers *n* 36
bull's-eye (US) *n* 140
bulldozer *n* 87
bullet train *n* 102
bulletin board (US) *n* 82
bullseye (UK) *n* 140
bumble bee *n* 162
bump *v* 112
bumper *n* 97
bumps *n* 96
bun *n* 12
bunch *n* 47
bungalow (UK) *n* 32
bungee jumping *n* 125
bunker *n* 115
Bunsen burner *n* 76
buoy *n* 106, 119, 134
bureau de change (UK) *n* 45
burgee *n* 119
burger *n* 70
burger bar *n* 70
burglar alarm *n* 25
burglary *n* 85
Burj Khalifa *n* 44
Burkina Faso *n* 149, 152
Burkinabe *adj* 152
Burkinabes *n* 152
Burma (Myanmar) *n* 150, 153
Burmese *adj* 153
Burmese *n* 164
Burmese people *n* 153
burn *n* 19, 29
burner *n* 27, 103
burrow *v* 159
Burundi *n* 149, 152
Burundian *adj* 152
Burundians *n* 152
bus, buses *n* 43, 99
bus driver *n* 90
bus shelter *n* 99
bus station *n* 42, 99
bus stop *n* 25
bus ticket *n* 99
bus transfer *n* 104
business class *n* 103
business deal *n* 81
business lunch *n* 81
business man *n* 81
business trip *n* 81
businesslike attitude *n* 93
businessman *n* 90
businesswoman *n* 81, 90
bust dart *n* 142
butcher *n* 46, 53, 89
butter *n* 61, 71
butter dish *n* 28
butter knife *n* 27
butterfly, butterflies *n* 77, 118, 162
buttermilk *n* 61
butternut squash *n* 56
buttock *n* 03
button, buttons *n* 15, 142
button acorn squash *n* 56
button hole *n* 15
buy *v* 32, 46
buy groceries *v* 09, 34
buying a house *n* 32
buzz *v* 162

C

cab *n* 50
cabbage *n* 55
cabbage white butterfly *n* 162
cabin *n* 32, 103, 105, 131
cabinet *n* 27
cable *n* 101
cable car *n* 122
cable TV *n* 137
cacti *n* 41
caddy *n* 115
caddy bin *n* 155
cadmium *n* 78
caesium (UK) *n* 78
café *n* 42, 46, 65–66
cafetière *n* 28
cage *n* 164
cake, cakes *n* 63
cake pan (US) *n* 28–29
cake shop (UK) *n* 46
cake tin (UK) *n* 28–29
cake topper *n* 63
calamari *n* 54
calcite *n* 156
calcium *n* 23, 49, 78
calculator *n* 73–74
calendar *n* 82, 172
calf *n* 01, 03, 165
californium *n* 78
call a friend *v* 09
call a plumber *v* 33
call in sick *v* 81
call off *v* 178
call up *v* 178
call your family *v* 09
calligraphy *n* 175
calm *adj* 06, 10, 93
calm down *v* 178
calorie-controlled diet *n* 23
calories *n* 23
Cambodia *n* 150, 153
Cambodian *adj* 153
Cambodians *n* 153
Cambrian *adj* 157
Cambrian *n* 157
camel pose *n* 24
camellia *n* 38
Camembert *n* 64
camera *n* [illegible]
camera crane *n* 84
camera mount *n* 123
camera operator *n* 84, 127
Cameroon *n* 149, 152
Cameroonian *adj* 152
Cameroonians *n* 152
camisole *n* 14
camomile tea (UK) *n* 66
camouflage *n* 88
camp *v* 135
camp bed *n* 135
camper van (UK) *n* 135
campfire *n* 135
campground (US) *n* 135, 148
camping *n* 135
camping equipment *n* 135
camping facilities *n* 135
campion *n* 168
campsite (UK) *n* 135, 148
campus *n* 80
can (US) *n* 52
can opener (US) *n* 28
Canada *n* 150, 152
Canada goose *n* 160

Canadian *adj* 152
Canadians *n* 152
canary *n* 160
Canary melon *n* 58
cancel *v* 69
Cancer *n* 144
candle *n* 26, 30
candle magic *n* 139
candlestick *n* 26
candy (US) *n* 48, 67
candy cane *n* 67
candy floss (UK) *n* 67
candy store (US) *n* 67
canes *n* 40
canines *n* 03
canned (US) *adj* 56
canned drink *n* 70
canned food *n* 48
canned tomato (US) *n* 71
cannelloni *n* 64
cannon *n* 79
Caño Cristales *n* 145
canoe *n* 105
canola oil *n* 60
canopy *n* 103, 125
canopy (US) *n* 97
cantaloupe *n* 58
canter *v* 120
canvas *n* 141
canyon *n* 146
cap *n* 118, 170
cap sleeve *n* 15
capacity *n* 174
cape *n* 147
cape gooseberry *n* 57
Cape Verde *n* 149, 152
Cape Verdean *adj* 152
Cape Verdeans *n* 152
capers *n* 64
capital letters *n* 175
capoeira *n* 117
cappuccino *n* 65
Capricorn *n* 144
capsize *v* 119
capsules *n* 49
captain *n* 105
capuchin monkey *n* 159
capybara *n* 159
car *n* 102
cars *n* 97–99
car exterior *n* 97
car hire (UK) *n* 104
car interior *n* 99
car park (UK) *n* 42
car rental (US) *n* 104
car stereo *n* 99
car theft *n* 85
car wash *n* 97
caravan *n* 135
caravan (UK) *n* 32
caraway seeds *n* 59
carbohydrates *n* 23
carbon *n* 78
carbon dioxide *n* 155
carbonated *adj* 52
Carboniferous *adj* 157
Carboniferous *n* 157
card (UK) *n* 141
card machine *n* 45, 48
cardamom *n* 59
cardboard (US) *n* 141
cardigan *n* 14
cardinal numbers *n* 173
cardiology *n* 21
cardiovascular *n* 04
care for *v* 178
cargo *n* 102, 106
cargo pants (US) *n* 12
cargo plane *n* 103
cargo trousers (UK) *n* 13
caribou *n* 159
caring *adj* 10
carnation *n* 38
carnelian *n* 156
carnival *n* 07
carousel *n* 133
carp *n* 54
carpenter *n* 89
carpentry bit *n* 36
carpet (UK) *n* 30
carpeting (US) *n* 30
carriage *n* 102
carriage race *n* 120
carrier *n* 100
carrier bag (UK) *n* 47, 48
carrot *n* 56
carry *v* 11
carry-on (US) *n* 103–104
carryout (US) *n* 70
cart (US) *n* 102, 104, 115
cartilage *n* 03
cartographer *n* 148
carton *n* 52
cartoon *n* 137
carve *v* 29, 35
carving fork *n* 28
case *n* 22
cash machine *n* 45
cash register (US) *n* 48, 68, 94
cashew, cashews (US) *n* 58, 68
cashew nut, cashew nuts (UK) *n* 58, 68
cashier *n* 45, 48
cassava *n* 56
casserole dish *n* 28
cassowary *n* 160
cast *n* 126–127
cast *v* 121
cast a spell *v* 139
cast-iron plant *n* 167
castle *n* 44
castor oil plant *n* 169
casual clothes *n* 14
casualty *n* 88
cat breeds *n* 164
catamaran *n* 105
catapult *n* 79
cataract *n* 22
catch *v* 11, 107, 113, 121
catch a train *v* 102
catch the bus *v* 09
catch the train *v* 09
catch up *v* 178
catch-up TV *n* 137
catcher *n* 113
catcher glove *n* 110
catering *n* 91
caterpillar *n* 77, 162
catfish *n* 54
cattail *n* 167
cattle *n* 165
cauldron *n* 139
cauliflower *n* 56
caulk *n* 37
cautious *adj* 10
caver *n* 146
caves *n* 146
caving *n* 146
cavity *n* 22
cavolo nero *n* 55
cayenne pepper *n* 59
CD *n* 136
CD player *n* 136
cedar of Lebanon *n* 167
cedilla *n* 175
ceiling *n* 26
ceiling fan *n* 33
celandine *n* 168
celebration cakes *n* 63
celebrations *n* 07
celebrity *n* 137
celeriac *n* 56
celery *n* 55
celery allergy *n* 23
cell *n* 85
cell membrane *n* 77
cell phone (US) *n* 82
cell wall *n* 77
cello *n* 128
Celsius *n* 154
cement *n* 87
cement mixer *n* 87
cemetery *n* 43
Cenozoic (new life) *adj* 157
Cenozoic (new life) *n* 157
centaur *n* 139
center (US) *n* 74, 107, 110, 112
center part (US) *n* 12
center speaker (US) *n* 136
centerboard (US) *n* 119
centimeter (US) *n* 174
centimetre (UK) *n* 174
centipede *n* 162
Central African *adj* 152
Central African Republic *n* 149, 152
Central Africans *n* 152
Central America *n* 150, 152
Central American *adj* 152
Central Americans *n* 152
central reservation (UK) *n* 96
centre (UK) *n* 74, 107, 110, 112
centre circle *n* 109
centre speaker (UK) *n* 136
centre parting (UK) *n* 12
centreboard (UK) *n* 119
centrifugal force *n* 75
centripetal force *n* 75
century *n* 172
CEO (chief executive officer) *n* 81
ceramic *adj* 176
ceramic *n* 176
ceramic hob (UK) *n* 27
ceramic stovetop (US) *n* 27
Cerberus *n* 139
cereal *n* 71
cereal bowl *n* 71
Ceres *n* 143
cerium *n* 78
cervical vertebrae *n* 03
cervix *n* 04
cesium (US) *n* 78
CFL (compact fluorescent lamp) bulb *n* 33
Chad *n* 149, 152
Chadian *adj* 152
Chadians *n* 152
chain *n* 16, 101
chair *n* 26, 82
chair pose *n* 24
chairlift *n* 122
chalet *n* 32, 131
chalk *n* 39, 156
challah *n* 62
chamomile tea (US) *n* 66
Champagne *n* 68
championship *n* 114
change *v* 14
change a light bulb *v* 35
change gear *v* 101
change money *v* 45
change the channel *v* 137
change the sheets *v* 34
change trains *v* 102
changing bag (UK) *n* 08
changing mat *n* 30
changing room (UK) *n* 124
changing rooms *n* 47
changing table *n* 30
channel *n* 137, 147
chanterelle *n* 56, 170
chapati *n* 62
chapter *n* 138
character *n* 138
charcoal *n* 135, 141
charentais *n* 58
charge *n* 50, 75, 85
charge *v* 165
charging cable *n* 83
chariot *n* 79
chase *v* 107
chassis *n* 123
chat *n* 83
chat online *v* 09
chat show (UK) *n* 137
chat with friends *v* 09
check (US) *n* 45, 69, 94
check in *v* 131, 178
check out *v* 131, 178
check the oil *v* 98
check the tires (US) *v* 98
check the tyres (UK) *v* 98
check your emails *v* 09
check-in desk *n* 104
check-up *n* 22
checked (UK) *adj* 13
checkered (US) *adj* 12
checkers (US) *n* 140
checking account (US) *n* 45
checkout *n* 48
cheddar *n* 64
cheek *n* 01
cheerful *adj* 06
cheerleader *n* 107
cheese, cheeses *n* 61, 64, 71
cheese platter *n* 69
cheeseburger *n* 70
cheesecake *n* 63
cheetah *n* 158
chef *n* 69, 90
chef's coat *n* 13
chef's hat *n* 13
chef's uniform *n* 13
Chelsea boots *n* 17
chemical equation *n* 76
chemical formula *n* 76
chemical industry *n* 91
chemical symbol *n* 76
chemist *n* 76
chemistry *n* 73, 76, 80
cheque (UK) *n* 45, 94
chequered flag *n* 123
cherry, cherries *n* 57, 169
cherry tomatoes *n* 55
chervil *n* 59
chess *n* 140
chessboard *n* 140
chest *n* 01
chest compressions *n* 20
chest expander *n* 124
chest of drawers (UK) *n* 30
chest press *n* 124
chest protection *n* 117
chest protector *n* 107
chestnuts *n* 58
chew *v* 52
chewing gum *n* 67
chicane *n* 123
chick *n* 165
chicken *n* 53, 165
chicken burger (UK) *n* 70
chicken coop *n* 86
chicken egg (US) *n* 61
chicken nuggets *n* 70
chicken of the woods *n* 170
chicken sandwich (US) *n* 70
chickenpox *n* 19
chicory *n* 55
chihuahua *n* 164
child *n* 05
child seat *n* 101
childcare provider *n* 90
child's meal (UK) *n* 69

child's pose *n* 24
childbirth *n* 08
childhood *n* 08
children's book *n* 138
children's department *n* 47
children's show (US) *n* 137
children's TV (UK) *n* 137
children's ward *n* 21
Chile (US) *n* 149, 152
chili (US) *n* 56, 60, 64
chili flakes (US) *n* 59
Chilean *adj* 152
Chilean fire bush *n* 167
Chileans *n* 152
chill *n* 19
chill out *v* 178
chilled *adj* 52
chilli (UK) *n* 56, 60, 64
chilli flakes (UK) *n* 59
chilies (US) *n* 59
chilly *adj* 154
chimney *n* 25, 32, 87
chimney pot *n* 25
chimpanzee *n* 159
chin *n* 01
chin strap *n* 107
China *n* 150, 153
Chinese *adj* 153
Chinese characters *n* 175
Chinese hibiscus *n* 169
Chinese hotpot *n* 72
Chinese lantern *n* 169
Chinese mahogany *n* 169
Chinese money plant *n* 38
Chinese people *n* 153
chip *v* 115
chipboard (UK) *n* 35
chipmunk *n* 159
chips (UK) *n* 70
chips (US) *n* 48, 68
chiropractic *n* 24
chisel *n* 36, 141
chives *n* 59
chlorine *n* 78
chloroplast *n* 77
chocolate bar *n* 67
chocolate cake *n* 63
chocolate chip cookie *n* 63
chocolate donut (US) *adj* 63
chocolate doughnut (UK) *adj* 63
chocolate milkshake *n* 61, 65
chocolate spread *n* 60
choir *n* 128
choker *n* 16
cholesterol *n* 23
choose *v* 46
chop *n* 53
chop *v* 29, 39, 117
chopped salad *n* 72
chopping board (UK) *n* 28
chopsticks *n* 27
chord *n* 128
chorizo *n* 53, 64
choux pastry *n* 63
christening *n* 07
Christmas *n* 07
chromium *n* 78, 156
chromosome *n* 77
chrysalis *n* 77
chrysanthemum *n* 38
chuck *n* 35
chukka boots *n* 17
church *n* 43–44
chutes and ladders (US) *n* 140
chutney *n* 60, 72
cider *n* 68
cider vinegar *n* 60
cilantro (US) *n* 59
cinder block (US) *n* 87
cinema (UK) *n* 42, 127
cinematographer *n* 127
cinnamon *n* 59
cinnamon rolls *n* 71
cinnamon stick *n* 59
circle *n* 74
circuit *n* 83
circuit board *n* 75
circuit training *n* 124
circular saw *n* 35
circulation desk (US) *n* 80
circumference *n* 74
circumflex *n* 175
cistern *n* 32
citrine *n* 156
citrus fruit *n* 57
city centre (UK) *n* 42
claimant (UK) *n* 85
clam *n* 54
clamp *n* 35, *n* 76
clap *v* 02
clapper board *n* 84
clarinet *n* 128
class *n* 73
classical *adj* 129
Classicism *n* 130
classroom *n* 73
clavicle *n* 03
claw *n* 161
clay *n* 39, 141
clean *adj* 176
clean the bathroom *v* 34
clean the car *v* 09
clean the oven *v* 34
clean the windows *v* 34
clean up *v* 34, 178
cleaned *adj* 54
cleaner *n* 89
cleaning *n* 34
cleanser *n* 18
clear the table *v* 09, 34
cleat *n* 119
cleaver *n* 28
clementine *n* 57
click *n* 83
client, clients *n* 81, 85
cliff *n* 147
climate *n* 155
climate change *n* 155
climb *v* 11
climber *n* 41
climbing frame (UK) *n* 43
clinch knot *n* 121
clipboard *n* 82
cloak *n* 15
cloakroom *n* 130
cloche *n* 16
clock *n* 44, 171
clock radio *n* 30
clockwise *adv* 148
clogs *n* 17
closed *adj* 48, 132
closed to bicycles *adj* 96
closed to pedestrians *adj* 96
closet (US) *n* 30
cloth *n* 34
clothes *n* 13–15
clothes moth *n* 162
clothes peg (UK) *n* 34
clothes pin (US) *n* 34
clothesline *n* 34
clothing *n* 100
cloud, clouds *n* 51, 154
cloudy *adj* 154
cloves *n* 59
clown *n* 89
clownfish *n* 166
club *n* 140
club sandwich *n* 70
clubhouse *n* 115
clumsy *adj* 10
clutch *n* 99–100
CMS (content management system) *n* 84
co-pilot *n* 103
co-worker *n* 81
CO_2 bubbles *n* 62
coach *n* 99, 112–113
coach's box *n* 113
coal *n* 51
coal mine *n* 51
coastal features *n* 147
coaster *n* 27, 68
coastguard *n* 106
coat hanger *n* 30
coats *n* 15
cobalt *n* 78
cobra pose *n* 24
coccyx *n* 03
cockatiel *n* 164
cockatoo *n* 161
cockerel (UK) *n* 165
cockle *n* 54
cockpit *n* 103, 123
cockroach *n* 162
cocktail *n* 68
cocktail glass *n* 68
cocktail shaker *n* 68
cocoa *n* 169
cocoa powder *n* 65
coconut *n* 58
coconut crab *n* 166
coconut oil *n* 60
coconut palm *n* 167
coconut shell *n* 57
coconut water *n* 65
cocoon *n* 162
cod *n* 166
cod fillet *n* 54
coelophysis *n* 157
coffee *n* 52, 65, 69, 71, 86
coffee cup *n* 27
coffee machine *n* 65, 68
coffee press *n* 28
coffee shop *n* 46
coffee table *n* 26
coins *n* 45, 94
cola *n* 52
colander *n* 28
cold *adj* 154, 176
cold *n* 19
cold frame *v* 39
cold front *n* 155
cold meats *n* 71
cold water *n* 31
collaborate *v* 92
collage *n* 141
collar *n* 15, 142
collarbone *n* 03
collards *n* 55
colleague *n* 07, 81, 92
collect (UK) *v* 11
collection *n* 130
college (US) *n* 43, 80
college departments *n* 80
college schools *n* 80
Colombia *n* 149, 152
Colombian *adj* 152
Colombians *n* 152
colon *n* 175
colored pencils (US) *n* 73
coloring book (US) *n* 138
Colosseum *n* 44
coloured pencils (UK) *n* 73
colouring book (UK) *n* 138
columbine *n* 168
column *n* 44, 146
comb *n* 12
combat aircraft *n* 88
combat sports *n* 117
combination *adj* 18
combine harvester *n* 86
combined events *n* 116
comedian *n* 89
comedy *n* 126–127, 137
comet *n* 143–144
comic *n* 48, 138
comma *n* 175
commence *v* 95
commercial break (US) *n* 137
commercial district *n* 42
commis chef *n* 69
commission *n* 94
common earthball *n* 170
common egg-eater *n* 163
common green iguana *n* 163
common houseleek *n* 168
common poppy *n* 168
common puffball *n* 170
common snake-necked turtle *n* 163
common toad *n* 163
community website *n* 84
commuters *n* 102
Comoran *adj* 152
Comorans *n* 152
Comoros *n* 149, 152
company *n* 81
compartment *n* 102
compass *n* 73–74, 119, 135, 148
competitive *adj* 93
complain *v* 46
complaint *n* 50
compose *v* 128
composer *n* 128
composite (US) *n* 85
compost *n* 40
compost bin *n* 40
compost heap *n* 41
compostable bags *n* 155
composter *n* 40
compound *n* 76
compressed-air cylinder *n* 50
computer, computers *n* 82–83
computer desk *n* 83
computer literacy *n* 93
computing *n* 93
concave lens *n* 75
concealer *n* 18
conceptual art *n* 130
concert hall *n* 43
conchiglie *n* 64
concourse *n* 102
concrete *adj* 176
concrete *n* 35, 176
concussion *n* 19
condensed milk *n* 61
condiment *n* 70
condiments *n* 60, 71–72
conduct *v* 128
conductor *n* 75, 102, 128
cone *n* 74, 87
confectionery (UK) *n* 48
conference *n* 95
confident *adj* 06, 10, 93
confused *adj* 06
confusing *adj* 177
conglomerate *n* 156
Congolese *adj* 152
Congolese people *n* 152
coniferous forest *n* 146
conifers *n* 41, 157, 167
connection *n* 104
conning tower *n* 105
conservation *n* 130
considerate *adj* 10
console *n* 136

constellation, constellations *n* 144
construction *n* 87, 91
construction ahead (US) *n* 96
construction site (US) *n* 87
construction waste *n* 33
construction worker (US) *n* 87, 90
contact *n* 83
contact lens, contact lenses *n* 22, 49
contact lens solution *n* 22
container *n* 105
container port *n* 106
container ship *n* 105–106
containers *n* 52
contents *n* 138
continent *n* 145
contours *n* 148
contract *n* 92
control tower *n* 104
controller *n* 136
controls *n* 100, 136
convenience food *n* 23, 48
conversion *n* 108
convert the attic *v* 35
convert the loft *v* 35
convertible *n* 97
convex lens *n* 73
conveyor belt *n* 48
cook dinner *v* 09
cookbook *n* 138
cooked *adj* 56
cooked breakfast *n* 71
cooked meat *n* 53, 64
cooked vegetables *n* 72
cookie *n* 63, 84
cooking *n* 29
cooking show *n* 137
cooksonia *n* 157
cool *adj* 154
cool down *v* 124
coolant reservoir *n* 98
cooler *n* 135
cooling rack *n* 29
cooling system *n* 98
cooling tower *n* 51
coordinate *v* 92
coordinates *n* 148
coot *n* 161
copernicium *n* 78
copper *n* 78, 156
copy *v* 11
copyright *n* 175
cor anglais (UK) *n* 128
coral *n* 166
coral reef *n* 118, 166
coral reef fish *n* 118
coral trout *n* 166
cordless drill *n* 35
core *n* 57
coriander (UK) *n* 59
coriander seeds *n* 59
cork *n* 60
corkscrew *n* 28, 68
cormorant *n* 160
corn *n* 55, 86
corn bread *n* 62
corn oil *n* 60
cornea *n* 22
corned beef (US) *n* 64
corner *n* 109
corner flag *n* 109
corner kick *n* 109
cornerback *n* 107
cornichons *n* 60
cornrows *n* 12
corpse pose *n* 24
correct *adj* 176
correction fluid *n* 82
corset (US) *n* 14
cortado *n* 65
cosmetics (US) *n* 47
Costa Rica *n* 150, 152
Costa Rican *adj* 152
Costa Ricans *n* 152
costume, costumes *n* 13, 126–127
costume drama *n* 137
cot (UK) *n* 30
cotoneaster *n* 169
cottage *n* 32
cottage cheese *n* 61
cottage garden *n* 41
cotton *adj* 176
cotton *n* 13, 86, 176
cotton balls *n* 18
cotton candy (US) *n* 67
cotton pads (US) *n* 20
cotton reel (UK) *n* 142
cotton wool (UK) *n* 20
couch *n* 26
couch potato *n* 137
cough *n* 19
cough *v* 20
cough medicine *n* 49
counsellor (UK) *n* 24
counselor (US) *n* 24
count *v* 11, 74
counter *n* 45, 131
counterclockwise (UK) *adv* 148
counterfeit money *n* 94
countertop (US) *n* 27
counterweight *n* 87
country, countries *n* 129, 149–150
countryside *n* 146
couple *n* 07
coupling rod *n* 102
coupon (US) *n* 48
courgette (UK) *n* 56
courier *n* 45
course book *n* 138
court *n* 85, 112
court case *n* 85
court date *n* 85
court officer *n* 85
court official *n* 85
court reporter *n* 85
courthouse (US) *n* 43
courtroom *n* 85
courtyard *n* 25, 41
cousin *n* 05
cover *n* 111, 138
coveralls *n* 13
cover letter *n* 92
cow *n* 165
cowcatcher *n* 102
co-worker *n* 92
cow's milk *n* 61
cowboy boots *n* 17
cowboy hat *n* 16
cowslip *n* 169
crab *n* 54, 134
crab apple *n* 58, 169
cradle *n* 50
craft market *n* 132
crafts *n* 141–142
cramp, cramps *n* 19, 118
cranberry *n* 57
cranberry juice *n* 65
crane *n* 106, 160
crash barrier (UK) *n* 96
crater *n* 143, 145
crawl *v* 11
crayfish *n* 54
cream *n* 49, 61, 71
cream cheese *n* 61
creative *adj* 93
credit card *n* 45, 94
creep *v* 11
creeper *n* 41
crème pâtissière *n* 63
crêpe *n* 70
crescent moon *n* 143
cress *n* 55
crest *n* 161
crested owl *n* 161
Cretaceous *adj* 157
Cretaceous *n* 157
crew *n* 119
crew cut *n* 12
crew hatch *n* 143
crib (US) *n* 30
cricket *n* 111, 162
cricket ball *n* 111
cricket equipment *n* 111
cricket pitch *n* 111
cricket positions *n* 111
cricket shoes *n* 111
crime *n* 85, 137
crime drama *n* 127
crime fiction *n* 138
crime scene *n* 50
criminal *n* 85
criminal record *n* 85
crisp *adj* 57
crispbread *n* 62, 71
crisper (US) *n* 27
crisps (UK) *n* 48, 68
critical *adj* 10
Croatia *n* 151, 153
Croatian *adj* 153
Croats *n* 153
crochet *n* 142
crochet hook *n* 142
crockery (UK) *n* 27
crocodile clip (UK) *n* 75
crocus *n* 38, 167
croissant *n* 62, 71
crop *n* 12
crop farm *n* 86
cropped *adj* 13
crops *n* 86
croquet *n* 133
cross-country skiing *n* 122
cross-section of tooth *n* 03
cross-trainer (UK) *n* 124
crossbar *n* 101, 108, 116
crosse *n* 110
crossroads (UK) *n* 43
crow *n* 160
crow *v* 165
crow pose *n* 24
crown *n* 22
crucible *n* 76
crudités *n* 72
cruise missile *n* 88
cruise ship *n* 105
cruiser *n* 88
crumpled *adj* 13
crunchy *adj* 52, 56
crust *n* 62, 145
crutches *n* 19
cry *v* 02
crystal *n* 76
crystal ball *n* 131
crystal healing *n* 24
crystalized honey (US) *n* 60
cub *n* 159
Cuba *n* 150, 152
Cuban *adj* 152
Cubans *n* 152
cube *n* 74
cubic meter (US) *n* 174
cubic metre (UK) *n* 174
Cubism *n* 130
cucumber *n* 55
cue *n* 125
cue ball *n* 125
cuff *n* 15, 21, 142
cufflinks *n* 16
cultivate *v* 39
cultivated mushrooms *n* 170
cumin *n* 59
cupcake *n* 63
curator *n* 130
curb (US) *n* 43
cured *adj* 72
cured meat *n* 53, 64
curious *adj* 06, 93
curium *n* 78
curlew *n* 161
curling *n* 122
curling brush *n* 122
curling iron (US) *n* 12
curling stone *n* 122
curly hair *n* 12
currant *n* 58
currency *n* 45, 94
currency exchange (US) *n* 45, 104
current account (UK) *n* 45
current affairs *n* 137
curry *n* 72
curry powder *n* 59
curtain, curtains *n* 26, 126
curved *adj* 74
cushion (UK) *n* 26
custard *n* 63
custard slice *n* 63
customer, customers *n* 45, 48, 65, 69
customer service *n* 47, 93
customer-focused *adj* 93
customs *n* 104
customs house (UK) *n* 106
customhouse (US) *n* 106
cut *n* 19
cut (US) *n* 53
cut *v* 29, 35, 142
cut down on *v* 23
cute *adj* 177
cuticle *n* 02
cutlery (UK) *n* 26, 27
cuts *n* 53
cuts of meat *n* 53
cutting board (US) *n* 28
CV (UK) *n* 92
cycad *n* 167
cycle *v* 101
cycle lane (UK) *n* 101
cycle parking *n* 43
cycle path *n* 43
cycling *n* 101, 133
cycling shoe *n* 17
cylinder *n* 74
cylinder head *n* 98
cymbals *n* 128
Cypriot *adj* 153
Cypriots *n* 153
Cyprus *n* 151, 153
Cyrillic alphabet *n* 175
cytoplasm *n* 77
Czech *adj* 153
Czech Republic *n* 151, 153
Czechs *n* 153

D

dachshund *n* 164
dad *n* 05
daffodil *n* 38
daily *adj* 172
daily *adv* 172
daily life *n* 178
daily routines *n* 09
dairy *n* 23, 48
dairy allergy *n* 23
dairy farm *n* 86
dairy produce *n* 61
dairy-free *adj* 23
daisy *n* 38
Dalmatian *n* 164
dam *n* 51
dance *n* 129

dance *v* 11
dance school *n* 80
dancer *n* 89
dandelion *n* 38, 55
dandruff *n* 12
Danes *n* 153
danger area *n* 117
Danish *adj* 153
dark *adj* 60, 176
dark chocolate *n* 67
darmstadtium *n* 78
darn *v* 142
dart, darts *n* 140, 142
dartboard *n* 140
Darwin's frog *n* 163
dash *n* 29, 175
dashboard and controls *n* 99
date *n* 57–58
date palm *n* 167
daughter *n* 05
daughter-in-law *n* 05
dawn *n* 171
day *n* 171–172
Day of the Dead *n* 07
dead ball line *n* 108
Dead sea *n* 145
deadhead *v* 39
deadly nightshade *n* 169
deal *v* 140
death angel *n* 170
death cap *n* 170
debit card *n* 45, 94
decade *n* 172
decay *n* 22
December *n* 172
decide *v* 11
deciduous *n* 41
decimals *n* 173
decision-making *n* 93
decisive *adj* 10
deck *n* 103
deck chair *n* 134
deck of cards *n* 140
decking *n* 41
decorate *v* 29, 63
decorating *n* 37
decoration *n* 63
decorator *n* 37
deep *adj* 176
deep diving *n* 118
deep end *n* 118
deep sea fishing *n* 121
deep-fried *adj* 72
deep-tread tire (US) *n* 100
deep-tread tyre (UK) *n* 100
deer crossing *n* 96
deerstalker *n* 16
defence (UK) *n* 85, 107
defendant (US) *n* 85
defender *n* 109
defending zone *n* 110
defense (US) *n* 85, 107
defensive specialist *n* 112
defibrillator *n* 50
deforestation *n* 155
defrost the freezer *v* 34
degree *n* 80
degrees *n* 154
delay *n* 102
delete *v* 83
deli *n* 48
delicatessen *n* 46, 64
delicious *adj* 52, 177
delighted *adj* 06
delivery *n* 45
delivery man *n* 48
delta *n* 147
deltoid *n* 03
Democratic Republic of the Congo *n* 149, 152
den (US) *n* 26
denim *n* 13
denim jacket *n* 15
Denmark *n* 151, 153
denomination *n* 74, 94
dental care *n* 49
dental floss *n* 22
dental floss *n* 31
dental history *n* 22
dental mirror *n* 22
dental hygienist *n* 22
dental surgery (UK) *n* 22
dental X-ray *n* 22
dentist *n* 22, 89
dentist chair *n* 22
dentist's office (US) *n* 22
dentures *n* 22
deodorant *n* 49
department store *n* 47
departments *n* 21, 91
departure, departures *n* 43, 104
departure board *n* 102
departure lounge *n* 104
deposit *n* 32
depressed *adj* 06
depth *n* 74
depth gauge *n* 118
Derby shoes *n* 17
derelict building (UK) *n* 44
dermatology *n* 21
derrick *n* 51
descaled *adj* 54
descent module *n* 143
describing abilities *n* 11
describing actions *n* 11
describing clothes *n* 13
describing fruit *n* 57
describing personalities *n* 10
describing things *n* 176–177
desert *n* 146
desert boots *n* 17
desert ironwood tree *n* 169
desertification *n* 155
design and technology *n* 73
designer *n* 89
designer labels *n* 47
desk *n* 73, 82
desktop computer *n* 83
dessert, desserts *n* 63, 69
dessert cart (US) *n* 69
destination *n* 104
destroyer *n* 88
detached house *n* 32
detective *n* 50
determined *adj* 93
detour (US) *n* 96
detox *n* 23
deuce *n* 114
Devanagari script *n* 175
Devonian *adj* 157
Devonian *n* 157
dewlap *n* 159
diabetes *n* 19
diagonal *adj* 74
diameter *n* 74
diamond *n* 140, 156
diamond back terrapin *n* 163
diaper (US) *n* 08
diaper bag (US) *n* 08
diaper rash cream (US) *n* 08
diarrhea (US)
diarrhoea (UK) *n* 19
diary (UK) *n* 82, 138
dice *n* 140
dice *v* 29
dictionary *n* 73, 138
didgeridoo *n* 129
die *v* 07
diesel *n* 97
diesel train *n* 102
diffraction *n* 75
diffusion *n* 76
dig *n* 79
dig *v* 11, 39, 112
digestif *n* 69
digestive *n* 04
digger *n* 87
digital *adj* 84
digital box *n* 136
digital currency *n* 94
digital projector *n* 73, 82
digital screen *n* 136
digital wallet *n* 94
Dijon mustard *n* 60
dill *n* 59–60
dimensions *n* 74
dimetrodon *n* 157
dimples *n* 12
dine *v* 52
dining car *n* 102
dining hall (US) *n* 80
dining room *n* 26
dinner *n* 26, 72
dinner menu (US) *n* 69
dinner party *n* 26
dinner plate *n* 27
dinnerware (US) *n* 27
diode *n* 75
diploma *n* 80
dipstick *n* 98
dire *adj* 177
direct current *n* 33, 75
direct debit *n* 45
direct flight *n* 104
direction of revolution *n* 143
direction to follow *n* 96
directions *n* 132, 148, 180
director *n* 84, 126–127
director's chair *n* 84
dirty *adj* 176
dirty clothes (US) *n* 34
dirty washing (UK) *n* 34
disabled parking *n* 96
disappointed *adj* 06, 177
disastrous *adj* 177
discharge *v* 21
discount voucher (UK) *n* 48
discus *n* 116
discuss *v* 73
disembark *v* 106
disgusted *adj* 06
disgusting *adj* 52, 177
dish rack *n* 27
dish towel (UK) *n* 28
dishcloth (US) *n* 28
dishes *n* 72
dishonest *adj* 10
dishwasher *n* 27, 34
dishwasher tablets *n* 34
dishwashing liquid (US) *n* 34
Disir *n* 139
dismount *v* 100
dispensary *n* 49
dispersion *n* 75
display *n* 21, 136
disposable razor *n* 31
dissertation *n* 80
distance *n* 174
distracted *adj* 06
distributor *n* [illegible]
districts *n* 42
dive *v* 118
diver *n* 118
diversion (UK) *n* 96
divide *v* 74
divided highway (US) *n* 96
dividends *n* 94
divider *n* 96
diving *n* 118
diving board *n* 118
diving tower *n* 118
division sign *n* 74
divorce *n* 07
divorced *adj* 05
Diwali *n* 07
DIY (do it yourself) *n* 47
DIY equipment *n* 35
dizzy *adj* 19
DJ *n* 84
DJ console *n* 129
Djibouti *n* 149, 152
Djiboutian *adj* 152
Djiboutians *n* 152
DM someone *v* 84
DNA *n* 77
do homework *v* 09, 11
do not bend *phr* 45
do the dishes *v* 09, 34
do the ironing *v* 34
do the laundry *v* 34
do the weeding *v* 39
do up *v* 178
Doberman *n* 164
dock *v* 106
docks *n* 106
doctor *n* 19–21, 89
doctor's surgery (UK) *n* 20
doctorate *n* 80
document *n* 79
documentary *n* 137
dog *n* 122
dog breeds *n* 164
dog rose *n* 169
dog sledding *n* 122
doghouse (US) *n* 164
dogsled *n* 122
doll *n* 08
doll's house (UK) *n* 08
dollhouse (US) 08
dolphin *n* 166
dolphin pose *n* 24
dome *n* 44
domestic flight *n* 104
Dominica *n* 150, 152
Dominican *adj* 152
Dominican Republic *n* 150, 152
Dominicans *n* 152
dominoes *n* 140
donation *n* 130
donkey *n* 165
donut (US) *n* 63, 70
door *n* 99, 102
door buzzer (UK) *n* 25
door chain *n* 25–26
door handle *n* 25–26, 97, 99
door knocker *n* 25
door lock *n* 99
doorbell *n* 25
doormat *n* 25–26
dorm *n* 131
dormer *n* 25
dorms (US) *n* 80
dosa *n* 72
dosage *n* 49
double *adj* 68
double bass *n* 128
double bed *n* 30
double burner camping stove *n* 135
double cream (UK) *n* 61
double espresso *n* 65
double fault *n* 114
double quotation mark *n* 175
double room *n* 131
double star *n* 144
double-decker bus *n* 99
doubles *n* 114
dough *n* 62
doughnut (UK) *n* 63, 70

downhill skiing *n* 122
download *v* 83
downpour *n* 154
downstairs *adv*, *n* 25
downtown (US) *n* 42
downward dog *n* 24
doze off *v* 178
draft *n* 83
drag racing *n* 123
dragon *n* 139
dragon tree *n* 38, 167
dragonfly *n* 162
drain *n* 31, 33, 43
drainage *n* 39
drama *n* 73, 127
draughts (UK) *n* 140
draw *v* 73
draw (UK) *v* 109
drawbridge *n* 44
drawer *n* 27, 30, 82
drawing *n* 141
drawing pin (UK) *n* 82
dreadful *adj* 177
dream *n* 30
drepanaspis *n* 157
dress *n* 14
dress circle (UK) *n* 126
dress pattern *n* 142
dress up *v* 178
dressage *n* 120
dressed *adj* 72
dresser (US) *n* 30
dressing *n* 20, 72
dressing gown (UK) *n* 14
dressing table (UK) *n* 30
dried apricots *n* 58
dried beans *n* 55
dried fig *n* 58
dried fruit *n* 58, 71
dried yeast *n* 62
drill *n* 22
drill *v* 35
drill bit, drill bits *n* 35–36
drilling rig *n* 51
drink *v* 52
drink tea or coffee *v* 09
drink water *v* 20
drinking *n* 52
drinks *n* 48, 52, 68
drip (UK) *n* 21
drip stand (UK) *n* 21
drive *v* 09, 95, 115
driver *n* 90, 99
driver's cab *n* 102
driver's seat *n* 99
driveshaft *n* 98
driving instructor *n* 89
drizzle *n* 154
dromedary *n* 158
drop anchor *v* 106
drop someone off *v* 98
dropper *n* 76
drops *n* 49
dropshot *n* 114
drought *n* 154
drug dealing *n* 85
drummer *n* 129
dry *adj* 18, 154
dry hair *n* 12
dry-cleaner's *n* 46
dry dock *n* 106
dry the dishes *v* 34
dry your hair *v* 09
dry yourself *v* 31
dry-cured meat *n* 64
dual carriageway (UK) *n* 96
dubnium *n* 78
duck *n* 53, 165
duck egg *n* 61
duckling *n* 165
due date *n* 08
duffel (US) *n* 16
duffle coat *n* 15
dull *adj* 176
dumbbell *n* 124
dummy (UK) *n* 08
dump truck (US) *n* 87
dumper truck (UK) *n* 87
dumplings *n* 70, 72
dumpster (US) *n* 25
dune *n* 147
dune buggy (US) *n* 97, 134
dungarees (UK) *n* 13
dunk *v* 112
duplex (US) *n* 32
dusk *n* 171
dust *v* 34
dustbin (UK) *n* 25
duster *n* 34
dustpan *n* 34
dustsheet *n* 37
Dutch *adj* 153
Dutch *n* 153
duty belt *n* 50
duty-free shop *n* 104
duvet *n* 30
DVD *n* 136
dwarf *n* 139
dwarf planets *n* 143
dynamo *n* 101
dysprosium *n* 78

E

e-reader *n* 83, 138
eagle owl *n* 161
ear *n* 01
ear muffs *n* 87
ear phone *n* 88
ear protectors *n* 87
ear thermometer *n* 20
early *adj* 171
early *adv* 171
early human *n* 157
earn *v* 81
earphones *n* 136
earrings *n* 16
Earth *n* 143, 145
earth tremor *n* 145
earthing (UK) *n* 33
earthquake *n* 145
easel *n* 82, 141
east *n* 148
East Timor *n* 151, 153
Easter *n* 07
eastern coral snake *n* 163
eat *v* 52
eat breakfast *v* 09
eat dinner *v* 09
eat in *v* 70
eat lunch *v* 09
eat out *v* 69, 178
eating *n* 52
eccentric *adj* 10
echidna *n* 158
éclair *n* 63
eclectus parrot *n* 161
economic downturn *n* 94
economics *n* 80
economy class *n* 103
ecosystem *n* 77, 155
ecotourism *n* 131
ecstatic *adj* 06
Ecuador *n* 149, 152
Ecuadorian *adj* 152
Ecuadorians *n* 152
eczema *n* 19
Edam *n* 64
editor *n* 89
education *n* 91
eel *n* 54
efficient *adj* 93
egg, eggs *n* 61, 77
egg allergy *n* 23
egg cup *n* 27, 61
egg slicer *n* 28
egg timer *n* 28
egg white *n* 61, 71
eggplant (US) *n* 56
eggshell *n* 161
Egypt *n* 149, 152
Egyptian *adj* 152
Egyptian goose *n* 160
Egyptians *n* 152
Eid al-Fitr *n* 07
Eiffel Tower *n* 44
eight *num* 173
eighteen *num* 173
eighth *num* 173
eighty *num* 173
einsteinium *n* 78
El Salvador *n* 150, 152
elbow *n* 01
elbow pads *n* 107
elderberry *n* 57
elderly *adj* 05
electric bike *n* 101
electric blanket *n* 30
electric car *n* 97
electric charge point (UK) *n* 97
electric drill *n* 35
electric field *n* 75
electric guitar *n* 129
electric guitarist *n* 129
electric hook-up *n* 135
electric kettle *n* 27
electric lines *n* 102
electric motorcycle *n* 100
electric pump *n* 135
electric razor *n* 31
electric scooter *n* 100
electric shock *n* 19
electric train *n* 102
electrical appliances *n* 47
electrical goods *n* 48
electrical waste *n* 33
electrician *n* 89
electricity *n* 33, 51, 75
electricity meter *n* 33
electrics *n* 33
electromagnetic spectrum *n* 75
electron *n* 76
electronics *n* 91
electronics store *n* 46
elements *n* 76
elevator (US) *n* 25, 47, 131
eleven *num* 173
elf *n* 139
elf owl *n* 161
elixir *n* 139
ellipsis *n* 175
elliptical (US) *n* 124
elliptical galaxy *n* 144
elm *n* 169
email *n* 83
embarrassed *adj* 06
embroidery *n* 142
embryo *n* 08
emerald *n* 156
emerald toucan *n* 160
emerald tree boa *n* 163
emergency brake (US) *n* 99
emergency department *n* 50
emergency exit *n* 103, 131
emergency signal *n* 102
emergency phone *n* 96
emergency room *n* 21
emergency services *n* 50
emergency vehicle beacon *n* 50
emigrate *v* 07
Emirati *adj* 153
Emiratis *n* 153
emissions *n* 51, 155
emoji, emojis *n* 84, 175
empanada *n* 70
emperor *n* 79
emperor moth *n* 162
emperor penguin *n* 161
empire *n* 79
Empire State Building *n* 44
employee *n* 81
employer *n* 81
employment *adj* 81
empress *n* 79
empty *adj* 176
emu *n* 160
emulsion *n* 37
en suite bathroom (UK) *n* 131
enamel *n* 03
encore *n* 126
encyclopedia *n* 73, 138
end line *n* 107
end zone *n* 107, 110
endangered species *n* 155
endive *n* 55
endline *n* 112
endocrine *n* 04
endocrinology *n* 21
endoskeleton *n* 77
energetic *adj* 93
energy *n* 23, 51, 91
energy drink *n* 52
engaged couple *n* 07
engine *n* 98, 100, 103
engine intake *n* 123
engine room *n* 105
engineer *n* 90
engineering *n* 80
English *n* 73
English bluebell *n* 167
English horn (US) *n* 128
English mustard *n* 60
engraving *n* 141
Enlightenment *n* 79
enoki mushroom *n* 56, 170
ENT *n* 21
enter *v* 11
entertainment *n* 91
enthusiastic *adj* 10
entrance *n* 130
entrance fee *n* 132
entrée (US) *n* 69
envelope *n* 45, 82, 103
environment *n* 155
environmental issues *n* 155
épée *n* 117
epiglottis *n* 04
episode *n* 137
equals *n* 74
equation *n* 74
Equator *n* 145
Equatorial Guinea *n* 149, 152
Equatorial Guinean *adj* 152
Equatorial Guineans *n* 152
equity *n* 94
eraser (US) *n* 73, 82
erbium *n* 78
Eritrea *n* 149, 152
Eritrean *adj* 152
Eritreans *n* 152
erupt *v* 145
escalator *n* 47, 104
esophagus (US) *n* 04
espadrilles *n* 17
espresso *n* 65
espresso maker *n* 27
essay *n* 73
essential oils *n* 24
estate (UK) *n* 97
estate agent (UK) *n* 32, 89
Estonia *n* 151, 153
Estonian *adj* 153
Estonians *n* 153

estuary *n* 147
Eswatini *n* 149, 152
Ethiopia *n* 149, 152
Ethiopian *adj* 152
Ethiopians *n* 152
Europe *n* 151, 153
European *adj* 153
European badger *n* 158
European common frog *n* 163
European robin *n* 160
Europeans *n* 153
europium *n* 78
EV charging station (US) *n* 97
eave *n* 32, 44
evening *n* 09, 171
evening dress *n* 15
evening menu (UK) *n* 69
evening primrose *n* 38
evergreen *n* 41
every day *adv* 172
every other day *adv* 172
evidence *n* 50, 85
evolution *n* 77
ewe *n* 165
ex-husband *n* 05
ex-wife *n* 05
exam *n* 73
excavation *n* 79, 87
excess baggage *n* 104
exchange *v* 46
exchange rate *n* 45, 94
excited *adj* 06
exciting *adj* 177
exclamation mark *n* 175
exercise *v* 09, 20
exercise ball *n* 124
exercise bike *n* 124
exercise book *n* 73
exercise class *n* 124
exercise mat *n* 124
exercises *n* 124
exhaust fan (US) *n* 27
exhaust pipe *n* 98, 100
exhausted *adj* 06
exhausting *adj* 177
exhibit *n* 130
exhibition *n* 130
exit *n* 48
exit *v* 11
exit ramp *n* 96
exoskeleton *n* 77
exosphere *n* 155
exotic shorthair *n* 164
expenditure *n* 94
experiment *n* 76
expiration date (US) *n* 49
expiry date (UK) *n* 49
extend *v* 124
extension cord (US) *n* 35
extension lead (UK) *n* 35
extra virgin *adj* 60
extraction *n* 22
extractor fan (UK) *n* 27
extraordinary *adj* 177
extras *n* 127
eye, eyes *n* 01, 121, 142
eye drops *n* 22
eye mask *n* 14
eyeball *n* 22
eyebrow *n* 01
eyebrow brush *n* 18
eyebrow pencil *n* 18
eyecup *n* 136
eyelashes *n* 01
eyelet *n* 17
eyelid *n* 01
eyeliner *n* 18
eyepiece *n* 77, 144
eyeshadow *n* 18

F

fabric *n* 142
fabric softener *n* 34
face *n* 01
face cream *n* 31
face mask *n* 18
face mask *n* 20, 107, 110
face powder *n* 18
face wash *n* 18
face-off *n* 110
face-off spot *n* 110
facemask *n* 111
facial *n* 18
facial hair *n* 12
facilities *n* 91
factory *n* 42
Fahrenheit *n* 154
fail *v* 73
faint *v* 20
fairway *n* 115
fairy *n* 139
fairy elephant's feet *n* 168
fairy ring *n* 170
fairy tale *n* 138–139
falafel *n* 70
fall (US) *n* 57, 172
fall *v* 11, 117
fall in love *v* 07
fall leaf *n* 169
fallopian tube *n* 04
fallow deer *n* 158
false teeth *n* 22
family *n* 05
family tent *n* 135
famous buildings *n* 44
fan *n* 33
fan belt *n* 98
fan space heater *n* 33
fans *n* 107, 109, 129
fantastic *adj* 177
fantastic creatures *n* 139
fantasy *n* 127, 138–139
far *adj* 176
fare *n* 99, 102
farm *n* 86, 165
farm animals *n* 165
farmer *n* 79, 86, 89
farmers' market *n* 23
farmhouse *n* 86
farming *n* 86, 91
farming terms *n* 86
farmland *n* 86, 146
farmyard *n* 86
farsighted (US) *adj* 22
fashion *n* 91
fashion accessories *n* 16
fashion designer *n* 90
fashion store *n* 47
fast *adj* 176
fast food *n* 47, 70
fast forward *v* 137
fast-food restaurant *n* 70
fasten *v* 14
fastening *n* 16
fat free *adj* 61
father *n* 05
father-in-law *n* 05
faucet (US) *n* 27, 31, 33
fault *n* 114
faun *n* 139
fava beans (US) *n* 55
feather duster *n* 34
feather *n* 161
feathers displayed *n* 161
February *n* 172
fedora *n* 16
feed *v* 86
feed the cat *v* 09
feed the dog *v* 09
feed the pets *v* 34
feel better *v* 20
feelings *n* 06
feet *n* 02
feet-first *adj* 118
feijoa *n* 58
female *n* 04
feminine hygiene *n* 49
femur *n* 03
fence *n* 41, 86
fencing *n* 116–117
feng shui *n* 24
fennec fox *n* 158
fennel *n* 55, 59
fennel seeds *n* 59
fenugreek leaves *n* 59
fermium *n* 78
fern, ferns *n* 41, 156, 167
ferret *n* 164
ferris wheel *n* 133
ferrule *n* 115
ferry *n* 105–106
ferry route *n* 148
ferry terminal *n* 106
fertilize *v* 39
fertilizer *n* 39
festivals *n* 07
feta *n* 64
fetus *n* 08
fever *n* 19
fez *n* 16
fiancé *n* 07
fiancée *n* 07
fiber (US) *n* 23, 57
fiberglass (US) *adj* 176
fiberglass (US) *n* 176
fibre (UK) *n* 23, 57
fibreglass (UK) *adj* 176
fibreglass (UK) *n* 176
fibula *n* 03
fiction *n* 138
fiddler crab *n* 166
field *n* 107, 113, 146
field (US) *n* 109
field *v* 111, 113
field events *n* 116
field hockey *n* 110
field hockey player *n* 110
field hospital *n* 88
field mushroom *n* 170
fielding positions *n* 111
fifteen *num* 173
fifth *num* 173
fifty *num* 173
fifty-yard line *n* 107
fig *n* 169
fighter *n* 88
figure skating *n* 122
Fiji *n* 150, 153
Fijian *adj* 153
Fijians *n* 153
filament *n* 38
file, files *n* 36, 82
filet (US) *n* 53
filing cabinet *n* 82
Filipino *adj* 153
Filipinos *n* 153
fill *v* 37
fill out *v* 178
fill out a form *v* 92
fill up *v* 98, 178
filler *n* 37
fillet (UK) *n* 53
fillet *n* 54
filling *n* 22, 63, 70
film set *n* 127
film star (UK) *n* 127
film studio *n* 127
films (UK) *n* 127
filo (UK) *n* 63
filter coffee *n* 65
filter paper *n* 76
fin *n* 103
final whistle *n* 109
finance *n* 91, 94
financial advisor *n* 94
finch *n* 160
finderscope *n* 144
finds *n* 79
fine *n* 85
fine leg *n* 111
fingernail *n* 02
fingerprint *n* 50
finish line *n* 116, 123
finish work *v* 09
Finland *n* 151, 153
Finnish *adj* 153
Finns *n* 153
fins *n* 118, 134
fir *n* 167
fire *n* 50
fire alarm *n* 50
fire brigade (UK) *n* 50
fire department (US) *n* 50
fire engine *n* 50
fire escape *n* 50
fire extinguisher *n* 50
fire salamander *n* 163
fire station *n* 42, 50
fire tree *n* 168
firefighter, firefighters *n* 50, 89
firefighter's uniform *n* 13
firelighter (UK) *n* 135
firepit *n* 135
fireplace *n* 26
firestarter (US) *n* 135
first *num* 173
first-aid bag *n* 50
first base *n* 113
first floor (UK) *n* 25, 47
first floor (US) *n* 25, 47
first-aid kit *n* 20, 49
fish *n* 48, 54, 164
fish and chips *n* 70
fish box *n* 54
fish farm *n* 86
fish sauce *n* 60
fish slice (UK) *n* 28
fish tank *n* 164
fisherman *n* 89
fishhook *n* 121
fishing *n* 91, 121
fishing license (US) *n* 121
fishing permit (UK) *n* 121
fishing port *n* 106
fishing rod *n* 121
fishing vest *n* 121
fishmonger *n* 18, 54, 89
fission *n* 75
fissures *n* 51
fist *n* 02
fit *v* 14, 46
fit a carpet (UK) *v* 35
fitted *adj* 13
five *num* 173
five hundred *num* 173
five past one *n* 171
five positions *n* 112
five spice *n* 59
five to two *n* 171
fix *v* 11
fix a fence *v* 35
fix a puncture *v* 101
fix up *v* 178
fixed menu (US) *n* 69
fizzy drink (UK) *n* 70
fjord *n* 147
flag *n* 115
flagstone *n* 35
flamenco dress *n* 15
flamingo *n* 160
flan *n* 64
flan pan (US) *n* 29
flan tin (UK) *n* 29
flap *v* 161
flare *n* 51, 119, 144
flashlight (US) *n* 135

flask *n* 76
flat *adj* 128
flat (UK) *n* 25
flat cap *n* 16
flat-head screwdriver *n* 36
flat race *n* 120
flat tire (US) *n* 98
flat tyre (UK) *n* 98
flat white *n* 65
flat wood bit *n* 36
flatbed truck *n* 87
flatbread *n* 62
flats *n* 17
flavored oil (US) *n* 60
flavoured oil (UK) *n* 60
flax *n* 86
fledgling *n* 161
flerovium *n* 78
flesh *n* 58
flex *v* 124
flexible *adj* 93, 176
flexitime (UK) *n* 81
flextime (US) *n* 81
flight attendant, flight attendants *n* 90, 103–104
flight instructor *n* 90
flight number *n* 104
flint *n* 156
flint tools *n* 79
flip *n* 118
flip chart *n* 82, 95
flip through *v* 138
flip-flops *n* 17, 134
flipper, flippers *n* 15, 118, 134
flipper (US) *n* 28
float *n* 118, 121
float *v* 118
floating crane *n* 106
flock of sheep *n* 165
flood *n* 154
flood plain *n* 147
floor *n* 25–26, 30
floor length *adj* 15
floor mat *n* 125
floor plan *n* 130, 132
floorboards *n* 26
Florentine *n* 63
floret *n* 55
florist *n* 46–47, 89
floss *v* 22
flours *n* 62
flower anatomy *n* 38
flower stall *n* 47
flowerbed *n* 41
flowering plants *n* 157
flowering shrub *n* 41
flu *n* 19
fluent in languages *adj* 93
fluid ounce *n* 174
fluorine *n* 78
flute *n* 128–129
fly *n* 121, 162, 168
fly *v* 11, 162
fly agaric *n* 170
fly fishing *n* 121
fly-half *n* 108
flying carpet *n* 139
flying fish *n* 166
flying kick *n* 117
flying reptiles *n* 157
flying squirrel *n* 158
flyover *n* 96
flysheet (UK) *n* 135
FM *adj* 84
foal *n* 120, 165
focusing knob *n* 77, 144
foetus (UK) *n* 08
fog *n* 154
foggy *adj* 154
foil *n* 117
fold *v* 14
fold clothes *v* 34
folders *n* 82
folding grill *n* 135
foliage *n* 47
folk blouse *n* 15
folk music *n* 129
follow *v* 84
follower *n* 84
food *n* 65, 91
food allergies *n* 23
food bowl *n* 26
food compost bin *n* 33
food court *n* 47
food delivery rider (US) *n* 70
food poisoning *n* 19
food preparation *n* 72
food processor (UK) *n* 27
food truck (US) *n* 70
food van (UK) *n* 70
food waste *n* 155
foot *n* 01, 174
foot board *n* 30
foot boot *n* 19
foot pedals *n* 99
foot stool *n* 26
foot strap *n* 119
football (UK) *n* 109
football (US) *n* 107
football boots (UK) *n* 17, 109
football cleats (US) *n* 107
football game (UK) *n* 109
football jersey (US) *n* 15
football player *n* 107
football rules *n* 109
football shirt (UK) *n* 15, 109
football timing *n* 109
footbridge *n* 104
foothill *n* 147
footrest *n* 82
forage mushrooms *v* 170
Forbidden City *n* 44
forearm *n* 01
forecourt (UK) *n* 97
forehand *n* 114
forehead *n* 01
foreperson *n* 85
forest *n* 147–148
forestay *n* 119
forewing *n* 162
forget *v* 11
fork *n* 27, 40, 101
forklift (US) *n* 87, 106
fork-lift truck (UK) *n* 87, 106
formal garden *n* 41
formal wear *n* 15
fortnight (UK) *n* 172
fortune cookies *n* 63
forty *num* 173
forty minutes *n* 171
forward (US) *n* 109
forward *v* 83
fossil *n* 77
fossil fuels *n* 51, 155
foul *n* 112
foul ball *n* 113
foul line *n* 112–113
foul pole *n* 113
foundation *n* 18
fountain *n* 41–42
fountain pen *n* 175
four *num* 173
four-wheel drive *n* 97
fourteen *num* 173
fourth *num* 173
fourth base *n* 113
foxglove *n* 38
fracking *n* 51
fraction, fractions *n* 74, 173
fracture *n* 19
fragile *adj* 45
frame *n* 26, 101, 130, 135
France *n* 151, 153
francium *n* 78
fraud *n* 85
freckles *n* 12
free weights *n* 124
free-range *adj* 53
free-throw lane *n* 112
free-throw line *n* 112
freesia *n* 47, 167
freeze *v* 29
freezer *n* 27
freezing *adj* 154
freezing point *n* 154
freight *n* 105
freight train *n* 102
freighter *n* 105
French *adj* 153
French beans (UK) *n* 55
French braid (US) *n* 12
French doors *n* 25
French horn *n* 128
French people *n* 153
French plait (UK) *n* 12
French toast *n* 71
frequency *n* 84
fresh *adj* 52, 54, 56
fresh cheese *n* 61
fresh chili (US) *n* 59
fresh chilli (UK) *n* 59
fresh fruit *n* 71
fresh yeast *n* 62
freshwater fishing *n* 121
fret *n* 129
Friday *n* 172
fridge (UK) *n* 27
fried *adj* 72
fried chicken *n* 70
fried egg *n* 61, 71
fried mushrooms *n* 71
friend *n* 07
friendly *adj* 10
fries (US) *n* 70
frigate *n* 88, 160
frightened *adj* 06
frightening *adj* 177
frill-necked lizard *n* 163
frisbee *n* 133
frisée *n* 55
frizzy hair *n* 12
frog eggs *n* 77
frog spawn *n* 77, 163
front *adj* 03
front *n* 88
front crawl *n* 118
front desk (US) *n* 131
front door *n* 25, 97
front entrance *n* 25
front kick *n* 117
front loader *n* 87
front speaker *n* 136
front suspension *n* 123
front view *n* 97
front wheel *n* 99
front wing *n* 97, 123
front-flip *n* 118
frontal *n* 03
frost *n* 154
frosty *adj* 154
froth *n* 65
frown *v* 02
frozen *adj* 54, 56
frozen food *n* 48
frozen yoghurt *n* 61
fruit *n* 48, 57–58
fruit bat *n* 158
fruit bowl *n* 26
fruit bread *n* 62
fruit farm *n* 86
fruit gummies (US) *n* 67
fruit gums (UK) *n* 67
fruit juice *n* 71
fruit tart *n* 63
fruit yoghurt (UK) *n* 71
fruit yogurt (US) *n* 71
fruitcake *n* 63
frustrated *adj* 06
fry *v* 29
frying basket *n* 28
frying pan *n* 28
fuchsia *n* 168
fuel rods *n* 51
fuel tank *n* 100
full *adj* 26, 135, 176
full back *n* 108
full moon *n* 143
full stop (UK) *n* 175
full time *n* 109
fullback *n* 107
fumble *v* 107
fun *adj* 177
funeral *n* 07
fungi *n* 77, 170
funnel *n* 76, 105
funny *adj* 10, 177
furious *adj* 06
furnished *n* 32
fuse box *n* 33, 98
fusilli *n* 64
fusion *n* 75

G

Gabon *n* 149, 152
Gabonese *adj* 152
Gabonese people *n* 152
gada *n* 79
gadgets *n* 83
gadolinium *n* 78
gain weight *v* 20
gain yards *v* 107
galah *n* 161
Galápagos turtle *n* 163
gale *n* 154
galia *n* 58
gall bladder *n* 04
gallery *n* 105, 130
gallium *n* 78
gallon *n* 174
gallop *v* 120, 165
Gambia *n* 149, 152
Gambian *adj* 152
Gambians *n* 152
game, games *n* 08, 53, 114, 140
game officials *n* 112
game show *n* 137
gaming *n* 91
gamma radiation *n* 75
Ganges *n* 145
gangway *n* 105
gannet *n* 160
garage *n* 25
garage (UK) *n* 98
garden center (US) *n* 46
garden centre (UK) *n* 46
garden features *n* 41
garden flowers *n* 38
garden gloves *n* 40
garden hose *n* 40
garden peas *n* 55
garden plants *n* 38
garden salad (US) *n* 72
garden tools *n* 40
garden types *n* 41
gardener *n* 89
gardenia *n* 38
gardening *n* 39, 133
gardening basket *n* 40
gardening book *n* 138
gardening features *n* 41
garland *n* 47

garlic *n* 56
garlic press *n* 28
garnet *n* 156
garnish *v* 29
garter *n* 14
garter belt *n* 14
gas *n* 51, 76
gas (US) *n* 99
gas giants *n* 143
gas pump (US) *n* 97
gas space heater *n* 33
gas station (US) *n* 42, 97
gasoline (US) *n* 97
gastornis *n* 157
gastroenterology *n* 21
gate *n* 32, 41, 86, 106, 122
gate number *n* 104
gateau *n* 63
gathered skirt *n* 142
gathers *n* 142
gauze *n* 20
gazelle *n* 158
gear lever *n* 101
gear stick (UK) *n* 99
gearbox *n* 98, 100
gears *n* 101
gearshift (US) *n* 99
gel *n* 49
Gemini *n* 144
gems *n* 156
gene *n* 77
general *n* 88
general appearance *n* 12
generator *n* 33, 51, 101
generous *adj* 10
genie *n* 139
genitals *n* 01
genoa *n* 119
genres *n* 138
Gentoo penguin *n* 161
geode *n* 156
geographical features *n* 146
geography *n* 73, 146–147
geological periods *n* 157
geometry *n* 74
Georgia *n* 150, 153
Georgian *adj* 153
Georgians *n* 153
geothermal energy *n* 51
geothermal power plant (US) *n* 51
geothermal power station (UK) *n* 51
geranium *n* 38
gerbera *n* 47
gerbil *n* 164
German *adj* 153
German shepherd *n* 164
germanium *n* 78
Germans *n* 153
Germany *n* 151, 153
get a job *v* 07
get changed *v* 14
get dressed *v* 09
get fired *v* 81
get into debt *v* 94
get married *v* 07
get off *v* 100, 178
get off a bike *v* 101
get on *v* 100, 178
get on a bike *v* 101
get the job *v* 92
get together *v* 178
get up *v* 09, 178
get your hair cut *v* 12
getting to know someone *n* 179
geyser *n* 146
Ghana *n* 149, 152
Ghanaian *adj* 152
Ghanaians *n* 152
gharial *n* 163
ghee *n* 61
gherkin *n* 60
ghost *n* 139
giant *n* 139
giant horsetails *n* 157
giant puffball *n* 170
giant sequoia *n* 167
giant slalom *n* 122
giant sloth *n* 157
giant squid *n* 166
gibbon *n* 159
gift shop *n* 46, 130
gila monster *n* 163
gills *n* 170
gin and tonic *n* 68
ginger *n* 59
gingerbread man *n* 63
ginkgo *n* 167
ginkgo nuts *n* 58
giraffe *n* 158
girder *n* 87
girl *n* 05
girlfriend *n* 05
girth *n* 120
give a presentation *v* 95
give away *v* 178
give back *v* 178
give notice *v* 32
give out *v* 178
give up *v* 23, 178
give way (UK) *v* 96
glacier *n* 146
gladiator sandals *n* 17
gladiolus *n* 47
glass *adj* 176
glass, glasses *n* 27, 52, 68, 155, 176
glass baking dish *n* 28
glass bottle *n* 76
glass rod *n* 76
glasses *n* 22
glassware *n* 27
glasswing butterfly *n* 162
glaze *v* 62–63
glide *v* 161
glider *n* 103, 125
glory of Texas *n* 168
gloss *n* 37
glossary *n* 138
glove, gloves *n* 16, 100, 110, 115, 117, 122, 107, 109
glue *n* 82, 101, 141
glue gun *n* 35
gluten intolerant *adj* 23
gluten-free *adj* 23
gluten-free flour *n* 62
gluteus maximus *n* 03
gneiss *n* 156
gnocchi *n* 64
gnome *n* 139
go *n* 140
go abroad *v* 104, 141
go away / get away *v* 178
go back *v* 148
go backpacking *v* 131
go down *v* 178
go on a cruise *v* 131
go on a diet *v* 23
go on a holiday (UK) *v* 131
go on a vacation (US) *v* 131
go on an excursion *v* 132
go on a tour *v* 132
go on Hajj *v* 07
go on maternity leave *v* 81
go out of business *v* 94
go out with friends *v* 09
go past (the restaurant) *v* 148
go straight ahead (US) *v* 96, 148
go straight on (UK) *v* 96, 148
go to a café *v* 09
go to bed *v* 09
go to nursery (UK) *v* 07
go to preschool (US) *v* 07
go to school *v* 09
go to sleep *v* 09
go to work *v* 09
go up *v* 178
go viral *v* 84
go-cart *n* 123
goal *n* 108–110
goal crease *n* 110
goal line *n* 107, 110
goal posts *n* 108
goalball *n* 125
goalie stick *n* 110
goalkeeper *n* 109–110
goalpost *n* 107–09
goat *n* 53, 165
goat's cheese *n* 61
goat's milk *n* 61
goatee *n* 12
goblin *n* 139
goggles *n* 15, 118, 122
goji berry *n* 57
gold *adj* 176
gold *n* 78, 116, 156, 176
gold-plated visor *n* 143
golden eagle *n* 160
golden guinea vine *n* 168
golden raisin (US) *n* 58
golf *n* 115
golf bag *n* 115
golf ball *n* 115
golf cap *n* 115
golf clubs *n* 115
golf course *n* 115
golf equipment *n* 115
golf push cart (US) *n* 115
golf shoe, golf shoes *n* 17, 115
golf trolley (UK) *n* 115
golfer *n* 115
gong *n* 128
good *adj* 177
good afternoon *phr* 179
good evening *phr* 179
good listener *n* 93
good morning *phr* 179
good night *phr* 179
goodbye *phr* 179
goose *n* 53, 165
goose egg *n* 61
gooseberry *n* 57
gorilla *n* 159
gosling *n* 165
gospel *n* 129
gossip magazine *n* 138
government building *n* 43
GPS *n* 99
grab bar *n* 31
graceful *adj* 177
grade *n* 73
grader *n* 87
graduate *n* 80
graduate *v* 07
graduation ceremony *n* 80
graffiti *n* 85
graft *v* 39
gram *n* 174
granary bread *n* 62
granddaughter *n* 05
grandfather *n* 05
grandmother *n* 05
grandparents *n* 05
grandson *n* 05
granite *n* 156
grapefruit *n* 57
grapes *n* 57
grapeseed oil *n* 60
grapevine *n* 168
graphite *n* 156
grass, grasses *n* 25, 41, 167
grass collector *n* 40
grass tree *n* 167
grasshopper *n* 162
grassland *n* 146
grate *v* 29
grated cheese *n* 61
grateful *adj* 06
grater *n* 28
grave accent *n* 175
gravel *n* 35, 40
gravity *n* 144
gray (US) *adj* 01, 141
gray (US) *n* 01, 141
gray hair (US) *n* 12
graze (UK) *n* 19
grease *v* 29
greasy hair *n* 12
great *adj* 177
Great Blue Hole *n* 145
great crested newt *n* 163
Great Dane *n* 164
great gray owl (US) *n* 161
great grey owl (UK) *n* 161
Great Mosque of Djenné *n* 44
Great Plains toad *n* 163
great white shark *n* 166
greater spotted woodpecker *n* 160
grebe *n* 161
Greece *n* 151, 153
Greek *adj* 153
Greek alphabet *n* 175
Greek mythology *n* 139
Greek salad *n* 72
Greeks *n* 153
green *adj* 01, 141
green *n* 115, 141
green basilisk *n* 163
green beans *n* 55
green energy *n* 51
green foliage *n* 172
green olives *n* 64
green sea turtle *n* 163
green tea *n* 66
green woodpecker *n* 160
greengrocer (UK) *n* 89
greengrocers (UK) *n* 46, 56
greenhouse *n* 39
greenhouse effect *n* 155
greenhouse gases *n* 155
greet *v* 179
greetings *n* 179
gremlin *n* 139
Grenada *n* 150, 152
grenade *n* 88
grenade launcher *n* 88
Grenadian *adj* 152
Grenadians *n* 152
grey (UK) *adj* 01, 141
grey (UK) *n* 01, 141
grey hair (UK) *n* 12
grey willow *n* 169
grid lines *n* 148
griddle pan *n* 28
griffin *n* 139
grill (UK) *v* 29
grill (US) *n* 41
grill pan *n* 28
grilled *adj* 72
grilled tomato *n* 71
grin *v* 01
grip *n* 115
grocer (US) *n* 89
grocery store (US) *n* 46, 56
groin *n* 01
groin protector *n* 117
groom *n* 07
groom *v* 120
groove *n* 115
ground (US) *n* 33
ground chili (US) *n* 59

ground chilli (UK) *n* 59
ground cinnamon *n* 59
ground cover *n* 41
ground floor (UK) *n* 25, 47
ground level *n* 47
ground maintenance *n* 89
ground meat (US) *n* 53
ground mince (UK) *n* 53
ground sheet *n* 135
groundnut oil (UK) *n* 60
group therapy *n* 24
grout *n* 37
grow up *v* 178
grow your hair *v* 12
growing up *n* 05
grunt *v* 165
guarantee *n* 47
Guatemala *n* 150, 152
Guatemalan *adj* 152
Guatemalans *n* 152
guava *n* 58, 168
guest *n* 26
guest house *n* 131
guest speaker *n* 95
guests *n* 131
guidebook *n* 131–132, 138
guided tour *n* 132
guillemot *n* 160
guilty *adj* 06, 85
Guinea *n* 149, 152
guinea pig *n* 164
Guinea-Bissau *n* 149, 152
Guinean *adj* 152
Guineans *n* 152
gulf *n* 147
gull *n* 134
gully *n* 111
gulp *v* 52
gulper eel *n* 166
gum *n* 03
gun, guns *n* 88
gunfire *n* 88
gunnera *n* 168
gutter *n* 25, 43
guy line (US) *n* 135
guy rope (UK) *n* 135
Guyana *n* 149, 152
Guyanese *adj* 152
Guyanese people *n* 152
gym *n* 124, 131
gym equipment *n* 124
gym machines *n* 124
gymnastics *n* 125
gynaecology (UK) *n* 21
gynecology (US) *n* 21
gypsophila *n* 47
gyrocopter *n* 103

H

habitat loss *n* 155
hacking *n* 85
hacksaw *n* 36
hadal zone *n* 166
haddock tail *n* 54
haemorrhage (UK) *n* 19
hafnium *n* 78
haggle *v* 46
hailstone *n* 154
hair *n* 01, 12
hair band *n* 16
hair curler (UK) *n* 12
hair dryer *n* 12
hair dye *n* 18
hair gel *n* 12
hair salon *n* 47
hair scissors *n* 12
hair spray *n* 12
hair straightener (UK) *n* 12
hair towel wrap *n* 18
hairbrush *n* 12
hairdresser *n* 89
hairpin turn *n* 123
Haiti *n* 150, 152
Haitian *adj* 152
Haitians *n* 152
hakama *n* 117
halal *adj* 72
half *num* 173
half an hour *n* 171
half moon pose *n* 24
half time *n* 109
half-court line *n* 112
half-liter (US) *n* 174
half-litre (UK) *n* 174
half-way line *n* 109
halfback *n* 107
halfway line *n* 108
halibut *n* 54
halloumi *n* 64
Halloween *n* 07
halls of
residence (UK) *n* 80
hallway *n* 25–26
halogens *n* 78
halter *n* 120
halter neck *n* 15
halva *n* 67
ham *n* 53, 71
hamburger *n* 70
hammer *n* 36, 116
hammer *v* 35
hammerhead
shark *n* 166
hammock *n* 135
hamper (UK) *n* 133, 134
hamster *n* 158, 164
hamstrings *n* 03
hand, hands *n* 01–02
hand cream *n* 18
hand drill *n* 36
hand fork *n* 40
hand grips *n* 124
hand in
your notice *v* 81
hand luggage (UK) *n*
103–104
hand out *v* 178
hand towel *n* 31
handbag (UK) *n* 16
handball *n* 125
handbrake (UK) *n* 99
handcuffs *n* 50
handful *n* 29
handicap *n* 115
handkerchief *n* 16
handle *n* 16, 28, 40, 87,
110, 113–114
handle with care *phr* 45
handlebar *n* 101
handouts *n* 95
handrail *n* 25, 99
handsaw *n* 36
handsome *adj* 12
handwriting *n* 175
hang *v* 37
hang clothes (US) *v* 34
hang glider *n* 125
hang out clothes (UK) *v* 34
Hang Son Doong *n* 145
hang up *v* 14, 178
hang-gliding *n* 125
hangar *n* 104
hanging basket *n* 41
hangman *n* 140
Hanukkah *n* 07
happy *adj* 06
harbor (US) *n* 106
harbour (UK) *n* 106
harbor master (US) *n* 106
harbour master (UK) *n* 106
hard *adj* 57, 176
hard candy (US) *n* 67
hard cheese *n* 61
hard drive *n* 83
hard hat *n* 87
hard shoulder *n* 96
hard-working *adj* 93
hardback *n* 138
hardboard *n* 35
hardware store *n* 46
hardwood *n* 35
hare *n* 53
hare's ear *n* 170
harissa *n* 60
harmless *adj* 177
harmonica *n* 129
harness *n* 115, 122
harness race *n* 120
harp *n* 128
harpoon *n* 121
harpy eagle *n* 160
harvest *v* 39, 86
hash browns *n* 70–71
hash marks *n* 107
hashtag *n* 83–84, 175
hassium *n* 78
hatch *v* 161
hatchback *n* 97
hatchling *n* 161
have a baby *v* 07, 09
have a break (UK) *v* 09
have a car accident *v* 98
have a conference
call *v* 95
have a day off *v* 81
have a shower *v* 09
have an interview *v* 92
have breakfast *v* 09
have dinner *v* 09
have lunch *v* 09
have tea or coffee *v* 09
have your hair cut *v* 12
hawk moth *n* 162
hawkfish *n* 166
hawksbill turtle *n* 166
hawthorn *n* 169
hay *n* 86
hay fever *n* 19
hazard *n* 96
hazard lights *n* 99
hazardous waste *n* 33
hazel *adj* 01
hazel *n* 01, 169
hazelnut *n* 58
hazelnut oil *n* 60
HDMI cable *n* 95
head *n* 01, 04, 162
head guard *n* 117
head injury *n* 19
head pocket *n* 110
head teacher *n* 73
head-first *adj* 118
headache *n* 19
headband *n* 16
headboard *n* 30
headlamp *n* 135, 146
headlight, headlights *n*
98, 99, 100
headlight controls *n* 99
headline *n* 138
headphones *n*
84, 95, 136
headquarters *n* 81
headrest *n* 99, 123
headset *n* 82
headstand *n* 24
headstock *n* 129
headwear *n* 16
heal *v* 20
health food
shop (UK) *n* 23, 46–47
health food
store (US) *n* 23, 46–47
healthcare *n* 91
healthy body *n* 24
healthy living *n* 23
healthy mind *n* 24
heart *n* 04, 53, 140
heart rate *n* 124
heat wave (US) *n* 154
heater controls *n* 99
heather *n* 38, 41
heatwave (UK) *n* 154
heavy *adj* 176
heavy cream (US) *n* 61
heavy metal *n* 129
hectare *n* 174
hedge *n* 41, 86, 146
hedgehog *n* 158
hedgehog
mushroom *n* 170
heel *n* 01–02, 17, 115
height *n* 74
helicopter *n* 103
helipad *n* 51
helium *n* 78
hello *phr* 179
helm *n* 119
helmet *n* 50, 100, 107, 111,
113, 123, 143, 146
help *v* 11
hem *n* 14, 142
hematite *n* 156
hemlock *n* 169
hemorrhage (US) *n* 19
hemp *n* 169
hen *n* 165
hen of the wood *n* 170
hen's egg (UK) *n* 61
henna *n* 168
herb garden *n* 41
herbaceous border *n* 41
herbal remedies *n* 49
herbal tea *n* 52, 66
herbalism *n* 24
herbicide *n* 86
herbs *n* 41, 59
herd *n* 86
herd of cows *n* 165
hermit crab *n* 134, 166
hero *n* 127, 139
heron *n* 160
herring *n* 54
Herzegovinian *adj* 153
Herzegovinians *n* 153
hex keys *n* 36
hexagon *n* 74
hi *phr* 179
hi-fi system *n* 136
hibernation *n* 77
hibiscus *n* 38
hide *v* 164
hide-and-seek *n* 133
high *adj* 176
high blood pressure *n* 19
high calorie *adj* 23
high chair *n* 08
high dive *n* 118
high jump *n* 116
high post *n* 112
high pressure *n* 155
high street (UK) *n* 46
high tide *n* 147
high-definition *adj* 137
high-heeled shoes *n* 17
high-speed train *n* 102
high-tops *n* 17
high-visibility jacket *n* 13
high-visibility vest *n* 87
higher pitch *n* 128
highland *n* 146
highlighter *n* 73, 82
highlighter pen *n* 175
highlights *n* 12
highway (US) *n* 96
hijab *n* 16
hiking *n* 133
hiking boots *n* 17
hiking map (UK) *n* 148

hilarious *adj* 177
hilt *n* 117
Himalayan *n* 164
Himeji Castle *n* 44
hindwing *n* 162
hip *n* 01
hip-hop *n* 129
hip pads *n* 107
hippopotamus *n* 158
historian *n* 79
historic building *n* 44, 132
historic quarter *n* 43
historical drama *n* 127
historical site *n* 79
history *n* 73, 79–80
hit *v* 11, 110
hive *n* 165
hob (UK) *n* 27
hobby horse *n* 08
hockey *n* 110
hockey stick *n* 110
hoe *n* 40
hold *v* 11, 117
hold your breath *v* 02
holdall (UK) *n* 16
hole *n* 115
hole in one *n* 115
hole punch *n* 82
Holi *n* 07
holiday (UK) *n* 104
holmium *n* 78
holy water *n* 07
home *n* 32, 107
home button *n* 83
home cinema *n* 136
home delivery *n* 48, 70
home entertainment *n* 136
home furnishings *n* 47
home improvements *n* 35
home office (US) *n* 26
home plate *n* 113
homeopathy *n* [illegible]
homestretch *n* 123
homework *n* 73
homogenized *adj* 61
Honduran *adj* 152
Hondurans *n* 152
Honduras *n* 150, 152
honest *adj* 10, 93
honey *n* 60, 71
honey badger *n* 158
honey bee *n* 162
honey dipper *n* 60
honeycomb *n* 60
honeydew melon *n* 58
honeymoon *n* 07
honeysuckle *n* [illegible]
hood *n* 13, 15
hood (US) *n* 97
hoof *n* 120, 158–159
hook *n* 87
hook and eye *n* 142
hooker *n* 108
hooliganism *n* 85
hoop *n* 16, 112, 125
hoot *v* 161
hop *n* 169
hop *v* 11, 164
hopeful *adj* 06
horizontal bar *n* 125
horn, horns *n* 99, 100, 158
hornbeam *n* 168
horoscope *n* 138
horrible *adj* 177
horror *n* 127
horse *n* 120, 165
horse chestnut *n* 169
horse race *n* 120
horse riding *n* 120
horse trail (US) *n* 133
horseback riding (US) *n* 120, 133
horseradish *n* 56
horseshoe *n* 120
horseshoe crab *n* 166
horsetail *n* 167
hose *n* 50
hose reel *n* 40
hospital *n* 21, 42
hospital bed *n* 21
hospital notes *n* 21
hospitality *n* 91
host (US) *n* 84, 137
host *n* 26
hostel *n* 131
hostess *n* 26
hot *adj* 52, 56, 154, 176
hot chocolate *n* 52
hot dog *n* 70
hot drink container (US) *n* 52, 135
hot sauce *n* 60
hot tub *n* 124
hot water *n* 31
hot-air balloon *n* 103
hot-water bottle *n* 30
hotel *n* 42, 131
hotel lobby *n* 131
hour *n* 171
hour hand *n* 171
hourly *adj, adv* 171–172
hourly rate *n* 81
house, houses *n* 25, 32, 148
house martin *n* 160
houseboat *n* 32
household chores *n* 34
household products *n* 48
household renovation *n* 37
household tasks *n* 34
housekeeper *n* 89
housemate (UK) *n* 32
houseplants *n* 38
hovercraft *n* 105
howler monkey *n* 159
hub *n* 51, 101
hubcap *n* 98
Hugin and Munin *n* 139
hula hoop *n* 08
hull *n* 105, 119
human body *n* 01
human resources (HR) *n* 91
humanities *n* 80
Humboldt penguin *n* 161
humerus *n* 03
humidity *n* 154
hummingbird *n* 160
hummingbird hawksmoth *n* 162
hummus *n* 72
humor (US) *n* 138
humour (UK) *n* 138
hump *n* 158
humpback whale *n* 166
Hungarian *adj* 153
Hungarians *n* 153
Hungary *n* 151, 153
hungry *adj* 26
hunt *v* 159
hurdles *n* 116
hurricane *n* 154
hurt *v* 20
husband *n* 05
hut *n* 32
hybrid *n* 97
Hydra *n* 139
hydrangea *n* 38
hydrant *n* 50
hydroelectric energy *n* 51
hydroelectric power station *n* 51
hydrofoil *n* 105
hydrogen *n* 78
hydrotherapy *n* 24
hyena *n* 158
hyphen *n* 175
hypnotherapy *n* 24
hypotenuse *n* 74
hyssop *n* 59

I

Iberian ham *n* 64
ibex *n* 158
ice *n* 68, 154
ice and lemon *n* 68
ice bucket *n* 68
ice climbing *n* 122
ice cream *n* 61, 70, 134
ice cream cone *n* 65
ice cream scoop *n* 65
ice cream sundae *n* 63
ice fishing *n* 121
ice hockey *n* 110
ice hockey player *n* 110
ice hockey rink *n* 110
ice maker *n* 27
ice skate *n* 110
ice-skating *n* 122
iceberg lettuce *n* 55
iceberg *n* 146
iced *adj* 52
iced bun *n* 63
iced coffee *n* 65
iced tea *n* 52, 66
Iceland *n* 151, 153
Icelanders *n* 153
Icelandic *adj* 153
ichthyostega *n* 157
icicle *n* 146
icing *n* 29, 63
icy *adj* 154
igloo *n* 32
igneous *adj* 156
ignition *n* 99
illness *n* 19
illustration *n* 138
imaginative *adj* 93
immature *adj* 10
immigration *n* 104
impala *n* 158
impatient *adj* 10
important *adj* 177
Impressionism *n* 130
impulsive *adj* 10
in brine *phr* 64
in credit *phr* 45
in debt *phr* 45
in field *n* 111
in front of *prep* 148, 180
in oil *phr* 64
in *prep* 180
in sauce *phr* 72
in the black *phr* 45
in the red *phr* 45
in town *n* 42
in-goal area *n* 108
inbox *n* 83
incandescent bulb *n* 33
inch *n* 174
inch plant *n* 167
incisors *n* 03
income *n* 94
incontinence pads *n* 49
incorrect *adj* 176
incredible *adj* 177
incubator *n* 08
independent *adj* 93
index *n* 138
index finger *n* 02
India *n* 150, 153
Indian *adj* 153
Indian cobra *n* 163
Indian pale ale (IPA) *n* 68
Indians *n* 153
indicate (UK) *v* 98
indicator (UK) *n* 97, 100
indifferent *adj* 06
indigo *n* 141
indium *n* 78
Indonesia *n* 151, 153
Indonesian *adj* 153
Indonesians *n* 153
industrial emissions *n* 155
industrial estate (UK) *n* 42
industrial revolution *n* 79
industrial zone (US) *n* 42
industries *n* 91
infection *n* 19
infield *n* 113
infielders *n* 113
inflatable boat *n* 134
inflatable dinghy *n* 105
influencer *n* 84, 93
information age *n* 79
information chart *n* 49
information screen *n* 104
information technology (IT) *n* 73, 91
infrared *n* 75
inhaler *n* 20, 49
initiative *n* 93
injera *n* 62
injury *n* 19
injury time (UK) *n* 109
ink *n* 141, 175
inline skating *n* 125
inner core *n* 145
inner tube *n* 101
inning *n* 113
innocent *adj* 85
innovative *adj* 93
inoculation *n* 20
insect repellent *n* 49, 135
insects *n* 162
insensitive *adj* 10
inside *prep* 180
inside center (US) *n* 108
inside centre (UK) *n* 108
inside lane *n* 96
insoles *n* 17, 49
insomnia *n* 19, 30
inspector *n* 50
install *v* 33
install a carpet (US) *v* 35
installation *n* 130
instep *n* 02
instruments *n* 129
insulated gloves *n* 143
insulating tape *n* 36
insulation *n* 35
insulin *n* 49
intelligent *adj* 10
intensive care unit *n* 21
intercity train *n* 102
intercom *n* 25
intercostal *n* 03
interdental brush *n* 22
interest rate *n* 45
interested *adj* 06
interesting *adj* 177
intermission (US) *n* 126
intern *n* 81
internal organs *n* 04
international flight *n* 104
interpersonal skills *n* 93
interpreter *n* 89
interrogation room *n* 50
interrupt *v* 95
intersection (US) *n* 43
interval (UK) *n* 126
interview *n* 81, 137
interviewer *n* 81
intolerant *adj* 23
intrigued *adj* 06
invertebrate *n* 77
investigation *n* 50
investment *n* 94

invoice n 94
iodine n 78
ionosphere n 155
Iran n 151, 153
Iranian adj 153
Iranians n 153
Iraq n 150, 153
Iraqi adj 153
Iraqis n 153
Ireland n 151, 153
iridium n 78
iris n 01, 38
Irish adj 153
Irish coffee n 65
Irish people n 153
iron n 23, 34, 49, 78, 115, 156
iron a shirt v 09
Iron age n 79
ironing board n 34
irritated adj 06
irritating adj 177
Islamic Golden Age n 79
island n 88, 145, 147
isobar n 155
Israel n 150, 153
Israeli adj 153
Israelis n 153
isthmus n 147
IT manager n 89
Italian adj 153
Italians n 153
italic adj 175
italic n 175
Italy n 151, 153
IV (US) n 21
IV pole (US) n 21
Ivorian adj 152
Ivorians n 152
Ivory Coast n 149, 152
ivy n 169

J

jack n 98, 140
jack connector n 129
jack-o'-lantern n 139, 170
jackal n 158
jacket n 15
jackfruit n 58
jackhammer (US) n 87
Jackson's chameleon n 163
jacuzzi n 25
jade n 156
jade pothos n 38
jaguar n 159
jalapeños n 59
jam n 71
jam doughnut (UK) n 63
Jamaica n 150, 152
Jamaican adj 152
Jamaicans n 152
janitor n 90
January n 172
Japan n 150, 153
Japanese adj 153
Japanese bobtail n 164
Japanese characters n 175
Japanese people n 153
jar n 27, 52, 60
jasper n 156
javelin n 116
jaw n 01, 03
jawed fish n 157
jawless fish n 157
jazz n 129
jealous adj 06
jeans n 14
jelly beans n 67
jelly donut (US) n 63
jelly sandals n 17
jellyfish n 166
Jerusalem artichoke n 56
jester n 79
jet n 156
jet engine n 103
Jet Ski n 134
jet skiing n 119
jetty n 106
jetway n 104
jeweler (US) n 46, 89
jeweller (UK) n 46, 89
jeweller's (UK) n 46
jewellery (UK) n 16
jewellery box (UK) n 16
jewellery making (UK) n 141
jewelry (US) n 16
jewelry box (US) n 16
jewelry making (US) n 141
jib n 87, 119
jigsaw n 35
jigsaw puzzle n 08, 140
job ads n 92
job applications n 92
job sheet n 92
job skills n 92
jobs n 89-90
jockey n 120
jockey pants (UK) n 14
jockey shorts (US) n 14
jodhpurs n 120
joey n 158
jog in place (US) v 124
jog on the spot (UK) v 124
jogging n 133
joint (UK) n 53
joker n 140
Jordan n 150, 153
Jordanian adj 153
Jordanians n 153
Joshua tree n 167
journal n 80
journalism n 91
journalist n 90
judge n 85, 90
judo n 117
jug, jugs (UK) n 27-29
juggle v 11
juice, juices n 52, 65
juicy adj 52
jujitsu n 117
July n 172
jumbo jet n 103
jump v 11, 117, 120
jump ball n 112
jump rope (US) n 08, 124
jumper (UK) n 14
jumping jacks (US) n 124
jumping ramp n 122
jumping spider n 162
junction n 96
June n 172
jungle gym (US) n 43
junk mail n 83
Jupiter n 143
Jurassic adj 157
Jurassic n 157
jury n 85
jury box n 85
jury deliberation n 85

K

K-pop n 129
kale n 55
kangaroo n 158
karaoke n 136
karate n 117
karate mat n 117
kayak n 105, 119
kayaking n 119
Kazakhstan n 151, 153
Kazakhstani adj 153
Kazakhstanis n 153
kebab n 70, 72
keel n 105, 119
keep n 44
keep net n 121
kefir n 61
kelp n 166
kendo n 117
kennel (UK) n 164
Kenya n 149, 152
Kenyan adj 152
Kenyans n 152
kerb (UK) n 43
kernel n 55
ketchup n 60, 70
kettledrum n 128
key, keys n 25, 32
key cutting shop n 46
keyboard n 83, 129
keyhole n 25-26
keypad n 45
kick n 108, 118
kick v 11, 107
kick flip n 125
kickboxing n 117
kickoff n 109
kickstand n 101
kid n 165
kidney, kidneys n 04, 53, 71
kids meal (US) n 69
kids' clothes n 13
kids' shoes n 17
killer whale n 166
kilogram n 174
kilometer (US) n 174
kilometre (UK) n 174
kilt n 15
kimchi n 60
kimono n 15
kind adj 10
king n 79, 140
kingdom n 79
kingfisher n 160
kiosk n 46-48
kippers n 71
Kiribati adj 153
Kiribati n 150, 153
Kiribati people n 153
kitchen n 27, 69
kitchen appliances n 27
kitchen equipment n 28
kitchen installer n 90
kitchen fitter n 90
kitchen knife n 28
kitchen scissors n 28
kitchenware n 28
kite n 08
kite surfing n 119
kitten n 164
kitten heels n 17
Kittitian adj 152
Kittitians n 152
kiwi n 160
kiwi/ kiwi fruit (UK) n 58
knead v 62
knee n 01, 126
knee joint n 03
knee pad n 107, 100
knee-high boots n
kneecap n 03
kneeler n 40
kneeling chair n 82
knickers (UK) n 14
knife n 27
knife sharpener n 28
knife stand n 28
knight n 79, 139-140
knitting n 142
knitting needle n 142
knob n 25-26, 113
knock down a wall v 35
knock out n 117
knots n 121
knuckle n 02
koala n 158
kohlrabi n 55
kola nuts n 58
Komodo dragon n 163
kookaburra n 160
kosher adj 72
krypton n 78
kumquat n 57
kung fu n 117
Kuwait n 151, 153
Kuwaiti adj 153
Kuwaitis n 153
Kwanzaa n 07
Kyrgyz adj 153
Kyrgyz people n 153
Kyrgyzstan n 151, 153

L

lab n 76
lab coat n 13
label, labels n 40, 130
laboratory n 76
labrador n 164
lace n 17, 107
lace bobbin n 142
lace-making n 142
lace-up boots n 17
lacrosse n 110
lacrosse player n 110
lactose free adj 61
lactose intolerant adj 23
ladder n 36, 50, 87
ladle n 27
lady n 79
ladybird (UK) n 162
ladybug (US) n 162
lager n 68
lagoon n 147
laid-back adj 10
lake n 146, 148
Lake Natron n 145
lamb n 53, 165
lamp n 26, 82, 101, 106, 135, 139
lampshade n 26
land n 145
land v 104
landfill n 155
landing gear n 103
landing hill n 122
landing net n 121
landlord n 32
landscape n 132
landscape v 39
landscape painting n 133
landslide n 146
lane n 116, 118
lane line n 112
lane rope n 118
languages n 73, 80
lantern n 135
lanthanum n 78
lanthanide series n 78
Laos n 150, 153
Laotian adj 153
Laotians n 153
lapel n 15
lapis lazuli n 156
laptop n 82-83
larch n 167
large adj 176
large intestine n 04
larynx n 04
lasagna n 64, 72
laser n 75
laser run n 116
late adj 171

later *adj* 171
later *adv* 171
Latin *n* 129
Latin alphabet *n* 175
latissimus dorsi *n* 03
latitude *n* 145, 148
Latvia *n* 151, 153
Latvian *adj* 153
Latvians *n* 153
laugh *v* 02
launch *n* 143
launch pad *n* 143
Launderette (UK) *n* 46
Laundromat (US) *n* 46
laundry *n* 34
laundry basket (UK) *n* 31, 34
laundry detergent *n* 34
laundry hamper (US) *n* 31, 34
laundry service *n* 131
laurel *n* 167
lava *n* 145
lava layer *n* 145
lavender *n* 38
law *n* 80, 85
law court (UK) *n* 43, 85
lawn *n* 41
lawn rake *n* 40
lawnmower *n* 40
lawrencium *n* 78
lawyer *n* 85, 90
lawyer's office *n* 85
laxative *n* 49
lay bricks *v* 35
lay sod (US) *v* 39
lay turf (UK) *v* 39
layer cake *n* 63
lazy *adj* 10
leaching *n* 39
lead *n* 78
lead (UK) *n* 164
lead singer *n* 129
leaded *n* 97
leader *n* 81
leadership *n* 93
leaf *n* 55
leaf blower *n* 40
leaf fall *n* 172
leafy *adj* 56
lean meat *n* 53
Leaning Tower of Pisa *n* 44
learn *v* 73
lease *n* 32
leash *n* 164
leather *adj* 176
leather *n* 13, 107, 176
leather suit (US) *n* 100
leatherback sea turtle *n* 163
leathers (UK) *n* 100
leave *v* 179
leave the house *v* 09
leave work *v* 09
Lebanese *adj* 153
Lebanese people *n* 153
Lebanon *n* 150, 153
lecture theatre *n* 80
lecturer *n* 80, 89
LED (light emitting diode) bulb *n* 33
lederhosen *n* 15
leek *n* 56
left defenceman (UK) *n* 110
left defenseman (US) *n* 110
left defensive end *n* 107
left defensive tackle *n* 107
left guard *n* 107
left safety *n* 107
left tackle *n* 107
left winger *n* 110
left-wing *n* 108
leg *n* 01, 26, 53
leg guard *n* 110
leg pad *n* 111
leg press *n* 124
legal *n* 91
legal advice *n* 85
legal system *n* 85
leggings *n* 14
legumes (US) *n* 23
lemon *n* 57
lemon balm *n* 59
lemon curd *n* 60
lemon squeezer *n* 28
lemonade *n* 52
lemongrass *n* 59
length *n* 71, 174
lens *n* 22, 75, 127, 136
lens case *n* 22
lens cleaning cloth *n* 22
lens solution *n* 49
Leo *n* 144
leopard *n* 159
leotard *n* 15
leprechaun *n* 139
Lesotho *n* 149, 152
lesson *n* 73
let *n* 114
let in *v* 178
let out *v* 142
letter *n* 45, 82
letterbox (UK) *n* 25, 45
letters *n* 175
lettuce *n* 55
level (US) *n* 35-36, 87
Liberia *n* 149, 152
Liberian *adj* 152
Liberians *n* 152
libero *n* 112
Libra *n* 144
librarian *n* 80, 90
library *n* 43, 80, 148
library card *n* 80
libretto *n* 126
Libya *n* 149, 152
Libyan *adj* 152
Libyans *n* 152
licence plate (UK) *n* 97
license plate (US) *n* 97
lick *v* 02, 11
licorice (US) *n* 67
lid *n* 28
lie down *v* 20
Liechtenstein *n* 151, 153
Liechtensteiner *adj* 153
Liechtensteiners *n* 153
life cycle *n* 77
life events *n* 07
life jacket *n* 105, 119
life preserver (US) *n* 105, 119, 134
life raft *n* 119
life ring (UK) *n* 105, 119, 134
life-support backpack *n* 143
lifeboat *n* 105
lifeguard *n* 118, 134
lifeguard tower *n* 134
lift (UK) *n* 25, 47, 131
lift *v* 11
ligament *n* 03
ligature *n* 175
light *adj* 60, 176
light, lights *n* 32, 50, 84, 101, 143
light a fire *v* 135
light aircraft *n* 103
light bulbs *n* 33
light cream (US) *n* 61
light shower *n* 154
light switch *n* 33
lighthouse *n* 44, 106
lighting *n* 47
lightning *n* 154
like *v* 84
lilac *n* 38
lily *n* 38, 167
lily of the valley *n* 38
lime *n* 57, 169
lime pickle *n* 60
limestone *n* 156
limousine *n* 97
limpet *n* 134, 166
linden *n* 169
line, lines *n* 74, 121
line (US) *n* 48, 132
line of play *n* 115
linen chest *n* 30
linesman *n* 109, 114
lingerie *n* 47
lining *n* 15
lining paper *n* 37
lintel *n* 87
lion *n* 158
lioness *n* 158
lip balm *n* 18
lip brush *n* 18
lip liner *n* 18
lips *n* 01
lipstick *n* 18
liqueur *n* 68
liquid *n* 76
liquid measure *n* 174
liquid measurements *n* 174
liquor store (US) *n* 46
liquorice (UK) *n* 67
listen *v* 11
listen to the radio *v* 09
liter (US) *n* 174
literary fiction *n* 138
literature *n* 73, 80
lithium *n* 78
Lithuania *n* 151, 153
Lithuanian *adj* 153
Lithuanians *n* 153
litre (UK) *n* 174
litter tray (UK) *n* 164
little finger *n* 02
little gem *n* 55
little toe *n* 02
litterbox (US) *n* 164
live *n* 33
live rail *n* 102
liver *n* 04, 53
livermorium *n* 78
liverwort *n* 167
living room *n* 26
living stones *n* 168
lizard *n* 164
llama *n* 158, 165
load the dishwasher *v* 34
loaf *n* 62
loafers *n* 17
loam *n* 39
loans desk (UK) *n* 80
lob *n* 114
lobster *n* 54
local produce *n* 23
lock *n* 101, 106
locker room (US) *n* 124
lockers *n* 118, 124
locksmith *n* 90
locust *n* 162
lodger (UK) *n* 32
log in *v* 83, 178
log out *v* 83, 178
loganberry *n* 57
logic game *n* 136
loin *n* 54
lollipop *n* 67
London plane *n* 168
lonely *adj* 06
long *adj* 176
long hair *n* 12
long jump *n* 116
long legs *n* 159
long-handled shears *n* 40
long-sighted (UK) *adj* 22
longitude *n* 145, 148
look after *v* 178
look at *v* 178
look for *v* 178
loom *n* 142
loose *adj* 13, 176
loosehead prop *n* 108
loppers *n* 40
lord *n* 79
lorikeet *n* 161
lorry driver (UK) *n* 90
lose *v* 109, 140
lose weight *v* 20, 23
lose your way *v* 148
lost and found *n* 104
lost property office *n* 102
lotus *n* 38
loudspeakers *n* 136
lovage *n* 59
love *n* 114
low *adj* 176
low calorie *adj* 23
low pressure *n* 155
low tide *n* 147
lower deck *n* 99
lower pitch *n* 128
lowercase *n* 175
loyalty card *n* 47
lucky *adj* 06
ludo *n* 140
lug nuts (US) *n* 98
luge *n* 122
luggage *n* 104, 131
luggage hold *n* 99
luggage rack *n* 102
luggage storage *n* 102
lumbar vertebrae *n* 03
lumber (US) *n* 87
luna moth *n* 162
lunar eclipse *n* 143
lunar module *n* 143
lunar rover *n* 143
lunch *n* 26, 72
lunch menu *n* 69
lung *n* 04
lunge *n* 117, 124
lupin *n* 38
lure *n* 121
lutetium *n* 78
Luxembourg *adj* 153
Luxembourg *n* 151, 153
Luxembourgers *n* 153
lychee *n* 57
lymphatic *n* 04
lynx *n* 159

M

macadamia, macadamias *n* 58, 168
macaque *n* 159
macaron *n* 63
macaroni *n* 64
mace *n* 59, 78
machine gun *n* 88
machine needle *n* 142
machinery *n* 87
mackerel *n* 54
macramé *n* 142
mad (US) *adj* 06
Madagascan *adj* 152
Madagascans *n* 152
Madagascar *n* 149, 152
magazine website *n* 84
maglev *n* 102
magma chamber *n* 145
magnesium *n* 49, 78, 156
magnet *n* 75
magnetic field *n* 75
magnolia *n* 167

maid *n* 89
maid service *n* 131
mail carrier (US) *n* 45, 90
mail slot (US) *n* 25, 45
mailbox (US) *n* 25, 45
main character *n* 127
main course (UK) *n* 69
main road *n* 148
main street (US) *n* 46
Maine coon *n* 164
mains supply (UK) *n* 33
mainsail *n* 119
maize (UK) *n* 86
make *v* 11
make a loss *v* 94
make a profit *v* 94
make a reservation *v* 69, 131
make a will (UK) *v* 07
make curtains *v* 35
make friends *v* 07
make the bed *v* 09, 34
make up *v* 178
makeup *n* 18
makeup bag *n* 18
malachite *n* 156
Malawi *n* 149, 152
Malawian *adj* 152
Malawians *n* 152
Malaysia *n* 151, 153
Malaysian *adj* 153
Malaysians *n* 153
Maldives *n* 150, 153
Maldivian *adj* 153
Maldivians *n* 153
male *n* 04
Mali *n* 149, 152
Malian *adj* 152
Malians *n* 152
mallard *n* 161
mallet *n* 36, 141
malt vinegar *n* 60
Malta *n* 151, 153
Maltese *adj* 153
Maltese people *n* 153
mammals *n* 158, 159
man *n* 05
manage *v* 92
manager *n* 81, 109
managing director *n* 81
manchego *n* 64
mandarin duck *n* 161
mandarin orange *n* 57
mandolin (UK) *n* 28
mandolin *n* 129
mandoline (US) *n* 28
mandrill *n* 159
mane *n* 120
manganese *n* 78
mangetout (UK) *n* 55
mango *n* 57
mango juice *n* 65
mangosteen *n* 58
mangrove *n* 169
manhole *n* 43
manicure *n* 18
mannequin (US) *n* 142
mansion *n* 32
mantis shrimp *n* 166
mantle *n* 145
mantlepiece *n* 26
manual *n* 99
manufacturing *n* 91
map *n* 132
maple *n* 169
maple syrup *n* 60
maps *n* 148
maracas *n* 128
marathon *n* 116
marble *adj* 176
marble *n* 156, 176
marble queen *n* 38
March *n* 172
mare *n* 120, 165
margarine *n* 61
marigold *n* 38
marina *n* 106
marinated *adj* 64, 72
marinated fish *n* 64
marine *n* 88
marine fishing *n* 121
marine iguana *n* 163
marine species *n* 166
marjoram *n* 59
mark *v* 112
marker *n* 175
market researcher *n* 89
marketing *n* 91
marmalade *n* 60, 71
marmoset *n* 159
marrella *n* 157
married *n* 05
married couple *n* 07
marrow *n* 56
Mars *n* 143
marsh *n* 147
Marshall Islands *n* 150, 153
Marshallese *adj* 153
Marshallese people *n* 153
marshmallow *n* 67
martial arts *n* 117, 127
Martini *n* 68
Mary Janes *n* 17
marzipan *n* 63
mascara *n* 18
mascot *n* 109
mash *v* 29
mashed *adj* 72
masher *n* 28
mask *n* 113, 117–118
masking tape *n* 37
Mason jar *n* 52
masonry bit *n* 36
massage *n* 24
mast *n* 105, 119
master's degree *n* 80
masterpiece *n* 130
mat *n* 24
matamata *n* 163
match *n* 114
materials *n* 35, 176
maternity *n* 21
maternity ward *n* 21
math (US) *n* 73
mathematical equipment *n* 74
mathematics *n* 74
maths (UK) *n* 73
matte *n* 37
mattress *n* 30
mature *adj* 10
matzo *n* 62
Mauritania *n* 149, 152
Mauritanian *adj* 152
Mauritanians *n* 152
Mauritian *adj* 152
Mauritians *n* 152
Mauritius *n* 149, 152
May *n* 172
mayonnaise *n* 60
MDF *n* 35
meal deal *n* 70
meals *n* 72
mean *adj* 10
measles *n* 19
measure *n* 68
measure *v* 174
measure out *v* 178
measurements *n* 74
measures *n* 174
measuring cup (US) *n* 27–29, 174
measuring jug (UK) *n* 27–29, 174
measuring spoon *n* 28, 49
meat *n* 48, 53
meat hook *n* 53
meat pies *n* 64
meat tenderizer *n* 28
meat thermometer *n* 28
meatballs *n* 72
mechanic *n* 89, 98
mechanics *n* 98
medal *n* 88, 116
media *n* 84, 91
median (US) *n* 96
medical chart *n* 52
medical examination *n* 20
medication *n* 20, 49
medicine *n* 20, 49, 80
mediocre *adj* 177
meditation *n* 24
medium height *adj* 12
medlar *n* 169
medley relay *n* 118
meerkat *n* 159
meet *v* 179
meet a deadline *v* 92
meet up *v* 178
meeting *n* 81, 82, 95
meeting-room equipment *n* 82
meganeura *n* 157
megaphone *n* 50
meitnerium *n* 78
melody *n* 129
melons *n* 58
melt butter *v* 29
melting ice caps *n* 155
membership *n* 124
memory card *n* 83
mendelevium *n* 78
men's decathlon *n* 116
menswear *n* 47
menu *n* 65, 70
meow *v* 164
merchant *n* 79
Mercury *n* 143
mercury *n* 78, 156
meringue *n* 63
mermaid *n* 139
merman *n* 139
mesa *n* 146
mesosphere *n* 155
Mesozoic (middle life) *adj* 157
Mesozoic (middle life) *n* 157
mess *n* 88
mess around *v* 178
metacarpals *n* 03
metal *adj* 176
metal, metals *n* 35, 155, 156, 176
metal bit *n* 36
metal detecting *n* 133
metamorphic *adj* 156
metamorphosis *n* 77
metatarsals *n* 03
meteor *n* 144
meteor shower *n* 144
meter (US) *n* 174
meter line (US) *n* 108
methane *n* 155
meticulous *adj* 10
metre (UK) *n* 174
metre line (UK) *n* 108
Mexican *adj* 152
Mexican axolotl *n* 163
Mexicans *n* 152
Mexico *n* 150, 152
mezzanine (US) *n* 126
mezzo-soprano *n* 126
mica *n* 156
microbiologist *n* 77
microbiology *n* 77
microlight *n* 103
Micronesia *n* 150, 153
Micronesian *adj* 153
Micronesian people *n* 153
microphone *n* 84, 95, 136
microscope *n* 77
microwave *v* 29
microwave oven *n* 27
microwaves *n* 75
mid-off *n* 111
mid-wicket *n* 111
midcourt area marker *n* 112
midday *n* 171
middle blocker *n* 112
middle finger *n* 02
middle lane *n* 96
middle level *n* 47
middle linebacker *n* 107
middle-aged *adj* 12
midfielder *n* 109
midnight *n* 171
midnight zone *n* 166
midwife *n* 08
migraine *n* 19
migrate *v* 161
mild *adj* 154
mile *n* 174
military *n* 88, 91
military ambulance *n* 88
military transport aircraft *n* 88
military truck *n* 88
military uniform *n* 13
military vehicles *n* 88
milk *n* 58, 61, 65, 71
milk *v* 86
milk carton *n* 61
milk chocolate *n* 67
milk products *n* 61
milk teeth (UK) *n* 22
milkshake *n* 52, 65, 70
milky conecap *n* 170
Milky Way *n* 144
millennium *n* 172
millet *n* 86
milligram *n* 174
milliliter (US) *n* 174
millilitre (UK) *n* 174
millimeter (US) *n* 174
millimetre (UK) *n* 174
millipede *n* 162
mimosa *n* 168
minaret *n* 44
mince *v* 29
mindfulness *n* 24
mine shaft *n* 51
miner, miners *n* 51, 89
mineral spirits (US) *n* 37
mineral water *n* 52, 68
minerals *n* 23, 156
minibar *n* 131
minibus *n* 99
mining *n* 91
minivan (US) *n* 97
Minotaur *n* 139
minstrel *n* 79
mint *n* 59, 67
mint tea *n* 66
minus sign *n* 74
minute *n* 82, 171
minute hand *n* 171
mirror *n* 18, 30, 77
miserable *adj* 06
miss a train *v* 102
mission control *n* 143
mist *n* 154
mistletoe *n* 168
misty *adj* 154
mitochondria *n* 77
mitt *n* 113
mittens *n* 13
mix *v* 29, 62

mixed salad (UK) *n* 72
mixing bowl *n* 28
mixing desk *n* 84
moat *n* 44
mobile *n* 30
mobile banking *n* 94
mobile home (US) *n* 32
mobile phone (UK) *n* 82
moccasins *n* 17
mochi *n* 63
mocktail *n* 68
model making *n* 141
modeling tool (US) *n* 141
modelling tool (UK) *n* 141
modern building *n* 44
modern pentathlon *n* 116
moisturizer *n* 18
molars *n* 03
mold *n* 170
molding (US) *n* 26
Moldova *n* 151, 153
Moldovan *adj* 153
Moldovans *n* 153
mole *n* 12, 159
molecule *n* 76
molt (US) *v* 164
molybdenum *n* 78
mom (US) *n* 05
Monacan *adj* 153
Monaco *n* 151, 153
monarch butterfly *n* 162
monastery *n* 44
Monday *n* 172
Monégasque *n* 153
money *n* 45, 94
Mongolia *n* 150, 153
Mongolian *adj* 153
Mongolians *n* 153
mongoose *n* 159
monkey puzzle *n* 167
monkey wrench *n* 36
monkfish *n* 54
mono *adj* 136
monocle *n* 22
monoplane *n* 103
monorail *n* 102
monster *n* 139
monster truck *n* 123
Montenegrin *adj* 153
Montenegrins *n* 153
Montenegro *n* 151, 153
month *n* 172
monthly *adj* 172
monthly *adv* 172
monument *n* 42, 44, 132
moods *n* 06
Moon *n* 143
moonstone *n* 156
moor *v* 106
mooring *n* 106
moorish idol *n* 166
moose *n* 159
mop *n* 34
mop the floor *v* 34
morel *n* 170
morning *n* 09, 171
morning glory *n* 169
morning show (US) *n* 137
Moroccan *adj* 152
Moroccans *n* 152
Morocco *n* 149, 152
mortar *n* 28, 35, 76, 87
mortar and pestle *n* 28
mortarboard *n* 80
mortgage *n* 32, 45
moscovium *n* 78
Moses basket *n* 08, 30
mosque *n* 44
mosquito *n* 162
mosquito net *n* 135
moss *n* 167
mother *n* 05
mother-in-law *n* 05
mother of thousands *n* 168
moths *n* 162
motion-sickness
medication (US) *n* 49
motivated *adj* 93
motor home (US) *n* 135
motor racing (UK) *n* 123
motor scooter *n* 100
motorbike (UK) *n* 100
motorbike
racing (UK) *n* 123
motocross *n* 123
motorcycle (US) *n* 100
motorcycle officer *n* 50
motorcycle
racing (US) *n* 123
motorsports *n* 123
motorway (UK) *n* 96
moulding (UK) *n* 26
moult (UK) *v* 164
mount *v* 100
mountain *n* 147
mountain ash *n* 169
mountain bike *n* 101
mountain biking *n* 133
mountain chain *n* 146
mountain goat *n* 159
mountain pose *n* 24
mountain range *n* 146
mountaineering *n* 133
mouse *n* 83, 158, 164
mouse mat (UK) *n* 83
mouse pad (US) *n* 83
moustache (UK) *n* 12
mouth *n* 01, 147
mouth guard *n* 107, 117
mouthwash *n* 31
movable panel *n* 82
move *v* 11, 140
move in *v* 32
move out *v* 32
movie camera *n* 127
movie star (US) *n* 127
movie
theater (US) *n* 42, 127
movies (US) *n* 127
moving truck (US) *n* 32
mow the lawn *v* 09, 39
Mozambican *adj* 152
Mozambicans *n* 152
Mozambique *n* 149, 152
mozzarella *n* 64
muck out *v* 120
mudguard *n* 100
mudskipper *n* 166
mudslide *n* 146
muesli *n* 71
muffin *n* 63, 70
muffin tin (US) *n* 29
muffin tray (UK) *n* 29
muffler (US) *n* 98, 100
mug *n* 27
mugging *n* 85
mulberry *n* 57
mulch *v* 39
mules *n* 17
multi-purpose knife *n* 135
multi-vitamins *n* 49
multiplayer game *n* 136
multiplex *n* 127
multiplication sign *n* 74
multiply *v* 74
mum (UK) *n* 05
mumps *n* 19
muscles *n* 03
museum *n* 43, 130, 132
museum curator *n* 89
musher *n* 122
mushroom *n* 56
mushroom picking *n* 133
mushrooms *n* 170
music *n* 73, 128, 129
music channel *n* 137
music school *n* 80
music stand *n* 128
music teacher *n* 90
music therapy *n* 24
musical *n* 126, 127
musician *n* 90
musk ox *n* 159
mussel *n* 54
mustache (US) *n* 12
mustard *n* 70
mustard allergy *n* 23
mustard seeds *n* 60
mute swan *n* 161
muzzle *n* 120
Myanmar
(Burma) *n* 150, 153
mycelium *n* 170
myrtle *n* 168
myths *n* 139

N

nacelle *n* 51
nachos *n* 70
nail *n* 36
nail clippers *n* 18, 49
nail file *n* 18
nail polish *n* 18
nail polish remover *n* 18
nail scissors *n* 18
nail varnish (UK) *n* 18
Namibia *n* 149, 152
Namibian *adj* 152
Namibians *n* 152
napkin *n* 27, 72
napkin ring *n* 27
nappy (UK) *n* 08
nappy rash
cream (UK) *n* 08
narrow *adj* 176
narwhal *n* 166
nasal spray *n* 20
nasturtium *n* 169
nasty *adj* 177
national park *n* 132, 133
nationalities *n* 152, 153
natural arch *n* 147
natural history *n* 157
nature documentary *n* 137
nature reserve *n* 133, 148
nature therapy *n* 24
nature writing *n* 138
naturopathy *n* 24
Nauru *n* 150, 153
Nauruan *adj* 153
Nauruan people *n* 153
nausea *n* 19
nautilus *n* 166
navel *n* 01
navigate *v* 119
navy *n* 88
navy blue *n* 141
navy vessels *n* 88
near *adj* 176
nearsighted (US) *adj* 22
nebula *n* 144
neck *n* 01, 115, 129, 161
neck brace *n* 19
neck pad *n* 107
necklace *n* 16
neckline *n* 142
nectarine *n* 57
needle *n* 20
needlefish *n* 166
needle-nose pliers *n* 36
needle plate *n* 142
needlepoint *n* 142
negative *adj* 75
negative electrode *n* 75
negotiate *v* 92
negotiating *n* 93
neighbor (US) *n* 07
neighbour (UK) *n* 07
neodymium *n* 78
Neogene *adj* 157
Neogene *n* 157
neon *n* 78
Nepal *n* 150, 153
Nepalese *adj* 153
Nepalese people *n* 153
nephew *n* 05
Neptune *n* 143
neptunium *n* 78
nerve *n* 03, 22
nervous *adj* 04, 06, 10
nest *n* 160
net *n* 109, 112, 114
net *v* 121
net curtain *n* 26
netball *n* 125
Netherlands *n* 151, 153
nettle *n* 169
neurology *n* 21
neutral *n* 33
neutral zone *n* 107, 110
neutron *n* 76
neutron star *n* 144
never *adv* 171, 172
Nevisian *adj* 152
Nevisians *n* 152
new *adj* 176
new leaves *n* 172
new moon *n* 143
new potato *n* 56
New Year *n* 07
New Zealand *adj* 153
New Zealand *n* 150, 153
New Zealanders *n* 153
newborn baby *n* 08
news anchor (US) *n* 137
news *n* 137
news website *n* 84
newsboy cap *n* 16
newsfeed *n* 84
newspaper *n* 48, 138
newsreader (UK) *n* 89, 137
newsstand *n* 46, 48
next to *prep* 148, 180
nib *n* 73, 175
nibble *v* 52
Nicaragua *n* 150, 152
Nicaraguan *adj* 152
Nicaraguans *n* 152
nice *adj* 177
nickel *n* 78, 156
niece *n* 05
nigella seeds *n* 59
Niger *n* 149, 152
Nigeria *n* 149, 152
Nigerian *adj* 152
Nigerians *n* 152
Nigerien *adj* 152
Nigeriens *n* 152
night *n* 171
nightgown *n* 14
night light (UK) *n* 30
night-light (US) *n* 30
nightclub *n* 42
nightdress *n* 14
nightie *n* 14
nightingale *n* 160
nightmare *n* 30
nightstand (US) *n* 30
nightwear *n* 14
nihonium *n* 78
Nile crocodile *n* 163
nine *num* 173
nine-to-five job *n* 81
nineteen *num* 173
ninety *num* 173
ninth *num* 173
niobium *n* 78
nipple *n* 01, 08
nitrogen *n* 78

no entry *n* 96
no overtaking (UK) *phr* 96
no passing (US) *phr* 96
no photography *phr* 130
no right turn *phr* 96
no U-turn *phr* 96
no vacancies *phr* 131
no-charge
semi-circle *n* 112
nobelium *n* 78
noble gases *n* 78
nobles *n* 79
nod *v* 02
noisy *adj* 176
non-blood relative *n* 05
non-carbonated *adj* 52
nonfiction (US) *n* 138
non-fiction (UK) *n* 138
nonmetals *n* 78
non-metals *n* 78
noodle soup *n* 72
noodles *n* 64, 70, 72
normal *adj* 18
normal hair *n* 12
north *n* 148
North America *n* 150, 152
North American *adj* 152
North Americans *n* 152
North Korea *n* 150, 153
North Korean *adj* 153
North Koreans *n* 153
North
Macedonia *n* 151, 153
North Macedonian *adj* 153
North Macedonians *n* 153
North Pole *n* 75, 145
northeast *n* 148
northern cardinal *n* 161
Northern
Hemisphere *n* 145
northwest *n* 148
Norway *n* 151, 153
Norwegian *adj* 153
Norwegians *n* 153
nose *n* 01, 103
nose clip *n* 118
nose cone *n* 123
noseband *n* 120
nosebleed *n* 19
nosewheel *n* 103
nostrils *n* 01
notation *n* 128
notebook *n* 73, 95
notepad *n* 82
notes (UK) *n* 45, 94
notes *n* 95, 128
notice board (UK) *n* 82
nougat *n* 67
nought point five (UK)
num 173
noughts and
crosses (UK) *n* 140
novel *n* 138
November *n* 172
now *adv* 171
nozzle *n* 40
nuclear energy *n* 51
nuclear power
plant (US) *n* 51
nuclear power
station (UK) *n* 51
nuclear waste *n* 51
nucleus *n* 76, 77
number *n* 112
number eight *n* 108
numbers *n* 173
numeracy *n* 93
numerals *n* 175
numerator *n* 74
nurse *n* 20, 21, 89
nursery *n* 30
nursing *n* 80
nut allergy *n* 23
nut, nuts *n* 36, 58, 68, 129
nutmeg *n* 59
nutrition *n* 23

O

oak *n* 169
oar *n* 119
oasis *n* 146
oatmeal (US) *n* 70
objective lens *n* 77
obliques *n* 03
oboe *n* 128
observatory *n* 144
obsidian *n* 156
obstetrician *n* 08
occupations *n* 89–90
occluded front *n* 155
ocean *n* 145, 134, 147
ocean life *n* 166
ocean ridge *n* 145
Oceania *n* 150, 153
Oceanian *adj* 153
Oceanians *n* 153
octagon *n* 74
October *n* 172
octopus *n* 54, 166
odd *adj* 177
odometer *n* 99
oesophagus (UK) *n* 04
off (UK) *adj* 52
off licence (UK) *n* 46
off the shoulder *adj* 15
off-piste *n* 122
off-road motorcycle *n* 100
offal *n* 53
offence (UK) *n* 107
offense (US) *n* 107
office *n* 82
office building *n* 42
office equipment *n* 82
office manager *n* 81
office reception *n* 81
office services *n* 91
office work *n* 81
often *adv* 172
oganesson *n* 78
ogre *n* 139
oil *n* 51, 60, 64, 97
oil field *n* 51
oil painting *n* 130
oil paints *n* 141
oil slick *n* 155
oil tank *n* 100
oil tanker *n* 105
oil terminal *n* 106
oil-filled radiator *n* 33
oily *adj* 18
ointment *n* 20, 49
okra *n* 55
old *adj* 12, 176
old man cactus *n* 168
old-fashioned *adj* 177
oleander *n* 169
oleaster *n* 169
olive *n* 68, 169
olive oil *n* 60
olm *n* 163
Oman *n* 151, 153
Omani *adj* 153
Omanis *n* 153
omelet (US) *n* 61, 71, 72
omelette (UK) *n* 61, 71, 72
on *prep* 180
on-demand boiler (US) *n* 33
on stage *adj* 126
on the corner *phr* 148
on the left *phr* 148
on the right *phr* 148
on time *adj* 171
once a week *adv* 172
oncology *n* 21
one *num* 173
one billion *num* 173
one hundred *num* 173
one million *num* 173
one o'clock *n* 171
one thirty *n* 171
one thousand *num* 173
one-way street *n* 96
one-way system *n* 42
one-way ticket *n* 131
onesie *n* 13
onion dome *n* 44
onion *n* 56
online banking *n* 45, 94
online check-in *n* 104
online
communication *n* 83
online delivery *n* 91
online map *n* 148
online media *n* 84
online retail *n* 91
online shopping *n* 48
only child *n* 05
only weekends *adv* 172
onyx *n* 156
opal *n* 156
open *adj* 48, 132
open sandwich *n* 70
open turn *n* 118
open-air activities *n* 133
open-air hobbies *n* 133
open-cast
mining (UK) *n* 51
open-pit mining (US) *n* 51
open-plan *n* 32
opening night *n* 126
opening times *n* 132
openside flanker *n* 108
opera *n* 126, 129
opera glasses *n* 22
opera house *n* 126
operating room (US) *n* 21
operating table *n* 21
operating theatre (UK) *n* 21
operation *n* 21
ophthalmology *n* 21
opinions *n* 177
opium poppy *n* 168
opponent *n* 117
opposite *prep* 112, 148
optician *n* 22, 46, 89
optics *n* 75
optimistic *adj* 10
optometrist *n* 22
orange *n* 57, 141
orange juice
with pulp *n* 65
orange peel fungus *n* 170
orange-cap boletus *n* 170
orangeade *n* 52
orangutan *n* 159
orb weaver *n* 162
orbit *n* 143
orc *n* 139
orchestra *n* 128
orchestra pit *n* 126
orchestra
seating (US) *n* 126
orchestral
instruments *n* 128
orchid *n* 38, 47
order *v* 46, 69
ordering online *n* 46
ordinal numbers *n* 173
Ordovician *adj* 157
Ordovician *n* 157
oregano *n* 59
organic *adj* 23, 39, 53
organic food section *n* 23
organic vegetables *n* 55
organization *n* 93
organize *v* 92
organized *adj* 93
oriental fire-bellied
toad *n* 163
orienteering *n* 133, 148
origami *n* 141
original *adj* 93
Orion *n* 144
ornamental plants *n* 41
orthodontist *n* 89
Orthodox church *n* 44
orthopaedics (UK) *n* 21
orthopedics (US) *n* 21
oryx *n* 159
osmium *n* 78
osprey *n* 160
osteopathy *n* 24
ostrich *n* 160, 165
otter *n* 158
Ottoman *n* 30
oud *n* 129
ounce *n* 174
out *adj* 113
out *adv* 180
out field *n* 111
out of bounds *adj* 112
outboard motor *n* 105
outbox *n* 83
outdoor activities *n* 133
outer core *n* 145
outfield *adj* 113
outfielders *n* 113
outgoing *adj* 10
outlay *n* 94
outpatient *n* 21
outside *adv, prep* 180
outside center (US) *n* 108
outside centre (UK) *n* 108
outside hitter *n* 112
outside lane *n* 96
outside linebacker *n* 107
outstanding *adj* 177
oval *n* 74
ovary *n* 04, 38
oven *n* 27
oven glove (UK) *n* 29
oven mitt (US) *n* 29
over par *adj* 115
overhanging eaves *n* 44
over-the-counter
drugs *n* 49
overalls *n* 13, 37
overcast *adj* 154
overdraft *n* 45, 94
overeat *v* 23
overfishing *n* 155
overhead compartment
n 103
overpass *n* 102
overtake (UK) *v* 98
overtime *n* 81
own *v* 32
Oxfords *n* 17
oxygen *n* 78
oxygen mask *n* 21, 50
oyster *n* 54
oyster mushroom *n* 56
mushrooms *n* 170
oyster sauce *n* 60
oystercatcher *n* 160
ozone depletion *n* 155
ozone layer *n* 155

P

PA (personal assistant) *n* 81
pacifier (US) *n* 08
pack *v* 11, 32
pack your bags *v* 131
pack your lunch *v* 09
package *n* 45, 48
packet *n* 52
paddle *n* 114, 119
paddleboarding *n* 119

paddling pool (UK) *n* 25, 133
paddock *n* 120
paediatrics (UK) *n* 21
paella *n* 72
page *n* 138
pail and shovel (US) *n* 134
pain au chocolat *n* 62
pain *n* 19
painkillers *n* 20, 49
paint *n* 37
paint *v* 37
paint a wall *v* 35
paint kettle (UK) *n* 37
paint bucket (US) *n* 37
paint stripper *n* 37
paint tray *n* 37
paint tube *n* 141
paintballing *n* 133
paintbrush *n* 37
painted lady butterfly *n* 162
painter *n* 89
painting *n* 26, 130, 141
paisley *adj* 13
pajamas (US) *n* 14
pak-choi (UK) *n* 55
Pakistan *n* 150, 153
Pakistani *adj* 153
Pakistanis *n* 153
palace *n* 132
palate *n* 04
Palau *n* 150, 153
Palauan *adj* 153
Palauan people *n* 153
Paleogene *adj* 157
Paleogene *n* 157
paleontologist *n* 77
Paleozoic (old life) *adj* 157
Paleozoic (old life) *n* 157
palette *n* 141
palette knife *n* 141
palladium *n* 78
pallet *n* 87
palm *n* 02, 41
palm hearts *n* 55
palm oil *n* 60
palm tree *n* 134
palomar knot *n* 121
pampas grass *n* 38, 167
Pamukkale *n* 145
pan *n* 174
panama *n* 16
Panama *n* 150, 152
Panamanian *adj* 152
Panamanians *n* 152
pancake *n* 65, 71
pancreas *n* 04
panda *n* 159
paneer *n* 64
pangolin *n* 159
panpipe *n* 129
pansy *n* 38
panther chameleon *n* 163
panties (US) *n* 14
pantograph *n* 102
pantry *n* 27
pants (US) *n* 15, 107
panty liner *n* 49
pantyhose (US) *n* 14
paparazzi *n* 127
papaya *n* 58
paper *adj* 176
paper *n* 82, 155, 176
paper clip, paper clips *n* 73, 82
paper napkin *n* 70
paperback *n* 138
papier-mâché *n* 141
paprika *n* 59
Papua New Guinea *n* 150, 153
Papua New Guinean *adj* 153
Papua New Guineans *n* 153
papyrus sedge *n* 167
par *n* 115
para athlete *n* 125
para ice hockey *n* 122
parachute *n* 125
parachuting *n* 125
paraglider *n* 125
paragliding *n* 125
Paraguay *n* 149, 152
Paraguayan *adj* 152
Paraguayans *n* 152
parallel *adj* 74
parallel bars *n* 125
parallelogram *n* 74
paramedic *n* 21, 50, 90
paramotor *n* 103
parasailing *n* 119
parasol *n* 65
parasports *n* 125
parcel (UK) *n* 45
Parcheesi (US) *n* 140
parchment *n* 175
parents *n* 05
park *n* 42, 133
park *v* 98
parking attendant *n* 96
parking enforcement officer (US) *n* 96
parking lot (US) *n* 42
parking meter *n* 96
parking space *n* 32
parkour *n* 133
Parmesan *n* 64
parole *n* 85
parry *v* 117
parsley *n* 59
parsnip *n* 56
parson's chameleon *n* 163
particle accelerator *n* 75
particle board (US) *n* 35
particle *n* 75
partner *n* 05, 07
parts of the body *n* 01
parts of the day *n* 171
pass *n* 112
pass *v* 73, 98, 107, 108, 110
passenger aeroplane (UK) *n* 103
passenger airplane (US) *n* 103
passenger port *n* 106
passenger seat (US) *n* 100
passengers *n* 102, 106
passing lane *n* 103
passion flower *n* 169
passion fruit *n* 58
passionate *adj* 10
Passover *n* 07
passport *n* 104
passport control *n* 104
password *n* 83
pasta *n* 64, 72
pasta shells *n* 64
pastels *n* 141
pasteurized *adj* 61
pasting table *n* 37
pastrami *n* 64
pastry *n* 63
pastry brush *n* 29
pasture *n* 86
patch *n* 101
patchwork *n* 142
pâté *n* 64, 71
patella *n* 03
path *n* 41
pathology *n* 21
patience (UK) *n* 140
patient *adj* 10, 93
patient *n* 19, 20, 21
patio *n* 25
patio doors *n* 25
patio garden *n* 41
patio umbrella *n* 65
patty pan *n* 56
pause *v* 137
pavement (UK) *n* 25, 43, 65
paving *n* 41
pavlova *n* 63
pawn *n* 140
pay *n* 81
pay *v* 46
pay by card *v* 94
pay cut *n* 81
pay in *v* 45
pay-per-view channel *n* 137
pay separately *v* 69
pay slip *n* 81
pay the bills *v* 09
pay with cash *v* 94
paying attention to detail *n* 93
pea *n* 55
peace lily *n* 38
peach *n* 57
peacock butterfly *n* 162
peacock *n* 161
peak *n* 147
peanut *n* 58, 68
peanut allergy *n* 23
peanut butter *n* 60
peanut oil (US) *n* 60
pear *n* 58, 169
peasants *n* 79
peat *n* 39
peat bog *n* 79
pecan *n* 58, 168
pectoral *n* 03
pedal *n* 101
pedal *v* 101
pedestrian crossing *n* 96
pedestrian zone *n* 42
pediatrics (US) *n* 21
pedicure *n* 18
pediment *n* 44
peel *v* 29
peeled prawn *n* 54
peeler *n* 28
peep toes *n* 17
pelican *n* 160
pelvis *n* 03
pen *n* 73, 82, 86
penalty area *n* 109
penalty bench *n* 110
penalty kick *n* 109
penalty spot *n* 109
pencil *n* 73, 82, 141, 175
pencil case *n* 73
pencil sharpener *n* 73, 82
pendant *n* 16
pendulous nose *n* 159
peninsula *n* 147
penis *n* 04
penne *n* 64
penny candy (US) *n* 67
pen pal *n* 07
penstock *n* 51
pentagon *n* 74
peony *n* 47, 168
people carrier (UK) *n* 97
pepper *n* 26
peppercorns *n* 59
peppered moth *n* 162
pepperoni *n* 64
pepper *n* 56
percent *n* 173
percentage, percentages *n* 74, 173
perch *n* 54
percussion *n* 128
peregrine falcon *n* 160
perennial *n* 41
performance *n* 126
performer *n* 126
performing arts *n* 91
perfume *n* 18
perfumery (UK) *n* 47
pergola *n* 41
period (US) *n* 175
period drama *n* 137
periodic table *n* 78
periodical *n* 80
permanent *adj* 81
permanent exhibition *n* 130
Permian *adj* 157
Permian *n* 157
perpendicular *n* 74
Persian *n* 164
persimmon *n* 58
personal assistant (PA) *n* 90
personal services *n* 91
personal trainer *n* 124
personality traits *n* 10
perspire *v* 02
Peru *n* 149, 152
Peruvian *adj* 152
Peruvians *n* 152
pescatarian *adj* 23
pescatarian *n* 23
pesticide *n* 40, 55, 86
pestle *n* 28, 76
pet *n* 164
pet food *n* 48
pet services *n* 91
pet shop (UK) *n* 46
pet store (US) *n* 46
pet supplies *n* 164
pet therapy *n* 24
petal *n* 38
petri dish *n* 77
petrol (UK) *n* 97
petrol pump (UK) *n* 97
petrol station (UK) *n* 42, 97
petroleum engineering *n* 91
pH level *n* 76
pharmaceuticals *n* 91
pharmacist *n* 49, 89
pharmacy *n* 42, 49
pharynx *n* 04
pheasant *n* 53, 161
Philippines *n* 151, 153
Phillips screwdriver *n* 36
philosopher *n* 79
philosophy *n* 80
phoenix *n* 139
phone *n* 82
phoropter *n* 22
phosphorus *n* 78
photo booth *v* 46
photo finish *n* 116
photocopier *n* 82
photofit (UK) *n* 85
photographer *n* 89
photosynthesis *n* 77
phrasal verbs *n* 178
phrasebook *n* 131
phyllo (US) *n* 63
physical education *n* 73
physical therapist *n* 89
physical therapy (US) *n* 21
physics *n* 73, 75, 80
physiotherapist *n* 89
physiotherapy (UK) *n* 21
piano *n* 128, 129
piano overture *n* 128
piccalilli *n* 60
piccolo *n* 128
pick *v* 57
pick 'n' mix (UK) *n* 67
pick mushrooms *v* 170
pick someone up *v* 98

pick up *v* 11, 178
pick-up *n* 129
pickax (US) *n* 87
pickaxe (UK) *n* 87
pickled *adj* 72
pickled beetroot *n* 60
pickled onions *n* 60
pickles *n* 60, 72
pickpocketing *n* 85
picnic *n* 133
picnic basket *n* 133, 134
picnic bench *n* 135
meat pie *n* 72
pie pan (US) *n* 29
pie dish (UK) *n* 29
pieces *n* 140
pier *n* 106
pig *n* 165
pig farm *n* 86
pigeon *n* 160
pigeon pose *n* 24
piglet *n* 165
pigtails *n* 12
pike perch *n* 54
Pilates *n* 124
pile up *v* 178
pileated
woodpecker *n* 160
pillion *n* 100
pillow *n* [illegible]
pillowcase *n* 30
pills *n* 20, 49
pilot *n* 90, 103
Pilsner *n* 68
pin *n* 16, 33, 142
PIN *n* 45
pin *v* 117
pinch *n* 29
pincushion *n* 142
pine nuts *n* 58
pineapple *n* 58, 167
pineapple juice *n* 65
ping pong *n* 114
pink *n* 141
pinking scissors (UK) *n* 142
pinking shears (US) *n* 142
pint *n* 174
pint glass *n* 27
pipe cutter *n* 36
pipe *n* 33, 87, 98
pipe organ *n* 128
pipefish *n* 166
pipette *n* 76
piping bag *n* 29
pirouette *v* 126
Pisces *n* 144
pistachio *n* 58
pistol *n* 88
pit lane *n* 123
pit stop *n* 123
pita bread (US) *n* 62, 72
pitch *n* 107, 109, 111, 128
pitch (UK) *n* 109, 135
pitch a tent *v* 135
pitch *v* 113
pitcher *n* 113
pitcher plant *n* 168
pitcher's mound *n* 113
pitches
available (UK) *phr* 135
pitta bread (UK) *n* 62, 72
pixie *n* 139
pizza *n* 70
pizza cutter *n* 28
pizza oven *n* 70
pizzeria *n* 70
place mat *n* 26
place setting *n* 27
place to live *n* 25
placenta *n* 08
placerias *n* 157
plaice *n* 54
plaid *adj* 13
plain *n* 146
plain *adj* 13
plain flour *n* 62
plaintiff (US) *n* 85
plait *n* 12
plan your route *v* 148
plane *n* 36
plane *v* 35
planets *n* 143
plank pose *n* 24
plankton *n* 77, 166
planner (US) *n* 82, 138
plant cell *n* 77
plant cutting *n* 39
plant food *n* 39
plant *n* 77, 167–169
plant pot *n* 40
plant *v* 39, 86
plantains *n* 86
plaque *n* 22
plaster *n* 37, 49
plaster *v* 37
plaster (UK) *n* 20
plastic *adj* 155, 176
plastic *n* 155, 176
plastic surgery *n* 21
plastic waste *n* 155
plate *n* 145
plate tectonics *n* 145
plateau *n* 146
plateosaurus *n* 157
platform *n* 84, 102, 118
platforms *n* 17
platform game *n* 136
platform number *n* 102
platinum *n* 78, 156
platypus *n* 158
play *n* 126
play *v* 11, 113, 137, 140
play a musical
instrument *v* 09
play suit *n* 13
play (the trumpet) *v* 128
play with your kids *v* 09
player *n* 108, 113, 114, 140
player's number *n* 107
players' bench *n*
107, 109, 110
players' dugout *n* 113
players' entrance/
exit *n* 109
playground *n* 43
playing cards *n* 140
playing surface *n* 108
playpen *n* 08
plead *v* 85
pleasant *adj* 177
pleased *adj* 06
pleat *n* 14
plié *v* 126
Plimsoll line *n* 105
plough (UK) *n* 86
Plough (UK) *n* 144
plow (US) *n* 86
plug *n* 31, 33, 83
plug in *v* 83
plug-in hybrid *n* 97
plughole (UK) *n* 31
plum *n* 57, 169
plum tomato *n* 56
plumb line *n* 37
plumber *n* 89
plumbing *n* 33
plunger *n* 31, 36
plus sign *n* 74
plush toy (US) *n* 08
Pluto *n* 143
plutonium *n* 78
plywood *n* 35
pneumatic drill (UK) *n* 87
poach *v* 29
poached *adj* 72
poached egg *n* 61, 71
pocket *n* 15, 125, 142
pod *n* 55
podcast *n* 84
podium *n* 116, 128
poetry therapy *n* 24
point *n* 111
point *v* 11
point guard *n* 112
point out *v* 178
points *n* 140
poison dart frog *n* 163
poisoning *n* 19
Poland *n* 151, 153
polar bear *n* 159
polar region *n* 146
Polaris *n* 144
pole *n* 121
pole position *n* 123
Pole Star *n* 144
pole stretcher *n* 50
pole vault *n* 116
Poles *n* 153
police *n* 50
police bike *n* 50
police car *n* 50
police cell *n* 50
police dog *n* 50
police hat *n* 50
police officer *n* 50, 89
police station *n* 42, 50
Polish *adj* 153
polish *n* 34
polite *adj* 10
politics *n* 80
polka dot (US) *adj* 13
polka dot plant *n* 38
pollock *n* 54
pollution *n* 155
polo *n* 120
polo shirt *n* 14
polonium *n* 78
pom pom beanie (US) *n* 16
pomegranate *n* 58, 168
pomelo *n* 57
Pomeranian *n* 164
pommel *n* 120
pommel horse *n* 125
poncho *n* 15
pond *n* 41, 86
ponytail *n* 12
poodle *n* 164
pool *n* 125
pool ring (US) *n* 134
pop *n* 129
Pop Art *n* 130
pop concert *n* 129
pop-up *n* 84
pop-up tent *n* 135
popcorn *n* 127
poplar *n* 168
popper (UK) *n* 13
popping crease *n* 111
poppy *n* 38
poppy seeds *n* 59
popular music *n* 129
porch *n* 25
porch light *n* 25
porcini *n* 170
porcupine *n* 158
porcupine fish *n* 166
pores *n* 12
pork *n* 53
porpoise *n* 166
porridge (UK) *n* 71
port *n* 68, 106
portable speakers *n* 95
portcullis *n* 44
porter *n* 21, *n* 131
portfolio *n* 92, 94
portion *n* 26
Portugal *n* 151, 153
Portuguese *adj* 153
Portuguese man-
of-war *n* 166
Portuguese people *n* 153
position markers *n* 129
positive *adj* 75
positive electrode *n* 75
post *v* 84
post office *n* 42, 45
post protector *n* 108
Post-Impressionism *n* 130
postal worker *n* 45
postbox (UK) *n* 45
postcard *n* 48, 132
postcode (UK) *n* 45
poster paint *n* 141
postgraduate *n* 80
postman (UK) *n* 45, 90
postmark *n* 45
postwoman (UK) *n* 45, 90
pot plant *n* 47
pot *v* 39
potassium *n* 78
potato *n* 56
potato cakes *n* 71
potato fork *n* 40
potatoes *n* 86
pothole *n* 101
potion *n* 139
potted plant *n* 41
potter *n* 141
potter's wheel *n* 141
pottery *n* 141
potting shed *n* 39
potty *n* 08
pouch *n* 158
poultry *n* 48, 53, 165
poultry farm *n* 86
pounce *v* 159
pound *n* 174
pour *v* 29
pour down *v* 178
powder *n* 49
powder puff *n* 18
powdered milk *n* 61
power *n* 33
power cord (US) *n* 83
power cut (UK) *n* 33
power forward *n* 112
power lead *n* 83
power outage (US) *n* 33
power station *n* 44
power supply *n* 51
practical *adj* 93
practice swing *n* 115
prairie *n* 146
pram (UK) *n* 08
praseodymium *n* 78
praying mantis *n* 162
Precambrian *adj* 157
Precambrian *n* 157
prefab house *n* 32
pregnancy *n* 08
pregnancy test *n* 08
pregnant *adj* 08
premiere *n* 127
premolars (UK) *n* 03
preparation *n* 54
prepositions *n* 148, 180
prescription *n* 20, 49
present *n* 07
presentation *n* 82, 95
presenter (UK) *n* 84, 137
presenter remote *n* 95
presenting *n* 95
preserved fruit *n* 60
preserving jar *n* 60
press ups (UK) *n* 124
presser foot *n* 142
pressure cooker *n* 28
pressure gauge *n* 33
pretty *adj* 177
pretzel *n* 62

preview *n* 137
price *n* 69
price list *n* 70
price tag *n* 47
prickly pear *n* 58, 168
prima donna *n* 126
primer *n* 37
prince *n* 79
princess *n* 79
principal *n* 73
print *v* 83
printer *n* 82
printing *n* 141, 175
priority traffic *n* 96
prism *n* 75
prison *n* 85
prison guards *n* 85
prisoners *n* 85
private bathroom *n* 131
private investigator *n* 89
private jet *n* 103
private room *n* 21
probe *n* 22
problem-solving *n* 93
proboscis monkey *n* 159
proceed to checkout *v* 46
processed food *n* 23
producer *n* 126, 127
production *n* 91
professional *adj* 93
professional attributes *n* 93
professional expertise *n* 93
program (US) *n* 126, 137
programme (UK) *n* 126, 137
project management *n* 93
projector *n* 82, 95
promenade *n* 134
promethium *n* 78
propagate *v* 39
propeller *n* 103, 105
property (UK) *n* 32, 91
proposal *n* 82
props *n* 126, 127
prosciutto *n* 64
prosecution *n* 85
prosecutor *n* 85
prostate gland *n* 04
protactinium *n* 78
protea *n* 38
protective padding *n* 110
protein *n* 23
proton *n* 76
protractor *n* 73, 74
proud *adj* 06
prove (UK) *v* 62
prow *n* 105
prowl *v* 159
prune *v* 39
pruners (US) *n* 40
prunes *n* 58
pruning knife *n* 40
pruning saw *n* 40
psychiatry *n* 21
psychologist *n* 90
psychotherapy *n* 24
public address
system *n* 102
public footpath *n* 148
public relations (PR) *n* 91
public speaking *n* 93
puck *n* 110
pudding (UK) *n* 69
puddle *n* 154
puff pastry *n* 63
pufferfish *n* 166
pug *n* 164
pull *v* 11
pull-along toy *n* 08
pulp *n* 03, 57
pulses (UK) *n* 23
pumice *n* 156
pumice stone *n* 31
pump *n* 101
pumpkin *n* 56
punch *v* 117
punchbag (UK) *n* 117
punching bag (US) *n* 117
punctual *adj* 93
puncture *n* 101
puncture repair kit *n* 101
punk *n* 129
pupil *n* 01, 73
puppet *n* 08
puppy *n* 164
purchasing *n* 91
purple *n, adj* 141
purple loosestrife *n* 168
purr *v* 164
purse *n* 16, 94
push ups *n* 124
push *v* 11
put away *v* 178
put on *v* 14, 178
put on makeup *v* 09
put the children to
bed *v* 09
put together *v* 178
put up shelves *v* 35
putt *v* 115
putter *n* 115
puzzle game *n* 136
puzzles *n* 138
pyjamas (UK) *n* 14
pylon *n* 51
pyramid *n* 74
pyramids of Giza *n* 44

Q

Qatar *n* 151, 153
Qatari *adj* 153
Qataris *n* 153
qibla prayer wall *n* 44
quack *v* 165
quad bike *n* 100
quad biking (UK) *n* 133
quadriceps *n* 03
quail *n* 53
quail egg *n* 61
qualifying *n* 123
quart *n* 174
quarter *num* 173
quarter of an hour *n* 171
quarter past one *n* 171
quarter to two *n* 171
quarterback *n* 107
quarterdeck *n* 105
quartz *n* 156
quartzite *n* 156
Quaternary *adj* 157
Quaternary *n* 157
quay *n* 106
queen *n* 79, 140
queen of the Andes *n* 167
quest *n* 139
question *v* 73
question mark *n* 175
queue (UK) *n* 48, 104, 132
queue (UK) *v* 104
quiet *adj* 176
quilt *n* 30
quilted jacket *n* 15
quilting *n* 142
quince *n* 58
quiver *n* 125
quiz show *n* 137

R

rabbit *n* 53, 158, 164
rabbit hutch *n* 164
raccoon *n* 158
race *n* 116
race car (US) *n* 97, 123
race car driver (US) *n* 123
race number *n* 100
race track *n* 123
racecourse *n* 120
racehorse *n* 120
racing bike *n* 100, 101
racing car (UK) *n* 97, 123
racing dive *n* 118
racing driver (UK) *n* 123
racing events *n* 116
racing overalls *n* 123
rack *n* 100, 125
racket *n* 114
racket games *n* 114
racquetball *n* 114
radar *n* 105
radar speed gun *n* 50
radiated tortoise *n* 163
radiator *n* 33, 98
radicchio *n* 55
radio antenna *n* 105
radio *n* 50, 84, 88, 136
radio DJ *n* 90
radio station *n* 84
radio telescope *n* 144
radio waves *n* 75
radioactivity *n* 75
radiology *n* 21
radish *n* 56
radium *n* 78
radius *n* 03, 74
radon *n* 78
raffia palm *n* 167
rafter *n* 87
rafting *n* 119
Ragdoll *n* 164
rail network *n* 102
railing *n* 65
railroad (US) *n* 148
railroad
terminal (US) *n* 106
railway (UK) *n* 148
railway
terminal (UK) *n* 106
rain *n* 51, 154
rain boots (US) *n* 17
rain forest *n* 146, 159
rain gear (US) *n* 135
rainbow *n* 154
rainbow trout *n* 54
raincoat *n* 15
raindrop *n* 154
rainfly (US) *n* 135
rainy *adj* 154
raise *n* 81
raise *v* 11
raised mudguard *n* 100
raisin *n* 58
rake *n* 40
rake (leaves) *v* 39
rake (soil) *v* 39
rally *n* 114
rally driving *n* 123
ram *n* 165
ramekin *n* 28
ramen *n* 64, 72
ramp (US) *n* 96
ranch house (US) *n* 32
rapeseed *n* 86
rapeseed oil *n* 60
rapids *n* 119, 146
ras el hanout *n* 59
rash *n* 19
raspberry *n* 57
raspberry jam *n* 60
rat *n* 158
rattle *n* 08
rattlesnake *n* 163
raven *n* 160
raw *adj* 56
raw meat *n* 53
ray *n* 166
razor blade *n* 31
razor-shell *n* 54
reach a consensus *v* 95
reach an agreement *v* 95
reaction *n* 76
reaction direction *n* 76
reactor *n* 51
read *v* 73
read a map *v* 148
read a newspaper *v* 09
reading *n* 138
reading a map *n* 148
reading glasses *n* 22, 49
reading light *n* 103
reading list *n* 80
reading room *n* 80
real estate (US) *n* 32, 91
real estate agent (US) 89
reality TV *n* 137
realtor (US) *n* 32
reamer *n* 36
rear light *n* 101
rear suspension *n* 123
rear wheel *n* 99
rear wing *n* 97, 123
reasonable *adj* 10
rebound *n* 112
receipt *n* 48, 69, 94
receptacle *n* 38
reception (UK) *n* 131
receptionist *n* 81, 90, 131
reconnaissance
aircraft *n* 88
reconnaissance
vehicle *n* 88
record player *n* 136
record shop (UK) *n* 46
record store (US) *n* 46
record *v* 137
recorder *n* 129
recording studio *n* 84
records *n* 136
recover *v* 20
recovery room *n* 21
recruiter (US) *n* 92
recruitment
agency (UK) *n* 92
rectangle *n* 74
recycling *n* 91, 155
recycling bin *n* 33, 34
red *n* 141
red blood cell *n* 77
red cabbage *n* 55
red card *n* 109
red carpet *n* 127
red currant (US) *n* 57
red deer *n* 158
red fox *n* 159
red giant *n* 144
red hair *n* 12
red line *n* 110
red meat *n* 53
red mullet *n* 54
red panda *n* 159
red salamander *n* 163
red wine *n* 52, 68
red-eyed tree frog *n* 163
redcurrant (UK) *n* 57
reed *n* 167
reef *n* 147
reel *n* 121
reel in *v* 121
refectory (UK) *n* 80
referee *n* 107–109, 112
referee crease *n* 110
reflected radiation *n* 155
reflection *n* 75
reflector 100, 101
reflector strap *n* 100
reflector telescope *n* 144
reflexology *n* 24
refraction *n* 75
refractor telescope *n* 144
refrigerator *n* 27

refund *v* 46
reggae *n* 129
registered mail *n* 45
registered trademark *n* 175
regulator *n* 118
reiki *n* 24
reindeer *n* 159
reins *n* 120
relationships *n* 05, 07
relaxation *n* 24
relaxed *adj* 06
relaxing *adj* 177
relay race *n* 116
release *v* 121
reliable *adj* 10, 93
remains *n* 79
remarkable *adj* 177
remember *v* 11
remote *n* 137
remote control *n* 26, 83, 136
removal van (UK) *n* 32
renew *v* 80
renewable energy *n* 51
rent *v* 32
rent a cottage *v* 131
rent out *v* 32
renting a house *n* 32
repair *v* 11, 33
reply *v* 83
reply to all *v* 83
report *n* 82
reporter *n* 137
reproduction *n* 77
reproductive *n* 04
reproductive organs *n* 04
reptiles *n* 163
Republic of the Congo *n* 149, 152
research *n* 91, 93
research and development (R&D) *n* 91
reserve *v* 80
reservoir *n* 51
residential area *n* 32
residential buildings *n* 44
residential district *n* 42
resign *v* 81
resit (UK) *v* 73
respectful *adj* 177
respiratory *n* 04
responsible *adj* 93
rest *v* 20
rest stop (US) *n* 148
restaurant *n* 42, 69, 131
restaurant manager *n* 69
restricted area *n* 112
restroom (US) *n* 47, 130, 131
résumé (US) *n* 92
resurfacing *n* 87
resuscitate *v* 20
retail *n* 91
retake (US) *v* 73
reticulated python *n* 163
retina *n* 22
retinal camera *n* 22
retire *v* 07, 81
retriever *n* 164
return *n* 114
return *v* 46, 80
return crease *n* 111
return ticket (UK) *n* 131
reusable cup *n* 70
rev counter (UK) *n* 99
reverb *n* 129
reverse *v* 96
reversible direction *n* 76
review *n* 138
review (US) *v* 73
revise (UK) *v* 73
rewind *v* 137
rewire the house *v* 35
rhenium *n* 78
rhinoceros *n* 158
rhinoceros beetle *n* 162
rhodium *n* 78
rhododendron *n* 38
rhombus *n* 74
rhubarb *n* 58
rib *n* 03, 53
rib cage *n* 03
ribs *n* 70
ribbon *n* 63, 125, 142
rice *n* 72, 86
rice bowl *n* 27
rice noodles *n* 64
rice pudding *n* 63
rich *adj* 52
ride *v* 11
ride passenger *v* 100
ride pillion *v* 100
rider *n* 100, 120
ridge *n* 146
ridge beam *n* 87
riding boot *n* 17, 120
riding crop *n* 120
riding hat *n* 120
rifle *n* 88
rig *n* 129
rigging *n* 119
right angle *n* 74
right bend *n* 96
right cornerback *n* 107
right defenceman (UK) *n* 110
right defenseman (US) *n* 110
right defensive end *n* 107
right defensive tackle *n* 107
right guard *n* 107
right of way *n* 96
right safety *n* 107
right side *n* 112
right tackle *n* 107
right wing *n* 108
right winger *n* 110
rim *n* 101
rind *n* 61, 64
ring *n* 16, 170
ring binder *n* 82
ring finger *n* 02
ring ties *n* 40
ring-tailed lemur *n* 159
rings *n* 125, 143
rinse *v* 22
rip out *v* 178
ripe *adj* 57
rise *v* 62
risotto *n* 72
river *n* 147, 148
river features *n* 147, 148
road *n* 96
road bike *n* 101
road construction (US) *n* 87, 96
road markings *n* 96
road signs *n* 96
roadmap *n* 95
roadmap (US) *n* 148
roadworks (UK) *n* 87, 96
roadworks ahead (UK) *n* 96
roar *v* 159
roast *n* 29, 72
robbers *n* 50
robbery *n* 50, 85
robe *n* 80
rock *n* 129
rock climbing *n* 125
rock garden *n* 41
rock pool (UK) *n* 134
rock star *n* 90
rocket *n* 143
rocket (UK) *n* 55
rockhopper penguin *n* 161
rocks *n* 147, 156
rocking chair *n* 26
rocking horse *n* 08
rodeo *n* 120
roe deer *n* 158
roentgenium *n* 78
role-playing game *n* 136
roll *n* 62
roll *v* 29
roll bar (US) *n* 97
roller *n* 37, 87
roller bar (UK) *n* 97
roller blind (UK) *n* 26
roller coaster *n* 133
roller extension pole *n* 37
roller shade (US) *n* 26
rollerblading *n* 133
rollerskating *n* 125
rolling pin *n* 29
romaine lettuce *n* 55
romance *n* 138
Romania *n* 151, 153
Romanian *adj* 153
Romanians *n* 153
romantic *adj* 10, 177
romantic comedy *n* 127
romper *n* 13
roof *n* 25, 98
roof garden *n* 41
roof ladder *n* 50
roof rack *n* 97
roof tiles *n* 87
rook *n* 140, 160
room service *n* 131
room with a view *n* 131
roomer (US) *n* 32
roommate (US) *n* 32
rooster *n* 165
root *n* 03
rope *n* 117, 119, 125
rose *n* 38
rosé *n* 68, 52
rose of Sharon *n* 38
rose-ringed parakeet *n* 161
rosemary *n* 38, 59
rotor *n* 51
rotor blade *n* 103
rotten *adj* 57
rough *n* 115
round *n* 117
round neck *n* 14
round-trip (US) *n* 131
roundabout *n* 96
route number *n* 99
router *n* 35, 83
rover *n* 143
row (US) *n* 32
row *n* 103, 126
rowboat (US) *n* 105
rower *n* 119
rowing *n* 119
rowing boat (UK) *n* 105
rowing machine *n* 124
royal circle (UK) *n* [illegible]
rubber (UK) *n* 73, 82
rubber *adj* 176
rubber *n* 176
rubber bands *n* 82
rubber boots (US) *n* 40
rubber gloves *n* 34
rubber plant *n* 38
rubber ring *n* 134
rubber tree *n* 169
rubbish bin (UK) *n* 27, 33
rubidium *n* 78
ruby *n* 156
ruck *n* 108
rucksack (UK) *n* 16, 135
rudder *n* 103, 119
rude *adj* 10
rug *n* 26
rugby *n* 108
rugby ball *n* 108
rugby jersey *n* 108
rugby pitch *n* 108
rugby positions *n* 108
rugby shirt *n* 108
ruler *n* 73, 74, 72, 174
rum *n* 68
rum and cola *n* 68
rump roast (US) *n* 53
rump steak (UK) *n* 53
run away *v* 178
run out (of) *v* 178
run out of time *v* 95
run *v* 11, 111, 113
rung *n* 36
runner beans *n* 55
runners *n* 122
running *n* 124
running back *n* 107
running blades *n* 125
running machine *n* 124
running shoes *n* 17
running spikes *n* 17
runny nose *n* 19
runway *n* 104
rush hour *n* 42, 102
rushes *n* 41
Russian *adj* 153
Russian Federation *n* 150, 151, 153
Russians *n* 153
rustic baguette *n* 62
rutabaga (US) *n* 56
ruthenium *n* 78
rutherfordium *n* 78
Rwanda *n* 149, 152
Rwandan *adj* 152
Rwandans *n* 152
rye bread *n* 62

S

saber (US) *n* 117
saber-toothed cat (US) *n* 157
sabre (UK) *n* 117
sabre-toothed cat (UK) *n* 157
sacred ibis *n* 160
sad *adj* 06
saddle *n* 101, 120
saddlebag *n* 120
safari park *n* 133
safe *adj* 113
safe *n* 131
safety area *n* 117
safety barrier *n* 122
safety glasses *n* 87
safety gloves *n* 87
safety goggles *n* 36, 76
safety notice board *n* 87
safety pin *n* 20
saffron *n* 59
sage *n* 59
Sagittarius *n* 144
sail *n* 119, 134
sail fish *n* 166
sailboat (US) *n* 105
sailing *n* 119
sailing boat (UK) *n* 105
sailor, sailors *n* 88, 99
sake cup *n* 27
salad *n* 55, 65
salad drawer (UK) *n* 27
salad vegetables *n* 55
salami *n* 53, 64
salary *n* 81
sale *n* 47
sale sign *n* 47
sales *n* 91
sales assistant *n* 89
salmon fillet *n* 54

saloon (UK) *n* 97
salt *n* 23, 26
salt beef (UK) *n* 64
salted *adj* 54, 61, 64
saltwater crocodile *n* 163
salty *adj* 52
Salvadoran *adj* 152
Salvadorans *n* 152
samara *n* 169
samarium *n* 78
Sammarinese *adj* 153
Sammarinese people *n* 153
Samoa *n* 150, 153
Samoan *adj* 153
Samoan people *n* 153
San Marino *n* 151, 153
sand *n* 35, 39, 134
sand *v* 37
sand dune *n* 146
sand martin *n* 160
sand rose *n* 156
sandals *n* 17
sandbox (US) *n* 43
sandcastle *n* 134
sander *n* 35
sandpaper *n* 36–37
sandpit (UK) *n* 43
sandstone *n* 156
sandstorm *n* 154
sandwich *n* 65, 70, 72
sandwich pickle *n* 60
sanitary pad (US) *n* 49
sanitary towel (UK) *n* 49
São Tomé and Príncipe *n* 149, 152
São Toméan *adj* 152
São Toméans *n* 152
sapphire *n* 156
sardines *n* 54, 64
sari *n* 15
sarong *n* 15
sash window *n* 25
satellite *n* 143
satellite dish *n* 25, 136
satellite TV *n* 137
satire *n* 137
satnav (UK) *n* 99
satsuma *n* 57
saturated fat *n* 23
Saturday *n* 172
Saturn *n* 143
sauce, sauces *n* 60, 64, 70
saucepan *n* 28
Saudi *adj* 153
Saudi Arabia *n* 151, 153
Saudis *n* 153
sauerkraut *n* 60
sauna *n* 124
sausage, sausages *n* 53, 71
sausage patties *n* 71
sauté *v* 29
savannah *n* 146, 158
save up *v* 32
savings *n* 45
savings account *n* 45
savoy cabbage *n* 55
savory (US) *adj* 52
savoury (UK) *adj* 52
saw *v* 35
sawfish *n* 166
saxophone *n* 128–129
scale *n* 54, 104, 128, 148
scales *n* 20, 29, 45, 76, 163, 174
scallop *n* 54
scalpel *n* 21, 77
scan *n* 21
scandium *n* 78
scanner *n* 48, 82, 104
scapula *n* 03
scarecrow *n* 86
scared *adj* 06
scarf *n* 16
scarlet *n* 141
scarlet ibis *n* 160
scarlet macaw *n* 161
scenic *adj* 132
schist *n* 156
scholarship *n* 80
school *n* 43, 73, 148
school bag *n* 73
school bus *n* 99
school equipment *n* 73
school shirt *n* 13
school students *n* 73
school tie *n* 13
school uniform *n* 13
school zone *n* 96
science, sciences *n* 73, 80
science fiction *n* 127, 138
scientist *n* 90
scimitar *n* 79
scissors *n* 20, 37, 82
scissors (UK) *n* 142
sconce (US) *n* 26
scoop *n* 28
scoop *v* 110
scootering *n* 133
score *n* 114, 128, 140
scoreboard *n* 107, 111
scorekeepers bench *n* 110
Scorpio *n* 144
scorpion *n* 162
Scotch and water *n* 68
scouring pad *n* 34
scrambled eggs *n* 61, 71
scrape (US) *n* 19
scraper *n* 37
scratch *v* 164
screen *n* 45, 83, 111, 127, 136–137
screen wash (UK) *n* 97
screen wash reservoir (UK) *n* 98
screenplay *n* 127
screenwriter *n* 127
screw *n* 36
screw base *n* 33
scribe *n* 79
script *n* 126
scroll *n* 79
scrotum *n* 04
scrub the floor *v* 34
scrubbing brush *n* 34
scrubs *n* 13, 21
scrum *n* 108
scrum-half *n* 108
scuba diving *n* 118
sculpting *n* 141
sculptor *n* 89
sculpture *n* 130, 141
sea *n* 134, 145
sea bass *n* 54
sea bed *n* 51
sea bream *n* 54
sea buckthorn *n* 169
sea cave *n* 147
sea krait *n* 163
sea lion *n* 166
sea serpent *n* 139
sea slug *n* 166
sea stack *n* 147
sea urchin *n* 166
sea vessels *n* 105
seaborgium *n* 78
seafood *n* 54
seafood allergy *n* 23
seafood platter *n* 54
seagull *n* 160
seahorse *n* 166
seal *n* 159, 166
sealant *n* 37
sealer *n* 37
seam *n* 111, 142
seamount *n* 145
seaplane *n* 103
seashore *n* 147
season (US) *n* 137
seasonal fruit *n* 57
seasons *n* 172
seat *n* 26, 33, 100, 102–103, 120
seat back *n* 103
seat belt, seat belts *n* 103, 123
seat post *n* 101
seated forward fold *n* 24
seated twist *n* 24
seating *n* 47, 126
seaweed *n* 134, 166
secateurs (UK) *n* 40
second *n* 171
second *num* 173
second base *n* 113
second floor (US) *n* 25, 47
second hand *n* 171
second row *n* 108
second-hand shop (UK) *n* 46
secondary road *n* 148
secretary *n* 90
secretive *adj* 10
sections *n* 48
security *n* 104
security (US) *n* 109
security bit *n* 36
security guard *n* 89–90, 130
sedan (US) *n* 97
sedative *n* 49
sedimentary *adj* 156
see *v* 11
seed, seeds *n* 40, 58 168
seed tray *n* 40
seeded bread *n* 62
seedless *adj* 57
seesaw *n* 43
segment *n* 57
selenium *n* 78
self checkout *n* 48
self management *n* 93
self-help *n* 138
self-inflating mattress *n* 135
self-raising flour (UK) *n* 62
self-rising flour (US) *n* 62
self-tanner (UK) *n* 18
selfish *adj* 10
sell *v* 46
semi-detached (UK) *n* 32
semi-hard cheese *n* 61
semi-metals *n* 78
semi-skimmed milk (UK) *n* 61
semi-soft cheese *n* 61
semicolon *n* 175
semiconductor *n* 75
semimetal *n* 78
seminal gland *n* 04
send *v* 83
send a package (US) *v* 09
send a parcel (UK) *v* 09
Senegal *n* 149, 152
Senegalese *adj* 152
Senegalese people *n* 152
sensitive *adj* 10, 18
sentence *n* 85
sepal *n* 38
September *n* 172
Serbia *n* 151, 153
Serbian *adj* 153
Serbs *n* 153
series (UK) *n* 137
serious *adj* 06, 10
serve *v* 65, 114
server (US) *n* 65, 59, 89
service charge *n* 69
service focused *adj* 93
service included *phr* 69
service line *n* 114
service not included *phr* 69
service station (UK) *n* 148
service the car *v* 98
service vehicle *n* 104
services *n* 131
serving spoon *n* 27
sesame allergy *n* 23
sesame oil *n* 60
set *n* 114, 126
set honey (UK) *n* 60
set menu (UK) *n* 69
set off *v* 98, 178
set sail *v* 106
set square (UK) *n* 73–74
set the alarm *v* 09
set the table *v* 26, 34
sets *n* 126
setter *n* 112, 164
seven *num* 173
seventeen *num* 173
seventh *num* 173
seventy *num* 173
sew *v* 142
sewer drain pipe (US) *n* 33
sewing *n* 142
sewing box *n* 142
sewing machine *n* 142
sewing needle *n* 142
Seychelles *n* 149, 152
Seychellois *adj* 152
Seychellois *n* 152
shade plants *n* 41
shaft *n* 115
shaggy bracket fungus *n* 170
shaggy mane mushroom *n* 170
shake *v* 11
shake hands *v* 92
shake your head *v* 02
shale *n* 51
shale gas *n* 51
shallot *n* 56
shallow *adj* 176
shallow end *n* 118
shaobing *n* 67
shapes *n* 74
share *v* 84
share price *n* 94
share your screen *v* 95
shares *n* 94
sharp *adj* 128
sharpening stone *n* 36
shave *v* 09, 12, 31
shaved head *n* 12
shaving cream (US) *n* 31
shaving foam (UK) *n* 31
shears *n* 40
shears (US) *n* 142
shed *n* 25, 39
sheep *n* 165
sheep farm *n* 86
sheep's milk *n* 61
sheep's milk cheese *n* 61
sheer *v* 165
sheer curtain *n* 26
sheet *n* 30, 119
shelf *n* 26–27
shell *n* 58, 61, 163
shelter *n* 44
shelves *n* 27, 48
sherry *n* 68
shiatsu *n* 24
shield *n* 40, 79
shih tzu *n* 164
shiitake mushroom *n* 56, mushrooms *n* 170
shin *n* 01
shin guard *n* 110
shingles (US) *n* 87

shiny *adj* 176
ship's captain *n* 89
shipping *n* 91
shipping container *n* 106
ships *n* 105
shipyard *n* 106
shirt *n* 15
shiver *v* 02
shocked *adj* 06
shocking *adj* 177
shoe accessories *n* 17
shoe brush *n* 17
shoe polish *n* 17
shoe shop (UK) *n* 46
shoe store (US) *n* 46
shoe trees *n* 17
shoelaces *n* 17
shoes *n* 17
shoe accessories *n* 17
shoot *v* 112
shooting guard *n* 112
shop (UK) *n* 42
shop window (UK) *n* 25
shoplifting *n* 85
shopper *n* 47
shopping *n* 46, 179
shopping bag (US) *n* 48
shopping cart (US) *n* 48
shopping
centre (UK) *n* 42, 47
shopping channel *n* 137
shopping list *n* 46
shopping mall *n* 42, 47
shopping spree *n* 46
short *adj* 12, 176
short corner *n* 112
short hair *n* 12
short-sighted (UK) *adj* 22
short-sleeved shirt *n* 14
shortbread *n* 63
shorts *n* 14
shot *n* 68
shot put *n* 116
shotgun *n* 88
shoulder *n* 01
shoulder bag *n* 16
shoulder blade *n* 03
shoulder pad *n* 15, 107, 110
shoulder strap *n* 16
shoulder-launched
missile *n* 88
shoulder-length hair *n* 12
shout *v* 11
shovel *n* 40, 87
show (US) *n* 137
show of hands *n* 95
show off *v* 178
shower *n* 31
shower block *n* 135
shower curtain *n* 31
shower door *n* 31
shower gel *n* 31
showjumping *n* 120
shredder *n* 82
shrinking glaciers *n* 155
shrubs *n* 41
shrug *v* 02
shuffle *v* 140
shutoff valve *n* 33
shutter *n* 25
shuttle bus *n* 99
shuttlecock *n* 114
shy *adj* 10
Siamese *n* 164
Siberian husky *n* 164
siblings *n* 05
side *n* 69, 74
side car *n* 100
side dishes *n* 72
side effects *n* 49
side order *n* 69
side part (US) *n* 12
side parting (UK) *n* 12
side plate *n* 27
side shuffles *n* 124
side street *n* 42
side view *n* 97
side-saddle *n* 120
side-view
mirror (US) *n* 97
sideboard *n* 26
sideburns *n* 12
sidedeck *n* 119
sideline *n* 107, 112, 114
sidestroke *n* 118
sidewalk (US) *n* 25, 43, 65
sidewinder *n* 163
Sierra Leone *n* 149, 152
Sierra Leonean *adj* 152
Sierra Leoneans *n* 152
sieve *n* 28
sieve *v* 39
sift *v* 62
sigh *v* 02
sightseeing *n* 99, 132
sign *n* 104
sign a contract *v* 92
signal *n* 102
signal (US) *v* 98
signature *n* 45, 83
signet ring *n* 16
silencer (UK) *n* 98, 100
silicon *n* 78
silk *n* 13
silk tree *n* 168
silly *adj* 10
silo *n* 86
silt *n* 39
Silurian *adj* 157
Silurian *n* 157
silver *adj* 176
silver *n* 78, 116, 156, 176
silverware (US) *n* 26, 27
sim card *n* 48
simmer *v* 29
simulation game *n* 136
sing *v* 11
Singapore *n* 151, 153
Singaporean *adj* 153
Singaporeans *n* 153
singer *n* 89
single *adj* 68
single bed (UK) *n* 30
single cream (UK) *n* 61
single parent *n* 05
single quotation
mark *n* 175
single room *n* 131
single-burner
camping stove *n* 135
singles *n* 114
sink *n* 27
sink (UK) *n* 33
sinus *n* 04
sip *v* 52
sippy cup *n* 27
sirloin steak *n* 53
sister *n* 05
sister-in-law *n* 05
sit down *v* 11
sit-up *n* 124
sitar *n* 129
sitcom *n* 137
site (US) *n* 135
site manager *n* 89
site manager's office *n* 135
sites available (US) *phr* 135
six *num* 173
sixteen *num* 173
sixth *num* 173
sixty *num* 173
skate *n* 54, 122
skate *v* 110
skate wing *n* 54
skateboard *n* 125
skateboarding *n* 125, 133
skein *n* 142
skeleton *n* 03, 122
sketch *n* 141
sketch pad *n* 141
skewer *n* 28
ski *n* 119, 122
ski boot *n* 17, 122
ski instructor *n* 89
ski jacket *n* 122
ski jump *n* 122
ski lodge *n* 122
ski pole *n* 122
ski resort *n* 122
ski run *n* 122
ski slope *n* 122
skier *n* 122
skiing *n* 122
skillet *n* 28
skim milk (US) *n* 61
skimmed milk (UK) *n* 61
skin *n* 01, 58
skin care *n* 49
skin type *n* 18
skip *v* 124
skipping
rope *n* 08, 124, 133
skirt *n* 14
skirting board (UK) *n* 30
skittles (UK) *n* 08
skull *n* 03
skunk *n* 158
skydiving *n* 125
skyscraper *n* 42
slalom *n* 122
slate *n* 156
sled (US) *n* 122
sledding (US) *n* 122
sledgehammer *n* 87
sledging (UK) *n* 122
sleep in *v* 178
sleeping bag *n* 135
sleeping
compartment *n* 102
sleeping mat *n* 135
sleeping pills *n* 49
sleepsuit *n* 13
sleet *n* 154
sleeve *n* 15
sleeveless *adj* 15
sleigh (UK) *n* 122
slice *n* 53, 114
slice *v* 29, 62
sliced bread *n* 62
slicer *n* 62
slide *n* 43, 77, 95
slide *v* 113
slides *n* 17
sling *n* 19–20
slingback heels *n* 17
slip *n* 14, 111
slip road (UK) *n* 96
slip-ons *n* 17
slippers *n* 11, 17
slit skirt *n* 15
sloth *n* 159
slotted spoon *n* 28
Slovakia *n* 151, 153
Slovakian *adj* 153
Slovaks *n* 153
Slovenia *n* 151, 153
Slovenian *adj* 153
Slovenians *n* 153
slow *adj* 176
slow down *v* 98
slug *n* 162
sluice gates *n* 51
small *adj* 176
small creatures *n* 162
small forward *n* 112
small intestine *n* 04
smartpen *n* 95
smartphone *n* 83
smartwatch *n* 83
smell *v* 11
smile *v* 02
smog *n* 154
smoke *n* 50
smoke alarm *n* 50
smoked *adj* 54, 72
smoked fish *n* 64
smoked haddock *n* 64
smoked mackerel *n* 64, 71
smoked meat *n* 53
smoked salmon *n* 64, 71
smooth orange juice *n* 65
smoothie *n* 52
smuggling *n* 85
snack bar *n* 48, 65
snacks *n* 65
snail *n* 162
snake plant *n* 38
snakes and
ladders (UK) *n* 140
snap (US) *n* 13
snap *n* 140
snare drum *n* 128
sneaker (US) *n* 17
sneeze *v* 02, 20
snell knot *n* 121
Snellen chart *n* 22
sniff *v* 164
snooker *n* 125
snore *v* 02, 30
snorkel *n* 118
snorkel and mask *n* 15, 134
snorkeling (US) *n* 118
snorkelling (UK) *n* 118
snort *v* 165
snow *n* 154
snow goose *n* 160
snow leopard *n* 159
snow peas (US) *n* 55
snow tires (US) *n* 97
snow tyres (UK) *n* 97
snowboarding *n* 122
snowdrift *n* 154
snowdrop *n* 167
snowflake *n* 154
snowmobile *n* 122
snowstorm *n* 154
snowsuit *n* 13
snowy *adj* 154
snowy owl *n* 161
soap *n* 31
soap dish *n* 31
soap opera *n* 137
soccer (US) *n* 109
soccer cleats (US) *n* 17, 107, 109
soccer game (US) *n* 109
soccer jersey (US) *n* 15, 109
social media *n* 84
social sciences *n* 80
sociologist *n* 89
sociology *n* 80
sock, socks *n* 14, 107
socket *n* 33
socket wrench *n* 36
soda (US) *n* 70
soda bread *n* 62
sodium *n* 78
sofa (UK) *n* 26
sofa bed *n* 26
soft *adj* 57, 176
soft candy (US) *n* 67
soft cheese *n* 61
soft down feathers *n* 161
soft drink *n* 70
soft sweets (UK) *n* 67
soft toy (UK) *n* 08
softwood *n* 35
soil *n* 39
soil tiller *n* 40
soil types *n* 39

solar charger *n* 83
solar energy *n* 51
solar farm *n* 51
solar panel *n* 51
solar radiation *n* 155
solar system *n* 143
solar water heating *n* 51
solder *n* 35–36
solder *v* 35
soldering iron *n* 35–36
soldier *n* 88–89
sole *n* 02, 17, 54, 115
solid, solids *n* 74, 76
solitaire (US) *n* 140
solo *n* 128
Solomon Island *adj* 153
Solomon Islanders *n* 153
Solomon Islands *n* 150, 153
soluble *adj* 49
solvent *n* 37
Somalia *n* 149, 152
Somalian *adj* 152
Somalians *n* 152
sombrero *n* 16
sometimes *adj* 172
sommelier *n* 69
son *n* 05
son-in-law *n* 05
song *n* 129
soprano *n* 126
sore throat *n* 19
sorrel *n* 55, 59
sort your
rubbish (UK) *v* 155
sort your trash (US) *v* 155
sorting unit *n* 33
soufflé *n* 72
soufflé dish *n* 28
soul *n* 129
sound bar *n* 136
sound boom *n* 84
sound engineer *n* 127
sound hole *n* 129
sound technician *n* 84
soundtrack *n* 127
soup *n* 69, 72
soup bowl *n* 27
soup spoon *n* 27
sour *adj* 52, 57
source *n* 147
sources *n* 79
sourdough bread *n* 62
sourdough starter *n* 62
south *n* 148
South Africa *n* 149, 152
South African *adj* 152
South Africans *n* 152
South America *n* 149, 152
South American *adj* 152
South Americans *n* 152
South Korea *n* 150, 153
South Korean *adj* 153
South Koreans *n* 153
South Pole *n* 75, 145
South Sudan *n* 149, 152
South Sudanese *adj* 152
South Sudanese
people *n* 152
southeast *n* 148
Southern Cross *n* 144
Southern
Hemisphere *n* 145
southwest *n* 148
souvenir *n* 132
souvenir stall *n* 132
sow *v* 39, 86
soy allergy (US) *n* 23
soy milk (US) *n* 61
soy sauce *n* 60
soy sauce dip *n* 72
soya allergy (UK) *n* 23
soya milk (UK) *n* 61
soybean oil *n* 60
space *n* 143–144
space exploration *n* 143
space probe *n* 143
space shuttle *n* 143
space shuttle launch *n* 143
space station *n* 143
space suit *n* 143
space telescope *n* 144
spacecraft *n* 143
spackle (US) *v* 37
spade *n* 40, 140
spaghetti *n* 64, 72
Spain *n* 151, 153
spam *n* 83
Spaniards *n* 153
Spanish *adj* 153
Spanish chestnut *n* 168
spanner (UK) *n* 36
spare tire (US) *n* 98
spare tyre (UK) *n* 98
spark plug *n* 98
sparkling *adj* 52
sparkling wine *n* 68
sparrow *n* 160
spatula *n* 28, 76
speak *v* 11
speaker, speakers *n* 83, 129
speaker stand *n* 136
spear *n* 79
spearfishing *n* 121
special *adj* 177
special effects *n* 127
special offer *n* 48
specials *n* 69
species *n* 77
species of birds *n* 160–161
species of fungi *n* 170
species of
mammals *n* 158–159
spectacled caiman *n* 163
spectators *n* 110, 115–116
speed boating *n* 119
speed camera *n* 96
speed limit *n* 96
speed skating *n* 122
speed up *v* 98
speedboat *n* 105
speeding *n* 85
speedometer *n* 99–100
speedway *n* 123
spell *v* 11, 73
spell book *n* 139
sperm whale *n* 166
sphere *n* 74
sphinx *n* 139, 164
spices *n* 59
spicy *adj* 52, 56
spicy sausage *n* 64
spider monkey *n* 159
spider plant *n* 38
spikes *n* 115
spin *n* 114
spinach *n* 55
spinal cord *n* 04
spine *n* 03, 138
spinning top (UK) *n* 08
spiral galaxy *n* 144
spirit dispenser *n* 68
spirit level (UK) *n* 35–36, 87
spit *n* 147
splashback (UK) *n* 27
spleen *n* 04
splinter *n* 19
split the bill (UK) *v* 69
split the check (US) *v* 69
spoiler *n* 97
spoke *n* 101
sponge *n* 31, 34, 37
sponge cake *n* 63
spontaneous *adj* 10
spores *n* 170
sport fishing *n* 121
sports bra *n* 15
sports car *n* 97
sports center (US) *n* 43
sports centre (UK) *n* 43
sports drink *n* 52
sports field *n* 80
sports game *n* 136
sports jacket *n* 15
sports
programme (UK) *n* 137
sports shoes *n* 17
sports show (US) *n* 137
sportsperson *n* 89
sportswear *n* 15
spotted (UK) *adj* 13
Spotted Lake *n* 145
sprain *n* 19
spray *n* 49
spray *v* 39
spray nozzle *n* 40
sprayer *n* 40
spring *n* 57, 172
spring a leak *v* 33
spring greens *n* 55
spring onion *n* 55
spring roll *n* 72
springboard *n* 118, 125
springbok *n* 158
sprinkle *v* 29
sprinkler *n* 40
sprinter *n* 116
sprocket *n* 101
spruce *n* 167
spy *n* 89
square *n* 42, 74, 140
square foot *n* 174
square
kilometer (US) *n* 174
square
kilometre (UK) *n* 174
square leg *n* 111
square meter (US) *n* 174
square metre (UK) *n* 174
square mile *n* 174
squash *n* 114
squat *n* 124
squeak *v* 164
squeegee *n* 34
squid *n* 54
squirrel *n* 158
squirrel monkey *n* 159
Sri Lanka *n* 150, 153
Sri Lankan *adj* 153
Sri Lankans *n* 153
St. Basil's cathedral *n* 44
St. Kitts and
Nevis *n* 150, 152
St. Lucia *n* 150, 152
St. Lucian *adj* 152
St. Lucians *n* 152
St. Vincent and The
Grenadines *n* 150, 152
stabilizers *n* 101
stable *n* 86, 120
staff *n* 81, 139
stag beetle *n* 162
stage *n* 126
stage lights *n* 129
stained glass window *n* 44
stair gate *n* 08
staircase *n* 25
stairs *n* 25
stake *v* 39
stalactite *n* 146
stalagmite *n* 146
stalk *n* 55
stall *n* 47
stallion *n* 120, 165
stalls (UK) *n* 126
stamen *n* 38
stamp, stamps *n* 45, 48
stance *n* 115
stand *n* 40, 109, 115, 121, 136
stand up *v* 11
standing ovation *n* 126
stapler *n* 73, 82
staples *n* 82
star, stars *n* 144
star anise *n* 59
star chart *n* 144
star cluster *n* 144
star jumps (UK) *n* 124
Star of David *n* 44
starfish *n* 134, 166
starfruit *n* 58
starling *n* 160
start school *v* 07
starter (UK) *n* 69
starting block *n* 116, 118
starting grid *n* 123
starting line *n* 116
statement *n* 85
station wagon (US) *n* 97
stationery *n* 82
status *n* 104
status update *n* 84
stay in a hotel *v* 131
steam *v* 29
steam dome *n* 102
steam train *n* 102
steamed *adj* 72
steel wool (US) *n* 36
steeplechase *n* 120
steering wheel *n* 99
stegosaurus *n* 157
stem *n* 38, 170
stemware *n* 27
stencil *n* 37
stenographer *n* 85
stepbrother *n* 05
stepladder *n* 37
stepmom (US) *n* 05
stepmother *n* 05
stepmum (UK) *n* 05
steppe *n* 146
steps *n* 25
stepsister *n* 05
stereo *adj* 136
stern *n* 105, 119
sternum *n* 03
stethoscope *n* 20
stew *n* 72
steward (UK) *n* 109
stick *n* 110
stick insect *n* 164
sticky notes *n* 82
sticky prong *n* 168
stiff *adj* 176
stifling *adj* 154
stigma *n* 58
stilettos *n* 17
still *adj* 52
stilt house *n* 32
sting *n* 19, 162
sting *v* 162
stinkhorn *n* 170
stir *v* 29
stir-fry *n* 29, 72
stir-fried *adj* 72
stirrer *n* 68
stirrup *n* 120
stitch *n* 142
stitches *n* 21, 113
stitch length selector *n* 142
stitch selector *n* 142
stock exchange *n* 94
stockbroker *n* 94
stockings *n* 14
stocks *n* 47, 94
stomach *n* 04
stomach ache (UK) *n* 19
stomachache (US) *n* 19
stone *adj* 176
stone *n* 16, 141, 176
Stone age *n* 79

stone fruit *n* 57
stool *n* 65
stop *v* 96, 137
stop at (the hotel) *v* 148
stop button *n* 99
stop light (US) *n* 43, 96
stop light ahead *n* 96
stoppage time (US) *n* 109
stopper *n* 76
storage *n* 32
store (US) *n* 42
store window (US) *n* 25
stories *n* 139
stork *n* 160
storm *n* 154
storm drain *n* 43
stormy *adj* 154
stout *n* 68
stove (US) *n* 27
straight *adj* 74
straight hair *n* 12
straightening iron (US) *n* 12
strainer *n* 28
strait *n* 147
strange *adj* 177
strapless *adj* 15
strategy game *n* 136
stratosphere *n* 155
straw *n* 70
strawberry *n* 57
strawberry jam *n* 60
strawberry milkshake *n* 61, 65
strawberry smoothie *n* 65
streaky bacon (UK) *n* 53
stream *n* 137, 147
street *n* 42
street corner *n* 42
street market *n* 46
street sign *n* 43
street stall *n* 70
streetlight *n* 25, 43
streetmap (UK) *n* 148
stress *n* 19
stressed *adj* 06
stretch *n* 124
stretcher *n* 21
strike *n* 113
strike *v* 117
strike out *v* 111
striker (UK) *n* 109
string *n* 129
string of pearls *n* 16
strings *n* 114, 128
strip *v* 37
striped *n* 13
stripes *n* 14
stroke *n* 118
stroller (US) *n* 08
strong *adj* 52
strong flour (UK) *n* 62
strontium *n* 78
stubble *n* 12
studs *n* 16, 111
study (UK) *n* 26
study *n* 73
studying the past *n* 79
stuffed *adj* 72
stuffed olives *n* 64
stuffed vine leaves *n* 64
stump *v* 111
stumps *n* 111
stunning *adj* 177
stunt *n* 127
style *n* 38
style your hair *v* 12
stylist *n* 89
subject *n* 83
submarine *n* 88, 105
submersible *n* 166
subscript *n* 76
subsoil *n* 39
substitutes *n* 109
subterranean stream *n* 146
subtitles *n* 137
subtract *v* 11, 74
suburb *n* 42
subway map (US) *n* 102
subway train (US) *n* 102
subwoofer *n* 136
succulents *n* 38, 41
suck *v* 02
suction hose *n* 34
Sudan *n* 149, 152
Sudanese *adj* 152
Sudanese people *n* 152
sugar *n* 23
sugar cane *n* 86, 167
suit *n* 15
suit (someone) *v* 14
suitcase *n* 16, 104
sulfite allergy (US) *n* 23
sulfur (US) *n* 78, 156
sulphite allergy (UK) *n* 23
sulphur (UK) *n* 78, 156
sultana (UK) *n* 58
sum up *v* 95
sumac *n* 59
summer *n* 57, 172
summer leaf *n* 169
summer roll *n* 72
summons *n* 85
sumo wrestling *n* 117
Sun *n* 143
sun *n* 154
sun bed (UK) *n* 18
sun cream (UK) *n* 134
sun hat *n* 14, 16, 134
sunbathing *n* 133–134
sunblock *n* 49, 134
sunburn *n* 19, 134
Sunday *n* 172
sundew *n* 168
sunflower, sunflowers *n* 38, 86
sunflower oil *n* 60
sunglasses *n* 22, 134
sunlit zone *n* 166
sunny *adj* 154
sunrise *n* 171
sunroof *n* 98
sunscreen (US) *n* 49, 134
sunset *n* 171
superb *adj* 177
superfoods *n* 23
supermarket *n* 48
supernova *n* 144
supervise *v* 92
supervisor *n* 81, 92
supplement *n* 23, 49
support *n* 87
support cane *n* 39
supportive *adj* 10
suppository *n* 49
surf *n* 119
surface *n* 39, 143
surface cleaner *n* 34
surface-to-air missile *n* 88
surfboard *n* 119, 134
surfcasting *n* 121
surfer *n* 119
surfing *n* 119, 134
surgeon *n* 21, 90
surgery *n* 21
surgical mask *n* 21
Suriname *n* 149, 152
Surinamese *adj* 152
Surinamese people *n* 152
surprised *adj* 06
Surrealism *n* 130
surround sound speaker *n* 136
surveillance camera *n* 130
surveyor *n* 90
sushi *n* 54
sushi set *n* 27
suspect *n* 50, 85
suspenders *n* 14
suspension *n* 98, 100
suspension line *n* 125
swallow *n* 160
swallow *v* 52
swallowtail butterfly *n* 162
swamp *n* 146
swarm *n* 162
Swazi *adj* 152
Swazis *n* 152
sweat *v* 02
sweatpants *n* 15
sweater *n* 14
sweatshirt *n* 14
Sweden *n* 151, 153
swede (UK) *n* 56
Swedes *n* 153
Swedish *adj* 153
sweep the floor *v* 34
sweet *adj* 52, 56–57
sweet chilli *n* 60
sweet potato *n* 56
sweet shop (UK) *n* 67
sweet spreads *n* 60
sweet trolley (UK) *n* 63, 69
sweetcorn (UK) *n* 55
sweets (UK) *n* 67
swift *n* 160
swim trunks (US) *n* 15, 134
swimmer *n* 118
swimming *n* 118
swimming pool *n* 118, 131
swimming trunks (UK) *n* 15, 134
swimsuit *n* 15, 118, 134
swing *n* 43, 115, 133
swing *v* 115, 159
Swiss *adj* 153
Swiss chard *n* 55
Swiss cheese plant *n* 38
Swiss people *n* 153
Switzerland *n* 151, 153
swoop *v* 161
sword *n* 79, 117
swordfish *n* 54
sycamore *n* 169
Sydney Opera House *n* 44
sympathetic *adj* 06
symphony *n* 128
symptoms *n* 19
synagogue *n* 44
synchronized swimming *n* 118
synthetic *n* 13
Syria *n* 150, 153
Syrian *adj* 153
Syrians *n* 153
syringe *n* 20, 49, 77
syrup *n* 49

T

T-shirt *n* 14
T-strap heels *n* 17
T11 (visual impairment) race *n* 116
tabard *n* 13
tabi boots *n* 17
table *n* 26, 65
table setting *n* 69
table tennis *n* 114
tablecloth *n* 26
tablespoon *n* 27
tablet *n* 83
tablets *n* 20, 49
tableware *n* 27
tachometer (US) *n* 99
tack *v* 119, 142
tackle *n* 108, 121
tackle *v* 107
tackle box *n* 121
taco *n* 70
tadpole *n* 77, 163
taekwondo *n* 117
tag *v* 113
tagine *n* 28
tai chi *n* 117, 133
tail *n* 54, 103, 120, 143, 158–160
tail feathers *n* 161
tail light *n* 100
tail plane *n* 103
tailbone sacrum *n* 03
tailgate *n* 97
tailor *n* 46, 89
tailor *v* 142
tailor's chalk *n* 142
tailor's dummy *n* 142
tailored *adj* 15
Taj Mahal *n* 44
Tajikistan *n* 151, 153
Tajikistani *adj* 153
Tajikistanis *n* 153
take *v* 11, 140
take a bath *v* 09, 31
take a break (US) *v* 09
take a nap *v* 09
take a penalty *v* 109
take a shower *v* 09, 31
take a test (US) *v* 73
take an exam (UK) *v* 73
take in *v* 142
take minutes *v* 95
take notes *v* 73
take off *v* 14, 98, 104, 178
take on *v* 81
take out the rubbish (UK) *v* 09, 34
take out the trash (US) *v* 09, 34
take questions *v* 95
take the first left *v* 96, 148
take the second right *v* 96, 148
take-away (UK) *n* 70
talented *adj* 10
talk *v* 11
talk show (US) *n* 137
talkative *adj* 10
tall *adj* 12
tamarillo *n* 58
tambourine *n* 128
tampon *n* 49
tandem *n* 101
tank *n* 88
tank top *n* 14
tanning bed (US) *n* 18
tanning cream (US) *n* 18
tanning goggles *n* 18
tanning mitt *n* 18
tantalum *n* 78
Tanzania *n* 149, 152
Tanzanian *adj* 152
Tanzanians *n* 152
tap (UK) *n* 27, 31, 33
tap *n* 33
tap water *n* 52
tape *n* 20, 32, 82
tape measure *n* 36, 142
tapir *n* 159
tarantula *n* 162
target *n* 125
target shooting *n* 125
taro root *n* 56
tarragon *n* 59
Tasmanian devil *n* 158
taste *v* 11, 29, 52
tasty *adj* 52
Taurus *n* 144
tawny owl *n* 161
taxi driver *n* 90
taxi rank (UK) *n* 104
taxi stand (US) *n* 104

tea *n* 52, 66, 71, 86
tea infuser *n* 66
tea strainer *n* 66
tea with lemon *n* 66
tea with milk *n* 66
teacher *n* 73, 90
teacup *n* 27
team *n* 107
team bench *n* 112
team jersey *n* 107
team leader *n* 92
team player *n* 93
teamwork *n* 92–93
teapot *n* 27, 66
tear *n* 22
tear duct *n* 01
tearful *adj* 06
teaspoon *n* 27
teat *n* 08
technetium *n* 78
technological
  revolution *n* 79
technology *n* 83
technology literate *adj* 93
teddy bear *n* 30
tee *n* 115
tee off *v* 115
teeing ground *n* 115
teenagers *n* 05
teepee *n* 32
teeth *n* 01, 03
telephone *n* 82
telephone banking *n* 94
telephone manner *n* 93
teleprompter *n* 84
telescope *n* 144
television *n* 26, 136–137
television studio *n* 84
telling the time *n* 171
tellurium *n* 78
temperate forest *n* 146
temperature *n* 154
temperature display *n* 33
temperature gauge *n* 99
temple *n* 01, 44
temporary *adj* 81
temporary exhibition *n* 130
ten *num* 173
ten past one *n* 171
ten to two *n* 171
tenancy
  agreement (UK) *n* 32
tenant *n* 32
tend *v* 39
tendon *n* 03
tennessine *n* 78
tennis *n* 114
tennis court *n* 114
tennis match *n* 114
tennis shoes *n* 114
tenon saw *n* 36
tenor *n* 126
tension control *n* 142
tent peg *n* 135
tent pole *n* 135
tenth *num* 173
terbium *n* 78
terminal *n* 104
termite *n* 162
terrace *n* 25, 65
terraced house (UK) *n* 32
terrible *adj* 177
terrified *adj* 06
terrifying *adj* 177
test *n* 73
test results *n* 20
test tube *n* 76
test tube rack *n* 76
testicle *n* 04
text *n* 138
textbook *n* 73, 138
textiles *n* 91
Thai *adj* 153
Thais *n* 153
thallium *n* 78
Thanksgiving *n* 07
thatched cottage *n* 32
thatched roof *n* 32
thawb *n* 15
theater (US) *n* 42, 126
theatre (UK) *n* 42, 126
theme park *n* 133
therapy *n* 24
thermal flask *n* 52, 135
thermals *n* 135
thermometer *n* 20, 76
thermosphere *n* 155
thesis *n* 80
thick *adj* 176
thigh *n* 01, 53
thigh-high boot *n* 17
thimble *n* 142
thin *adj* 176
think *v* 11
third *num* 173
third base *n* 113
third man *n* 111
thirteen *num* 173
thirty *num* 173
this way up *phr* 45
thistle *n* 38, 169
thoracic vertebrae *n* 03
thorium *n* 78
thorny devil *n* 163
thoughtless *adj* 10
thread *n* 84, 142
thread *v* 142
thread guide *n* 142
thread reel (US) *n* 142
three *num* 173
three times a week *adv* 172
three-course meal *n* 69
three-second area *n* 112
three-wheeler *n* 100
thrift shop (US) *n* 46
thrilled *adj* 06
thriller *n* 127, 137
thrilling *adj* 177
throat *n* 04
throat lozenge *n* 49
throttle *n* 100
throw *n* 26, 30
throw *v* 11, 107–108, 113, 117
throw away *v* 178
throw-in *n* 109, 112
throw-in line *n* 112
thrush *n* 160
thruster *n* 143
thulium *n* 78
thumb *n* 02
thumbtack (US) *n* 82
thunder *n* 154
thundery *adj* 154
Thursday *n* 172
thyme *n* 59
thyroid gland *n* 04
tiara *n* 16
tibia *n* 03
tic-tac-toe (US) *n* 140
ticket *n* 102, 104, 130
ticket barrier *n* 102
ticket inspector *n* 102
ticket office *n* 102, 102, 130
tidal barrage *n* 51
tidal energy *n* 51
tide pool (US) *n* 134
tidy (UK) *v* 34
tie *n* 15–16
tie (US) *v* 109
tie bar (US) *n* 16
tie your hair back *v* 12
tie-break *n* 114
tie-pin (UK) *n* 16
tiger *n* 157, 159
tiger's eye *n* 156
tight *adj* 13, 176
tighthead prop *n* 108
tights (UK) *n* 14
tilde *n* 175
tile, tiles *n* 25, 35
tile *v* 35, 37
till (UK) *n* 48, 68, 94
tiller *n* 119
timber (UK) *n* 87
time *n* 104, 107, 171
time management *n* 93
time out *n* 107
timer *n* 28, 76, 95
timetable *n* 102, 132
Timorese *adj* 153
Timorese people *n* 153
tin *n* 78, 156
tin (UK) *n* 52
tin opener (UK) *n* 28
tinned (UK) *adj* 56
tinned food *n* 48
tinned tomato (UK) *n* 71
tip *n* 69, 122
tiramisu *n* 63
tire (US) *n* 97, 100–101
tire lever (US) *n* 101
tired *adj* 06
tiring *adj* 177
tissue *n* 49
tissue box *n* 30
titanium *n* 78
title *n* 138
toadstools *n* 170
toast *n* 71
toasted sandwich *n* 71
toaster *n* 27
tobacco *n* 86
Tobagonian *adj* 152
Tobagonians *n* 152
toco toucan *n* 160
toddler *n* 05, 08
toe *n* 02, 115
toe box *n* 126
toe clip *n* 101
toe strap *n* 101
toenail *n* 02
toffee *n* 67
Togo *n* 149, 152
Togolese *adj* 152
Togolese people *n* 152
toilet *n* 31, 33
toilet block *n* 34, 135
toilet brush *n* 31
toilet cleaner *n* 34
toilet float *n* 33
toilet paper *n* 31
toilet paper holder *n* 31
toilet seat *n* 31
toiletries *n* 18, 48
toilets (UK) *n* 47, 130–131
tollbooth *n* 96
tomato *n* 56
tomato juice *n* 65
tomato sauce *n* 70
tomb *n* 79
tombolo *n* 147
ton *n* 174
toner *n* 18
Tonga *n* 150, 153
Tongan *adj* 153
Tongan people *n* 153
Tonghi bottlebrush *n* 168
tongs *n* 28, 68, 76
tongue *n* [illegible]
tonne *n* 174
tonsillitis *n* 19
tool belt *n* 36, 87
tool rack *n* 35
toolbox *n* 36
tools *n* 35–36, 40, 87
toothache *n* 22
toothbrush *n* 31
toothpaste *n* 31
top (US) *n* 08
top dress *v* 39
top tier *n* 63
topaz *n* 156
topiary *n* 41
topping *n* 70
topsoil *n* 39
torc *n* 16
torch (UK) *n* 135
torch lily *n* 167
tornado *n* 154
tortellini *n* 64
tortilla *n* 62
tortoise *n* 164
touch-in goal line *n* 108
touchdown *n* 107
tour bus (US) *n* 99, 132
tour guide *n* 90, 130, 132
tourer *n* 100
touring bike *n* 101
tourism *n* 91
tourist *n* 132
tourist attraction *n* 132
tourist bus (UK) *n* 99, 132
tourist information (UK) *n* 42, 132
tourist map *n* 48, 132
tourist office (US) *n* 42
tourmaline *n* 156
tournament *n* 115
tow away *v* 96
tow truck *n* 98
towel bar *n* 31
towels *n* 31
tower *n* 44, 51
tower crane *n* 87
town *n* 43, 148
town features *n* 42–43
town house *n* 32, 43
toy car *n* 08
toy shop (UK) *n* 46
toy store (US) *n* 46
toybox *n* 08
toys *n* 08, 164
trachea *n* 04
track *n* 102, 116
track your order *v* 46
tracksuit *n* 15
tractor *n* 86
traditional clothes *n* 15
traffic *n* 96
traffic barrier (US) *n* 96
traffic jam *n* 43, 96
traffic light (UK) *n* 43, 96
traffic light ahead *n* 96
traffic warden (UK) *n* 96
tragedy *n* 126
trail map (US) *n* 148
trailer *n* 135
train, trains *n* 15, 102
train *v* 39, 124
train driver *n* 90
train set *n* 08
train station *n* 42, 102, 148
trainer (UK) *n* 17
training cane *n* 39
training wheels *n* 101
tram *n* 99, 102
trampoline *n* 08, 125
transfer money *v* 45
transformer *n* 33, 75
transition metals *n* 78
transmission *n* 98
transplant *v* 39
transport helicopter *n* 88
transportation *n* 91
trap *n* 33
trapezium (UK) *n* 74
trapezius *n* 03
trapezoid (US) *n* 74
trapped insect *n* 168
trapped radiation *n* 155

trash *n* 83
trash bag (US) *n* 33–34
trash can (US) *n* 25, 27, 33, 82
travel *n* 131
travel agent *n* 46, 90
travel card *n* 48
travel writing *n* 138
travel-sickness pills (UK) *n* 49
traveler's tree (US) *n* 168
traveller's tree (UK) *n* 168
trawler *n* 105
tray *n* 69–70
tray table *n* 103
trays *n* 82
tread *n* 101
tread water *v* 118
treadmill *n* 124
treasure *n* 139
treatment *n* 20–21
treatments *n* 24
treats *n* 164
treble clef *n* 128
treble fishhook *n* 121
tree, trees *n* 41, 167–169
tree climbing *n* 133
tree house *n* 32, 133
tree pose *n* 24
tree pruner *n* 40
trekking *n* 120
trellis *n* 41
trench *n* 145
trench coat *n* 15
trend *v* 84
trial *n* 85
triangle *n* 74, 128
triangle (US) *n* 74
triangle pose *n* 24
Triassic *adj n* 157
Triassic *n* 157
triathlon *n* 116
tributary *n* 147
triceratops *n* 157
trilobite *n* 157
trim *v* 39
trimmer *n* 40
Trinidad and Tobago *n* 150, 152
Trinidadian *adj* 152
Trinidadians *n* 152
trip over *v* 178
trip switch (UK) *n* 33
triple bar vertical *n* 120
triple jump *n* 116
triplets *n* 05
tripod *n* 76, 144
trivia game *n* 136
troll *n* 139
troll *v* 84
trolley (UK) *n* 48, 102, 104
trolley *n* 102, 104, 131
trolley bus *n* 99
trolling *n* 84
trombone *n* 128
Tropic of Cancer *n* 145
Tropic of Capricorn *n* 145
tropics *n* 145
troposphere *n* 155
trot *v* 120, 165
trousers (UK) *n* 15
trout *n* 54
trowel *n* 40, 87
truck driver (US) *n* 90
truck-mounted crane *n* 87
truffle *n* 56, 170
trug (UK) *n* 40
trumpet *n* 128–129
trumpetfish *n* 166
truncheon (UK) *n* 50
trunk *n* 159
trunk (US) *n* 97
try *n* 108
try line *n* 108
try on *v* 46
try something on *v* 14
tsunami *n* 145
tuba *n* 128
tubular bells *n* 128
Tuesday *n* 172
tuff *n* 156
tugboat *n* 105
tulip *n* 38
tumble dryer *n* 34
tumble turn *n* 118
tumbler *n* 27
turmeric *n* 59
tuna *n* 54
tundra *n* 146
tune in *v* 136
tuner *n* 129, 136
tungsten *n* 78
tuning buttons *n* 136
tuning peg *n* 129
Tunisia *n* 149, 152
Tunisian *adj* 152
Tunisians *n* 152
turban *n* 16
turbine *n* 51
turbot *n* 54
turkey *n* 53, 161, 165
Türkiye *n* 150, 151, 153
Turkish *adj* 153
Turkish delight *n* 67
Turkish people *n* 153
Turkmen *adj* 153
Turkmenistan *n* 151, 153
Turkmens *n* 153
Turks *n* 153
turle knot *n* 121
turn *v* 35, 118, 126
turn down *v* 136, 178
turn down the volume *v* 137
turn left *v* 96, 148
turn off *v* 83, 137, 178
turn on *v* 83, 137, 178
turn right *v* 96, 148
turn signal (US) *n* 97, 100
turn up *v* 14, 136, 178
turn up the volume *v* 137
turner *n* 28
turnip *n* 56
turntable *n* 129
turquoise *n* 141, 156
turret *n* 44
tutu *n* 126
Tuvalu *n* 150, 153
Tuvaluan *adj* 153
Tuvaluan people *n* 153
tuxedo *n* 15
TV *n* 26, 136
TV channels *n* 137
TV guide *n* 137–138
TV schedule *n* 137
TV set *n* 137
TV shows *n* 137
tweeter *n* 136
tweezers *n* 18, 20, 77
twelve *num* 173
twentieth *num* 173
twenty *num* 173
twenty-five past one *n* 171
twenty-five to two *n* 171
twenty minutes *n* 171
twenty past one *n* 171
twenty thirty-three *n* 172
twenty to two *n* 171
twenty-first *num* 173
twenty-one *num* 173
twenty-two *num* 173
twice a week *adv* 172
twilight zone *n* 166
twin bed (US) *n* 30
twin room *n* 131
twine *n* 40
twins *n* 05
twist bar *n* 124
twist ties *n* 40
two *num* 173
two hundred *num* 173
two o'clock *n* 171
two percent milk (US) *n* 61
two weeks *n* 172
two-person tent *n* 135
typeface *n* 175
types of aircraft *n* 103
types of buildings *n* 44
types of buses *n* 99
types of cars *n* 97
types of fishing *n* 121
types of houses *n* 32
types of meat *n* 53
types of motorcycles *n* 100
types of motorsports *n* 123
types of plants *n* 41
types of soil *n* 39
types of trains *n* 102
tyrannosaurus rex *n* 157
tyre (UK) *n* 97, 100–101
tyre lever (UK) *n* 101

U

udon *n* 64
Uganda *n* 149, 152
Ugandan *adj* 152
Ugandans *n* 152
ugli fruit *n* 57
ugly *adj* 177
Ukraine *n* 151, 152
Ukrainian *adj* 153
Ukrainians *n* 153
ukulele *n* 129
ulna *n* 03
ultrasound *n* 08
ultraviolet *n* 75
ultraviolet rays *n* 155
umbilical cord *n* 08
umbrella *n* 16
umbrella pine *n* 167
umbrella plant *n* 38
umlaut *n* 175
umpire *n* 111, 113–114
umpire's chair *n* 114
unanimous vote *n* 95
unapproachable *adj* 10
unblock the sink (UK) *v* 35
unblock the toilet (UK) *v* 35
uncle *n* 05
unclog the sink (US) *v* 35
unclog the toilet (US) *v* 35
under *prep* 180
under par *adj* 115
undercoat *n* 37
undergraduate *n* 80
underground map (UK) *n* 102
underground train (UK) *n* 102
underpass *n* 96, 102
underscore *n* 175
undersea features *n* 145
undershirt *n* 14
understand *v* 11
underwater camera *n* 118
underwater diving *n* 118
underwear *n* 14
unemployment benefit *n* 81
unenthusiastic *adj* 06
uneven bars *n* 125
unfasten *v* 14
unfriendly *adj* 10
unfurnished *adj* 32
unhappy *adj* 06
unicorn *n* 139
unicycle *n* 101
uniform, uniforms *n* 13, 50, 88
unimpressed *adj* 06
United Arab Emirates *n* 151, 153
United Kingdom *n* 151, 153
United States of America *n* 150, 152
universe *n* 144
university (UK) *n* 43, 80
university departments *n* 80
university schools *n* 80
unkind *adj* 10
unleaded *n* 97
unload the dishwasher *v* 34
unpack *v* 11, 32
unpasteurized *adj* 61
unpeeled prawn *n* 54
unpick *v* 142
unpleasant *adj* 177
unreasonable *adj* 10
unreliable *adj* 10
unsalted *adj* 61
unsaturated fat *n* 23
upload *v* 83
upmarket (UK) *adj* 47
upper deck *n* 99
upper level *n* 47
uppercase *n* 175
upscale (US) *adj* 47
upset *adj* 06
upstairs *adv, n* 25
uranium *n* 78
Uranus *n* 143
urinary *n* 04
urology *n* 21
Uruguay *n* 149, 152
Uruguayan *adj* 152
Uruguayans *n* 152
USB drive *n* 83
useful *adj* 177
useful expressions *n* 179–180
useless *adj* 177
usher *n* 126
uterus *n* 04, 08
utility knife *n* 36–37
utility power (US) *n* 33
UV tubes *n* 18
Uzbekistan *n* 151, 153
Uzbekistani *adj* 153
Uzbekistanis *n* 153

V

V-neck *n* 14
vacancies *n* 92, 131
vacation (US) *n* 81, 104
vaccination *n* 08, 20
vacuole *n* 77
vacuum *n* 75
vacuum cleaner *n* 34
vacuum the carpet *v* 34
vagina *n* 04
Vaisakhi *n* 07
valance *n* 30
valley *n* 146
valve *n* 101
vampire *n* 139
vanadium *n* 78
vandalism *n* 85
vanilla milkshake *n* 61
vanity (US) *n* 30
Vanuatu *n* 150, 153
Vanuatuan *adj* 153
Vanuatuan people *n* 153
varnish *n* 37
vase *n* 26

Vatican City *n* 151
vault *n* 125
veal *n* 53
vegan *adj* 23
vegan *n* 23
vegetable garden *n* 41, 86
vegetable plot (UK) *n* 86
vegetables *n* 48, 55–56
vegetarian *adj* 23
vegetarian *n* 23
veggie burger *n* 70
veil *n* 15
vein *n* 04
Venetian blinds *n* 26
Venezuela *n* 149, 152
Venezuelan *adj* 152
Venezuelans *n* 152
venison *n* 53
vent *n* 145
Venus *n* 143
Venus fly-trap *n* 168
verdict *n* 85
vermilion flycatcher *n* 160
vertebrate *n* 77
verticals *n* 120
vest *n* 14
vest (US) *n* 15
vet *n* 89
veteran *n* 88
vial *n* 36
vibraphone *n* 128
Victoria Falls *n* 145
vicuña *n* 158
video chat *n* 83
video conference *n* 83
video games *n* 136
video on demand *n* 137
Vietnam *n* 150, 153
Vietnamese *adj* 153
Vietnamese people *n* 153
view a house *v* 32
viewing platform *n* 44
viewpoint *n* 148
villa *n* 32, 131
village *n* 43
villain *n* 127
Vincentian *adj* 152
Vincentians *n* 152
vinegar *n* 60, 64
vineyard *n* 86
vintage *adj* 13
vintage *n* 97
vinyl records *n* 129
viola *n* 128
violet *n* 38
violin *n* 128–30
violin sonata *n* 128
Virginia creeper *n* 168
Virgo *n* 144
virus *n* 19, 77
visa *n* 104
visible light *n* 75
vision *n* 22
visitor *n* 107
visor *n* 100
vitamins *n* 23, 49
vivarium *n* 164
vlog *n* 84
vlogger *n* 84
vocal cords *n* 04
vodka *n* 68
vodka and orange *n* 68
voice recorder *n* 83
volcano *n* 145
volley *n* 114
volleyball *n* 112
volleyball positions *n* 112
volt *n* 75
voltage *n* 33
volume *n* 74, 136, 174
volunteer *v* 92
vomit *v* 20
vote *n* 85
vulture *n* 160

W

waders *n* 121
wading pool (US) *n* 25, 133
waffle, waffles *n* 65, 70–71
wages *n* 81
waist *n* 01, 129
waistband *n* 15, 142
waistcoat (UK) *n* 15
wait in line (US) *v* 104
wait on *v* 178
wait up *v* 178
waiter (UK) *n* 69, 89
waiting room *n* 20, 102
waitress (UK) *n* 65, 69, 89
wake up *v* 09, 178
walk *v* 120
walk the dog *v* 09
walkie-talkie *n* 50
walking boots *n* 135
walking trail *n* 148
wall *n* 25, 44, 87
wall light (UK) *n* 26
Wallace's flying frog *n* 163
wallet *n* 94
wallet (US) *n* 16
wallflower *n* 169
wallpaper *n* 37
wallpaper *v* 37
wallpaper border *n* 37
wallpaper brush *n* 37
wallpaper hanger *n* 37
wallpaper paste *n* 37
wallpaper roll *n* 37
wallpaper stripper *n* 37
walnut *n* 58, 168
walnut oil *n* 60
walrus *n* 166
wand *n* 139
want *v* 46
war *n* 79, 88
war elephant *n* 79
ward *n* 21
wardrobe *n* 30
warehouse *n* 44, 106
warfare *n* 79
warhorse *n* 79
warm *adj* 154
warm front *n* 155
warning track *n* 113
warp thread *n* 142
warrant *n* 85
warrior *n* 79
warrior pose *n* 24
warthog *n* 159
wasabi *n* 60
wash the car *v* 34
wash up *v* 09
wash your face *v* 09
wash your hair *v* 09, 12
washer *n* 36
washer fluid (US) *n* 97
washer fluid reservoir (US) *n* 98
washing line (UK) *n* 34
washing machine *n* 34
washing-up liquid (UK) *n* 34
wasp *n* 162
wasp nest *n* 162
waste *n* 33
waste disposal *n* 135
waste pipe (UK) *n* 33
watch *n* 16
watch TV *v* 09
watching television *n* 137
water *n* 48, 91, 118
water *v* 39
water bottle, water bottles *n* 101, 135
water carrier *n* 135
water chestnut *n* 56
water cooler *n* 82
water features *n* 145
water garden *n* 41
water hazard *n* 115
water jet *n* 50
water lilies *n* 167
water phenomena *n* 145
water plants *n* 41
water polo *n* 119
water rail *n* 161
water shoes *n* 17
water skier *n* 119
water skiing *n* 119
water sports *n* 119
water the plants *v* 09, 34
water vapor (US) *n* 51
water vapour (UK) *n* 51
watercolor (US) *n* 130
watercolor paints (US) *n* 141
watercolour (UK) *n* 130
watercolour paints (UK) *n* 141
watercress *n* 55
waterfall *n* 146
waterfront *n* 132
watering *n* 40
watering can *n* 40
watermark *n* 94
watermelon *n* 58
waterproof fishing gear *n* 121
waterproofs (UK) *n* 121, 135
wave *n* 75, 119, 134, 147
wave *v* 02
wavelength *n* 75
wavy hair *n* 12
wax *adj* 176
wax *n* 18, 176
waxcap *n* 170
weapons *n* 79, 88
wear *v* 14
weasel *n* 158
weather *n* 137, 154
weather forecaster *n* 137
weather map *n* 155
weaver *n* 142
weaverbird *n* 160
weaving *n* 142
webcam *n* 83
wedding *n* 07
wedding cake *n* 63
wedding dress *n* 15
wedge *n* 115
wedge sandals *n* 17
Wednesday *n* 172
weedkiller *n* 39
weeds *n* 41
week *n* 172
weekends *n* 172
weekly *adj* 172
weekly *adv* 172
weevil *n* 162
weft thread *n* 142
weigh *v* 174, 178
weigh out *v* 178
weight, weights *n* 121, 174
weight bar *n* 124
weight belt *n* 118
weight training *n* 124
well qualified *adj* 93
wellies (UK) *n* 40
wellington boots (UK) *n* 17
werewolf *n* 139
west *n* 148
western *n* 127
wet *adj* 154
wet suit *n* 118, 134
wet wipe, wet wipes *n* 08, 49
wetlands *n* 146
wharf *n* 106
wheat allergy *n* 23
wheat beer *n* 68
wheel *n* 97, 101
wheel nuts (UK) *n* 98
wheel pose *n* 24
wheel roller (UK) *n* 124
wheelbarrow *n* 40
wheelchair *n* 21
wheelchair access *n* 99
wheelchair basketball *n* 125
wheelchair curling *n* 122
wheelchair race *n* 116
wheelchair ramp *n* 130
wheelchair rugby *n* 108, 125
wheelie bin (UK) *n* 25
whiplash *n* 19
whipped cream *n* 61
whisk *n* 28
whisk *v* 29
whiskers *n* 158
whiskey (US) *n* 68
whisky (UK) *n* 68
whisper *v* 11
white *adj* 140–141
white *n* 140–141
white blood cell *n* 77
white bread *n* 62
white chocolate *n* 67
white coffee *n* 65
white currant *n* 57
white dwarf *n* 144
white flour *n* 62
White House *n* 44
white meat *n* 53
white mustard *n* 59
white spirit (UK) *n* 37
white tea *n* 66
white vinegar *n* 34
white wine *n* 52, 68
whiteboard *n* 73, 95
whitening *n* 22
whiting *n* 54
whole milk *n* 61
whole-grain mustard (US) *n* 60
whole-wheat flour (US) *n* 62
wholegrain mustard (UK) *n* 60
wholemeal flour (UK) *n* 62
whooper swan *n* 161
Wi-Fi *n* 83
wicket *n* 111
wicket-keeper *n* 111
wide *adj* 176
wide range *n* 48
wide receiver *n* 107
widow *n* 05
width *n* 74
wife *n* 05
wig *n* 12
wigwam *n* 32
wildcat *n* 159
wildebeest *n* 158
wildlife photography *n* 133
willow *n* 169
win *v* 11, 109, 115, 140
win a prize *v* 07
wind *n* 51, 154
wind energy *n* 51
wind farm *n* 51
wind turbine *n* 51
windbreak *n* 134
windlass *n* 105
windmill *n* 44
window cleaner *n* 90
window shopping *n* 46
windscreen (UK) *n* 97, 100
windshield (US) *n* 97, 100

windsurfer *n* **119**
windsurfing *n* **119, 134**
windy *adj* **154**
wine *n* **68**
wine list *n* **69**
wine vinegar *n* **60**
wineglass *n* **27**
wing *n* **53, 103, 112, 161**
wing mirror (UK) *n* **97**
wings *n* **49, 126**
wink *v* **02**
winners' cup *n* **109**
winter *n* **172**
Winter Olympics *n* **122**
winter sports *n* **122**
winter tires (US) *n* **97**
winter tyres (UK) *n* **97**
wipe the surfaces *v* **34**
wiper *n* **97**
wire *n* **35, 83**
wire cutters *n* **36**
wire strippers *n* **36**
wire wool (UK) *n* **36**
wireless *adj* **83**
wireless headphones *n* **136**
wires *n* **33**
wiring *n* **33**
wisteria *n* **38**
witch *n* **139**
witches' brew *n* **139**
with ice *adj* **68**
withdraw money *v* **45**
without ice *adj* **68**
witness *n* **85**
wizard *n* **139**
wok *n* **28**
wolf *n* **159**
woman *n* **05**
womb *n* **04, 08**
wombat *n* **158**
women's heptathlon *n* **116**
womenswear *n* **47**
wonderful *adj* **177**
wood *adj* **176**
wood *n* **35, 115, 141, 146, 176**
woods *n* **176**
wood duck *n* **161**
wood glue *n* **35**
wood preserver *n* **37**
wooden spoon *n* **28**
woodwind *n* **128**
woodworking *n* **141**
woofer *n* **136**
wool *adj* **176**
wool *n* **142, 176**
woolen (US) *n* **13**
woollen (UK) *n* **13**
woolly mammoth *n* **157**
woolly rhinoceros *n* **157**
work *n* **81**
work *v* **11**
work bench *n* **35**
work boots *n* **17**
work from home *v* **81**
work full-time *v* **81**
work part-time *v* **81**
work shifts *v* **81**
workclothes *n* **13**
worker *n* **81**
working out *n* **124**
working well under pressure *n* **93**
workplace skills *n* **93**
workstation *n* **82**
worktop (UK) *n* **27**
worm *n* **162**
worried *adj* **06**
wound *n* **19**
wrap *n* **70**
wrap up the meeting *v* **95**
wren *n* **160**
wrench (US) *n* **36, 98**
wrestling *n* **117**
wrinkles *n* **12**
wrist *n* **01-02**
wrist band *n* **107**
wrist weights *n* **124**
wristband *n* **114**
writ *n* **85**
write *v* **73**
write a will (US) *v* **07**
writer *n* **90**
writing *n* **175**
writing equipment *n* **175**
written communication *n* **93**

X

X-ray, X-rays *n* **19, 21, 75**
X-ray machine *n* **104**
xenon *n* **78**
xylophone *n* **128**

Y

yacht *n* **105, 119, 134**
yak *n* **159**
yam *n* **56, 86**
yard *n* **174**
yard line *n* **107**
yarmulke *n* **16**
yawn *v* **02**
year *n* **172**
yellow *n* **141**
yellow box fish *n* **166**
yellow card *n* **109**
yellow mustard *n* **60**
yellow surgeonfish *n* **166**
yellow tang *n* **166**
Yemen *n* **151, 153**
Yemeni *adj* **153**
Yemenis *n* **153**
yew *n* **167**
yield (US) *v* **96**
yo-yo *n* **08**
yoga *n* **24**
yoga class *n* **24**
yoga pants *n* **24**
yoga teacher *n* **90**
yoghurt (UK) *n* **61**
yogurt (US) *n* **61**
yolk *n* **61, 71**
young *adj* **12**
young frog *n* **77**
ytterbium *n* **78**
yttrium *n* **78**
yucca *n* **38**
yurt *n* **32**

Z

Zambia *n* **149, 152**
Zambian *adj* **152**
Zambians *n* **152**
zebra *n* **158**
zero carbon *adj* **155**
zero point five (US) *num* **173**
zest *n* **57**
ziggurat *n* **44**
Zimbabwe *n* **149, 152**
Zimbabwean *adj* **152**
Zimbabweans *n* **152**
zinc *n* **78, 156**
zip (UK) *n* **17, 142**
zip code (US) *n* **45**
zipper (US) *n* **17, 142**
zirconium *n* **78**
zodiac *n* **144**
zodiac constellations *n* **144**
zodiac symbols *n* **144**
zombie *n* **139**
zoo *n* **133**
zookeeper *n* **90**
zoologist *n* **77**
zoology *n* **77, 80**
zucchini (US) *n* **56**

Acknowledgments

The publisher would like to thank:
Dr. Steven Snape for his assistance with hieroglyphs. Elizabeth Blakemore for editorial assistance; Mark Lloyd, Charlotte Johnson, and Anna Scully for design assistance; Simon Mumford for national flags; Sunita Gahir and Ali Jayne Scrivens for additional illustration; Adam Brackenbury for art colour correction; Claire Ashby and Romaine Werblow for images; William Collins for fonts; Lori Hand and Kayla Dugger for Americanization; Christine Stroyan and Justine Willis for proofreading; Elizabeth Blakemore for indexing; Christine Stroyan for audio recording management and ID Audio for audio recording and production.

DK India
Senior Art Editors Vikas Sachdeva, Ira Sharma; **Art Editor** Anukriti Arora;
Assistant Art Editors Ankita Das, Adhithi Priya; **DTP Designer** Manish Upreti